Seventh Edition

Child, Family, School, Community

SOCIALIZATION AND SUPPORT

Roberta M. Berns

University of California, Irvine

Saddleback College

(Emeritus)

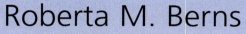

Australia • Brazil • Canada • Mexico • Singapore • Spain
United Kingdom • United States

Child, Family, School, Community: Socialization and Support,
Seventh Edition
Roberta M. Berns

Publisher: Vicki Knight
Editor: Dan Alpert
Development Editor: Tangelique Williams
Assistant Editor: Dan Moneypenny
Editorial Assistant: Ann Richards
Technology Project Manager: Amanda Kaufmann
Marketing Manager: Terra Schultz
Marketing Communications Manager: Tami Strang
Project Manager, Editorial Production: Mary Noel
Creative Director: Rob Hugel
Executive Art Director: Maria Epes

Print Buyer: Barbara Britton
Permissions Editor: Kiely Sisk
Production Service: Anne Draus, Scratchgravel Publishing Services
Text Designer: Ellen Pettengell
Photo Researcher: Laura Molmud
Copy Editor: Margaret C. Tropp
Illustrators: Richard Sheppard, Greg Draus
Cover Designer: Bill Reuter
Cover Images (top to bottom): Kevin Levit/ Alamy; Corbis; Corbis; Corbis
Compositor: Integra Software Services Pvt. Ltd.
Printer: Transcontinental Printing/Louiseville

Library of Congress Control Number: 2005936427
ISBN-13: 978-0-495-00758-6
ISBN-10: 0-495-00758-7

Thomson Higher Education
10 Davis Drive
Belmont, CA 94002-3098
USA

For more information about our products, contact us at:
Thomson Learning Academic Resource Center
1-800-423-0563
For permission to use material from this text or product, submit a request online at
http://www.thomsonrights.com.
Any additional questions about permissions can be submitted by e-mail to
thomsonrights@thomson.com.

I dedicate this book to significant people in my life:

My Children—Son, Gregory & Kathleen (his wife), and daughter, Tamara

My Grandchildren—Helen and Madeline

My Family—husband, Michael, brother, parents, and grandparents

My School—Cornell University (in memory of Dr. Urie Bronfenbrenner),
University of California, Irvine, and Saddleback College
(my colleagues and students)

My Community—New York (past) and California (present)

Brief Contents

Contents

Chapter 8   Ecology of the Peer Group 297

Chapter 9 Ecology of the Mass Media 348

Chapter 10 Ecology of the Community 399

Chapter 11   Emotional and Cognitive Socialization Outcomes 447

Chapter 12   Social and Behavioral Socialization Outcomes 494

Preface

Purpose

Dear Reader,

When I was a freshman in college, I had the good fortune of having a professor who not only had a unique view of child development, but an engaging teaching style as well. He would begin his lecture with a research study on a topic, such as the development of personality or intelligence. He would then leave the podium and walk up and down the aisle of the lecture hall, which seated 300 students, and throw out questions to whoever happened to be in the seat near where he stopped: "What other factors besides parents might influence personality development?" "Why did the researcher choose this method to do the experiment?" "How else could the results have been interpreted?" That professor was Dr. Urie Bronfenbrenner.

Having come to the university from a large public high school where the curriculum was based on state educational goals and where achievement was measured by standardized tests, critical thinking skills were not well-nurtured. So, being asked to muster my own ideas by my professor in front of fellow students was horrifying. Even more horrifying was saying something dumb. I had no option but to adapt to this Socratic method of having to examine the logic behind my answer. Eventually, I learned how to synthesize various facts I had memorized in high school and other college courses, relating to them in new ways. I even gained confidence in critiquing research studies assigned as required reading.

I have revised this 7th edition of Child, Family, School, Community *to engage you as I was when I began my college experience. Because socialization has always occurred through storytelling, for a prologue, I begin each chapter with a folktale related to the subjects explored. I sprinkle thought-provoking questions throughout the chapter to introduce each main section. For an epilogue, I end the chapter with a plausible conclusion to tie the information discussed back to the beginning folktale. I encourage you to come up with other epilogues.*

Prologue

What does it mean to be human?

The quote from John Milton suggests that the paths of childhood lead to maturity. These paths or challenges are exemplified by the developmental tasks (discussed in this chapter) to be accomplished by each child in order to become a man or a woman.

The following Italian classic children's tale, *The Adventures of Pinocchio* by Carlo Collodi (1882/1972), illustrates the trials and tribulations of a little boy growing up and the agents who contribute to his socialization.

Once Upon a Time There was a woodcutter named Gepetto who wanted a son very much, so he carved a little boy out of a block of wood and named him Pinocchio. When Gepetto goes to sleep, the Blue Fairy appears and gives the wooden boy life.

DIVERSITY AND EQUITY

How can the school meet the diverse needs of individuals while also providing everyone with equal opportunities?

All the macrosystem influences previously discussed relate to how diverse groups in society, such as those characterized by gender, ethnicity, religion, or disability, are enabled to have equitable opportunities to achieve. Here we examine the effects of those macrosystem influences; in the next chapter, we examine how such diverse groups are treated as part of the student population in the classroom.

Epilogue

The school's basic function in society is to develop future contributing citizens. What is important to impart to children varies as societies change. Philosophies on teaching and learning also vary regarding the best way to accomplish this. Rousseau's philosophy was learner-directed (let the child's natural curiosity determine what is learned); formal traditional schooling is teacher-directed (the teacher determines what the child learns); home schooling can be either or both.

For the school to be an effective socializer, the family and community must be involved in the child's education.

Related Readings

Aries, P. (1962). *Centuries of childhood: A social history of family life*. New York: Knopf.

Bremner, R. H. (1971). *Children and youth in America: A documentary history*. Cambridge, MA: Harvard University Press.

Bronfenbrenner, U. (1979). *The ecology of human development*. Cambridge, MA: Harvard University Press.

Campbell, J. (1968). *The hero with a thousand faces* (2nd ed.). Princeton, NJ: Princeton University Press.

Chess, S., & Thomas, A. (1987). *Know your child*. New York: Basic Books.

Cleverly, J., & Philips, D. C. (1986). *Visions of childhood: Influential models from Locke to Spock*. New York: Teachers College Press.

Elkind, D. (1998). *Reinventing childhood*. Rosemont, NJ: Modern Learning Press.

For those of you who want to pursue a more specific, or in-depth, study of the chapter topics, I include a list of related readings. For those of you who would like a dramatization of concepts in the whole book, either as an overview before you begin its study or as a summary to "gel" what you've learned, I recommend the following movies that document the process of socialization and support:

- *Mad Hot Ballroom (2005)*
- *Spellbound (2003)*
- *Whale Rider (2003)*
- *Bend It Like Beckham (2003)*
- *Hoop Dreams (1994)*

All these movies are about kids from vastly different family backgrounds (in terms of composition, socioeconomic status, ethnicity, and culture) who, with the support of caring adults, try their very best to achieve. They all illustrate the message provided by this book—that children need adults, adults need each other, and we all need a sense of community to optimally live in this world.

Sincerely,

Roberta M. Berns

Audience

Child, Family, School, Community is for anyone who deals with children—parents, teachers, and professionals in human services, home economics, public health, psychology, and social work. It is an introductory text for the combination of disciplines that most affect a child's development. It can be used for both lower- and upper-division courses, such as child and community relationships and child socialization. I have used it at the community college level as well as at the university level by varying the type and depth of assignment.

Distinguishing Features

Child, Family, School, Community is distinctive because of its comprehensive coverage. It integrates the contexts in which a child develops, the relationships of the people in them, and the interactions that take place within and between contexts. It also addresses the need for parents and professionals who work with children to enable all children to adapt optimally to a changing world.

The title of the book indicates that when one is concerned about children's development one must also be concerned with the contexts in which children develop. For example, the

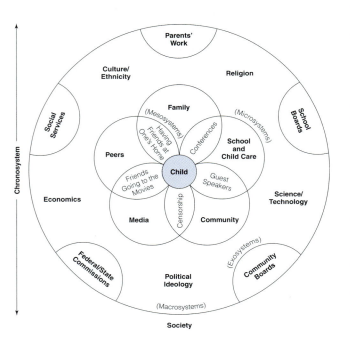

teacher is concerned with children's families because when children come to school, they bring with them their attitudes toward learning, experiences in dealing with others, and self-concepts, all of which germinated in the family. To enhance a child's development, the teacher must work with the child's family and communicate goals, be supportive of the family's values, and enlist the family's cooperation for providing optimal learning experiences.

The professional is concerned with the child's family because when the child has a problem, whether it is emotional, intellectual, social, or physical, the professional must work with the family to determine the probable cause, to develop an effective treatment plan, and to evaluate the results.

Parents, teachers, and professionals are concerned with communities (including the peer group, media, and neighborhood) because communities make certain decisions that affect children. For example, a community shows its support for children in the way that it allocates its tax money for schools, services, libraries, and safety. A community also shows support for children via its business policies, such as maternal or paternal leave, flextime, and child care.

Ancillaries to this book include a student study guide, instructor's manual, and a website.

Themes and Pedagogy

I have analyzed the socialization influences of the family, child care, the school, the peer group, the mass media, and the community on children's development. I have explained how the dynamic and reciprocal interactions of these agents with the child and with each other contribute to the outcomes of socialization—values, attitudes, motives and attributions, self-esteem, self-regulation/behavior, morals, and gender roles. I also have illustrated how children with special needs due to maltreatment, disability, and/or diverse family background, can be empowered via socialization supports.

I have organized classic research as well as contemporary studies on children, families, schools, and communities according to the ecological approach to enable students to understand the many settings and interactions influencing development. The ecology of human development encompasses the disciplines of biology, psychology, sociology, anthropology, and education as they affect the person in society.

Whenever one analyzes something, one takes it apart and evaluates its components. Occasionally, in the process, one loses sight of the whole. I have tried to avoid this by including chapter outlines, prologues as advance organizers (stories

IN PRACTICE

Recommendations for Community Support of Single Parents

- Extend availability of day-care facilities to evening hours.
- Form babysitting cooperatives in neighborhoods or places of employment.
- Make transportation available for children to and from day care to parent's home or work.
- Provide classes on single parenthood and opportunities for support groups.
- Provide Big Sister programs (for girls from mother-absent homes) as well as Big Brother programs (for boys from father-absent homes).

You and School

What was the *most* significant thing you learned or experienced in school and why?

What was the *least* significant you learned or experienced in school and why?

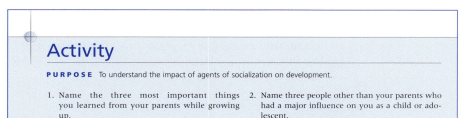

Activity

PURPOSE To understand the impact of agents of socialization on development.

1. Name the three most important things you learned from your parents while growing up.

2. Name three people other than your parents who had a major influence on you as a child or adolescent.

with questions to stimulate critical thinking about the chapter), case studies, examples, open-ended questions in main sections of chapters to engage the reader, boldface glossary terms, epilogues as conclusions to the prologues, and summaries. I have also included applications and activities in each chapter to enable students to experience the relationship between theory and practice. For further study, related readings are listed.

Because our society is changing so rapidly, a major concern of parents, professionals, and politicians is how to socialize children for an unknown future. What skills can we impart? What knowledge should we teach? What traditions do we keep? The impact of historical changes on society is discussed to help us deal with future ones.

Supportive Socialization Influences

The seeds for this book were sown more than 45 years ago. I was a freshman in the College of Human Ecology at Cornell University taking a child development course taught by Dr. Urie Bronfenbrenner. Dr. Bronfenbrenner, who died in 2005, was a distinguished professor of psychology, human development, and family studies. His human ecology theory has stimulated much new research on children and families in various settings as well as advocacy of government and business policies to support families.

To sum up Dr. Bronfenbrenner's philosophy: (1) A child needs the enduring, irrational involvement of one or more adults in care and joint activity with the child, and (2) for one or more adults to provide such care and involvement, public policies and practices are required that provide opportunity, status, resources, encouragement, examples, and, above all, time for parenthood, primarily by parents, but also by other adults in the child's environment, both within and outside the home.

Dr. Bronfenbrenner's enthusiasm for children and families, his dynamic lecture style, and his probing questions regarding the current state of human development research, as well as public policy, provided me with an analytic perspective to examine whatever else I read or heard thereafter.

The seeds for this book could not have flowered had it not been for the care their host (the author) received in her growth and development. My family, my teachers, my friends, the neighborhood in which I grew, and my experiences growing up all contributed to this book. Even as I reached adulthood, the seeds for this book are still being nurtured along by others—my husband (Michael), my children (Gregory and his wife, Kathleen, and Tamara), my grandchildren (Helen and Madeline), my friends, my neighbors, my students, and my colleagues.

As flowers grow, to maintain their shape and stimulate new growth they must be pruned and fertilized. I would like to thank my reviewers of all editions and my editors for their valuable input in this process. Specific thanks to the reviewers of this edition: John Chavez, California State University, East Bay; Jennifer Fererro, Palomar College; Phil Freneau, College of the Redwoods; Gail Goldstein, Southwestern Indian Polytechnic Institute; Charlotte Metoyer, National-Louis University; Robert Schirrmacher, San Jose City College; Susan Schuller Friedman, California State University, Los Angeles; and Andrea Zarate, Hartnell College. I would also like to thank Alison Clarke-Stewart, University of California, Irvine, for the support she provided.

For the fruit of the harvest, this seventh edition, I would like to thank my editor, Dan Alpert, for plowing this version with me. Also many thanks to the rest of the book team: Vicki Knight, Publisher; Tangelique Williams, Development Editor; Dan Moneypenny, Assistant Editor; Ann Richards, Editorial Assistant; Mary Noel, Project Manager; and Anne and Greg Draus of Scratchgravel Publishing Services.

Chapter 1

FogStock, LLC/Index Stock Imagery

Ecology of the Child

The more things change, the more they remain the same.

— **ALPHONSE KARR**

What does "then" have to do with "now"?

Humans pass on their history, knowledge, values, beliefs, and morals through the stories they tell. Although these stories (oral, printed, or visual) reflect the culture of the storyteller, they also represent universal themes regarding human nature (people's needs, desires, and how they cope with challenges). I have chosen to begin each chapter with a classic or modern tale to illustrate the traditional role of such stories, many of which have varied versions in different countries, in the socialization of children. A **folktale** is a legendary or mythical story originating and handed down among the common people. Folktales can serve as a link with your heritage and a gateway to your future. These stories transcend time, illustrating the notion that "the more things change, the more they stay the same."

The following Native American folktale, "How Medicine Came to the People," illustrates the concepts of **ecology**, the science of interrelationships between organisms and their environments, and **adaptation**, the modification of an organism or its behavior to make it more fit for existence under the conditions of its environment. The process of adapting to environmental change will be elaborated throughout the book as we discuss the child's near, or proximal, environments such as the family, and far, or distal, environments such as culture.

Once Upon a Time a long time ago, all the animals and people

lived happily together. But the people grew quickly in number and spread all over the earth. The animals began to feel crowded in their beautiful world. Soon the people made weapons, and used them to hunt the animals for their hides and meat.

The animals grew to hate and fear the people. It was no longer safe to wander through the woodlands as they had always done. At last came the day when they decided to fight back. All over the world, the animals gathered in their councils, and they devised ways to defeat the people.

Chief White Bear led the council of bears. They argued over many plans and schemes, but could agree on only one. The bears would use the people's own weapon, the bow, to destroy them. They brought out a bow and an arrow, left by some careless hunter in the forest.

"First we should see how this weapon is used," White Bear advised.

"I'll show you how!" a young bear named Big Head laughed as he picked up the bow.

He had seen men shooting arrows before. Aiming an arrow at a pumpkin a few yards away, he pulled back the bowstring and let go. But the string caught in his long claws. The arrow wobbled tin the air and fell to the ground.

"My claws are in the way," Big Head complained. "I will cut them off and try again."

folktale a legendary or mythical story originating and handed down among the common people

ecology the science of interrelationships between organisms and their environments

adaptation the modification of an organism or its behavior to make it more fit for existence under the conditions of its environment

And that is what he did. This time the arrow split the pumpkin in two halves. The bears shouted with joy. They were ready to make bows and arrows and cut off all their claws. But above their cheering came a loud roar. Chief White Bear had something to say.

"Listen to yourselves!" he cried. "You would cut off your own claws to use a man's weapon. How will you dig for roots, or climb the wild honey trees? What good is it to kill the people with the bow if we go hungry and die?"

The bears had no answer. Sleepy and tired, they wandered away from the council grounds.

The deer council wasted no time making their plan. They had discovered a terrible weapon. It was a sickness that would bring pain to the hunter each time he tried to move. The disease got into the knees, ankles, elbows, and shoulders, all the joints of the body. It had a name, "Rheumatism."

All the fish and reptiles came together for a great council. They had plenty of reasons to seek revenge on human beings. The people speared the fish for food, and tormented the snakes and lizards with sticks and rocks.

"When it is time to build my nest," Catfish said, "the young men of the village will not leave me alone. They grab me and pull me from my riverbank hole. From this day on, I will sting them with my sharp spines."

"I will bring the people dreams of raw fish," vowed Black Perch. "They will lose their appetites for food, and they will weaken and die."

"My husband and I will visit the people in their dreams," hissed Copperhead. "They will feel us coiled around their necks. Each time they close their eyes, they will feel our cold breath on their faces. The people will be afraid to go to sleep. They will stay awake until they are too weak to hunt us down."

"If a man injures my wife, I will be hiding nearby to strike him," Copperhead's husband swore. "I will spread my poison around him, and he will turn against his friends and family."

This is why human beings have dreams about fish and frightful snakes. We know to watch out for Copperhead's mate, for he is always near her, and the smell of his poison warns us to leave her in peace.

Grubworm presided as chief of the birds and insects and all the small creatures of the earth. Everyone there was allowed to speak and to cast a vote. They would decide whether the people were guilty. If seven guilty votes were counted, then the people would be punished.

Frog jumped up and showed the spots on his back to the crowd.

"They call me ugly and kick me until I am covered with bumps," he said. "I vote guilty!"

"So do I," Turkey agreed. "The people roast off our feet and feathers over their cooking fires. We must punish them!"

"The votes are counted," Grubworm announced. "All but one vote guilty. Now we must decide what we will do to the people."

The little creatures followed the example of the deer. They began at once to create new illnesses and diseases. They made coughs and colds and aches and pains. They made fevers and swellings and rashes and allergies. They did not stop working until there was enough sickness to destroy all the human beings living on the earth.

Things were looking bad for the people as diseases spread from village to village. The human race might be lost forever. All through the animal world, the story was passed from one to another. The people would soon be destroyed! All over the earth, the animals danced and sang and feasted.

The people who lived in the Cherokee villages got sicker and sicker. No hunter could be found tracking animals through the woods. No hunter had the strength to pull the bowstring or throw the fishing gig. The hunters were first to come down with the diseases, and now all of them were sick.

The women of the villages called a council among themselves to plan what must be done to save the people. Around their fire, each in turn told the story of the great sickness that had befallen their husbands and sons. But none knew the way to stop its spreading. The women went back home with no decision. Beyond the firelight, eyes were watching the council with great interest. Now the animals knew that they had truly won.

From above, another was watching and listening. Yellow Poplar immediately told his whole family about the women's council and the sickness among the people. They spread the word to all the other tress and plants who lived in the forest. The plants called a council of their own to decide what to do.

"Keep in mind," said River Willow, chief of the council, "no animal has ever cared for us the way the people do."

Se-lu, the corn plant, stood up and said, "The people work the earth around my roots, and I grow tall and straight. They keep my seeds safe and dry over the winter, and my family prospers. I vote to save the people."

After the voting, River Willow declared, "Everyone agrees. We will help the people overcome these new diseases. I will make medicine in my bark. When the people chew it, their pains and fevers will leave them."

"My white flower tops will take the poison from their wounds and insect bites," Yarrow pledged.

Spearmint and Peppermint made leaves to be picked and boiled into a tea to cure ailments of the stomach. Dandelion made medicine flow from her yellow flower to her roots. Every bush, tree, vine, grass, mushroom, and moss created a healing remedy for some disease.

Each plant in turn agreed, "Whenever the human beings call on me in their time of need, I shall appear to help them."

That was how medicine came to the people. The ancient cures have been passed down through generations of healers. If our medicine people cannot find the cure a sick person needs, they can ask the spirits of the plants to tell them. And the answer will be given, just as they promised long ago.

Source: Duvall, D. L. (2003). *How medicine came to the people: A tale of the Ancient Cherokee's grandmother stories* (Vol. 2). Albuquerque: University of New Mexico Press.

This simple folktale illustrates the challenges that living things faced to survive. Competition for resources in their crowded environment led humans to kill animals for food, clothing, and shelter. This led to retaliation by the animals, who fought back first with weapons, then with bioterrorism, and finally through mind control. This chaos led, in turn, to the plants' offering of remedies for the ailments brought upon the humans by the animals, fish, and reptiles. Now, harmony and health among those who shared the earth became a possibility.

- **What natural occurrences or historical events have affected your ability to survive, or at least to lead the life you had planned?**

- **How have you or your family adapted to reductions in resources (physical, economic, social)?**

- **What are some ways you would try to achieve harmony and equity in your community (among those who share your environment)?**

Ecology, Change, and Children

How does growing up in a changing world affect how children are socialized?

The concept of ecology can be applied to humans. Human ecology involves the biological, psychological, social, and cultural contexts in which a developing person interacts and the consequent processes (for example, perception, learning, behavior) that develop over time (Bronfenbrenner & Morris, 1998). As humans develop, they must continually adapt to change, on a personal, social, and societal level. For example, such forces as demographics, economics, politics, and technology present challenges to human adaptation. The purpose of this book is to examine how growing up in a changing world affects the development of children through socialization. Children are socialized and supported by their families, schools, and communities, in that these significant agents accept responsibility for ensuring children's well-being. These socializing agents nurture children's development, enabling them to become contributing adults.

Kids Today: Are They . . .

computer chippers?	button pushers?
phone fans?	cash commandos?
frightened by war and violence?	bombarded by commercialism?
confused by choices?	too busy?
too distracted?	too stressed?

Socialization and Child Development

What is socialization?

Socialization is the process by which individuals acquire the knowledge, skills, and character traits that enable them to participate as effective members of groups and society (Brim, 1966).

- Socialization is what every parent does: "Help your brother button his jacket." "We use tissues, not our sleeves, to wipe our noses."
- Socialization is what every teacher does: "Study your spelling words tonight." "In our country we have the freedom to worship as we choose."
- Socialization is what every religion does: "Honor your father and mother." "Do not steal."
- Socialization is what every employer does: "Part of your job is to open the store at eight o'clock and put the merchandise on the tables." "Your request must be in writing."
- Socialization is what every government does through its laws and system of punishment for violations.
- Socialization is what friends do when they accept or reject you on the basis of whether or not you conform to their values.
- Socialization is what the media do by providing role models of behavior and solutions to common problems.

The concept of socialization, including parenting or child rearing, social development, and education, really goes back in time as far as human life: "Train up a child in the way he should go: and when he is old, he will not depart from it" (Proverbs 22:6). As we shall see, many forces in society contribute to children's development—as do the children themselves. Socialization takes place in the family, school, peer group, community, as well as via the media. While socialization enables a person to participate in social groups and society, it also enables the very existence of a society and its consequent social order. In sum, according to Elkin and Handel (1989, p. 27), socialization occurs over time

- through interaction with significant others,
- by means of communication,
- in emotionally significant contexts,
- which are shaped by social groups of varying scopes.

socialization the process by which individuals acquire the knowledge, skills, and character traits that enable them to participate as effective members of groups and society

SOCIALIZATION AS A UNIQUE HUMAN PROCESS

What makes socialization unique to humans?

Most social scientists agree that socialization is unique to human beings. More than 70 years ago George Mead (1934) wrote that it is language that sharply separates humans from other animals. Mead goes on to say that language makes ideas and communication of these ideas possible, and language also makes it possible to replace action with thoughts and then use thoughts to transform behavior. A little boy who breaks his mother's favorite vase and encounters her anger understands her threat the next day when she says, "If you don't hold your glass with both hands, it might fall and break, and then I will be very angry." The child now well understands what *break* and *angry* mean.

Language enables humans to develop *mind*, the ability to reason, and *self*, one's characteristic pattern of behavior. It is reason and behavior that enable us to internalize the attitudes of others. *Internalization* is the process by which externally controlled behavior shifts to internally controlled, or self-controlled, behavior. The ability of humans to self-regulate behavior and emotions is the basis for expecting the same of others with whom they interact. So, the development of a society wherein citizens behave appropriately requires social control.

> Four-year-old Helen's thought one day was to try out Mom's makeup. In the process, the eye shadow got on her fingers, and she wiped it on her shorts. She then sat down on Mom's bed to look in the mirror, leaving a smudge of blue shadow where her bottom touched. She soon got bored with this activity, wiped her moist, red mouth on Mom's yellow towel, and went outside to play. Fifteen minutes later, tears were streaming down Helen's cheeks, indicating her feeling of remorse for her behavior. Mom pointed to the trail of evidence while scolding her for taking other people's things without permission (not to mention the mess that had to be cleaned).

Helen's thoughts led to behavior that caused her mother to vehemently express her feelings regarding taking other people's things without permission. Her mother's communication of values such as this to Helen will lead to Helen's internalization of self-control. If other children, too, learn to internalize behavioral control (for example, respect each other's property), then a human society is possible.

SOCIALIZATION AS A RECIPROCAL DYNAMIC PROCESS

What role does the child play in his or her socialization over time?

Socialization begins at birth and continues throughout life. It is a *reciprocal* process in that when one individual interacts with another, a response in one usually elicits a response in the other. It is also a *dynamic* process in that interactions change over time, with individuals becoming producers of responses as well as products of them (Collins, Maccoby, Steinberg, Hetherington, & Bornstein, 2000). These reciprocal dynamic processes become more complex throughout development. As we will see throughout the book, they can influence children's competence, coping skills, and resilience, serving as a buffer when the child is at risk due to harmful events (Bronfenbrenner & Morris, 1998).

Maturation

Newborn human biological organisms with inherited characteristics come into the world with certain needs that change as they mature or develop. They are given names, which indicates that they are members of society. They are clothed in the manner appropriate to the society into which they are born. In the United States they are diapered, dressed in stretch suits, and kept in cribs. In certain African societies they are swaddled and put on their mothers' backs. The way their parents respond to their cries and their needs, the way their parents communicate expectations, the people with whom their parents allow them to spend time (babysitter, relatives, and so on) all contribute to infants' socialization and consequent development.

As children develop and change, so do parental expectations for behavior. Toddlers may need adult assistance when eating; preschoolers can eat independently using some utensils; school-agers are capable of taking some responsibility in meal preparation (such as making sandwiches, using a microwave, or cleaning utensils).

Throughout development, children play a role in their own socialization. As most parents will tell you, children sometimes instigate how others treat them. You know that if you smile, you are more likely to get a smile back than if you frown. The way you socialize children is often influenced by their reaction to you. For example, I needed only to look sternly at my son or speak in an assertive tone, and he would comply with what was asked of him. My daughter, however, would need to experience consequences (usually several times)—being sent to her room, withdrawal of privileges, having to do extra chores—before she would comply with my rules. Thus, not only do children actively contribute to interactions, but in so doing, they affect their own developmental outcomes, transforming themselves in the process and influencing how others reciprocate (Bugental & Goodenow, 1998; see Figure 1.1).

Genes

genotype the total composite of hereditary instructions coded in the genes at the moment of conception

The role played by biology in the child's contribution to his or her developmental outcomes begins with the child's **genotype**, the total composite of hereditary instructions coded in the genes at the moment of conception. According to Plomin and Asbury (2002) as well as Scarr and McCartney (1983), parents not

Figure 1.1

How Children Affect Their Own Developmental Outcomes

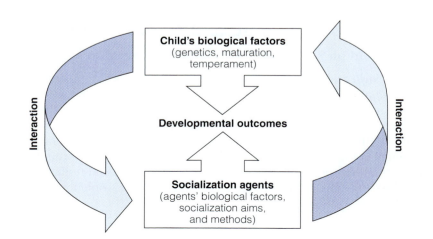

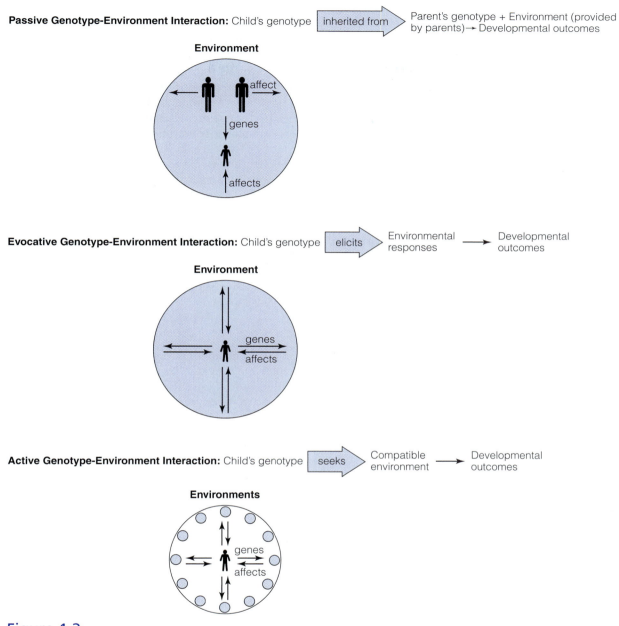

Figure 1.2

Genotype–Environment Interactions

only pass on genes to children but also provide environments, or contexts for development (see Figure 1.2). In other words, there is a correlation between the influence of one's genotype and one's environment on developmental outcomes. Because children inherit genes from their parents, children are "prewired'" or predisposed to be affected by the environments their parents provide. This type of genotype–environment interaction is referred to as *passive*. For example, a child born to intelligent parents will, most likely, possess the genes involved in intelligence. The parents, because of their genotypes and their developmental experience, will likely provide intellectually stimulating things and activities in the home. The child's "prewiring" will enable him or her to benefit from such stimulation.

Another type of genotype–environment interaction is *evocative*, meaning an individual's genotype will tend to evoke, or elicit, certain responses from the environments in which they interact. For example, a happy, sociable child is more likely to engage others in social activities than is a moody, shy child. Consequently, the happy child tends to experience more warm, responsive environments growing up.

Still another type of genotype–environment interaction is *active*, meaning an individual's genotype will tend to motivate that person to seek out environments most compatible with his or her genetic "prewiring." For example, a shy child might prefer solitary activities to group ones, consequently influencing the path of that child's development. My yoga teacher describes herself as an introspective person. As a child she grew up in a beach community in Southern California. Rather than join the extroverted beach culture, she preferred to daydream, making castles in the sand. Her high school activities were dance and gymnastics. Having those skills, she tried the cheerleading squad, but did not feel comfortable in the "rah-rah" role, so years later chose yoga.

Temperament

Another aspect of one's biological makeup, in addition to genes, is **temperament**— the innate characteristics that determine an individual's sensitivity to various experiences and responsiveness to social interaction. Research supports what parents have known for centuries: babies are born with different temperaments (Chess & Thomas, 1987; Kagan, 1994; Thomas, Chess, & Birch, 1970; Wachs & Bates, 2001). That is, they respond differently physiologically to various experiences. This is evident soon after birth in the individual differences in activity level, distractibility, adaptability to new situations, mood, and so on (see Figure 1.3). Children's physiological responses fall into three broad temperamental categories: "easy," "slow-to-warm-up," and "difficult."

How caregivers respond to their children's temperaments influences the social-ization process. If there is a "goodness of fit" between the child's temperament and his or her caregivers, then socialization is likely to proceed smoothly (Chess & Thomas, 1987). For example, if the child does not adapt easily to new situations (is a "slow-to-warm-up" child), and the caregivers understand this and are patient (not pushing the child, yet encouraging him or her to get used to new things slowly), then socialization is likely to be smooth. In a longitudinal (long-term) study on the socialization of conscience, or internal monitor, Kochanska (1995, 1997) found that the use of gentle parenting techniques such as persuasion ("Why don't you _____ because _____"), rather than harsh power assertion ("Do _____ or else _____"), was more effective in getting timid children than assertive children to comply.

If, on the other hand, the fit between the child's temperament and the care-givers' is poor, socialization is likely to be rough. For example, if the child is very active, responds intensely to people and things, and is moody (a "difficult" child), and the caregivers force him or her to sit still, punish him or her for crying or being frightened, and demand a smile much of the time, then social-ization may become a battleground of wills. A longitudinal study of more than

temperament the innate characteristics that determine an individual's sensitivity to various experiences and responsiveness to patterns of social interaction

Temperamental Quality	Easy Child	Slow-to-Warm-Up Child	Difficult Child
Rhythmicity	Very regular	Varies	Irregular
Approach/withdrawal	Positive approach	Initial withdrawal	Withdrawal
Adaptability	Very adaptable	Slowly adaptable	Slowly adaptable
Intensity of reaction	Low or mild	Mild	Intense
Quality of mood	Positive	Slightly negative	Negative

Figure 1.3

Temperament and Socialization

Source: Based on Chess & Thomas, 1987

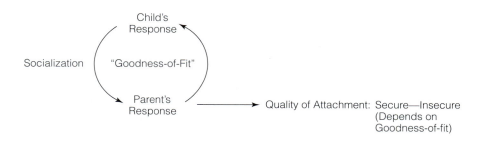

1,000 twins and their families showed that genetically influenced antisocial behavior (difficult temperament) was a significant provoker of parental use of harsh discipline (Jaffee, Caspi, Moffitt, Polo-Thomas, Price, & Taylor, 2004). The impact of temperament on parenting styles is discussed in more detail in Chapter 4.

As infants become children, adolescents, and then adults, they interact with more people and have more experiences. In so doing, they acquire skills, knowledge, attitudes, values, motives, habits, beliefs, interests, morals, and ideals. You may learn to read from your first-grade teacher. You may learn to appreciate music from an uncle who takes you to concerts. You may learn about sportsmanship from your coach and about love from the girl or boy down the street.

Thus, from the point of view of society, individuals are socialized to fit into an organized way of life (a *social identity*). And from a personal point of view, socialization enables them to discover themselves—their potentialities for personal growth and fulfillment (a *personal identity*). The environment (including various genotype–environment interactions, discussed earlier) also plays its part in the socialization process. The environment is what the child experiences—the setting, the roles, and the interactions. For example, a child growing up in a large family on a farm has different socialization experiences than does a child growing up in a single-parent family in the city. Over time, children choose and are exposed to many different environments that affect their development (Bronfenbrenner & Morris, 1998). By going to school, children not only gain knowledge; they also find out in what subjects they do best. As members of a peer group, they not only learn to cooperate; they find out whether they are leaders or followers. One child may discover that he or she likes art, another likes dance, still another prefers sports. As these children are enabled to pursue their interests and their abilities are encouraged, they have different socialization experiences.

INTENTIONAL AND UNINTENTIONAL SOCIALIZATION

Is all socialization deliberate?

Much socialization is intentional, done on purpose. When an adult tells a 6-year-old to share a toy with a 4-year-old sibling, that is intentional socialization. Or when an adult reminds a 10-year-old to write a thank-you note to Grandma, that too is intentional socialization. Thus, when adults have certain values that they consistently convey explicitly to the child, and when they back these up with approval for compliance and negative consequences for noncompliance, it is referred to as *intentional socialization.*

Much of socialization, however, takes place spontaneously during human interaction, without the deliberate intent to impart knowledge or values. *Unintentional socialization* may be the product of involvement in human interaction or observation of interaction. For example, a 4-year-old approaches two teachers conversing and excitedly says, "Miss Jones, Miss Jones, look!" One teacher says, "Sally, don't interrupt; we're talking." Later that morning Sally and her friend Tanya are busily playing with Legos. Sally is explaining and demonstrating to Tanya how to fit the pieces together. Miss Jones comes over to the block corner and interrupts with, "Girls, please stop what you're doing and come see what Rene has brought to school." It is very likely that the message Sally received from the morning's interactions was that it is *not* OK to interrupt adults, but it *is* OK for adults to interrupt children.

Sometimes, a socialization goal can be intentional on the part of the parents, but have both intentional and unintentional outcomes on the child. For example, toilet training is usually purposeful and deliberate in Western cultures. A popular book, *Toilet Training in Less Than a Day* (Azrin & Foxx, 1976), gives specific behavior-learning techniques for using the potty. To condition children to associate the urge to urinate or defecate with using the potty, reinforcement (praise and juice) is used for effort and success. Although Azrin and Foxx contend that their method is successful, not all parents execute it appropriately, not all children respond as intended, and sometimes the outcome of being "toilet-trained" is short-term because of other events in the child's life. For example, if a new baby enters the family, the "toilet-trained" child, who has gotten much attention for his or her achievement, may perceive the new baby as getting attention for wetting its diaper. The "toilet-trained" child may then regress to wetting his or her pants in order to regain attention.

In sum, children take cues and learn from others' behavior as well as from their verbal statements. This information is all processed (constructed, interpreted, transformed, and recorded) in the brain to influence future behavior. Bronfenbrenner (1979) contends that the influence of a setting (such as the family) on a child's development is not exerted by the "objective" or "real" qualities of the activities, roles, and interpersonal relations observed there, but rather by the child's perception or interpretation of them. Thus, intentional socialization can end up being unintentional in that "unreal" elements, such as the child's imagination, fantasies, or fears, may be involved. When a parent hurriedly tells a child to get dressed, the child may interpret anger, whereas the parent may actually be in a rush.

Omni Photo Communications Inc./Index Stock Imagery

Sometimes parents are more eager for their child to participate in sports than is the child.

Socialization, Change, and Challenge

How do you socialize children for the future?

Children are socialized by many people in society—parents, siblings, grandparents, aunts, uncles, cousins, friends, teachers, coaches, and role models on television, in the movies, and in books. These agents of socialization use many techniques, which will be discussed, to influence children to behave, think, and feel according to what is considered worthy. What all these agents believe is worthy are outcomes of their own socialization—their values, morals, attitudes, and self-concepts.

Socialization is a very complex process indeed. The more technological and diverse the society, the more children have to learn in order to adapt effectively, the more socializing agents and experiences contribute to the process, and the more time the socialization process takes. As society changes, more and more challenges are posed to the socializing agents because there are more choices to be made. How should the period of childhood be adjusted to accommodate all the opportunities that exist?

When societal change occurs as, for example, rapid technological and scientific advances that result in economic fluctuations, socializing agents are affected. Adults are affected *directly* by the uncertainty that change produces, as well as by the new opportunities and challenges it may present. Economic fluctuations can affect job security and can have a major negative impact on family finances. Family members may have to work longer hours; purchasing power may decrease; the family may have to move. However, sometimes such stresses uncover positive strengths in the family members—for example, spousal emotional support and children's cooperation in assuming more responsibilities for household chores. How adults adapt to societal change *indirectly* affects children. For example, two parents in the workforce usually require child care, and family time becomes the "second shift" (Hochschild, 1989, 1997). Parents learn to adapt by performing several tasks simultaneously. New technology helps (talking on a speaker-phone while folding clothes), but the efficiency gained in doing multitasks may contribute to diminished attentiveness to family members.

One result of societal change is seen in the goals of child rearing and education. Many psychologists (Elkind, 1988, 1994; Kluger & Park, 2001) see today's parents as being very concerned with developing their children's intellectual abilities. This concern is evidenced by the growth of preschools and kindergartens with academic programs; the development of infant stimulation programs such as "Mommy and Me" classes; the availability of "how-to" books on teaching your baby to read, do math, and be brighter; and the proliferation of computer software for children and after-school activities. The concern is also evidenced by the pressure on elementary schools to emphasize formal instruction involving passive listening and memorization rather than a *developmentally appropriate* curriculum, which involves understanding children's normal growth patterns and individual differences and exposing them to active, hands-on, age-appropriate, meaningful experiences. Developmental appropriateness is discussed in more detail in Chapter 5.

As a consequence of this parental concern with nourishing the intellect, children are under pressure to become "intellectually independent" and "intellectually successful" at an early age. This is measured by test scores, performance in various activities such as athletics and music, and being accepted by certain prestigious schools (even preschools!). Elkind (1988) cited an example of this push for having superkids. A mother complained to her son's first-grade teacher, "How is he going to get into M.I.T. if you only give him a 'satisfactory'?" Elkind believes such a push for excellence is causing an increase in stress symptoms in children.

Carol's parents were very proud of their daughter. Considered a "gifted" student, she did very well in school while juggling a full schedule that included ice skating, gymnastics, and piano lessons. At age 10, Carol won her elementary school's outstanding student award, placed first in an ice-skating competition, and gave a solo piano recital. At age 13, she was selected as a candidate for admission to a prestigious private girls' high school. Two days before the scheduled entrance exam, Carol took an overdose of sleeping pills.

Why did Carol choose suicide? Other adolescents face varying degrees of pressure and stress, yet develop coping strategies. Was it her family situation? friends? school? community? or a combination of these complex relationships?

That children are pressured to know more than their parents is really not a new phenomenon; it is part of evolution or societal change. As new knowledge is discovered, it is the children who learn it in school. For example, children in many schools use computers for learning tasks. There is likely to be tension in the parent–child relationship when children can figure things out more efficiently with computers than their parents can with traditional paper-and-pencil methods. As another example, children of immigrants learn to be Americanized in school whereas their parents may cling to the traditional attitudes and behavior patterns learned in their countries of origin. Thus, societal change can produce family tensions; it can also produce challenges. To reduce tension in the parent–child relationship resulting from an imbalance of knowledge, parents can be challenged to become knowledgeable in the very activities their children are pursuing. For example, parents can share activities; they can provide the opportunity for children to teach them; they can read books, talk to experts, and request adult education courses (for example, on how to use a computer); they can volunteer to help in the classroom in order to learn along with their children. There needs to be a distinction between encouraging and motivating children to succeed and pressuring them with inappropriate expectations. Schools can also be challenged to involve parents more in their children's developmentally appropriate learning. Parent involvement in school will be discussed in Chapter 6.

Another result of societal change, according to Elkind (1994), has been a shift in the value of the child's place in the family. There has been a move away from "child-centeredness." Traditionally, parents sacrificed for their children—their energy and resources went to their children. They may have saved money for their children's college education instead of buying a new car. Today, however, some parents see their needs and rights as being at least equal to their children's, rather than subordinate.

Elkind sees this trend evidenced in the pressure placed on children to attain emotional independence at an early age. For example, after school many children come home to a place devoid of adults. They often have to be responsible for younger siblings as well as for themselves. Even though they are independent for part of the day, many are fearful of staying alone. Some are resentful that they cannot play with their friends, for many such children are not permitted to let anyone into the home for safety reasons. Most spend their time watching television. What sorts of adults will these "independent" children become?

CHANGE AND THE CONCEPT OF CHILDHOOD

What is "childhood"? Is it static or dynamic? How is it different from adulthood?

One of the challenges brought on by change is the society's concept of childhood. We assume childhood to be a special period of time when we are cared for, taught, and protected because we are not mature enough to do these things for ourselves. Does the period of childhood change—lengthen or shorten—when society changes?

Renaissance. Before the Renaissance (14th through 16th centuries) there was no concept of childhood, only infancy and adulthood. If a child lived beyond age 7, the child was treated as a miniature adult (Aries, 1962). There was no distinction in the clothing worn by children and adults. Children were treated harshly, not lovingly. They were expected to work and were included in all adult activities, even drinking and partying. Seven-year-olds could even be punished the same way adults were (put in jail or hanged) for a crime such as pilfering.

Printing Press. With the development of the printing press in the middle of the 15th century came a new conception of adulthood, based on reading competence, and of childhood, based on reading incompetence. Prior to the printing era, infancy ended at age 7 and adulthood began at once; there was no intermediary stage (Postman, 1985, 1994). In the 16th century, schools were created so that children could be taught to read. Because school was intended to prepare literate adults, children came to be perceived not as "miniature adults" but as "unformed adults" (Postman, 1985). Thus, the concept of childhood as we know it evolved over the following three centuries. It came to be regarded as the bridge between infancy—total dependence—and adulthood—total independence.

Children working in factories was a common sight prior to child labor laws prohibiting such practices.

© CORBIS

Industrial Revolution. As society became more complex, the need for an education preparatory to adulthood became more apparent. For example, one consequence of the Industrial Revolution (18th to 20th centuries) was the passage by many Western countries of compulsory education laws. Children *had* to attend school to prepare themselves to be functioning members of society.

The need to protect children also became more apparent. Another consequence of the change that took place during the Industrial Revolution was the recognition of children's rights. Before the 19th century, children could be exploited to work in factories for long hours under harsh conditions. The 19th and 20th centuries saw the passage of labor laws that limited the age at which children could be employed and the conditions under which they could work. Thus, from the Renaissance until today, the span of childhood has lengthened and, gradually, the special needs of children have been recognized.

Today. Today, however, a common concern in the United States revolves around the loss of childhood (Elkind, 1994; Garbarino, 1986; Kluger & Park, 2001; Weissbourd, 1996). Gone are many of the physical consequences of growing up in a changing society—toiling in the sweatshops, trekking five miles to school, dying from influenza. But ushered in instead have been psychological consequences: pressure to achieve, stress, substance abuse, violence, eating disorders, teen pregnancies, depression, and suicide (Children's Defense Fund, 2004; Elkind, 1994). The childhood that had evolved from the time of the Renaissance—a romanticized time of fantasy, play, freedom from responsibility, and freedom to develop at one's own pace—has now been reversed into a time of reality, work, and hurrying to develop to fit the pace of societal change. The time of childhood is once again shortening.

Children today must cope with a world in which both parents work, drugs are readily available, sex is as close as the TV or Internet, and violence is just around the corner (Children's Defense Fund, 2004; Elkind, 1994; Weissbourd, 1996). Children are regarded as consumers. From the numerous ads for toys, food, and clothing, you would think children had major purchasing power. Sports are rarely played for amusement as they were a generation ago; learning specific skills and how to compete have become goals. Soccer, football, and Little League games are now analyzed and even commercialized, just like professional sports. The video camera and computer have enabled games to be rehashed the next day and the next, instead of being tossed aside in the name of fun. Businesses often fund team uniforms, equipment, and travel in return for advertising, putting more pressure on children to compete and win.

In sum, the age of protection for children has been undermined by societal pressures on parents. Today's children are increasingly thrust into independence and self-reliance before they have the skills and ability to cope (Elkind, 1994; Garbarino, 1995b; Weissbourd, 1996). Some consequences are the rise in psychosomatic ailments such as stomachaches, headaches, wheezing, dizziness, and chest pains among school-age children and the rise in emotional problems such as depression, substance abuse, eating disorders, and suicide among adolescents (Hewlett & West, 1998; Zill & Schoenbom, 1990). Even the law—the Freedom of Information Act, for example—has certain consequences for children. If you are 18 years old, the law allows you to have privacy rights. That means your parents are not entitled to get any information about you without your consent. They are not privy to your grades, your personal bank account, your credit history, or your health. Although some young people might consider this positive, some parents who are helping their child make the transition to adulthood, perhaps by financing their education, might consider this application of the law's intent counterproductive to their parenting role.

What can we do to cope with these consequences of change? Can we meet the challenge? We need to understand the process of socialization whereby human beings, beginning at birth, acquire the skills to function as social beings and participants in society. We also need to understand the impact of change on socialization. Finally, we need to be able to make choices that will support and prepare today's children for tomorrow's challenges.

SOCIALIZATION AND ADAPTATION

How can socialization help children adapt to change?

Socialization is elaborate; it involves many variable and reciprocal experiences, interactions, and environments that affect children's development. Analyzing some of the variables involved in the socialization process can help people adapt to change. For instance, understanding how the "input"—socialization interactions in various settings and situations—affects the "output" of socialization—values, attitudes, motives and attributions, self-esteem, self-regulation of behavior, morals, and gender roles—may enable us to manipulate that input to induce the desired output (see Table 1.1).

A simplified example of this kind of manipulation is described in a classic book, *Walden Two*, by B. F. Skinner (1948). *Walden Two* is a utopian community founded on behavioral principles. To learn self-control, young children (age 3 to 4) are given lollipops dipped in sugar at the beginning of the day, to be eaten later, provided that they have not been licked (reinforcement). There are practice sessions in which the children are urged (instruction) to examine their own behavior in

Table 1.1

Socialization Variables

EXAMPLES OF INPUT	EXAMPLES OF OUTPUT
Instruction	Values
Setting standards	Attitudes
Learn-by-doing	Motives and attributions
Feedback	Self-esteem
Reinforcement	Self-regulation of behavior
Punishment	Morals
Group pressure	Gender roles

the following situations: when the lollipops are concealed, when the children are distracted from thinking about the candy by playing a game, and when the lollipops are in sight. Thus, when the children are given the lollipops again for a real exercise in self-control (learn-by-doing), they have at their disposal some adaptive behaviors to use (put them out of sight or keep busy) to help them avoid the temptation.

Another example of how input can be used to affect output is Sherif's (1956) classic Robber's Cave experiment, in which manipulation of the environment was used first to bring about antisocial behavior (hostility) via competitive strategies between two groups of young boys, and then to reverse that pattern via cooperative strategies. How was this done? To produce friction, competitive tournaments were held—baseball, tug-of-war, touch football, and so on. Frustration led to name-calling, raids, and aggressive behavior. To eliminate this friction, the counselors rigged a series of crises that forced all the boys to work together in order to solve the problem. Once, the water line was deliberately broken; another time, the camp truck broke down just as it was going to town for food. Thus antisocial behavior gave way to prosocial behavior when a compelling goal for all concerned had to be achieved. Anti- and prosocial behavior will be discussed in more detail in Chapter 12.

The previous examples are illustrations of *intentional socialization*, in which input affected desired output. In reality, all of us have unique biological characteristics; we come into the world with different "wiring." As a result, we perceive and interact with the world differently, resulting in a range of outputs. A muscular, coordinated child will tend to be attracted to sports, while a frail, timid child will tend to avoid competitive activities. Thus, children play a role in their own socialization (Scarr, 1992), which sometimes makes intentional socialization difficult. In contrast to the scientifically shaped utopian society described in *Walden Two* or the manipulated situation in the Robber's Cave experiment, in reality each human being is exposed to many different environments in which many different interactions and experiences, both intentional and unintentional, take place. Therefore, individuals reflect both their biological characteristics and their socialization experiences (Bugental & Goodenow, 1998; Collins et al., 2000). As the child changes, so must the process of socialization. Socialization is not static; it is dynamic, transactional, and bidirectional, or reciprocal (Sameroff, 1987). Ideally, as children develop, control over their behavior gradually shifts from the adult to the child. More specifically, infants and toddlers require much adult direction.

Preschoolers are developmentally capable of directing some of their activities and are exhibiting some self-control of their behavior. School-agers can direct most of their activities with adult support and some direction. Adolescents who have been socialized by nurturant adults exhibit much self-control and self-directed behavior, even though they still need some adult guidance.

Some of the effects of various socialization experiences, interactions, and environments will be examined in later chapters when such questions as these are discussed: What are the effects of divorce on the child? What is the impact of both parents' working outside the home? Is child care helpful or harmful? What type of schooling will raise students' academic achievement? How influential are friends? Should children participate in organized sports? How do the media influence child development? Should children with disabilities be included in the mainstream? Should children from ethnically diverse groups be Americanized, or should societal institutions be modified to meet their special needs? How can communities become more caring?

Theories Relating to Socialization

What are some explanations of how children are socialized?

A **theory** is an organized set of statements that explains observations, integrates different facts or events, and predicts future outcomes. Theories provide a framework for interpreting research findings and give direction for future study. Some theories explain a particular aspect of development, such as genetics. Others describe settings that influence many aspects of the child's development, such as culture. Still others examine the interaction between the child and his or her environment, such as ecology.

> Man is a model exposed to the view of different artists; everyone surveys it from some point of view, no one from every point. (Claude Adrien Helvetius, 1715–1747)

Some categories of theories discussed in this book as they apply to relevant chapters are biological, behavior-learning, sociocultural, psychoanalytical, cognitive developmental, information processing, and systems. The general framework for the whole book is the ecological model of developmental psychologist Urie Bronfenbrenner (1979, 1989, 1995).

What features of the ecological model make it especially appropriate for understanding "the whole picture" of human development, including both nature and nurture?

The ecological model represents the evolving character of science because it can accommodate other theories and old research while providing a conceptual scheme to assimilate new research. Many theories tend to focus on patterns or similarities among individuals to explain human development, but the ecological model can also incorporate differences among individuals to explain human variation and adaptation. Computer technology, enabling multifaceted analyses, and communication technology, enabling collaboration among researchers, have made it possible to conduct integrative and complex studies. A comprehensive study, begun in 1996, on the effects of nonparental care ("child care") on children, families, and communities (discussed in Chapter 5), sponsored by the National Institute of Child Health and Development (NICHD), is one example. This study

theory an organized set of statements that explains observations, integrates different facts or events, and predicts future outcomes

has examined the links between nonparental care and child health, security of attachment to mother, self-control, compliant and problem behavior, peer interactions, cognitive and language development, adjustment to kindergarten, and more (NICHD, 2005).

The ecological model represents a composite of bits and pieces of information about human development designed to foster understanding. It is like a mosaic—a composite arranged out of bits and pieces to form an artistic or a graphic design, as in a website (actually, Mosaic was the first computer software to provide a multimedia graphic user interface). The bits and pieces of the ecological composite can be organized according to person, process, context, and outcome. This book follows such a pattern, discussing (1) the child as a biological organism, (2) socialization processes, (3) significant contexts of development, and (4) socialization outcomes.

Examining Socialization in an Ecological Context

What ecological contexts and interactions influence the process of socialization?

The social context of individual interactions and experiences determines the degree to which individuals can develop their abilities and realize their potentials, according to Bronfenbrenner (1979, 1989, 1995). His conceptual model (see Figure 1.4) for studying humans in their various social environments—the ecology of human development—allows for a systematic study of interactions and serves as a guide for future research on the very complicated process of socialization.

Bronfenbrenner's complicated but inclusive definition of the ecology of human development is as follows:

> the scientific study of the progressive, mutual accommodation, throughout the life course, between an active, growing, highly complex biopsychological organism characterized by a distinctive complex of evolving interrelated dynamic capacities for thought, feeling, and action—and the changing properties of the immediate setting in which the developing person lives as this process is affected by the relations between these settings, and by the larger contexts in which the settings are embedded. (1993, p. 7)

More simply, ecology involves interrelationships between humans and their environments, including the consequent psychological, social, and cultural processes over time.

According to Bronfenbrenner's bioecological theory, there are four basic structures—the *microsystem*, the *mesosystem*, the *exosystem*, and the *macrosystem*—in which relationships and interactions take place to form patterns that affect human development. Such a conceptual framework enables us to study the child and his or her family, school, and community as dynamic evolving systems that are influenced by broader social change (the *chronosystem*), as in economics, politics, and technology. A computer analogy might be a website with links to other sites on the Internet: economic changes can affect the extent of the linkages; political changes can affect what is permissible to post on the website; and technological changes can affect the media interfaces.

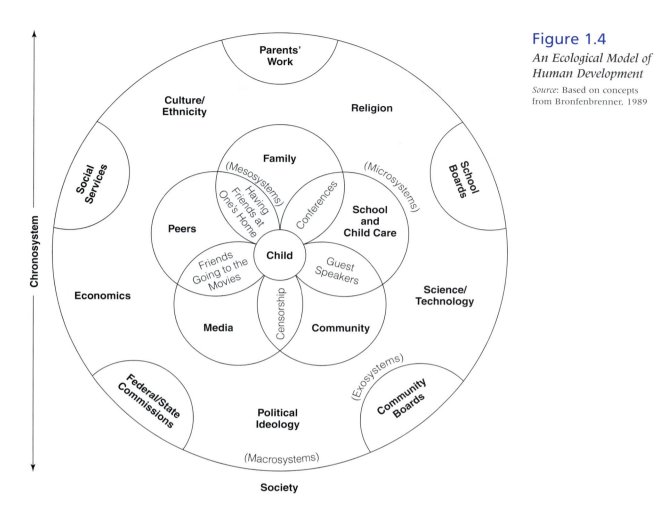

Figure 1.4

An Ecological Model of Human Development

Source: Based on concepts from Bronfenbrenner, 1989

MICROSYSTEMS

What are the most significant contexts in which a child interacts?

The first basic structure, the **microsystem** (*micro* meaning small) refers to the activities and relationships with significant others experienced by a developing person in a particular small setting such as family, school, peer group, or community (see Figure 1.5).

Family. The *family* is the setting that provides nurturance, affection, and a variety of opportunities. It is the primary socializer of the child in that it has the most significant impact on the child's development. According to James Garbarino (1992), the child who is not adequately nurtured or loved, such as one who grows up in an abrasive or dysfunctional family, may have developmental problems. Also, children who do not have sufficient opportunities to manipulate objects, to model desirable behaviors, to initiate activity, and to be exposed to a language-rich environment will be at a disadvantage when they reach school. This early disadvantage will persist and even worsen as the

microsystem activities and relationships with significant others experienced by a developing person in a particular small setting such as family, school, peer group, or community

Figure 1.5
Microsystems

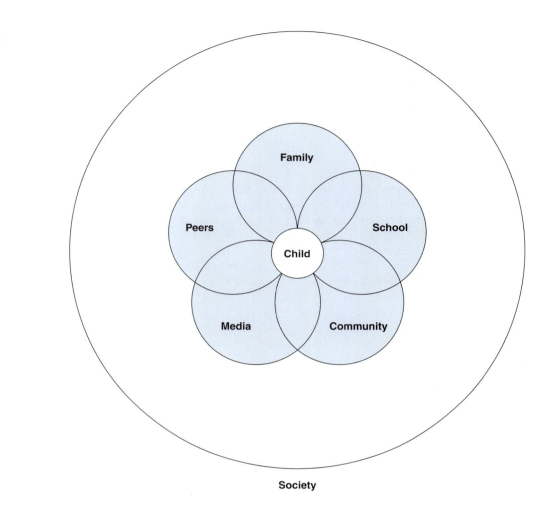

child progresses through school unless intervention, such as that provided by some quality child-care programs, can modify the opportunities at home and in school.

School. The *school* is the setting in which children formally learn about their society. The school teaches reading, writing, arithmetic, history, science, and so on. Teachers encourage the development of various skills and behaviors by being role models and by providing motivation for children to succeed in learning.

Peer Group. The *peer group* is the setting in which children are generally unsupervised by adults, thereby gaining experience in independence. In the peer group, children get a sense of who they are and what they can do by comparison with others. Peers provide companionship and support as well as learning experiences in cooperation and role taking.

Community. The *community*, or neighborhood on a smaller scale, is the main setting in which children learn by doing. The facilities available to children determine what real experiences they will have. Is there a library? Are stores and workplaces nearby where children can observe people at work? Are the people with whom children interact in the community similar or diverse? Are the people in the community advocates for children? These questions relate to the significance of the community as a socializer.

Media. The *media*—television, movies, videos, books, magazines, music, and computers—are not regarded as a microsystem by Bronfenbrenner because they are not a small, interactive setting for reciprocal interaction. However, I consider the media as significant a socializer as those just described because they present a setting in which a child can view the whole world—past, present, future, places, things, roles, relationships, attitudes, values, and behaviors to emulate. Many TVs have interactive capabilities. In addition, because computers are interactive and can be combined with any media, they provide the potential for relationships (e-mail and chat groups, for example).

The child's development is affected in each of the aforementioned settings not only by the child's relationships with others in the family, school, peer group, or community, but also by interactions among members of the particular microsystem. For example, the father's relationship with the mother affects her treatment of the child. If the father is emotionally supportive of the mother, she is likely to be more involved and to have more positive interactions with the child (Cox, Owen, Henderson, & Margand, 1992). For another example, a child's classroom performance varies as a function of whether or not the teacher has taught the child's older sibling and how well that sibling performed (Seaver, 1973). A teacher who has taught a high-achieving older sibling tends to have high expectations for the younger sibling. The younger sibling, in turn, is more likely to perform as expected.

MESOSYSTEMS

How are the child's significant contexts of development linked to one another?

The second basic structure, the **mesosystem** (*meso* meaning intermediate), consists of linkages and interrelationships between two or more of a developing person's microsystems, such as the family and the school, or the family and the peer group (see Figure 1.6). The concept of linkages was introduced by Guglielmo Marconi, inventor of the wireless telegraph and winner of the 1909 Nobel Prize in physics. He posited the principle of "six degrees of separation," meaning it would take no more than six connections to link any two people in the world. Marconi was referring to telegraph stations, but today social scientists apply the idea to personal linkages. By having subjects send letters to people they knew in the United States, Stanley Milgram (1967) found that two random people were connected by an average chain of six acquaintances.

The impact of mesosystems on the child depends on the number and quality of interrelationships. Bronfenbrenner (1979) uses the example of the child who goes to school alone on the first day. This means that there is only a single link between home and school—the child. Where there is little linkage between home and school "in terms of values, experiences, objects, and behavioral style," there also tends to be little academic achievement for the child. In contrast, where all these links are strong, there is likely to be academic competence.

mesosystem linkages and interrelationships between two or more of a person's microsystems (for example, home and school, school and community)

Figure 1.6

Mesosystems

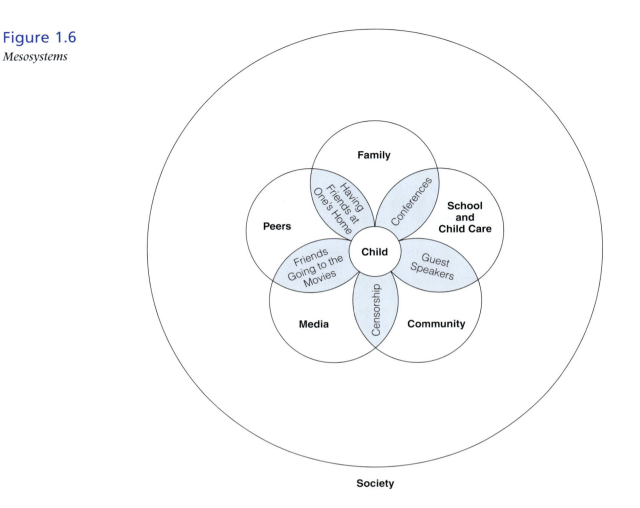

To illustrate, a longitudinal study following adolescents from their last year of middle school through their first year of high school found a relationship between academic performance and the joint effects of family and school (Epstein, 1983). When the style of family interaction was similar to the school's, in that both settings encouraged child participation, academic performance was enhanced (Ginsburg & Bronstein, 1993). Thus, the more numerous the qualitative links or interrelationships between the child's microsystems, the more impact they have on socialization. Mesosystems, then, provide support for activities going on in microsystems. For example, when parents invite a child's friends to their home, or when parents encourage their child to join a certain club, team, or youth group, the socialization impact of the peers is enhanced through parental approval.

Another example of mesosystem impact occurs when a community censors the movies that can be shown in local theaters; the impact of the media as a socializing agent is then reduced because of lack of sponsorship. However, censorship may actually motivate some individuals to see a movie, thereby increasing its influence.

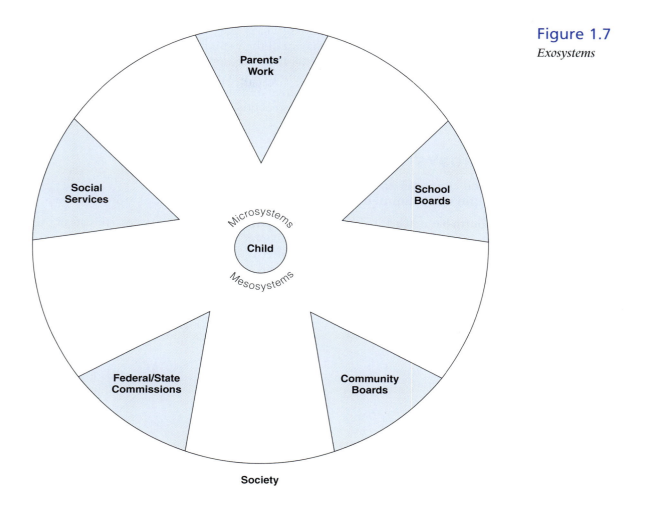

Figure 1.7
Exosystems

EXOSYSTEMS

How do settings in which the child does not participate influence his or her development?

The third basic structure, the **exosystem** (*exo* meaning outside), refers to settings in which children are not active participants, but that affect them in one of their microsystems—for example, parents' jobs, the city council, parental social support networks (see Figure 1.7). The effects of exosystems on the child are indirect via the microsystems. To illustrate, when parents work in settings that demand conformity rather than self-direction, they reflect this orientation in their parenting styles, tending to be more controlling than democratic. This orientation, in turn, affects the child's socialization. When the city planning commission approves a freeway through a neighborhood or an air traffic pattern over a school, children's socialization is affected because the noise interferes with learning. Studies show that parental employment, income, and setting affect child development outcomes. For example, low-income parents involved in work-based antipoverty programs (ones that provide sufficient family income, child

exosystem settings in which children do not actually participate, but which affect them in one of their microsystems (for example, parents' jobs, the school board, the city council)

care, health insurance, and support services) have been shown to enhance the school performance and social behavior of their children (Huston et al., 2001). On the other hand, high-income parents living in upwardly mobile suburban communities have been shown to have children who exhibit a relatively high rate of lower-than-expected school performance and negative social behavior (anxiety, depression, and substance abuse) as a reaction to achievement pressure (Luthar & Becker, 2002).

MACROSYSTEMS

macrosystem the society and subculture to which the developing person belongs, with particular reference to the belief systems, lifestyles, patterns of social interaction, and life changes

How do characteristics of the larger society influence the child's development?

The fourth basic structure, the **macrosystem** (*macro* meaning large), consists of the society and subculture to which the developing person belongs, with particular reference to the belief systems, lifestyles, patterns of social interaction, and life changes (see Figure 1.8). Examples of macrosystems include the United States, the middle or lower class, Hispanic or Asian ancestry, Catholicism or Judaism, urban or rural

Figure 1.8
Macrosystems

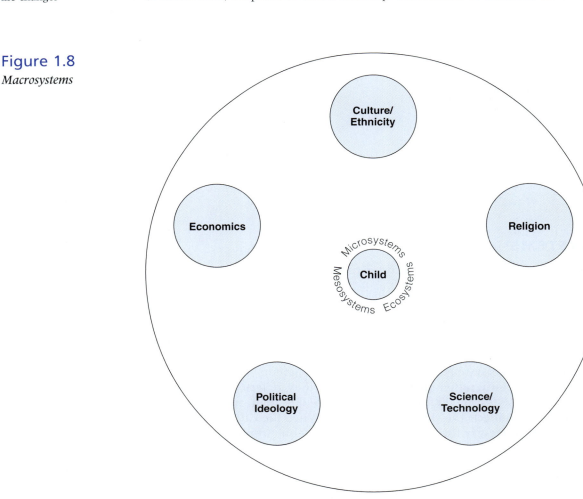

Low-context cultures value cultivating the land, whereas high-context cultures value living in harmony with it.

areas. Macrosystems are viewed as patterns, or sets of instructions, for exosystems, mesosystems, and microsystems. Democracy is the basic belief system of the United States and so is considered a macrosystem. Democratic ideology affects the world of work, an exosystem—for example, employers cannot discriminate in hiring. Democratic ideology also affects school–family interaction, a mesosystem—for example, schools must inform parents of policies, and parents have the right to question those policies. Finally, democratic ideology affects what is taught in schools, a microsystem—for example, children must learn the principles upon which the United States was founded.

A person who lives in the United States and subscribes to its basic belief system of democracy, and consequently is influenced by that macrosystem, may also be part of other macrosystems, such as his or her ethnic group. **Ethnicity** refers to an attribute of membership in a group in which members identify themselves by national origin, culture, race, or religion. Because the United States is becoming more and more ethnically diverse, we need to understand some basic effects of various macrosystems. More details on specific ethnic groups will be discussed throughout the book.

According to cultural anthropologist Edward T. Hall (1964, 1966, 1976, 1983), people from different macrosystems, or cultures, view the world differently, unaware that there are alternative ways of perceiving, believing, behaving, and judging. Particularly significant are the unconscious assumptions people make about personal space, time, interpersonal relations, and ways of knowing. These assumptions can interfere with communication, a point on which Hall focuses to illustrate differences as well as similarities among cultures.

Hall classifies macrosystems as being low or high context. Generally, **low-context macrosystems** are characterized by rationality, practicality, competition, individuality, and progress; **high-context macrosystems** are characterized by intuitiveness, emotionality, cooperation, group identity, and tradition (see Table 1.2).

Communication. In a low-context macrosystem, such as Anglo-American, urban, middle class, meaning from a communication is gleaned from the verbal message—a spoken explanation, a written letter, or a computer printout. *What* is said is generally more important than *who* said it. For example, employees in

ethnicity an attribute of membership in a group in which members identify themselves by national origin, culture, race, or religion

low-context macrosystem culture generally characterized by rationality, practicality, competition, individuality, and progress

high-context macrosystem culture generally characterized by intuitiveness, emotionality, cooperation, group identity, and tradition

Table 1.2

Worldviews

	LOW-CONTEXT MACROSYSTEMS	HIGH-CONTEXT MACROSYSTEMS
GENERAL CHARACTERISTICS	Rationality Practicality Competition Individuality Progress	Intuitiveness Emotionality Cooperation Group identity Tradition
SIGNIFICANT VALUES	Emphasis on concrete evidence and facts Efficient use of time Achievement Personal freedom Humans can control nature and influence the future Change is good	Emphasis on feelings Build solid relationships through human interaction Character Group welfare Nature and the future are governed by a power higher than human Stability is good

- What if these views represented two individuals wanting to marry?
- What if one view represented a teacher's and the other a student's?
- What if one view represented an employer's and the other an employee's?

government, business, or education routinely communicate by phone or memorandum without ever meeting the other individuals involved. In a high-context macrosystem, on the other hand, such as Native American, Hispanic American, Asian American, or rural United States, meaning from a communication is gleaned from the setting in which the communication takes place. For example, a Spanish-speaking person can communicate familiarity by whether he or she uses the formal or informal word for "you." A person raised in traditional Japanese culture can communicate degree of respect by how deeply he or she bows.

Relationship to Natural and Social Environment. In general, people in low-context macrosystems tend to try to control nature (for example, irrigating desert areas) and to have more fragmented social relations—that is, they may behave one way toward friends, another way toward business colleagues, and yet another way toward neighbors. Members of high-context macrosystems tend to live in harmony with nature and with other humans who are part of their social network. Whereas individuals in low-context macrosystems usually develop an identity based on their personal efforts and achievements, people in high-context macrosystems tend to gain their identity through group associations (lineage, place of work, organizations). Members of low-context cultures expect personal freedom, openness, and individual choice. Members of high-context cultures are less open to strangers, make distinctions between insiders and outsiders, and are more likely to follow traditional role expectations.

Adaptivity. Both low- and high-context macrosystems illustrate adaptiveness for human survival. Low-context cultures, valuing progress, provide ways of changing and using new knowledge that can benefit society; high-context cultures, valuing tradition, provide a strong human support network that helps guard against the alienation of a technological society. Different parenting styles influence the child's degree of interdependence on others and curiosity to explore new things.

On a daylong cruise to see the glaciers in Alaska, I had the opportunity to observe the contrast in parenting styles in a high- and low-context family. The high-context family consisted of a mother and father, a baby (about 10 months old), and a grandmother and grandfather. The baby was continually held and played with by one of the adults. She was kissed and jiggled and spoken to. There were no toys to amuse her. When it was lunchtime, the mother, after distributing the food she had brought to the adults, took some food from her plate, mashed it between her fingers, and put it in the baby's mouth. After lunch the grandmother and grandfather took turns rocking the baby to sleep. The baby never cried the whole day. The care she received fostered a sense of interdependence.

In contrast, the low-context family, consisting of a mother, a father, and a baby (about 15 months old), had brought a sack of toys for the baby to play with while the parents enjoyed the sights through a nearby window. After a while, the baby began to fuss; the father picked him up and brought him to the boat's window, pointing out seals and birds and glaciers. Later, when the baby tired of his toys, the mother held his hands and walked him around the deck. The baby was given crackers and a bottle to soothe him when he cried. The care he received fostered a sense of independence.

Interaction of Ecological Systems Over Time: The Chronosystem

What role does time play in how environmental conditions affect the child and how the child affects his or her environments?

The **chronosystem** involves temporal changes in ecological systems, or within individuals, producing new conditions that affect development. For example, changes in computer software technology may result in your having to purchase new equipm ent or having to learn different passwords for Internet access and security. For another example, significant societal events can produce a variety of effects on children. The school shootings at Columbine High School in Littleton, Colorado, affected many schools' on-campus security procedures; schools installed metal detectors, hired guards, and initiated "zero-tolerance" policies whereby aggressive students are expelled for one offense. Certainly, the fear for safety at school has increased. As a final example, the physical changes experienced during puberty can affect self-esteem, depending on how the child's developing body compares to his or her friends' as well as to the cultural ideal body type.

IMPACT OF SIGNIFICANT HISTORICAL EVENTS

To illustrate that changes in a macrosystem can result in changes in exosystems, mesosystems, and microsystems, sociologist Glen Elder (1974, 1979, 1998) and his colleagues (Elder & Hareven, 1993; Elder, Van Nguyen, & Casper, 1985) conducted a very thorough, longitudinal study of 167 California children born 1920–1929. They compared the life-course development of children whose

chronosystem temporal changes in ecological systems or within individuals, producing new conditions that affect development

families had experienced a change in their socioeconomic status during the Great Depression (a period of widespread economic insecurity in the United States) and those who had not. The immediate exosystem effect was loss of a job. This in turn caused emotional distress, which was experienced in the home and affected the children (effect on a microsystem). There were also secondary exosystem effects: In families hit by the Depression, the father lost status in the eyes of the children and the mother gained in importance. The affected father's parenting behavior became more rejecting, especially toward adolescent girls. Children, especially boys, from affected families expressed a stronger identification with the peer group. Children from affected families also participated more in domestic roles and outside jobs, with girls being more likely to do the former and boys the latter.

The fact that longitudinal data were available over a period of more than 60 years gave Elder the opportunity to assess the impact of childhood experience, within and outside the family, on behavior in later life (effects of chronosystem). He found that the long-term consequences of the Depression varied according to the age of the child at the time. Children who were preadolescents when their families suffered economic loss did less well in school, showed less stable and less successful work histories, and exhibited more emotional and social difficulties, even in adulthood, than did those of the same socioeconomic status from families who did not suffer economically. Such adverse effects have been explained (Conger, Xiaojia, Elder, Lorenz, Simons, & Whitebeck, 1994) as due to the impact of economic hardship on the quality of parenting and hence on the psychological well-being of children.

In contrast, those who were teenagers when the Depression hit their families did better in school, were more likely to go to college, had happier marriages, exhibited more successful work careers, and in general were more satisfied with life than youngsters of the same socioeconomic status who were not affected by the Depression. These favorable outcomes were more pronounced for teenagers from middle-socioeconomic-status backgrounds but were also evident among their lower-status counterparts.

Interestingly, adults whose families escaped economic ruin turned out to be less successful, both educationally and vocationally, than those whose families were deprived. Why was this so? According to Elder (1974):

> It seems that a childhood which shelters the young from the hardships of life consequently fails to develop or test adaptive capacities which are called upon in life crises. To engage and manage real-life (though not excessive) problems in childhood and adolescence is to participate in a sort of apprenticeship for adult life. Preparedness has been identified repeatedly as a key factor in the adaptive potential and psychological health of persons in novel situations. (pp. 249–250)

Thus, a major consequence of the Depression was that economic loss changed the relation of children to the family and the adult world by involving them in work that was necessary for the welfare of others. This early involvement contributed to deprived children's socialization for adulthood. Elder hypothesized that the loss of economic security forced the family to mobilize its human resources. Everyone had to take on new responsibilities.

With regard to the effect of today's abundance on the socialization of our youth, Elder (1974) expressed the following concern:

Since the Depression and especially World War II various developments have conspired to isolate the young from challenging situations in which they could make valuable contributions to family and community welfare. Prosperity, population concentration, industrial growth with its capital-intensive formula, and educational upgrading have led to an extension of the dependency years and increasing segregation of the young from the routine experiences of adults. In this consumption-oriented society, urban middle-class families have little use for the productive hands of offspring, and the same applies to community institutions. . . .

This society of abundance can and even must support "a large quota of nonproductive members," as it is presently organized, but should it tolerate the costs, especially among the young; the costs of not feeling needed, of being denied the challenge and rewards which come from meaningful contributions to a common endeavor? (pp. 291–293)

Elder's challenge calls for bringing adults back into the lives of children and children back into the lives of adults. His study shows how ecological change over time can have varying impacts on a child's socialization depending on other variables, such as the age and gender of the child, the existing family relationships, and the socioeconomic status of the family before the change, thereby illustrating the multiplicity of variables interacting to affect socialization.

IMPACT OF ONGOING EVENTS

Socialization must pass on the cultural heritage to the next generation while also enabling that generation to become competent adults in society. Thus, every socializing agent engages in preparing children for both stability and change. Training for stability, which is implemented by passing on the cultural heritage and the status quo to children, involves making their behavior somewhat predictable and conforming; but paradoxically, preparation for change, enabling children to become competent for a future society, very likely involves disrupting some stable patterns and encouraging new ways of thinking and behaving. The challenge of successful socialization in today's society, then, is to rear children to maintain certain values, morals, attitudes, behaviors, and roles while, at the same time, being adaptable to change, so that they will become responsible, caring, and competent human beings.

What is it that makes some people responsible for their actions and others not? Does the answer lie in the way they were socialized? Did the responsible individuals become that way because their parents were loving and these individuals grew up wanting to please them? Or were these individuals punished from a very early age when they did not behave responsibly (for example, did not call to say they would be home late)? Or were they trusted to take on tasks involving responsibility, such as babysitting, gardening, money management, and so on, at an early age and expected to take the consequences for their mistakes (not being hired again as a sitter or a gardener) as well as the rewards for their successes (more jobs, higher pay)? Did they have responsible adults to emulate, or did they spend most of their time with friends or watching television? Did their teachers have certain standards and demand responsibility (for example, homework to be turned in on time or not accepted), or were the standards and evaluation procedures vague?

We live in a society in which the lines of responsibility are often fuzzy. Years ago, if I got sick, I was responsible for paying the doctor. Today it is primarily my insurance company's responsibility (my employee benefits include health coverage). Years ago, when a carpenter was hired to build some cabinets, the carpenter took responsibility for the quality of materials and work. Today, because of diversification and specialization, it is rare for one person to be responsible for a whole job—there is the bank that may loan money for the materials, the lumberyard that supplies the materials, and the delivery trucks that bring the materials to the lumberyard and to the customer. If a job is not completed on time, perhaps it is due to the bank's taking longer than expected to approve the loan, or the lumberyard's ordering the wrong materials, or the delivery trucks' not operating because of a union strike. Who is really responsible?

Do the technological advances in society, then, lessen responsibility? How are children affected by such advances? Children experience toys that do not work as they were advertised, textbooks that do not arrive on time, adults who abdicate responsibility (do not pay child support, become substance abusers, or simply do not care). So children who may be reared to be responsible—by their families, their religion, their culture, their school—are still exposed to many situations in which irresponsibility is evident. Some situations even seem to reward irresponsibility. For example, people who default on their bills may be able to get a loan to pay them, as well as being able to deduct from their taxes the interest on certain loans. As one can see, the outcomes of socialization influenced by microsystems and mesosystems are extremely complicated, and they become even more so when we also consider the ongoing effects of change on a child's exosystems and macrosystems.

Contemporary Ecology

What are some societal trends affecting children?

Some contemporary societal trends (Naisbitt & Auburdene, 1990; Toffler Associates Inc., 2000–2003) affecting the future of families and children are discussed in the following paragraphs.

Biotechnology. Genetic engineering can potentially cure inherited diseases by substituting normal genes for defective ones; but what about using such techniques to increase intelligence? Will children have "designer" genes? Assisted reproductive techniques (sperm donation, egg donation, in-vitro fertilization, frozen embryos, surrogacy) enable adults who have fertility problems to become parents; but what about medical, legal, and ethical risks? For example, if a male and female contribute sperm and egg for conception to take place in a dish, several resulting embryos are frozen, one or two are implanted in a surrogate who is paid to carry through with the pregnancy, and the biological parents die, to whom do the babies and embryos belong? What makes one a parent—genes, prenatal environment, postnatal environment?

Reconceptualization of Societal and Individual Responsibilities. Political ideology is shifting from "paternalistic" policies (a strong authority takes care of less able citizens) to "empowerment" policies (any individual can learn to care for him- or herself). For example, government welfare support is waning while "workfare" is waxing. Government funding of Social Security plans is yielding to private insurance and investment programs. How will children whose parents must become more economically responsible be affected?

Information Technology The concept of information technology (IT) is broadening to include not only traditional computer hardware and software but also a wide range of communication tools (such as cell phones, palm pilots, and scanners), media (such as television, cameras, and recorders), and data. Wireless networks allow users to work, play, and shop anytime, anyplace. For businesses, operations can be streamlined and efficiency increased by enabling workers to make plans, make decisions, and generate sales reports without going to the office. For consumers, mobile commerce offers the ability to shop for tickets, books, or pizza while waiting on line or at the doctor's office. People can download music, videos, and games, also on handheld devices. How do individuals cope with even more choices, advertising, and distractions? What about privacy issues, personal security, and information errors? Will IT foster closer connections among family and friends, or come between them, competing for time and space?

According to social forecaster John Naisbitt (2001), in his book *High Tech/High Touch*, technology has accelerated our lives at such a frenetic pace that we crave satisfaction and authenticity from human relationships. Naisbitt describes the ecosystem of technology:

> The introduction of any technology alters life, relationships, and societies, on a macro and micro level. We know from nature that the introduction of something new into a habitat—a new species, a climatic change—will alter most relationships within that habitat. But humans have introduced technology without thinking about how relationships will change, about what exactly will be enhanced, what will be displaced, what will be diminished. . . . High tech/high touch means what place technology should have in our lives and in society. (p. xv)

Globalism/Nationalism. Telecommunications and transportation facilitate a global economy. Labor, production, marketing, and consumption can occur in different places in the world. Do these changes—in competition for jobs, location of job, skills needed—affect the work families do?

As people throughout the world are exposed to greater homogeneity through travel, media, and telecommunications, they sometimes cling to their religious/ethnic traditions for identity. In *Jihad vs. McWorld* (Barber, 1996), the author defines *McWorld* as the "universe of manufactured needs, mass consumption, and mass infotainment." It is motivated by profits and consumer preferences. *Jihad*, or holy war, is shorthand for the "fundamentalist politics of religious, tribal, and other zealots." It is motivated by faith in a spirit that governs all aspects of life. The terrorist attacks in the United States on September 11, 2001, were an extreme example of the fanatically defended beliefs in spiritual determinism versus self-determination. How has the fear of terrorism changed our lives?

Shift in Decision-Making Responsibility. New advances in science, medicine, education, economics, communications, media, transportation,

HIRB/Index Stock Imagery

As technology increases, humans compensate by finding new ways to interact, as exemplified by beepers and cellular phones.

security, privacy, and ecology require skills to cope with massive amounts of information. Recently an exterminator asked me to decide which of several available pesticides should be used in my house to get rid of ants. Even though I was informed of the varying effectiveness and safety of each, I did not really have the appropriate background knowledge on which to base such a decision; yet the responsibility for consequences was shifted to me.

Another example is the shift in responsibility for children's learning. Children are subjected to standardized achievement testing. Schools and teachers are held accountable for children's learning in that political leaders make decisions regarding funding based on test scores—schools producing low scores are at risk of losing public funding. Does such a system influence teachers to "teach to the test" rather than the child?

Information Intermediaries. One way the business world has capitalized on today's information glut is to offer endorsements (celebrity), enticements (rewards), and services (consulting) to help consumers make decisions. When you buy a book, isn't it easier to choose one from "The New York Times Bestseller List" or "Amazon's Book Recommendations" than to read the jackets? Do you choose an airline because of its rewards program or the convenience of its schedules and destinations? Do you need to hire a wedding planner or an investment counselor?

A challenge resulting from these societal trends is the need to create caring communities in which children can learn to think—to apply, analyze, synthesize, and evaluate information, not just regurgitate facts (Fiske, 1992). The ability to think and use knowledge becomes critical in a world plugged into machines and bombarded with information and choices (Postman, 1992). Because of new technology and new information, children will have to learn to solve problems not previously encountered. They will have to extrapolate from previous experiences. How will we teach them?

IN PRACTICE

Ecology in Action: A Reality Show

How did Michael Jackson, one of the most successful African American popular music singers of all time, go from superstar to suspect?

While Michael Jackson's singing career has gained him legions of devoted fans, his changing physical appearance and "eccentric" lifestyle have made him fodder for the media. He has been subjected to repeated accusations of sexual abuse of children, all of which he denies. Recently, he was acquitted of them in a court of law. Is Michael a product of his biology, his family, his community (including media and fans), societal change, or all of them and then some?

How can the ecological model can be applied to analyze Michael's behavior?

Microsystems

- What parenting styles characterized Michael's *parents*?
- How was Michael treated by his *siblings*?

- How would Michael's *peer* relations be described?
- What was the effect on Michael of being in the *media* limelight early in life?

Mesosystems

- What *links to role models* were available and significant in Michael's childhood?
- What *links to opportunities* were available to explore activities other than music?

Exosystems

- What sort of pressures from *work* (the recording business) affected Michael?

Macrosystems

- To what *values—moral, religious, cultural*—was Michael exposed?

Chronosystem

- What was the effect on Michael's self-esteem *over time* of his childhood experiences as well as his adult ones?

In sum, these contemporary societal trends affect how people use available resources—economic, social, and psychological—in their daily lives. Next, we examine ecological trends specific to children and the impact on their well-being.

What is happening to U.S. children today?

- Children as a proportion of the population has decreased.
- The proportion of children with mothers in the labor force has grown dramatically.
- The proportion of children living with both biological parents has declined while those living in single-parent families has grown.
- The number of children with parents who divorce and remarry has risen. The effects of divorce on children are often long-lasting.
- The number of children who are abused or neglected has increased.
- Children are more likely than other age groups to live in poverty. Children under age 6 living in a female-householder family are particularly at risk. Poor children are more likely to have health problems and physical or mental disabilities.
- The number of children who have no health insurance has increased.
- Low birth weight and infant mortality have increased.
- The number of overweight children ages 6–18 has increased.
- There is wider acknowledgment of cultural diversity.
- Children with disabilities must be included in educational programs for all children.
- Fewer children ages 3–5 are attending early childhood education programs. (Children's Defense Fund, 2004; Federal Interagency Forum on Child and Family Statistics, 2004)

What is being done to address children's well-being?

To monitor the effects of change on children, the federal government has issued a report, *America's Children: Key National Indicators of Well-Being, 2004* (Federal Interagency Forum on Child and Family Statistics, 2004), showing the overall status of the nation's children. Political leaders use the following indicators to make decisions regarding what services for children will be funded and what new programs need to be developed to address their needs. Examples of such services will be discussed in Chapter 10.

- **Population and family characteristics** document the number of children as a proportion of the population, racial and ethnic composition, family structure and children's living arrangements, births to unmarried women, and child care.
- **Economic security indicators** document poverty and income among children and basic necessities such as housing, food, and health care.
- **Health indicators** document the physical health and well-being of children, including immunizations and probability of death at various ages.
- **Behavior and social environment indicators** document the number of youths who are engaged in illegal, dangerous, or high-risk behaviors such as smoking, drinking alcohol, using drugs, or committing violent crimes.
- **Education indicators** document success in educating the nation's children, including preschool, reading, overall achievement, completion of high school, and college attendance.

James Garbarino, professor and author of *Raising Children in a Socially Toxic Environment* (1995b), believes that government and business need to do more to optimize children's well-being. He asserts that violence, drugs, uncaring communities, poverty, abusive families, and custody battles are poisoning children's lives and are responsible for the less-than-optimal well-being of America's children. As pollution has toxified our physical environment, our social environment is being toxified by the breakdown of family and community support systems, resulting in alienation, depression, vengeance, and/or paranoia.

Violence in the community is a reality many children face.

© Michael Newman/PhotoEdit

According to Garbarino (1995b), society must revise its conception of childhood; childhood should be viewed as "the social space in which to lay the foundation for the best that human development has to offer" (p. 12). All children should "be shielded from the direct demands of adult economic, political, and sexual forces" (p. 8). Children have a right to be protected from poverty. They have a right to be protected from excessive consumerism and commercial advertising that preys upon their immaturity. They have a right to be protected by laws against situations deemed harmful.

Garbarino discusses what can be done to strengthen children's "social space":

- Children need stability; government and business must therefore have policies that are supportive of families, such as personal leaves.
- Children need security; law enforcement policies must therefore ensure that their physical and social environments are safe from violence.
- Children need affirmation and acceptance; they must therefore have opportunities to spend time with caring adults who enable them to be part of the larger community and who give them a sense of values and spirituality.

Epilogue

The Cherokee folktale at the beginning of this chapter illustrates how organisms adapt to survive in changing environments. To survive, humans hunted and fished. In turn, the animals and fish developed poisons in the hope of stopping humans from killing them. Humans then turned to the plants for a remedy. The plants provided the needed resources to enable the earth's inhabitants to attain balance and harmony. This process is the gist of ecology.

Summary

Ecology involves studying humans in their physical, social, and cultural environments, all of which are affected by societal change. The purpose of this book is to examine how growing up in a changing world affects the development of children via socialization—the process by which individuals acquire the knowledge, skills, and character traits that enable them to participate as effective members of groups and society.

Socialization is unique to humans because of our capacity for language. Language enables us to communicate ideas; it lets us replace action with thought and then use thought to transform behavior. Self-regulation and self-control come from the internalization of thoughts.

Socialization begins at birth and continues throughout life. Biological factors (genetics, maturation, temperament) influence developmental outcomes. Socialization occurs through human interaction; it is reciprocal, or bidirectional, with children playing a role in their own socialization. Thus, genotype–environment interactions also affect developmental outcomes. Socialization may be intentional or unintentional.

Society's concept of childhood has changed over time. The period of protection for children has gone from being short during the Renaissance to long during the Industrial Revolution. As societal pressures increase, many fear that today's concept of the period of childhood will have to be adjusted.

When societal change occurs, the agents that socialize children are affected and children bear the consequences. The agents of socialization are the family, the school, the peer group, the media, and the community. These agents employ different socialization techniques. Children play a transactional role in their own socialization, too, eliciting different techniques as they develop. Generally, however, "outputs" of socialization (values, attitudes, attributions, motives, self-regulation of behavior, morals, gender roles, self-esteem) are affected by "inputs" (reinforcement, instruction, learning-by-doing, competitive strategies, cooperative strategies).

A theory is an organized set of statements that explains observations, integrates different facts and events, and predicts future outcomes. Theories provide a framework for research. Bronfenbrenner's model of human ecology—the child's development in microsystems, mesosystems, exosystems, and macrosystems, with relationships and interactions that take place over time (the chronosystem)—is the framework used in this book to explain socialization processes and outcomes.

The microsystem is the immediate small setting where the child is at a particular time. The mesosystem consists of the intermediate interrelationships between two or more of a person's microsystems. The exosystem refers to outside settings in which children do not actually participate, but that affect them in one of their microsystems. The macrosystem refers to the larger society and its ideology in which a child grows up. Macrosystems can be classified as high context or low context, each type having different influences on a person's perspectives on the world. The chronosystem refers to changes in ecological systems as well as in individuals producing new conditions that affect development.

Effects of change in the macrosystem on exosystems, mesosystems, and microsystems are exemplified in Elder's study comparing families who were deprived during the Depression and those who were not. A major influence for children growing up in deprived families was their involvement in the adult world of work necessary for the welfare of others. The long-term consequences of the Depression were found to depend on the gender and age of the child, the existing family relationships, and the socioeconomic status of the family at the time when economic hardship hit.

The interaction of micro-, meso-, exo-, and macrosystems over time make socialization very complex. The challenge is to pass on the cultural heritage to the next generation while also enabling that generation to adapt to change.

Contemporary societal trends affecting children include biotechnology, reconceptualization of societal and individual responsibility, a shift in decision-making responsibility, information technology, and globalism/nationalism. Accompanying societal change are consequences for children's well-being, such as being exposed to an increasingly socially toxic environment. For parents and other adults to fulfill their commitments and caring roles, they need support from government and business.

Activity

PURPOSE To understand the impact of change (chronosystem) on microsystems and mesosystems.

1. Describe one to three changes you observed:
   - In your family as you grew up
   - In your school
   - In your peer group
   - In the media—television or books
   - In your community

2. Pick one change for each microsystem and discuss:
   - Why you think it occurred
   - How it affected you
   - What impact, if any, it had on the other microsystems (mesosystem)

Related Readings

Aries, P. (1962). *Centuries of childhood: A social history of family life*. New York: Knopf.

Bremner, R. H. (1971). *Children and youth in America: A documentary history*. Cambridge, MA: Harvard University Press.

Bronfenbrenner, U. (1979). *The ecology of human development*. Cambridge, MA: Harvard University Press.

Campbell, J. (1968). *The hero with a thousand faces* (2nd ed.). Princeton, NJ: Princeton University Press.

Chess, S., & Thomas, A. (1987). *Know your child*. New York: Basic Books.

Cleverly, J., & Philips, D. C. (1986). *Visions of childhood: Influential models from Locke to Spock*. New York: Teachers College Press.

Elkind, D. (1998). *Reinventing childhood*. Rosemont, NJ: Modern Learning Press.

Garbarino, J. (1995). *Raising children in a socially toxic environment*. San Francisco: Jossey-Bass.

Moen, P., Elder, G. H., Jr., & Luscher, K. (Eds.). (1995). *Examining lives in context: Perspectives on the ecology of human development*. Washington, DC: American Psychological Association.

Naisbitt, J. (2001). *High tech/high touch: Technology and our accelerated search for meaning*. London, UK: Nicholas Brealey.

Plomin, R., DeFries, J. C., McClearn, G. E., & McGuffin, P. (2001). Behavioral genetics (4th ed.). New York: Worth.

Postman, N. (1992). *Technopoly: The surrender of culture to technology*. New York: Vintage.

Skinner, B. F. (1948). *Walden two*. New York: Macmillan.

Chapter 2

FogStock, LLC/Index Stock Imagery

Ecology of Socialization

The childhood shows the man, as morning shows the day.

— JOHN MILTON

The quote from John Milton suggests that the paths of childhood lead to maturity. These paths or challenges are exemplified by the developmental tasks (discussed in this chapter) to be accomplished by each child in order to become a man or a woman.

The following Italian classic children's tale, *The Adventures of Pinocchio* by Carlo Collodi (1882/1972), illustrates the trials and tribulations of a little boy growing up and the agents who contribute to his socialization.

Once Upon a Time there was a woodcutter named Gepetto who wants a son very much, so he carves a little boy out of a block of wood and names him Pinocchio. When Gepetto goes to sleep, the Blue Fairy appears and gives the wooden boy life.

The Blue Fairy tells Pinocchio that if he wants to become a real boy, he must prove himself to be brave, truthful, and unselfish: "Be a good son to Gepetto—make him proud of you! Then, some day, you will wake up and find yourself a real boy."

However, the Blue Fairy warns Pinocchio that the world is full of temptations and that he must learn to choose between right and wrong in order to become human. Pinocchio asks how he will know the difference. The Blue Fairy explains he must rely on his conscience to tell him. Pinocchio, who does not know what a conscience is, remains perplexed. Fortunately, a little cricket, Jiminy Cricket, who had been observing the whole scene, volunteers to serve as Pinocchio's conscience. The Blue Fairy leaves Pinocchio in Jiminy Cricket's hands, asking him to give Pinocchio the benefit of his advice and experience.

The story of Pinocchio tells of his adventures and inability to resist temptation. One time he starts off to school, but sells his books in order to go to a marionette show. Another time he wanders off and meets with thieves, who steal his money and try to kill him. He is saved by the Blue Fairy, who then puts a spell on him that makes his nose grow long every time he tells a lie—which is supposed to remind Pinocchio not to do wrong. Eventually, however, Pinocchio succumbs to the temptation of going off to Playland, where boys can be lazy and play all day. There he finds out that laziness can last for just so long. Good-for-nothing boys end up making jackasses of themselves. Without Jiminy Cricket, who helps him escape from Playland before it is too late, Pinocchio would have turned completely into a jackass.

Full of remorse, Pinocchio searches for Gepetto, only to find out that the woodcarver has been swallowed by a whale, and the boy goes to sea to save him. Pinocchio vows to work hard at his studies to become someone of whom Gepetto can be proud. Pinocchio has learned that to be human is to make mistakes; but to be worthy, one must correct them. Because Pinocchio has risked his life, thereby demonstrating bravery and unselfishness, the Blue Fairy turns him into a real boy. And so Pinocchio finally becomes socialized into the human race.

The story of Pinocchio's struggle to become a real boy parallels any child's struggle to become socialized, hence its timelessness. The Blue Fairy's warnings are like those of any parent. Jiminy Cricket's advice is like that of a teacher. Pinocchio's adventures with the lazy boys are like those with one's peer group. Finally, Pinocchio's triumph of learning the difference between good and evil represents a most significant outcome of socialization—a conscience.

- Why did Pinocchio finally put others' desires before his own (giving up the pleasures and freedom of play for the hard work and responsibilities of school)?
- Was the change in Pinocchio's behavior motivated by his love for Gepetto? the fear of punishment? the desire to be rewarded by the Blue Fairy? Did he learn from his experiences?
- What role did self-determination, or choice, play in Pinocchio's transformation?

Socialization Processes

How do you get a helpless infant to eventually become a contributing adult?

This chapter explores the process of socialization, including its aims or goals, its agents, their methods, and its outcomes. Figure 2.1 shows an ecological model of the bidirectional interactive systems involved in the process. Because socialization outcomes are affected by many variables (biological, sociocultural, interactional), they will be discussed more specifically in the concluding chapters.

In the past, socialization research focused on the effect of forces *outside* the child (for example, the influence of significant adults on the child's moral development) or forces *inside* the child (for example, the influence of unconscious motives on aggressive behavior). Today, because of advances in computer and medical technology as well as the increase in collaborative activities among diverse disciplines, socialization processes have come to be regarded as dynamic and reciprocal—dynamic in that the aims and methods change as does the child; reciprocal in that the child contributes to his or her own developmental outcomes.

Socialization processes are affected by biological, sociocultural, and interactive factors such as individual life history (Bugental, 2000). Biological factors (genetics, evolution, hormones) are thought to influence basic neural circuitry of the brain during early development. These connections, referred to as **experience-expectant**, develop under genetic influence independent of experience, activity, or stimulation (Bruer & Greenough, 2001). For example, our brains are equipped at birth to receive visual, auditory, tactile, and other stimuli from the environment. One-month-old infants can distinguish different speech sounds and prefer to listen to sounds falling within the frequency range of the human voice (Aslin, Jusczyk, & Pisoni, 1998).

Sociocultural factors are also thought to influence the development of brain neural circuitry. These connections, referred to as **experience-dependent**, develop in response to experience. This mutual facilitation between the environment and the brain is thought to be significant in learning to adapt (Bruer & Greenough, 2001). For example, a child's language development depends on being spoken to and participating in conversation, beginning with eye contact, then babbling, single words, and finally sentences.

experience-expectant the neural connections that develop under genetic influence, independent of experience, activity, or stimulation

experience-dependent the neural connections that develop in response to experience

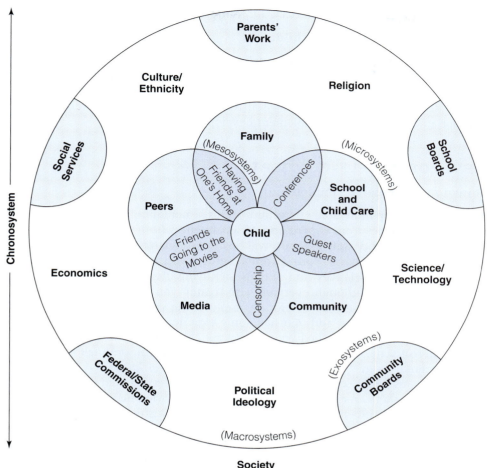

Figure 2.1

An Ecological Model of Human Development

Socialization involves bidirectional interactions between the child and significant others in microsystems, mesosystem links, exosystems, macrosystems, and over time (the chronosystem).

Interactional, or individual life history, factors involve the child's receptivity to socialization. For example, a child with a difficult temperament may react rebelliously to parental demands for compliance (Dodge & Pettit, 2003). For another example, a child exposed to extreme stress, such as maltreatment, war, or natural disaster, may be at risk for developmental problems (Chisholm, 1998); or the child may be resilient in the face of adversity (Rutter & O'Connor, 2004) because of his or her biology or supportive social networks in his or her life.

Parental Script Messages

What comes to mind, like a tape recording, when you think about what your parent(s) said about . . .

Doing work?   Fighting for what you believe is right?
Getting an education?   Achieving success?
Using money?   Developing talents?
Being sexual?

Aims of Socialization

What are society's goals for children?

Socialization enables children to learn what they need to know in order to be integrated into the society in which they live. It also enables children to develop their potentialities and form satisfying relationships. More specifically, socialization aims to develop a self-concept, enable self-regulation, empower achievement, teach appropriate social roles, and implement developmental skills.

DEVELOP A SELF-CONCEPT

How do you perceive yourself and why?

Self-concept is an individual's perception of his or her identity as distinct from that of others. It emerges from experiences of separateness from others. The value one places on that identity, **self-esteem**, will be discussed later in the chapter.

When you were born, your parents named you and may have sent out announcements to relatives and friends signifying that a new individual had entered the world. Although everyone else treated you as a separate being, you were unaware of where your environment ended and you began.

As the months passed and you had some experiences using your senses, you noticed that when you touched your hand you felt something in your fingers and hand, whereas when you touched your mother's hand, you only felt sensation in your fingers.

Gradually, as people met your needs, you realized they existed even when you could not see them. As you developed language, you learned that objects have names and so did you, and each had an independent existence. Language enabled you to describe and compare. Sometime around 15 to 18 months, you put it together and understood that you are you. You could recognize yourself in a mirror. You could assert your wants ("Me do it!"), especially when you perceived that someone else was controlling you.

As you got older, your concept of self—your identity, your understanding of who you are—was influenced by significant others. If your needs were met consistently and you were given opportunities to discover things on your own, you developed a sense of autonomy, or self-regulation and control. If, on the other hand, your needs were not met consistently and you did not get to explore your environment, you developed a sense of doubt. These significant others also acted as a mirror. Your parents, teachers, and friends provided constant feedback on your achievements and failures. Thus, in developing a self-concept or identity, you also develop self-esteem.

As you entered adolescence, your self-concept included how you related to others. Being a member of a group was important to your identity. In the later part of adolescence, your self-concept expanded to include how you related to the larger community. Self-concept involves not only "who am I?" but "where am I going?" and "how will I get there?"

Charles Horton Cooley (1909/1964), one of the founders of sociology, observed that through the experiences of interacting with others, children begin to distinguish themselves from others. Children call themselves "I" or "me"—"I hungry," "Me go." As they begin to act independently, they gradually become aware that others are evaluating them, saying "Good boy/girl" or "No, don't do that." Thus, their behavior is being judged according to certain rules and standards. These rules and standards must be learned and understood before the individual is capable of

self-concept an individual's perception of his/her identity as distinct from others

self-esteem the value one places on his/her identity

self-evaluation. As children gradually learn these criteria, each develops a self-concept; this concept, which reflects the attitudes of others, is termed the "looking-glass self." George Herbert Mead (1934) referred to this gradually maturing way of looking at the self as the "generalized other." When children refer to themselves as "shy" or "hardworking," they have incorporated the standards of others into the description.

Thus, a self-concept develops when the attitudes and expectations of significant others with whom one interacts are incorporated into one's personality, making it possible to regulate one's behavior accordingly. One's perceived competence in self-regulation/control is part of one's self-esteem. Susan Harter (1998, 1999) studied various types of competence involved in self-esteem—behavioral, academic, physical, and social—which will be discussed in Chapter 11.

Psychologist Erik Erikson (1963, 1980) has explained the personality development of individuals as the outcome of their interactions in their social environment. He identified eight critical stages of psychosocial development in a human's life that affect the self-concept: trust versus mistrust, autonomy versus shame and doubt, initiative versus guilt, industry versus inferiority, identity versus identity diffusion, intimacy versus isolation, generativity versus self-absorption, and integrity versus despair (see Figure 2.2). How one copes with these normal challenges at one stage of development affects one's ability to overcome difficulties in the next stages.

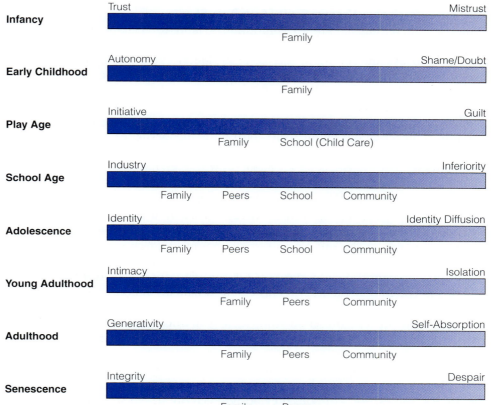

Figure 2.2

Erikson's Stages of Psychosocial Development

Note that an individual's development could be described as being at any point on the horizontal dimension lines, rather than at one extreme or the other. The importance of interactions with one's social environment in the development of a self-concept is indicated by the socializing agents that are most significant at various stages.

Infancy: Trust Versus Mistrust (Birth to Age 1)

The first "task" of infants is to develop the "cornerstone of a healthy personality"—a basic sense of trust in themselves and of the people in their environment. The quality and consistency of care the infant receives determines the successful outcome of this stage. A child whose basic needs for nourishment and physical contact are met will develop a sense of trust. This sense of trust lays a foundation for positive self-esteem. A child whose care is negligent or inconsistent will develop a sense of mistrust, which may persist throughout life and result in negative self-esteem. Some mistrust, however is healthy in that it can guard against danger and manipulation. Contemporary research shows a positive relationship between parental nurturance and self-worth (Harter, 1998, 1999; Hopkins & Klein, 1994).

Early Childhood: Autonomy Versus Shame and Doubt (Age 2 to 3)

Physical and cognitive maturation enables children to behave autonomously—to walk without help, feed themselves, get things off the shelf, assert themselves verbally. If children are allowed to be self-sufficient according to their ability, the outcome of this stage will be a feeling of autonomy. If children are deprived of the opportunity to develop a will, if they are continually being corrected or reprimanded, later they may feel shame when being assertive and self-doubt when being independent. However, some shame is healthy in that it can prevent certain socially unacceptable behaviors such as picking one's nose in public.

Play Age: Initiative Versus Guilt (Age 3 to 5)

Children's increasing ability to communicate and to imagine leads them to initiate many activities. If they are allowed to create their own games and fantasies, to ask questions, to use certain objects (a hammer and wood, for example) with supervision, then the outcome of this stage will be a feeling of initiative. If they are made to feel that they are "bad" for trying new things and "pests" for asking questions, they may carry a sense of guilt throughout life. Probably the reason "Pinocchio" has remained a favorite story is that, like all children, Pinocchio was continually learning which activities he initiated were OK and which ones were not. Thus, some guilt is healthy in that it can control misbehavior.

School Age: Industry Versus Inferiority (Age 6 to Puberty)

During school age, while learning to accept instruction and to win recognition by showing effort and by producing "things," the child is developing the capacity to enjoy work. The outcome of this stage for children who do not receive recognition for their efforts, or who do not experience any success, may be a feeling of incompetence and inferiority. Children who are praised for their efforts will be motivated to achieve, whereas children who are ignored or rebuked may give up and exhibit helplessness. Yet, some feelings of inferiority are healthy in that they can prevent the child from feeling invincible and taking dangerous risks.

Adolescence: Identity Versus Identity Diffusion (Puberty to Age 18 +)

With rapid growth and sexual maturity, the young person begins to question people, things, values, and attitudes previously relied on and to struggle through the crises of earlier stages all over again. The developmental task during adolescence, then, is to integrate earlier childhood identifications with biological and social changes occurring during this time. The danger in this stage is that while young people are trying out many roles, which is a normal process, they may be unable to choose an identity or make a commitment and so will not know who they are or what they may become (identity diffusion). Because adolescence is a time for exploration, some diffusion is healthy in that it can allow for learning what is suitable and what is not for an individual.

Young Adulthood: Intimacy Versus Isolation (Age 18+ to Middle Adulthood)

Individuals who have succeeded in establishing an identity are now able to establish intimacy with themselves and with others, in both friendship and love. The danger here is that those who fear losing their identity in an intimate relationship with another may develop a sense of isolation. Some isolation is healthy, however, in that it can enable one to learn about oneself and provide time for individual pursuits.

Adulthood: Generativity Versus Self-Absorption (Middle Adulthood to Late Adulthood)

From the development of intimate relationships comes **generativity**, an interest in establishing and guiding the next generation. This interest can be manifested by becoming a parent; by being involved with the development of young people through teaching, religion, Scouts, or other means; or through productivity and creativity in one's work. In this stage, a lack of generativity may result in self-absorption, which may show up as depression, hypochondria, substance abuse, or promiscuity. Yet, some self-absorption is healthy in that it can lead to creativity and the development of hobbies.

Senescence: Integrity Versus Despair (Late Adulthood to Death)

The individual who has achieved an identity, has developed a satisfying intimacy with others, and has adapted to the joys and frustrations of guiding the next generation reaches the end of life with a certain ego integrity or positive self-esteem—an acceptance of responsibility for what one's own life is and was and where it fits in the continuum of life. For those who have not achieved that integrity, this stage may produce despair or extremely negative self-esteem.

generativity interest in establishing and guiding the next generation

Despairing individuals tend to be in ill health, to abuse drugs and/or alcohol, or to commit suicide. They may become burdens to their families physically, financially, or psychologically. On the other hand, individuals with a sense of integrity are likely to have friends, to be active (physically and mentally), and to look at life positively even though they know that death is imminent. Exemplifying an integral self-concept, or sense of integrity, Rose Kennedy, who lived to be 104, said before she died, "I find it interesting to reflect on what has made my life, even with its moments of pain, an essentially happy one; I have come to the conclusion that the most important element in human life is faith" (Goldman, 1994, p. 20). Probably the only characteristic of despair that could be considered healthy is that which leads to change or greater appreciation of life.

HIRB/Index Stock Imagery

A sense of initiative is influenced by having opportunities to produce things.

ENABLE SELF-REGULATION

How did you learn to control your feelings and behavior?

Self-regulation involves the ability to control one's impulses, behavior, and/or emotions until an appropriate time, place, or object is available for expression. This can be interpreted as routing our feelings through our brains before acting on them according to the situation. Regulated behavior often involves postponing or modifying immediate gratification for the sake of a future goal. This implies being able to tolerate frustration. For example, you curb your urge to spank a child who has just thrown a plate of food on the floor in a tantrum because you want to set an example of how to deal with frustration. When you are trying to maintain your weight, you postpone satisfying those hunger pangs until mealtime. You postpone sexual intercourse until marriage because of your religious or personal goals. Even though you hate to wake up early, you set your alarm in order to be at work on time because your supervisor depends on you.

Early relationships, especially attachment to parents, play a significant role in the development of emotional regulation (Bridges & Golnick, 1995; Eisenberg, 2002) and "emotional intelligence" (Goleman, 1995). As the child progresses from infancy to childhood, emotional and behavioral regulation gradually shifts from external socializing agents to internal, self-induced mechanisms (Eisenberg, 1998). Caregivers provide children with information (body language, facial expressions, verbal instructions and explanations) to help them deal with situations. As children develop cognitively and have more real experiences, they learn how to interpret events and how to express emotions appropriately. They develop strategies for coping with disappointment, frustration, rejection, and anger. Self-regulation/control is related to moral development, an outcome of socialization to be discussed in Chapter 12.

EMPOWER ACHIEVEMENT

How did you decide what you were going to do as an adult?

Socialization furnishes goals for what you are going to be when you become an adult—a teacher, a police officer, a business executive. These goals provide the rationale for going to school, getting along with others, following rules, and so on. In other words, socialization gives meaning or purpose to adulthood and to the long process a child has to go through to get there. In order for Pinocchio to become a real boy, he had to go to school as well as learn right from wrong.

Significant adults and peers influence one's motivation to succeed. For example, adults who understand child development and provide the appropriate challenge at the "right" time with the "right" amount of support are likely to produce highly competent and motivated children (Eccles, Wigfield, & Schiefele, 1998). The motive to achieve and attributions of achievement (explanations for success and failure) are among the socialization outcomes discussed later in the chapter.

TEACH APPROPRIATE SOCIAL ROLES

How do we learn to act according to what is required in different social settings?

self-regulation the ability to control one's impulses, behavior, and/or emotions until an appropriate time, place, or object is available for expression

In order to be part of a group, one has to have a function that complements the group. For example, in a group of employees, the supervisor's function or role is to lead the employees; in a family group, the parents' role is to nurture the child; in a peer group, the role of friends is to provide emotional support. We have many social roles throughout life, some of which occur simultaneously, and we must assume the appropriate behavior for each at the appropriate time. I am a wife, a parent, a child, a teacher, and a friend—all at the same time. As a wife, I am a confidante; as a parent, I am nurturant; as a child, I am submissive; as a teacher, I am a facilitator; as a friend, I am emotionally supportive.

Gender is a social role, too, in that boys and girls learn gender-appropriate behavior from significant members of their society (Ruble & Martin, 1998; McHale, Crouter, & Whiteman, 2003). What is appropriate (Maccoby, 2000) is affected by culture, ethnicity, and religion (macrosystem influences), as well as time (chronosystem influence).

IMPLEMENT DEVELOPMENTAL SKILLS

How do you meet your own needs while accommodating to society's expectations?

Socialization aims to provide social, emotional, and cognitive skills to children so that they can function successfully in society. Social skills may involve learning how to obtain information from other people, use the telephone, or conduct business negotiations. Emotional skills may involve controlling aggressive impulses, learning to deal with frustration by substituting another goal for one that is blocked, or being able to compensate for mistakes. Cognitive skills may include reading, mathematics, writing, problem solving, geography, history, and science.

Niyati Reeves/Getty Images

This child is having difficulty controlling his temper.

Psychologist Robert Havighurst (1972) examined how society's expectations with regard to certain behavioral skills change according to the maturation of the individual (chronosystem influence), using the term *developmental task* to explain this aspect of socialization. According to Havighurst, "a **developmental task** is midway between an individual need and a societal demand." The developmental tasks of life are those things one must learn if one is to get along well in society (macrosystem influence). As we grow, we develop physically, intellectually, and socially. Our physical development will enable us to walk, control our bladders, and use a pencil. Our intellectual development will enable us to learn to read, do arithmetic, and solve problems. Our social development will enable us to cooperate, empathize, and interact with others. And our emotional development will enable us to regulate our impulses and express our feelings. Developmental tasks categorized according to societal demands for certain behaviors are listed below; how they change for the individual from birth to death can be found on the *Child, Family, School, Community* companion website at http://www.thomsonedu.com//berns.

1. Achieving an appropriate dependence/independence pattern
2. Achieving an appropriate giving–receiving pattern of affection
3. Relating to changing social groups
4. Developing a conscience
5. Learning one's "psychosociobiological" role

developmental task a task that lies between an individual need and a societal demand

6. Accepting and adjusting to a changing body
7. Managing a changing body and learning new behavioral patterns
8. Learning to understand and control the physical world
9. Developing an appropriate symbol system and conceptual abilities
10. Relating oneself to the cosmos

As we develop along these dimensions, we face new expectations from significant socializing agents in the surrounding society. We are expected to learn to walk, talk, use the toilet, and dress ourselves. We are expected to read, write, add, and subtract. We are expected to share, develop a conscience, and achieve an appropriate gender role. We are expected to love other people and be responsible for our actions.

Thus, developmental tasks arise from societal pressures on individuals according to their development: "If the task is not achieved at the proper time, it will not be achieved well, and failure in this task will cause partial or complete failure in the achievement of other tasks yet to come" (Havighurst, 1972, p. 3). If children do not have experiences in language, such as being spoken to and making sounds during the critical stage of language development (first year), their ability to communicate will be handicapped for the remainder of their lives. A child who is not socialized to develop a conscience may engage in delinquent behavior in adolescence. A child who does not have experiences receiving and giving affection may not succeed in a marriage or family relationship.

Those who do not succeed in a developmental task face the disapproval of others because they have not behaved as expected. As a reminder of the Blue Fairy's disapproval, Pinocchio's nose grew long whenever he did not tell the truth. Developmental tasks differ from society to society, and each group in a society has its own developmental definitions and expectations. For example, a common developmental milestone for Euro-American, middle-class infants is to "sleep through the night." This expectation is usually fulfilled by about age 4 to 6 months and is often facilitated by parents' feeding the baby just before they go to sleep and/or playing with the baby and putting him or her to sleep for the night as late as possible. However, in many other ethnic groups, in which the infant sleeps with the mother and nurses on demand, "sleeping through the night" is not pushed as a developmental milestone.

Differences in developmental definitions and expectations may account for some of the social adjustment problems in school among children from diverse ethnic or cultural groups. For example, the developmental task for achieving an appropriate dependence/independence pattern may be interpreted differently by various groups. Most middle-class American mothers, as well as American teachers, expect children to be independent of adults by school age in that they can take care of personal needs and learn on their own with some directions. Japanese mothers, on the other hand, expect some of their child's dependency needs to be transferred to the teacher when the child goes to school, and Japanese mothers generally remain very involved in their child's learning throughout school. Hispanic and Hawaiian mothers expect their child's dependency needs to be transferred to older siblings, and interdependence, rather than independence, is encouraged. Thus, Japanese, Hispanic, Hawaiian, and children from other high-context cultures may experience conflicts between developmental skills taught by their families and those taught in American schools (Bennett, 2003).

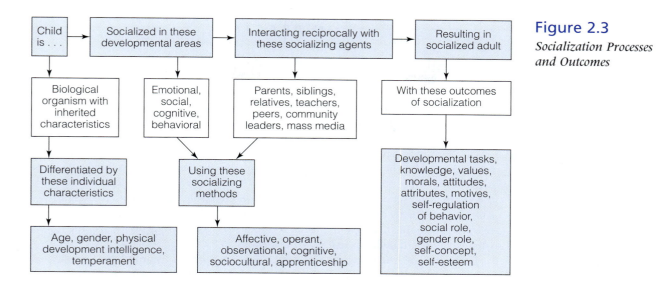

Figure 2.3

Socialization Processes and Outcomes

Every individual in a society is the outcome of the process of socialization (along with his or her genetic traits). The success of this outcome in terms of society's expectations will depend on a series of interactions with significant socializing agents, such as parents, teachers, peers, and media, that constitute the community in which this individual lives (Collins et al., 2000). Figure 2.3 illustrates the processes and outcomes of socialization.

Agents of Socialization

Who shaped you?

The generalized community is made up of many groups that play a part in socializing an individual. These agents of socialization exert their influence in different ways and at different times.

In the early years, the family assumes the primary role of nurturing the child. As the child gets older, the peer group becomes a primary source of support. In primitive societies, training for competency occurs in the family in the form of learning to hunt or build a shelter, whereas in industrial societies it occurs in the school in the form of learning to read, write, compute, and master a wide range of subject matter.

Each agent has its own functions in socialization. Sometimes the agents complement each other; sometimes they contradict each other. The value of getting along with others is usually taught in the family, the school, the religious community, the peer group, and perhaps in the media, with the agents complementing each other. The value of academic achievement, however, may be supported by some families and the school, but scorned by the peer group—an example of contradiction among the agents of socialization. The media and the peer group may support sexual experimentation, while the family and religious group condemn it.

IN PRACTICE

Socializing Agents and Their Messages: The Reality

Typical American children start the day with some instructions and expectations from their parents about finishing breakfast, setting an after-school schedule, cleaning their rooms, and so on. A few additional remarks may be added by older siblings regarding the condition of the bathroom when they went to use it.

On the way to school the bus driver may refuse to allow loud talking or changing seats once the bus has begun moving. At school, one teacher may stress independence and competition, and another may emphasize cooperation and dependence on the group. After school, teachers may assume different roles, perhaps as coaches or club leaders. The team or club members may value the best athlete or the one who sells the most raffle tickets, but in the classroom setting peers may dislike the one who gets the best grades or reads the most books.

Back at home, the television sends messages via the various programs. One day a child may watch *Sesame Street* and feel empathic and altruistic. Another day the child may watch *Spiderman* and come away feeling powerful and aggressive. Video or computer games provide for the interactive expression of emotions without real adult involvement.

In reality, children receive many demands from socializing agents as well as conflicting messages. As we discussed in Chapter 1, the process of socialization is reciprocal and dynamic, with children playing a role in their own socialization. A child's temperament—the innate characteristics that determine an individual's sensitivity to various experiences and responsiveness to patterns of social interaction—can elicit different reactions in caregivers. For example, a relaxed, happy baby tends to elicit smiles; a tense, crying baby tends to elicit concern or anxiety. As children develop and change, so, too, do others' reactions to them. My son and I have similar temperaments, which made the management of socialization goals and methods easier than for my daughter, whose temperament is different from mine. What role do you think your temperament played in the bidirectionality of socialization interactions in your family?

FAMILY

How did your family contribute to who you are?

The family is the child's introduction to society and has, therefore, borne the major responsibility for socializing the child. The family into which a child is born places the child in a community and in a society; newborns begin their social lives by acquiring the status their families have, which influences their opportunities. For example, children in low-income families not only have fewer material things, they also have less opportunity to develop their abilities. Because they perceive that they cannot compete with others of their age who have more things and more opportunities, children from families with low incomes are likely to believe that they have little control over the future and, therefore, try less hard in school, accomplishing less. Characteristics of families and possible outcomes for children will be discussed in Chapter 3.

The family also passes on its socioeconomic status through its ability to afford higher education for its children. Children from middle- and upper-income families are more likely to go to college after high school, whereas children from low-income families are more likely to go to work. And those who have not achieved in high school, perhaps from lack of motivation, have fewer job opportunities. Educational level, then, is a strong determinant of future occupation and income.

The family exposes the child to certain cultural experiences available in the society—perhaps religious instruction, Scouts, music lessons, Little League, or soccer. Parents buy certain toys for their children and arrange certain activities together such as games, outings, and vacations. These depend to a large extent on socioeconomic status.

The family functions as a system of interaction, and the way it conducts personal relationships has a very powerful effect on the psychosocial development of children. Through various interactions with family members, such as siblings, grandparents, and other relatives, the child develops patterns for establishing relationships with others. These patterns are expressed and further developed in relationships with peers, authority figures, co-workers, and ultimately a spouse and children.

> Marie, the oldest of three children, was responsible for helping her mother care for her younger siblings. She often had to play a game with her younger sister while her mother nursed the baby, or she had to watch the baby while her mother drove her sister to pre-school. In her relations with her friends, Marie was the one always saying, "Let's play this" or "Let's play that" or "This is the way you're supposed to draw a house (or dog or cat)." In school she was often appointed to be a monitor. As an adult, Marie got a managerial position in her office.

"The family into which a child is born is the child's first reference group, the first group whose values, norms, and practices one refers to in evaluating one's behavior" (Elkin & Handel, 1989, p. 143). For example, there is now evidence that marital conflict and distress are related to children's difficulties with peers (Rubin, Bukowski, & Parker, 1998; Rubin & Thompson, 2003). For another example, it has been found that children of employed mothers from kindergarten age through adulthood have less restricted views of gender roles (Ellis, 1994). In passing on values, expectations, and practices, families also pass on to children certain behavior patterns toward others. These behavior patterns tend to vary by culture and ethnicity (Greenfield, Keller, Fuligni, & Maynard, 2003; Greenfield & Suzuki, 1998). Diverse parenting styles will be discussed in Chapter 4.

How can we better understand ethnic behavior patterns that differ from our own?

The following dimensions of ethnic behavior patterns represent extremes; usually, however, there is individual variation within groups (Trumbull, Rothstein-Fisch, Greenfield, & Quiroz, 2001).

Orientation: Collectivistic–Individualistic. At one extreme of this dimension is collectivism (orientation toward the group), as commonly exhibited by families representing such ethnic groups as Japanese, Hawaiian, Mexican, and Middle Eastern. These groups tend to emphasize affiliation, cooperation, and interpersonal relations. At the other extreme of this dimension is individualism (orientation

Babies are born into a culture and learn appropriate social roles.

HIRB/Index Stock Imagery

toward the individual), which is commonly exhibited by many families representing middle-class American and Western European groups. They tend to focus more on individual accomplishment, competition, and independence from the group. One's orientation on this dimension becomes significant in situations in which one has to choose between obligation to family and personal ambition, such as remaining geographically close to kin rather than relocating to earn more money or prestige. One's orientation on this dimension also influences risk taking and innovation versus conservatism and conformity in entrepreneurship (Hayton, George, & Zahra, 2002).

Coping Style: Active–Passive. An active coping style is associated with "doing" and "getting things done," a passive coping style with "being" or "becoming." An active coping style also involves a future time orientation, a perception that time moves quickly and one can control and change the environment. A passive coping style is associated with a belief that all events are determined by fate and are, therefore, inevitable. Generally, those with Hispanic backgrounds are less active in coping style than are those with Euro-American backgrounds (Bennett, 2003). Coping style becomes significant in motivating families to seek social services, such as psychological support, when problems occur (McGoldrick, Giordano, Pearse, & Giordano, 1996).

Attitude Toward Authority: Submissive–Egalitarian. This dimension can be observed in children: Do they regard their parents and teachers as clear authority figures whom they respect and obey without question, or do they see them as more nearly equal figures with whom they may disagree and question? Young children with Hispanic or Asian backgrounds have been found to be more obedient, respectful, and accepting of authority than are children with Euro-American backgrounds (Bennett, 2003). One's attitude toward authority on this dimension becomes significant in such situations as workplaces that reward assertiveness (Hofstede, 1991).

Communication Style: Open/Expressive–Restrained/Private. Generally, children with African heritage have been found to be more openly and freely expressive, both positively and negatively, in a wide variety of situations, than children with Euro-American heritage; the latter, in turn, are more direct and open in social interactions than are children with Asian heritage, who tend to be more polite and ritualistic (Bennett, 2003). One's communication style on this dimension becomes significant in relating to those whose way of interacting differs.

In Chapter 1, socialization outcomes of different worldviews were discussed. Likewise, these examples of behavior patterns from diverse ethnic groups passed on by families are important, as will be seen throughout the book, especially when they differ from the standards socialized by the school.

According to extensive cross-cultural research done by Kagicibasi (1996), family behavioral patterns and consequent socialization practices can be categorized as *interdependent* (stress on family loyalty, intergenerational dependency, control, and obedience) or *independent* (stress on individual achievement, separateness of generations, egalitarianism, and consensus). A child brought up with interdependent values would *give* his or her parent money if needed; a child brought up with independent values might *lend* the parent money, perhaps even charging interest.

Many immigrants have brought their cultural behavior patterns to the United States. The following is an excerpt from a family analysis done by a college student from a Persian Jewish family in Los Angeles (quoted in Greenfield & Suzuki, 1998, p. 108).

> Being a first-generation immigrant I have had to deal with . . . adjusting a collectivistic upbringing to an environment of individualism. In my home my parents and family coming from a country and culture . . . [with] beliefs of family as the central and dominant unit in life, endeavored to instill in us a sense of family in the collectivistic sense.
>
> We were brought up in a home where the "we" consciousness was stressed, rather than the "I" consciousness. We were taught that our behavior not only had implications for . . . ourselves but also for the rest of the family; for example, if I stayed out late at night, not only would I be taking the chance of getting robbed, raped, and/or murdered (implications of that experience for me), but also my younger brother and sister who looked up to me would also be jeopardized (implications of my actions for others). . . .
>
> We were also taught to be responsible not only for ourselves, but also responsible for every other family member, thereby sharing the responsibility for both good and bad outcomes and playing a major part in each other's lives. For example, if my brother did bad in school, I was also responsible because as his older sister I was responsible to help him and take care of him and teach him right from wrong. I was, to an extent, as responsible for his actions as he, and my parents were.

SCHOOL AND CHILD CARE

How did your teachers and/or caregivers influence your life?

The school acts as an agent of society in that it is organized to perpetuate that society's knowledge, skills, customs, and beliefs. The school's part in the transmission of culture is continually under debate because knowledge and technology expansion make it impossible to convey all information. Thus, difficult choices have to be made as to what is most important—with consequent conflicting opinions. All education springs from some image of the future.

Socializing children for a society of rapid change is a continual challenge. In such changing conditions, when educators become unsure of what is right for the next generation to learn in order to be adequately prepared for the future, the trend becomes education for adaptability. What is education for adaptability? Is it teaching basic skills or problem solving? Is it an individual or group enterprise? Computers can facilitate individualized learning; cooperative activities can foster group learning. Schools must choose how to balance them. While schools must encourage the creative capacities of the young to adapt to a changing physical and social environment, they still have the task of maintaining the status quo and ensuring cultural continuity. Ideally, the school must act as an agent to foster respect and adherence to the existing social order of society, but reality proves this is not a constant.

Education professor John Goodlad (1984) studied documents related to the purposes of schooling spanning 300 years of U.S. history. He found four broad categories of goals: academic (reading, writing, arithmetic); vocational (preparation for the world of work); social and civic (preparation to participate in a democracy); and personal (development of individual talent and self-expression). Schooling goals and outcomes will be discussed in Chapter 6.

The social order of society is communicated to the child largely in the classroom—a setting in which children are evaluated by the teacher's comments, report cards, marks on papers, charts, classmates' judgments, and self-judgments. "Who can help Sally with that problem?" "Who has read the most books?" "Only papers with the best handwriting will be displayed for parents' night." Evaluation contributes to socialization in that the norms and standards of society are learned via the criteria of the evaluation. The self-concept emerges from how well the child meets the expectations of others, the evaluators (Harter, 1999).

The political ideology of society is communicated to the child through textbooks and how subjects are taught. How is the classroom setting organized? Do students compete with one another, participate in discussion, or pursue activities independently? Do they collaborate and help each other on projects?

Socialization outcomes in teacher-centered and learner-centered classrooms are different (Wells, 2001). Teacher- and learner-centered classrooms will be discussed in more detail in Chapter 7. The teacher in the school also contributes to the socialization process by serving as a model for children to imitate. Teachers who are involved in their subject matter tend to have active, curious students who want to learn (Brophy, 1992).

As a result of societal changes, child care has become an important socialization agent. The specific effects of care from someone other than a parent are controversial, involving many variables such as a child's temperament, type of care, and parents' involvement (Belsky & Rovine, 1988; Clark-Stewart, 1987). Specifics will be discussed in Chapter 5.

PEERS

Who was your best friend and why?

The peer group comprises individuals who are of approximately the same age and social status and who have common interests. Experiences in child-care facilities can expose children to peer relations months after birth. However, reciprocal interactions in the peer group don't usually begin until about age 3, when the child starts to understand the views of others and, therefore, is able to cooperate, share, and take turns. Cognitively, the child is beginning to move away from **egocentrism**, the inability to look at the world from any point of view other than one's own. As the child matures and develops new interests, his or her peer groups change. Some may be based on proximity, such as the children in the neighborhood or the classroom, and others on interest, such as those on the soccer team or in Scouts.

> The peer group gives children experience in egalitarian types of relationships. In this group they engage in a process of give-and-take not ordinarily possible in their relationships with adults. . . . In the peer group they gain their first substantial experience of equality. Children entering a peer group are interested in the companionship, attention, and good will of the group (particularly of the members of the group who are significant for them), and the group is in a position to satisfy this interest. For behaving in the appropriate or valued manner, the group rewards its members by bestowing attention, approval, or leadership or by giving permission to participate or to employ certain symbols. For behaving otherwise, the peer group punishes by disdain, ostracism, or other expressions of disapproval. (Elkin & Handel, 1989, p. 184)

Thus, children come to look at themselves from the point of view of the group. The peer group rewards sociability, or getting along, and rejects deviations, such as eccentricity, aggression, and showing off (Kindermann, 1998). The child learns to obey the "rules of the game" and how to assume the various roles required in the game, such as batter, pitcher, or catcher. The peer group exerts control by simply refusing to include those who do not conform to its values or rules.

> An example of the power of peer group pressure is the classic children's story by Hans Christian Andersen, "The Emperor's New Clothes." The emperor, who was very vain about his clothes, bought some cloth that—according to the merchants who sold it—was invisible only to those not worthy of their positions in life. He proudly wore his new outfit made of this unique cloth in a parade before the entire town. No one dared admit to others that the emperor really hadn't any clothes on, for fear of being judged unworthy. It took the astonished cry of an innocent child to make everyone realize the truth.

The peer group functions as a socializing agent in that it provides information about the world and oneself from a perspective other than that of the family (Hartup, 1996; Rubin et al., 1998). It is a source of social comparison. From the peer group children receive feedback about their abilities. Through interaction with their equals, people find out whether they are better than, the same as, or worse than their friends in sports, dating, grades, and other areas of life. Within the peer group the child can experiment with various roles—leader, follower, clown, troublemaker, or peacemaker—and discover how the others react.

Peers also serve as a support group for the expression of values and attitudes (Hartup, 1996; Schneider, 2000). Members often discuss situations with parents, siblings, and teachers. Beyond that, friends may offer sympathy and/or advice in handling problems. That children spend an increasing amount of time with their peers was illustrated in a study of children ages 2 to 12 (Ellis, Rogoff, & Cromer, 1981). It was observed that by age 8, children were interacting with other children six times more than with adults. Internet and cell phone capabilities for instant messaging provide infinite opportunities to connect to peers. Such technology provides a means for school-agers and adolescents to relate to one another virtually any time and any place, and anonymously if they so choose. The peer group, then, as an

egocentrism the cognitive inability to look at the world from any point of view other than one's own

agent of socialization exerts a strong influence on children's ideas and behavior, especially those who need social approval and fear rejection. The quality of the parent–child relationship is the most important factor affecting peer group influence (Collins et al., 2000). Peer group influences will be discussed in Chapter 8.

MASS MEDIA

What was your favorite book or movie and why?

Mass media include newspapers, magazines, books, radio, television, videos, movies, computers, and other means of communication and information technology that reach large audiences via an impersonal medium between the sender and the receiver. Unlike other agents of socialization, the mass media do not ordinarily involve direct personal interactions; the interactions are of a more technical nature. The mass media must be considered socializing agents, however, because they reveal many aspects of the society and elicit cognitive processes in children that affect their understanding of the real world (Harris, 1999; Huston & Wright, 1998; Perse, 2001). Newspapers report such items as current baseball scores or government policy; magazines illustrate the latest fashions or suggest things to do with free time in the summer; radio stations play popular songs; books discuss issues such as sex and drugs; television gives glimpses of hospitals, courtrooms, and family situations. Television, videos, and movies also show relationships between people in various settings, providing children with images or patterns of how to behave or interact in similar situations.

Television, movies, books, and computers (the Internet) provide information about society. Through them children come to learn about parts of the world they might not otherwise encounter or experience. They are taken under the sea, to outer space, to the jungles, to other times, and to other countries. The media also provide role models—the hero, the villain, the detective, the doctor, the lawyer, the mother, and the father. They reflect social attitudes—beliefs about political issues, such as war or taxes, social issues such as abortion or child abuse, occupations, sex, and minority groups.

Children, because of cognitive immaturity, are of special concern regarding media influence (Roberts & Foehr, 2004; Perse, 2001). They process the content they see and hear and transform it into something meaningful to them, which may or may not be accurate or desirable. One concern is that young children may come to think of all people in a group as having the same characteristics as the people in that group presented on TV or in books, and this may influence their attitudes. For example, in the majority of television shows and movies, the white male is portrayed as dominant, brave, powerful, and competent (Berry & Asamen, 2001; Huston & Wright, 1998; Signorielli, 2001). This is true in textbooks as well. These images are especially influential for children who do not have the real experience to evaluate the attitude portrayed.

Another concern is children's susceptibility to advertising (Huston & Wright, 1998; Kunkel, 2001). Many children demand that parents buy products and toys seen on TV. Children often imitate well-known media characters, especially active, powerful ones. They role-play, they bring the toys to school, and they wear clothing decorated with the media characters. The problem with marketed media-related toys, clothing, and supplies is not only the materialistic and competitive values they foster, but the aggressive acting-out behavior they inspire in children's play (Levin, 1998). Commercialism abounds in children's sports and schools, as well as on TV.

With the introduction of new technology to mass media, such as modems connecting to the Internet and cell phones connecting to friends, children can play a greater role in their own socialization. They can, for example, access any information that is on the Internet (unless access to a site is blocked). They also have more opportunities to interact with media independent of adult mediation, as many households have more than one TV, and cell phones, pagers, and e-mail provide opportunities for instant communication. Various media influences will be discussed in Chapter 9.

COMMUNITY

What kind of neighborhood(s) did you grow up in?

The term **community** is derived from the Latin word for fellowship. It refers to the affective relationships expected among closely knit groups of people having common interests. It also refers to people living in a particular geographical area who are bound together politically and economically. The function of the community, then, is to provide a sense of belonging, friendship, and socialization of children (Etzioni, 1993). A survey by the National League of Cities cited five characteristics that make a city "family-friendly": education (accessible quality school programs), recreation, community safety, citizen involvement, and physical environment (Meyers & Kyle, 1998). Many sociologists and psychologists are concerned with the erosion of community ties as we move toward the future (Garbarino, 1992; Schorr, 1997). The factors contributing to this erosion, such as fear of violence, technology, and "busyness," as well as coping strategies, will be discussed in Chapter 10.

The size, population, and mobility pattern of a community determine the pattern of human interaction. In a town with a small and stable population of a few thousand, most people know each other, in contrast to a larger, more mobile town of many thousands. Small-town interaction involves more intimate details of people's lives than does large-town interaction. In a small town, people see each other in many settings—at the store, at school, at the movies, at church. In a large town, relationships are more fragmented—it is unlikely that one would just by chance see a friend at a restaurant, simply because there are so many restaurants available in a large town. Similarly, a large town provides more activities than does a small town. Thus, one's interactions focus on the community groups to which one belongs—Scouts, Little League, the "Y," and so on.

One function of such community groups is to give children different perspectives on life—to broaden their range of experience and give them new statuses or roles. In this respect, community agencies and organizations contribute to the socialization of children. In Scouting, for example, children learn about various occupational roles through a badge program. The Scout is supervised by a designated community "sponsor"—perhaps by a veterinarian in caring for an animal. A church or temple youth group might participate in a project of visiting people in a home for the elderly on a regular basis. Community libraries open the world of reading to children; museums open the worlds of art, science, and natural history.

Neighborhoods are often stratified by economic status (Leventhal & Brooks-Gunn, 2000). Lower-economic-status families may live in less-desirable sections, whereas upper-economic-status families may live in large homes surrounded by green lawns or in apartments with doormen. The location of these neighborhoods in the larger community influences interaction patterns. If children from different neighborhoods

community a group of people sharing fellowship and common interests; a group of people living in the same geographic area who are bound together politically and economically

attend a particular school, or share community services such as recreation and library, all the children have an opportunity to interact with many diverse individuals. On the other hand, if the neighborhoods are segregated, each having its own school and recreational facilities, the children generally interact with those like themselves.

People in the neighborhood, adults and older children, are the ones with whom the young child interacts and "probably stand second only to parents in terms of their power to influence the child's behavior" (Bronfenbrenner, 1979, p. 161; Schorr, 1997). The adults in the neighborhood are role models. They may be carpenters, engineers, entrepreneurs, teachers, or recreation leaders. The older children are models of behavior and interaction. Children often learn games and cues about getting along with certain people from older children: "Mrs. Grady is an old grouch; she won't give your ball back if it goes in her yard."

A community can offer an *informal social support system*—relatives, friends, neighbors who can be counted on to help in a crisis. For example, when Mrs. Cooper went to the hospital, her mother-in-law came to care for the children, and the neighbors took turns cooking meals and doing errands for the family. A community can also have a more *formal social support system,* such as institutionalized child care, Big Brothers/Big Sisters, Meals on Wheels, and Parents Without Partners. These formal support systems may be funded by tax dollars, donations, or membership fees.

Formal support systems in a community usually emerge through the process of advocacy. **Advocacy** means speaking or writing in support of something—for example, setting goals on behalf of children and seeing that politicians or governmental agencies implement them. It is a long and arduous process, however, to go from goals to laws. Thus, if community members want to improve opportunities for their children, they must get involved in politics. Politics begins locally, in one's own community. If community members want their children to have "the right to full opportunity for play and recreation," they can communicate this desire to their city council members and follow through by examining how their local tax dollars are distributed. For example, one city doubled the money previously budgeted for programs such as child care, youth activities, senior citizens' food, and a shelter for victims of domestic violence. Most of the money had been previously allocated to street repair. The most effective community services supporting children and families involve collaboration between informal and formal networks providing empowerment (Epps & Jackson, 2000).

Methods of Socialization

How do people learn the ways of the society in which they live?

Given that socialization is the process by which people learn the ways of society so that they can function effectively within it, we now turn to examine the various methods by which these ways are transmitted to children (see Table 2.1). These socialization methods vary according to culture, family, child, and situation (Bugental, 2000).

AFFECTIVE METHODS (EFFECT EMERGES FROM FEELING)

Why do you have to be attached to someone to be socialized?

Affective refers to feelings or emotions, such as love, anger, fear, or disgust. Affective mechanisms include responses to others, feelings about self, feelings about others, and expression of emotions. Affect emerges from person-to-person interaction, which leads

advocacy speaking or writing in support of a person, a group, or a cause

affective having to do with feelings or emotions

METHOD	TECHNIQUES
AFFECTIVE (effect emerges from feeling)	Attachment
OPERANT (effect emerges from acting)	Reinforcement Extinction Punishment Feedback Learning by doing
OBSERVATIONAL (effect emerges from imitating)	Modeling
COGNITIVE (effect emerges from information processing)	Instruction Setting standards Reasoning
SOCIOCULTURAL (effect emerges from conforming)	Group pressure Tradition Rituals and routines Symbols
APPRENTICESHIP (effect emerges from guided participation)	Structuring Collaborating Transferring

Table 2.1

Methods of Socialization

to attachment. The socialization of the child, whether intentional or unintentional, is accomplished through person-to-person interaction. When people are attached to one another, they interact often; thus, attachment and interaction are bidirectional (Thompson, 1998).

Attachment is an "affectional tie that one person forms to another specific person, binding them together in space and enduring over time" (Ainsworth, 1973, p. 1). Socialization begins with personal attachment (Elkin & Handel, 1989; Collins et al., 2000). The human infant is born helpless, requiring care. In the process of caring for the infant, the parents or caregivers hold, play with, and talk to the infant. They respond to the feelings evoked in them by the child. This sensitive, responsive caregiving is the foundation for social interaction, and it is this interaction that contributes to many socialization outcomes for the child (Kuczynski, 2003; Thompson, 1998).

Infants who are responded to when they cry, who are fed, held, and spoken to, will develop a *secure attachment* and a sense of trust toward the world. On the other hand, infants who receive minimal or inconsistent care will develop an *insecure attachment* and a sense of mistrust (Erikson, 1963). Our first human relationship, then, provides the basis for our later expectations regarding other relationships.

An outcome of attachment, other than feelings of trust or mistrust for future social interactions, is the feeling of competence. Paradoxically, the more securely attached children are to a nurturing adult, the safer they feel to explore the environment. On the other hand, the more insecurely attached they are, the less likely they are to leave their caregivers and try out new things (Ainsworth, 1973). Follow-up observations in preschool showed that infants who were judged to be securely attached at age 1.5 years were more enthusiastic, sympathetic to others, cooperative, independent, and competent than those who displayed insecure attachment at that age (Sroufe, 1978). Several studies have found insecurely attached children to exhibit disruptive, hostile, or aggressive behavior in preschool (Sroufe, 1996; Waters,

attachment an affectional tie that one person forms to another person, binding them together in space and enduring over time

Mother–child interaction is the basis for attachment and a sense of trust.

Posada, Crowell, & Kengling, 1993). A child's difficult temperament has been found to contribute to such negative externalizing behavior (Burgess, Marshall, Rubin, & Fox, 2003). Attachment to the primary caregiver is the first of many important emotional relationships with significant others that the child will form in the future. These significant others may include relatives, teachers, friends, and coaches. Because each of these others is unique and because each situation the child encounters with these others is unique, each will contribute in a different way to the child's socialization.

David Elkind (1981b) discusses the importance of attachment in determining how children learn: "In children's early years, adults predigest experience for them much as mothers predigest food to provide milk for their babies" (p. 20). Adults, then, communicate to children their own learning experiences. The adults are mediators. Elkind cites an example of a teacher who always had children around her when she used various art materials. She showed them different ways paper could be folded and how to use a brush, and she joyfully produced new colors when she mixed the paints. The children not only acquired the ability to fold paper, make brush strokes, and mix paint; they also acquired an attitude of appreciation, enjoyment, and respect for art materials. Elkind refers to this kind of learning as the acquisition of mediating structures. Personal attachment to adults enables children to abstract mediating structures from them.

Reuveen Feurstein (1980) describes an example of mediating structures. In comparing children who immigrated to Israel from Yemen and Morocco, Feurstein found that even though both groups of children attended school in Israel, the Yemenite children were better learners than the Moroccan children. Case histories of the children revealed that, as part of their religious training, the Yemenite children had studied with their fathers. Feurstein called this kind of interaction a "mediated learning experience," in which the adult provides the mechanisms for the acquisition of learning. Thus, by becoming attached to an adult who enjoys learning, the child's attitude toward future learning is acquired.

When the child is attached to a caregiver, socialization takes place in many ways. Some of these result from the child's action (an *operant method*); some of them result from the child's imitating (an *observational method*); some of them result from the child's information processing (a *cognitive method*); some of them result from the child's cultural traditions (a *sociocultural method*); and some of them result from guided participation (an *apprenticeship method*).

OPERANT METHODS (EFFECT EMERGES FROM ACTING)

What influences whether your behavior will be repeated or modified?

operant producing an effect

Operant refers to producing an effect. When one's behavior is followed by a favorable outcome (reinforcement), the probability of that behavior's occurring again is increased. When one's behavior has no favorable outcome (for example, it does not get attention, it is ignored) or has an unfavorable outcome (punishment), the probability of that behavior's occurring again is decreased. Operant methods take into account the participatory role of individuals in their own socialization.

Several socialization techniques can be used to increase desired behavior: positive reinforcement, negative reinforcement, and shaping.

Reinforcement

A **reinforcement** is an object or event that is presented following a behavior and that serves to increase the likelihood that the behavior will occur again. Reinforcement can be positive or negative. **Positive reinforcement** is a reward, or pleasant consequence, given for desired behavior; examples are food, physical contact, and praise. **Negative reinforcement** is the termination of an unpleasant condition following a desired response—for example, allowing children to come out of their rooms when they stop a temper tantrum, or stopping a spanking when the child apologizes.

To reinforce a behavior that is complex, involving many steps, such as writing the alphabet, we often use shaping. **Shaping** is the systematic immediate reinforcement of successive approximations of the desired behavior until the desired behavior occurs and is maintained. Writing the alphabet involves holding a pencil and copying lines and circles in a specific way on a piece of paper. The lines and circles must be a certain size and a certain distance from one another. At a child's first attempt, the teacher may reward a line of any size that resembles the letter. Then the teacher may reward only straight lines, then straight lines of a certain size, and so on, until the child reaches the desired level of performance. Shaping is an effective socializing mechanism to teach various skills.

The following is a summary of conditions under which reinforcement can be effective as a socializing technique (Martin & Pear, 2003):

- The desired behavior must first be exhibited before it can be reinforced. In training a child to defecate in the toilet, the caregiver must put the child on the seat and wait for the behavior to occur before reinforcing it. The main unresolved question accompanying the technique of positive reinforcement is: How do you get children to make the desired response in the first place so that they can be rewarded?
- The desired behavior must be reinforced immediately the first time it occurs. If you want children to verbalize their requests rather than point to or grunt for desired objects, you must reward them when they say, for example, "Juice."
- Initially, the desired behavior must be reinforced each time it is exhibited. Every time children verbalize their requests, they should get what is asked for. Every time children defecate in the toilet, they should be rewarded.
- When the newly acquired behavior is being performed relatively frequently, reinforcement can then become intermittent. Reward or praise can be given every few times the behavior is performed, or it can be given every few days instead of every time. "I'm glad you're asking for what you want." "I'm proud you're using the toilet now."
- Because the long-range goal is self-reward, subjective reinforcers, such as privileges and praise, should be used in conjunction with objective reinforcers, such as food, toys, or money.

Using reinforcement as a socializing technique has several problems, besides having to wait for the desired behavior to occur: (1) Individuals respond differently to reinforcers. For some children, a toy is an effective reinforcer; for

reinforcement an object or event that is presented following a behavior and that serves to increase the likelihood that the behavior will occur again

positive reinforcement a reward, or pleasant consequence, given for desired behavior

negative reinforcement the termination of an unpleasant condition following a desired response

shaping the systematic immediate reinforcement of successive approximations of the desired behavior until the desired behavior occurs and is maintained

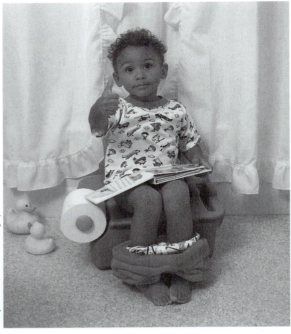

Behavior, such as using the toilet, that is reinforced will likely be repeated.

others, adult approval is more effective. It is sometimes difficult to find the best one. (2) The child may become bored with the reinforcer, so its effectiveness diminishes. (3) Being human, it is difficult for adults to constantly reward children's desired behavior, even during the initial stages. If parents want to train a child to urinate in the toilet, they must be present as well as ready to put the child on the toilet at certain intervals. They also must wait patiently for the desired behavior to occur. (4) Adults sometimes unintentionally reinforce the very behaviors they want to eliminate. When children who have been toilet trained begin to urinate in their pants again, perhaps because they see their baby brother or sister do it, and the mother says "I thought you were a big boy (girl)," it is highly likely that the undesired behavior will occur again because negative attention is better than no attention. (5) Although the goal is for the child to internally regulate his or her behavior, reinforcement is externally regulated and may reduce the motivation for self-control.

Other socialization techniques that can decrease or eliminate undesired behavior include extinction, punishment, feedback, and learning by doing.

Extinction

If reinforcement increases the likelihood that a response will occur again, then removal of the reinforcement should decrease and eventually eliminate, or extinguish, the likelihood of that response. **Extinction** is the gradual disappearance of a learned behavior following the removal of the reinforcement. Basically, it involves ignoring undesirable responses. For example, to extinguish the habit of nail biting, a father decides to ignore his daughter every time she bites her nails instead of nagging her to stop, as he used to do. Thus, he removes the previous reinforcement of attention. When she does not bite her nails for a 10-minute stretch, however, he praises her. Gradually the interval between nail-biting episodes becomes longer and longer, with the father giving praise every half-hour for not nail biting, but still ignoring his daughter when she does bite her nails.

Extinction must be used in conjunction with reinforcement to be effective as a socializing method. Annoying behaviors such as tantrums, dawdling, and tattling respond well, but more complex or deep-seated behaviors such as aggression, stealing, and overeating do not.

Timeout is a type of extinction in which all reinforcement is removed. Usually, the child spends a specified amount of time in his or her room, in a corner, or in any place where behavior can be ignored. A timeout can give a child time and space to better manage emotions and behavior. Reasons for the timeout should be given, so the child can use them for self-control in the future.

extinction the gradual disappearance of a learned behavior following the removal of the reinforcement

Punishment

According to David Ausubel (1957), it is impossible to guide behavior effectively using only positive reinforcement and extinction; children cannot learn what is not approved or tolerated simply by making a reverse generalization from the approval

Nancy Sheehan/Index Stock Imagery

they receive for acceptable behavior. Children must be enabled to process what they are *not* supposed to do, as well as what they *are*. Thus, nonhostile punishment or constructive responses designed to correct misbehavior can have an informative effect.

Punishment consists of physically or psychologically painful stimuli or the temporary withdrawal of pleasant stimuli when undesirable behavior occurs. A physically painful stimulus might be a spanking; a psychologically painful stimulus might be a scolding or harsh criticism causing shame; withdrawal of a pleasant stimulus might be removing a privilege such as TV. Punishment is used as an intervention technique to discourage undesirable behavior. It is probably most valuable when a child's behavior must be stopped quickly for safety reasons. A 2-year-old who runs out into the street is more likely to be stopped from doing it in the future by a quick swat on the rear end than by a reward for staying on the sidewalk. A 2-year-old also cannot really understand the logical reasons for not running into the street. Thus, a more concrete physical reminder may be necessary.

For punishment to be useful as an effective socializing technique, the following summary applies (Martin & Pear, 2003):

- **Timing.** The closer the punishment is to the behavior, the more effective it will be.
- **Reasoning.** Punishment accompanied by an explanation is more effective than punishment alone. "We do not play in the street because cars might hurt us."
- **Consistency.** If children are consistently punished for repeating a behavior, they are more likely to stop it than if they are sometimes punished, sometimes ignored, and sometimes rewarded. Aggression is an example of a behavior sometimes handled inconsistently. It may be punished at home or at school when the child is caught, yet may be rewarded in the peer group.
- **Attachment to the person doing the punishing.** The more nurturant the relationship between the punisher and the punished, the more effective the punishment will be. A child whose parent denies a privilege for undesired behavior, such as coming home late, is less likely to repeat that behavior than if an acquaintance, such as a babysitter, administers the punishment.

The use of punishment as an effective technique in modifying behavior has been criticized for the following reasons (Martin & Pear, 2003):

- Punishment may stop the undesirable behavior immediately, but by itself it does not indicate appropriate or desired behavior.
- Punishment may merely slow the rate at which the undesirable behavior is emitted, rather than eliminate it entirely. Or it may change the form in which the undesirable behavior is emitted. People who stop smoking often report they begin eating more. Children who are punished for physical aggression may engage in verbal aggression ("I hate you," "You big doody head").
- Punishment by an adult may have an undesirable modeling effect on the child. Parents who abuse their children are likely to have been abused by their parents.
- The emotional side effects of punishment (fear, embarrassment, shame, low self-esteem, and tenseness) may be psychologically more damaging than the original behavior.

In sum, punishment can function as a socializing technique when used appropriately (Martin & Pear, 2003). It can provide an opportunity to reestablish attachment or affection following emotional release; it can provide vicarious learning by observation of others being punished; it can reduce guilt in that it can provide an

punishment physically or psychologically painful stimuli or the temporary withdrawal of pleasant stimuli when undesirable behavior occurs

opportunity to correct the misbehavior; and, when combined with reasoning, it can enable the internalization of moral standards. Thus, when using punishment, be aware of the negative, as well as the positive, consequences for the child.

> When a group of 10-year-old boys wrote on the wall of their camp cabin, their counselor required them to spend the afternoon scrubbing walls instead of going swimming. This type of punishment is referred to as a "logical consequence"—one that is arranged by the parent or another adult and that is logically related to the misbehavior (Dreikurs & Grey, 1968). For a logical consequence to be effective, however, it must make sense to the child. For example, Todd continually left his clothes around his room after repeatedly being told to put them in the hamper. His mother finally said, "Clothes that do not get picked up do not get washed." Todd still did not pick up his clothes. Finally, when Todd wanted to wear his favorite shirt and realized it was not washed because he had not put it in the hamper, the consequence became effective—he picked up his clothes.

For a summary of behavioral consequences, see Table 2.2.

Feedback

Feedback is evaluative information, both positive and negative, about one's behavior. It is an example of a dynamic, bidirectional relationship between teacher and learner in that the teacher modifies his or her response according to that of the learner. Feedback responses may include an approving nod, a questioning look, a comment, further instructions, or a reminder. Feedback provides knowledge of results and how to improve them, factors shown to be important to learning (Bangert-Drowns, Kulik, Kulik, & Morgan, 1991; Bransford, Brown, & Cocking, 1999).

An example of a classical feedback experiment illustrates the value of knowing the results while learning a simple skill (Baker & Young, 1960). The task to be learned was to reproduce on paper the length of a 4-inch piece of wood. The subjects were blindfolded. However, they could feel the piece of wood. One group of subjects was told after each performance whether they were within .20 inch of the correct length. The other group received no feedback. When both groups were tested, the group receiving feedback consistently improved, whereas the group receiving no knowledge of results made no consistent progress. When the feedback was stopped, that group's accuracy dropped abruptly.

This experiment demonstrated that in order to increase accuracy of performance, individuals must change incorrect responses. In this case, unless the individuals were made fully aware of their incorrect behavior, change was unlikely to occur.

The effects of feedback on performance can be summarized as follows (Good & Brophy, 1986):

- Feedback generally increases motivation.
- Feedback usually improves subsequent performance.
- Generally, the more specific the knowledge of performance, the more rapidly performance improves.
- Feedback given punctually is usually more effective than feedback given long after a task has been completed.
- Noticeable decreases in feedback often result in a marked decline in performance.
- When knowledge of results is not provided, individuals tend to develop substitutes. For example, they may compare their performance to that of peers to determine whether it is better or worse.

feedback evaluative information, both positive and negative, about one's behavior

TYPE	DEFINITION	EFFECT
Positive reinforcement	Present a stimulus (give attention)	Increases desirable response
Negative reinforcement	Remove aversive stimulus (stop scolding)	Increases desirable response
Extinction	Remove pleasant stimulus (stop giving attention)	Decreases undesirable response
Punishment	Present aversive stimulus (start scolding)	Decreases undesirable response

Table 2.2
Summary of Behavioral Consequences

Thus, feedback provides children with information on how they are measuring up to standards of behavior and performance: "Susie, your letters need to go on the line. I've circled your best one; make five more just like it." "Jack, that frown on your face is most unpleasant; what is your problem?" "Garth, next time you have a friend over, say 'Thank you for coming.'" "Terry, that outfit looks very good on you."

Learning by Doing

Sometimes socialization occurs through experiencing and interacting. As an ancient Chinese proverb says, "I hear and I forget, I see and I remember, I do and I understand." Psychologist Jean Piaget (1952), known for his developmental theory of cognitive development, states that children learn through their own activity. Likewise, psychologist Jerome Bruner (1981) believes that children learn through discovery. Learning is a slow process of construction and transformation of experience into meaning. Learning to ride a bicycle is an example of learning by doing. It involves experimenting and discovering how to shift your weight while pedaling, holding on, and watching where you are going, all at the same time. Albert Bandura (2000) relates learning by doing to the attribution of **self-efficacy**—the belief that one can master a situation and produce positive effects. For example, children who are encouraged and given opportunities to become competent (as by helping to cook, putting a puzzle together, or creating artwork) tend to be motivated to achieve on other tasks.

Offering developmentally appropriate choices, meaningful activities that create opportunities for children to succeed, enables children to learn by doing because they can experience what works and what doesn't (Schank, 2004). Evidence from studies on children supports the relationship between learning by doing and successful problem solving. For example, in one study (Smith & Dutton, 1979), a group of children was given the opportunity to play with materials involved in a problem. Another group received instruction on how to solve the problem, but was not given the opportunity to play with the materials. The group that played with the materials ended up solving the problem as easily as the children who had had instruction. On a more complex problem, requiring innovative thinking, the group that had the opportunity to play with the materials did better in solving the problem than the group that had received instruction. Thus, as Piaget and Bruner said, experience leads to discovering ways to tackle problems. Learning by doing, then, transforms the individual in some way, affecting future development.

The computer is an interactive tool that provides opportunities for experiential learning—problem solving, creativity, simulations, and personal tutoring

self-efficacy the belief that one can master a situation and produce positive outcomes

© Superstock

This child learns to roller-blade by doing it.

(Schank, 2004). It also is capable of supporting many different learning styles while enabling the user to learn how to learn (Papert, 1993), an example of transformation. Every time I get new software for my computer, I learn how to use it by doing it—seeing what works and what doesn't.

Problem solving can involve interacting with others. Most interactional skills are learned by doing. When one smiles and says "Hi," one usually gets a positive response. When one sulks after losing a game, one may not be invited to play again, another example of transformation.

When children play, they are learning by doing (Hughes, 1998). They are being socialized in that they are practicing physical, intellectual, and social skills—physical skills such as climbing, jumping, writing, and cutting; intellectual skills such as remembering, reasoning, making decisions, and solving problems; social skills such as communicating, sharing, cooperating, competing, and having empathy. For example, as children experiment with different behaviors and social roles, they are finding out what it feels like to be Mom, or baby brother; they are experiencing what it is like to wash the car, or to play doctor; they are feeling the joy of approval and the despair of disapproval. They are constructing views of the world that will influence future thinking and behavior.

OBSERVATIONAL METHODS (EFFECT EMERGES FROM IMITATING)

How can you learn complicated behavior by observing it?

> Six-year-old Vicky went on her first boat ride in her uncle's new boat. She watched the waves ripple on the lake as her uncle joyfully demonstrated the power of his boat's new motor to her parents. When they docked, Vicky's uncle tied up the boat. The next day Vicky could not wait to go for another ride. She besieged her uncle with questions while motoring around the lake, and when they pulled up to the dock, to her uncle's amazement Vicky jumped out, grabbed the rope, and tied up the boat.

Vicky's behavior, her attitude about boating, and her performance in tying up the boat illustrate socialization through observational learning, or modeling.

Modeling

Modeling is a form of imitative learning that occurs by observing another person (the model) perform a behavior and experience its consequence. It enables us to learn appropriate social behavior, attitudes, and emotions vicariously or second-hand. The models can be parents, siblings, relatives, friends, teachers, coaches, or television characters. Jerome Kagan (1971, 1984) explains how the child assumes complex patterns of behavior through identification with a model:

modeling a form of imitative learning that occurs by observing another person (the model) perform a behavior and experience its consequence

> Identification is, in fact, the belief of a person that some attributes of a model (for example, parents, siblings, relatives, peers, and fictional figures) are also possessed by the person. A boy who realizes that he and his father share the same name, notes that they have similar facial features, and is told by relatives that they both have

lively tempers, develops a belief that he is similar to his father. When this belief in similarity is accompanied by vicarious emotional experiences in the child that are appropriate to the model, we say that the child has an identification with the model. (Kagan, 1971, p. 57)

Modeling is a significant socializing method. As children mature, they acquire a wide range of behaviors through modeling from parents, siblings, teachers, and friends, which become part of their repertoire for future interactions.

Modeling (observational learning) involves the ability to abstract information from what is observed, store it in memory, make generalizations and rules about behavior, retrieve the appropriate information, and act it out at the appropriate time. Thus, modeling enables one to develop new ways of behaving in situations not previously experienced. Vicky, for example, "knew" how to tie up the boat without having previously tried it or been instructed on how to do it. The probability that children will imitate a model is a function of their (1) attention, (2) level of cognitive development, (3) retention, (4) type of activity being observed, (5) motivation, (6) ability to reproduce the behavior, and (7) repertoire of alternative behaviors (Bandura, 1989, 2001).

Many ethnic groups, especially high-context cultures such as Native Americans, emphasize observation and modeling as socialization methods. These methods enable children to participate in chores alongside adults or older siblings according to their developmental abilities. For example, in some African tribes girls as young as age 3 are given their own hoes to work in the gardens with their mothers and older sisters (Whiting & Edwards, 1988).

Various factors affect the extent to which children will imitate modeled behavior. Models who are perceived as similar (physically and/or psychologically) to the observer are likely to be identified with and imitated: "I have yellow hair, just like Mommy." "You have a strong will just like your grandfather." Models who are perceived as nurturant are more likely to be identified with and imitated: "My daddy always brings me presents when he comes back from a trip." "My coach always has time to listen to me." Models who are perceived as powerful or prestigious are more likely to be identified with and imitated (Bandura, Ross, & Ross, 1963): "My grandmother won first prize in the fair for her chocolate cake!" "My teacher is the smartest person in the whole world!"

Children's behavior is also influenced by whether the model with whom they identify is punished or reinforced. It has been demonstrated that children who see a model being punished for aggressive behavior are less likely to imitate that behavior than children who see a model being rewarded or experiencing no consequences (Bandura, 1965).

Television provides an excellent example of a context in which observational learning and consequent modeling take place. There is much evidence that children learn both prosocial and antisocial behavior by watching TV (Comstock & Paik, 1991; Perse, 2001; Roberts & Foehr, 2004). For example, children who watched an episode of *Lassie* in which the master risks his life to rescue Lassie's puppy were more helpful in a task following the show (Sprafkin, Liebert, & Poulos, 1975). For another example, studies of preschool children have shown a relationship between violent television viewing and aggressive behavior during free play at preschool (Levin & Carlsson-Paige, 1995; Singer & Singer, 1980).

The reason that televised behavior, whether prosocial or antisocial, is likely to be modeled is that children observe someone being rewarded for an act. Prosocial behavior on TV is generally reinforced by the person's getting lots of attention or becoming a hero. Antisocial behavior is generally reinforced on TV by the person's "getting away with it" or obtaining a desired object.

COGNITIVE METHODS (EFFECT EMERGES FROM INFORMATION PROCESSING)

What socialization methods coincide with the ways you process information best?

Socialization techniques using cognitive methods specifically focus on how an individual processes information, or how the individual abstracts meaning from experiences. Strategies used by socialization agents are instruction, setting standards, and reasoning.

Instruction

Instruction provides knowledge and information and is a useful socializing mechanism. For instruction to be effective, however, the child must be able to understand the language used as well as remember what was said. In other words, instruction must provide specific information at a child's level. "Bring me your shoes" would be appropriate for a 2-year-old. "Get your jacket out of the closet, turn out the pockets, and bring it to me" would not. Even a 2-year-old who knows what a jacket is will probably forget the second part of the instruction ("turn out the pockets") because a child at that age simply cannot remember to do three things at once.

"Instructions" conjures up the image of the piece of paper that comes at the bottom of the box with 20 bicycle parts. Instructions usually communicate how to do something, but they can also communicate directions or orders. "Don't sit on the coffee table, sit on the chair."

> "Greg [age 9], please clean up your room," says Mom.
>
> An hour later, Mom goes into Greg's room and observes that his bedspread is rumpled, books are on his desk, and his model airplanes are strewn among his shoes on the floor of his closet.
>
> Mom yells, "I told you to clean up your room!"
>
> Greg replies, "But I did; I put all my books and toys away."
>
> And that he had.

The problem here is that the instructions are not specific enough for Greg. (If the instructions for putting the bicycle together were as vague as Mom's, the parts would still be in the box.) Mom probably has an image of a clean room that includes an unrumpled bed, books on the bookshelf, and toys on the appropriate closet shelf. Greg's image of a clean room, on the other hand, may simply include space to walk and lie down. Thus, Mom's instructions, to be effective, must say, "Greg, please clean your room—straighten your bedspread, put your books on the bookshelf, and your toys on the shelf in your closet." If Greg were younger—for example, age 4— he might answer, "But I don't know how to straighten my bed." Then Mom would know what parts of the instructions could and could not be followed independently. Thus, for instructions to be effective, they must be understood. To be understood, the instructor must be willing to rephrase, to demonstrate, and to repeat. Exemplary coaching techniques involving instruction, explanations, practice, and feedback have been used successfully with preschool and school-age children to enable them to make friends (Mize & Ladd, 1990; Spence, 2003).

Setting Standards

A **standard** is a level of attainment or a grade of excellence regarded as a goal or a measure of adequacy. When parents set standards for children, they are telling children what they should do: "You are 3 years old now; I want you to dress yourself." "I expect only A's and B's on your report card." Setting standards provides children with advance notice of what is expected or not expected of them, thus helping them become socialized. The laws of a country, driver's license requirements, school achievement tests, and a city's building code are all examples of standards. A contract, or written agreement, specifying goals for learning or behavioral expectations can be a vehicle by which standards are communicated.

Standards are set by many socializing agents. In *Are You There, God? It's Me, Margaret* by Judy Blume (1970), to be a member of the secret sixth-grade club you had to wear a bra, tell when you got your period, and keep a Boy Book (a list of boys you liked). The standards are set in this example by a peer group. Standards are also set by teachers. Some accept only good handwriting and perfect spelling on papers to be graded. Others may set standards regarding content and creativity. Good and Brophy (2003) noted that teachers tend to demand better performances from high-achieving students; for example, they are less likely to accept an inadequate answer from high achievers than from low achievers. Standards are set by coaches: "You will do 10 sit-ups every day, get eight hours of sleep a night, and eat a balanced diet." Standards are set by employers regarding job performance. Thus, setting standards is a recurring method of socialization throughout life.

Reasoning

Reasoning is giving explanations or causes for an act. The purpose of giving reasons in the process of socialization is to enable the child to draw conclusions when encountering similar situations, thereby internalizing self-regulatory mechanisms.

When a teacher says to a preschool child who has just spit on another child, "Keep your spit in your mouth; spitting spreads germs and is rude. How would you like that?" that teacher is using reason to influence the child's behavior.

The problem with giving reasons is that children may not understand the words used (for example, "spreads germs," "is rude"), and often they are not able to generalize a reason to another situation. Because, according to Piaget (1974), children under age 3 are generally egocentric—that is, they lack the cognitive ability to take another's point of view—the child in the previous example may not be able to mentally take the view of the child who has been spit upon and so may not relate to the teacher's reasons.

Some children under age 3 do react to others' emotions with altruistic behavior. **Altruism** refers to actions that are intended to aid or benefit another person or group of people without the actor's anticipation of external rewards. Such actions often entail some cost, self-sacrifice, or risk on the part of the actor. A team of researchers (Radke-Yarrow & Zahn-Waxler, 1986; Radke-Yarrow, Zahn-Waxler, & Chapman, 1983; Zahn-Waxler, Radke-Yarrow, & King, 1979) interviewed mothers of 15- and 20-month-old children. The mothers were trained to observe and report incidents of their children's altruism when others were distressed, such as efforts at reparation when someone was hurt, trying to comfort a victim, offering a toy, or going to find someone else to help. The researchers found that the way the mother

standard a level or grade of excellence regarded as a goal or a measure of adequacy

reasoning giving explanations or causes for an act

altruism actions that are intended to help or benefit another person or group of people without the actor's anticipation of external rewards

interacted with her child when another was in distress was clearly related to her child's degree of altruism. The mothers of highly altruistic children did not simply offer cognitive reasoning of the other's distress; they reacted emotionally, sometimes quite strongly, and stated forcefully that socially responsible behavior was expected, such as "You made Shawna cry; you must never bite." Consequently, for children under age 3, if reasoning is to be used as a socializing technique, it must be combined with other methods—for example, an emotional reaction—to be effective.

Children between age 4 and 7 are moving away from egocentrism and toward **sociocentrism**—the ability to understand and relate to the views and perspectives of others. These children may be able to understand how another person feels or views things, but may not be able to generalize the reason to another situation. At this age, a child's ability to reason is **transductive** (connecting one particular idea to another particular idea based on appearance rather than logic) rather than **inductive** (connecting a particular idea to a more general idea based on similarities) or **deductive** (connecting a general idea to a particular idea based on similarities and differences). The following examples help to illustrate these different types of reasoning:

- **Transductive reasoning:** "Kyle has red hair and hits me; therefore all boys with red hair hit."
- **Inductive reasoning:** "I can't hit Kyle; therefore, I can't hit any other children."
- **Deductive reasoning:** "I can't hit other children; therefore, I can't hit Kyle."

Around age 7, children begin to think less intuitively and more concretely (Piaget, 1952); that is, they can understand reasons if they are associated with real, concrete events, objects, or people. The 7-year-old understands "You must not hit people with blocks because it hurts very much; look how Kyle is crying," because 7-year-olds can *see* that hitting Kyle with a block caused Kyle to cry. Children who think concretely, however, cannot yet reason in terms of abstract principles; they cannot yet understand "The law punishes people who hit." Since they cannot visualize it, the law is an abstraction of which they as yet have no concept.

Around age 11 or 12, children begin to think less concretely and more abstractly. They are able to perform formal, or logical, operations (such as those involved in science); they are capable of rational thought (Inhelder & Piaget, 1958). They can think in terms of past, present, and future and can deal with hypothetical problems: "If everyone went around hitting everyone else whenever angry, then the world would end up in a war."

Reasoning as a socializing mechanism is most effective when children exhibit the ability to think logically and flexibly. This occurs after age 11 or 12, as the child enters adolescence. At this stage, reasoning ability allows for adaptation to whatever problem is presented, thus enabling adolescents to benefit and learn from concepts imparted to them as young children. Reasoning tends to be used more often as a socializing method in ethnic groups that value verbal skills, abstract thought, assertiveness, and self-reliance (Peterson, Steinmetz, & Wilson, 2003).

Baumrind (1971, 1989) distinguishes parents who are willing to offer reasons behind the directives they issue (**authoritative** parents) from parents who do not offer directives at all, relying on manipulation to obtain compliance (**permissive** parents), and parents who expect the child to accept their word as right and final without any verbal give-and-take (**authoritarian** parents). According to Baumrind, the authoritative approach may best enable children to conform to social standards with minimal jeopardy to "individual autonomy or self-assertiveness." In one study, preschool children from authoritative homes were consistently and significantly

sociocentrism the ability to understand and relate to the views and perspectives of others

transductive reasoning reasoning from one particular fact or case to another similar fact or case

inductive reasoning reasoning from particular facts or individual cases to a general conclusion

deductive reasoning reasoning from a general principle to a specific case, or from a premise to a logical conclusion

authoritative a style of democratic parenting in which authority is based on competence or expertise

permissive a style of child-centered parenting characterized by a lack of directives or authority

authoritarian a style of parent-centered parenting characterized by unquestioning obedience to authority

more competent than other children (Baumrind, 1989). In another study (Elder, 1963), it was shown that 7th- to 12th-graders were more likely to model themselves after their parents if their parents explained the reasons behind their decisions and restrictions.

Thus, it would seem that even though reasoning as a socializing mechanism is not as effective for young children as it is for adolescents, the continual use of reasoning by parents is habit-forming. Children who are habitually given reasons for directives benefit more and more from reasoning as they mature, becoming increasingly able to rationalize and regulate their own behavior (Hoffman, 2000).

SOCIOCULTURAL METHODS (EFFECT EMERGES FROM CONFORMING)

What socialization methods ensure that you conform to your social or cultural group?

Culture involves learned behavior, including knowledge, beliefs, art, morals, law, customs, and traditions, that is characteristic of the social environment in which an individual grows up. The sociocultural expectations of those around an individual continually influence that individual's behavior and ensure conformity to established precedents. Some of the socializing techniques by which sociocultural expectations influence behavior are group pressure, tradition, rituals and routines, and symbols.

Group Pressure

Group pressure is a sociocultural method of socialization because it involves conforming to certain norms. Communities are made up of social groups, including family, neighborhood, religious community, peers, clubs, and school. The groups to which one belongs influence one's behavior. Because humans have a need to affiliate with other humans, and because social approval determines whether or not one is accepted by the group, humans will tend to conform to the group's expectations (group pressure).

In a classic study by Solomon Asch (1958), male subjects were asked to judge the length of lines. In each experimental session, only one of the participants was an actual subject; the others had been previously coached to express certain opinions. Thus, the real subject often faced a situation in which his eyes told him that one line was the longest while the others in the group all said another line was the longest. Several of the subjects consistently yielded to the pressure of the group, even when the group's opinion was clearly erroneous. In later interviews, those who conformed to the majority opinion explained that they thought something was wrong with their eyesight and that the majority were probably correct.

In a similar experiment by other researchers (Hamm & Hoving, 1969), children age 7, 10, and 13 were asked to judge how far a light moved—a perceptually ambiguous task. Before the subjects made their decisions, however, two other children gave their answers. Just as Asch discovered, many of the subjects patterned their answers on the group estimates.

Does history repeat itself? Did group pressure compound the obedience to authority displayed by the Nazis in World War II? Did it play a role in the abuse of Iraqi prisoners by U.S. Marines in 2004? Philip Zimbardo (www.zimbardo.com), who conducted the famous Stanford Prison Experiment in 1971 (Haney, Banks, & Zimbardo, 1973), believes individuation and reason can succumb to deindividuation and impulsivity in certain group pressure situations.

culture the knowledge, beliefs, art, morals, law, customs, and traditions acquired by humans as members of society

Individuals are influenced by group pressure because they desire social identity, they seek social approval, and/or they believe the group's opinions are probably correct (Bugental & Goodenow, 1998). The influence of the social group varies according to several factors (Bukowski, Newcomb, & Hartup, 1996):

1. **Attraction to the group.** The more people want to belong to a group, the more likely they will be to conform to group pressure. In elementary school and junior high school, attraction to the group becomes very important. Children of this age may have the same hairstyles, wear the same kind of shoes, and even talk alike.
2. **Acceptance by the group.** The role or status a person has—leader versus follower—in a group affects the degree of influence. A follower is more subject to group pressure than is a leader. One study found that boys who were anxious, dependent, and not sure where they stood in the group were more susceptible to group influence (Harrison, Serafica, & McAdoo, 1984).
3. **Type of group.** The degree of influence a group has depends on the affective relationships among the members. Groups in which the ties are very close, such as family or friends, exert a stronger influence than groups in which the affective ties are more distant, such as Scouts or Little League.

When individuals are influenced by group pressure because they believe the group's opinions are probably correct, it is usually because they lack confidence in their own judgment. For example, if you like a movie and later find out everyone else dislikes it, or if you have a certain political opinion and find out the rest of the group believes differently, you may begin to question your own judgment. Children who lack the experience and knowledge to have faith in their own judgment are more likely to succumb to group pressure, especially if the group is older, because they are more likely to trust the group's opinion.

Certain ethnic groups that value a sense of dependence on the group and community, such as Japanese, emphasize group pressure ("What will other people think?") as a socializing technique to control nonconforming behavior and foster achievement (Rogoff, 2003).

Tradition

Tradition is the handing down of customs, stories, and beliefs from generation to generation. In an ethnic group, tradition refers to all the knowledge, beliefs, customs, and skills that are part of that ethnic group's heritage. In religion, tradition refers to the unwritten religious code handed down from the Buddha, Moses, Jesus and the Apostles, or Mohammed. In a family, tradition is implemented in the way it celebrates holidays and tells stories. The stories that families tell represent perspectives on events and relationships that are passed on from one generation to the next. These stories give meaning to the family (Fiese, Sameroff, Grotevant, Wamboldt, Dickenstein, & Fravel, 1999).

Because tradition represents humans' ways of having solved certain problems in the past, through socialization the offspring of each generation receive a "design for living" from their ancestors—how to get shelter, how to feed themselves, how to dress, how to get along with one another. Traditional beliefs, attitudes, and values are also transmitted from one generation to another—the belief in God, the attitude that children should be protected, the value of hard work.

Tradition is a sociocultural method of socialization in that it sets the pattern for the way one satisfies basic biological needs—eating, sleeping, elimination, and sexual behavior. Some ethnic groups traditionally eat with chopsticks, others with forks

tradition customs, stories, and beliefs handed down from generation to generation

Alan Brigish/Index Stock Imagery

Traditions help remind us of socialized values, as in this celebration of independence.

and knives. Some ethnic groups sleep on the ground, others in beds. Some cultures eliminate outdoors; others have enclosed toilets. Some ethnic groups have premarital sexual taboos; others do not.

Tradition also sets the patterns by which people interact with one another. Social interaction refers to who does what in the society (roles) and how it is done (behavior). In some ethnic groups, it is traditional for the women to do the cooking; in other ethnic groups, the men do it. In some ethnic groups, the elderly are considered the wisest and are revered; in other ethnic groups, they are considered obsolete and useless. In some ethnic groups, a price is fixed in advance for an exchange in the marketplace; in other ethnic groups, the exchange is accomplished by an agreed-upon price only after a certain amount of bargaining. In some ethnic groups, people greet one another by surnames; in other ethnic groups, first names are used. Traditions become unquestioned ways of doing things that stay with us, even though we may forget the reasons behind them.

> A bride served baked ham, and her husband asked why she cut the ends off. "Well, that's the way Mother always did it," she replied.
>
> The next time his mother-in-law stopped by, he asked her why she cut the ends off the ham. "That's the way my mother did it," she replied.
>
> And when Grandma visited, she too was asked why she sliced the ends off. She said, "That's the only way I could get it into the pan." (James & Jongeward, 1971, p. 97)

Rituals and Routines

Rituals connect us with our past, define our present, and give us a future direction (Dresser, 1999; Pleck, 2000). A **ritual** is a ceremonial observance of a prescribed rule or custom. The symbols or symbolic actions embrace meaning that cannot

ritual a ceremonial observation of a prescribed rule or custom

always be easily expressed in words. Some familiar examples of rituals are the baptism or naming ceremony; the communion, signifying acceptance of a church's beliefs; the bar or bas mitzvah, signifying the age of responsibility; graduation, signifying an accomplishment; and the Navajo ritual called the Blessing Way, signifying "for good hope." Rituals serve not only a socialization function but a protective one as well, because they provide stability, something the child can "count on" in spite of change (Parke & Buriel, 1998).

The ritualization of behavior is a way of creating respect for traditions (Fiese, 2005). A ritual evokes appropriate feelings. The ritual of saying the Pledge of Allegiance evokes feelings of loyalty and reaffirms national identity. The ritual of saying grace evokes feelings of humility and thankfulness. The ritual of marriage signifies faithfulness and procreation.

Rituals that signify changes in individuals' status as they move through the cycle of life are called **rites of passage**. The most common rite of passage occurs at puberty to acknowledge passage from the state of childhood to adulthood and celebrate the transformation. Some rites involve a circumcision ceremony, as in some African or Australian tribes; some involve parties, such as a debutante ball; some involve the recitation of knowledge, as in the bar mitzvah. Graduation from high school is an American rite of passage. The ritual serves as a mechanism of socialization in that it announces to the rest of society that a certain individual has a new position and will fill a new role in the society, and it makes the individual aware of the new status and its accompanying roles and responsibilities.

Routines are repetitive acts or established procedures. In families, they may include bedtime, mealtime, and anything else done on a regular basis. They play a part in socialization because children come to know what to expect, giving them security and a chance to practice appropriate behaviors.

Symbols

Symbols are acts or objects that have come to be generally accepted as standing for or representing something else (Vander Zanden, 1995), especially something abstract. The dove is a symbol of peace; the cross is a symbol of Christ's death; the circle is a symbol of the Great Spirit.

Symbols are a powerful code or shorthand for representing and dealing with aspects of the world (Hewitt, 2003). The significance of symbols as socializing mechanisms lies in the attitudes they conjure up and the accompanying behavior they stimulate. A crown conjures up the image of authority and all the attitudes associated with it. The resultant behavior would be respect and obedience. A country's flag conjures up feelings of patriotism. A salute might be the socialized behavior. Certain ways of dressing may serve as symbols of status and role in society. A uniform may indicate a police officer; a BMW may symbolize wealth; a sarong may symbolize virginity. Symbols, then, as socializing mechanisms, serve as cues to behavior.

According to anthropology professor Leslie White (1960, p. 73):

> All culture (civilization) depends upon the symbol. It was the exercise of the symbolic faculty that brought culture into existence and it is the use of symbols that makes the perpetuation of culture possible. Without the symbol there would be no culture, and man would be merely an animal, not a human being.

The symbol to which White is referring is language. Language makes it possible to replace behavior with ideas and to communicate these ideas to the next generation.

rites of passage rituals that signify changes in individuals' status as they move through the cycle of life

routines repetitive acts or established procedures

symbols acts or objects that have come to be generally accepted as standing for something else

APPRENTICESHIP METHODS (EFFECT EMERGES FROM GUIDED PARTICIPATION)

How do you learn a behavior from someone who has already mastered it?

Apprenticeship is a process in which a novice is guided by an expert to participate in and master tasks. According to Rogoff (1990, 2003), all the methods of socialization discussed so far are imparted in the child's macrosystem by means of various apprenticeships. In other words, the child, or novice, is guided to participate in various social activities and master tasks by someone who has more expertise. This person could be a parent, a sibling, a relative, a teacher, a peer, a coach, or some other member of the community.

To illustrate how apprenticeship as a socializing method works, we look at how children learn to feed themselves. First, the child is totally dependent on his or her mother for nourishment. As the child matures physically and cognitively, he or she observes others feeding themselves and wants to try the activity independently. The mother, or caregiver, structures the feeding activities according to the capability of the child—at first providing soft food the child can grasp with the fingers, such as fruit or crackers. Then the caregiver might give the child a utensil, such as a spoon, a cup, or a pair of chopsticks, at first guiding it into the child's mouth until the child can handle it alone, offering support when needed. Thus, the caregiver and the child participate or collaborate in the activity together. When the child exhibits appropriate mastery, the caregiver transfers the responsibility for independent feeding to the child.

In sum, apprenticeship as a method of socialization progresses from the expert's *structuring* activities for the novice according to ability, to *collaborating* in joint activities so that support can be provided when needed, to *transferring* responsibility for the management of the activity when the activity is appropriately mastered.

The ages at which these progressions in apprenticeship take place vary according to the macrosystem in which the child grows up. For example, in Euro-American ethnic groups, self-feeding (drinking from a cup and using a spoon or fork) is expected by age 2, whereas in some Asian American ethnic groups, the child is breast-fed until age 2 (and in some groups, age 4), thereby extending the apprenticeship progression from dependence to independence.

Outcomes of Socialization

How would you describe your emotional, rational, social, and behavioral characteristics?

A brief overview of major socialization outcomes follows. Each will be discussed in more detail in Chapter 11 (affective/cognitive outcomes—values, attitudes, motives and attributions, and self-esteem) and Chapter 12 (social/behavioral outcomes—self-regulation/behavior, morals, and gender roles).

VALUES

What matters most to you in life?

Values are qualities or beliefs that are viewed as desirable or important. Socializing agents in microsystems influence the internalization of values. For example, what message did your parents give you about money? about

apprenticeship
a process in which a novice is guided by an expert to participate in and master tasks

values qualities or beliefs that are viewed as desirable or important

work? about spirituality? What message did your teachers or coaches give you about succeeding? What message did your friends give you about being liked?

Significant societal events (chronosystem and macrosystem influences) also affect values. For example, the Depression in the 1930s made people aware of the need to be thrifty. World War II in the 1940s evoked feelings of patriotism. In the postwar years, the prosperity of the 1950s brought forth the value of materialism. The social upheaval of the 1960s stimulated people to critically evaluate traditional systems. Acts of violence and terror in the 2000s caused people to reexamine the values of privacy versus security.

ATTITUDES

Should children have rights? If so, what?

Attitudes are tendencies to respond positively or negatively to certain persons, objects, or situations. Like values, attitudes are learned from socializing agents. Some methods by which they are acquired are via instructions ("Don't play with Sam; he doesn't go to our church"), modeling (the teacher shows concern when Juan says his father is sick), and direct experience (Leslie plays with Helena, who has cerebral palsy).

The macrosystem influences attitudes, too. During World War II, Japan was an enemy of the United States. Japanese immigrants were interned. Now Japan is a political and economic ally. What groups are currently being racially profiled and why?

MOTIVES AND ATTRIBUTIONS

What do you work hard at in order to be successful?

Motives are needs or emotions that cause a person to act, such as the need for achievement. **Attributions** are explanations for one's performance, such as "I failed the test because there were trick questions" (*external* attribution) or "I failed because I didn't study" (*internal* attribution).

Most developmental psychologists agree that there is an inborn motive to explore, understand, and control one's environment (Mayes & Zigler, 1992; White, 1959), known as **mastery motivation**. Some children are also motivated to achieve mastery of challenging tasks, known as **achievement motivation** (McClelland, Atkinson, Clark, & Lowell, 1953).

The motive to achieve, however, is not necessarily a reliable prediction of successful performance. Atkinson (1964) found that successful performers pursued challenging tasks because the desire to master them was greater than the fear of embarrassment for not doing so (motive to avoid failure). Thus, expectancies of success or failure influence achievement.

Weiner (1992) explains the role of attributions in achievement expectancies, and hence motivation. He says that people interpret past successes and failures in terms of whether they think they can control the outcomes of performance. Was success/failure due to personal ability (or lack thereof), the amount of effort expended, the level of difficulty of a task, or luck? Bandura (2000) cites the important attribute of *self-efficacy* (the belief that one can master a situation and produce positive effects) in motivating achievement.

attitude a tendency to respond positively (favorably) or negatively (unfavorably) to certain persons, objects, or situations

motives needs or emotions that cause a person to act

attributions explanations for one's performance

mastery motivation the inborn motive to explore, understand, and control one's environment

achievement motivation the motivation to achieve mastery of challenging tasks

SELF-ESTEEM

How do you feel about yourself?

Recall that *self-esteem* is the value one places on his or her identity. Why do some children come to view themselves as competent and worthy, whereas others view themselves as incompetent and unworthy?

As pointed out earlier in this chapter, Cooley's (1909/1964) "looking-glass self" and Mead's (1934) "generalized other" described the process of evaluating the self as involving the ability to perceive the opinions of significant others. Interactions with parents, peers, and significant adults who communicate approval, validation, and support influence self-esteem.

Until recently, self-esteem has been viewed as a unitary, global construct. Susan Harter (1999) has examined more specific domains, including physical competence, academic competence, behavioral competence, and social acceptance.

It is generally agreed that self-esteem begins to develop with a secure attachment to a caregiver who is sensitive and responsive to the infant's needs. Parenting styles that are warm and supportive, setting clear standards for behavior with discussions of reasons, are also influential. Peer acceptance and generally favorable social comparisons ("I can run faster than you even though you're better at math") have an impact on global self-esteem as well as on its specific domains. Finally, the influence of significant adults (relatives, teachers, coaches) who are accepting plays a role as well.

SELF-REGULATION/BEHAVIOR

How do you keep yourself "under control"?

Self-regulation is the process of bringing emotions, thoughts, and/or behavior under one's control. **Behavior** consists of what one does or how one acts in response to a stimulus.

Behavior in infancy consists mostly of biological reflexes (sucking to get nourishment, defecating to rid the body of waste), but as the child matures physically and cognitively, he or she becomes more capable of directing external behavior and internal thought processes (eating at regular intervals rather than on demand, using the toilet instead of diapers). A number of theories have been offered to explain the influence of socialization on the development of self-regulation (Bronson, 2000).

According to *psychoanalytic theory* (Freud, 1938), the ego (decision maker) develops self-regulatory capacities as a result of trying to meet the demands of the id (biological needs and instincts) and the standards of the superego (conscience, or societal ideals).

Behavioral learning theory (Skinner, 1948) views self-regulation as the learned ability to delay gratification. Self-regulation is a response that results from having been reinforced for waiting for an appropriate time and place to express a need, desire, or emotion. Children who are praised for waiting their turn to go on the swing will more easily adapt to waiting their turn at bat in a baseball game.

Social cognitive theory (Bandura, 1986) explains self-regulation as the result of internalizing observed standards of models who were reinforced for such behavior and the consequent self-reinforcement for imitating those standards.

Cognitive developmental theory (Piaget, 1952) considers self-regulation to be adaptive behavior. As children mature and interact with their environments, they assimilate and accommodate standards of behavior, adding them to existing cognitive structures and modifying the structures as their understanding changes.

behavior what one does or how one acts in response to a stimulus

Vygotskian theory focuses on the role of social and cultural factors in the development of self-regulation and behavior. Vygotsky (1978) believed that language enables the child to learn social rules and cultural roles. The language of others ("social speech") becomes internalized ("private speech"), enabling the child to think and regulate behavior accordingly.

A socialization goal of self-regulation is the development of *prosocial,* or helpful, behavior rather than *antisocial,* or aggressive, behavior (Bronson, 2000). Socialization methods associated with the development of prosocial behavior are attachment (warmth), instruction (clear rules), reasoning (discussing standards), modeling, and learning by doing (participation in activities that involve helping and cooperating) (Eisenberg & Fabes, 1998). Socialization methods associated with antisocial behavior are rejection, punishment, and group pressure (Patterson, DeBaryshe, & Ramsey, 1989).

MORALS

Why do you do "the right thing"?

Morals are an individual's evaluation of what is right and wrong. Morals involve acceptance of rules and govern one's behavior toward others.

Theories of moral development involve (1) an *affective,* or emotional, component (moral feelings such as guilt, shame, and empathy); (2) a *cognitive* component (moral reasoning, such as a conceptualization of right and wrong and related decision making); and (3) a *behavioral* component (moral action, how one responds to temptations to violate moral rules such as lying, cheating, or stealing).

Turiel (1983, 2002) distinguishes between two types of rules governing moral behavior: *moral rules,* focusing on the welfare and rights of others (no hitting, stealing, lying); and *social-conventional rules,* focusing on conduct in social situations (no talking without raising your hand, saying thank you). Although general moral reasoning is linked with cognitive development (Kohlberg, 1984; Piaget, 1965), specific perspectives on rules differ by age, gender, and culture. For example, children as young as 2-1/2 or 3 consider moral-rule misbehavior to deserve more punishment than social-conventional-rule misbehavior (Smetana, 1985).

Some theorists believe that different cultural and social experiences growing up influence different moral perspectives. For example, according to Triandis (1995), in individualistic cultures, morality is generally oriented toward *justice* (principles of equality, fairness, rights), whereas in collectivistic cultures, morality is generally oriented toward *care* (principles of welfare, compassion, relationships).

Cultural values regarding right and wrong influence children's moral perspectives. For example, one study compared children ages 5 to 13 in the United States with children in India (Shweder, Mahapatra, & Miller, 1987) on responses to 39 moral transgressions. The Indian children, who were Hindu, believed that it was morally worse for the eldest son in a family to eat chicken and get a haircut the day after his father died (thereby showing disrespect) than it was for a husband to beat his wife for going to a movie without his permission after having been warned (thereby fulfilling his duty as head of the family). Hindus believe that respect for father and husband is a universal moral rule, not an arbitrary social convention created by members of a society.

morals an individual's evaluation of what is right and wrong

Thus, differences in socialization contribute to moral development—specifically, parents' affect and attachment, their use of reasoning (Laible & Thompson, 2000), modeling of appropriate behavior and reinforcement, peer interaction, and real experiences in school and community with diverse viewpoints, necessitating discussion and compromise.

GENDER ROLES

Are males and females really psychologically similar?

Gender roles are qualities that an individual understands to characterize males and females in his or her culture. The term *gender* usually refers to psychological attributes, whereas the term *sex* usually refers to biological ones.

Biologically, males and females differ in their chromosomes (male—XY, female—XX), their hormones, and their physiques. They also differ in the social roles they assume based on societal expectations. The female's biological capacity to bear children is associated in many societies with the expectation that she will assume a nurturing, cooperative role. The male's hormones (testosterone) and his muscular physique are associated in many societies with the expectation that he will assume an assertive, dominant role.

Theories of gender-role development, explaining how children are socialized to assume behaviors, values, attitudes considered appropriate for their sex, will be discussed in more detail in Chapter 12. *Psychoanalytic theory* focuses on how one learns to *feel* like a male or a female based on identification with the same-sex parent. *Behavior learning theory* focuses on how one learns to *act* like a male or a female based on reinforcement of expected gender-appropriate behavior. *Social cognitive theory* focuses on how one learns to *imitate* gender-role models. *Gender schema theory* focuses on how one *processes* gender-related information and selects what is appropriate and worthy for him or her.

gender roles the qualities that an individual understands to characterize males and females in his or her culture

Epilogue

To be human is to be caring and to have a conscience. Socialization of the child into a "human being" is multifaceted, dynamic, and reciprocal. Socialization methods vary in effectiveness according to the person implementing them, the situation, and the child to whom they are directed.

Pinocchio was influenced by Gepetto, Jiminy Cricket, the Blue Fairy, and others. Gepetto provided love and acceptance; Jiminy Cricket provided instructions, feedback, support, and encouragement; the Blue Fairy provided standards and rewards; the others provided experiences for learning by doing. After experiencing many consequences, both positive and negative, Pinocchio determined to adopt Gepetto's values to be "good," put himself at risk to save Gepetto's life, and was rewarded by turning into a "real boy."

Summary

Socialization involves aims, goals, methods, and outcomes. It is a reciprocal, dynamic process, with children playing a role in their own socialization as a result of their biology, their culture, and their individual life experiences.

Socialization aims to develop a self-concept. Erikson's eight stages of psychosocial development are trust versus mistrust, autonomy versus shame and doubt, initiative versus guilt, industry versus inferiority, identity versus identity diffusion, intimacy versus isolation, generativity versus self-absorption, and integrity versus despair.

Socialization aims to enable self-regulation/control and to empower achievement by teaching appropriate social roles and developmental skills (social, emotional, and cognitive). A developmental task is "midway between an individual need and a societal demand." Developmental tasks differ from society to society.

Every individual in society represents outcomes of the socialization process. The success of this outcome in terms of society's expectations depends on a series of interactions with significant socializing agents that are components of the community in which the individual lives. The significant agents of socialization discussed in this chapter are the family, the school, the peer group, the media, and the community.

The family is the child's introduction to society and therefore bears major responsibility for socializing the child. The family is a system of interaction. The relationships have a powerful effect on the psychosocial development of children. The family is the child's first reference group for values.

The school acts as an agent of society in that it is organized to perpetuate that society's knowledge, skills, customs, and beliefs. It also acts as an agent to foster respect for and adherence to the existing social order while educating for adaptability.

Child care has become an important socialization agent because of societal changes in the amount of time children spend being cared for by individuals outside the family.

The peer group gives children experience in egalitarian types of relationships. Children learn to look at themselves from the group's point of view. Peers also serve as a support group for the expression of values and attitudes. They exert a strong influence on those who need social identity and approval.

The media, unlike other agents of socialization, do not involve direct personal interaction. The media are considered to be socializers, however, because they teach many of the ways of the society. Children process media information, constructing meaning and transforming it into behavior.

The community provides a sense of belonging and friendship. The population distribution of a community affects the interactions a child will have. The types of agencies, such as Scouts, the "Y," and Little League, that a community provides affect the experiences a child has while growing up. The services a community provides, such as libraries, museums, and cultural events, affect which parts of society are opened to the child. Communities can be support systems for families. Advocacy is the process by which this occurs.

Socialization is the process by which individuals learn the ways of a given society so that they can function effectively within it. These ways are transmitted through a number of different methods: affective (attachment); operant (reinforcement, extinction, punishment, feedback, learning by doing); observational (modeling); cognitive (instruction, setting standards, reasoning); sociocultural (group pressure, tradition, rituals and routines, symbols); and apprenticeship (structuring, collaborating, transferring).

The outcomes of socialization outlined here are affective/cognitive (values, attitudes, motives and attributions, self-esteem) and social/behavioral (self-regulation of behavior, morals, gender roles).

Activity

PURPOSE To understand the impact of agents of socialization on development.

1. Name the three most important things you learned from your parents while growing up.

2. Name three people other than your parents who had a major influence on you as a child or adolescent.

3. Describe each one's influence, using specific examples.
4. What methods of socialization did your parents and the significant others in your life use?
5. Whom are you influencing in ways similar to the ones you have described?
6. What are your aims and methods of socialization?

Related Readings

Bandura, A. (1986). *Social foundations of thought and action: A social cognitive theory.* Englewood Cliffs, NJ: Prentice-Hall.

Bjorklund, D. P., & Pelligrini, A. D. (2002). *The origins of human nature: Evolutionary developmental psychology.* Washington, DC: American Psychological Association.

Bowlby, J. (1988). *A secure base: Parent–child attachment and healthy human development.* New York: Basic Books.

Brazelton, T. B. (1984). *To listen to a child.* Reading, MA: Perseus Books.

Cialdini, R. B. (2001). *Influence: Science and practice* (4th ed.). Boston: Allyn and Bacon.

Erikson, E. (1963). *Childhood and society.* New York: Norton.

Golding, W. (1954). *Lord of the flies.* New York: Putnam.

Goleman, D. (1995). *Emotional intelligence.* New York: Bantam.

Pleck, E. H. (2000). *Celebrating the family: Ethnicity, consumer culture, and family rituals.* Cambridge, MA: Harvard University Press.

Rogoff, B. (2003). *The cultural nature of human development.* New York: Oxford University Press.

Chapter 3

DesignPics Inc./Index Stock Imagery

Ecology of the Family

My soul knows that I am part of the human race, . . . as my spirit is part of my nation. In my very own self, I am part of my family.

— **D. H. Lawrence**

Reproduction is a basic part of human nature, as is the care of the young. To perpetuate human society, the family as a social system has evolved. D. H. Lawrence's quote implies that one's self is part of one's family, which is part of one's community, which is part of the human race.

Until recently, families chose marriage partners for their children; love was assumed to develop later. Arranged marriages still exist in many ethnic groups and cultures. The purpose of the arrangement might be economic, political, religious, or cultural. Nevertheless, marriages were ties that bound the families of the spouses together, creating alliances with certain rights and obligations. The following biblical story illustrates how families evolved.

Once Upon a Time At the beginning of the human race, God told Adam and Eve to "be fruitful and multiply." About 4,000 years ago, God told one of their descendents, Abraham, that he was chosen to be the father of many generations to come. He is credited with being the first biblical patriarch of the Jews, Christians, and Muslims. Abraham's wife, Sarah, however, does not conceive, so she tells Abraham to take their slave, Hagar, into his bed. Hagar bears him a son, Ishmael, who becomes the father of Islam. Meanwhile, after many years of infertility, Abraham and Sarah are promised a son in return for a covenant with God. Their son, Isaac, then becomes the destined ancestor of many future generations of Jews and Christians.

To assure that the family line will continue as agreed, Abraham selects his son's future wife from another land, sending gifts with a servant to be given to the betrothed's family. Rebekah, the bride-to-be, leaves her family to live with Isaac and his family in his land and bear his children. Hence, the pattern of traditional family formation was born, a family based on kinship and community ties with certain rights and obligations of its members, under the father's authority. The goal was security and continuance; "happiness" was secondary.

- **What are the personal and family consequences (positive and negative) of subscribing to a value of obligation to the self on one end of the spectrum versus obligation to others on the other end of the spectrum?**

- **Who has the most at stake in the marriage or family union—adults or children?**

- **How are one's views on societal change and how children should be socialized related to the family system (structure, functions, relationships)?**

Family Systems

What is the purpose of families and how do they work?

This chapter provides an understanding of what a family is, what a family does, how different families adapt to change, and how different families cope with external forces. Figure 3.1 shows an ecological model of the systems involved in the process. *Family systems theory* views the family as a whole, in terms of its structure and organizational patterns, and at the individual level, in terms of how members interact with one another (Parke & Buriel, 1998).

In Chapters 1 and 2, the aims, methods, and outcomes of socialization were discussed, and the agents of socialization identified. Here, the family, the primary agent of socialization, is explored. A family is a microsystem. The classic (structural-functional) definition of a family, according to sociologist George Murdock (1962, p. 19), is "a social group characterized by common residence, economic cooperation, and reproduction. It includes adults of both sexes, at least two of whom maintain a socially approved sexual relationship, and one or more children, own or adopted, of the sexually cohabiting adults."

Figure 3.1

An Ecological Model of Human Development

The family is a primary influence on the child's development.

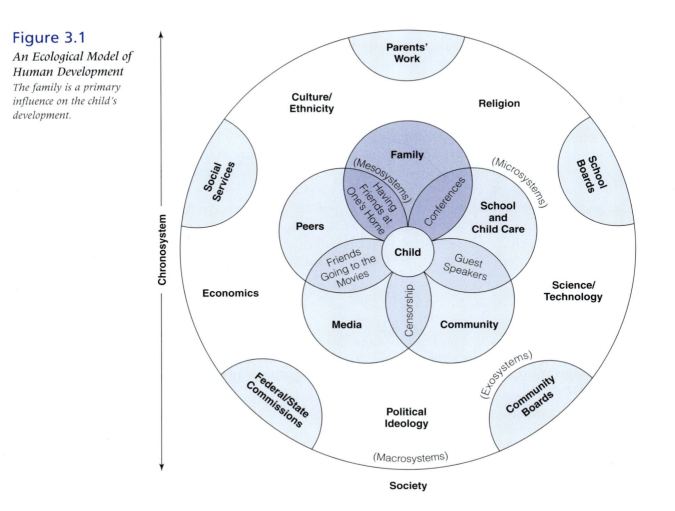

How many families do you know that fit this classic definition? Today, relationships that do *not* conform to Murdock's definition are more common than those that do, illustrating the impact of societal change on the family system's form and function.

To accommodate changes in family patterns, the U.S. Bureau of the Census defines a **family** as "two or more persons related by birth, marriage, or adoption, who reside together." Thus, a family can be two or more adult siblings living together, a parent and child or children, two adults who are related by marriage but have no children, or adults who adopt a child.

Some states (Vermont, for example) and cities have legally recognized certain unrelated people in caring relationships who live together in a household as a "family." These laws pertaining to "domestic partnerships," "reciprocal partnerships," or "civil unions" are intended to provide gay couples, foster parents, related pairs (mother/daughter, two brothers), and stepfamilies with rights and privileges related to health insurance policies, medical and educational decisions, employment leave policies, employment benefits, annuities, and pensions.

It is important to understand the changes in the concept of the definition of family structure because these changes affect the functions that families perform, the roles its members play, and the relationships its members have with one another, thereby affecting the socialization of children.

Family—Romantic or Real?

Is family a structure or function?
What were some of your family traditions?
What about your family was healthy/unhealthy?

BASIC FAMILY STRUCTURES

What is your concept of a family?

Families are organized in different ways around the world. A family consisting of a husband and wife and their children is called a **nuclear family**. For the children, such a family is the **family of orientation**, which means the family into which one is born. For the parents, the nuclear family is the **family of procreation**, the family that develops when one marries and has children (see Figure 3.2). In the nuclear family, the wife and husband depend on each other for companionship and the children depend on their parents for affection and socialization.

The significance of the nuclear family structure is that it is the main source of children and so provides the basis for the perpetuation of the society. Most societies assign responsibility for the care and socialization of children to the couple that produces or adopts them and sanction the sexual union of a male and a female by law or tradition—in our society, by legal marriage. The institution of marriage, then, serves not only to legalize a sexual union but also to fix the obligation toward children who result from that sexual union.

The **extended family** pattern consists of relatives of the nuclear family who are economically and emotionally dependent on each other. They may or may not live nearby (see Figure 3.3).

family any two or more related people living in one household

nuclear family a family consisting of a husband and wife and their children

family of orientation the family into which one is born

family of procreation the family that develops when one marries and has children

extended family relatives of the nuclear family who are economically and emotionally dependent on each other

Figure 3.2
Nuclear Family

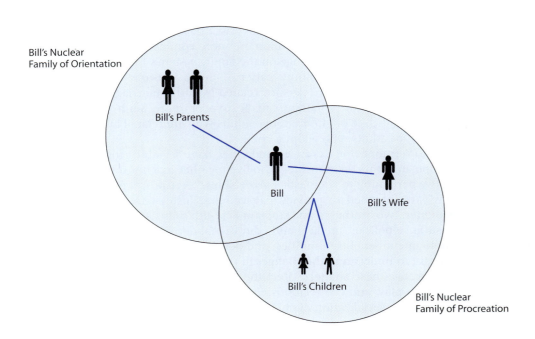

In some cultures or ethnic groups, such as Native Americans, Asian Americans, and Italian Americans, great emphasis is placed on the extended family (obligation to family supersedes obligation to the self). In these ethnic groups, tradition assigns certain obligations and responsibilities to various members of the extended family—for example, who socializes the children, who decides how the family resources are allocated, and who cares for needy family members. Some cultures emphasize the mother's side of the family as having the responsibility for socialization, authority, and resources. These families are known as **matriarchal**. A contemporary example would be the royal family in Great Britain headed by Queen Elizabeth II. Other cultures emphasize the father's relatives as having responsibility for care of the family's members, authority, and resources. These families are known as **patriarchal**. This organizational pattern is much more common in the world than is the matriarchal. Examples of patriarchal families can be found in the Bible and in the popular television series *The Sopranos*.

In the United States, both sides of the extended family are generally regarded as equal, or **egalitarian**. Your mother's parents have as much legal authority and responsibility over you as do your father's parents. If something happened to your parents and they could no longer care for you, both sets of grandparents would have equal claim to your custody. Because we live in an egalitarian society, whose parents' house you go to for holidays after you are married sometimes has to be negotiated. In traditional societies, the rules are set; in modern ones like ours, the rules are ever changing (Silverstein & Auerbach, 2001).

Regardless of whether your extended family is matriarchal, patriarchal, or egalitarian, its main function is support; relatives are the people you turn to when you need help or when you have joys to share. Because, in today's society, many nuclear families do not have an extended family for support (for reasons that include moving, divorce, remarriage, and death), the people they turn to for help might be friends, neighbors, co-workers, or children's teachers (see Figure 3.4). These people assume some of the traditional support functions of the extended family and become one's

matriarchal family
family in which the mother has formal authority and dominance

patriarchal family
family in which the father has formal authority and dominance

egalitarian family
family in which both sides of the extended family are regarded as equal

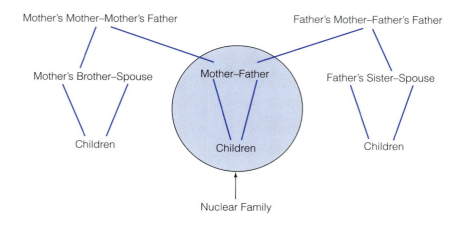

Figure 3.3
Extended Family

personal network (Dean, 1984). People who have no such personal network have to rely on the *formal network* of society—professionals or government agencies—for support (Garbarino, 1992). Support services provided by the formal network are influenced by politics, economics, culture, and technology. For a political example, the federally funded preschool program, Head Start, was launched by the Democrats and later experienced a reduction in funding by the Republicans. For an economic example, the cultural norm of working for a living was a significant factor in changing government financial support for needy families—from welfare to workfare. For a technology example, cell phones and computers compete for family members' time together.

BASIC FAMILY FUNCTIONS

What do families do?

In general, the family performs certain basic functions that enable society to survive and continue generation after generation, although how these functions are implemented may vary by culture. Family functioning can be seen as a continuum, with "healthy," or functional, at one end and "unhealthy," or dysfunctional, at the other (keeping in mind that no family is "healthy" all the time). Economic, health, and social stresses can upset some or all of the following basic family functions:

- **Reproduction**. The family ensures that the society's population will be maintained; that is, a sufficient number of children will be born and cared for to replace the members who die.
- **Socialization/education**. The family ensures that the society's values, beliefs, attitudes, knowledge, skills, and techniques will be transmitted to the young.
- **Assignment of social roles**. The family provides an identity for its offspring (racial, ethnic, religious, socioeconomic, and gender roles). An identity involves behavior and obligations. For example, a Jewish person may not eat pork and may feel obliged to give to charity. A Chinese person may eat with chopsticks and defer to the authority of his or her elders. A person born into a high socioeconomic status may be pressured to choose a spouse from a similar family background. In some families, girls are socialized to do housework and be caregivers and boys to be breadwinners.
- **Economic support**. The family provides shelter, nourishment, and protection. In some families, all members except very young children contribute to the economic function by producing goods. In other families, one or both parents earn the money that pays for goods the entire family consumes.

Figure 3.4

Sources of Family Support

Source: Adapted from Dean, 1984

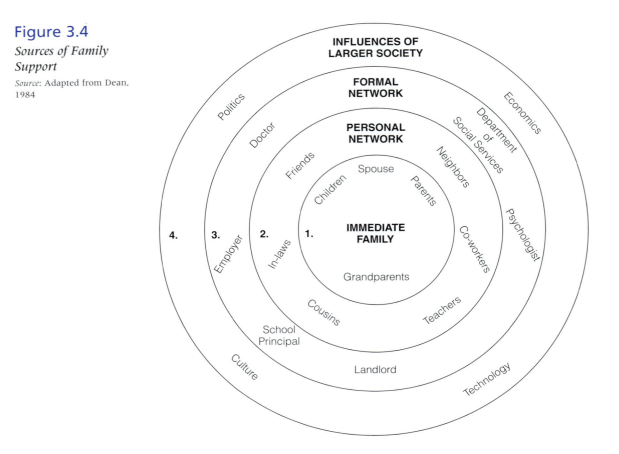

- **Nurturance/emotional support**. The family provides the child's first experience in social interaction. This interaction is intimate, nurturing, and enduring, thus providing emotional security for the child. The family cares for its members when they are ill, hurt, or aging.

Family Transitions

How has the family adapted to societal change?

Throughout history, family structure has adapted to accommodate economic, social, political, and technological influences. Examples of such chronosystem influences include the Industrial Revolution, no-fault divorce, welfare reform, and birth control.

STRUCTURAL FAMILY CHANGES

What influences family composition?

Structural family changes can include the addition of family members to the household, as by birth, adoption, remarriage, or relatives (kin) moving in; or the removal of family members, as by death, divorce, or children becoming adults and moving out.

Library of Congress

Early American farm life required everyone's participation for family survival.

Family Ties
What events affect family ties?

Although families are always in a process of transition (marriage, childbirth, death), certain events affect the socialization of children more than others. These are divorce, single parenting, and stepparenting.

Changes in family ties are documented by the increase in divorce and in the proportion of children living with only one parent. According to the U.S. Bureau of the Census (2003), the number of children living with one parent (divorced or never married) at some point in childhood is 1 out of 2.

Parental divorce is not a single event but rather represents a series of stressful experiences for the entire family that begins with marital conflict before the actual separation and includes many adjustments afterward. Families must often cope with a reduction in family resources, assumption of new roles and responsibilities, establishment of new patterns of interaction, reorganization of routines, and probably the introduction of new relationships into the existing family (Hetherington & Clingempeel, 1992). More specifically, parents in conflicted marriages are less able to help their children regulate emotions and behavior, as well as self-soothe their own stress (Kelly, 2000).

As the divorce rate has risen in the 1990s, so has the frequency of remarriage (U.S. Bureau of the Census, 2003). When a divorced person remarries, the children gain a stepparent. With the stepparent come additional kinship relationships. New roles and obligations, not derived from custom and tradition, have to be established.

Divorce and the Law
How have changes in the macrosystem affected divorce?

Divorce laws have adapted to such societal changes as increased cost of living, employment of women, and the father's role in child care. Formerly, the law permitted divorce only if one spouse committed such serious marital misconduct as adultery, cruelty, or desertion. Traditional divorce proceedings involved a determination of who was guilty and who was innocent. Child custody arrangements and financial settlements were intended to reward the innocent party and punish the guilty one. For example, a woman, deemed to be the innocent party, would not have to agree to a divorce unless her husband, deemed to be the guilty party, provided adequate support for her and the children. Further, judges would often divide property in accordance with family need. The mother and children retained the family home and enough support to avoid sudden poverty (Skolnick, 1987). Divorce cases were often costly financially and emotionally—to both parents and children.

Criticisms of existing laws led to the passage of no-fault divorce laws. These laws do away with assigning blame and allow divorces on the basis of "irreconcilable differences" or "marital breakdown." Today, in most states, the family's assets are divided equally between the spouses. Often the family home must be sold in order to divide the couple's tangible assets. The husband and wife each usually retain their intangible assets such as education, career, future earning power, pension(s), and insurance. Thus, today's divorce laws have had a tremendous influence on how the family is able to adjust to inevitable changes accompanying the dissolution of a marriage.

Divorce and the Family
How does the family adapt to divorce?

Functions. Divorce has certain consequences for family functioning and the socialization of children. Barring external social support, the effect of divorce on the custodial parent is that the responsibilities double. The single parent is responsible for financial support, child care, and home maintenance. Because the parent is usually under great stress, parenting is likely to diminish (Goodman, Emery, & Haugaard, 1998). The children may have to take increased responsibility for themselves and may have less time available to spend with the parent to receive love and security. In an attempt to prevent the consequences of divorce, some states are enacting mandatory waiting periods, mediation, and marital counseling before legalizing an application for divorce.

Roles. To assess the effect of divorce, one must examine how all the various members of the family deal with the transition, reestablish their role obligations to one another, and perform such functions as the following (Hetherington & Clingempeel, 1992):

- **Socialization/education.** Child rearing must continue; behavior must be monitored, values and morals imparted.
- **Assignment of social roles/authority**. Power for decision making within the family must be allocated and responsibilities for tasks assigned.
- **Economic support/domestic responsibilities**. The family must obtain enough money to provide for the support of its members. The physical well-being of the children must be provided for, and the residence must be maintained in a safe and healthy manner.
- **Nurturance/emotional support.** Caring and involvement toward one another are necessary to provide for the emotional well-being of family members.

The ability of the family going through a divorce to carry on its former functions is affected not only by the coping skills of its members but also by macrosystem forces. These forces include economic disparity for females, societal attitudes regarding the ideal two-parent family, and available informal or formal support services (Coontz, 1997; Hetherington, 1989).

Regardless of their marital status, women do not earn income on the same scale as men. Although men are legally required to support their children following divorce, and in some cases their wives too, evidence shows that the majority of men do not continue to provide support even when the court orders them to do so (Children's Defense Fund, 2004). Sometimes a woman who heads a family must turn to her own family of orientation or to the government for economic assistance. Evidence shows that children who live in mother-only families have almost a 1-in-2 chance of being in poverty, in contrast to a less than 1-in-10 chance for children living with two parents (Children's Defense Fund, 2004).

Economics. The change in the economic status of the family resulting from divorce means not only a change in family consumption habits, but often a change in housing. Moving in itself is a source of stress to the family; for one thing, former neighborhood supports are no longer available. Also, maintaining two households is costly when a parent lives in one place but must contribute to another.

Authority. Divorce affects the distribution of authority within the family. Before the divorce, the father may have had more authority because traditionally he had been regarded as the primary breadwinner, or authority may have been shared by both parents. After the divorce, however, the custodial parent assumes day-to-day authority over the children, and the noncustodial parent becomes restricted to areas spelled out in the divorce agreement. Hetherington and Kelly (2002) found that both fathers' and mothers' authority over children, as indicated by their parenting practices, tended to deteriorate in the first two years following the divorce. There was less consistency, control, and affection.

Domestic Responsibility. Divorce affects the distribution of the domestic functions of the family. Before the divorce, both parents performed chores related to family functioning. If the mother was not employed outside the home, it was likely that she was primarily responsible for household duties and child care while the father was earning the money. In such cases, after the divorce, the mother is more likely to have custody of the children (Hetherington & Kelly, 2002). Generally, she has to find work outside the home because of a reduction in the father's economic contribution to her and the children. In addition, she has to find someone to care for the children. For his part, the father has to assume the domestic duties associated with his separate household or else hire someone to clean, cook, shop, and do laundry. If the mother was employed outside the home before the divorce, the father may have shared domestic responsibilities with her. This means that after the divorce she has to assume his chores as well.

Emotional Support. The isolation of the nuclear family from relatives compounds the dilemma of the burdens thrust upon the single-parent family—relatives cannot be called upon for help with child care, household duties, or emotional support. Because emotional support is one of the functions of the family, and divorce removes one adult from the context, the remaining adult no longer has someone with whom to share the burdens and joys of child rearing. Neither is there some-one with whom to share the daily decision making and to provide needed psycho-logical support.

Effects of Divorce on Children
How do children experience parental divorce?

According to the U.S. Bureau of the Census (2003), almost one out of two marriages ends in divorce. Most divorces occur within the first 10 years for both first marriages and remarriages. Children experience a deep sense of loss, develop divided loyal-ties, and often feel helpless against forces beyond their control. In summarizing the last three decades of research on the effects of divorce, Hetherington and Kelly (2002) report that although children of divorced parents, as a group, have more adjustment problems than do children of never-divorced parents, the divorce per se is not necessarily the major cause of these problems; rather, the negative effects of conflict in troubled marriages can be observed in children years before the divorce takes place.

Parental divorce involves a series of stressful interactions between children and their environment as the family restructures. However, not all children react to divorce in the same way (Sandler, Tein, & West, 1994). Children's reactions depend on the various personalities involved, their coping skills, and the parents' relations with their children (Cowan, Powell, & Cowan, 1998). Reactions also depend on such factors as age and gender, how much family disharmony existed before the divorce, and how available other people are to the parents for emotional support and to the children for role models (Kelly & Emery, 2003; Hetherington & Stanley-Hagan, 2002). Studies by Hetherington (1988, 1989, 1993) show that during and after parental divorce, children often exhibit marked changes in behavior, such as acting out, particularly in school. An analysis of academic achievement of high school students showed that those from divorced families had significantly lower achievement levels than those from intact families (Hetherington & Kelly, 2002).

Age.   Wallerstein and Kelly (1996) found that divorce affected the self-concept of the preschool child. In particular, the child's views of the dependability and pre-dictability of relationships were disrupted. Some children blamed themselves for the breakup. For example, one 5-year-old child said, "If only I didn't whine like Daddy said, he wouldn't have left me." Even a year later, in a follow-up study, almost half the children in the sample still displayed heightened anxiety and aggression. These authors also found that school-age children responded to divorce with sadness, fear, feelings of deprivation, and some anger (Wallerstein, Corbin, & Lewis, 1988; Wallerstein & Kelly, 1996). They, like the preschool children, were still struggling after a year with the changes in their lives. School-age children had difficulty focusing their attention on school-related tasks.

In various studies (Amato, 2000; Hetherington & Clingempeel, 1992), young children of divorce were found to be more dependent, aggressive, whiny, demand-ing, unaffectionate, and disobedient than children from intact families. They feared abandonment, loss of love, and bodily harm. The behavior and fears expressed were due, in part, to the parents' preoccupation with their own needs, as well as to the ensuing role conflicts. When compared to parents of intact families, divorced par-ents of preschoolers were less consistent in their discipline and less nurturant. Also, communication was not as effective, and they made fewer demands for mature behavior from their children.

Adolescents, unlike younger children, feel little sense of blame for the separation of their parents, but they feel resentment. They are often pawns in each parent's bid for loyalty: "She tells me terrible things about my dad; when I'm with him, he tells me terrible things about her." They are also still burdened by painful memories of the divorce 10 years later (Wallerstein et al., 1988).

Gender. Gender influences the impact of divorce, with research showing that boys are harder hit. Hetherington (1988, 1993), in attempting to explain this difference, suggested that boys receive less support from their mothers, teachers, and peers than do girls. Girls tend to cry and whine to vent their sadness—and this gets them help—whereas boys tend to bully other children and cry only when hit back.

According to Lamb (2004), the father's role in the socialization of children is very important. He not only models and teaches gender roles, he also models and teaches other values and morals. As children grow, each parent interprets society to them. Children from a single-parent family lack the live-in gender role model of the parent, usually the father, who has left. Single parents can, however, provide opportunities for children to have opposite-sex role models in the form of relatives, teachers, coaches, or community service personnel.

Disharmony. Children involved in custody battles are the most torn by divorce (Kelly, 2000). To avoid this win/lose situation, some parents are turning to joint custody, sharing responsibility for their children. The effects of various custody arrangements are discussed later in the chapter.

Emotional Support. Although divorce is upsetting to everyone involved, it is probably worse for a child to live in an embattled household. For parents, divorce is a very stressful time, and feelings of depression, loss of self-esteem, and helplessness interfere with parenting abilities. Parents must find support outside the family to bolster their confidence in themselves and their ability to parent. They must tell the child that even though they are divorcing each other, they are not divorcing the child.

Role Models. A serious long-range effect of divorce is the removal of marriage models. Unrealistic expectations of future mates occur. Children may grow up idealizing the absent parent. Ideals are wishes for perfection; they are untempered by reality. For example, a child growing up in a two-parent home may experience Daddy's illnesses (Daddy needs to be cared for, too), disagreements (that may or may not be worked out), and physical affection from both parents. The child growing up in a single-parent home may fantasize situations and relationships regarding the missing parent; reality inevitably brings disappointment.

Single-Parent Custody
What is the effect on children of being raised by one parent?

In the United States, the percentage of children living with a single parent has more than doubled since 1970. The number of single mothers raising children has increased more than threefold, and the number of single fathers raising children has quadrupled (U.S. Bureau of the Census, 2003).

Single parenthood can occur through death, divorce, desertion, births outside marriage, adoption without marriage, or even artificial insemination. Some people believe that having a husband is no longer a prerequisite for raising children.

However, "children in female-headed homes are often deprived of two types of resources a father might provide—economic and socioemotional" (McLanahan & Carlson, 2002, p. 151). Apparently, motherhood is not a prerequisite for raising a child, either. The Uniform Parentage Act of 1973, a law in about 20% of the states, awards custody based on care, rather than biology, when appropriate.

Female heads of households often have to work outside the home as well as care for the children and maintain the household. They are likely to depend on other caregivers. Frequently, female-headed families are poor; at the least, a drop in the family's standard of living occurs if the woman was previously married. Thus, single-parent mothers experience economic as well as emotional and physical strain (Hetherington & Clingempeel, 1992; Peterson, 1996).

Generally, preadolescent boys show more intense and enduring problems in response to their parents' divorce than do girls. Two years after the divorce, many boys have trouble concentrating, do poorly on intelligence tests, and have difficulty with math. Also, they interact aggressively with their mothers, their teachers, and boys their own age. Monitoring of boys was lower in divorced nonremarried households, and the boys engaged in more antisocial behavior (Hetherington, 1993; Hetherington & Clingempeel, 1992). Although preadolescent girls seem to adjust to the divorce within two to three years, evidence has accumulated showing problems related to feminine gender role development emerging at adolescence. Problems include difficult heterosexual relationships, precocious sexual activity, and confrontational exchanges with the mother (Ellis et al., 2003; Hetherington, 1993). Studies (Coontz, 1997; Miller, Forehand, & Kotchick, 1999) that control for family process (monitoring of children, communication) have found that single parenthood is *not* related to early teen sexual behavior, but *rules* about dating are; ethnicity was not influential. Apparently, it is harder to establish and enforce such rules when one parents alone, without support.

In sum, the effect of the father's absence on boys and girls depends on the age of the child at the time of separation from the father, how long the father is absent, the quality of the mother–father relationship before separation, the availability of substitute appropriate male models, and the emotional state of the mother during and after the separation (Biller, 1993; Kelly, 2000; Wallerstein & Kelly, 1996).

Because children under age 18 are much more likely to be living with their mothers than with their fathers, little research has been done on children being raised by single-parent fathers, and most studies have involved school-age children. Until recently, custody of the children of divorcing parents was usually awarded automatically to the mother. Now, however, many courts are taking into consideration the actual needs of the children involved when custody is awarded, and more fathers are getting custody.

Another reason that little research has been done on children being raised by single-parent fathers is that fathers with custody, more than mothers, tend to use additional caregivers, such as babysitters, friends, relatives, and day-care centers. Thus, children growing up in single-father homes are likely to have opportunities to interact with female role models, which makes it more difficult to research the effect on children of the mother's absence. Also, father-custody children have more contact with their mothers than mother-custody children have with their fathers (Parke & Buriel, 1998; Santrock & Warshak, 1979).

Studies done by Santrock and associates (Santrock & Warshak, 1979; Santrock, Warshak, & Eliot, 1982) compared families in which the mother was awarded custody, families in which the father was awarded custody, and two-parent families. They found that girls who live with their fathers and boys who live with their mothers tend to be less well adjusted than those who live with the same-sex parent. Boys who live with their fathers tend to be less demanding, more mature, independent, and sociable, and to have higher self-esteem than girls in father-custody situations. Likewise, girls who live with their mothers tend to be less demanding, more mature, independent, and sociable, and to have higher self-esteem than boys in mother-custody situations. However, another study (Downey & Powell, 1993) of 400 eighth-grade boys and girls failed to find any evidence that boys and girls benefit significantly from living with their same-sex parent.

Problems for fathers raising children are similar to those of mothers. In general, fathers find it difficult to obtain child-care help (day care, after-school care, housekeepers). Sometimes day-care centers' hours do not coincide with work hours, and the cost of a housekeeper or nanny is prohibitive. There is also role overload in having to work, care for children, and maintain the house. Social life suffers.

A common problem among fathers is that they tend to receive little preparation for homemaking and parenting. Buying groceries, mending, ironing, doing dishes, and keeping the house clean are difficult adjustments. Many fathers have little knowledge regarding the normal developmental stages of children or about parenting (Biller, 1993). Fathers' *economic* responsibility for their children has been the focus of public policy and consequent legislation; fathers' *emotional* responsibility has been ignored until recently (Amato, 1998, 2000). Fathers are now being included in prenatal, preschool, and elementary school programs.

IN PRACTICE

Recommendations for Community Support of Single Parents

- Extend availability of day-care facilities to evening hours.
- Form babysitting cooperatives in neighborhoods or places of employment.
- Make transportation available for children to and from day care to parent's home or work.
- Provide classes on single parenthood and opportunities for support groups.
- Provide Big Sister programs (for girls from mother-absent homes) as well as Big Brother programs (for boys from father-absent homes).

Joint Custody

Joint custody is a modern-day solution to the quandary facing many judges: Which adult claimant should be given custody of a child? It also provides the rationale for father–mother involvement in child rearing, which enables the child to relate to both male and female role models (Biller, 1993). A concern expressed by Mary Ann Mason (1998), in her book *The Custody Wars*, is that the legal shift to "equal treatment" of men and women has translated into parents' rights taking precedence over children's needs.

Joint custody can refer to legal and/or physical custody arrangements. Joint *legal* custody divides decision-making authority for the child between the divorced parents. Typical areas requiring decisions include discipline, education, medical care, and religious upbringing. Sometimes *physical* custody is divided as well. For example, a child may spend weekdays with one parent and weekends and holidays with the other, or 6 months with one and 6 months with the other.

As the number of divorces has climbed, so has the number of states giving legal sanction to some form of joint custody. As a result, some nuclear families split by divorce are evolving into a new form, called the **binuclear family**, in which the children are part of two homes and two family groups. Binuclear families are not limited to joint custody cases, but parents without legal custody eventually tend to become less involved in the child's life.

Joint custody has as many negatives as positives, depending on the individuals and situations involved (Maccoby & Mnookin, 1992). The main advantage is that it requires that the parents' top priority be the child. Parents have to set aside their differences and make decisions based on the child's welfare, not their own. Joint custody is supposed to encourage continued child-support payments and mutual sharing of parental responsibilities. An analysis of studies on children in joint physical or legal custody showed they were better adjusted than children in sole-custody settings and no different from intact families (Bauserman, 2002).

The realistic disadvantage to joint custody, however, is that usually the parents are divorcing because they can no longer communicate or cooperate with one another. So what may happen is that parents divide authority, and the joint-custody child, instead of having two decision-making parents, ends up having none because the parents can't agree. Lack of consensus or inconsistency is confusing to a child and may undermine discipline.

If the divorce was bitter, then the increased communication between the parents required by joint custody is likely to become more hostile, thereby exposing the children to even more conflict and psychological damage (Maccoby & Mnookin, 1992). Another problem occurs when parents use the child to communicate messages between them (Furstenburg & Cherlin, 1991)—"Tell your father to send the check or he won't get to see you next weekend"—and to inform each parent of the other's activities (Parke & Buriel, 1998).

Although joint custody gives children access to both parents, thereby avoiding the feeling of being abandoned by the noncustodial parent, some children, especially younger ones, are actually harmed by the inevitable continual separation and reattachment. Preschool children have a very difficult time understanding why everyone can't live in the same house and "Why, if Mommy loves me and Daddy loves me, don't they love each other anymore?" School-age children express confusion and anxiety over their schedules, anxiety that spills over into school performance and relationships with friends (Francke, 1983). For example, a 6-year-old became obsessed with carrying his backpack everywhere because he was afraid of leaving his homework at one parent's house while he stayed at the other's. An 11-year-old girl felt that she could never be anyone's "best" friend because she didn't stay in one house long enough. To her, being a best friend meant being around all the time.

A remaining question regarding joint custody is, What happens over time? Children grow and change. Some parents remarry, take new jobs, or relocate. What works today may not work tomorrow.

Kin Custody

An increasing number of children are being raised by relatives (kin) other than parents, the most common being grandparents raising grandchildren. Some of these families have informal arrangements (without legal custody or guardianship); others are part of the formal foster care system (Children's Defense Fund, 2004). Family relationships beyond the nuclear family are becoming increasingly important in American society (Bengston, 2001). Extended family members help care for children and provide emotional support.

binuclear family
family pattern in which children are part of two homes and two family groups

About 6% of children under age 18 are cared for by their grandparents. This represents a 76% increase from 1970 (U.S. Bureau of the Census, 2003). Some reasons are that the child's parents are deceased, the child was abandoned, or the court granted legal custody to the grandparent(s) because the parents were deemed unfit to nurture and support. Substance abuse, teen pregnancy, divorce, physical and mental illness, abuse, neglect, and incarceration are reasons cited (Children's Defense Fund, 2004). Many custodial grandparents do not fit the stereotype of senior citizens enjoying retirement activities (Smith, Dannison, & Vach-Hasse, 1998). Their median age is 53, and some have to care for their own parents in addition to their grandchildren. The constant challenge leaves many grandparents physically, emotionally, and financially drained. The challenges faced by parenting grandparents are changes in relationships with their spouse and other family members, financial stress, possible feelings of uncertainty, isolation, anger, grief, fear, and worries about health or death (deToledo & Brown, 1995; Minkler & Roe, 1993; Smith & Drew, 2002).

The challenge faced by children being raised by grandparents is to develop a sense of belonging and stability amid the transition from their own homes. Common feelings are grief, fear, anger, guilt, and embarrassment. Sometimes these feelings are exhibited in such acting-out behaviors as physical or verbal aggression, regression to immature behavior (crying, whining, bed-wetting), manipulation, withdrawal, and hyperactivity (deToledo & Brown, 1995; Minkler & Roe, 1993).

Many grandparents today are raising their grandchildren. This grandfather shares his love of fishing with his granddaughter.

Step Families

Because of the changing nature of families, as well as budgetary constraints, the U.S. Bureau of the Census no longer provides statistics on the number of children residing in stepfamilies. However, projections based on earlier data suggest that one out of three Americans is now a stepparent, a stepchild, a stepsibling, or a cohabiting member of a stepfamily (Larson, 1992; Stepfamily Association of America, 2000).

Because of the increase in the number of stepfamilies, the concept of family needs reexamining, according to the Stepfamily Association of America. Institutions such as schools, hospitals, and courts must adapt to the special needs of stepfamilies (Kantrowitz & Wingert, 1990). Most societal institutions have policies based on intact families. Although they may be full-time parents to their spouses' kids, stepparents, in many cases, have no legal rights. For example, if a child needs emergency surgery, hospitals almost always require the consent of a biological parent or legal guardian.

In addition to legal issues, psychosocial issues present special problems for the stepfamily. Each family member has experienced the trauma of divorce, death, or separation from a parent or spouse. When a new family is formed, new problems are likely to arise. The impact of remarriage on a family is second only to the crisis of divorce (Hetherington & Kelly, 2002).

The interactions in stepfamilies are similar to those in any other family, which means they are sometimes tainted with anger, jealousy, value conflicts, guilt, and unrealistic expectations. One of the most common unrealistic expectations is the belief in instant love. Stepfamily relationships are, generally, instant; they do not evolve as they do in a family of orientation, where a child is born and grows.

Children in a stepfamily may feel abandoned by the parent with whom they have formed a close bond since the divorce. Having to live with new rules and values, while still trying to deal with the old rules and values from both parents, places an enormous burden on the child. Also, the stepfamily often adds more children to the household. This involves adjustments in relating to new siblings. Thus, when families blend, all members are very much affected. In the early months of remarriage, there is likely to be less family cohesion, more poorly defined family roles and relationships, poorer family communication, less effective problem resolution, less consistency in setting rules, less effective disciplining, and less emotional responsiveness. Both stepmothers and stepfathers take a considerably less active role in parenting than do custodial parents (Bray, 1988). Even after two years, disengagement is the most common parenting style (Hetherington & Stanley-Hagan, 2002). Stepfamilies also may suffer from a lack of external support, fueled by a history of media myths—the wicked stepmother, the molesting stepfather (Rutter, 1994).

In general, families in which the custodial father remarries and a stepmother joins the family experience more resistance and poorer adjustment for children than do families in which the custodial mother remarries and a stepfather joins the family (Hetherington & Stanley-Hagan, 2002). The introduction of a stepparent may also strain the child's relationship with the noncustodial parent. Remarriage often presents children with loyalty dilemmas that they are too inexperienced to solve (Francke, 1983). If they like the stepparent, is that disloyal to their noncustodial parent? Or worse, will they lose the love of their biological parent? Does the noncustodial parent compete with the stepparent for the child's loyalty by buying the child things or by "putting the stepparent down"? Does the child view the stepparent as usurping the biological parent's role? ("She wants us to call her 'Mother.' I won't," said a 10-year-old girl. "He can't tell me what to do; he's not my real father," said a 7-year-old boy.)

Families in which both parents bring children from a previous marriage tend to be associated with the highest level of behavior problems (Santrock & Sitterle, 1987). The addition of instant siblings to the family constellation is both bewildering and taxing to the children (Francke, 1983; Rutter, 1994). For example, overnight the birth-order hierarchy may shift. The child who has been the oldest may inherit an older brother; the child who has been the youngest may inherit a baby sister. Children often compete for attention, especially with the biological parent. Children who have differing histories of upbringing must now live under the same roof with new sets of rules. For example, children who were given choices at mealtime must now adapt to having to eat everything that is put on their plates or "no dessert." A child who has had to make his or her bed and clean his or her room now has to share a room with a child who has never had those responsibilities.

At least half of children living in stepfamilies are likely to face an additional strain—the birth of a half-sibling to their biological parent and the new spouse (Kantrowitz & Wingert, 1990). Not only is there yet another threat to securing parental love, but common sibling rivalry is intensified by half-versus full-blooded relationships (Francke, 1983; Rutter, 1994).

The complications in roles and relationships faced by the stepparents are evidenced by the increased risk of divorce among remarriages, especially those with children from a previous marriage. Whereas about 50% of first marriages end in divorce, for second marriages the estimated divorce rate is 60% (Kantrowitz & Wingert, 1990). Divorce is most likely to occur in remarried families during the first five years, the time in which the new stepfamily is trying to restructure and "refunctionalize" (Parke & Buriel, 1998). After five years, stepfamilies are as stable as intact families of the same duration (Rutter, 1994).

Of course, not all stepchildren have behavioral or emotional problems. Studies have indicated that younger children and older adolescents are most likely to accept a stepparent, whereas preadolescent and early adolescent children from about age 9 to 15 do the poorest (Hetherington & Clingempeel, 1992; Hetherington & Stanley-Hagan, 2002). In the first two years following remarriage, conflict between mothers and daughters was found to be high. Hostility, coercion, and demandingness were exhibited toward both mother and stepfather. Interestingly, although boys tended to exhibit more antisocial behavior following divorce, two years after remarriage their behavior was no different from that of boys from intact families (Hetherington, 1989). It may be that for girls a stepfather is an intrusion on the relationship with the mother, whereas for boys the stepfather is a support and a role model. The six-year follow-up of one ongoing study of stepfamilies found that when the stepparent was firm but warm, and when the children's biological parents maintained close relationships with them, the children were functioning better than those in either single-parent families or conflict-ridden intact families (Hetherington, 1989).

In sum, the effect of remarriage on the child depends on several factors (Hetherington & Clingempeel, 1992; Hetherington & Stanley-Hagan, 2002):

- The presence of additional stressors (moving, finances, stepsiblings)
- The age, developmental status, and sex of the child
- The quality of the child's relationship with both biological parents (custodial and noncustodial)
- The quality of the child's relationship with the stepparent and siblings
- The temperament, personality, and emotional stability of the child and the parents
- The availability of parent substitutes or other social supports for the child
- The parenting styles of biological parents and stepparents
- The availability of social supports for the parents

A majority of all divorced adults remarry within a few years to form a stepfamily (Stepfamily Association of America, 2000). A positive consequence is that children who have seen the disruption of adult relationships, either through death or divorce, can then have the opportunity of seeing a couple working together in a constructive way. Communicating and allowing feelings to be vented, perhaps in family meetings or in private discussions with each parent, can help blended-family members adjust to one another and form positive relationships. Knowing what the pitfalls are can help stepparents deal with them when they arise. Counseling and/or self-help support groups, such as the Stepfamily Association, can be very beneficial.

Families of Unmarried Parents

Marriage is a legal contract with certain rights and obligations. It is society's institution for founding and maintaining a family. Families of unmarried parents include heterosexual adults who choose to live together without legal sanction and homosexual adults who live together unwed because society doesn't legalize their relationship. Such unconventional families are increasing (Kantrowitz & Wingert, 2001) and are discussed here because of their impact on children.

Unconventional families can give children love and stability, but it is more difficult because of the general absence of community supports. What makes things more challenging for unconventional families is the fact that traditional rights and obligations are not necessarily expected or implemented. For example, financial

marriage a legal contract with certain rights and obligations

requirements for support of children under age 18 are not legalized for the cohabiting partner. The cohabitating partner is not automatically included in the child's school or social functions.

Most research on children growing up without a married mother and father reports a higher incidence of poverty, poor academic performance, emotional or behavioral problems, and substance abuse (U.S. Department of Health and Human Services, 2001). However, numerous factors are involved in the circumstances under which children are born to unmarried parents that affect developmental outcomes. These factors include socioeconomic status, relationship of biological parents to each other and to the child, relationship of cohabiting adults (if not biologically related) to the child, child's characteristics (age, temperament, cognitive development), mother's and father's characteristics (age, temperament, education, parenting style, history of substance abuse, domestic violence, and/or child abuse), relationships with other children in the household or family, extended family relationships, and neighborhood characteristics (safety, supports, services) (Vosler & Robertson, 1998). What makes these factors more salient in nonmarried households with children is the lack of legal sanctions that accompany the marriage contract to ensure child protection.

Families with homosexual parents are becoming more visible in society today (Goodman, Emery, & Haugaard, 1998; Patterson, 2002). Most common are two lesbian women living together raising children of one or both from their previous relationships with men. There are also lesbian relationships in which one of the women becomes artificially inseminated or adopts a child, as well as two gay men living together with custody of their own or adopted children.

Many issues faced by families with homosexual parents are similar to those faced in divorced, stepparent, and various custodial arrangements (Patterson, 2002). Overriding these, however, is how the homosexual family manages the stigmatizing attitude of society. Society does not legally sanction homosexual marriages or families. Some cities and businesses, however, have implemented policies for domestic partnerships or civil unions; otherwise housing, insurance benefits, emergency room visits, and school permission forms exclude the cohabiting partner.

Attitudes about homosexuality generally stem from one's personal feelings about one's own sexuality. These attitudes include fear, disgust, indifference, and acceptance. Because of perceived negative attitudes, many homosexuals, especially those raising children, hide their relationship by pretending to be heterosexual (Kantrowitz, 1996). Being open about their homosexuality renders them vulnerable to discrimination and ostracism.

The initial reactions of children of gay and lesbian parents to learning about their parents' homosexuality are confusion, lack of understanding, worry, shame, disbelief, anger, and guilt (Harris & Turner, 1986). Children in homosexual homes may be afraid to bring friends home or become involved in school activities because contact with others threatens exposure (Ross, 1988). Children of those who are open about their homosexual relationship may be teased by other children (Gollnick & Chinn, 2005)—"Why do you have two mommies?" or "Your dad is a ——." However, being secret, although arguably adaptive, is accompanied by the consequences of self-betrayal and disconnectedness from social support (Ross, 1988). New associations must be continually evaluated regarding the safety of disclosure. Many homosexual parents fear they will lose custody of their children if their sexual orientation is known (Kantrowitz, 1996).

Research on children living with homosexual parents and their partners has focused on three fearful attitudes held by society in general: (1) that the children will become homosexual, (2) that they will be sexually molested, and (3) that psychological damage will result from the stigma of being raised by homosexuals. This research (Anderssen, Amlie, & Ytteroy, 2002; Goodman, Emery, & Haugaard, 1998) has found no higher incidence of homosexuality among children raised by homosexuals than by heterosexuals, nor have there been any reported incidents of sexual abuse; also, children reared by homosexuals are not necessarily more psychologically troubled than children reared by heterosexuals.

However, as children approach adolescence and become concerned about their identities and sexual orientation, any family deviations from the norm among their peers can be magnified. The normal developmental changes that occur during adolescence, coupled with the problem of having to cope with a stigmatized parent, can multiply the potential problems facing the adolescent and his or her family (Ross, 1988).

Variables affecting the adolescent's perception of the situation include his or her relationship with the biological parents, the partner, and friends; level of acceptance in the community; and self-confidence. The adolescent who is struggling to achieve an identity and sexual orientation may feel the need to prove that he or she is not homosexual by engaging in sexual acts with the opposite sex. He or she may become panicked by his or her own homosexual feelings, which are common in adolescence, yet potentially more threatening to one being raised by homosexuals (Ross, 1988).

Families of Adopted Children

Families adopt children for many reasons, including an inability to conceive, the desire to care for a child without the sanction of marriage, the desire to care for a child with special needs (one who has been abused or neglected, has disabilities, or comes from another country), or the desire to make a foster care arrangement permanent. Regardless of the reason, the American Academy of Child and Adolescent Psychiatry [AACAP] (1999) recommends that the adoptive parent(s) tell the child about the adoption in a way the child can understand based on age and maturity. This enables the child to feel that his or her adoption was wanted by the family and is a positive experience.

Adoptive parents need to be prepared for child interpretations of the adoption even years after the situation was explained (AACAP, 1999). The child may create fantasies about the birth parents and may even deny the reality of the adoption (Pavao, 1999). The child may believe he or she did something bad and was sent away. Some children believe they were kidnapped by the adoptive parent(s). In adolescence, when identity formation is a normal challenge, the adopted child faces more complex issues, such as whether to tell friends, whether to contact the birth parent(s), what medical history is relevant, and loyalty. The identity issues are even greater in transracial adoptions. Some other issues may be fear of abandonment, painful reminders of identity at birthdays, a need to grieve for what is perceived to be lost, and dealing with the unknown (Eldridge, 1999).

FUNCTIONAL FAMILY CHANGES

How are family functions affected by societal change?

Throughout history, families have been changing in the ways they execute their various functions, including reproduction, socialization/education, assignment of social roles, economic support, and nurturance/emotional support. Such changes in family functioning are adaptations to macrosystem influences, such as economics, political ideology, and technology.

Reproduction
How have reproductive ability and family size changed?

Technological changes, such as birth control and reproductive assistance (donation of egg and sperm, in vitro fertilization, embryo transfer, surrogacy) have affected family size. Economics, too, has played a role. Many young people have chosen to postpone childbearing until they achieve financial stability. However, delaying conception until the late 30s affects fertility. Couples who have difficulty conceiving may then turn to technology for assistance or choose to adopt. In any case, family size has decreased in the past century compared to the past, when families had many children hoping some would survive to reproduce the next generation (Federal Interagency Forum on Child and Family Statistics, 2004).

Socialization/Education
How have the socialization and education of children by families changed?

The socialization/education domain of the family has decreased in the past century. Until the 19th century, children were educated at home. Education consisted of religious teachings and training to work on the farm or in the family business, or to perform household chores. The Industrial Revolution provided work outside the home and farm for women and children as well as men. Thus, the family could no longer be totally responsible for their children's education and training for the adult world. Gradually, schools took over this function.

The public, or "common," school emerged in the middle of the 19th century under the leadership of Horace Mann. The main rationale for compulsory, free public education was that families could no longer socialize their children for a productive role in the increasingly complicated U.S. economy. Schools were expected to teach good work habits and basic reading, writing, and arithmetic skills, as well as form good character. Today many states require that, in addition to these basics, schools teach such topics as sex education, substance abuse prevention, and anger management, things previously assumed to be the domain of the family.

Assignment of Social Roles
How have the various roles performed by family members changed?

Social roles within the family are defined by which members perform what jobs, as well as the distribution of authority. Changes in family roles over time, as discussed here, illustrate chronosystem influences.

Wife/Mother. When the family was agrarian and self-sufficient, the wife was responsible for preparing food, making clothes, caring for the children, managing the house, caring for the animals, and cultivating the garden. Her husband had the authority in the family. When the economy began to change from agriculture to industry, and farms started to sell produce and animal products, men took over the responsibilities of making contacts for sales and transporting the goods, and the woman's role diminished.

Industrialization provided an opportunity for the expansion of women's roles, but few jobs were open to women initially. In the 19th and early 20th centuries in the United States, women were usually employed only as seamstresses, laundresses, maids, cooks, housekeepers, governesses, teachers, and nurses. Not until World War II did this pattern change. Today, more than half of all mothers with children under 18 are employed outside the home, occupying work roles similar to men.

Husband/Father. Traditionally, a man was responsible for economically support-ing his wife and children; a wife was responsible for maintaining the household. This division of labor between husband and wife affected their parental roles (Mintz, 1998). In colonial families, children learned appropriate gender roles from both father and mother, because there was no sharp split between work and home. In 19th-century families, however, mothers assumed more child-rearing tasks because fathers worked in industry and were away from home much of the time.

Today, the role of father is being redefined by technological and ideological changes in our society. In many families, men are assuming more household and child-care responsibilities (Parke, 2002; Tamis-LeMonda & Cabrera, 1999). This is especially true in families in which the mother is employed. It is also true in cases where the parents are divorced and the father has custody, or partial custody, of the children. Today, many fathers are active participants in the socialization of their children.

Children. In preindustrial times, children contributed to the family work by help-ing adults on the farm, in the business, and in the home. Today, most adult family members work for pay outside the home and children rarely work at all. Work and family life are separate entities. Families have become consumption units rather than production units. Children used to be an economic asset, contributing to the family by doing chores or contributing wages earned outside the family. Now they have become an economic liability; they not only have to be sheltered, clothed, and fed until age 18 but have to be educated as well. In dual-earner families, the cost of child care must be added to the economic liability. Not only are children expensive to raise, but most cannot be counted on to provide economic support when their parents reach old age.

Authority Patterns

Authority patterns in the family can be traced back in time. The biblical family pat-tern was patriarchal and extended. Thus, Abraham, Isaac, and Jacob had several wives who, along with their children, constituted their families. In ancient Rome, the father had absolute authority, known as *patria potestas* (paternal power), over his children. The father was guardian over his sons as long as he lived, and even had the right to kill them. When the sons married, they lived with their families in the father's household, forming an extended family. Families, to continue their lin-eage, arranged marriages for their sons with women of equal status. The bride-to-be often came with a dowry that was negotiated between her family and that of her husband-to-be. The dowry signified her worth. Marriage was monogamous; the commitment was to one person at a time (usually for life). The marital union really constituted a binding tie between extended families, rather than just the couple. This arrangement still applies in many cultures around the world today.

In the United States, similar patterns were evident during colonial times. Fami-lies were patriarchal and extended. The father was responsible for not only the eco-nomic survival of the family, but the socialization of the children as well. It was not until the 20th century that mothers gained status as family providers, influenced by political events. Their help was needed in the workforce while many men were engaged in the war effort (Coontz, 1997). It took implementation of the Civil Rights Act of 1964, which outlawed ethnic and gender discrimination, for women to gain more equal authority in the workplace and, consequently, at home. Now authority patterns in many families approach an egalitarian pattern, or some sort of collabo-rative one negotiated between the parents, with the father responsible for some tasks and the mother for others (Kaslow, 2001).

Economic Support
How has economic responsibility for family functioning changed?

A major function of the family remains the economic support of its members, but the scope of this responsibility has changed, as well as which family members contribute.

Until the 18th century, most American families were extended. They owned and occupied farms and plantations that were self-sufficient, producing most of what the family needed. Families built their own houses, grew their own food, and made their own furniture and clothing. Things the family needed but did not produce were usually obtained through barter. These early American families were economic units in which all members, young and old, played important productive roles. Thus, children were essential to the prosperity of the family. The boys helped cultivate the land and harvest crops; the girls helped cook, sew, weave, and care for domestic animals and younger children.

During the 19th century, farm families had begun raising crops to sell and using the proceeds to buy goods produced by others. Thus, families gradually became less and less self-sufficient. As industries grew, family members began to work for wages in factories and businesses. Money, then, became the link between work and family. The nuclear family became more common as houses were smaller and family providers had to be willing to move to where the work was (Coontz, 1997).

Today, most families require the economic contributions of both parents in order to afford food, clothing, shelter, services and other goods needed for themselves and their children.

Dual-Earner Families

Ideology in the United States has been influenced by a deep-seated view that a woman's role is in the home (Brazelton, 1984; Hochschild, 1989). She should be there for her children; if she is not, they will suffer in some way. This biased attitude has contributed to society's reluctance to give employed women the support they need, including child care, parental leave, and other services.

About two-thirds of mothers with children younger than age 6 work outside the home. Labor force participation rates for these mothers have increased about 50% since 1975 (Children's Defense Fund, 2004).

Mother employment almost always improves the economic well-being of families with children, and often makes the difference between whether or not they can make ends meet. To the extent that mothers' working keeps children out of poverty and ensures that their basic material needs are met, it has important benefits (Federal Interagency Forum on Child and Family Statistics, 2004). Other benefits of dual-earner families include personal stimulation for the mother (if she enjoys her job), a closer relationship between father and children (because of his increased participation in family matters), and greater sense of responsibility for the children.

The main socialization effect of dual-earner families is the reallocation of household and child-care responsibilities (Gottfried, Gottfried, & Buthurst, 2002). A common dual-earner family liability is "role overload," resulting from the parents' increased responsibilities and the sacrifice of social relationships. Most employed mothers have less time to visit relatives and friends, or be part of community and school organizations.

Reviews of the research on maternal employment (Gottfried et al., 2002; Hoffman, 1989, 2000) reveal that a variety of effects, depending on individual factors, result when a mother is employed outside the home. Individual factors influencing the impact of a mother's employment are the age, gender, and temperament of the child;

the socioeconomic status of the family; the quality of the parents' marriage; the mother's satisfaction with her job; the father's satisfaction with his job; and the father's involvement with the children and support of the mother.

In general, employed mothers provide different role models than do mothers who remain at home. Also employment affects the mother's emotional state—sometimes providing satisfactions, sometimes stress, and sometimes guilt—and this, in turn, influences the mother–child interaction. When the mother is satisfied with her career and does not feel guilty about working, her relations with her children are similar to those of nonemployed mothers who are content with their homemaking role.

One finding that has occurred frequently in various studies is that children of mothers employed outside the home, from kindergarten age through adulthood, have less stereotyped views of gender roles (Gottfried et al., 2002; Parke & Buriel, 1998). These views are influenced by the mother's discussion of her work, as well as the father's participation in household tasks and child care.

Some evidence suggests that mothers employed outside the home use different child-rearing practices than do mothers not so employed. Generally, employed mothers tend to be more authoritative, or democratic, in that there is discussion about expectations and responsibilities (Greenberger & Goldberg, 1989). This parenting style will be discussed in more detail in Chapter 4.

The trend today is toward dual-earner families. The impact of this trend on the family really depends on the adaptive and coping strategies of the particular family: What are the parents' attitudes toward each other's jobs, as well as their own? How are work and family life coordinated? Who cares for the children, and what kind of care are they receiving? Who does the household chores? How are unexpected problems (machine breakdowns, illness) handled? How flexible is each parent's work schedule?

IN PRACTICE

Coping Strategies for Dual-Earner Families

- Think of themselves as household managers who delegate and supervise rather than do.
- Determine their priorities as well as what is really essential—clothes ironed or a game played with the children.
- Set aside routine "quality" time for each other and the children. For each other, uninterrupted time away from household and child-care duties will do. For children, any activity that raises the child's self-esteem is quality time—for example, talking about their day, reading to them, or playing a game with them.
- Establish traditions and rituals to which they and their children can regularly look forward.
- Schedule time alone, time to pursue an interest, time to refresh their energies.
- Learn to say "no" sometimes. When invited somewhere or asked to help on a committee, they might respond, "Let me check and get back to you." This response gives them time to evaluate the invitation and see if it fits in with other commitments to family members.
- Advocate for family-responsive corporate policies such as leaves, flexible work hours, job sharing, child-care support, and seminars dealing with work/family issues.

Note: The American Psychological Association gives "Psychologically Healthy Workplace Awards" (www.apapractice.org/apo/psychologically_healthy.html).

Nurturance/Emotional Support
How has family nurturance and emotional support changed?

The nurturing and emotional support function of families for the young (and sometimes the old) has remained fairly stable, but the range of the caregiving has diminished. For example, as medicine advanced, the family turned to doctors and nurses to provide health care. In the 19th century, health care as we know it today did not exist. There were no preventive inoculations (except for smallpox in the latter part of the century), no clinics, few hospitals, few medications, and doctors were few and far between. The sick were cared for by their families, as were the elderly. Today, we have insurance plans to cover costs of long-term care in residential facilities; we have disability plans; we have hospices to care for the dying. Because of the expense of caregiving outside the family, however, the importance of multigenerational bonds and links to extended kin needs to be reassessed (Bengston, 2001).

Macrosystem Influences on Families, Socialization, and Children
How do features of the macrosystem influence the socialization of children?

Specific effects of macrosystems (socioeconomic status, ethnic orientation, and religious orientation) on socialization are examined to better understand how larger contexts can affect the way family systems operate.

SOCIOECONOMIC STATUS

On what basis are families ranked in society?

All societies have their own ways of ranking people, and they differ in the criteria used for placing people in certain classes or statuses. Some societies stratify members by **ascribed status**; that is, family lineage, gender, birth order, or skin color determines a person's class. For example, in the British royal family marriages can occur only with members of the nobility, and the firstborn son is automatically heir to the throne.

Other societies stratify members according to **achieved status**; that is, education, occupation, income, and/or place of residence determine an individual's class. The United States exemplifies a society in which status can be attained by achievement—Abraham Lincoln, the sixteenth president of the United States, was the son of a farmer. Academic achievement, trade skills, and athletic talent enable some youths from lower-class families to attain high status.

Traditional societies, those that rely on customs handed down from past generations as ways to behave, tend toward *ascribed status* for stratification; **modern societies**, those that look to the present for ways to behave and are thus responsive to change, tend toward *achieved status*. Stratification is based on the importance of individuals' contributions to a particular society's ability to function. For example, one person makes jewelry; another sells shoes; another is a doctor. Jewelry may be important to those who can afford it; shoes may be necessary for everyone in cold climates; a doctor contributes to the well-being of everyone in the society. Thus people in societies are not equally dependent on one another; some people are therefore more important to society than others and so are ranked higher in terms of social class or status. How a society stratifies or ranks people in social classes is

ascribed status social class, rank, or position determined by family lineage, gender, birth order, or skin color

achieved status social class, rank, or position determined by education, occupation, income, and/or place of residence

traditional society a society that relies on customs handed down from past generations as ways to behave

modern society a society that looks to the present for ways to behave and is thus responsive to change

This child learns the traditional skill of weaving as her mother supervises and provides help when necessary.

© Paul Conkin/PhotoEdit

shown by income earned and prestige acquired. In the United States, doctors are ranked high, whereas salespeople are ranked low.

It is more difficult for people to change their rank, or social class, in societies using ascribed criteria than in societies using achieved criteria. In societies using ascribed criteria, however, it is possible for achievements to change a person's ranking. For example, a person born into a lower-class family could become a soldier or a priest and thereby attain higher status. In contrast, in societies using achieved criteria, individuals' ascriptions (conditions of birth) affect their status. For example, those born into upper-class families will receive a head start on achievement because of their families' ability to educate them, live in certain neighborhoods, and buy certain material things.

When statuses are ascribed, roles are set in tradition. In other words, when one is born into a certain status, children are socialized primarily by modeling their elders and being instructed in the traditional ways. When statuses are achieved, however, as is the case in modern societies undergoing change, "the established system for assigning individuals to recognized statuses may break down. Wholly new statuses may come into existence" (Inkeles, 1969, p. 616). Thus, in societies that stratify by achievement, members may find themselves inadequately socialized to play the roles of the statuses they seek or have been assigned. For example, farmers who want to be competitive and profitable have to seek more technical knowledge than they learned from their parents. Society must then compensate for gaps in socialization by the family and rely on other institutions, such as the school or business, to prepare individuals for their new roles. Farmers may choose from courses such as plant pathology, genetics, animal husbandry, and economics for further expertise.

According to sociologist William Goode (1982), it is the family, not just the individual, that is ranked in society's class structure. This is an illustration of the macrosystem's influence on a child's development, because the social class and status of the family help determine an individual's opportunities for education and occupation, as well as for social interaction. The members of the community in which the family lives, the children's friends, and the guests invited to the home generally come from the same social class. Even though U.S. citizens play down the existence of social classes, social scientists recognize that different groups in our society possess unequal amounts of money, prestige, influence, and "life chances" (Bornstein & Bradley, 2003). Despite its egalitarian principles, the United States has been widening the gap between rich and poor (Children's Defense Fund, 2004).

Social class membership begins exerting its influence before birth and continues until death. Health care and diet of the mother affect the birth of the child. The incidence of birth defects is higher in the lower classes than in the middle and upper classes. Economic pressure and lack of opportunities affect the mental health of the lower-class family, as well as determine socialization practices (Parke & Buriel, 1998). Lower-socioeconomic-status parents have been found to be more dominant, controlling, and punitive than higher-socioeconomic-status parents, who have been found to be more verbal and democratic and to use various techniques. Economics, or lack of money, prevents lower-social-class parents from using an allowance as a reward. Children from lower-class families cannot be sent to their rooms as a punishment, because there may be no room they can call their own to which they can be sent. Neither can such children have privileges removed for noncompliance, such as going to the movies, because they do not have those opportunities anyway. Thus, lower-class families frequently use physical punishment as a socializing technique, whereas middle- and upper-class families have more options available (Hart & Risley, 1995).

Socioeconomic classes can be described in terms of averages; that is, they differ, *on average*, by income, occupation, housing, education, social interaction, and values. It is these defining criteria that influence socialization. Sociologists vary in the way they see the social structure in the United States. Some sociologists believe that although differences in rank exist, true class lines cannot be drawn because the United States is an open society with much mobility up and down and numerous informal social interactions.

Class Descriptions

The following descriptions apply to the majority of people in a given socioeconomic class, but not to every person in the class (Levine & Levine, 1996; Macionis, 2005). See Figure 3.5 for a distribution of social classes in the United States.

Upper Class. In general, upper-class families have inherited their wealth and have a family tradition of social prominence that extends back several generations. Much emphasis is placed on the extended family, which is often either patriarchal or matriarchal.

Many upper-class families believe proper rearing is more important than formal schooling in preparing to fulfill adult roles. If children do go to school to train for an occupation, it must be a high-status one such as medicine, law, or business. Upper-class children generally attend private schools and prestigious private colleges.

Middle Class. In general, middle-class families have earned their status by achievement (education and/or hard work): "It is not who you are, but what you are." Much emphasis is placed on the nuclear family, even though ties are still maintained, often loosely, to the extended family. These families tend to be egalitarian.

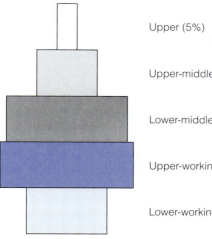

Figure 3.5

Social Class Structure in the United States

About 13.7% of the total population are considered "poor" by government standards.

Source: Based on data from the U.S. Bureau of the Census, 2003

A high value is placed on achievement, respectability, and harmonious interpersonal relationships within the family. Education and the ability to get along with others are considered essential to adult success.

The upper-middle class generally includes business executives and professional people.

The lower-middle class generally includes salespeople, small business owners, contractors, craftspeople, and farmers.

Lower Class. In general, lower-class families are composed of semiskilled and unskilled workers. Much emphasis is placed on the extended family; close ties with relatives are maintained. Patriarchal patterns are more common (except where the father is absent), as is the distinction between male and female roles.

Many lower-class families emphasize respect for elders and the importance of survival. These families are most affected by economic fluctuations. Many experience being in debt, being laid off, and/or being on welfare. Often, children must help the family rather than further their own education. Some don't complete high school.

Historically, the lower class includes the newest immigrants to the United States, who are willing to work at menial jobs while learning the ways of American society.

Underclass. In recent years, many social scientists have begun to identify another class: the underclass. This class differs from the others in its degree of hopelessness regarding upward mobility. People in the underclass are stuck at the bottom of the social structure and perceive themselves as having little chance of ever escaping from a pervasively poverty-ridden environment (Wilson, 1987).

The underclass is composed of many faces: female-headed families; street-living homeless alcoholics, drug users, and the mentally ill who have been "deinstitutionalized"; the destitute elderly, illegal aliens, and rural families from economically depressed areas; and any other group who, for whatever reason, cannot get an adequate education, job, or housing. Because of the hopelessness of getting out of such extreme poverty, the underclass has become a culture of illegitimacy, drugs, and crime, as well as joblessness. The underclass, in essence, represents a contradiction to the concept that social mobility is available to anyone in America who is willing to work hard enough for it.

How the underclass developed and what should be done about it remain debated issues among social scientists and public policymakers. The problems for underclass children include exposure to drugs and AIDS, child abuse, poor housing or homelessness, crime, insufficient health care, inferior education, insufficient child-care programs and other community services, and economic dependency on government (Children's Defense Fund, 2004). The federal government's response since 1996 has been to provide Temporary Assistance to Needy Families (TANF) while the parent(s) get job training and learn coping skills to become self-sufficient.

Effects of Class
How does socioeconomic status influence socialization?

Children from lower-class families are often identified in school as slow learners, aggressors, and truants. Studies comparing the relative intelligence of children from high- and low-socioeconomic-status families show that those from high-status homes score higher on IQ tests and achievement tests than do children from low-status homes (Patterson, Kupersmidt, & Vaden, 1990). The differences are more marked in later childhood and adolescence than in infancy (Levine & Levine, 1996; Tozer, Violas, & Senese, 2002).

Various theories have been advanced to explain this contrast in intelligence. One of these is based on heredity—intelligence is inherited, and brighter persons achieve higher statuses (Jensen, 1969, 1988). Another emphasizes the environment—the limited resources of lower-status families prevent them from providing intellectual stimulation, especially verbal, for their children. Brain research concludes that the influence of environmental stimulation and stressors during infancy is significant and long lasting for cognitive development (Bransford et al., 2000). Evidence shows that if special schooling is provided, especially in the preschool years, the IQ scores of children from lower-status families improve (Bereiter & Engelmann, 1966; Spitz,

Families that have many responsibilities without adequate resources negatively impact the present and future opportunities for their children.

© Tony Freeman/PhotoEdit

1992). A third theory is that of the self-fulfilling prophecy. It suggests that IQ tests are biased toward the middle class, so children from lower-class families, who have a different set of experiences, do not score as well. These scores, in turn, cause teachers to have lower expectations: "Since Johnny has a low IQ, I won't give him as many math pages as the others." Thus, Johnny does not learn as much as the others, and his intellectual potential decreases (Brophy & Good, 1986).

The belief that improving the environment of children from lower-class families could reduce the difference in achievement levels between the classes led to the War on Poverty in the 1960s. Under the leadership of President Lyndon Johnson, many government programs were instituted, including "compensatory education" and Head Start. Compensatory education included hiring remedial reading specialists, counselors, and truant officers. Head Start, a preschool program for children considered to be disadvantaged, was designed to enable children to be more successful when they entered elementary school. The program provided various learning experiences, with an emphasis on language experiences and abstract thinking skills, in an attempt to overcome significant social-class differences in the use of language and concept development (Levine & Levine, 1996; Tozer et al., 2002).

The structure and syntax of language used by the upper-middle class is far more complex than that used by the lower class (Bernstein, 1961; Hoff, Laursen, & Tardiff, 2002). Use of complex language indicates a more abstract, as opposed to concrete, perception of reality. Bernstein uses the following example to illustrate this concept: "I'd rather you made less noise, dear" might be what a mother from the middle class would say to her boisterous child, whereas "Shut up!" might be what a mother from the lower class would say. Thus, the child from a middle-class family learns the abstract meanings of words like *rather* and *less*; the child from a lower-class family gets a simple, concrete message, directly to the point.

Other experiences provided for Head Start children are opportunities to be successful and to be rewarded for this success. It has been shown that the socializing technique of reinforcement or reward for desired behavior given by significant people in a child's life is very effective in motivating the child to repeat the behavior. Parents from the middle class usually reward children, especially sons, for ambition, high levels of aspiration, and long-range goals. To achieve one's ambitions and long-range goals, one must defer gratification. Generally, children from middle-class families learn from their parents to defer gratification ("Save for a rainy day," "Study hard now so you'll be able to get a good job in the future"), whereas children from lower-class families do not.

Parents from the middle class generally train their children to be achievement-oriented. Self-discipline, initiative, responsibility, academic achievement, and restraint of aggression are encouraged. Parents from the lower class, on the other hand, generally focus on the behavior rather than the attitudes or motivation of the child. Perhaps this is because they tend to view the world in terms of concrete events and practical outcomes. Faced with the realities of substandard housing, overcrowded neighborhoods, and inadequate services from public institutions, the lower classes' apparent lack of achievement motivation reflects a profound lack of trust in the social system that has excluded them from its benefits (Wilson, 1987, 1995).

Various studies (Levine & Levine, 1996; McLanahan, 2005) have examined the relationship between lower-social-class socialization and achievement as well as behavior. Levels of achievement depend on what people believe can be attained. More important than achievement to those struggling to survive is security. Toughness in boys is generally admired as an ability to get ahead of other people; intellectualism tends to be regarded as "unmasculine." Students grouped according to their abilities are likely to reinforce each other's attitudes and behavior. Living for the present is the norm, perhaps because opportunities to "live it up" are so rare. Skills in budgeting time and money tend to be lacking.

In upper-class families, the child is generally regarded as the carrier of the family's name, its heritage, and its status. The family is able to bear the maximum costs of child rearing (material goods, private schooling, setting up in business or career). Children are expected to meet family standards for behavior and for educational and vocational attainment. Socializing children in upper-class families to be responsible and to achieve is a challenge when such children already "have everything." Pressures to conform to family standards come not only from the nuclear family, but from the extended family (even the dead relatives) as well: "What would Grandfather Smith say?"

Whereas relatives play a large role in the socialization of children from upper-class families to conform to family standards, children from middle-class families are reared more by their families of orientation; relatives are expected not to interfere. Children and their parents from the lower class tend to rely on their kin for support, mostly emotional, rather than for the intentional purpose of socialization, even though much unintentional socialization does take place through the social interactions occurring among relatives. Besides using relatives as a network to adapt to poverty, individuals from the lower class tend to believe in fate and luck as explanations for their destiny.

Lower-class families, in rearing their children, generally put emphasis on not being a nuisance. Physical punishment is the form of discipline most likely to be used. Children must be trained to adjust to the conditions of many people occupying the same small space. They are also usually taught early to assume responsibility for doing chores around the home, caring for smaller children, and running errands. Middle-class families are more likely to use reasoning and nonphysical forms of discipline (Bornstein & Bradley, 2003; Parke & Buriel, 1998). They tend to emphasize conformity to "what people will say" or "how it would look." Children are usually taught early to look toward the future. ("Eat your vegetables so you'll grow big and strong," "When you can use the potty, you'll be able to wear big-boy pants like Daddy instead of diapers.")

Reasons for the social-class differences in socializing children are that lower-class families are so burdened with survival concerns in the present that they tend to have difficulty teaching their children to delay gratification or be oriented to the future, as our society's education system is structured. They have inadequate resources, such as income, education, and good jobs, to meet their needs in life. They are often plagued with sickness, injuries, and entanglements with the law, and lack the money, knowledge, and access to support services to cope with these problems. The pessimistic view that "things will turn out as badly as they generally have in the past" often pervades their lives. Their relatively low level of skill makes them easily replaceable in their jobs. Because they have previously experienced little success in shaping their lives, they tend to expect nothing else in the future (Levine & Levine, 1996).

However, generalizations about the influence of socioeconomic status on socialization do not always apply. In her book *Common Purpose*, Lisbeth Schorr (1997) describes support programs that have strengthened families and neighborhoods in the United States. For example, a program called Youth Build, begun in Harlem, New York, recruits adolescents from poor families to build and renovate low-cost housing. The youth are trained by journeymen in construction skills and the personal habits and qualities that contractors seek in entry-level workers. They also attend school and are trained in leadership skills that, together with job skills, will help them rebuild their own lives and provide them with the prospect of moving out of the lower class. What makes Youth Build successful is the caring support and commitment of its staff, as well as the sense of family and community among its members. They help each other and impose consequences for disruptive behavior, absences, and substance abuse. Building something tangible and useful in one's own neighborhood provides a sense of pride and respect, which, in turn, leads to a sense of personal responsibility for life's outcomes.

IN PRACTICE

What Are the Implications of Socioeconomic Status for Professionals?

Professionals whose experiences have been typically middle class must understand the differences in various social class behavior and motivations if they are to work effectively with children from all socioeconomic statuses.

The ability to delay gratification is generally a middle-class value; immediate gratification is generally the norm among the lower class. Professionals can provide children feedback on their behavior with cues or specific instructions and tangible, immediate rewards, such as small tokens (stickers, toys), rather than giving hypothetical reasons—for example, "You must do well in school so that you'll get a good job" or "You must take turns on the slide so the others will be your friends."

When a teacher tells a 5-year-old child not to hit "because it hurts" and the 5-year-old replies, "That's why I hit him," the teacher needs to learn that lower-class values may include "Stand up for yourself," "Fight for your territory," and "Don't ask for help." That teacher cannot rely on reasoning in this case to modify the child's aggressive behavior. A more effective socializing technique in this case might be setting standards with reinforcement for compliance and consequences for noncompliance. In other words, the teacher would tell all the children the standard or expectations in advance, as well as the consequences for deviation: "We use our words to tell someone our angry feelings." "When I hear words, I will give you a sticker." "We do not hit anyone. If you hit someone, you get a warning; if you hit someone again, you will have to sit in the hall outside the room for five minutes."

For professionals who work with groups outside their own class experience, the challenge is not to make everyone into upper- or middle-class people, but rather to downplay those aspects of class socialization that hamper personality development (limited language, experiences, and cognitive stimulation) and enhance those aspects of class socialization that make the individual a unique, contributing member of society (helpfulness of kin, responsibilities given to children, ability to cope with adversity).

ETHNIC ORIENTATION

What does ethnicity have to do with how parents interact with children?

Ethnicity, as discussed previously, is an attribute of membership in a group in which members identify themselves by national origin, race, or religion. Ethnic distinction can be based on physical and/or cultural attributes. Physical attributes include such things as skin color, body build, and facial features. Cultural attributes include a shared history, language, traditions, rituals, customs, beliefs, attitudes, and values. Ethnic orientation, then, constitutes a macrosystem.

Ethnic groups differ in the way they deal with basic questions of living (Harrison, Wilson, Pine, Chan, & Buriel, 1990). The need to eat is universal, but the kind of food one eats and how one eats it are determined by the ethnic group to which one belongs. The need for shelter is also universal, but the types of dress and housing depend on the particular culture. Ethnic groups also differ in child-rearing practices—in their methods of socialization of the child. Another variable introduced into families' ecologies is the immigration history: Which family members came to the United States and when? Which have adopted American values for child rearing, which maintain those of their culture, and which are bicultural (Parke & Buriel, 1998; Rogoff, 2003)?

In some immigrant families, children may serve as "language and cultural brokers" for their non- or limited-English speaking parents, assuming responsibility for translation and interpretation of transactions with U.S. society. The challenge for the parents is to maintain authority while depending on the child to transmit and receive information. The challenge for the child is to maintain respect and not cause the parents to lose face (Orellana, Dorner, & Pulido, 2003).

Because children are socialized by various methods of communication and interaction, examining differences in the way parents relate to children can provide insight into general socialization outcomes according to ethnic orientation (Greenfield & Suzuki, 1998). For example, a study that compared Euro-American and Japanese mother–infant interaction found that Euro-American mothers interacted more vocally with their infants than did Japanese mothers. In contrast, Japanese mothers exhibited more body contact with their infants and, in so doing, soothed them into physical quiescence. A comparison of the infants revealed that Euro-American infants tended to be more vocal, more active, and more explorative of their environments than were the Japanese infants, who tended to be more passive (Caudill, 1988).

Parents socialize children to encourage the development of those qualities and attributes required for their expected adult roles in their particular society or according to their specific ethnic orientation. To illustrate, in a classic study, Barry, Child, and Bacon (1959) evaluated 104 societies to find out whether the child-rearing practices of parents in industrialized societies, such as the United States, differed from those of parents in agricultural societies, such as India. They found that parents in industrialized societies socialized children for achievement and independence, whereas parents in agricultural societies socialized children for obedience and responsibility. In a different study examining attitudes toward family obligations, it was found that Asian and Latin American adolescents possessed stronger values and greater expectations regarding their duty to respect and assist their families than did their peers with European backgrounds. These differences were large and consistent across socioeconomic status and gender (Fuligni, Tseng, & Lam, 1999).

Another socialization outcome affected by ethnic orientation is the way in which children learn to adapt to their environment. One way of adapting is to be actively independent and struggle to master problems and challenges; another is to be passively obedient, cooperative with others, and accept environmental stresses rather than change them. Socialization outcomes for children are implemented by sleeping arrangements, feeding practices, parenting styles, and peer, school, and community experiences, all of which vary by culture (Greenfield & Suzuki, 1998).

SOCIALIZATION AREAS	MAJORITY ETHNIC ORIENTATION	MINORITY ETHNIC ORIENTATION
INTERPERSONAL	Competition and individual accomplishment; take risks; active learning style	Cooperation and group relationships; save face; passive learning style
ORIENTATION TOWARD TIME	Plan for the future. work and save now for a better future for yourself; efficiency, punctuality, time should not be "wasted"	Focus on the present. trust that the future will be provided for; units of time are undifferentiated; value the past, tradition, and ancestors
VALUED PERSON	Busy, materialistic, practical, assertive	Relaxed, spiritual, emotional, quiet
RELATIONSHIP OF HUMANITY TO NATURE	Control nature, use science and technology to "improve" nature	One with nature, respect and live with nature; belief in fate
MOST CHERISHED VALUES	Independence, individual freedom, achievement	Dependence, loyalty to the group and tradition

Table 3.1

Some Areas of Diverse Socialization Patterns in the United States

Sources: Kluckhohn, 1961; Maehr, 1974; Thiederman, 1991

For example, an important socialization outcome generally valued by American parents is for children to learn to make their own decisions and establish separate individual existences. Children are taught to assert themselves and stand up for their own rights. They are encouraged to verbalize their needs and disagree, even with an elder. In contrast, Japanese parents generally value self-control, compliance with adult authority, and cooperation. Children are taught to depend on parents, defer to elders, and sacrifice personal goals for those of the family. They are encouraged to keep their feelings to themselves and not cause another embarrassment by disagreeing.

There are many ethnic groups in the United States, and not all have the same status and power as the majority group (white, Anglo-Saxon, Protestant, or Euro-American), even though equality is a value subscribed to in the United States. These other ethnic groups are commonly referred to as "minorities," even though, in reality, these groups are beginning to outnumber Euro-Americans. Being socialized in a family of a different orientation from that of the school, which represents the majority orientation, can be problematic for the child (Trumbull et al., 2001). Table 3.1 outlines some areas of diverse socialization patterns, keeping in mind that there is variation within groups.

How do ethnic norms and values influence socialization?

Part of one's ethnic orientation involves **norms**—the rules, patterns, or standards that express cultural values and reflect how individuals are supposed to behave. Some dimensions of differing ethnic behavioral patterns were introduced in Chapter 2. This discussion examines ethnic or cultural norms from the perspective of variations in human ways of adapting. In the 1960s, Florence Kluckhohn (1961; Kluckhohn & Strodbeck, 1961) developed a way of analyzing the seemingly limitless variety of cultural lifestyles. She suggested that there are five basic questions that humans in all places and circumstances must

norms rules, patterns, or standards that express cultural values and reflect how individuals are supposed to behave answer. These questions greatly help our understanding of ethnic diversity and socialization:

1. How do humans relate to each other? Do relationships have an individualistic orientation, where importance is placed on what one accomplishes and on personal rights and freedom? Or is importance placed on belonging to a group, such as family, peers, or community (a collectivistic orientation)? The Euro-American norm generally, as exemplified by the Bill of Rights, is personal freedom, whereas the Japanese norm generally, as exemplified by family loyalty, is commitment to the group.

2. What is the significant time dimension? Is it past, present, or future? Some cultures associate time with religious beliefs; for example, some Hispanics live each day as it comes, believing that God will provide for the future. Other cultures, such as Euro-American and German, generally associate time with progress, and therefore generally plan for the future, even though it may require sacrifice in the present. Still others view the concept of time as subordinate to activities and interactions instead of dominating them. For example, some African Americans and Latin Americans may approximate when an event will start or end (the party takes place when everyone gets there), whereas Anglos generally tend to put events on a precise schedule (the party takes place from 8:00 to 12:00).

3. What is the valued personality type? Is it simply "being"? Is it "being in becoming"? Or is it "doing"? Asians generally believe that a person "is being in becoming"—that one's deeds in this life determine the quality of one's next life. Anglos generally stress "doing" to enhance the quality of one's present life.

4. What is the relationship of humans to nature? Are humans subjugated to nature? Are humans seen as existing in nature? Do humans have power over nature? Western cultures generally assume that nature can be controlled. An example is our use of pesticides, irrigation, and various technologies that make farming more efficient. Other cultures, such as Native American, however, are generally taught that land and all that grows on it are only lent, to be cared for and shared, not exploited.

5. What are the innate predispositions of humans? Are they evil? Neither good nor bad? Good? If one believes that humans are essentially bad, one assumes that the child's will must be broken and tends to use punitive and controlling measures to socialize the child—as was done by Calvinist and Puritan parents, for example. If one believes that humans are neither good nor bad, one assumes that the child can be molded and shaped by experiences provided by the adult. This philosophy was advocated by British philosopher, John Locke (1632–1704). If one believes that humans are essentially good, one assumes that the child will seek out appropriate experiences and develop accordingly. Jean Jacques Rousseau (1712–1778), a French philosopher, advocated such a belief.

RELIGIOUS ORIENTATION

What role does religion play in life?

Religion is a "unified system of beliefs and practices relative to sacred things, uniting into a single moral community all those who adhere to those beliefs and practices" (Durkheim, 1947, p. 47). Understanding some basic purposes of religion also helps us be more sensitive to diversity.

religion a unified system of beliefs and practices relative to sacred things

About 85% of the population in the United States and Canada identify with one of five major faiths: Protestant (58%), Catholic (25%), Jewish (2%), Latter-Day

Saints (2%), and Orthodox (1%) (U.S. Bureau of the Census, 2003). Although these religious groups share the same Old Testament heritage, their interpretations and beliefs differ. Other major world religions found in the United States include Islam, Buddhism, and Hinduism.

Religion is a macrosystem in that it influences patterns of gender roles, sexual behavior, marriage, divorce, birthrates, morals, attitudes, and child rearing. It also may affect one's dress, dietary habits, alcohol consumption, health care, and social interactions, including ethics (Gollnick & Chinn, 2005).

Generally, religion provides people with "a way of facing the problems of ultimate and unavoidable frustration, of 'evil,' and the generalized problem of meaning in some nonempirical sense, of finding some ultimate why" (Williams, 1960b, p. 327). Religion, its followers, and its influence on nonreligious dimensions of human life will likely continue as a significant force in American society (Greely, 2001).

How does religion influence socialization?

If the family subscribes to an organized religion, at birth children are often inducted into it via a public naming ceremony. The family's religious beliefs determine what is selected from the environment to transmit to the child. The family also interprets and evaluates what is transmitted. For example, Roman Catholics believe in strict obedience to authority and do not believe in divorce or birth control. Thus, children from Roman Catholic families are brought up to obey their parents and the church. They are also reared to believe in the sanctity of marriage and to believe that sex is for producing children.

Not only does religion influence families and their socialization of children, but it influences the community as well, in respect to values and behavior. The dominant religious group in the United States (Protestants) has undoubtedly influenced the political and economic foundations of our country (Weber, 1930). The **Protestant ethic** is a religiously derived value system that defines the ideal person as individualistic, thrifty, self-sacrificing, efficient in use of time, strong in personal responsibility, and committed to productivity. By following this value system, believers feel one can reach salvation. An example of the Protestant ethic's influence on politics is welfare reform—laws passed to require welfare recipients to work (be self-sufficient) after a certain amount of time receiving government assistance. Religious beliefs can affect communities when religious groups elect members to government offices and school boards to influence policies such as abortion laws, school prayer, and science curriculum.

Every religion includes some beliefs that are shared by all its adherents. For example, Judaism teaches that a "good life" can be led only in a community; good Jews must always view their actions in terms of their effect on others. They believe in responsibility for others and regard charity as a virtue. Muslims give a percentage of their annual income to the poor. The ultimate goal of Buddhism is to be fully in the world and relate compassionately to others.

Most religions provide an ideology that enables individuals to comprehend events that happen to them; death, illness, financial crises, and injustices make sense if these are seen as part of a divine plan. Religion helps fill the gap between scientific and technical knowledge and the unknown.

Religious beliefs and practices help individuals accept and cope with crises without overwhelming psychological costs. For example, prayer helps people feel that they are "doing something" to meet the crisis. If the crisis is resolved, the individual's faith in prayer is confirmed. If the crisis is not resolved, the individual can explain

Protestant ethic
belief in individualism, thrift, self-sacrifice, efficiency, personal responsibility, and productivity

Miro Vintoniv/Index Stock Imagery

A bar mitzvah celebrates this 13-year-old boy's studies of Jewish history, culture, and prayer.

the outcome as part of God's plan. Thus, one can avoid feeling that life's catastrophes are senseless.

Most religions have beliefs about death. Some preach hell for those who transgress in life on Earth and heaven for those who lead a good life. The hope of a blissful immortality makes the death of a loved one more tolerable and the thought of one's own death less terrifying.

Religion helps people establish an identity and gives meaning to their lives. Many religious activities reflect pride and celebration. Religious rituals symbolize faith, honor God, or remind members of the group of their religious responsibilities. Rituals may include observing holidays, saying prayers, tithing, handling sacred objects, wearing certain clothing, and eating certain food (or fasting). For example, Holy Communion commemorates the climactic meal of Jesus' life and his sacrifice for humankind. In partaking of the holy bread and wine, the communicant partakes of Christ.

Carl Jung (1938) wrote that religion provides individuals who have a strong commitment to traditional norms and values with moral strength and behavioral stability. In other words, religious people are more likely to comply with societal norms, especially if they believe that those norms are divinely sanctioned. They look upon social deviance as a form of religious deviance. This has been confirmed in research (Furrow, King, & White, 2004; Gorsuch, 1976) showing that moral behavior was consistently related to religious commitment.

Chronosystem Influences on Families, Socialization, and Children

How has societal change affected the socialization of children in families?

"Families are not static but dynamic and are continuously confronted by challenges, changes, and opportunities" (Parke & Buriel, 1998, p. 511). Some families can develop coping styles to adapt to changes and remain healthy and functional, but others may become victims of the consequences of change. They may experience stress, dissolution, or an unanticipated lifestyle. They are at risk for becoming unhealthy, or dysfunctional. Chronosystem influences affecting the health of families include political changes, such as changes in the law (for example, welfare to workfare); economic changes, such as certain jobs becoming obsolete (for example, telephone operators); and technological changes, such as computers completing tasks faster, enabling more work to be done and hence increasing performance standards.

The general chronosystem effect on families is stress. Change, in itself is not good or bad; how we react to it determines its worth. Stress is a concept from physics that refers to physical forces and the ability to withstand strain. Dr. Hans Selye applied the concept to refer to the human ability to adjust to danger signals. He was interested in the biochemical changes that occur when an individual reacts to stress. Selye (1956) defined stress as "the nonspecific response of the body to any demand" (p. 54). Others have defined **stress** as any demand that exceeds a person's ability

stress any demand that exceeds a person's ability to cope

to cope (Honig, 1986). *Physical stressors* include disease, overexertion, allergies, and abuse; *sociocultural stressors* include crowding, traffic, noise, bureaucracies, and crime; *psychological stressors* include personal reactions to real or imagined threats and reactions to real or imagined pressure to achieve (Kuczen, 1987).

Stress is not new. In hunting-and-gathering societies, the fear of not finding food or shelter was a stressor. In agricultural societies, the unpredictability of the weather was a stressor. In industrial societies, working long hours was, and still is, a stressor. In information societies, information overload and excessive choice are stressors. One must make decisions in areas in which one has little or no expertise, and often facts and opinion are blurred. Children today face many of the same stressors of growing up that children a generation ago faced: separation anxiety, sibling rivalry, coping with school, peer pressure, being independent. However, children today also face stressors that were practically nonexistent a generation ago (Elkind, 1994; Hewlett & West, 1998). Examples include the escalation of violence in families and communities, terrorism in the world (National Association of School Psychologists, 2001), and the bombardment of consumerism into homes, schools, extracurricular activities, and the media. Another stress is that family life has become fragmented. People are pressured by occupational and community demands for their time. Pagers, cellular phones, wireless computers, and e-mail have all contributed to merging the boundaries between family and other commitments, thus jeopardizing time for family.

SOCIOPOLITICAL CHANGES

What are the consequences for families of social and political changes?

Sociopolitical changes influencing family functioning include foreign policy regarding immigration and war, and domestic policy regarding security, privacy, and social services. Newcomers to this country usually occupy the lower-income jobs, require English language training, may need housing assistance, health care, and other services until they adapt to American life. Children of immigrants have to accommodate to the culture of their parents as well as to that of their new country, and as mentioned earlier, serve as intermediaries between the two cultures.

War obviously affects the functioning of military families when one parent is called to duty. War and terrorism also affect the functioning of society as a whole. For example, terrorism has affected travel rules, communication procedures, and racial profiling. Flexibility in travel has diminished, affecting family visits and vacations. Mail is subject to inspection for fear of biological warfare (anthrax, for example). Families who have ethnic backgrounds similar to that of terrorists are subjected to more searching and interrogation in public places. Some children have been ostracized and treated cruelly.

Children victimized by war or terrorism who have experienced loss of a loved one may react with emotional detachment or a seeming lack of feeling, by exhibiting regressive or immature behavior, by acting out or exploding, or by continually asking the same questions because they cannot understand what happened (National Association of School Psychologists, 2001). All of us are affected in some way by political uncertainty. There have been documented increases in substance abuse, people seeking therapy, and individuals turning to spirituality for comfort (Kaslow, 2001).

Social services, such as government financial assistance, have decreased. Welfare reform has brought changes in family structure and functions. Recognizing that most poor families are headed by single parents, lawmakers in 1996 emphasized the responsibility of both parents to support their children. In addition to strengthening the child support enforcement system, the law included provisions designed to decrease childbearing outside of marriage and promote two-parent families (McLanahan & Carlson, 2002). What are the long-term consequences for parents, children, community support services, and society in general of these new welfare regulations, stronger paternity establishment, and stricter child support enforcement?

ECONOMIC CHANGES

What economic changes affect families and children?

Economic changes influencing family functioning may involve job uncertainty because of company buyouts, downsizing, and layoffs; the cost of living, requiring both parents to be employed; and the erosion of employee benefits, such as health insurance (Gallay & Flanagan, 2000).

Reduced levels of economic well-being have been found to increase parental stress, resulting in less affection toward children and less effective disciplinary interactions. Children in such families were more likely to be reported by teachers as having behavior problems and negative social relations with peers (Mistry, Vandewater, Huston, & McLoyd, 2002).

When both parents are employed, their family life may be at risk for fragmentation. The father works, the mother works, and the children go to child care or school, all requiring coordination. If working hours are staggered, the family may not eat together. Household tasks have to be done after work. If children have after-school activities, they have to be coordinated with the parents' already busy schedules. Then there are meetings—school, work, and community meetings. Hardly any time is left for family communication or shared leisure. Needless to say, this can cause stress. Children may feel rushed, tense, or out of control. And what happens when one parent is transferred to another city or state and the other parent's job doesn't allow for similar mobility? For single parents, the risk of fragmentation may be greater unless there is another supportive adult to assist with family functioning and buffer stress. Support and buffering have been shown to enable parents to perform multiple roles that, if they enjoy them, can contribute to their emotional well-being (Barnett & Hyde, 2001).

TECHNOLOGICAL CHANGES

What technological changes affect families and children?

Technological changes influencing family functioning include designed obsolescence—things have to be replaced because the parts are no longer available or they're not compatible with newer things. Obsolescence causes added expenses for family consumption and can influence people's jobs.

Technological changes also include things that enable "multitasking" and "instantaneousness." "Generation Y—the nearly 60 million children born after 1979—are the first to grow up in a world saturated with networks of information, digital devices, and the promise of perpetual connectivity" (Montgomery, 2000). I see individuals doing multiple tasks—shopping while talking on their cell phones, eating while driving, working while watching TV or a computerized movie. There is so much to do that we feel we have to maximize our time. Businesses have changed to help us adapt. We have superstores with "one-stop" shopping; we have fast foods; we have fast lanes. Because we hurry through experiences so fast, we look for more ways to spend our time, so we have mega-theaters with mega-movie choices; we have cable or satellite TV with hundreds of channels; we have new sports added to the old ones every year, with their accompanying new equipment for sale.

Some parents react to the time bind by "overscheduling" their children's activities. With the increase in homework that has occurred today, every minute must be used to allow for participation in the many activities now available for children, such as team sports or Scouts. Does "busyness" cause family members and friends to get the short shrift of our attention? Some phone and Internet providers have been able to capitalize on that concern by offering free or low-cost services such as call waiting, caller ID (you only have to talk to those you choose), unlimited calls to preselected individuals, and instant e-mail messaging.

What is the effect of constantly being "turned on" and "tuned in"? Does our "fast-forward" world with its multiple, simultaneous activities (for example, several screen images or pop-up messages on your TV or computer) make us talk faster, interrupt more, bore easily, and continually seek novelty or stimulation? What is the effect of being constantly exposed to virtual reality, as provided by media, on our perception of reality and our ability to cope with it?

Meeting the Challenge of Change: Family Empowerment

How can families be enabled to deal with the stress of change?

As we have discussed, the family is a dynamic social system that has structure, functions, roles, and authority patterns. The way the system operates and adapts to change affects the relationships within it. Change can produce stress that affects all the individual members of the family. Stressors other than death, illness, divorce, and moving that have been found to cause significant problems in family functioning include the following (Curran, 1985):

1. Economics
2. Children's behavior
3. Insufficient couple time
4. Lack of shared responsibility in the family
5. Communicating with children
6. Insufficient "me" time
7. Guilt for not accomplishing more
8. Spousal relationship
9. Insufficient family play time
10. Overscheduled family calendar

An effective way for families to meet the challenge of adapting to societal change is to examine the characteristics of functional or successful families as models to emulate, rather than clinging to some family pattern that worked in the past (Coontz, 1997). How families cope with stress can be assessed by how they solve problems, how they communicate, how they adapt to change, their social supports, their spiritual beliefs, their self-esteem and personal adjustment, and absence of pathology, deviance, or drug use (Curran, 1985; Stinnett & Defrain, 1985). These studies have shown that functional families that are resilient to stress are more likely to exhibit certain key characteristics—behaviors and values—than are

HIRB/Index Stock Imagery

The physical closeness between father and child is important to foster attachment and interdependence.

families that are at risk for dysfunction when stressed. The strength of each characteristic and the combination of characteristics, as well as how they are demonstrated, may vary from one family to another and may be influenced by ethnic orientation. But, in general, the overall picture of functional families is as follows:

- **Display of love and acceptance**. Members of strong families show their love and appreciation for one another. This acceptance and warmth is expressed spontaneously—physically (smile, touch, hug) or verbally ("I love you," "You're a good son/daughter"). Family members cooperate rather than compete with one another.
- **Communicativeness**. Family members are spontaneous, honest, open, and receptive to one another. This means expressing negative as well as positive feelings. Conflicts are faced and handled, rather than repressed into resentment. However, some ethnic groups such as Asians believe it is better not to express negative feelings in order to avoid conflicts.
- **Cohesiveness**. Family members enjoy spending time together. Sharing chores, resources, and recreational activities is considered important. There is also respect, however, for individual differences, autonomy, and independence. It is common in Anglo-American families for members to engage in individual as well as family pursuits, whereas this is not necessarily the pattern among other ethnic groups.
- **Communication of values and standards**. Parents in strong families have definite and clear values and make them known to their children. These values and standards are discussed and practiced. There is also tolerance and respect for individual differences. Parents are models as well as teachers.
- **Ability to cope effectively with problems**. Stress and crises are faced optimistically with the purpose of finding solutions. Alternatives are explored, and family members are mutually supportive.

How can families develop resilience to stress? **Empowerment** is enabling individuals to have control over resources affecting them. Giving families access to knowledge and skills that enhance their ability to influence their personal lives and the community in which they live is the first step toward resiliency (Vanderslice, 1984). Empowerment is a process that evolves from analyzing one's own strengths and resources, becoming educated in skills one is lacking, and participating in the community. Empowerment is part of current U.S. social policy. For example, government funding to families is tied to becoming self-reliant instead of dependent. Rather than viewing families with problems as helpless, the government has various programs to help people help themselves, such as financial aid for a college education, vocational rehabilitation, child care, and health services. Public and private community agencies that help empower families will be discussed in Chapter 10.

empowerment
enabling individuals to have control over resources affecting them

Epilogue

Family structure and function are affected by historical changes. Family systems vary and are influenced by larger contexts, or macrosystems, including culture, politics, economics, and technology. Macrosystem values, such as obligation to self or others, affect family functions. Values affect child developmental outcomes. Security and continuance family values provide stability for children, while personal happiness family values may result in uncertainty for children.

Summary

The family is viewed as a system affected by external and internal factors. The concept of family has changed from "a social group characterized by common residence, economic cooperation, and reproduction including adults of both sexes, at least two of whom maintain a socially approved sexual relationship and one or more children, biological or adopted, of the sexually cohabiting adults" (Murdock, 1962) to "any two or more related persons by birth, marriage, or adoption who reside together" (U.S. Bureau of the Census, 2003).

The basic structures of a family are the nuclear and the extended family. A nuclear family consists of husband, wife, and children. An extended family consists of kin related to the nuclear family who are emotionally, and perhaps economically, dependent on each other. Extended families can be matriarchal, patriarchal, or egalitarian.

In general, the family's basic functions are reproduction, socialization/education, assignment of social roles, economic support, and nurturance/emotional support. Functional families maintain resilience and adaptability; dysfunctional families are at risk for breakup or problems. The scope of the specific family functions have changed.

Family transitions affect family structure and functions. Divorcing parents affect children. All children do not react to divorce the same way; variables include the temperaments and personalities involved, coping skills, parents' relations with their children, age and gender of the child, and availability of others for support. Divorce affects the custodial parent, too—responsibilities double, and stress increases. Joint custody arrangements may give the children access to both parents, but may also cause confusion.

Stepfamilies and the impact of remarriage on children are stressful. Children in a stepfamily have to form new relationships and accept new rules and new values, while still having to deal with the old relationships, rules, and values. Reestablishing an effective functioning family system is a challenge.

Kin custody, usually grandparent, is another arrangement affecting children, especially with regard to their sense of belonging and stability. Community support is beneficial.

Families with parents who are unmarried by choice may affect children's stability, depending on variables such as economics and relationships within the family. Families with homosexual parents, on the increase, can influence children if they become concerned about their sexual identities. How the community responds is also a factor in a child's development.

Families of adopted children vary according to the reasons they choose to adopt. Adopted children may have misunderstandings about their adoption, fears of abandonment, and identity issues.

Functional changes related to family transitions include the roles of various family members. In dual-earner families, work, household responsibilities, child care, and leisure time must be coordinated. The effects of maternal employment outside the home depend on the age, gender, and temperament of the child, the socioeconomic status of the family, the quality of the parents' marriage, the mother's satisfaction with her job, the father's satisfaction with his job, and the father's involvement with the children, as well as the availability of quality child care and social supports.

Macrosystem influences on families, socialization, and children are socioeconomic status, ethnic orientation, and religious orientation. Socioeconomic status involves stratification. In traditional societies, status is usually ascribed; in modern societies, status is usually achieved. One's status or social class influences how one is socialized. The different socioeconomic classes rear children differently; academic performance and behavior are affected.

Ethnicity involves identification with a group based on national origin, race, or religion. Ethnic attributes can be physical, cultural, or both. Members of an ethnic group share a history, a language, and a set of traditions, rituals, customs, beliefs, attitudes, and values. People of different ethnic orientations differ in the ways they deal with basic questions of living, which affects socialization and consequent behavior patterns.

Religion is a unified system of beliefs and practices relative to sacred things, uniting into a single moral community all those who adhere to those beliefs and practices. Families that practice an organized religion usually induct their children into it at birth. The family's religious beliefs influence its socialization practices. Religion provides an ideology that enables individuals to comprehend events that happen to them and gives them an identity and a support system for traditional norms and values.

Chronosystem influences on families, socialization, and children are sociopolitical changes such as war, economic changes such as job security, and technological changes such as computers and cell phones.

Activity

PURPOSE To understand the influence of certain family characteristics on socialization and development.

1. Of what socioeconomic status was your family of orientation? On what criteria did you base your answer?
2. List the values, beliefs, or attitudes supported by your ethnic group.
3. List the values, beliefs, or attitudes supported by your religion.
4. What were some stresses your family of orientation experienced, and how did your family adapt?
5. What were three socialization goals communicated by your family of orientation? (Were they successful or unsuccessful?)
6. List three goals you have for yourself.
7. List three goals you have for your family of procreation.
8. Is there any connection between your family of orientation's socialization goals and your goals for your family of procreation?

Related Readings

Barnett, R. C., & Rivers, C. (1996). *She works; he works.* Cambridge, MA: Harvard University Press.

Blankenhorn, D. (1995). *Fatherless America.* New York: Basic Books.

Bria, G. (1998). *The art of family: Rituals, imagination, and everyday spirituality.* New York: Dell.

Coleman, M., & Ganong, L. (1994). *Remarried family relationships.* Newbury Park, CA: Sage.

Coontz, S. (1997). *The way we really are: Coming to terms with America's changing families.* New York: Basic Books.

Cummings, E. M., & Davies, P. (1994). *Children and marital conflict. The impact of family dispute and resolution.* New York: Guilford Press.

Elkind, D. (1994). *Ties that stress: The new family imbalance.* Cambridge, MA: Harvard University Press.

Galinsky, E. (1999). *Ask the children: What America's children really think about working parents.* New York: William Morrow.

Gilbert, D., & Kahn, J. A. (1987). *The American class structure: A new synthesis* (3rd ed.). Chicago: Dorsey Press.

Hareven, T. (1999). *Families, history, and social change: Life course and cross-cultural perspectives.* Boulder, CO: Westview Press.

Hetherington, E. M., & Kelly, J. (2002). *For better or worse: Divorce reconsidered.* New York: Norton.

Kornhaber, K., & Forsythe, K. (1995). *Grandparent power: How to strengthen the vital connection among grandparents, parents, and children.* New York: Crown.

Martin, A. (1993). *Lesbian and gay parenting handbook: Creating and raising our families.* New York: HarperCollins.

Mason, M. A. (1998). *The custody wars: Why children are losing the legal battle—and what we can do about it.* New York: Basic Books.

McAdoo, H. P. (Ed.). (1993). *Family ethnicity: Strength in diversity.* Newbury Park, CA: Sage.

Pavao, J. M. (1999). *The family of adoption.* Boston: Beacon Press.

Stinnett, N., & Defrain, J. (1985). *Secrets of strong families.* Boston: Little, Brown.

Wilson, J. (1978). *Religion in American society: The effective presence.* Englewood Cliffs, NJ: Prentice-Hall.

Chapter 4

DesignPics Inc./Index Stock Imagery

Ecology of Parenting

You are the bows from which your children as living arrows are sent forth.
— KAHLIL GIBRAN

What makes a good parent?

Being a parent is probably the most difficult job in the world. Sometimes when parents try to do what they think is best for their children, circumstances prove them wrong. The following ancient Greek myth is an example of the danger of a parent's greed and materialism.

Once Upon a Time In ancient Greece, there lived a very rich king, whose name was Midas. He was fonder of gold than of anything else in the whole world, except perhaps his young golden-haired daughter, Marygold. As a parent, he thought the best thing he could do for his beloved child would be to bequeath her the largest pile of yellow glistening coins that had ever been heaped together since time began. Whenever he saw the gold-tinted clouds of a sunset, or yellow dandelions in the fields, or orange roses growing in his garden, he wished they would turn into gold coins. He became so obsessed with his desire to possess gold that he forgot the reason why he wanted it was to show his love for his daughter concretely.

One day while he was in his treasure room admiring his gold collection, a stranger, named Dionysus, dressed all in white appeared.

"You are indeed a wealthy man, King Midas," observed the stranger.

"Yes," said the king, "but think how much more gold is out there in the world."

"Are you not satisfied?" asked the stranger.

"No, of course not. I often lie awake at night planning of new ways to get more gold. Sometimes I even wish that everything I touch would turn to gold."

"Do you really wish that, King Midas?"

"Yes, nothing would make me happier."

"Then you shall have your wish. Tomorrow when the sun rises, you shall have the golden touch," proclaimed the stranger. And with that, he vanished.

Midas thought he had dreamed the whole encounter, but went to sleep that night hoping it was true. When he awoke the next morning and touched his slippers, they turned to gold! Excitedly, he began touching things in his room; they all turned to gold.

He looked out the window at the garden where his daughter Marygold loved to play and run outside to touch all the flowers. "Won't Marygold be happy," he thought. When Marygold saw the garden, she cried. "I won't be able to smell the flowers anymore; I won't be able to play in the garden, either!"

Not knowing how to comfort her, King Midas ordered breakfast to be served. However, as soon as Midas's lips touched the food, it turned to gold. He sputtered and spat. Marygold, thinking her father had burned his mouth, went to hug him, but alas, as her arms went about his chest, she, too, turned to gold. King Midas began to sob; his beloved daughter was now a statue who couldn't laugh, or play, or kiss him. He had robbed her of her essence.

The stranger appeared again and asked, "Are you happy now, King Midas?"

"How can I be happy? I am miserable. I can't eat, I can't smell, I can't touch my daughter . . ."

"But you have the golden touch . . ."

"Please give me back my little Marygold and I'll give up all the gold I have. I've lost all that was worth having."

"You have become wise," said the stranger. "Go plunge in the river and take from it water to sprinkle on whatever you wish to transform."

King Midas learned that being the best parent to his daughter did not mean giving her all the gold in the world. Such materialism only served to turn her into a material being herself; and statues are without spirit and have no love to give.

- **Where do we get our values and information about how we should parent?**

- **What is a "good" parent (in terms of society, the child, the self)?**

- **How do children influence parenting?**

Parenting

What is involved in parenting?

As a complement to Chapter 3, this chapter explores a major task of families, which is the physical protection, emotional nurturing, and socialization of children—commonly referred to as parenting. Parenting is a relationship that unfolds over time (Bornstein, 1995) and is affected by children themselves, as we will see.

Parenting means implementing a series of decisions about the socialization of your children (Kagan, 1975)—what you do to enable them to become responsible, contributing members of society, as well as what you do when they cry, are aggressive, lie, or do not do well in school. Parents sometimes find these decisions overwhelming. One of the reasons parenting can be confusing is that there is little consensus in the United States today as to what children should be like when they grow up or what you do to get them there. Another reason parenting is confusing is that it is *bidirectional* and *dynamic*—an adult's behavior toward a child is often a reaction to that child's temperament and behavior, changing with time as the child develops (Lerner, 1998; Putnam, Sanson, & Rothbart, 2002). Thus, by influencing adults, children influence their own development. Causes for behavior are viewed from a circular rather than a linear perspective (Cowan et al., 1998). The concept of the *bidirectionality* of parenting is exemplified throughout the chapter.

Whereas *parenthood* is universal, *parenting* is highly variable among different cultures and groups within societies. We will examine macrosystem influences on parenting styles, such as political ideology, culture, socioeconomic status, ethnicity, and religion, and chronosystem influences, such as historical trends and family dynamics.

parenting the implementation of a series of decisions about the socialization of children

Figure 4.1

An Ecological Model of Human Development

Parenting is the means by which the family socializes the child.

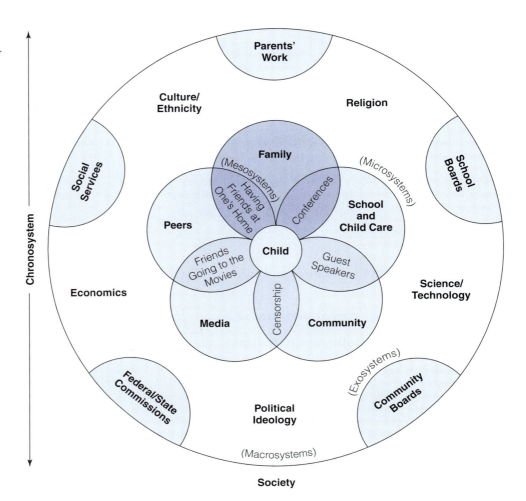

Is Parenting a Fad or a Fact?

What parenting practices worked best for you?

What kinds of behavior did you engage in to manipulate your parents? Get attention? Get revenge?

Macrosystem Influences on Parenting

How have societal values and practices influenced parenting?

The purpose of examining the macrosystem influences on parenting is to provide an understanding of political, cultural, socioeconomic, and ethnic/religious values or practices that, indirectly, have contributed to children's socialization and development.

POLITICAL IDEOLOGY

What does politics have to do with child rearing?

Political ideology refers to theories pertaining to government. It influences parenting styles because children must be raised to function as citizens in society. Most traditional societies subscribe to an aristocratic political ideology, or government by the highest ranking class of individuals in a society. Some traditional examples are tribes in Africa, New Zealand, and Australia. Some modern examples, still based on tradition, are the United Kingdom, Japan, and Spain, which have hereditary monarchs as heads of state. An **autocracy** such as this is a society in which one person has unlimited power over others. Many modern societies, such as the United States, subscribe to a democratic political ideology. A **democracy** is a society in which those ruled have power equal to those who rule; the principle is equality of rights. In an autocracy, relationships between people are understood in terms of a pecking order. The autocratic traditional family system follows such an order. The father is the authority who has power over the mother and the children; women and children have few rights. In a democracy, relationships between people are based on consensus and compromise. The democratic modern family system considers the rights of all members.

Fifty years ago, parenting decisions were easier to make because it was assumed that one's main purpose in life was to serve God by being faithful and following the teachings of one's religion. Children were constantly exhorted to overcome their base natures in order to please God (Spock, 1968). This concept is still preached by some of the fundamentalist religious sects around the world.

In some countries, one's purpose in life was held to be to serve one's country—for example, in France under Napoleon Bonaparte and in Germany under Hitler. This still holds true today in China. Parents and teachers are expected to agree with the country's leaders about what values and attitudes to instill in children.

In other places in the world, it is assumed that children are born and raised to serve the purposes of the family—for example, in rural India children are trained to work at jobs considered of value to their particular family; children defer to their elders and marriages are often arranged for the benefit of the family.

In the United States, few children are brought up to believe that their principal destiny is to serve their family, their country, or God. Euro-American children are generally given the feeling that they are free to set their own goals in life. However, other ethnic groups in the United States, ones that subscribe to the value of interdependence, generally bring up their children to be obligated to their families (Fuligni et al., 1999; Trumbull et al., 2001). Some examples are Mexican Americans and Asian Americans.

As U.S. society has undergone social and economic change, people have questioned the inadequate implementation of democratic ideals written in the Constitution, particularly those regarding equality. In the 1960s, people were especially concerned with unfair opportunities for ethnic minorities and women. As a result, Congress passed the Civil Rights Act of 1964, which required that ethnic minorities and women be treated equally in housing, education, and employment. Similar legislation was extended to individuals with disabilities in 1990. Such legislation has had beneficial economic effects in terms of opportunities to earn a living, as well as beneficial psychological effects on minorities' self-concept.

The notion that unlimited authority is no longer appropriate in U.S. society, because it is incongruent with democracy, has filtered down to children. Parents find it difficult to raise children by the "do it because I said so" method. Also, children

political ideology theories pertaining to government

autocracy a society in which one person has unlimited power over others

democracy a society in which those ruled have equal power with those who rule

learn democratic ideals in school and from the media, so they are not willing to be ruled autocratically. Appropriate child rearing in a democratic society becomes a challenge, especially for parents who were raised autocratically.

CULTURE

How does culture affect child rearing?

Culture, introduced in Chapter 2, includes the knowledge, beliefs, art, morals, law, customs, and traditions acquired by members of a society. Culture encompasses the way people have learned to adapt to their environment, their assumptions about the way the world is, and their beliefs about the way people should act (Triandis, 1994). The culture in which one grows up has indirect effects on parenting attitudes and consequent parenting styles (Greenfield & Suzuki, 1998; Parke & Buriel, 1998; Rogoff, 2003). To illustrate, Garcia-Coll (1990) reviewed the literature on cultural beliefs and care-giving practices and concluded that parenting goals and techniques depend to some extent on the nature of the tasks that adults are expected to perform or competencies that adults are supposed to possess in a given population. For example, in the United States adults are expected to read, write, compute, and be economically self-sufficient. American children are thus expected to achieve in school, are given an allowance to learn the value of money, and are pressured to get a job at least by the time they finish their schooling. In the Fiji Islands, however, adults are expected to farm, fish, and be able to make economic exchanges with relatives on the bigger islands (West, 1988). Fijian children are thus expected to relate to others in the community, to learn to help adults work, and to share resources.

LeVine (1977, 1988) proposes a set of universal parenting goals:

- Ensuring physical health and survival
- Developing behavioral capacities for economic self-maintenance
- Instilling behavioral capacities for maximizing cultural values, such as morality, prestige, and achievement

However, cultures vary in the importance they place on these goals as well as how they implement them. Also, if one goal is threatened, it becomes the foremost concern and overrides the need to implement the others. To illustrate, if a society has a high rate of infant mortality, parents will concentrate more on the goal of physical health and survival; the pursuit of learning to participate economically and learning cultural values will be postponed until a later age, when the child's survival is relatively certain. Societies with bare resources for subsistence place emphasis on training children in skills that will be economically advantageous in adulthood, thereby minimizing survival risks. Once society has tested and adopted various methods for survival, these methods become part of the folk tradition and get passed on to children.

How various cultures prioritize these universal parenting goals may explain differences in maternal behavior toward infants (Richman, LeVine, New, & Howrigan, 1988). For example, the Gusii of Kenya prioritize the parenting goal of physical health and survival. They interpret holding the child as a form of protection from physical hazards such as cooking fires and domestic animals, and have no alternatives like cradle boards, playpens, or infant seats. The Gusii mothers also soothe their infants through rapid physical comforting when they cry. This close physical contact enables the mother to know when her baby is becoming sick, as opposed to being hungry or temporarily distressed, because a sick baby will not be comforted by physical contact or food.

For another example, American mothers prioritize the parenting goal of developing capacities for economic self-maintenance. They verbalize with and gaze at their infants more frequently than do the Gusii. This reflects the belief that infants can communicate socially. By the time the American infant can walk, holding declines rapidly; infant seats, playpens, and high chairs are used to protect the locomotive infant from harm. This reduction in human physical contact reflects the value Americans put on separateness and independence.

What does the way in which a culture has adapted to survive have to do with child rearing?

Economics involves the production, distribution, and consumption of goods and services. Cultural anthropologists Beatrice Whiting and John Whiting (1975) wanted to see the relationship between a society's economic system, family structure, and parenting styles. Did the way the society governed and supported itself to survive relate to the way it reared its children?

The Whitings classified socioeconomic systems as *simple* or *complex*. *Simple* societies had economies based on subsistence gardening. Roles for men, women, and children were clearly defined, and cooperation was emphasized for survival. *Complex* societies, on the other hand, had economies based on occupational specialization. They had a class system and centralized government, and competition was emphasized. Family structure was classified as extended or nuclear, depending on whether there were specified relations with kin or whether the family was free to do "its own thing."

The Whitings observed the behavior of 134 children between the ages of 3 and 11 in Kenya, the Philippines, and Mexico (representing simple socioeconomic systems) and in Okinawa, India, and the United States (representing complex socioeconomic systems). The categories of social behavior that were found in the children of all six cultures, in varying degrees, included nurturance, responsibility, dependence, dominance, sociability, intimacy, authoritarianism, and aggressiveness. Because some of these categories consistently occurred together in the six cultures, they were organized into two dimensions in order to investigate the effect of culture on children's social behavior. One dimension was *nurturant/responsible* (offered help, offered support, suggested responsibility) versus *dependent/dominant* (sought help, sought attention, sought dominance). The other dimension was *sociable/intimate* (acted sociably, teased sociably, touched) versus *authoritarian/aggressive* (reprimanded, assaulted).

The societies having a relatively simple socioeconomic structure with little or no occupational specialization, no class or caste system, a localized, kin-based political structure, and no professional priesthood had children who were more nurturant/responsible and less dependent/dominant. The societies with a more complex socioeconomic structure, characterized by occupational specialization, social stratification, a central government, and a priesthood, had children who scored low on nurturance/responsibility but high on dependence/dominance.

The children of societies whose family structure was nuclear and egalitarian scored high on sociability/intimacy and low on authoritarianism/aggressiveness. The children of societies whose family structure was based on the extended family and was patriarchal scored high on authoritarianism/aggressiveness and low on sociability/intimacy (see Figure 4.2).

In societies having a patrilineal, extended family structure, the male head of the family must exercise authority over other family members. He must be able to express aggression when necessary, a skill learned in reprimanding younger siblings

economics the production, distribution, and consumption of goods and services

Figure 4.2

Dimensions of Sociocultural Characteristics and Socialized Behavior

The behavior emphasized in children is related to the social and economic structure of the culture.

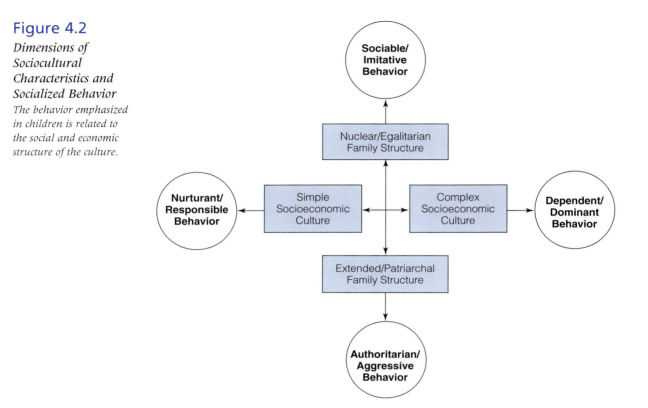

during childhood. In societies having a nuclear, neolocal (newlyweds set up a new place or residence) family system, authoritarianism and aggressiveness are not as necessary as sociability and intimacy.

> Formulas for appropriate adult social behavior dictated by the socioeconomic and family system are embedded in the value system of the culture. Nurturance and responsibility, success, authority, and casual intimacy are types of behavior that are differentially preferred by different cultures. These values are apparently transmitted to the children before the age of six. (Whiting & Whiting, 1975, pp. 178–179)

In another study, Whiting and Edwards (1988) examined the ideologies of the same six cultures in regard to expectations of children by age and gender. They examined the social behavior of girls and boys ages 2 to 10 who lived in communities in India, Okinawa, the Philippines, Mexico, Kenya, and the United States. With whom did the children interact? Did they go to school, or did they have responsibilities at home? What activities occupied their time—caring for siblings, doing errands, or playing?

They found that different societies varied in their expectations of behavior according to age. In some societies, 6-year-olds were expected to learn the ways of their culture by taking on household responsibilities and caring for younger siblings, whereas in others, 6-year-olds were expected to go to school. Different societies also varied in their expectations of behavior according to gender. Some societies had different ideologies for boys and girls, and assigned children to settings or activities accordingly. Boys were allowed more autonomy and expected to exhibit more dominant behavior with others; girls were kept in close proximity and expected to engage in more nurturing activities with younger siblings.

Thus, the social behavior of the children of each culture type was found to be compatible with the adult role requirements of the society. In societies based on a simple socioeconomic structure, reciprocity among kin and neighbors is essential. People offer help and support to one another; dominance and attention-seeking are frowned upon. Children take on helping responsibilities early on. In societies based on a more complex socioeconomic structure, dominance and attention-seeking are behaviors that may enhance a person's chance to rise in social status; help and support of others are regarded as counterproductive. Children's autonomous behavior is encouraged.

SOCIOECONOMIC STATUS

How does socioeconomic status affect child rearing?

A family's **socioeconomic status** is its rank or position within a society based on social and economic factors, such as income, occupation, and education of the parents. In general, parents of *high socioeconomic status* have high incomes, engage in highly respected occupations, and are well educated; parents of *low socioeconomic status* have low incomes, hold unskilled or semiskilled jobs, and are poorly educated; parents of *middle socioeconomic status* have medium incomes, business or professional occupations, and a good education. It must be remembered that not all families can be classified according to the criteria listed here; some parents are very well educated and have very low incomes (graduate students, for example), and some parents have very high incomes and are not well educated (some businesspersons, for example). Also, there is as much variation within socioeconomic status groups as between them. For example, in a study of lower-class, blue-collar families, LeMasters (1988) found that fathers had different ideas about raising their children, especially their sons, than did the mothers. According to the blue-collar fathers in the study, to become a "man" a boy has to learn to fight, to defend himself, and to give back at least as much punishment as he takes. If a boy doesn't learn this, he will be weak and tend to be "victimized" all his life, not only by men, but also by women. The blue-collar mothers in the study, on the other hand, were trying to raise their boys for family roles—to be more sensitive and cooperative rather than "macho."

The following descriptive (not evaluative) generalizations are made on the basis of many research studies that compare the parenting styles of families of high and low socioeconomic status (Hart & Risley, 1995; Hoff et al., 2002; Parke & Buriel, 1998), keeping in mind that variations exist within each class:

- Parents of low socioeconomic status are more likely to emphasize obedience, respect, neatness, cleanliness, and staying out of trouble; parents of high socioeconomic status are more likely to emphasize happiness, creativity, ambition, independence, curiosity, and self-control.
- Parents of low socioeconomic status are likely to be more controlling, authoritarian, and arbitrary in their discipline and are apt to use physical punishment; parents of high socioeconomic status are more likely to be democratic, using reason with their children and being receptive to their children's opinions.
- Parents of high socioeconomic status are more likely to show warmth and affection toward their children than are parents of low socioeconomic status.
- Parents of high socioeconomic status are more likely to talk to their children, reason with them, and use complex language than are parents of low socioeconomic status.

socioeconomic status rank or position within a society, based on social and economic factors

A major reason why parenting styles differ according to socioeconomic status is that families tend to adapt their interactional patterns to the level of stress they are experiencing. Families of high as well as low socioeconomic status experience stress, such as work problems, health problems, and relationship problems. However, low income and other stressors related to poverty (housing, unsafe neighborhoods, job turnover) influence parents' well-being, the tone of their marriage, and the quality of their relationship with their children (Cowan et al., 1998). According to several studies (Dodge, Pettit, & Bates, 1994; McLoyd, 1998), economic hardship experienced by lower-class families is associated with anxiety, depression, and irritability. This emotional stress increases the tendency of parents to be punitive, inconsistent, authoritarian, and generally nonsupportive of their children. The emotional strain encourages the parent to adopt parenting techniques, such as physical punishment and commanding without explanation, that require less time and effort than other methods, such as reasoning and negotiating. Expecting unquestioning obedience from children is more efficient than trying to meet the desires of all family members when one is experiencing stress.

What is the relationship between parental occupation and children's behavior?

So far we have discussed *macrosystem* influences, such as political ideology, culture, and socioeconomic system, on parenting styles. Now we examine an *exosystem* influence—parents' work—which is a factor in socioeconomic status. Complex societies in which there are many roles to perform have complex stratification systems, or many criteria on which status is based, such as income, occupation, education, and place of residence. The more complex the society and the more roles that exist, the more complex the job of socialization becomes. When one performs a role, one takes on the behavioral expectations of that role through the process of socialization. For example, army officers will behave in an authoritarian manner, giving commands, whereas lawyers will use logic, reason, and explanation in performing their roles. Do the socialized role behaviors performed in one's occupation carry over into parenting styles?

To find out, Miller and Swanson (1958) examined the child-rearing practices of American parents who had different occupational roles, which they classified as *bureaucratic* versus *entrepreneurial*. Bureaucratic occupations were characterized by a direct salary and relatively high job security—for example, civil service employees, public school teachers, military personnel, and some corporate employees. Entrepreneurial occupations were classified as those in which a person is self-employed or works on the basis of a direct commission—for example, physicians, owners of businesses, and certain salespeople such as real estate agents. Miller and Swanson found that bureaucratic families tended to stress egalitarian practices and to emphasize social adjustment or "getting along"; entrepreneurial families tended to emphasize independence training, mastery, and self-reliance. The entrepreneurial parents also tended to depend heavily on psychological techniques of discipline, such as "You've disappointed me with your behavior," rather than "No television for the rest of the night for you."

HIRB/Index Stock Imagery

People who work in bureaucratic jobs, like those in a hospital, tend to incorporate the value of following the rules in their parenting styles.

Sociologist Melvin Kohn (1977, 1995) analyzed the ways in which middle-class occupations in general differ from lower-class occupations. Middle-class occupations typically require the individual to handle ideas and symbols, as well as be skilled in dealing with interpersonal relations, whereas lower-class occupations typically involve physical objects rather than symbols and do not involve as many interpersonal skills. Also, middle-class jobs often demand more self-direction in the prioritizing of job activities and in the selection of methods to get the job done than do lower-class jobs, which are more often routinized and subject to stricter supervision.

Kohn's (1977, 1995) subsequent research on differences in parent–child relationships in middle- and lower–class families indicated that lower-class parents were likely to judge their children's behavior in terms of its immediate consequences and its external characteristics, whereas middle-class parents were more concerned with their children's motives and the attitudes their behavior seemed to express. Kohn explained these differences as due to the different characteristics required in middle- and lower-class occupations.

Kohn (1977, 1995) found that middle-class parents were more likely than lower-class parents to want their children to be considerate of others, intellectually curious, responsible, and self-controlled; lower-class parents were more likely to want their children to have good manners, to do well in school, and to be obedient. Thus, the middle-class parent tends to emphasize self-direction for the child, whereas the lower-class parent tends to emphasize conformity. Kohn also found that fathers whose jobs entail self-direction, who work with ideas instead of things, who are not closely supervised, and who face complexity on the job value self-direction in their children; whereas those whose work requires them to conform to close supervision and a highly structured work situation are more likely to want their children to conform.

Similarly, Bronfenbrenner (1979) and others (Bronfenbrenner & Crouter, 1982; Crouter & McHale, 1993) suggest that parents' workplaces affect their perceptions of life and the way they interact with family members. Therefore, parenting styles tend to be extensions of the modes of behavior that are functional for parents. In dual-earner families, so prevalent today, it is possible for mothers and fathers, due to the nature of their jobs, to come to favor different parenting practices and these, in turn, may further vary according to their children's age and gender (Crouter, Bumpus, Maguire, & McHale, 1999; Crouter & McHale, 1993; Greenberger, O'Neil, & Nagel, 1994).

In sum, the differences in socialization practices related to differences in socioeconomic status are due not only to variations in physical resources but also to the types of adult models available to children for patterning behaviors, the breadth and quality of learning experiences provided for children, and the kinds of child-rearing practices implemented by the parents as influenced by their occupations.

ETHNICITY/RELIGION

How do ethnicity and religion affect child rearing?

Ethnicity, introduced in Chapter 1, refers to membership in a group in which members identify themselves by national origin, culture, language, race, or religion. *Religion*, introduced in Chapter 3, refers to a unified system of beliefs and practices relative to sacred things. Ethnicity and religion affect one's values, perceptions, attitudes, and behavior. Here we examine some aspects of ethnic and religious influences on child-rearing goals and practices. The purpose is not to stereotype by the examples provided, but rather to sensitize us to the power and pervasiveness of traditional beliefs and practices that have been developed as adaptive survival strategies and passed from generation to generation. As various ethnic and religious groups become part of the mainstream, their values may change, as may those of the mainstream. This process can be observed in generational differences among grandparents, parents, and children (Parke & Buriel, 1998).

To begin to understand differences in group values, we examine the work of Tonnies (1957), a German sociologist, who analyzed the reasons for this diversity as being tied to how societies adapt to political, social, and economic changes. The social order of society is based largely on the customs and traditions of groups sharing the same ethnicity or religion. He classified groups according to *gemeinschaft* characteristics on one end of the spectrum and *gesellschaft* on the other. In **gemeinschaft** groups, interpersonal relationships tend to be communal, cooperative, close, intimate, and informal. Social sanctions and political control are based on an established hierarchy with ascribed rights and obligations. Personal opinions and beliefs are private; the customs of the community are adhered to and respected. In **gesellschaft** groups, on the other hand, interpersonal relationships tend to be associative, practical, objective, and formal. Social sanctions and political control are achieved through public discussions and consensus, emphasizing fairness and equal rights. The concepts of gemeinschaft and gesellschaft community relations will be discussed further in Chapter 10.

Because families are embedded in larger social groups, such as ethnic or religious communities, they can be similarly categorized, albeit generally, as *cooperative/interdependent (collectivism)* on one end of the spectrum (more likely found in gemeinschaft societies) and *competitive/independent (individualism)* on the other end (more likely found in gesellschaft societies). **Collectivism** emphasizes interdependent relations, social responsibilities, and the well-being of the group—"fitting in"; **individualism** emphasizes individual fulfillment and choice—"standing out" (Trumbull et al., 2001). Collectivism includes a "we" consciousness, group solidarity, sharing, duties and obligations, group decisions, and particularism or partiality toward group members; individualism includes an "I" consciousness, autonomy, individual initiative, right to privacy, pleasure seeking, and universalism or impartiality toward group members (Hofstede, 1991). About 70% of the world cultures could be described as collectivistic (Trumbull et al., 2001).

Collectivistic and individualistic orientations are exhibited by diverse parenting values and child-rearing practices in families, specifically in the authority roles, the communication that takes place, how emotion is displayed, how children are disciplined and guided, and what skills are emphasized. For example, children socialized in a collectivist context are amused by people—by being held, teased, or *shown* how to do something; children socialized in an individualistic context are amused by things—by being given space, given toys, or *told* how to do something (Trumbull et al., 2001). For example, at our fall picnic to welcome faculty and graduate students in our department, I observed an Israeli parent trying to keep her $2\frac{1}{2}$-year-old child occupied and away from the cooking area by continually talking to him. He was quite verbally adept for his age, and the attentive conversation seemed to distract him from examining the barbeque. The preschool children of the parents from the United States were given toys to play with while their parents talked and cooked.

What impact do collectivistic and individualistic parenting orientations have on children?

Some generalizations on ethnic/religious patterns of parenting follow, organized by collectivistic versus individualistic orientations, as well as by specific family dynamics regarding (1) authority roles, (2) communication, (3) display of emotion, (4) discipline/guidance of

gemeinschaft
communal, cooperative, close, intimate, and informal interpersonal relationships

gesellschaft
associative, practical, objective, and formal interpersonal relationships

collectivism emphasis on interdependent relations, social responsibilities, and the well-being of the group

individualism emphasis on individual fulfillment and choice

children, and (5) skills emphasized (Garcia-Coll, Meyer, & Britton, 1995; Parke & Buriel, 1998; Rogoff, 2003; Thiederman, 1991). Affecting the homogeneity or heterogeneity within the generalizations is the degree of assimilation into, and adoption of, mainstream ways. For example, European Americans tend to be more oriented toward individualism than collectivism; Native Americans tend to be more oriented toward collectivism than individualism; African Americans tend to be more oriented toward collectivism than European Americans, but more oriented toward individualism than Native Americans (Trumbull et al., 2001).

Cooperative/Interdependent (Collective) Orientation

Authority Roles. Generally, authority roles in groups with collective orientations are hierarchical. Children are taught to respect age and status. Appropriate behavior is ascribed in social roles—mothers do certain things, as do grandparents, as do teachers. Different treatment of individuals according to rank and/or situation is known as *particularism*. Authority figures are expected to have more rights and privileges than other group members because they have more obligations and responsibilities to protect and care for other group members.

Asian American family structure and roles are generally based on Confucian religious principles of order, relationships, and harmony. The structure is hierarchical. Typically, Asian American families are patriarchal and members place family needs above individual needs. Children show obedience and loyalty to parents and are expected to take care of elderly parents (Bugental & Goodenow, 1998).

Native American families "may be characterized as a collective cooperative social network that extends from the mother and father union to the extended family and ultimately the community and tribe" (Bugental & Goodenow, 1998, p. 504). Children are socialized by the extended, as well as the nuclear, family. Generally, there are strong bonds of affection between family members. Traditionally, it is the old people who pass on the cultural heritage to the younger ones. It is not acceptable for children to communicate their opinions to older people. Children are taught to respect elders (age is a "badge of honor"—if you have grown old, you have done the right things). Respect is taught by example as well as by instruction.

Hispanic American parents generally encourage children to identify with the family and community. Children are close to members of the extended, as well as the nuclear, family. This fosters a sense of obligation to the family. The religious principles of Catholicism, such as God's will and childbearing, are commonly followed. Respect for parents is emphasized, as is obedience and fear of authority. Typically, age and gender are important determinants of roles and status. Hierarchical relationships tend to assure that people keep their appropriate roles and behave accordingly. Older children are given responsibility for socialization of younger ones. The family is viewed as the main source of one's sense of self, and its honor in the community is highly valued. To set up a life separate from the family is considered irresponsible; in adulthood, offspring owe allegiance and support to parents and extended family members.

Some African Americans derive a sense of community and identity from an organized religion rather than race or national origin. Authority roles in the family follow those of the religious group. For example, those Muslim immigrants and their families who follow the practices of Islam believe that all things belong to God and that wealth held by men is held in trust. Islam, like other religions, requires that a portion of one's accumulated wealth be given to those in need.

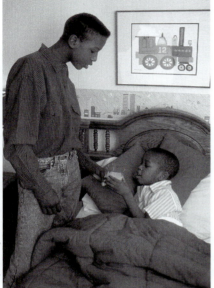

In some cultures, children are given important responsibilities that contribute to the welfare of the family.

Communication. Patterns of communication vary among collectivistic groups, but reliance on nonverbal communication (body language, gestures, touch, facial expression, eye contact) is generally greater than in individualistic groups. Compared to European Americans, for example, Asian Americans use relatively restrained verbal communication; instead, they use nonverbal communication, such as facial expressions and body language.

Some groups value silence and pauses in communication, whereas others value interruptions. For example, Asian Americans and Native Americans use silence and pauses in conversations to contemplate what was said and to think about how to respond. Middle Eastern Americans, Italian Americans, and Hawaiians tend to interrupt as a means of getting involved (Thiederman, 1991).

African Americans tend to encourage body contact (embraces in greeting or to thank). Mothers are physically close to their infants, often sleeping with them. Babies tend to be fed on demand rather than on a schedule. Mothers become involved early on in bowel and bladder training. Nonverbal communication with babies is common, such as caressing and rubbing their feet (Hale, 1994).

Shirley Brice Heath (1989) observed African American communication styles in low-income families. She found that adults asked children different types of questions than those typically heard in middle-class European American families. European American parents tended to ask "knowledge-training" questions, such as "What is this story about?" African American parents in Heath's sample asked only "real" questions—those to which they did not know the answer—such as "What's in that box?" Often conversations were acted out with body language and contained a lot of teasing. Sometimes speakers coin words if doing so enhances and furthers communication. It's not what is said, but how it is said that is important (Hale, 1994). Eye contact is important, too. When speaking, European Americans often look away from the listener, glancing at them from time to time; yet when they listen, they look directly at the speaker. African Americans, on the other hand, generally do the opposite; when they speak, they tend to stare at the listener, whereas when they listen, they mostly look away (Dresser, 1996).

Displays of Emotion. Some groups display their emotions outwardly and others, inwardly. Emotions kept inside can be expressed through a change in personal distance (an African American stepped backward while engaged in a loud conversation), shunning (a Native American ignored and avoided his friend for boasting), or deviations in performing routines (a Japanese American husband knew his wife was angry because she filled his teacup only halfway with lukewarm tea).

Generally, African Americans tend to show emotions outwardly, through facial expressions, sound, and body movement (Thiederman, 1991). On the other hand, Native Americans and Japanese Americans rarely show their feelings publicly (Triandis, 1994). In Japan, a smile can disguise embarrassment, mask bereavement, or conceal rage, whereas a straight face can hide happiness (Stewart & Bennett, 1991).

Discipline/Guidance of Children Hierarchical groups consider age to be of high status because age is equated with knowledge. Children, who are of low status in such groups, are not asked their desires nor are they expected to communicate their opinions to older people. Instead, they are expected to be guided by the wisdom of adults; children obey and imitate. Even when children in such collectivistic groups play, an adult or older sibling is nearby to guide them as needed (Rogoff, 2003).

Asian American children are generally nurtured closely in the early years by the mother. Parenting of infants can be described as responsive: infants are seldom allowed to cry for prolonged periods before they are picked up; they are fed on demand; they are weaned at a later age than European Americans; the child is allowed to sleep with the parents; and toilet training is gradual. Thus, the Asian American child becomes dependent on the mother to satisfy his or her needs. This dependency, as well as the physical closeness, fosters in the child a sense of obligation, which is continually reinforced as the child grows older. Consequently, the mother is able to use shame and guilt to control behavior by appealing to this sense of duty when the child deviates from her expectations. The power of shame is expressed in a Chinese proverb: "If you disregard the question of face, life is pointless." Avoiding shame, or "saving face," is part of the desire to maintain harmony and balance in the group—no one should be caused embarrassment. Related socialized behaviors to avoid shame and save face are a reluctance to admit lack of understanding or to ask questions, a reluctance to take initiative or do something a new way, and avoiding confrontation or disagreement. A Japanese proverb says: "The nail that sticks out gets hammered down."

Asian American parents are generally not overtly affectionate with children, but show their love in indirect ways, such as by sacrificing their own needs for their children's. As children reach school age, they are subjected to stricter discipline and taught that their actions reflect not only on themselves but on their families. Fathers usually assume the role of disciplinarian.

Native American adults show that approval is indicated through a smile, a pleasant tone of voice, or a friendly pat. Children are typically corrected by the adult lowering his or her voice. Generally, there is no physical punishment, nor is there verbal praise. Frowning, ignoring, withdrawal of affection, and shaming are forms of social control, as is group pressure. Criticism of another is traditionally communicated indirectly through another family member, rather than directly.

Hispanic American children are encouraged to learn by observation, by doing, and by the reactions of others, and children are normally included in many adult activities. Self-regulation occurs by building new behaviors onto old. Feedback is used to help children improve. As in other collectivistic groups, overly praising performance is frowned upon because it may make the individual feel more important than others (Trumbull et al., 2001).

Although African American parents use a variety of discipline techniques, those living in poor neighborhoods tend to demand strict obedience from their children and use physical punishment as a consequence for noncompliance because, knowing the dangers of ghetto life, they want to protect their children (Ogbu, 1994; Pinderhughes, Dodge, Bates, Pettit, & Zelli, 2000).

Skills Emphasis. Different groups place different emphasis on skills they believe important for children to learn to get along in the group as well as to become a contributing adult.

Native American children are taught brotherhood, sharing, spirituality, and personal integrity. Spirituality is taught through rites and rituals. Personal items are readily shared because the boundaries of property ownership tend to be permeable. Cooperation is highly valued. Generally, there is no competition within the group, nor is there majority rule; rather, consensus is sought based on the needs of the group overriding the needs of the individual. Modesty and moderation are stressed: don't talk for the sake of talking; don't boast when one achieves; don't show emotions. Children are not expected to be perfect, only to do what they are capable of for their age. Therefore, failure is not a concept. The goal is to improve on one's past performance.

Hispanic American children are not usually encouraged to exhibit curiosity or independence; rather, cooperation and helpfulness are emphasized. Children are socialized to be sensitive to the feelings and needs of others.

African American families generally value close family ties and a strong sense of familial obligation. Children relate to many people of all ages in the household. Commonly, there is more emphasis on interaction with people than with things.

Competitive/Independent (Individualistic) Orientation

Authority Roles. Individualistic groups tend to value *achieved* authority, whereas collectivistic groups tend to value *ascribed* authority. For example, in an equal opportunity work environment, employees recognize that authority is usually achieved by hard work and is so respected; in a hierarchical work environment, employees recognize that authority is usually related to one's privileged status and so obedience and respect are required (Thiederman, 1991). Individualistic and equal opportunity settings assume that the rules are universal, the same for everyone; collectivistic and hierarchical settings assume that the rules are particular, flexible according to one's status and the situation. The particularistic approach, wherein rules are malleable, affects parenting styles and how children are socialized. To illustrate, I have students who never question the policies and procedures set forth in the course outline because they accept that the standards are universal, the same for all. Then I have students who are most creative in their rationale to bend the requirements to fit their particular situation.

Communication. Communication of a message can be direct and independent of context (as in a memorandum), or it can be indirect and dependent on context (as in a face-to-face meeting).

Compared to other groups, European Americans tend to use direct communication. With their pragmatic style, they are specific and come to the point quickly. They are comfortable with written and electronic messages because what is stated is the message; the context in which it is said is not important. Compared to other groups, Middle Eastern Americans or Japanese Americans tend to be more indirect. They might inquire about family members, health, or other matters seemingly unrelated to the purpose of the conversation. However, such questions are necessary for assessing the choice of language to be used and the degree of familiarity with which certain topics can be discussed (Stewart & Bennett, 1991).

Some groups, such as Native Americans, who tend to rely on the context to fully understand the communication (including nonverbal behavior and relational cues), may not be comfortable with written or electronic messages.

Displays of Emotion. Some groups of individuals openly express their feelings to others; some close their feelings to others; and some are open with those people with whom they are intimate and closed with others. This display of emotions (open or closed) is likely an adaptive strategy developed and passed on regarding how best to get along with others—share your feelings with all, hide your feelings from all, or be selective.

> An example of how people differ in their display of emotions comes from a story in the business section of the *Los Angeles Times* (Pham, 2002). Two engineers, Hinton and Marr, paired up for a project to design a computer chip that performed multiple tasks. Hinton was loquacious, constantly throwing out ideas, talking to everyone he met in the hall about the project. Marr was quiet, focused, and methodical. She recruited her allies in advance of crucial meetings and hated surprises, developing strategies to know how a meeting would turn out before it began. Marr came to believe in Hinton's ideas, and Hinton respected Marr's ability to get things done. Both styles were necessary to design the chip and to convince the thousand engineers working on the project to implement every step, every mathematical algorithm.

African Americans generally are openly expressive, as are Latin Americans and Middle Eastern Americans. Asian Americans tend to be more closed and European Americans typically fall in between, being warm to relatives and close friends and neutral to acquaintances.

Discipline/Guidance of Children. Among individualistic groups, children are socialized to solve problems they encounter. Some groups guide children by instruction or modeling; others expect children to learn by doing and by asking questions (Rogoff, 2003). Providing children with reasons for desirable behavior so that they will internalize them and be self-directive is common practice.

European Americans believe there is a rational order in the world and see themselves as individual agents of action ("Take the bull by the horns"). They assume that problems and solutions are the nature of reality. Major emphasis is on taking action in the present to avoid problems in the future ("A stitch in time saves nine"). Thus, children are trained in prevention. For example, in the area of health, children get vaccinated so they won't succumb to certain illnesses; in the area of safety, parts are tested and periodically inspected before they wear out. Children get a lot of socialization to avoid risks (Stewart & Bennett, 1991). However, they are also encouraged to engage in trial and error ("If at first you don't succeed, try, try again").

Native Americans tend to learn all the ramifications of a problem before attempting to try and solve it, if it is deemed solvable. Children are therefore taught to think before they act (Trumbull et al., 2001).

Chinese Americans who subscribe to the Confucian belief in strict discipline, respect for elders, and socially desirable behavior expect children to achieve academic and social competence to make their families proud (Chao, 1994, 2001).

Skills Emphasis. Skills emphasized with children can come from religious beliefs, traditional beliefs, or beliefs in self-determination. Many European Americans believe that the self is "located solely within the individual and the individual is definitely separate from others. From a very young age, children are encouraged to make their own decisions" (Lustig & Koester, 1999, p. 95). They are also expected to maintain clear boundaries between the self and others. Emphasis is placed on individual achievement, self-expression, and personal choice. A tenet of Judaism is personal choice. If one chooses to live a good life, being kind to others and sharing

Table 4.1

Summary: Collectivistic and Individualistic Parenting Orientations

	COLLECTIVISTIC ORIENTATION	INDIVIDUALISTIC ORIENTATION
AUTHORITY ROLE	Ascribed Hierarchal	Achieved Egalitarian
COMMUNICATION	Indirect More emphasis on nonverbal (facial & body language) Dependent on context	Direct Verbal (face-to-face) Independent of context
DISPLAYS OF EMOTION	Outward (facial & body) or inward (personal distance)	Open with all or open with intimate others
DISCIPLINE OF CHILDREN	Obedience Imitation Sense of obligation	Learn by doing Instruction & reasoning Sense of independence
SKILLS EMPHASIS	Sharing Helping Interaction with people Group loyalty	Decision making Individual achievement Self-expression Personal choice & responsibility

with those less fortunate, one will experience self-reward. Judaism is one of the world's oldest religions and the first to teach the existence of one God, giving birth to both Christianity and Islam.

European Americans tend to judge achievement in terms of comparisons with self and others. "You swam faster today than you did yesterday." "You got the highest grade in the class on the math test." Praise is given generously, not only for achievement, but to enhance self-esteem (Trumbull et al., 2001). Competition between groups is believed to promote performance and "team spirit"; competition within the group is believed to promote creativity and productivity ("The early bird catches the worm").

European American parents generally teach children personal responsibility for learning, behavior, and possessions. Personal responsibility for success or failure is ingrained: "The buck stops here" is a common saying in organizations (Thiederman, 1991). Our legal system is inundated with assigning responsibility for wrongdoings.

A significant religious influence on the individualistic orientation and the inherent socialized skills comes from Protestantism. The "Protestant ethic" is the belief that salvation is achieved through hard work, thrift, and self-discipline: "Where there's a will, there's a way." "God helps those who help themselves."

Table 4.1 summarizes the differences between collective and individualistic parenting orientations.

Chronosystem Influences on Parenting

How has parenting changed over time?

Parenting today raises new questions that previous generations seldom had to face. Should we have children? How many and how far apart? Terminate the unexpected or the imperfect? Should we be strict or permissive? Should we stress competitiveness or cooperation? What activities should be encouraged? Because society is changing so rapidly and because of new advances in science and technology, parents cannot look to experience for answers as their parents could.

Several social scientists (Bronfenbrenner, 1989; Hewlett & West, 1998) are concerned that a number of developments—many beneficent in themselves— have conspired to isolate the family and to reduce drastically the number of relatives, neighbors, and other caring adults who used to share in the socialization of American children. Among the most significant forces are occupational mobility, the breakdown of neighborhoods, the separation of residential from business areas, consolidated school districts, separate patterns of social life for different age groups, and the delegation of child care to outside institutions. What today's parents lack is a support system.

Because of the nature of today's rapidly changing society, parents spend less time with their children. A majority of mothers hold jobs outside the home. Fathers often must travel in connection with their work and are away for days or even weeks at a time. Parents may have meetings to attend in the evenings and social engagements on the weekends. Various studies have found that lack of time together is perceived as the greatest threat to the family (Hochschild, 1997; Leach, 1994). Given the changing nature of society and its pressures on the family's ability to function optimally, parenting today has become a "journey without a road map."

HISTORICAL TRENDS

How have children been treated throughout history?

A brief history of trends in the United States concerning the treatment of children and the role of parents follows.

Eighteenth Century

Before this time, it was not uncommon for children to be considered significant only if they contributed to their elders' welfare; no thought was given to their individual needs. If parents could not afford to care for them, they could be abandoned. Parenting was adult-centered.

Beginning in the 18th century, however, there was some improvement in the way children were treated. Contributing to this reform was a reexamination of the writings of Locke, Rousseau, and Pestalozzi, all advocates of **humanism**—a system of beliefs concerned with the interests and ideals of humans rather than of the natural or spiritual world (Berger, 2003). British philosopher John Locke's (1632–1704) best-known concept was that a newborn's mind is a **tabula rasa**, a blank slate before impressions are recorded on it by experience, and that all thought develops from experience. Children are neither innately good nor innately bad. The influence of this concept on contemporary parenting has been to encourage parents and teachers to mold children's minds by providing them with optimal experiences.

During the 18th century in colonial America, children were needed to do endless chores. The father was the primary authority. Children were to be seen and not heard; immediate obedience was expected. Discipline was strict; those who disobeyed were believed to be wicked and sinful and were severely punished. Tradition and religion influenced child-rearing practices: "He that spareth his rod, hateth his son: but he that loveth him chasteneth him betimes" (Proverbs 13:24). "Train up a child in the way he should go: and when he is old, he will not depart from it" (Proverbs 22:6). There was also much emphasis on manners and courtesy (Berger, 2003). Early Americans viewed early childhood "as a negative period of life, a sort of necessary evil full of idle deviltry and cantankerous mischief; the child survived it and his parents endured it as best they could until late adolescence, when life hesitatingly began" (Bossard & Boll, 1954,

humanism a system of beliefs concerned with the interests and ideals of humans rather than of the natural or spiritual world

tabula rasa the mind before impressions are recorded on it by experience; a blank slate

p. 526). Childhood was regarded as a foundation period of great importance, a period of bending the twig to affect the shape of the future tree.

Parenting was also influenced by French philosopher Jean Jacques Rousseau (1712–1778), who believed that children are innately good and need freedom to grow because insensitive caregivers might otherwise corrupt them. Rousseau's writings influenced Johann Pestalozzi (1746–1827), who emphasized the importance of the mother as the child's first teacher. The mother is more likely than other adults to be sensitive to her child's needs. That the mother was most important in the upbringing of the child was corroborated by Robert Sunley's (1955) analysis of child-rearing literature from early-19th-century magazines, books, and journals.

Nineteenth Century

During the 19th century, parents were exposed to the ideas of psychologist G. Stanley Hall (1846–1924) who, like Rousseau, believed that young children are innately good and will grow naturally to be self-controlled adults, if not overdirected (Berger, 2003). This idea influenced many contemporary attitudes on child development and parenting. Parenting was becoming child-centered. Unlike the traditional emphasis on the needs of the parent, contemporary ideas of child rearing placed paramount importance on the individual needs and welfare of the child. However, parents still directed the child-rearing practices.

Although at the end of the 19th century, parenting literature was espousing love and affection for children in order to mold their characters, at the beginning of the 20th century, the discipline method advocated to mold character emphasized rewards and punishment. *Infant Care*, published in 1914 by the Children's Bureau, recommended strict child rearing. For example, thumb-sucking and masturbation were believed to damage the child permanently (Wolfenstein, 1953). At the beginning of the 20th century, the parenting literature advocated rigid scheduling of infants. Mothers were told to expect obedience, ignore temper tantrums, and restrict physical handling of their children (Stendler, 1950).

Twentieth Century

In the 1920s, the influences of John B. Watson's theory of **behaviorism**, which held that only observable behavior, rather than what exists in the mind, provides valid data for psychology, and Sigmund Freud's theory of personality development, which dealt with nonobservable (unconscious) forces in the mind, began to appear in books and magazines. Watson's theoretical view defined learning as a change in the way an individual responds to a particular situation: behavior that is reinforced or rewarded will be repeated; behavior that is not reinforced will be extinguished or eliminated. Both Watson and Freud believed in the importance of the early years in setting the stage for later development. Watson believed in the importance of firmness early in a child's life, because behavior is conditioned by specific stimuli; if parents give in to bad behavior, that bad behavior will persist. Thus, good habits must be conditioned from the beginning. Freud believed that harmful early experiences can harm children's development (especially when these experiences are buried in the unconscious mind); that **fixations**, or arrested development, can occur at any time in life; and that children's growing personalities must therefore not be repressed, or else children will inevitably be marked as adults. The scientific methods described by Watson gave credibility to behaviorism. Freud's writings regarding the need to express—rather than repress—emotions were also extremely influential.

behaviorism   the theory that observed behavior, rather than what exists in the mind, provides the only valid data for psychology

fixation   a Freudian term referring to arrested development

In the 1940s, mothers were told that children should be fed when hungry and be toilet trained when they developed physical control. This was very different from the rigid scheduling of feeding and toilet training previously advocated. Even handling of genitals was considered natural, whereas years before parents were warned to take every precaution to prevent it (Wolfenstein, 1953). Benjamin Spock, in the 1946 edition of *The Common Sense Book of Baby and Child Care*, advised parents to enjoy their children and their roles as parents. He advocated self-regulation by the child rather than strict scheduling by the parents. Spock wanted to encourage parents to have a greater understanding of children and to be more flexible in directing their upbringing. He based his recommendations on the writings of educators such as John Dewey (who believed children should learn by doing) and psychoanalysts such as Sigmund Freud (who believed children's psychological development occurred in natural stages and that healthy outcomes were influenced by parents).

Jerry Bigner (1979) analyzed the child-rearing literature in several women's magazines from 1950 to 1970. He found that in the early 1950s physical punishment—spanking—was condoned, but by the end of that decade it was discouraged on the grounds that physical punishment does no more than show a child that a parent can hit. Most articles encouraged self-regulation by the child. Parents were advised to hold, love, and enjoy their children and to emphasize the importance of children feeling loved. Parents were also urged to recognize individual differences, to realize that development is natural and maturation cannot be pushed. The extensive work of Arnold Gesell (Gesell & Ilg, 1943) influenced this view. He published norms, or average standards, of child development based on observations of children of all ages. He concluded that the patterns for healthy growth were biologically programmed within the child and that if the parents would relax, growth would occur naturally.

Toward the end of the 1950s, after the Soviet Union's successful launch of the first satellite into space, the concern for intellectual development in children became urgent. Jean Piaget's theories on cognitive development were of interest to professionals working with children. He emphasized that knowledge comes from acting in one's environment. Thus, the importance of giving children a stimulating environment and many experiences was reinforced.

The movement from a *parent-centered* approach to child rearing, with its strict discipline, to a more *child-centered* approach, with more flexibility, is partially the result of parents' turning to the mass media, which publicized scientific and humanitarian views on child rearing. It is interesting to note that Spock revised the 1946 edition of his book on child care, which advocated a child-centered approach, to reflect a change in his attitude. The 1957 edition read, "Nowadays there seems to be more chance of a conscientious parent's getting into trouble with permissiveness than with strictness" (Spock, 1957). Spock realized the consequences of parents' focusing exclusively on what children need from them, rather than what the community will need from children when they grow up. Even though Spock continued to maintain his belief that children's needs should be attended to, subsequent editions of his book addressed the rights of parents—children need to feel loved, yet parents have the right to demand certain standards of behavior (Spock, 1968, 1985). Other contemporary parenting views concur (Baumrind & Thompson, 2002; Parke & Buriel, 1998).

In sum, the trend in parenting attitudes in the United States over time has swung from parent-centeredness to child-centeredness to more of a balanced approach.

FAMILY DYNAMICS

How do family members influence each other?

Family dynamics refers to what activities are going on, with whom, and how they "play out." As discussed in Chapter 3, the structure and functioning of the family as a whole affect parenting. Here we discuss the particular characteristics of family members and how these members relate to one another, which also affect parenting (Bornstein, 2002).

Parenting involves a continuous process of reciprocal interaction that affects both the parents and the children. When one becomes a parent, one rediscovers some of one's own experiences in childhood and adolescence—for example, making snowmen, playing hopscotch, playing hide-and-seek, and running through the sprinklers on a hot day. When one becomes a parent, one's experience is expanded. Not only do children have a unique way of looking at the world (for example, they believe the moon follows them at night when they go for a ride in the car, that dreams come through the window when they are sleeping, and that you can walk on clouds); they also open new doors for parents. My son became interested in astronomy and opened up a world of telescopes, stars, planets, and galaxies to our family. My daughter became interested in running and opened up a world of track-and-field events to us. When children bring their work home from school, new information, ideas, and values are shared with their parents.

Like a game involving strategies and counterstrategies, parenting requires continual adaptation to children's changing capacities. As children grow, parents need to adapt to the increased amount of time they are awake. As children learn to walk, parents need to set limits for their safety. When the child goes to school, decisions have to be made about achievement, friends, television, activities outside of school, and so on. When the child approaches adolescence, parenting involves determining which decisions are to remain the parents' and which are to be assumed by the adolescent.

Parenting is time-consuming and difficult; it is also joyful and satisfying. Children are loving, open, and curious. What could be more gratifying than the first hand-made card your child gives you that says "I luv u," or when your grownup child asks for your advice?

As parenting styles influence children, and children influence parenting styles, both parents and children interact in a dynamic family system that itself has certain influential characteristics (children's ages and family's size, for example) that we will examine here.

Children's Characteristics
What characteristics of children influence family dynamics and parenting practices?

Characteristics of children that influence family dynamics and parenting style in a bidirectional way include age and cognitive development, temperament, gender, and presence of a special need, such as a disability.

Age and Cognitive Development. As the child gets older and more mature physically and cognitively, parent–child interactions change. During infancy, parenting tasks are primarily feeding, changing, bathing, and comforting. As the child is awake more, play is added to the repertoire of activities. During the second year of life, physical and verbal restraint must be introduced for the child's safety. The child must be prevented from going into the street, from eating poisonous materials, from handling sharp objects, and so on.

During the preschool years, parenting techniques may expand to include reasoning, instruction, isolation (timeout), withdrawal of privileges (negative consequences), and reinforcement or rewards. As the children mature during school age, parents may encourage them to become more responsible for their behavior by allowing them to make certain decisions and to experience the positive as well as the negative consequences. For example, if a child requests a pet fish for his or her birthday, then the parents should allow the child to have the responsibility of feeding it. If a child chooses to bounce a ball off the side of the house and breaks a window accidentally, then the child should be given the responsibility of paying for the damage.

As children enter adolescence, parents may deal with potential conflicts by discussion, collaborative problem solving, and compromise. My son neglected to clean his room. It was "a waste of time" to make his bed and put his things away, since he would just be using them again. Because I like order and neatness, his behavior caused me to nag. After discussing his reasons for not complying with my standards and my reasons for him to do so, we agreed on a compromise: the day I cleaned house, he was to tidy his room; other days, he could keep the door closed, but not locked.

Researchers (McNally, Eisenberg, & Harris, 1991; Parke & Buriel, 1998) have found that although specific parenting practices change according to the age of the child, basic parenting styles remain quite stable over time. For example, a parent might isolate a preschooler who is hitting a younger sibling until some self-control is established. That parent might use reasoning and/or withdrawal of privileges for a school-ager who fights. Parenting practices may also change according to the situation. For example, a parent who usually gives a child instruction on how to behave in advance, may resort to yelling when rushed. Thus, even though the methods may change, the goal of self-control and the emotional climate or style of attaining that goal remain stable.

IN PRACTICE

Parenting and Prevention of Adolescent Problem Behavior

Studies have shown that adolescents whose parents are warm, affectionate, communicative toward them, and have certain standards for behavior are less likely to abuse drugs or engage in delinquent acts or join gangs than children who do not have good parental relationships (Baumrind, 1991; Greenberger & Chen, 1996; Grotevant, 1998; Steinberg & Morris, 2001).

Adolescence is a time when parent–child relations are tested. Many of the everyday demands of family life—doing one's assigned chores, being considerate of other members, communicating, adhering to standards (coming home on time, keeping appointments, writing thank-you notes, doing homework)—can become areas of conflict.

When parents react negatively to an adolescent's push for autonomy and become overly strict or overly permissive, the adolescent is more likely to rebel by exhibiting problem behavior (Collins & Laursen, 2004; Patterson et al., 1989).

The research also suggests that the effect of conflict between a child and one parent can be offset by a positive relationship with the other parent. Positive parent–child relationships can also negate the influence of a peer group that abuses drugs or alcohol and engages in delinquent behavior. Thus, parenting styles established in childhood have an impact on adolescent problem behavior.

Temperament. *Temperament*, introduced in Chapter 1, is the combination of innate characteristics that determine an individual's sensitivity to various experiences and responsiveness to patterns of social interaction. It is a central aspect of an individual's personality, and has been shown to be stable over time (Rothbart & Bates, 1998). For example, Kagan (1998) and his colleagues (Kagan, Reznick, & Gibbons, 1989) have studied shyness and sociability. Children who were classified as shy, or inhibited, at age 21 months, exhibiting timidness with unfamiliar people and cautiousness in strange surroundings, exhibited similar behavior when they were examined at age 7.5. Children who were rated as sociable, or uninhibited, as toddlers were talkative and outgoing with strange adults and peers in unfamiliar settings at age 7.5.

Temperament influences one's interactions with others—how infants respond to their caregivers and how caregivers respond to children—thereby illustrating the concept of bidirectionality. Thus, certain parenting styles may be elicited by a child's temperament (Putnam et al., 2002; Sameroff, 1994). For example, a very active child may have to be told more than once to sit still at the table or may have to be removed from the table to eat alone, whereas a less active child may only have to be told "Sit still at the dinner table so the food won't spill off the plate." Some methods of child rearing may have to be modified to suit a child's temperament. A child who has irregular patterns of hunger and sleep would be better suited to a more flexible "demand" feeding schedule, whereas a child who exhibits regularity is more suited to feeding at scheduled intervals.

In a classic longitudinal study of 136 children from infancy to adolescence (Chess & Thomas, 1987; Thomas et al., 1970), the following nine temperamental characteristics were isolated. This model is still used by researchers today.

1. *Activity level*: the proportion of inactive periods to active ones
2. *Rhythmicity*: regularity of hunger, excretion, sleep, and wakefulness
3. *Distractibility*: the degree to which extraneous stimuli alter behavior
4. *Approach/withdrawal*: the response to a new object or person
5. *Adaptability*: the ease with which children adapt to their environments
6. *Attention span and persistence*: the amount of time devoted to an activity and the effect of distraction on the activity
7. *Intensity of reaction*: the energy of response, regardless of its quality or direction
8. *Threshold of responsiveness*: the intensity of stimulation required to evoke a response
9. *Quality of mood*: the amount of friendly, pleasant, joyful behavior, as opposed to unpleasant, unfriendly behavior

Thomas and Chess (1977; Chess & Thomas, 1987) found that the 136 behavioral profiles clustered into three general types of temperament. *Easy* children displayed a positive mood and regularity in body function; they were adaptable and approachable, and their reactions were moderate or low in intensity. At the other extreme, *difficult* children were slow to adapt and tended to have intense reactions and negative moods; they withdrew in new situations and had irregular body functions. The group in the middle, the *slow to warm up* children, initially withdrew but slowly adapted to new situations; they had low activity levels and tended to respond with low intensity. These temperamental types could be recognized by the second or third month of life.

Although individual temperament seems to be established at birth, environmental factors play an important role in whether or not a person's style of behavior can be modified. Regarding this interplay of heredity and environment, if the two influences blend together well, one can expect healthy development of the child; if they are incompatible, behavioral problems are almost sure to ensue (Thomas & Chess, 1977, 1980).

Thomas and Chess recommend that parents adjust parenting styles to their offspring's temperament, although they emphasize that "a constructive approach by the parents to the child's temperament does not mean an acceptance or encouragement of all this youngster's behavior in all situations" (1977, p. 188). *Difficult* children need consistent, patient, and objective parents who can handle their instability. For example, instead of expecting very active, distractible children to concentrate for long periods of time on their homework, parents can reward them for shorter periods of work with pleasurable breaks in between, as long as the task is finished. *Slow to warm up* children do best with a moderate amount of encouragement coupled with patience; parents and teachers should let these children adjust to change at their own pace. *Easy* children tend to adapt well to various styles of child rearing. Thomas and Chess refer to the accommodation of parenting styles to children's temperaments as **goodness-of-fit**.

Infant temperament determines what kinds of interactions parents and infants are most likely to find mutually rewarding. For example, *difficult* children are more likely to accept change and enjoy new experiences if their parents are accepting, encouraging, and patient, rather than critical, demanding, and impatient. Just because infants are born with certain temperaments does not preclude them from adapting to certain behaviors demanded of them; the key is how the parents do it.

Initially, temperament mediates environmental input and individual responsiveness by setting the tone for interaction. Children who are sociable will communicate a different mood when they encounter people than will children who are more reserved. Next, temperamental differences will determine the kinds of behaviors children may initiate. Active children will experience more things because they are constantly doing and on the go. They will probably have more social interactions because of their activities. Their temperamental differences may either encourage or discourage the responses of others. For example, if a parent accepts a child's frequent emotional expressions of joy, sadness, or even anger as normal behavior, that parent is likely to reinforce those behaviors by being attentive. On the other hand, if a parent disapproves of overt displays of emotion, that parent is likely to punish those expressions by disapproval (Putnam et al., 2002).

Not only is a child's temperament influential, but the parents' temperament affects their parenting styles and how they respond to their child's behavior as well (Lerner, 1993). An active parent may be impatient with an inactive infant; a sociable parent may feel rejected by a withdrawn child; a reserved parent may feel intimidated by an aggressive child. Thus, parents, because of their own temperaments, may encourage, ignore, or discourage certain exhibitions of their children's temperament.

Heredity is partly responsible for our abilities and interests. As we discussed in Chapter 1, some believe that we seek out certain environments because of our genes (Scarr & McCartney, 1983). For example, a person who has musical ability might become involved in playing an instrument, singing, and listening to music. When that person creates a home environment for his or her child, in turn, music will be part of the parenting environment.

Gender. Parents provide different socializing environments for boys and girls (Leaper, 2002; Ruble & Martin, 1998), most likely because of their own socialization. Parents give children different names, different clothing, and different toys.

goodness-of-fit accommodation of parenting styles to children's temperaments

Fathers, in particular, are more likely to act differently toward sons and daughters than are mothers (Fagot, 1995; Lamb, 2004; Parke, 2002). Also, fathers tend to be more demanding of their children than are mothers (Doherty, Kouneski, & Erikson, 1998; Lamb, 2004). Parents of school-age children were interviewed regarding parenting techniques used with their sons and daughters. Parents reported being more punishing and less rewarding with same-gendered children. Parents of girls emphasized cooperation and politeness; parents of boys emphasized independent and self-reliant behaviors (Power, 1987).

The types of play activities that are encouraged differ for boys and girls. There is also some evidence that parents encourage girls to be more dependent, affectionate, and emotional than boys. In addition, as boys get older, they are permitted more freedom than girls—for example, they are allowed to be away from home without supervision more than are girls (Huston, 1983). Besides parental effects on gender-role socialization, siblings and the child's own cognitive development have been found to be influential (McHale, Crouter, & Tucker, 1999). Gender-role socialization will be discussed more specifically in Chapter 12.

Presence of a Disability   The presence of a disability in a child influences family dynamics and parenting styles. The nature, onset, and severity of the disability as well as the availability of support systems are factors in how the parents cope.

Parental reactions to the diagnosis of a disability vary enormously; they may include grief, depression, and/or guilt (Meadow-Orlans, 1995). Another common reaction is anger—anger with God, fate, society, professionals, oneself, the other parent, or even the child. In addition, parents may also experience frustration as they seek an accurate diagnosis or referral of a child who has a problem that is not so readily identifiable.

Parenting a child with disabilities is a challenge.

© Jose Carillo/PhotoEdit

Society expects parents to love their children. When a parent experiences negative feelings at the birth of a child, that parent commonly feels guilt. Unable to accept their own feelings of rejection or hostility, parents may blame themselves for experiencing emotions unbefitting a good and loving parent, especially a parent of a child so in need of love and special care. Guilt may also be related to a parent's feeling that something he or she did, or failed to do, caused a child's disability.

Parenting is a difficult and complicated task. Parenting a child with a disability is even more so. Although most people will tolerate a 2-year-old's temper tantrum in a grocery store, they are apt to stare, or even make remarks, at a 10-year-old behaving in the same manner. Many parents have difficulty from time to time getting responsible babysitters, but parents of children with disabilities have even more. It is a challenge to change the diapers on a preadolescent, or care for a blind preschooler, or calm down a hyperactive child.

Not only is parenting a child with a disability more complicated and difficult, it is also more likely to cause major psychological stress in the parent, resulting in disturbed family interactions. According to Ann Turnbull and H. Rutherford Turnbull (2001), the parents of children born with disabilities may lose self-esteem. This can be transmitted to the child as overprotection, rejection, or abuse. The child may experience ambivalence, sometimes feeling love and sometimes anger. The frustrations of parenting a child with disabilities can tax anyone's patience. Parents worry about the care, the expense, and the future of their child. Some parents dedicate themselves totally to their child with disabilities. This pattern can lead to marital conflicts, neglect of other children, and family disruption.

Children with disabilities also have some psychological hurdles to overcome. They must adapt to being different: "Why do I have to use crutches?" "Why am I this way and my brother isn't?" "Will I still have to use crutches when I grow up?" Children may feel guilty about the inconveniences they perceive themselves to have caused—the financial burden (for example, the cost of special equipment), the extra work and care, the inability to measure up to parental aspirations. The attention given children with disabilities may be resented by siblings, who may make these children feel guilty.

Siblings may also experience emotions such as sorrow, anger, and guilt. In addition, they may feel embarrassment and resentment and, as a result, not want to be identified as a relative of the child with disabilities. According to studies on siblings (Simeonsson & Bailey, 1986), the most central concern of siblings of children with disabilities is avoiding identification with them because they may be ashamed, they may fear others questioning their normality, and they may wonder about themselves.

Siblings may also resent the amount of time and/or money directed toward a brother or sister with disabilities. They may feel deprived of attention or resources they want and feel they need. Although sibling responses to having a brother or sister with disabilities may be negative in certain respects, positive reactions are common. These include increased maturity, compassion, tolerance for individual differences, patience, sense of responsibility, and greater appreciation for family and health (Heward, 2002).

Family Characteristics
What characteristics of families influence its dynamics and parenting practices?

Characteristics that influence family dynamics and consequent parenting style are size (number of siblings) and configuration (birth order, spacing, and gender of siblings), as well as parents' stage of life, marital quality, and abilities to cope with stress (Bornstein, 2002; Cowan et al., 1998).

Size. Both parents and children are affected by the number of children in the family. The more children there are, the more interactions within the family, but the less likely are individual parent–child interactions. Children in large families may have many resources to draw on for company, playmates, and emotional security. They may also have increased responsibility in the form of chores or caring for younger siblings. Parents in larger families, especially those with limited living space and economic resources, tend to be more authoritarian, tend to be more likely to use physical punishment, and tend to be less likely to explain their rules than are the parents of smaller families. The emphasis is on the family as a whole rather than the individuals within it (Bossard & Boll, 1956; Elder & Bowerman, 1963; Furman, 1995). However, it has also been found that the effects of family size on parenting style are mediated by parental education, occupation, social class, intactness of the family, and ethnic orientation (Blake, 1989).

Configuration. Not only does the number of children in a family affect child-rearing practices, but the spacing and gender of the siblings also influence parent–child interactions. With the birth of each sibling come different temperaments, different ages, and new relationships for parents to handle.

A number of studies (Furman, 1995; Sutton-Smith, 1982) have shown parenting practices with regard to firstborn and later-born siblings to differ even at the same age. Firstborns receive more attention, affection, and verbal stimulation than their later-born siblings. They also are disciplined more restrictively and are coerced more by their parents. More mature behavior is expected of them than of their siblings. Other findings have shown that mothers help their firstborns in solving problems more frequently than they do their later-borns. And mothers of firstborns apply more pressure for achievement than they do on their later-borns (Zajonc, 1976).

It is much more difficult to predict the sibling effects on later-borns than on firstborns because with later-borns there are more variables to take into account, such as number of siblings, the space between them, and the gender distribution. For example, the interactions of the youngest male born after two females differ from the interactions of the youngest male born after two males. The patterns change, too, if there are six years between siblings versus two years.

Judy Dunn (1988, 1992, 1993) has examined the socialization effects siblings have on each other. While most studies, some of which have been discussed, investigate bidirectional influences of siblings on parenting behavior and differential parenting on siblings (McHale, Updegraff, Jackson-Newsom, Tucker, & Crouter, 2000), Dunn has added the perspective of social understanding to what goes on inside families. Siblings provide opportunities for cooperation, competition, empathy, aggression, leading, following, and so on. Older siblings function as tutors or supervisors of younger brothers or sisters (Parke & Buriel, 1998). Dunn has shown that from 18 months on, children understand how to hurt, comfort, and exacerbate a sibling's pain. They understand what is allowed or disapproved in their families. They can even anticipate responses of adults to their own and others' misbehavior as well as comment on and ask about the causes of others' actions and feelings. Dunn concludes that the ability to understand others and the social world is closely linked to the activities and relationships with siblings and parents. It is important that parents monitor sibling interactions and intervene in conflicts. By explaining rights and fairness, as well as interpreting differences in abilities according to age, parents can enhance positive relationships between siblings. A longitudinal study of sibling influences on gender development in middle childhood and early adolescence confirms the modeling influence of older siblings on younger siblings' gender-related behavior (McHale, Updegraff, Helms-Erikson, & Crouter, 2001).

What about only children? Are they more pressured to grow up or are they babied? Do they suffer socially and emotionally from not having sibling relationships that involve closeness, compromises, and conflicts?

Only children experience more parent–child interaction, and their relationships with their parents are reported to be more positive and affectionate than those of children with siblings (Falbo & Polit, 1986). In a study of 2-year-olds with an unfamiliar peer in a laboratory room, Snow, Jacklin, and Maccoby (1981) observed that only children were more advanced socially than children with siblings, showing more positive behavior as well as assertive/aggressive behavior. Second-borns showed the least. Only children have also been shown to perform better academically in school than children who have siblings (Falbo & Polit, 1986).

Thus, being an only child does not seem to be harmful to development; rather, it may be beneficial. There are disadvantages, however, such as too much pressure from parents to succeed, loneliness, or not having anyone to help care for aging parents.

Parents' Life Stage. The need for parenting practices to change in response to children's changing over time has already been discussed. According to Ellen Galinsky (1981), parents go through six stages of changes in their expectations and practices for children from infancy to adolescence: (1) image making, (2) nurturing, (3) authority, (4) interpretive, (5) interdependent, and (6) departure. Parents, too, are in the process of development over time (Cowan et al., 1998). As they get older, parents experience health concerns, career changes, responsibilities toward their parents, and other changes.

An area of generational research is the impact of parents' childhood and adulthood relationships with their parents on their own parenting practices (Cowan et al., 1998). For example, mothers who reported having had an insecure childhood relationship with their parents have less effective parenting strategies with their preschool children than mothers who reported having had a secure relationship. Apparently, having a good "working" model to emulate influences parenting.

Marital Quality. Marital quality contributes to children's development in that the parents form a co-parenting alliance, cooperating with and supporting each other (Cowan et al., 1998). United parents are less subject to manipulation by their child. What child hasn't tried to get one parent to give in when the other parent has refused a request?

Research shows that children whose fathers are involved in their care do better socially and academically than children whose fathers play a marginal parenting role (Lamb, 2004; Parke, 2002). McHale (1995) found that marital distress observed in a two-way problem-solving discussion was associated with hostile/competitive co-parenting with sons, and differing levels of involvement with daughters.

Marital conflict culminating in divorce imposes a major disruption in relationships among all members of the family (Kelly & Emery, 2003). As was discussed in Chapter 3, divorce affects the parenting style of both the custodial and the noncustodial parent, with the custodial parent (usually the mother) becoming more authoritarian and restrictive, and the noncustodial parent (usually the father) becoming more permissive and indulgent, at least initially. Such a major stress also affects children's behavior, with children becoming more aggressive, rebellious, and manipulative.

There is evidence that stressors outside the family, such as economics, work problems, illness, and peer relationships, disrupt the parent–child relationship, thereby interfering with children's optimal development (Evans & English, 2002; Patterson & Capaldi, 1991). Conversely, the availability of social support has a buffering effect and lessens the strain (Cowan et al., 1998).

Ability to Cope with Stress. Parents who are tired, worried, or ill and those who feel they have lost control of their lives are likely to be impatient, lacking in understanding, and unwilling to reason with their children. To see whether and how stress affects child rearing, Zussman (1980) created a stressful situation in which parents were observed interacting with their toddlers and preschool-age children. A laboratory playroom was equipped with play materials that were complex enough to require the children to request help. It was also equipped with such items as a breakable vase, a filled ashtray, and a stack of index cards. The parents were given mental tasks to perform while the children played in the room. Zussman found that when the parents were preoccupied with their task, they became less responsive to their preschool children (less likely to play with them, talk to them, help them) and more interfering, critical, and authoritarian with their toddlers.

What are the effects of real-life stress, such as divorce, illness, death, abuse, or financial problems, on parental interaction with children? In one study, Patterson (1982) obtained daily reports from a group of mothers concerning the occurrence of crises of varying magnitudes, including an unexpectedly large bill, a car breaking down, illness of a family member, and quarrels between spouses. The mothers were also asked to describe their moods, and family interactions were observed. The number of crises experienced was found to be a positive predictor of maternal irritability. Patterson found that the more often a mother becomes irritable, the less likely she is to deal with family problem solving, and that unsolved problems accumulate and lead to increased stress. Further, disrupted family interaction leads to an intolerant discipline style that in turn fosters antisocial behavior in the child (Patterson & Dishion, 1988).

Unemployment, with its consequent economic deprivation, is another cause of family tension. A considerable body of research has shown an association between paternal job loss and intrafamily violence, including partner abuse and child abuse (Luster & Okagaki, 1993; McLoyd, 1998). The possible explanations offered are the greater amount of time the father spends at home, which increases the possibility of conflict; an increase in the father's discipline role; a reaffirmation of the father's power in order to save face; and tension from diminished economic resources.

Finally, it has been shown that crises or stress do not always disrupt family functioning. The type of stressor, personalities, and relationships within the family, as well as the presence of social support networks outside the nuclear family, are influential factors (Cochran, 1993; Yogman & Brazelton, 1986).

Parenting Styles

How do parents implement their jobs?

Parenting style encompasses the emotional climate in which child-rearing behaviors are expressed (Cowan et al., 1998). Parenting styles are usually classified by the dimensions of *acceptance/responsiveness* (warmth/sensitivity) and *demandingness/ control* (permissiveness/restrictiveness) (Maccoby & Martin, 1983). Parents who are accepting/responsive give affection, provide encouragement, and are sensitive to their children's needs; parents who are unaccepting/unresponsive are rejecting, critical, and insensitive to their children's needs. Parents who are demanding/

Authoritarian:	↑ Demandingness/Control	↓ Acceptance/Responsiveness
Authoritative:	↑ Demandingness/Control	↑ Acceptance/Responsiveness
Permissive:	↓ Demandingness/Control	↑ Acceptance/Responsiveness
Uninvolved:	↓ Demandingness/Control	↓ Acceptance/Responsiveness

Figure 4.3

Dimensions of Parenting Styles

Source: Based on Maccoby and Martin, 1983

controlling set rules for children and monitor their compliance; parents who are undemanding/uncontrolling make few demands on children and allow them much autonomy. Parents who are neither responsive nor demanding are considered to be indifferent, or *uninvolved*. See Figure 4.3 for variations on the major dimensions of parenting styles.

MICROSYSTEM INFLUENCES: BETWEEN PARENT AND CHILD

What significant child outcomes are affected by the parent–child interaction?

A microsystem effect on children is the bidirectional parent–child relationship within the family. Research has shown parenting styles to have an impact on children's behavior, and vice versa, in such areas as attachment, self-regulation, prosocial behavior, competence, and achievement motivation. *Attachment*, introduced in Chapter 2, is an affectional tie that one person forms to another person, binding them together in space and enduring over time. *Self-regulation*, also introduced in Chapter 2, is the process of bringing one's emotions, thoughts, and/or behavior under control. **Prosocial behavior** involves behavior that benefits other people, such as altruism, sharing, and cooperation. **Competence** involves behavior that is socially responsible, independent, friendly, cooperative, dominant, achievement-oriented, and purposeful. *Achievement motivation*, introduced in Chapter 2, refers to the tendency to approach challenging tasks with confidence of mastery.

Parenting styles, as we saw in Chapter 2, are usually described in terms of major dimensions or degrees: *authoritative* (democratic), *authoritarian* (parent-centered), and *permissive* (child-centered). More detailed definitions of the basic parenting styles can be found on the *Child, Family, School, Community* companion website at http://www.thomsonedu.com/author/berns. A fourth parenting style, **uninvolved**—insensitive, indifferent parenting with few demands or rules—is discussed later with inappropriate parenting practices.

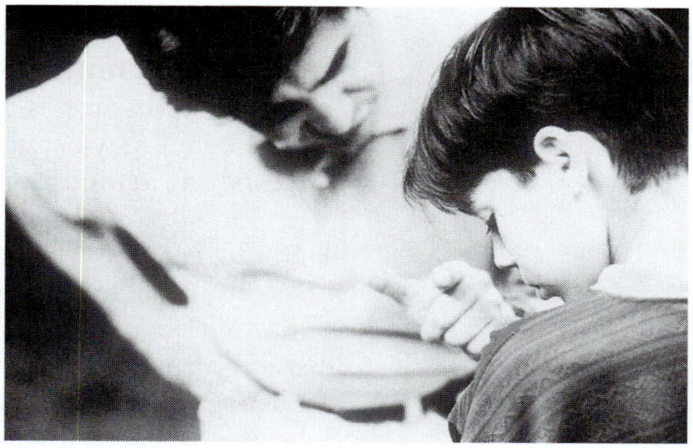

It must be realized that parents seldom fall into one category or one extreme; they are often a mixture. Parenting is so complex that it is often influenced by such factors as the particular situation (including stress); the child's age, gender, birth order, and siblings; the child's temperament (including how the child

prosocial behavior behavior that benefits other people, such as altruism, sharing, and cooperation

competence involves behavior that is socially responsible, independent, friendly, cooperative, dominant, achievement-oriented, and purposeful

uninvolved a style of insensitive, indifferent parenting with few demands or rules

© Tony Freeman/PhotoEdit

The scolding a child gets from a parent for wrongdoing exemplifies the authoritarian *parenting style.*

responds to parental demands); the parent's previous experience (Dunn, Davies, O'Connor, & Sturgess, 2000), including how the parent was parented; and the parent's temperament. In order to better understand the effects of parenting styles on children's behavior, researchers base their findings on the parenting styles observed most frequently in various situations.

Attachment

As mentioned in Chapter 2, attachment is an outcome of sensitive, responsive caregiving. It provides the basis for socialization because infants who are securely attached are willing to comply with parental standards.

Parenting behavior toward the baby influences attachment (Cummings & Cummings, 2002). When a parent responds appropriately, being sensitive and responsive to the baby's signals, the baby forms a *secure* attachment; when a parent responds inappropriately, inconsistently, or not at all, the baby tends to form an *insecure* attachment. According to Ainsworth and colleagues (Ainsworth, Blehar, Waters, & Wall, 1978), appropriately responsive caregiving involves paying attention to the baby's signals, interpreting them accurately, giving appropriate feedback, and responding promptly (enabling the baby to learn that his or her stimuli cause a response).

Parents of securely attached babies also synchronize their interactions according to the baby's activity (DeWolff & van IJzendoorn, 1997). When the baby is alert and active, they stimulate. When the baby is fussy, they soothe. When the baby is tired, they put him or her to sleep. Parents of insecurely attached babies may ignore the baby's signals; they may respond ineffectively or inappropriately. For example, a mother may give her baby a bottle or her breast when the baby is hungry, but be talking on the phone or reading rather than gazing at the infant to adjust to his or her needs.

To measure the quality of attachment in infants ages 1 to 2, researchers commonly use a classic experiment known as the *strange situation* (Ainsworth et al., 1978). In the strange situation, the parent brings the child to a laboratory playroom equipped with toys. Does the infant explore the room, using the parent as a secure base? The parent leaves the room briefly and the infant's behavior is monitored. Does the infant continue to explore, do nothing, or cry? A stranger enters the room and the infant's behavior is recorded. Does the infant ignore the stranger, seek comfort, or cry? The stranger leaves and the parent returns. How does the infant react?

The following types of attachment that have been observed in the strange situation:

- **Secure attachment (secure).** The infant actively explores the environment in the mother's presence, is upset when she leaves, and seeks contact when she returns. (The infant may accept the stranger's attention when the mother is present.)
- **Resistant attachment (insecure).** The infant stays close to the mother, doesn't explore, becomes upset when the mother leaves, is wary of strangers, and resists physical contact with the mother when she returns.
- **Avoidant attachment (insecure).** The infant shows little distress when the mother leaves, may ignore or avoid the stranger, and ignores the mother when she returns.
- **Disorganized/disoriented attachment (insecure).** The infant is very upset by the strange situation and appears confused about whether to approach or avoid the stranger; when the mother returns, the infant may seek contact and then withdraw (Main & Solomon, 1990).

Frank Siteman/Index Stock Imagery

The verbal give-and-take discussion between this father and son exemplifies the authoritative *parenting style.*

The significance of the quality of attachment is that it correlates with later intellectual and social development (Lamb, Hwang, Ketterlinus, & Fracasso, 1999). Securely attached infants tend to be more attentive, curious, and confident, exploring various physical environments, exhibiting more social competence with peers, and being more compliant with adults in the preschool years.

Self-Regulation and Prosocial Behavior

Diana Baumrind (1966, 1967, 1971a, 1973) studied parenting practices by observing the behavior of preschool children. She rated their behavior according to degree of impetuosity, self-reliance, aggressiveness, withdrawal, and self-control.

The parents of groups of preschool children were observed and interviewed to determine how their parenting styles differed. Baumrind found that parents of children rated as "competent" and "contented" were controlling and demanding as well as warm, rational, and receptive to the child's communication. She labeled this combination of high control and positive encouragement of the child's autonomous and independent strivings *authoritative*. Parents of children rated as "withdrawn" and "discontented" were detached, controlling, and somewhat less warm than the other parents. Baumrind labeled this group *authoritarian*. Parents of children rated as "immature" and "impulsive" were noncontrolling, nondemanding, and relatively warm. Baumrind labeled this group *permissive*. (See Table 4.2.)

Later studies (Brophy, 1989; Forman & Kochanska, 2001; Hart, DeWolf, & Burts, 1992) have supported Baumrind's findings that parenting style affects children's behavior. For example, children of authoritarian parents showed little independence and scored in the middle range on social responsibility. Children of permissive parents conspicuously lacked social responsibility and were not very independent. Children of authoritative parents were independent and socially responsible. In sum, children of affectionate, responsive parents want to please them and, therefore, are motivated to learn and behave according to parental expectations.

Table 4.2

Relationship of Parenting Styles to Children's Behavior

PARENTING STYLE	CHARACTERISTICS	CHILDREN'S BEHAVIOR
AUTHORITATIVE (democratic) "Do it because . . ."	Controlling but flexible Demanding but rational Warm Receptive to child's communication Values discipline, self-reliance, and uniqueness	Self-reliant Self-controlled Explorative Content Cooperative
AUTHORITARIAN (adult-centered) "Do it!"	Strict control (self-will curbed by punitive measures) Evaluation of child's behavior and attitudes with absolute standard Values obedience, respect for authority, and tradition	Discontent Aimless Withdrawn Fearful Distrustful
PERMISSIVE (child-centered) "Do you want to do it?"	Noncontrolling Nondemanding Acceptance of child's impulses Consults with child on policies	Poor self-reliance Impulsive Aggressive Hardly explorative Poor self-control
UNINVOLVED (insensitive & indifferent) "Do what you want."	Noncontrolling Nondemanding Indifferent to child's point of view and activities	Deficits in attachment, cognition, emotional & social skills, and behavior Poor self-control Low self-esteem

Source: Based on Baumrind (1967, 1971a, 1971b, 1991)

According to Baumrind, both the authoritarian and permissive parents in her studies had unrealistic beliefs about young children. Whereas the strict or authoritarian parents thought the child's behavior must be constrained, the permissive parents tended to look at the child's behavior as natural and refreshing. Neither group seemed to take into account the child's stage of development—for example, the desire in early childhood to model parental behavior or the inability in early childhood to reason when given a parental command. Thus, Baumrind and others (Steinberg, 2001; Steinberg, Lamborn, Darling, Mounts, & Dornbusch, 1994) endorsed the authoritative parenting style for adapting to the European American values of independence, individualism, achievement, and self-regulation. Authoritative parents take into account their children's needs as well as their own before deciding how to deal with a situation. They exert control over their children's behavior when necessary, yet they respect their children's need to make their own decisions. Reasoning is used to explain parenting policies, and communication from the children is encouraged. Children experience democracy at home.

Most early parenting research involved young children, but more recent studies have included adolescents in order to reveal the long-term effects of parenting styles (Baumrind, 1991; Holmbeck, Paikoff, & Brooks-Gunn, 1995; Steinberg, 2001). Dornbusch and his colleagues (Dornbusch, Ritter, Leiderman, & Roberts, 1987) found that authoritative parenting is positively correlated, and authoritarian and permissive parenting negatively correlated, with adolescent school performance. Steinberg and his colleagues (Steinberg, Elmen, & Mounts, 1989; Steinberg, Mounts, Lamborn, & Dornbusch, 1991) confirmed the relationship between authoritative parenting and academic performance. They explained it as being due to the effects of authoritativeness on the development of a healthy sense of autonomy and, more specifically, on the development of a healthy psychological orientation toward work. Thus, authoritative parenting influences not only how a child behaves in the early years but also how a child deals with responsibility, as exhibited in adolescence.

Authoritative parenting is *not* the norm among various socioeconomic and ethnic groups in the United States and other countries. More common is the authoritarian style utilized by Asian Americans, Hispanic Americans, and African Americans (Greenfield & Suzuki, 1998). Certain conditions, such as lack of social supports or living in dangerous neighborhoods, may make strict discipline necessary to protect children from becoming involved in antisocial activities (Brody & Flor, 1998; Ogbu, 1994). Certain values, such as respect for elders and the need for social order, may influence child-rearing methods. For example, whereas authoritarian parenting is perceived by Americans and Europeans to be strict and regimented, stressing adult domination, it is perceived by Chinese people to be a means of training (*chaio shun*) and governing (*guan*) children in an involved and physically close way (Chao, 1994, 2001). The Chinese concept of authoritarianism comes from the Confucian emphasis on hierarchical relationships and social order. Standards exist, not to dominate the child, but to preserve the integrity of the family unit and assure harmonious relations with others (Greenfield & Suzuki, 1998). Thus, Baumrind's definition of authoritarian parenting (see companion website for definitions of basic parenting styles) and child development outcomes (discontent, withdrawal, distrust, lack of instrumental competence) do *not* always apply cross-culturally.

Competence and Achievement Motivation

Burton White (1971) and his colleagues at Harvard (White & Watts, 1973) studied the relationship between parenting styles and the development of *competence* versus *incompetence* in preschoolers. First, they had preschool teachers rate children ages 3–6, representing different socioeconomic statuses, as "competent" or "incompetent" (see Table 4.3). Then, to find out when the differences in competence appeared, the researchers went into the homes of the competent and incompetent children who had younger siblings and observed the mother–child interaction from infancy to age 3.

No differences in competency were found between infants who were siblings of competent versus incompetent children. Yet by 10 months of age, differences in competency began to show up; by age 2, and often as early as 18 months, children could be classified as competent or incompetent. What is so significant about the period of development between 10 and 18 months? This period is the time when children begin to talk, walk, explore, and assert themselves. It is during this time that the parenting style is revealed—a good example of the bidirectionality of the parent–child relationship.

How did the parenting styles differ? The mothers of the competent children designed a safe physical environment at home so their children could explore and discover things on their own. They also provided interesting things to manipulate; these could be pots and spoons as well as commercial toys. Surprisingly, these mothers spent

Table 4.3

The Harvard Preschool Project: Differences in Learning

COMPETENT CHILDREN	INCOMPETENT CHILDREN
Get attention in socially acceptable ways	Remain unnoticed or are disruptive
Use adults as resources	Need a lot of direction to complete a task
Get along well with others	Have difficulty getting along with others
Plan and carry out complicated tasks	Lack ability to anticipate consequences
Use and understand complex sentences	Have a simplistic vocabulary

no more than 10% of their time deliberately interacting with their children, yet they were always "on call" when needed. They made themselves available to share in their children's exciting discoveries, answer their children's questions, or help their children in an activity for a few minutes here and there while they went about their daily routines. They enjoyed their children and were patient, energetic, and tolerant of messes, accidents, and natural curiosity. They set limits on behavior and were firm and consistent in their discipline. The mothers of the competent children used distraction with infants under age 1; distraction and physical removal of either the child or the object from age 1 to $1\frac{1}{2}$; and distraction, physical distance, and firm words after age $1\frac{1}{2}$.

The mothers of the incompetent children were diverse. Some spent little time with their children; they were overwhelmed by their daily struggles, and their homes were disorganized. Others spent a great deal of time with their children; they were overprotective and pushed their children to learn. Still others provided for their children materially, such as giving them toys, but restricted their children's instinct to explore by ruling certain places and possessions out of bounds. The mothers of the incompetent children used playpens and gates extensively.

In sum, White's research has shown that human competence develops between 10 and 18 months, and it is the parenting style that fosters competence. Parenting style includes arrangement of the environment, shared enthusiasm with the child, having a lot of energy, setting reasonable limits according to the child's developmental level, and being available as a resource when needed. According to White (1995), the informal education provided by families for their children has more of an impact on a child's total educational development than does the formal educational system. Such an informal initial education essentially enables the child to "learn how to learn," or be motivated to achieve. Research on school-age children confirms the connection between parenting style and competence/achievement in school (Grolnick & Ryan, 1989; Wigfield & Eccles, 2002).

To assess the relationship of the environment provided by families to the achievement motivation and consequent intellectual development of the child, Caldwell, Bradley, and colleagues (Bradley, 2002; Bradley, Caldwell, & Rock, 1990; Caldwell & Bradley, 1984) developed an assessment scale to determine the quality of the home environment for children under age 3. This scale, called HOME (Home Observation for the Measurement of the Environment), contains 45 items in the following six areas:

1. **Emotional and verbal responsiveness**. The parent responded to the child's vocalizations with verbal response.
2. **Avoidance of restriction and punishment**. The parent did not interfere with the child's actions or prohibit him or her more than three times during the observation.

3. **Organization of the physical and temporal environment**. The child's play environment was accessible to him or her and was safe.
4. **Provision of appropriate play materials**. The child had toys that were safe and age-appropriate, and that stimulated play.
5. **Parental interaction with the child**. The parent kept the child within visual range and looked at, touched, or talked to the child frequently.
6. **Opportunities for variety in daily stimulation**. The parent read stories or played games with child.

Studies examining the relation between young preschoolers' HOME scores and their IQ scores, as well as later academic achievement in middle school (Wen-Jui, Leventhal, & Linver, 2004), showed a strong positive correlation (Bradley et al., 1990). Also, as White's group discovered, the most critical time for influencing a child's achievement motivation and intellectual development is the first two years of life.

Does the same relationship between home environment and children's achievement motivation and intellectual development apply in non-Western cultures? To find out, Sigman and her colleagues (Sigman, Neumann, Carter, & Cattle, 1988) observed the home interactions experienced by 110 Embu children ages 15–30 months growing up in a rural Kenyan community. The results were similar to those of White and Watts (1973) and Bradley, Caldwell, and Rock (1990). Children who were talked to frequently, whose vocalizations were responded to, and who engaged in sustained social interactions passed more items on the Bayley Mental Scale at 24 months and 30 months than did those who did not receive such attention. Children who were carried a great deal between 15 and 30 months of age scored poorly. The researchers suggest that carrying a child after he or she can walk may restrict exploration of the environment.

MESOSYSTEM INFLUENCES: BETWEEN PARENT AND OTHERS

How do links between parents and significant others affect child outcomes?

The impact of parental socialization techniques is enhanced by supportive links with other microsystems, such as the school and the community (Bronfenbrenner & Morris, 1998; Cochran & Niego, 2002). (See Table 4.4.) Collaborative values are more likely to have positive child outcomes than conflicted values. When family and school or community values differ, the child is at risk for school failure, delinquency, and substance abuse (Wang, 2000). An example of where family and community (especially business community) values are likely to differ is in the amount of consumerism thrust at children through advertising, promotional games and rewards, and product displays.

School

Families' links to schools via parent education, conferences with children's teachers, and participation in school activities can have positive effects on parenting (Epstein, 1995; Epstein & Sanders, 2002). Even parents of adolescents who take time to talk to their children about school, homework, and activities, and who show support and confidence in their abilities, have adolescents who are achievement oriented (Wang & Wildman, 1995). Aspects of family involvement in schools are discussed in Chapters 6 and 7.

An example of how school and family have worked together on the value of not abusing substances is when parents and teachers plan a special graduation party or event allowing only those not partaking of alcohol or drugs to attend. Perhaps parents

Table 4.4

Ecological Influences on Parenting Styles

CHILD CHARACTERISTICS	FAMILY CHARACTERISTICS	COMMUNITY CHARACTERISTICS
Age and cognitive development	Size (number of siblings)	Supportive social environments
Temperament (easy, slow to warm up, difficult)	Configuration (birth order, spacing, gender of siblings)	Informal network: gemeinschaft relationships
Gender	Marital quality	Formal network: gesellschaft relationships
Presence of a special need	Abilities to cope with stress	

and teachers could work together to devise a plan for consumer education for children, helping children learn how to spend money wisely and not feel they have to compete with their peers for possessions. Some lesson ideas might include comparative shopping, studying advertising techniques, and reaching consensus on the role of an allowance as a reward for chores accomplished.

Community

The community is considered here to include social environments outside the family context of parenting. They can be supportive in helping parents cope with stress (Crnic & Acevedo, 1995). Relatives and friends are examples of *informal* supports; psychologists and employers are examples of *formal* supports. Each of these types of social support systems can provide instrumental (physical and financial) support, emotional support, and informational support (Bugental & Goodenow, 1998). Formal support systems are discussed in Chapter 10.

The neighborhood in which a family resides can influence parenting practices by the response to various neighborhood ecologies (Bugental & Goodenow, 1998), such as rural or urban, safe or unsafe, stable or mobile. It has been found that when parents perceive their neighborhoods to be dangerous and low in social control, they place more restrictions on their children's activities (Cebello & McLoyd, 2002). To illustrate, residence in a neighborhood with high levels of crime, low levels of economic opportunity, poor transportation, and weak marital support can affect a single mother's commitment to seek employment and find child care (Duncan & Raudenbush, 2001). On the other hand, parents in lower-risk neighborhoods with neighbors who have similar norms, expectations, and values about child rearing are less likely to need so many restrictions (Parke & Buriel, 1998) because they feel connected and are more likely to intervene for the common good (Small & Supple, 2001).

Appropriate Parenting Practices

What constitutes appropriate parenting behavior?

Influences on parenting in general and specific parenting styles have been discussed so far. This section examines which parenting practices are *appropriate* for optimal child development; the next section discusses practices that are *inappropriate*, resulting in negative childhood outcomes.

Appropriate parenting practices involve knowledge of child development—what a child is capable of physically, emotionally, cognitively, and socially—as well as preventive and corrective methods for misbehavior.

Child protection agencies use objective, standardized risk-assessment instruments, such as Child at Risk Field (CARF), to define parenting practices on a continuum from appropriate at one end to inappropriate at the other. Appropriate parenting is that "which takes into account the child's age capacity; possesses reasonable expectations for the child; understands and acts on the child's strengths/limitations/needs; uses varied and acceptable disciplinary approaches; provides basic care, nurturing, and support; demonstrates self-control" (DePanfilis, Holder, Corey, & Olson, 1986, p. 273; Dubowitz & DePanfilis, 1999).

The National Institute of Child Health and Human Development (2002) has put decades of parenting research into an easy-to-read booklet, *Adventures in Parenting*, that enables parents to make informed decisions based on the applicability of child development principles to their child. The main principles are as follows:

- Respond to your child in an appropriate manner.
- Prevent risky behavior or problems before they arise.
- Monitor your child's contact with his or her surrounding world.
- Mentor your child to support and encourage desired behaviors.
- Model your own behavior to provide a consistent and positive example for children.

DEVELOPMENTAL APPROPRIATENESS

Developmental appropriateness involves knowledge of children's normal growth patterns and individual differences. Appropriate parenting practices are influenced by parents' understanding of what is developmentally appropriate behavior in their child. Appropriate parenting practices can also reflect a knowledge of socialization methods (described in Chapter 2). For example, when is it appropriate to use *guidance*, a preventive socialization method, and *discipline*, a corrective socialization method?

Mother and son exhibit close physical contact and face-to-face interaction.

© Myrleen Ferguson Cate/PhotoEdit

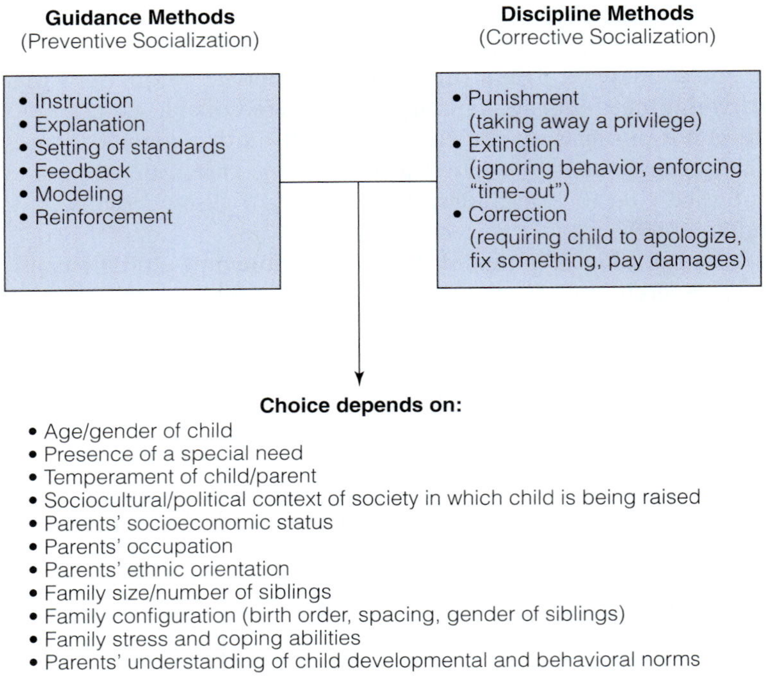

Figure 4.4

Parental Practices: Guidance and Discipline

Guidance Methods (Preventive Socialization)	Discipline Methods (Corrective Socialization)
• Instruction • Explanation • Setting of standards • Feedback • Modeling • Reinforcement	• Punishment (taking away a privilege) • Extinction (ignoring behavior, enforcing "time-out") • Correction (requiring child to apologize, fix something, pay damages)

Choice depends on:

- Age/gender of child
- Presence of a special need
- Temperament of child/parent
- Sociocultural/political context of society in which child is being raised
- Parents' socioeconomic status
- Parents' occupation
- Parents' ethnic orientation
- Family size/number of siblings
- Family configuration (birth order, spacing, gender of siblings)
- Family stress and coping abilities
- Parents' understanding of child developmental and behavioral norms

Understanding why children misbehave can help parents choose an effective method. Children sometimes misbehave because they are tired, hungry, uncomfortable, or sick. Sometimes children don't understand what is expected of them or why they did something wrong. Children may react to parental demands with anger, such as when they are told they can't have the candy displayed at the supermarket. They may misbehave when they are fearful, such as when left in a new and strange place. They may be jealous when a new sibling arrives and misbehave to get attention. They may feel hurt or disappointed when an adult lets them down, as by not fulfilling a promise or when parents divorce, and react with revenge.

GUIDANCE AND DISCIPLINE

developmental appropriateness involves knowledge of children's normal growth patterns and individual differences

guidance involves direction, demonstration, supervision, and influence

discipline involves punishment, correction, and training to develop self-control

Guidance involves direction, demonstration, supervision, and influence. One who guides "leads the way." **Discipline** involves punishment, correction, and training to develop self-control. One who disciplines enforces obedience or order. Both guidance and discipline are necessary socialization methods in child rearing. Sensitivity to the situation, the child's temperament, and the desired outcome are some of the factors involved in deciding which is appropriate at a particular time. (See Figure 4.4.)

Inappropriate Parenting Practices

What constitutes inappropriate parenting behavior?

Inappropriate parenting practices include uninvolved parenting and child maltreatment. Uninvolved parenting is characterized by insensitivity, indifference, and distancing. Usually parents who display this style are so overwhelmed by their own stresses and problems that they have little energy left to devote to the demands of child rearing (Maccoby & Martin, 1983). Preschool children of uninvolved parents display aggressive and externalizing behaviors such as temper tantrums; school-agers perform poorly academically and display conduct disorders; adolescents tend to be hostile, selfish, and rebellious, to commit antisocial acts such as delinquency and vandalism, and to abuse substances (Weiss & Schwarz, 1996).

Inappropriate parenting, as objectively defined by CARF criteria to determine potential risk, "is based on the parent's needs; demonstrates expectations that are impossible for the child to meet; ignores the child's strengths/limitations/needs; shows an aversion to parenting; employs extreme/harsh disciplinary approaches, including violence, threats and verbal assaults; generally does not provide basic care and/or support; deliberately takes frustrations out on the child; is self-righteous" (DePanfilis et al., 1986, p. 273; Dubowitz & DePanfilis, 1999).

CHILD MALTREATMENT: ABUSE AND NEGLECT

Maltreatment is any intentional harm to or endangerment of a child. It includes unkindness, harshness, rejection, neglect, deprivation, abuse, and/or violence (Barnett, Manley, & Cicchetti, 1993). It is a broader term than abuse and neglect and can be viewed as a continuum, with homicide at one extreme and parental force for disciplinary purposes at the other (Kalichman, 1999; Pagelow, 1982). Cultures differ in what constitutes maltreatment (Goodman et al., 1998). However, it is generally agreed that maltreating parents fail to meet the physical or emotional needs of the developing child, and in many cases the trust the child places in the parent is betrayed (Starr, 1990). Child maltreatment constitutes inappropriate parenting in that it may result in child maladaptation (Bolger & Patterson, 2001; Maughan & Cicchetti, 2002; Rogosch, Cicchetti, Shields, & Toth, 1995). Child maltreatment occurs in all economic, social, ethnic, and religious groups. Estimates of the number of children who are neglected, physically abused, sexually abused, or psychologically abused varies according to who is reporting; however, it is agreed that abuse and neglect are marks of risk for later development of aggressive behavior, emotional or psychological problems, and competency defects (Goodman et al., 1998; Shonk & Cicchetti, 2001).

Research suggests that maltreatment during childhood has far-reaching consequences in adulthood (Cicchetti & Lynch, 1993; Starr, 1990), such as inability to trust, low self-esteem, depression, relationship problems, sexual problems, learning difficulties, eating disorders, and alcohol or drug problems. The lack of normal nurturing during childhood may result in the adult need to replace the missing love and security with externals, such as drugs, alcohol, food, material objects, sex, gambling, and relationships (Farmer, 1989).

> Ellen's addictions began when she was a teenager. "In high school, I used alcohol and drugs to numb myself just so I wouldn't have to feel anything," she states flatly. "I just couldn't deal with the pain, with the insanity of it all. I'd walk around all the time depressed." (Farmer, 1989, p. 7)

What can be done to help children who are maltreated? Although parents in our society have the fundamental right to raise their children as they see fit, the Fourteenth Amendment of the United States Constitution, which states that *everyone* has equal protection under the law, warrants legal intervention when the safety of the child is in jeopardy. Intervention may involve the filing of criminal charges,

maltreatment
intentional harm to or endangerment of a child

referral to community agencies for counseling and treatment, and/or removal of the child from the care and custody of the parent, guardian, or caregiver. Every state has child protective laws with varying procedures.

To better understand the forms child maltreatment may take, they are examined separately even though they may occur simultaneously. **Abuse** is defined as maltreatment that includes physical abuse, sexual abuse, and psychological or emotional abuse. **Neglect** is defined as maltreatment involving abandonment, lack of supervision, improper feeding, lack of adequate medical or dental care, inappropriate dress, uncleanliness, and lack of safety.

Physical Abuse

Physical abuse is maltreatment involving deliberate harm to the child's body. Physically abused children include those who are intentionally bruised, wounded, or burned. Some physical abuse takes place under the guise of discipline. The places on children's bodies where they are wounded and the shape of the wound can give clues that indicate abuse rather than accident. Physical beating with a hand or an object, such as a belt or hairbrush, is the most common cause of physical abuse; other sources include kicking, shaking, choking, burning with cigarettes or scalding in hot water, freezing, and throwing the child around.

Physical abuse of children is more likely to occur in families where there is domestic violence—verbal conflict or physical aggression between partners (Dodge, Bates, & Pettit, 1990). Research shows a direct relation between physical abuse, aggressive behavior in children, and juvenile delinquency in adolescents (Rogosch et al., 1995). These effects may be due in part to modeling and in part to deficient abilities to process social information (Dodge et al., 1990). In other words, adolescents attribute hostile intentions to others, and they lack strategies to solve interpersonal problems.

Sexual Abuse

Sexual abuse occurs whenever any person forces, tricks, or threatens a child in order to have sexual contact with him or her. This contact can include such non-touching behaviors as an adult's exposing himself or herself, or asking a child to look at pornographic material. It includes behaviors ranging from the sexual handling of a child (fondling) to genital contact, intercourse, and violent rape. In all instances of child sexual abuse, the child is being used as an object to satisfy the adult's sexual needs or desires.

Children who are sexually abused often go through phases of (1) secrecy; (2) helplessness; (3) entrapment and accommodation; (4) delayed, conflicted, and unconvincing disclosure; and (5) retraction (Goodman et al., 1998). These phases can be explained by realizing that the child is vulnerable to a more powerful and knowledgeable adult. The adult demands secrecy and threatens the child if he or she tells—"I'll take your cat away." "Your mom will spank you." Thus, to enable the child to share, one must ensure a supportive and nonpunitive response.

The most common forms of sexual abuse of children are fondling and oral stimulation. Physical injury is rare. The offender often uses bribery, manipulation to secrecy with threats, and psychological power over the child because most sexual abuse occurs with an adult the child knows and trusts (Finkelhor, 1984). Although some sexual abuse occurs between adult women and children, in a majority of cases it is the adult male who is the perpetrator of child sexual abuse. Both young girls and boys are victims.

abuse maltreatment that includes physical abuse, sexual abuse, and psychological or emotional abuse

neglect maltreatment involving abandonment, lack of supervision, improper feeding, lack of adequate medical or dental care, inappropriate dress, uncleanliness, and lack of safety

physical abuse maltreatment involving deliberate harm to the child's body

sexual abuse maltreatment in which a person forces, tricks, or threatens a child in order to have sexual contact with him or her

Because children, by their very nature, are trusting and obedient, and because of their age and lack of experience as well as their dependence on adults, they are vulnerable to incest and molestation. Most sexual assaults follow a gradually escalating pattern in which the perpetrator first attempts to gain the child's trust and affection before attempting sexual contact (Koblinsky & Behana, 1984).

Child victims may experience guilt, anxiety, confusion, shame, embarrassment, fear, sadness, and a sense of being bad or dirty. Every child reacts differently. Some child victims do not understand that the abuse is "sexual" in nature; therefore, they may find some elements of the abuse pleasant if the abuse was not forceful or scary.

The way certain adults view children provides a clue to why sexual abuse takes place. These adults feel that children in their care are their property to do with as they wish. A great myth of child abuse is that the child wants sex (O'Brien, 1984). Child sexual abusers also exhibit characteristics of low self-esteem, poor impulse control, and childish emotional needs (Koblinksy & Behana, 1984). They themselves were likely to have been abused as children.

Incest, or sexual relations between persons closely related, deserves special attention. The closer the victim and offender are emotionally, the greater trauma the victim experiences. Ongoing incest, or sexual abuse by someone close to the family, can disrupt necessary psychological developmental tasks of a child. Victims may develop poor social skills with peers their own age, often feel unable to trust people—yet desperately want to trust—and may become depressed, suicidal, self-destructive, and confused about their sexuality. A high percentage of drug abusers, juvenile runaways, and prostitutes have been sexually abused as children.

Psychological or Emotional Abuse

Psychological or emotional abuse is maltreatment involving a destructive pattern of continued attack by an adult on a child's development of self and social competence, taking the forms of rejecting, isolating, terrorizing, ignoring, and corrupting (Garbarino, Guttman, & Seely, 1986). Psychological or emotional abuse can occur when parents are inconsistent in their talk, rules, or actions; when they have unrealistic expectations of their children; when they belittle and blame their children; when they do not take an interest in any of their children's activities; or when they do not ever praise their children. For example, a mother leaving a dance class with her sobbing 5-year-old daughter said, "Why can't you learn the positions like the others? You always embarrass me. Sometimes I can't believe you're really my daughter."

Parents who psychologically abuse their children are prompted not by the child's misbehavior, but by their own psychological problems. They are usually people who received inadequate love and nurturing from their own parents (Helfer, Kempe, & Krugman, 1999). Parents may use a steady stream of verbal abuse that discounts the child's achievements and blows out of proportion every sign of misbehavior. Words like *always, never,* and *should* imply that a child invariably fails to live up to a parent's expectations. Psychologically abusive parents may display irrational expectations so that normal behavior is seen as a deficiency on the part of the child and a failure on the part of the parent. For example, forgetting to give the parent change from lunch money may be viewed as stealing rather than a mistake.

Psychological abuse is also associated with physical and sexual abuse as well as is neglect. Exposure to domestic violence, a form of psychological abuse, also results in emotional, social, behavioral, and learning problems (Margolin, 1998; Maughan & Cicchetti, 2002).

incest sexual relations between persons closely related

psychological or emotional abuse maltreatment involving a destructive pattern of continual attack by an adult on a child's development of self and social competence, including rejecting, isolating, terrorizing, ignoring, and corrupting

IN PRACTICE

Things Parents Should Never Do

- Never call children derogatory names.
- Never threaten to leave your child.
- Never say, "I wish you were never born!"
- Never sabotage the parenting efforts of your spouse.
- Never punish when you've lost control of yourself.
- Never expect a child to think, feel, or behave like an adult.

CORRELATES AND CONSEQUENCES OF CHILD MALTREATMENT

Why does child maltreatment occur?

To understand the causes of child abuse and neglect, one has to examine not only the family interactions, but also the cultural attitudes sanctioning violence and aggression as well as the community support system (Rogosch et al., 1995). Figure 4.5 provides a model to illustrate the interaction among child, family, community, and cultural factors involved in maltreatment. For example, some influences on child maltreatment include temperament of the child, marital distress, unemployment, and lack of community support, as well as cultural values such as tolerance for violence and a view of the child as property (Belsky, 1993; Emery, 1989).

Before predicting maltreatment, risk and resilient factors must be weighed (Cicchetti & Lynch, 1993; Kalichman, 1999). *Risk* factors include those that are ongoing, such as parental history of being abused, and those that are transient, such as parent's loss of a job. *Resilient* factors include ongoing ones such as the child's easy temperament and transient ones such as an improvement in the family's financial status.

The Family and Maltreatment

As has been discussed, the process of parenting is very complex. It can be stressful and frustrating, as well as rewarding. Parenting involves the ability to continually give love, support, and guidance. Some individuals, because they themselves were never given love, support, or guidance, do not know how to give them to their own children.

Many abusers have a family history of being maltreated (Rogosch et al., 1995; Starr, 1990). A person who is maltreated feels unworthy, inadequate, and unacceptable. This results in low self-esteem. The next generation tends to model the parenting and attitudes to which it has been exposed. Therefore, unless it can be broken, maltreatment becomes a self-perpetuating cycle.

When children grow up under negative conditions, are scapegoated, belittled, and under constant criticism, they cannot develop their full potential or grow to be competent adults. They live out all the negative feelings they have developed as a result of the self-image they have received from their parents or caretakers and are thus prone to character and behavior disorders, self-doubt, and internal anger. They also have difficulty regulating their emotions and may avoid displaying their feelings; they have difficulty forming attachments and tend to avoid intimacy; they display more aggressive behaviors; and their cognitive development is often impaired (Lowenthal, 1999).

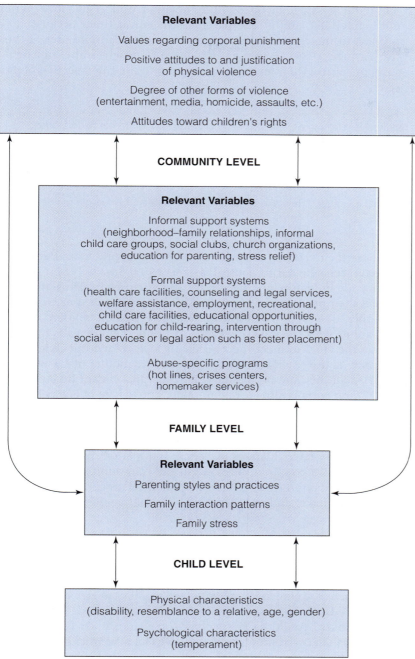

Figure 4.5

An Ecological Model of Risk and Resilient Factors in Child Maltreatment

Sources: Adapted from Parke and Lewis, 1981, p. 171; Cicchetti and Lynch, 1993

When life's stresses are added to feelings of inadequacy and lack of parenting skills, child abuse and neglect may be the result. Parents who face emotional problems, financial problems, and stress, who lack knowledge about child development, and who are immature may neglect or abuse their children. Abusive parents lack understanding of child development and consequently often have unrealistic expectations (Azar, 2002). They expect their children to eat when they are fed, not to be messy, to be obedient, to be quiet, and to give love. When children do not behave like adults, the parents lash out at them because their inability to conform to their parents' expectations serves as a reminder of their own inferiority (Farmer, 1989). When parents were themselves abused as children, their ability to control their feelings, in addition to their perspective of parenting, is affected.

> Vicky was reported for child abuse. She had tied her 3-year-old son to the bed because, earlier that morning, he had gone to his friend's house and had not telephoned his mother to report his whereabouts. The little boy sobbed, "But Mommy, I forgot my number." Often, abusive parents believe that their child's behavior is deliberate and purposeful (Helfer et al., 1999). "She spit up on my new blouse because she was mad at me," said a mother of her 1-month-old daughter. "He ran in the street just to frighten me," said a mother of her 2-year-old son.

Parents who abuse their children often have psychological problems. Depression and alcoholism have been linked to abuse (Farmer, 1989; Small, 1987). Abusive parents are emotionally immature and need nurturing themselves. Thus, they look to the child to meet their needs (Farmer, 1989). This behavior, called *role reversal*, is the most commonly observed psychological characteristic in abusive parents (Farmer, 1989). Parents who are abusive, instead of seeing themselves as nurturers of the child, expect the child to meet their needs for love. When the child fails to meet this expectation, abuse results (Belsky, 1993). As one mother of a 3-week-old said, "When he cried all the time no matter what I did, that meant he didn't love me, so I hit him." These parents also lack appropriate knowledge of behavior management and developmental norms. Physical, or corporal, punishment is their only source of control.

Parents who are abusive often have a low threshold of stress and frustration (Farmer, 1989). They may have financial problems and marital discord; they may suffer from overload and lack support networks in the community (Belsky, 1993). Many of these parents are unprepared for possible financial indebtedness, the constant demands children make, and the responsibilities that keep them from other activities.

The Child and Maltreatment

Certain physical and psychological characteristics have been associated more often with children who are abused than with those who are not (Belsky, 1993)—for example, behaviors such as crying, hyperactivity, and inability to give an acceptable response to the parent. Disabilities, such as mental retardation, were also found to be associated with abuse. Additionally, a child's appearance or behavior that reminds the parents of their own parents or of negative characteristics of themselves was found to contribute to a negative parent–child relationship. Such children may become scapegoats for buried negative feelings.

In sum, children who are more difficult than average to care for seem to be the objects of more maltreatment (Rogosch et al., 1995). These children may be demanding, whiny, crying, stubborn, resistive, sickly, or negative. High rates of mistreatment of premature babies, as well as those with developmental difficulties, have been reported (Fontana, 1992). Such children are commonly sensitive to all stimuli; they are restless, distractible, prone to anoxia and colic, and are disorganized sleepers (Maidman, 1984). Not only do these children require more care than average, it is likely that their parents have received less support, encouragement, and advice in caring for them. Also, parents who do not have the opportunity to form an attachment with the child immediately after birth (as in the case of premature babies or babies with medical problems who must remain in the hospital for a time) are at greater risk for neglect or abuse (Kennell, Voos, & Klaus, 1976). The main reason is that children who require more than average nurturance, such as children who are premature, sickly, or colicky, tend to make their parents feel less successful.

When babies are irritable, difficult to soothe, and difficult to engage in eye contact, parents tend to blame themselves and may project their anger onto the child or withdraw from relating to the child. Depending on the parents' knowledge about child development and the parents' emotional needs, such child behaviors may weaken the initial attachment process.

An older child's reaction to discipline may in turn evoke harsher discipline, possibly culminating in abuse. Studies have shown that of the various responses children make to being disciplined (ignoring, pleading for another chance, apologizing, defiance), defiance is most likely to lead to harsher discipline (Dodge & Pettit, 2003; Patterson et al., 1989).

The Community and Maltreatment

Researchers have reported that a significant characteristic of families who are abusive is their isolation from the rest of the community (Emery, 1989; Garbarino, 1977) and consequent lack of support. Frequently, they have no close relatives nearby or have few friends. Therefore, they have no one to turn to for guidance, comfort, or assistance when they need advice or have a problem. They have no one to relieve them of child-care responsibilities when they need to get away from the house occasionally.

The line between physical abuse and acceptable discipline sometimes depends on the interpreter (Kalichman, 1999). Society expects parents to socialize their children to behave acceptably, so to foster acceptable behavior, some parents use physical, or corporal, punishment. Although occasional spankings could not legally be classified as child abuse, parental use of corporal punishment as a means of dealing with behavioral problems may have future undesirable consequences, such as teaching the child to be aggressive to resolve conflicts. To help determine whether corporal punishment should be interpreted as abuse, James Garbarino has defined maltreatment as "acts of omission or commission by a parent or guardian that are judged by a mixture of community values and professional expertise to be inappropriate and damaging" (Garbarino & Gilliam, 1980, p. 7).

Poverty, unemployment, social isolation of families, transient lifestyle, lack of recognition of children's rights, cultural acceptance of corporal punishment, and limited help for families in crisis are environmental factors that correlate highly with abuse (Garbarino & Gilliam, 1980; Thompson, 1994). The most frequently reported environmental stressors for families who are abusive and/or neglectful is their lower socioeconomic status (McLoyd, 1998) and their exposure to community violence (Garbarino & Eckenrode, 1997). Community support programs for child and family maltreatment are discussed in Chapter 10.

Epilogue

Parenting occurs in context. It is affected by cultural, family, and personal values. It is also affected by knowledge of child development and socialization methods as to what is appropriate for different ages and situations. King Midas's parenting style was influenced by his materialistic values. Apparently, Midas lacked knowledge of child development and developmentally appropriate practices. However, Midas eventually learned appropriate parenting through his daughter, illustrating bidirectional socialization.

Summary

Parenting means implementing a series of decisions about the socialization of a child. There is little consensus today in the United States about what children should be like when they grow up and what parents need to do to get them there.

Parenting is conducted within various macrosystems, such as political ideology, culture, and economics. Political ideology affects parenting because children have to be raised to function as citizens in society when they become adults. All cultures have parenting goals, which vary in importance. Different economic systems have different family structures and different formulas for appropriate adult social behavior, which are transmitted to children.

The socioeconomic status of a family influences parenting style. It has been found that, generally, parents of lower socioeconomic status are more punitive, emphasizing obedience, whereas parents of higher socioeconomic status use more reasoning, emphasizing independence and creativity.

Parental occupations (exosystems) influence parenting styles because skills required at work tend to be emphasized at home; for example, bureaucratic jobs tend to emphasize getting along, whereas entrepreneurial jobs tend to emphasize self-reliance.

Various ethnic and religious groups differ in certain parenting styles and practices. They can be classified as cooperative/interdependent (collectivistic) on one end of the spectrum and competitive/independent (individualistic) on the other. These orientations differ in their socialization of children regarding authority roles, communica-

tion, display of emotions, discipline guidance, and emphasis on skills.

Parenting is affected by chronosystem influences, such as historical trends and evolving family dynamics. Historically, children were regarded as existing solely for their contribution to their family's welfare. Parenting styles were strict. Contemporary ideas of parenting regard the child as an individual whose development must be nurtured and protected by the family. Parenting practices in the 20th century were influenced by "experts," ranging from strict to permissive to democratic.

Family dynamics involve the continuous and evolving bidirectional interactions affecting parents and children. Some variables involved are child characteristics (age and cognitive development, temperament, gender, presence of a disability) and family characteristics (size, configuration, parents' stage of life, marital quality, ability to cope with stress).

Parenting styles include microsystem influences (between parent and child) and mesosystem influences (between parent and others). There are four basic types of parenting styles: authoritarian (adult-centered), permissive (child-centered), authoritative (democratic), and uninvolved. Parenting styles affect children's attachment, self-regulation, prosocial behavior, competence, and achievement motivation. Mesosystem influences on parenting styles include links with the school and the community, which can be collaborative or conflicted.

Appropriate parenting practices are influenced by parental understanding of developmental appropriateness as well as guidance/discipline techniques.

Parents respond to their child's development by changing their expectations and parenting tasks; thus, socialization is bidirectional. Parents need to know when it is appropriate to use guidance and discipline. Guidance techniques are preventive, whereas disciplinary techniques are corrective.

Inappropriate parenting is maltreatment—intentional harm to or endangerment of a child, including abuse and neglect. Parents who maltreat their children fail to meet the physical or emotional needs of the developing child. Whether families resort to maltreatment depends on ongoing and transient risk and resilient factors.

Children who are neglected are those who are abandoned, lack supervision, do not receive proper nutrition, need medical or dental care, are frequently absent or late for school, do not have appropriate or sufficient clothing, are unclean, or live in unsafe or filthy homes.

Children who are physically abused are those who are intentionally bruised, wounded, or burned. Physical abuse is often related to domestic violence. Children who are sexually abused are those who are forced, tricked, or threatened to have sexual contact with an individual. Children who are psychologically or emotionally abused are those who are exposed to unreasonable demands that are beyond their capabilities; this type of abuse may include persistent teasing, belittling, or verbal attacks.

The parents in families that abuse tend to have been abused as children. These parents also tend to have unmet emotional needs. Generally, they have unrealistic expectations for children and often lack knowledge of child development. In many cases, they believe that their children's behavior is deliberate and meant to hurt them. These parents also often have very low self-esteem. Depression and alcoholism have been linked to abuse.

Parents who are abusive tend to be isolated from the community, lacking a supportive network of relatives and/or friends on whom they can rely when needed. They also have a low tolerance for handling stress, in addition to financial, emotional, and health problems. Corporal punishment is often their only means of dealing with misbehavior. There is a documented relationship between poverty and neglect.

Activity

PURPOSE   To examine your values relating to parenting.

1. Write the appropriate requirements for a parenting license. Include (a) physical requirements (health status, age, etc.); (b) psychological requirements (temperament, educational status, etc.); (c) social requirements (marital status, finances, etc.); and (d) experience with children.
2. What would you do?
   - Your 2-year-old has been coming into your bedroom for the past three nights about 3:00 A.M.
   - Three-year-old Charles spills his milk all over the table and begins to cry.
   - Your 4-year-old daughter tells you the 6-year-old boy next door likes to play "doctor."
   - Just as you walk out of the grocery store, you notice your 5-year-old son eating a candy bar that you did not purchase.
   - Your 6-year-old daughter does not want to go to school. You talk to the teacher to find out what the problem is; the teacher says your daughter is shy and will not participate in class or interact with the other children.
   - Your 7- and 9-year-old children have lately been arguing about everything. When they have nothing specific to argue about, like a toy, a game, or a television show, they tease each other.
   - Your 9-year-old son is watching the news on television and asks, "What does 'rape' mean?"
   - Bill, age 10, has recently begun to ignore your requests to put his things away. He also has been "forgetting" to do his regular chores.
   - Your 11-year-old daughter asks to spend the night at a school friend's house, and you have never met the friend's parents.
   - Your 12-year-old son makes an online purchase using your credit card.

Related Readings

Brazelton, T. B. (1992). *Touchpoints*. Reading, MA: Addison-Wesley.

Christophersen, E. R., & Mortweet, S. L. (2003). *Parenting that works: Building skills that last a lifetime*. Washington, DC: American Psychological Association.

Cleverly, J., & Phillips, D. C. (1986). *Visions of childhood: Influential models from Locke to Spock* (rev. ed.). New York: Teachers College Press.

Dodson, F. (1974). *How to father*. New York: New American Library.

Dodson, F. (1987). *How to single parent*. New York: Harper & Row.

Dreikurs, R. (1964). *Children: The challenge*. New York: Hawthorn.

Faber, A., & Mazlish, E. (1982). *How to talk so kids will listen and listen so kids will talk*. New York: Avon.

Faber, A., & Mazlish, E. (1988). *Siblings without rivalry*. New York: Avon.

Garbarino, J., & Eckenrode, J. (1997). *Understanding abusive families: An ecological approach to theory and practice*. San Francisco: Jossey-Bass.

Gordon, T. (1991). *Discipline that works: Promoting self-discipline in children at home and at school*. New York: Plume.

Ilg, F. L., Ames, L. B., & Baker, S. M. (1991). *Child behavior* (rev. ed.). New York: Harper & Row.

Satir, V. (1988). *The new peoplemaking*. Mountain View, CA: Science and Behavior Books.

Snow, R. L. (1997). *Family abuse*. Boulder: Perseus.

Steinberg, L. (2004). *Ten basic principles of good parenting*. New York: Simon & Schuster.

Steinberg, L., & Levine, A. (1997). *You and your adolescent: A parent's guide for ages 10–20* (2nd ed.). New York: Harper Perennial.

Turecki, S., & Wernick, S. (1994). *Normal children have problems, too*. New York: Bantam Books.

White, B. L. (1995). *The new first three years of life*. New York: Simon & Schuster.

Chapter 5

BananaStock/Jupiterimages

Ecology of Child Care

Give a little love to a child, and you get a great deal back.

—JOHN RUSKIN

What kind of support is most appropriate for families in caring for children?

Collaborative caregiving involves working together cooperatively. It generally refers to the relationship between the child's caregiver and parent(s). The following English tale, *Mary Poppins*, by Pamela Travers (1934/1997), tells of a nanny with magical powers to address children's needs and imaginations. This extraordinary caregiver was actually quite bossy, but commanded children's respect by having strict standards and by being consistent with rewards and consequences for behavior. The socialization of her charges involved providing them with love, fun, and a sense of security.

Once Upon a Time A long time ago, there lived a fairly wealthy family who could afford to have help with child care. The father, Mr. Banks, worked long hours in the city and the mother, Mrs. Banks, was loving but a bit inept at taking care of four children. The older children, Jane and Michael, were particularly sullen and spoiled, and the younger twins were well on their way toward becoming so.

Everything changes when nanny extraordinaire, Mary Poppins, arrives via a windstorm to Cherry Tree Lane; she is firm, strict, and demanding . . . but she is also attentive and playful. After the children complete their schoolwork or chores, she takes them on fantastic adventures, like stepping into the drawings made with chalk on the sidewalk. She also does silly things with them, like having tea upside down on a ceiling. But when the children misbehave, the magic goes awry. Have a tantrum, and you might end up in an antique plate—trapped inside with no way out. Be rude, and your world will become unpleasant. Whining or stubbornness are not tolerated by Mary Poppins; yet be nice and you might be rewarded by being taken to the zoo to celebrate your birthday. The Banks family learned that giving love did not mean "giving in."

When Mary feels confident that Mr. and Mrs. Banks have absorbed the caregiving skills they need and that the children have achieved some self-reliance, she leaves to become a nanny at another family's home.

- **Should parents seek caregiving help (full- or part-time babysitter, nanny, day care)?**

- **How can parents and caregivers collaborate for optimal socialization and developmental outcomes?**

Child Care

What is nonparental child care?

day care the care given to children by persons other than parents during the parts of the day that parents are absent

Child care, or as it is sometimes called, **day care**, refers to the care given to children by persons other than parents during the parts of the day when parents are absent. Nonparental child care can begin as early as birth and extend into the school years until children are old enough to care for themselves. Most states have laws regarding the age at which children can legally be left unsupervised by an adult. Child care provided for children before or after school hours or during vacations is referred to as **extended day care**.

The care of children today, for a significant part of the day, is likely to be provided by caregivers other than parents. Approximately 80% of children age 5 and younger with employed mothers are in a child-care arrangement for an average of almost 40 hours a week with someone other than a parent, and about 60% of these children ages 6 to 14 spend an average of 21 hours per week in nonparental care before and after school (Smolensky & Gootman, 2003). Because children are spending significant socialization time in nonparental care settings, and at very young ages, this chapter examines the influence of such child-care settings on development. Figure 5.1 shows an ecological model of the systems involved in the process.

The availability, affordability, and adequacy of child care has become an increasingly serious concern over the past 30 years. In the mid-1970s, approximately 30% of mothers with children under age 6 were employed, as were more than 50% of mothers of school-age children. By the year 2000, these percentages had grown to about 65% and 77%, respectively (Smolensky & Gootman, 2003). In the twenty-first century, these numbers will climb even further as the rising cost of living forces more parents to contribute to the family income jointly.

extended day care care provided for children before or after school hours or during vacations

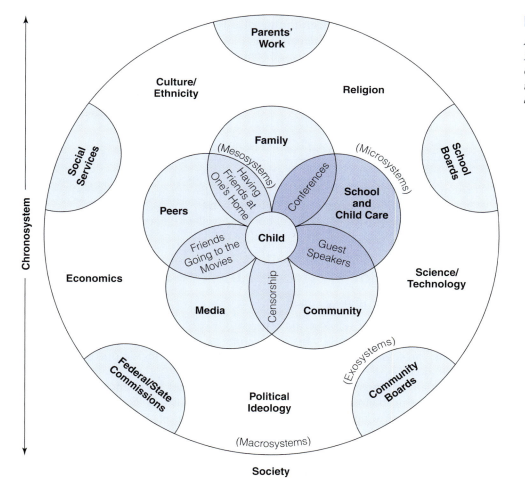

Figure 5.1
An Ecological Model of Human Development
Child care is a significant influence on the child's development.

Only 45% of parents working in the private sector have guaranteed unpaid parental leave under the Family and Medical Leave Act (FMLA) of 1993; less than 5% have access to paid parental leave. Many parents do not have the right to more than the 12 weeks of leave mandated by the FMLA (Smolensky & Gootman, 2003).

There are several different types of nonparental child care. A friend, relative, or sitter may come to the home and care for the child. The family may hire a nanny (someone who has received child-care training) to live in. Families may cooperate and provide care by taking turns. Independent caregivers may provide care for children in their homes (family day care). Parents may take children to a center for care during the day. According to Clarke-Stewart & Allhusen (2002), children ages 3–5 are more likely than children younger than 3 to be cared for in a center-based program; children under the age of 3 are more likely to be cared for by parents, relatives, or independent caregivers in the child's home or the caregiver's.

Regardless of the type, *quality* child care involves certain basics: a caregiver who provides warm, loving care and guidance for the child and works with the family to ensure that the child develops in the best way possible; a setting (home or center) that keeps the child safe, secure, and healthy; and developmentally appropriate activities that help the child develop emotionally, socially, mentally, and physically (Clarke-Stewart, 1993; National Institute of Child Health and Development [NICHD], 2005). Many states require fingerprinting of caregivers so that background checks can be made through the police department.

The terms *nursery school, preschool, early childhood education*, and *child development program* are sometimes used to describe certain types of programs for young children. Because all care for children has an impact on their socialization or education, the terms *child care* or *day care* will be used to refer to nonparental caregiving.

Your Care as a Child

Who cared for you in your early years?
Will you be the primary caregiver for your children?
Are you and your present or future spouse employed, or do you plan to be?

COMPONENTS OF OPTIMAL QUALITY CARE

What is involved in quality care?

Given the patchwork of services that currently exists and the projected need for future child care, quality child care has become an issue of concern among working parents, professionals who deal with children, and legislators (Ghazvini & Mullis, 2002; Lamb, 1998, 2000).

Since "quality" tends to be a subjective evaluation of excellence, research has approached the problem of an objective definition by closely examining the many aspects, both physical and social, of the child-care setting. For example, the federal government initiated the National Day-Care Study (Ruopp, Travers, Glantz, & Coelen, 1979) for the purpose of ultimately constructing national child-care standards. The task was to identify key child-care components that best predicted good outcomes for children and to develop cost estimates for offering those components within programs. The study found the components of optimal quality child care—that is, the most significant predictors of positive classroom dynamics and child outcomes—to be:

- The size of the overall group
- The caregiver–child ratios
- Whether the caregiver had specialized training in child development or early childhood education

In classrooms that had smaller groups and whose teachers had specialized training, teachers could engage in more social interaction with the children. As a result, the children were more cooperative, more involved in tasks, more talkative, and more creative. They also made greater gains on cognitive tasks.

Today, measures such as the Early Childhood Environment Rating Scale (Harms & Clifford, 1980) are available to assess quality. More recent studies have confirmed and expanded the National Day-Care Study findings (Ghazvini & Mullis, 2002; NICHD, 1996, 2005). Caregivers with specialized training in child development and developmentally appropriate practices have a more authoritative, rather than authoritarian, attitude toward child rearing, use more planned activities, are less stressed, and tend to communicate regularly with parents (Ghazvini & Mullis, 2002; NICHD, 2005).

In spite of such research on child-care quality and positive child outcomes, studies of child-care centers reveals that typical quality is still considerably below what is considered good practice by child development, psychology, and education specialists (Fragin, 2000; Cost, Quality, and Child Outcomes Study [CQO], 1995, 1999; NICHD, 2005).

What factors contribute to *less* than optimal quality child care?

- The education credentials of caregivers who work in child-care centers are often inadequate relative to the skills required (Fragin, 2000; NICHD, 1996).
- Staff turnover is high, ranging from 25% to 50% each year. This means that children are continually adapting to new caregivers, and administrators are constantly training new staff (Fragin, 2000; Whitebook, Howes, & Phillips, 1989).
- Staff compensation, including wages and benefits, is exceptionally low. Worker compensation is significantly related to quality of care provided (Whitebook et al., 1989).

A number of studies have examined the effects of varying levels of quality on children's behavior and development. Conclusions were similar in finding a significant correlation between program quality (safe, stimulating environment) and socialization outcomes for children (Frede, 1995; Fragin, 2000; NICHD, 2005). Outcomes related to quality include cooperative play, sociability, ability to resolve conflicts, self-control, and language and cognitive development.

Most studies on quality care have focused on the effects on the child, but a few have examined effects on parental sense of well-being. The emotional state of the parents influences choice of child care, satisfaction at work, and parenting (Phillips, 1992). For example, Mason and Duberstein (1992) found that the objective factors of availability and affordability of care overshadow the subjective factor of quality in parental sense of well-being and, hence, choice of child care. Also affecting parental sense of well-being is ease of communication with caregivers. Parents favored informal, frequent communication, such as a daily face-to-face chat, over formal, infrequent communication, such as a written monthly report (Ghazvini & Mullis, 2002).

What is involved in advocacy for quality child care?

Advocacy, introduced in Chapter 2, is the process of supporting a person, group, or cause. An example of the process of advocacy is the work of the National Association for the Education of Young Children (NAEYC), an organization of professionals involved in early childhood education. Because national standards of quality do not exist, NAEYC took on the task of setting its own criteria, publishing a position statement on criteria for high-quality early childhood programs in 1984. Briefly, a high-quality program is

> one which meets the needs of and promotes the physical, social, emotional, and cognitive development of the children and adults—parents, staff, and administrators—who are involved in the program. Each day of a child's life is viewed as leading toward the growth and development of a healthy, intelligent, and contributing member of society. (National Association for the Education of Young Children, 1984, p. 7)

Child-care programs that meet the criteria can voluntarily apply to the National Academy for Early Childhood Programs (a division of NAEYC) for accreditation, thereby receiving national recognition for high-quality standards and performance. Accreditation specifics will be discussed later.

In 1986, NAEYC expanded its position on quality. With the proliferation of programs for young children and the introduction of large numbers of infants and toddlers into group care, NAEYC felt the need for a clear definition of *developmentally appropriate practice*, a term often used in the criteria for quality early childhood programs. In response to the trend (seen in many programs) toward increasing emphasis on formal instruction in academic skills, NAEYC published specific guidelines for developmentally appropriate practices for programs servicing children from birth through age 8 (Bredekamp, 1986, 1993; Bredekamp & Copple, 1997).

Developmental appropriateness, as introduced in Chapter 4, involves knowledge of children's normal growth patterns and individual differences. Research in human development indicates that universal, predictable sequences of growth and change occur in childhood, adolescence, and adulthood. These predictable changes occur in all domains of development—physical, emotional, social, and cognitive. Knowledge of typical development of children within the age span served by the program provides a framework within which caregivers can plan an appropriate learning environment and appropriate experiences. Play is viewed as the primary indicator of children's development. Each child is viewed as a unique person with an individual pattern and timing of growth, as well as individual temperament, learning style, and family background. Both the program and interactions should be responsive to individual differences. Learning in a developmentally appropriate program emerges as a result of the interaction between the child's thoughts and experiences and the materials and people available. The curriculum should match the child's developing abilities while also challenging the child's interest and understanding (Bredekamp, 1986, 1993).

After much hard work, debate, and compromise involving numerous child advocate organizations, a federal child-care bill was eventually passed in 1990. The bill included a Child Care and Development Block Grant to state governments, requiring

Sally Moskol/Index Stock Imagery

This preschool child is engaged in a developmentally appropriate "hands-on" activity.

them to designate a lead agency to direct their child-care programs, to set health and safety standards, and to allow eligible low-income families to choose any licensed child-care provider. In addition, the child-care bill included tax credits for working families with children if they have child-care expenses for one or more children under age 13 and pay for child care in order to work.

Voluntary systems exist nationally to establish higher quality standards than are required by law for both child-care centers and family day-care homes (Helburn & Howes, 1996).

Child-Care Centers. In 1984, the National Association for the Education of Young Children (NAEYC) developed an accreditation system for child-care centers involving self-evaluations by staff and parents. Professional validators from NAEYC conduct visits to determine whether standards have been met; if they have, the program is accredited for three years. Standards are designed for programs serving children from infancy through age 8 in centers caring for more than 10 children; school-age programs are eligible if a majority of the children are age 8 or younger.

The NAEYC accreditation standard criteria (see Figure 5.2), based on research and professional consensus, include staff qualifications and training, administration and staffing patterns (group size and adult–child ratios), physical environment, health and safety, and nutrition and food service. For example, for children ages 0 to 12 months, the standard is 6 to 8 children per group with an adult–child ratio of 1:3 to 1:4; for children ages 4 to 5 years, the standard is 16 to 20 children per group with an adult–child ratio of 1:8 to 1:10.

Family Day-Care Homes. In 1988, the National Association for Family Day Care (now the National Association for Family Child Care, or NAFCC) began a program for voluntary accreditation of family child-care homes. The process includes self-evaluation as well as external validation of aspects of program operation including

Figure 5.2

Conceptual Framework of Early Childhood Program Standards for NAEYC Accreditation

Source: National Association for the Education of Young Children, 1984—Promoting excellence in early childhood education

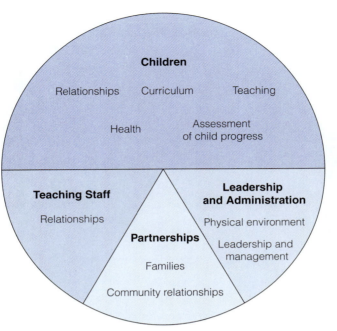

Reprinted with permission from the National Association for the Education of Young Children. From 'Introduction' in NAEYC Early Childhood Program Standards and Accreditation Criteria: The Mark of Quality in Early Childhood Education (Washington, DC: NAEYC, 2005).

health and safety, nutrition, indoor and outdoor play environments, interactions, and professional responsibility. Continuing education for the caregiver, such as cardiopulmonary resuscitation (CPR), is also required.

In-Home Care: Nannies. The oldest professional nanny organization in the United States is the International Nanny Association (INA). It includes nannies, nanny employers, nanny placement agencies, and nanny educators. Since 1987, INA has worked to professionalize the nanny industry by maintaining high standards of conduct, respecting and supporting families in their task of nurturing children, and promoting continuing professional growth. Background checks, referrals, conferences, and newsletters are some of their services.

Macrosystem Influences on Child Care

What aspects of society have influenced child care?

Generally, child care and educational practices have been affected by three macrosystems: political ideology, economics, and science and technology. *Political ideology* is seen in values such as social responsibility (e.g., fostering adaptation of immigrants); competition (e.g., providing young children with learning opportunities to prepare for the future); and equal opportunity (e.g., assisting poor families and including ethnically diverse children and children with disabilities). *Economics* can be seen in the need for both parents to work. *Science and technology* are reflected in the pressure to impart academic skills to all children as early as possible. To illustrate macrosystem influences, child care has been used during the twentieth century for the following purposes:

- Social service for immigrants who are poor
- Enrichment for preschoolers of middle- and high-income families

- Employability of parents
- Intervention to equalize learning opportunities for preschoolers who may be disadvantaged because of low income, ethnicity, disability, or abuse
- Readiness for elementary school

Social Service. The first day nurseries were established to care for the children of masses of immigrants to the United States during the mid-19th century. Day nurseries were also established to care for the children of women who worked in factories and hospitals during wartime. The motivation to establish these day nurseries was social service to care for neglected children, and the care provided was essentially custodial (Clarke-Stewart, 1993).

Enrichment. The first cooperative nursery school was inaugurated at the University of Chicago in 1915. The purpose was to give the children of faculty wives opportunities to play in a supervised environment where they could develop impulse control, verbal skills, and knowledge about the world. Parent participation was required. Such nursery schools were popular with middle-class families from the 1930s to the 1960s. In the late 1960s, as a result of child development research and political pressure for the United States to compete globally—specifically to keep pace with Russian scientific advances—a new purpose was incorporated into nursery school programs: to stimulate intellectual growth (Clarke-Stewart, 1993).

Employability. Child-care services are used to enable women to seek job training and/or employment outside the home (Lamb, 2000). Economic necessity, including increases in the cost of living and in the number of single-parent families, has led to a growing reliance on nonparental care. Recent welfare reforms to increase employability have also contributed to this trend. The 1996 welfare law allows recipients of Temporary Assistance to Needy Families (TANF) to collect federally funded benefits for a maximum of 60 months. States can modify requirements with state funds. Recipients of TANF must be engaged in work-related activities (training, job search, job) within their state's time limit. The immediate effect of the imposed time limit for welfare was to increase the demand for available, accessible, affordable child care.

Intervention. In the 1960s, civil rights groups demanded equal opportunities in education, jobs, and housing. The Economic Opportunity Act, passed in 1964, funded preschool programs designed to compensate for the perceived physical, social, and academic disadvantages of children who came from low-income families, were members of ethnic minorities, had various disabilities, or were identified as abused. The purpose of such intervention was to provide children with skills they would be unlikely to get at home, enabling them to succeed in school and avoid poverty in adulthood. Intervention programs are usually comprehensive, including health and nutrition services, social services, and parental involvement. An example of a federally funded comprehensive preschool intervention program is Head Start. Its goal is to enable children from qualified families to enter school ready to learn. Public money spent to enhance the early childhood years would be more beneficial than public money spent to correct a deficiency in later childhood.

In addition to child development research, the political climate in the 1960s was also part of the rationale for early intervention. President Lyndon Johnson felt that the only way to break the cycle of poverty was through education. Intervention programs seemed to be a solution that would equalize opportunities through education.

Education would ultimately enable people to get jobs to support themselves, rather than depend on welfare. Today, part of welfare reform is government funding of child care to enable mothers of young children to work.

Readiness. Those who advocate that child care should be synonymous with early childhood education also believe the period in a child's life from birth to age 5 is a critical time for developing the physical, emotional, social, and cognitive skills they will need for the rest of their lives. That the formation of neural connections in the brain is most susceptible to stimulating experiences in the early years has been documented by scientific research (Shonkoff & Phillips, 2000). Such findings have influenced political policy. For example, President George W. Bush, in his State of the Union Address of 2002, outlined his plan for educational reform—the "No Child Left Behind Act"—whereby public schools teach students what they need to know to be successful in life. The Bush administration has also proposed a new early childhood initiative—"Good Start, Grow Smart"—to help states and local communities fund programs that will ensure young children are equipped with skills they will need to be ready to learn in school, such as prereading and language skills.

In sum, as a result of macrosystem influences, child care has become a service to families with children to provide custodial care, stimulating learning experiences, and socialization, to enable parents to work, and to implement early childhood education principles.

Chronosystem Influences on Child Care: Correlates and Consequences

What controversies surround the issue of child care?

The 1971 White House Conference on Children pointed to the need for quality child care as the most serious problem confronting families and children. Unfortunately, as the twenty-first century begins, we still have no official national policy or federal standards aimed at establishing a system of child care that is of good quality. Child-care standards continue to vary widely from state to state and family to family. Why is this so?

One reason is that traditional views of parenting in this country have delegated the primary responsibility for child care to the family. Some people in government and business support the "individualist" view that each family should be able to care for its own without outside assistance (Schorr, 1997).

Another reason is the fear of government involvement in what is considered a basic personal right: to bring up one's children according to one's values, one's religion, and one's culture. Federal involvement in private matters is seen by some as teetering on the brink of socialism. Is the underlying fear that if the government foots the bill for child care, then the government will call the shots?

In general, the federal government has not committed itself to implement child-care standards (except in programs where federal funds are involved). This means the task is left to the states, local communities, private enterprise, professional organizations, and the consumer (see "How to Choose a Good Early Childhood Program" on the *Child, Family, School, Community* website at http://www.thomsonedu.com/author/berns.

Now that nonparental child care has become a fact of life, the question from the 1980s and 1990s—"Is day care helpful or harmful to children?"—needs to be reframed as "What ecological model of child care is most supportive of children and families?" (Ghazvini & Mullis, 2002; NICHD, 2005).

There are a variety of opinions among professionals and laypeople as to whether or not children should be enrolled in day care. There are also opinions on the age at which children should be enrolled and whether such care should be full- or part-time. There are even opinions on the types of program that should be offered. For example, some believe the preschool experience should focus on learning how to get along with others, exploring the environment, and dealing with feelings; others believe the preschool experience should focus on academic skills, such as reading and math. The debate goes on.

Much of the early controversy regarding the effects of child care on the child's development was centered on the fear that separation from the mother, especially in infancy, would disrupt the natural mother–child bond of attachment and would result in psychological and social problems. Thus, most of the original research studies examined the effects of separation on the child. It should be noted that the infant separation studies were done in residential institutions, rather than in child-care centers as we know them today. More recent studies have examined the overall effects of different child-care settings (home versus alternative) on children's social relationships with other children, their relationships with their mothers, and their intellectual development. The most recent studies have used an ecological approach, combining family factors and child-care factors (Clarke-Stewart & Allhusen, 2002; NICHD, 2005), as well as cultural factors (Lamb, 2000), that work together to affect children's development. It is now well accepted that "childrearing has become a collaborative endeavor with children moving back and forth . . . between their homes and child care" (Phillips & Howes, 1987, p. 9). The mesosystem links may be supportive, competitive, or neutral. In examining these issues, both classical and modern studies will be examined.

CHILD CARE AND PSYCHOLOGICAL DEVELOPMENT

What are the effects of separating infants from their mothers?

One of the first studies to report the detrimental effects of separating infants from their mothers was done by Rene Spitz in 1946. He compared the development of infants raised by caregivers in a foundling home (a home for illegitimate and abandoned babies) to that of infants raised by their mothers in a prison. Each caregiver in the foundling home was responsible for at least eight infants. The mothers, who were all either mentally retarded or emotionally disturbed, were responsible for caring for their own infants in the prison. The infants raised in the foundling home had poor appetites and lacked interest in their surroundings; they exhibited severe depression, according to Spitz. As a result, they were retarded in their growth and mental development. The infants raised by their mothers in prison, on the other hand, developed normally. Even though the mothers in the prison were socially deviant, the one-on-one care and nurturance they gave their infants enabled the infants to exhibit normal development; whereas even though the caregivers in the institution were professionally trained, they had eight babies to nurture and probably could not establish emotional attachments with each one. Spitz supported "nature" care.

In 1952, John Bowlby (1966, 1969, 1973) wrote that maternal love and care are the most important influences on an infant's future development. After reviewing studies on infants separated from their mothers, he concluded that any break in the early mother–child relationship could have severe emotional, social, and intellectual consequences. What Bowlby meant by "any break" was loss of the mother in infancy due to death or separation from the mother because of hospitalization, employment, or other circumstances such as neglect—being physically present but emotionally absent. He went on to say that being deprived of the early mother–child relationship would cause the infant to become depressed, physically and mentally retarded, or delinquent. Bowlby, too, supported "nature" care.

A 30-year longitudinal study completed in 1966 by Harold Skeels demonstrated that it is the quality of care (nurture) that affects children's development, not the relationship of the person who provides it (nature). Thus, the care can come from someone other than the child's mother. Skeels studied 25 infants who were institutionalized because they were deemed mentally retarded. Of these, 13 were later transferred to the institution for retarded women, where the infants were "adopted" by small groups of residents, who lavished care and attention on them. The remaining 12 infants stayed where they were. After two years, the transfer group had gained an average of 28.5 points on an IQ test, but the control group had lost an average of 26.2 points.

Thirty years later, Skeels did a follow-up study on the original 25. He found that 11 of the 13 children who were transferred to the institution for retarded women had been adopted by families; 12 out of the 13 had achieved an education and become self-supporting adults with responsible jobs. Their own children had average IQs. Of the control group of 12 children who had remained institutionalized, 11 had survived; 4 were in institutions, 1 was a vagrant, 1 was a gardener's assistant at an institution, 3 were dishwashers, 1 was a part-time worker in a cafeteria, and 1 was a domestic worker.

This study showed that children need care and nurturance to develop normally (in this respect, Skeels agrees with Spitz and Bowlby); that the care and nurturance can be provided by someone other than the mother (here Skeels disagrees with Spitz and Bowlby); and that infants who are initially deprived can grow up normally if intervention by a caring, nurturing person is provided (Spitz and Bowlby did not even consider this possibility). Skeels supported "nurture" care.

Skeels's study has implications for society. If deprivational effects caused by neglect in infancy can be reversed by intervention, then we can enable many children to grow up to be independent, self-sufficient, responsible adults who are assets to society rather than liabilities. There are still many unresolved questions. Which children qualify for intervention? When do you intervene? What type of intervention is best? What kind of program do you provide, and for how long? Is day care worth paying for? Does the government or some other agency have the right to intervene? Is society willing to pay the cost of intervention? These questions will be discussed in more detail later.

Selma Fraiberg (1977), a psychologist and author, defends mothering: The mother is the primary caretaker of the infant; good maternal care "is every child's birthright"; society's intervening role should be to help inadequate mothers improve their relationships with their infants, rather than subsidize alternatives to mothering such as day care. Sandra Scarr (1984), another psychologist and author of *Mother Care/Other Care*, provides evidence that babies and young children can be successfully reared by qualified others.

What exactly is so special about the early mother–child relationship? During the first year of life children become attached to their primary caregiver—the person who holds them, comforts them, feeds them, and plays with them. This caregiver is usually the mother, but it can be the father, a grandparent, an older sibling, or another person not related to the child. Feelings of attachment distinguish this caregiver from others. When children are in strange situations or not feeling well, they want to be near the person they are attached to; no one else will do.

As was discussed in Chapter 4, researchers assess the level of attachment to the mother by putting children in a strange or stressful situation—for instance, leaving them in a room with a stranger and observing their reactions to their mother's presence, her departure, and her return. An *insecure attachment* is usually indicated when the child clings to the mother when she leaves or cries hysterically until the mother returns. An insecure attachment is also usually indicated when the child ignores the mother when she leaves and avoids her when she returns, or when a child clings to the mother one moment and rejects her the next. A *secure attachment* is indicated when the child is able to leave the mother's side to explore the toys in the room—obviously, however, preferring the mother's company to the stranger's. When the mother leaves, the child shows concern or becomes mildly upset, but gets over it quickly. When she returns, the child greets her happily (Ainsworth, 1973, 1979; Ainsworth & Bell, 1970).

Jay Belsky (1988, 1992) showed that babies less than 1 year old who receive nonmaternal care for more than 20 hours a week are at a greater risk of developing insecure

This child clings to his mother when left at child care because he is attached to her.

relationships with their mothers; they are also at increased risk of emotional and behavioral problems in later childhood. Youngsters who have weak emotional ties to their mothers are more likely to be aggressive and disobedient as they grow older.

Others (Clarke-Stewart, 1988, 1992; Phillips & Howes, 1987) take issue with Belsky, saying the evidence is insufficient to support the claim that infants in full-time day care are at risk for emotional insecurity. That day-care infants exhibit different attachment behaviors than home-care infants may mean they have developed a coping style to adapt to the different people who care for them as well as the daily separations and reunions. In addition, the assessment of attachment procedures commonly used may not be an accurate way of comparing differences in attachment between infants reared in such diverse environments. Not all children who begin day care in infancy are insecurely attached, aggressive, or noncompliant, nor are they intellectually advanced. There are individual differences for day-care children just as there are for children reared at home (Clarke-Stewart, 1989, 1992; Honig, 1993).

Finally, recent data on psychological functioning of children who have attended day care in infancy are often confounded by the child's temperament and gender, family socioeconomic status, marital status, parent–child relationships, number of hours daily in care, and quality of care, including sensitivity and responsiveness of the caregiver (Langlois & Liben, 2003; NICHD, 1997, 2005). According to Michael Lamb (1998), who reviewed the research, it now appears that day care in itself does not reliably affect mother–child attachment. Adverse effects occur only when poor-quality day care concurs with such risky conditions as insensitive and unresponsive maternal behavior (NICHD, 1997). In sum, children in a quality child-care program, compared to children cared for at home, attach to their mothers similarly.

CHILD CARE AND SOCIAL DEVELOPMENT

What is the effect of putting infants, toddlers, and preschoolers with peers in child care?

Children in day care may be with peers from infancy. Infants stare at each other and touch each other. Toddlers may smile at each other, share toys, and fight over toys. Three-year-olds may play games, share, take turns, argue, and fight. Four-year-olds may also role-play. ("Let's play house. You be the mommy, and I'll be the baby.")

Results of a substantial number of studies on the social development of preschool children conclude that children attending some form of child-care program interact more with peers, positively and often negatively, and that they are less cooperative and responsive with adults than children in home care (Clarke-Stewart et al., 2002; Field, Masi, Goldstein, & Perry, 1988; NICHD, 1998).

Specifically, children who have had experience in a child-care program seem to be more socially competent than those who have not had such an experience. They are more self-confident, more outgoing, and less fearful. They are also more assertive and more self-sufficient. They know more about the social world—gender roles, taking the perspective of others, solving problems regarding getting along with another child, and emotional labels ("cheater," "crybaby," "bully"). While they are more socially competent, they have also been observed to be less polite, less respectful of others' rights, and less compliant with adult demands, as well as more aggressive and hostile to others (Clarke-Stewart, 1989; Clarke-Stewart et al., 2002; Lamb, 2000). Early individual differences in social competence have been found to remain stable through school age and early adolescence (Campbell, Lamb, & Hwang, 2000).

CHILD CARE AND COGNITIVE DEVELOPMENT

What is the effect of child care on intellectual outcomes?

Generally, the intellectual performance of children who attend a quality day-care program is higher than that of children from similar family backgrounds who do not attend a day-care program or who attend one of poor quality. For example, it has been shown that children, especially from low-income families, who attend a quality preschool program, even part-time, are more verbally expressive and more interactive with adults than children who do not (Burchinal, Peisner-Feinberg, Bryant, & Clifford, 2000; Clarke-Stewart, 1993; Honig, 1993; Shonkoff & Phillips, 2000). It has also been demonstrated that children who attend quality child-care programs are better able to meet the requirements in the primary grades of elementary school and function at an increased intellectual capacity during their initial years of schooling; IQ scores show an increase of up to 10 points at the end of program implementation. Academic achievement in these children continues to be better through high school than for those who did not attend a quality preschool (CQO, 1999; Karoly, 1998; Schwienhart, Montie, Xiang, Barnett, Belfield, & Nores, 2005). Although longitudinal studies have shown that the increase in IQ scores is not permanent, there is a significant reduction in grade retention as well as in the need for placement in a special education program (CQO, 1999; Karoly, 1998; Schweinhart et al., 2005).

This father is influencing his son's competency and total educational development through his interest and involvement in his son's learning.

Scholastic Studio 10/Index Stock Imagery

What child care programs have been developed to modify the consequences of growing up disadvantaged?

Traditional preschool programs usually provide enrichment activities to children who already get basic intellectual stimulation at home. For children who do not have such an advantage, intervention programs were developed to provide compensation, or amends, for skills these children lack to succeed in U.S. public schools. Most research on the effects of day care on children's cognitive development has focused on intervention programs.

Many types of intervention programs were implemented in the 1960s and 1970s, using different curriculum models (discussed later). Although children enrolled in such programs fared better academically, socially, and emotionally than their nonparticipant counterparts (Karoly, 1998), the debate as to which type of intervention is best, for whom, for how long, and where (home or school) remains ongoing.

Even though intervention programs vary widely, most investigators concur that to enable the child to become a competent member of society, the child's family must be involved. Thus the best type of intervention (among government-funded programs) is one that reinforces the strengths of the family as a child-rearing system—that enables the family to be the primary educator of its children, links the family to the formal educational system through involvement, and links the family to resources in the community so that the family can receive needed health and social services. These are known as family support programs. An example of such a program is the Child and Family Resource Program (CFRP), which began in 1973 as part of Head Start. It enrolled qualified families of children from birth through age 8, rather than just the children. It provided diagnostic medical, dental, nutritional, and mental health services as well as treatment. It also provided prenatal care and education for pregnant mothers.

It assisted parents in promoting the development of infants and toddlers, as well as providing preschool comprehensive Head Start services for children ages 3 to 5. It eased the transition from preschool to elementary school and offered special development programs for children with disabilities. Finally, it provided services such as counseling, referrals to community agencies, family planning assistance, and help in dealing with emergencies or crises.

Family support programs exist today under the Comprehensive Child Development Program (CCDP). These programs foster more developmentally appropriate behavioral expectations for children by the mothers and more prosocial behavior by the children (Greenfield & Suzuki, 1998).

In sum, accurately predicting the socialization outcomes of intervention programs is difficult because of the numerous variables that must be taken into account, including quality of the mother–infant relationship, socioeconomic status of the family, educational level of the parents, stress on the family and coping skills, available family supports, temperament and gender of the child, spacing of the siblings, age at which the child enters the program and for how many hours per day, quality of the caregiver–infant relationship, caregiver–parent communication, and quality of the program (see Table 5.1).

Table 5.1

Variables Influencing Child-Care Socialization Outcomes

CHILD-CARE VARIABLES	FAMILY VARIABLES	CHILD VARIABLES
Type of care (in-home, family day care, center care)	Socioeconomic status	Age at entry into day care
Type of program (compensatory, enrichment)	Ethnicity	Gender
Compensation of caregivers	Family structure (two-parent, single, step, kin)	Health
Caregiver stress	Parental educational level	Temperament
Stability of caregivers	Mother employed part- or full-time	Security of attachment to mother
Adult–child ratio	Mother's attitude toward work	
Quality of day-care setting	Mother's attitude toward child care	
Sensitivity and responsiveness of caregiver to child	Mother's sensitivity and responsiveness to child	
Caregiver education/training	Roles and relationships between parents	
Caregiver ideology and attitudes toward child rearing	Father's involvement in child care	
Caregiver–parent communication	Parenting styles	
Part- or full-time day care	Stress/coping strategies	
	Availability of social supports in community	

Mesosystem Influences on Child Care

What collaborative links are available for child-care services?

The challenge of the future will be for society to provide more choices in quality child-care services because of the increased need. Links with school, community, government, and business must occur on a greater scale to increase the availability, accessibility, and affordability of child care options (Smolensky & Gootman, 2003).

The types of child care most often used for infants and toddlers (younger than age 3) are relatives, family day-care homes (care in the home of a nonrelative), and day-care centers. Preschoolers (age 3 to 4) are most frequently cared for in a child-care center or by relatives. The most common types of care (excluding self-care) for school-age children (ages 6 to 12) are family day-care homes and relatives (see Figure 5.3). A most striking trend, however, is the substantial growth in use of center-based care for children of all ages, especially by mothers who are employed full-time (Hofferth, 1996; Smolensky & Gootman, 2003).

If center-based care is the trend, how can such child-care options be increased? For families, the communities in which they live, the government to which they pay taxes, and the businesses where they are employed must make a commitment to provide quality child care.

SCHOOL AND COMMUNITY INVOLVEMENT IN CHILD CARE

One way to increase child-care options is for the elementary school to extend the hours it is normally in session and extend its services to include children younger than age 5. A majority of school-age children whose parents are employed care for themselves before and after school. Other children may be cared for by a neighbor. Still others may participate in a community program. Unsupervised children, contrary to popular belief, are not most likely to be found in impoverished, minority communities; rather, self-care is most common when mothers work full-time and parents are divorced or separated, regardless of income (Lamb, 2000). Indeed, extended day care can be an

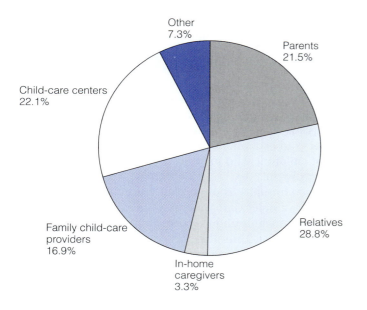

Other
7.3%

Parents
21.5%

Child-care centers
22.1%

Family child-care
providers
16.9%

In-home
caregivers
3.3%

Relatives
28.8%

Figure 5.3

Who's Caring for the Children?

Source: Children's Defense Fund, 2005

effective link among child, family, and school as it complements, supports, and extends the school's educational purposes and supports the family in its education and nurturance of children. To illustrate, according to Schorr (1997), Edward Zigler, one of the founders of Head Start, envisioned the schools of the 21st century to include full day care and be the hub of social services for families. Bowling Park Elementary School in Norfolk, Virginia, is such a school. It includes infants and preschoolers and their parents, responding to family needs. A breakfast club provides an opportunity for parents to discuss parenting issues, children's books, and other matters, and adult education courses are offered. The concept is for children to feel connected to people who care.

Another extended day-care program that is a cooperative community venture involves the public schools in some cities and the YMCA. The school district provides several schools as sites for the program. The Y provides the trained recreational leaders and transportation—if an extended program is not available at their school, children are bused to a nearby extended day-care site after school. The male and female recreational leaders provide care that promotes the physical, social, emotional, and cognitive development of children. Games, crafts, and help with homework are some of the activities. An added bonus of this program for some children is the opportunity to develop a relationship with a male role model. Such opportunities are important for children living with single mothers.

Adult-supervised extended day care is important in light of research that found both boys and girls in fifth through ninth grade to be more susceptible to peer pressure when they were in an after-school situation in which there was no consistent adult control (Lamb, 2000; Smolensky & Gootman, 2003; Steinberg, 1986).

It is often assumed that children in home settings are experiencing caregiving from one or more adults who are committed to meeting the child's needs and capable of supervising safe, developmentally appropriate activities. This assumption is invalid in many homes. Data from the U.S. Census Bureau (2003) indicate that about 5 million children ages 5 to 14 are left alone to care for themselves outside of school hours while their parents work. There is no exact number of children under age 5 who are left alone all day, but a significant number are cared for by a sibling under age 14. Children who are unsupervised by adults after school (sometimes referred to as **latchkey children** because they carry keys to let themselves into their homes) are more likely to become involved in antisocial acts in their neighborhoods than children who attend an after-school program (Levanthal & Brooks-Gunn, 2000; Steinberg, 1986; Vandell & Su, 1999). Children involved in self-care are discussed in Chapter 10.

Child care affects not only the child and the family but the community as well, exemplifying mesosystem linkages. Thus, when examining the effects of child care on the community, one must ask the question: How does day care affect those children whose families' other alternatives are no care or inadequate care? Only then can one make a responsible decision regarding the economic cost of child care to the community versus the social (and economic) costs to the community resulting from inadequate socialization of children, who may need government social services such as welfare when they grow up.

The quality of family life in a community is often elevated by the provision of child care (Garbarino, 1992). For example, Garbarino and Sherman (1980) found that support for child care in certain neighborhoods correlated significantly with a lower incidence of child abuse and neglect. Thus, the effect of child care on the community was that it helped prevent child maltreatment and, in so doing, resulted in a reduced need for more costly government social services to protect at-risk children, such as foster care.

latchkey children
children who carry their own key and let themselves into their homes

Finally, child care affects the economics of the community by enabling adults to work. In some societies—for example, China, France, and Belgium—the government totally supports, through tax funds, child care for this purpose. Likewise, some American businesses have become involved in supporting child care to attract and keep their employees (Smolensky & Gootman, 2003).

The question "Is child care a public, private, or individual concern?" remains unresolved in the United States. Who will pay? If child-care needs in the United States are so great, why is cost such a problem? Child-care costs depend on the age of the child, whether the care is part- or full-time, and the type of care. Next to housing, food, and taxes, child care is parents' biggest expense.

GOVERNMENT AND BUSINESS INVOLVEMENT IN CHILD CARE

The current official policy in the United States is that the government will pay for child care for disadvantaged families (defined by specific criteria) and will give tax credits to other families up to a maximum set by Congress. It is less costly for the government to fund child care than to fund other services such as special education, welfare, or programs for juvenile delinquents. Government-subsidized child care enables the parents to work. Also, research shows that certain types of child care have the potential to break the cycle of poverty in which families in need find themselves (Lamb, 2000; Smolensky & Gootman, 2003).

For example, Lynn Karoly (1998) and her colleagues examined nine early intervention programs, including Perry Preschool Project in Ypsilanti, Michigan (Schweinhart & Weikart, 1993). Beginning in 1962, they followed 123 poor African American children for 25 years, from age 3 or 4 to age 27. Compared to nonparticipating peers (children were randomly assigned to groups), children who had attended a "quality preschool" significantly outperformed those who had not. Specifically, the major findings of Karoly's review were the following:

- Gains in emotional or cognitive development for the child, typically in the short run, or improved parent–child relationships
- Improvements in educational process and outcomes for the child
- Increased economic self-sufficiency, initially for the parent and later for the child, through greater labor force participation, higher income, and lower welfare usage
- Reduced levels of criminal activity
- Improvements in health-related indicators, such as child abuse, maternal reproductive health, and maternal substance abuse

Thus, preschool, or early child care, does have lasting effects. It is beneficial for children because it starts them off on a more positive track. From the beginning, they experience greater success in school, which leads to pride in themselves, a greater commitment to school, and less disruptive behavior. Preschool is cost efficient, according to Schweinhart and colleagues (Schweinhart & Weikart, 1993; Schweinhart et al., 2005) and others (Karoly, 1998), because it reduces the need for special education and the likelihood of dropping out of school and ending up on welfare or becoming delinquent (see Figure 5.4). In terms of tax dollars, child care appears to be worth the expense (Karoly, 1998; Schweinhart et al., 2005). Government and business are beginning to agree with the research.

The federal government has recently committed to expanding existing programs, such as Head Start, to include more children. It has given block grants to states to

Figure 5.4

High/Scope Perry Preschool Project: Lifetime Effects

Source: Schweinhart et al., 2005

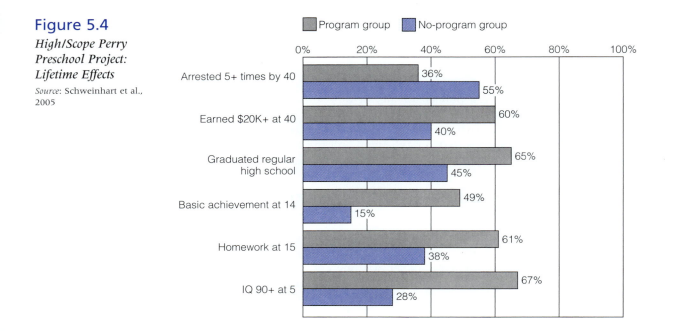

develop programs according to need. For example, North Carolina has the Abcedarian Project, providing individualized learning for children, links with the public schools, and services for families; Georgia has initiated public preschool for all 4-year-old children.

Some businesses provide child-care assistance for their employees, such as parental leaves, flexible scheduling, a list of community resources for parents to choose from (known as "resource and referral"), start-up funds or contributions to a community child-care center in return for preferential admission for employees' children, financial assistance to pay for child care, or on-site child care. It has been found that employer-sponsored day care has several benefits: new employees are easier to recruit, employee absenteeism is lower, employees have a more positive attitude toward their work, and the job turnover is lower (Galinsky, 1981, 1992). In addition, day-care facilities located at a parent's place of work can provide a beneficial link between family and community for children. For example, parents can visit children during breaks, and children can learn about the work their parents do by touring the workplace and meeting employees. Some of the innovations businesses have implemented to support family life are outlined in Table 5.2.

Child Care and Socialization

How do different types of child care and different curriculum affect socialization?

curriculum the goals and objections of an educational program, the teacher's role, the equipment and materials, the space arrangement, the kinds of activities, and the way they are scheduled

As has been discussed, there are different types of child care: care provided by an individual in the child's own home (in-home care), care provided in someone else's home (family day care), and care provided in a center either part- or full-time (center-based care). See Table 5.3 for a summary of the socialization effects of types of child care. Children who care for themselves (latchkey children) are discussed in Chapter 10.

1. Child-care, elder-care, and ill-dependent assistance programs
2. National resource and referral service networks
3. Flextime programs to allow employees to adjust their workdays by as much as two hours in either direction
4. Extended leave-of-absence policies permitting up to a three-year break from full-time employment with part-time work in the second and third years
5. Work-at-home programs
6. Family-issues sensitivity training for managers and supervisors
7. School partnerships, including donations of equipment, time for employees to volunteer, or time for parent–teacher conferences
8. On-site employee-staffed child-care centers
9. Job-sharing programs
10. Parent education seminars

Table 5.2

*Exosystem Link:
Business Support for
Families*

There are also different educational practices, or curriculum models, that are implemented in center-based care. A **curriculum** includes the educational goals and objectives of the program, the teacher's role, the equipment and materials, the space arrangement, the kinds of activities, and the way they are scheduled.

SOCIALIZATION EFFECTS OF DIFFERENT PRESCHOOL PROGRAMS

What are some socialization effects of different preschool programs?

Because many child-care programs, especially center-based ones, follow a curriculum, some examples are briefly described in this chapter, keeping in mind that some programs select only certain facets of the various curriculum models. A curriculum translates theories about learning into action; consequently, different curricula have different socialization effects. Curricula can be generally categorized as **teacher-directed** (learning activities are planned by the teacher for all the children), or **learner-directed** (learning activities emerge from individual interest and teacher guidance). The curriculum models used in child-care programs that we will briefly discuss are the *cognitively oriented curriculum, direct instruction, Montessori,* and *developmental interaction.*

The Cognitively Oriented Curriculum (Learner-Directed)

The **cognitively oriented curriculum**, developed by David Weikart and associates at the High/Scope Educational Research Foundation in Ypsilanti, Michigan, represents an application of Jean Piaget's theory of cognitive development to an educational program. It is classified as "learner-directed" because it attempts to blend the virtues of purposeful teaching with open-ended, child-initiated activities.

Piaget believed that humans adapt mentally to their environments through their interactions or experiences with people, objects, and events. He viewed the child as an active learner who explores, experiments, and plans, thereby constructing knowledge. Learning, or mental adaptation to one's environment, occurs by **assimilation** (incorporating experiences) and by **accommodation** (reconciling differences of experiences). An example of *assimilation* is seeing a bluebird for the first time. The experience is incorporated into one's mental concept of a bird. An example of *accommodation* is seeing a butterfly, calling it a bird, and being told it is not a bird but a butterfly. The experience results in adjusting the original mental concept of butterfly and accommodating the concept that all things that fly are not always

**teacher-directed
curriculum**
a curriculum in which
the learning activities
are planned by the
teacher for all the
children

**learner-directed
curriculum**
a curriculum in which
the learning activities
emerge from individual
interests and teacher
guidance

**cognitively oriented
curriculum**
a curriculum that
attempts to blend the
virtues of purposeful
teaching with
open-ended,
child-initiated activities

assimilation
a Piagetian term for
mental adaptation to
one's environment by
incorporating
experiences

accommodation
a Piagetian term for
mental adaptation to
one's environment by
reconciling differences
of experiences

Table 5.3
Socialization and Types of Quality Child Care[a] for Young Children[b]

	IN-HOME CARE (PRIVATELY FUNDED OR RELATIVE)	FAMILY DAY CARE (PRIVATELY FUNDED)	CENTER-BASED CARE (PRIVATELY AND PUBLICLY FUNDED)
PHYSICAL SETTING	Adult-oriented (valuable and breakable items moved)	Adult-oriented but some specific child materials and play areas	Child-oriented (toys, educational materials, specific areas for play)
CAREGIVER SPECIAL TRAINING	Unlikely	Some	More likely to have had college courses related to and experience with children (especially in public centers)
ADULT–CHILD INTERACTION	Frequent and personal	Close	Mostly adult-directed and shared with other children
ACTIVITIES	Mostly unplanned (generally around housekeeping chores)	Some planned	Planned curricula (group and individual)
PEER INTERACTION	Little	Varied	Much
DEVELOPMENTAL DIFFERENCES (BASED ON A SERIES OF TESTS DONE IN A LABORATORY PLAYROOM AND OBSERVATIONS AT HOME)	Scored lowest on assessments of cognitive ability, social understanding (taking another's perspective and empathy), cooperation, friendliness, and independence from mother	Scored highest on assessments of friendliness; lowest on independence from mother	Scored higher on assessments of cognitive ability, social understanding (taking another's perspective and empathy), cooperation, friendliness, and independence from mother
SOCIALIZATION OUTCOMES (INTERPRETATION OF RESULTS)	One-to-one interaction and training by adult	Experience in complex interactions with children of different ages	Increase in social competence, maturity, intellectual development

[a] These are general differences *between* types of care; there are also differences *within* each type of care (Clarke-Stewart, 1987; Clarke-Stewart & Allhusen, 2002).
[b] Ages 2 to 4.

birds. When one can assimilate *and* accommodate new information, according to Piaget, one is in **equilibrium**, a state of balance, thereby allowing the information to be incorporated. We continually assimilate and accommodate throughout our lives. However, we do not always reach equilibrium. When we cannot accommodate some new information at the time we encounter it, we reject it.

To minimize rejection in a child's learning experiences, Piaget recommends that all new experiences be planned in such a way that a child can make a connection or relationship to previous experiences. The implications of this recommendation for education are significant. If teachers can assess children's cognitive structures through parent conferences, observation, interviews, and tests, they can select appropriate learning activities and tasks that will promote cognitive growth. Otherwise, if a child lacks the cognitive structure for a given task, the child will fail; the new information

equilibrium
a Piagetian term for the state of balance between assimilation and accommodation, thereby allowing knowledge to be incorporated

will be rejected because the child cannot accommodate it at that particular time. For example, 4-year-olds generally have a poor understanding of equality. Thus, trying to convince a preschooler that the piece of cake on his plate is the same size as his sister's, even though a smaller plate makes her piece look larger, will be useless.

In addition to experiences or interactions with people, objects, and events, motivation is also a factor in intellectual development. According to Piaget, all children mature in a certain order. At first, they understand their environment only through their senses and motor abilities that enable them to explore. He called this stage **sensorimotor** (*thinking is action*). It involves only understanding the here and now. As children develop language, they understand that words symbolize objects, but they think everyone understands things as they do. They can also consider only one characteristic of a thing at a time. Piaget called this stage **preoperational** (*thinking is based on appearances*). Children in this stage make judgments based only on how things appear. By the time children reach school age, their understanding of the world expands to incorporate concepts about time, equality, weight, distance, and so on, but their understanding is limited to concrete, or actual, things they can see or manipulate. Piaget called this stage **concrete operations** (*thinking is based on reality*). Whereas children in this stage can apply logical, systematic principles to specific experiences, they still cannot distinguish assumptions or hypotheses from facts or reality. It is not until adolescence that children come to understand abstract concepts such as government and are able to use logical thinking. Piaget called this stage **formal operations** (*thinking is based on abstractions*). In this stage, children can think logically about abstract ideas and hypotheses as well as concrete facts.

In the cognitively oriented curriculum, children are encouraged to become actively involved in constructing their own learning. The teacher observes the children individually, questions and evaluates them, in order to identify their developmental level. Knowing their developmental level enables the teacher to involve children in appropriate activities that they will be capable of accommodating. The teacher organizes the environment so that children can choose from an array of developmentally appropriate materials and activities. The teacher encourages goal setting and problem solving by asking the children to plan what they are going to do and how it is to be done. Meanwhile, the teacher is enabling the children to have key experiences that stimulate thinking processes, language development, and social development. Thus the child learns to make decisions, to set goals, and to solve problems by finding alternatives to plans that did not work out as anticipated (Hohmann & Weikart, 1995). A preschool child's goal might be to build a road with blocks. A third-grader's goal might be to make a book of the planets, with descriptions and drawings.

In a cognitively oriented program, the children's emerging abilities are "broadened and strengthened" rather than "taught." In other words, once an ability is recognized by the teacher, it is nourished by the activities the teacher then provides. Children are not pushed to achieve at another developmental level. They also are not taught facts per se; they learn to think for themselves. Emphasis is placed on self-direction, rather than external reinforcement from others (as emphasized in behavioral programs). For example, a child may choose to make an airplane at the workbench. The teacher asks the child what materials are needed to carry out the project. When the airplane is complete, the teacher asks the child to tell how the airplane was made. A discussion about how airplanes fly might follow.

The Direct Instruction Curriculum (Teacher-Directed)

The **direct instruction curriculum** is based on behaviorist principles of dividing learning tasks into small progressive segments and reinforcing mastery of them.

sensorimotor the first stage of Piaget's theory of cognitive development (ages $1\frac{1}{2}$–2), in which the child uses senses and motor abilities to interact with the environment and understands only the here and now

preoperational the second stage in Piaget's theory of cognitive development (ages 2–7), in which the child uses symbols to represent objects, makes judgments based on appearances, and believes that everyone has the same viewpoint as he or she

concrete operations the third stage in Piaget's theory of cognitive development (ages 7–11), in which the child can apply logical, systematic principles to specific experiences, but cannot distinguish between assumptions or hypotheses and facts or reality

formal operations the fourth stage in Piaget's theory of cognitive development (ages 11 and up), in which the child can think logically about abstract ideas and hypotheses as well as concrete facts

direct instruction curriculum a curriculum based on behaviorist principles

This activity exemplifies one typically found in a teacher-centered classroom, such as direct instruction.

Frank Siteman/Index Stock Imagery

The behaviorist theory of B. F. Skinner (1954) provides the foundation for the direct instruction curriculum. *Behaviorism*, introduced in Chapter 4, is the doctrine that observed behavior, rather than what exists in the mind, provides the only valid data for psychology. The direct instruction curriculum would be classified as "teacher-directed." Also known as academic preschool, the curriculum was initially developed at the University of Illinois by Carl Bereiter and Siegfried Engelmann. It was later elaborated by Engelmann and Wesley Becker at the University of Oregon. The program was based on the idea that waiting for children to become academically ready was not a very sound educational practice, especially for children from lower socioeconomic groups. Those who subscribe to behaviorism believe that it is possible to ensure learning and that the school can create readiness through behavioral principles of reinforcement and individualized instruction, whatever the IQ or background of the child. Therefore, in the behavioral approach to education, learning is mastery of specific content. The content and sequence are determined by the teacher or the school—whoever is responsible for planning the curriculum. Learners receive immediate feedback for their responses. Incorrect responses require repetition of the task; correct responses are reinforced, and the learner progresses to the next task.

The Bereiter–Engelmann (1966) preschool program, which was specifically designed for children from low-income families, implements the behavioral approach to learning. Bereiter and Engelmann believe that children from low socioeconomic levels are behind in language development. This lag causes them to have difficulty understanding what is required of them in school. To catch up with their age-mates, they need intense instruction in structured, detailed, sequential skill building. Concepts are organized explicitly and concisely in presentation books for teacher use. All the teacher needs to do is teach the lessons exactly as they are presented in the book. The Bereiter–Engelmann program also prescribes classroom management techniques, such as rewarding students for correct responses, instructional pacing techniques (how much time to spend on a topic or with a child), and group management—for example, using hand signals to cue students to respond. The program is designed to foster IQ gain and improve achievement test performance in the early school years (Horowitz & Paden, 1973).

A revised form of the Bereiter–Engelmann program for use in elementary schools is the Engelmann–Becker program. It stresses hard work, focused attention, and achievement in reading, language, and arithmetic. The direct instruction curriculum uses few of the play materials normally seen in many early childhood programs. The reason for this is to minimize environmental distractions that could tempt the children to leave the task at hand and explore. Children are expected to be quiet, respond to the teacher, and not interrupt or leave their seats without permission.

The Montessori Curriculum (Learner-Directed)

Dr. Maria Montessori was a physician in Italy at the turn of the century. She developed methods of working with children who were mentally retarded and later adapted them for use with children of normal intelligence in her *Casa del Bambini*.

Her principles of education were described in a journal in the United States in 1909 and eventually became very popular in many parts of the world. Trainers were sent to her school to learn her methods and apply them in early childhood programs. However, philosophical differences in the United States prevented Montessori's curriculum from "taking off." In the 1960s, interest in the Montessori curriculum by parents and teachers was renewed.

Montessori (1967) believed that children should be respected and treated as individuals and that adults should not impose their ideas and wishes on them. Children must educate themselves. The Montessori curriculum is classified as "learner-directed."

Children naturally absorb knowledge just by living. However, there are sensitive periods when children absorb knowledge most easily. The role of the adult should be to recognize these sensitive periods and prepare the children's environment for the optimum use of these periods of learning (Montessori, 1967). In order for teachers to take advantage of these sensitive periods, they must be keen observers of children's behavior. They also have to know when to encourage the child, when to divert the child, and when to leave the child alone.

A **Montessori curriculum** involves children of different ages. The teacher, called a directress or director, prepares the classroom environment for the children so that the children can do things independently, thereby facilitating individual self-directed learning. Sometimes the younger children learn from the older ones. The teacher introduces materials to the children by demonstrating the correct way to use them. The children are then free to choose any materials with which they wish to work. Children work on the floor or on child-sized furniture. The Montessori program provides material designed for exercises in daily living, sensory development, and academic development (Miller & Dyer, 1975). Exercises in daily living include gardening, setting the table, buttoning buttons, and folding clothes. Sensory development includes work with shapes, graduated cylinders, blocks, and puzzles. Academic materials include large letters, beads and rods for counting, and equipment for learning about size, weight, and volume. All the materials are designed in such a way that children can determine whether they have succeeded in using them properly. Reward for success or reprimand for failure is nonexistent in a Montessori school (unlike behavioral programs). Rather, each child is encouraged to persist as long as possible on a chosen task because each child is respected as a competent learner.

The Montessori curriculum fosters reality training. For example, toys such as replicas of furniture or dress-ups are not included. Children use real things instead of play things and do real tasks, such as setting the table with real silverware and ironing with a real iron.

Only one of each type of equipment is provided in a Montessori classroom. A child must wait until the child using a particular piece of equipment is finished. The intent of this is to help children learn to respect the work of others and cope with the realities of life.

The Developmental Interaction Curriculum (Learner-Directed)

The Bank Street curriculum, developed by Elizabeth Gilkeson and associates at the Bank Street College of Education in New York City in 1919, focuses on the development of self-confidence, responsiveness, inventiveness, and productivity (Gilkeson & Bowman, 1976). It is classified as "learner-directed." The program is also referred to as the **developmental interaction curriculum** because it is individualized in relation to each child's stage of development, while providing many opportunities for children to interact and become involved with peers and adults. The curriculum was influenced by the writings of John Dewey (1944), who believed that children are

Montessori curriculum
a curriculum based on individual self-directed learning with the teacher as facilitator; materials provide exercises in daily living, sensory development, and academic development

developmental interaction curriculum
a curriculum that is individualized in relation to each child's stage of development while providing many opportunities for children to interact with peers and adults

naturally curious and learn by exploring their environment, and Sigmund Freud (1938), who believed the interactions in the first five years of a child's life are significant in forming the child's personality.

The curriculum is designed to help children understand more fully what is already known to them. Learning is organized around children's own experience bases. Gradually, children's orbit of knowledge and understanding is enlarged by enabling children to explore in greater depth things already familiar to them. Teachers must continually assess children's progress in order to challenge children to experience new levels of complexity (a feature similar to the Montessori curriculum).

The classroom is arranged to include a variety of interest centers where children can pursue special projects, ample storage space giving children easy access to materials, a quiet area for reading, a library, musical instruments, and art materials. There are also places for the care of animals and plants.

All areas of the curriculum are integrated through the development of themes or units—for example, community helpers, animals, seeds, and so on. Concepts are built around the theme. For example, seeds grow into plants such as wheat; plants such as wheat are used to make ingredients for food such as flour; ingredients are combined and cooked to make food such as bread. Activities are built around the concepts. For example, children might plant seeds and bake bread. The activities lead to other learning engagements. For example, cooking leads to math—measuring, counting, adding, weighing. Children might look at books about seeds, take a trip to a bakery, and so on. Motivation to learn comes from the pleasure inherent in the activities themselves; extrinsic rewards, such as praise or tokens commonly used in behavioral programs, are generally not used in the Bank Street curriculum to influence children's learning, choice of activities, or behavior. The teacher gains the children's cooperation by showing care, concern, and support.

How do the child outcomes of the different curriculum models compare?

Research results showed that children from the *teacher-directed programs* (where there was more drill, practice, direct praise for good work, and time spent in reading and math activities) scored higher on reading and math achievement tests. They also showed more persistence in the ability to do this kind of work. They took responsibility for their failures. Children from the *learner-directed programs* (where there were more varied materials, more opportunities for choice and exploration, and more interpersonal contact) scored higher on the nonverbal reasoning and problem-solving tasks. They also expressed responsibility for their successes. The children from these classrooms were involved in more cooperative work with other children and were more independent (Miller & Dyer, 1975; Schweinhart & Weikart, 1993; Schweinhart, Weikart, & Larner, 1986a; Stallings, 1974).

SOCIALIZATION EFFECTS OF CHILD-CARE IDEOLOGIES

How do concepts of child rearing affect socialization practices in child care?

ideology concepts about human life and behavior

An **ideology** involves concepts about human life and behavior. It has been well documented, as discussed in past chapters, that cultural or ethnic ideology influences socialization practices. People from different cultural and economic backgrounds hold different views of what constitutes appropriate child care (Epps & Jackson, 2000; Honig, 2002); yet much of the existing literature on child-care practices has been focused on a monocultural model of optimum care (Bromer, 1999; Greenfield, Keller, Fuligni, & Maynard, 2003; Miller, 1989).

In a study examining the nature of early socialization in quality day-care centers serving infants and toddlers from families of different social classes, Miller (1989) found differences in language and social interaction according to the socioeconomic status of the center's clientele. She also discovered that parents tend to seek out and employ caregivers outside the family whose child-care ideologies generally match theirs.

Miller's study included Center A (Alphabet Academy), which served a relatively low-income clientele, mostly working-class; Center B (Balloons and Bunnies Learning Center), which served a clientele with modest incomes, mostly middle-class; Center C (Color-Coordinated Country Day School), which served a highly educated professional clientele with affluent means; and Center E (Le Exclusive Enfants School), which served an elite, very wealthy clientele, mostly executives. Miller focused on the verbal interactions and role expectations between adults and children because language, according to Bernstein (1961), mediates and is mediated by one's perception of reality as well as one's social role. Thus, the language of caregivers who spend much of the day talking and responding to children has an impact on the development of values, roles, and culture-specific behaviors.

Caregivers in the centers gave evidence of differing perceptions of babies' needs (Miller, 1989). In Centers A and E, crying was not necessarily perceived to indicate a need, so it wasn't responded to as such. For example, in Center A, a baby who cried for days was said to have just wanted her mama. A bottle or pacifier was not given to soothe the baby because it was not allowed. The attitude was that the children "holler for a few days and then they forget about them [their mothers]." In Center E, crying was perceived as a simple annoyance typical of babies; it was sometimes indulged and sometimes ignored. In Centers B and C, crying was almost always perceived to indicate a need. In Center B, whenever several babies started to cry, they were said to be either hungry or tired, although not much was done except telling the babies to stop. In Center C, when a baby cried, the adults were responsible for finding a solution; if nothing they came up with worked, the parents were called.

According to Miller, the caregivers' response to babies' crying represents the world as they perceive it. If the world appears to be warm, gentle, and compliant, that is the way they interact with the children—meeting their needs, comforting, and giving verbal encouragement ("You'll be fine; I'm here now"). If, on the other hand, caregivers perceive the world to be cold, hard, and unbending, they respond to children with epithets ("You scaredy-cat," "You naughty boy"), pointing out their failures and denying indulgences as a way of habituating and protecting them from future hurts and disappointments and avoiding false expectations. A child socialized to existence in a setting of poverty and inequality may have low expectations and low self-esteem but highly effective coping skills. The child socialized to exist in a protected, middle-class environment may be confident, verbal, and creative, but unprepared for life's daily hazards, especially when the real world proves colder and harder than expected.

That humans replicate for their children their own perceptions of social reality, based on their experiences in the larger society, was demonstrated by the different expectations communicated to children by caregivers in Miller's study (1989). For example, although both the low-socioeconomic and the high-socioeconomic day-care providers reported that they would have toddlers "clean up" spilled milk, the low-socioeconomic caregiver said she would "make" them clean it up and the high-socioeconomic caregiver said she would "invite" them to do it.

In Center C—the center serving affluent, highly educated professional/managerial parents (doctors, lawyers, professors)—there was a high level of give and take among caregivers and children. Children negotiated with caregivers for autonomy when caregivers made demands. Caregivers regarded a child's resistance as an indication that perhaps their expectations were unwarranted or the child's primary needs were not being met. Thus, the caregiver adjusted her expectations and demands to gain the child's cooperation. Children were treated with respect. Since achievement of responsible independence was a goal for children in Center C, the rights and interests of individual children were the focal point of curriculum decisions. These children were being socialized to fit into the world of their privileged parents, who were primarily employed in self-directed, creative, and highly respected occupations.

In Center E—the center serving primarily very wealthy, elite, executive parents—children's measurable performance on academic tasks was the focal point of curriculum decisions. Children were positively reinforced for absorbing as much memorized information as they could reasonably handle via abstract symbols for quantities, etters, and geometric shapes. Adults controlled most of the use of time, space, and objects. Children who resisted authority demands were at first ignored, then firmly redirected if they persisted. Caregivers valued compliance, receptivity, and attentiveness, as well as high-quality performance. These caregivers were socializing the children to fit into their parents' world, in which compliance, loyalty to the company, and ability to perform on cue help one rise through the hierarchy of power and money.

In Center B—the center serving families of middle socioeconomic status—children were expected to depend on caregivers, compete with peers for attention, and take circumstances in stride. Children's resistance to caregivers' demands was tolerated. Safety, avoidance of conflict, adherence to set routines, and maintenance of the status quo seemed to be the criteria for curriculum decisions. The attitude was that development and learning would take their normal courses in a safe, nurturing environment. Here again, these caregivers were socializing the children to fit into their parents' world. These parents were middle-level supervisors in factories, small business owners, and participants in other occupations in which one may be less able to control one's work circumstances and more at the mercy of one's superiors or economic trends. Occupational success in such circumstances may depend on avoidance of conflict and adherence to set procedures.

In Center A—the center serving mainly semiskilled and unskilled, working-class families—children were treated as underlings with few rights. Teachers were to be obeyed without question, even though resistance was expected. Resistance was arbitrarily punished. Conformity and group cohesion along with rote memorization were the bases for curriculum decisions. The children were not overprotected or directly controlled during rowdy physical playtimes. These children were adept in dealing with the physical environment. They had learned to cope with environmental dangers, long periods of boredom, and lack of material resources. They learned to tolerate discomfort, care for the physical needs of one another, suppress impulses, and passively resist authority. They also became used to punishment, becoming impervious to it. Academic work was passive and drudging. These children were being socialized to live in their parents' world, which generally consisted of doing menial and repetitive work while being at the mercy of forces outside their grasp.

The significance of Miller's description of socialization in child-care facilities for children under age 3 is its attempt to analyze different cultural ideologies that may be typical of various socioeconomic statuses and may unwittingly contribute to structures of social inequity in the larger society. Also, when nonparental child care complements family ideology and behavior, it is more likely to be beneficial for the child; when it differs, it is more likely to be harmful (Lamb, 2000). This was also found to apply to differences between caregiver and parental attitudes regarding child-rearing practices—for example, authoritative versus authoritarian (Ghazvini & Mullis, 2002).

Developmentally Appropriate Caregiving

What does knowledge of child development have to do with teaching?

Maturation refers to developmental changes associated with the biological process of aging. There are individual differences within the "average" ages at which children reach certain developmental milestones, such as walking, talking, and controlling bladder and bowels. Maturation is a significant factor in being "ready" to learn.

Caregivers or teachers who implement developmentally appropriate practices "must know about child development and the implications of this knowledge for how to teach, the content of the curriculum—what to teach and when—how to assess what children have learned, and how to adapt curriculum and instruction to children's individual strengths, needs, and interests. Further, they must know the particular children they teach and their families and be knowledgeable as well about the social and cultural context" (Bredekamp & Copple, 1997, p. 16). Some aspects of developmentally appropriate caregiving involve observation, sensitivity to children's needs, and responsiveness. Teachers create a stimulating environment, plan engaging activities, enable children to initiate learning, and facilitate self-regulatory behavior in children. In order to enhance children's development, ongoing assessment of their learning must take place and be reflected in the planned activities. Collaboration with families is essential.

COLLABORATIVE CAREGIVING

How can caregivers work with parents for optimal child outcomes?

To provide a beneficial caregiving environment for children, it is critical for professionals who care for infants and children to collaborate with families regarding ideologies and socialization goals (Bromer, 1999; Greenfield & Suzuki, 1998). At opposite ends of a continuum are cultural frameworks (ideologies) for socialization, *individualism* versus *collectivism* (see Figure 5.5). The primary goal in an individualistic society is independence. Children are encouraged to be autonomous and self-fulfilled; social responsibilities are motivated by personal choice. The primary goal in a collectivistic society is interdependence. Children are encouraged to be subordinate and responsible in relating to others; achievements are motivated in terms of service to the group, usually the family (Greenfield & Suzuki, 1998). In a diverse society, such as the United States, both parents and caregivers represent different degrees of individualism and collectivism. These differences can be observed in such attitudes as sleeping arrangements (Should the baby sleep alone or with its parents?), carrying (Should the baby be carried in a baby carrier close to the mother's body or in an infant seat physically separate from but in view of the mother?), feeding (Should the baby be fed whenever it cries, or should a certain schedule be adhered to?) (Bhavnagri, 1997).

maturation
developmental changes associated with the biological process of aging

Figure 5.5

Dimensions of Cultural Frameworks for Socialization in Caregiving Settings

Source: Adapted from Bromer, 1999

Independence Oriented   **Interdependence Oriented**

	Values	
Individual achievement is valued.		Group cohesiveness is valued.
• Competition is encouraged. • Toys promoting individual enjoyment or mastery are provided. • Self-help skills are reinforced.		• Mutual help is encouraged. • Toys promoting turn taking or collaboration are provided. • Helping others is reinforced.

	Activities	
Object-focused activities are emphasized.		People-focused activities are emphasized.
• Children are stimulated and learn from playing with toys and things. • Babies are put on mats or in playpens to play with things.		• Children are stimulated and learn from observing and interacting with people. • Babies are held by adults most of the time.

	Communication	
Communication of feelings is openly expressive.		Communication of feelings is restricted.
• Children are encouraged to talk about feelings of happiness, sadness, fear, or anger. • Children are permitted to question rules and authority figures.		• Children are expected to subordinate their feelings to promote the harmony of the group. • Children are not permitted to question rules or authority figures.

In this classroom parents and teachers are collaborating in an activity with the children.

Diversity in socialization goals can also be observed in communication styles with infants. An American mother is likely to label objects verbally so the child will learn the names of things in the environment ("That's a car. It's red. Look! It has four wheels."). A Japanese mother is likely to focus more on the sharing of an object than on labeling it ("Here's the car. I give it to you; you give it to me. Thank you!") (Greenfield & Suzuki, 1998).

Perhaps parents and nonparental caregivers should set aside "transition time" when the child enters a child-care setting. During this time, parent and caregiver observe each other interact with the child and discuss socialization goals, methods, and outcomes. Observation and discussion should take place at regular intervals. Evidence for this recommendation comes from a study of child-care facilities in three Canadian cities of major immigrant influx (Bernhard, Lefebvre, Kilbride, Chud, & Lange, 1998). The investigators found that parents and teachers were unaware of their basic differences in socialization goals, particularly regarding respect for authority, social skills, and learning. Also, there were substantial differences over what constitutes appropriate parenting at home. Thus, there need to be more linkages between home and child care in order to provide developmentally appropriate practices for diverse groups of children (Bredekamp & Copple, 1997).

Collaborative caregiving also refers to the support child caregivers can provide to parents because of their knowledge of child development and developmentally appropriate practices. Support includes the following:

- Listening to parents
- Empathizing
- Translating emotional responses into concrete ones that can be acted on
- Modeling methods of guidance and discipline
- Providing opportunities for support groups and parent education
- Enabling the family to link with services in the community

CAREGIVERS AND CHILD PROTECTION

What is the caregiver's legal responsibility in suspected cases of child maltreatment?

Political ideology in the United States (a macrosystem) regarding children is that they should be protected from harm and maltreatment. If the family doesn't do this, then the government must. Child protection laws, such as the Child Abuse Prevention and Treatment Act (CAPTA) of 1974, have been passed. CAPTA defines maltreatment and lists professionals who must report suspected cases to their local child protective agency. Child caregivers and educators are among the mandated reporters. Sometimes caregivers notice that a child's appearance, behavior, or way of interacting differs from that of the other children. Caregivers with child development training and experience are able to recognize deviations from what is considered normal development. Although states vary in their specific definitions of maltreatment and their procedures as to when and how to report it, Table 5.4 lists some general indications of possible maltreatment. Intervention programs are discussed in Chapter 10.

Children who are maltreated do not usually "tell." They may be distrustful of all adults. They are even unlikely to express hatred toward abusing parents. They have little understanding of the parents' behavior.

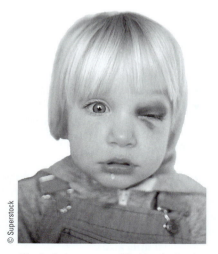

© Superstock

Physical abuse, exemplified by the bruise on this child's eye, must be reported to child protective services.

Table 5.4

Indications of Possible Maltreatment

PHYSICAL ABUSE
Physical Indicators
Bruises
- Unexplained bruises and welts on the face, lips, mouth, torso, back, buttocks, or thighs, which often reflect the shape of the object used to inflict the injury, such as electric cords, belts, buckles, and sticks. ("Normal" bruises or welts do not usually cause lacerations, deep discoloration, or other trauma to the extent that injuries from abuse do.)
- Bruises that regularly appear after absences, weekends, or vacations

Burns
- Burns in unusual places, especially on the soles of the feet, palms of the hands, the back, and the buttocks. (These are often caused by cigars or cigarettes.)
- Burns resembling sock-like or glove-like markings on the hands or feet or "doughnut" burns on the buttocks or genital area. (These burns are caused by forced immersion in scalding liquids.)
- Appliance or tool burns that leave a pattern mark of the object (iron, electric burner, fireplace tool, etc.)
- Rope burns on the arms, legs, neck, or torso. (These appear when children are tied to beds or other structures.)

Fractures and Other Injuries
- Unexplained fractures (particularly to the nose or facial structure) in various stages of healing. Fractures that are a result of child abuse frequently cannot be explained by one episode of trauma. They often have not healed properly and have some additional patterns of stress in terms of growth that are evident upon examination.
- Multiple fractures appearing in different parts of the body (ribs, vertebral compression or spinal fractures)
- Injuries that are in various stages of healing, are clustered, or form regular patterns over the same injured area
- Unexplained swelling of the abdomen, localized tenderness, and constant vomiting
- Human bite marks, especially when they are recurrent and/or appear to be adult size

Behavioral Indicators
- Unexplained behavior patterns, such as fear of adult contact, apprehension when other children cry, fear of parents, or fear of going home
- Chronic tardiness, poor attendance, increased withdrawal, preoccupation, or simply the need to talk to someone
- Inability to establish good peer relations and, often, aggressive acting-out behavior
- Restlessness or inability to sit down

PHYSICAL NEGLECT
Physical Indicators
- Constant hunger
- Poor hygiene
- Inappropriate dress for weather conditions
- Unattended physical or medical needs
- Lack of supervision in especially dangerous situations or activities over long periods of time

Behavioral Indicators
- Alcohol or drug abuse
- Begging for or stealing food; making statements that indicate there is no guardian or parent at home
- Extended stays at school (early arrival or late departure)
- Constant fatigue, listlessness, or falling asleep in class

SEXUAL ABUSE AND EXPLOITATION
Physical Indicators
- Difficulty in walking or sitting
- Torn, stained, or bloody underclothing
- Complaints of pain or itching in the genital area

- Bruises or bleeding in external genital, vaginal, or anal area
- Venereal disease in the genital area, mouth, or eyes

Behavioral Indicators
- Unwillingness to change clothes for gym class or to participate in physical education class
- Bizarre, sophisticated, or unusual sexual behavior or knowledge in younger children, including withdrawal, fantasy, or infantile behavior
- Verbal reports by the child of sexual relations with a caretaker or parent
- Fear of certain people or places
- Withdrawal
- Clinging to parent more than usual
- Behaving like a younger child
- Acting out the abuse with dolls or peers
- Excessive masturbation

Even though sexual abuse is often deceptively nonviolent, it is disabling and emotionally harmful. It involves the employment, use, or coercion of any child to engage in sexually explicit conduct. It includes indecent exposure, obscene phone calls, pornographic pictures (viewing or taking), fondling, oral or genital stimulation, and sexual intercourse. It may begin gradually and continue over a long period of time, or it may occur as rape.

EMOTIONAL ABUSE

Just as physical injuries can scar and incapacitate a child, emotional cruelty can cripple and disable a child emotionally, behaviorally, and intellectually. Individual incidents of emotional abuse are difficult to identify and/or recognize and are, therefore, not mandated reporting situations. However, the interests of the child should be primary, and if it is suspected that the child is suffering from emotional abuse, it should be reported. Furthermore, if there is an indication that emotional abuse is being inflicted willfully and causing unjustifiable mental suffering, reporting is required. Regardless of whether or not the situation is one requiring mandatory reporting, cases should be diverted to some sort of treatment as soon as possible.

Behavioral Indicators
- Withdrawn, depressed, apathetic behavior
- Antisocial or "acting out" behavior
- Displaying other signs of emotional turmoil (repetitive, rhythmic movements, inordinate attention to details, no verbal or physical communication to others)
- Unwittingly making comments about own behavior: "Daddy always tells me I'm bad"

EMOTIONAL DEPRIVATION

Like emotional abuse, emotional deprivation can leave serious scars on a child. It, too, is difficult to recognize or identify, and is only a mandated reporting situation if willfully intended and if serious mental suffering results. However, the same precautions apply. In the best interests of the child, suspected emotional deprivation should be reported and/or referred for some type of intervention treatment.

Physical Indicators
- Speech disorders
- Lag in physical development, frailty, refusal to eat
- Failure to thrive

Behavioral Indicators
- Thumb or lip sucking (habit disorders)
- Constantly "seeking out" or "pestering" other adults for attention and affection
- Attempted suicide
- Antisocial or destructive behavior
- Sleep disorders, inhibition of play, neurotic traits
- Behavior extremes (such as compliant/demanding, passive/aggressive)
- Hysteria, phobias, or compulsive traits

Table 5.4
(continued)

PARENT ATTITUDES

Some noticeable indicators in parental behavior that may indicate abuse are as follows:

- Blaming or belittling the child
- Having an overly defensive or abusive reaction when approached about problems concerning the child
- Exhibiting an apathetic or unresponsive attitude
- Showing little concern about the child, as evidenced by a lack of interest in what child is doing in school and lack of participation by parent or child in school activities
- Finding nothing good or attractive in the child

Sources: Crime Prevention Center, 1988; National Clearinghouse on Child Abuse and Neglect, 2002

Often children believe the abuse occurred because they did something wrong. Thus, they may be confused and even frightened by another adult's concern. They may also worry about their parents' retaliation if they tell (O'Brien, 1984). With this understanding, child caregivers and educators can be involved in identifying, supporting, providing a stable environment, and modeling ways to express feelings appropriately and to resolve conflicts.

Epilogue

Child care is a significant socialization setting. Family involvement is essential to the caregiver in socializing the child; it is thus a collaborative effort. Mary Poppins modeled appropriate practices with the Banks children. Mary was available to the parents as a consultant. She was sensitive, responsive, and stimulating to the children in her care, enabling psychological, social, and cognitive development.

Summary

Child care, or day care, refers to care given to children by persons other than parents during the day or part of the day. It can be at the child's home, at another home, or in a center.

Components of optimal quality care include (1) a caregiver who provides warm, loving care and guidance for the child and works with the family to ensure that the child develops in the best way possible; (2) a setting that keeps the child safe, secure, and healthy; and (3) activities that help the child develop emotionally, socially, mentally, and physically. Quality care is also judged by whether the program is developmentally appropriate.

Objective measures of quality include size of the overall group, caregiver–child ratios, and caregiver training in child development. Voluntary accreditation systems exist nationally to establish higher-quality standards than are required by law for both child-care centers and family day-care homes.

Child care and early childhood educational practices have been affected by macrosystems—political ideology, culture/ethnicity, economics, and science/technology.

Chronosystem influences in child care are evidenced by historical changes in the United States. Child care began in this country as a social service for immigrants who were poor and for mothers employed outside the home. It was mainly custodial. By the 1960s, child-care programs began to flourish because of the increase in mothers of young children entering the labor force and the recognition of the importance of the early childhood years for later development. The focus became more educational. Giving children from low-income families an opportunity to develop learning skills before entering public school also became a priority.

Studies have examined the emotional, social, and intellectual correlates and consequences of child care for the child. Basically, children who attend quality day-care programs do not differ in their attachment to their mothers from children cared for at home. Children in day-care programs differ somewhat from children who are not in day care in their relationships with peers; those in day-care programs tend to be more self-sufficient, outgoing, and aggressive with others. Generally, the intellectual performance of children who attend day care is higher than that of children from similar family backgrounds who did not attend a quality child-care program. This is especially true of children from families of lower socioeconomic status.

A federally funded program for children who are disadvantaged, Head Start, provides intervention to enable such children to enter school ready to learn. The rationale for government intervention comes from research on the importance of early experience for intellectual development, as well as political attitudes regarding prevention of poverty. There are many kinds of intervention programs, but most investigators agree that for the child to become a competent member of society, the child's family must be involved. Also, the earlier and longer the intervention, the better the results.

Mesosystem influence on child care includes links with the school and community. Schools can extend hours to care for children and include those under the age of 5. Child care affects the community as well as families. Child care fosters future contributors to society. Economically, it is less costly to fund child-care programs with tax dollars than it is to fund other services such as special education, welfare, or programs for juvenile delinquents. Child care provides work for adults in the community, thereby contributing economically.

Another mesosystem influence on child care involves links with government and business. Government provides funding of child care and tax credits to families using child care. Business may provide services for their employees, such as leaves, flextime, financial assistance for child care, resources and referrals, in-kind contribution to child-care facilities in the community, and/or on-site care.

Different types of child care (in-home care, family day care, center-based care) have different effects on socialization because of the varying opportunities for interacting with adults, other children, and materials. Having several adults as well as children with whom to interact in a safe, orderly, stimulating environment is related to intellectual and social competence.

Some curriculum models found in preschool programs are cognitively oriented, direct instruction, Montessori, and developmental interaction. Curriculum influences socialization in that the specific skills a program emphasizes are likely to be the ones exhibited by the child. Teacher-directed curricula, such as direct instruction, generally produce children who score higher on achievement tests. Learner-directed curricula, such as Montessori and developmental interaction (as well as the cognitively oriented curriculum), generally tend to foster autonomy, problem-solving skills, and cooperation.

Caregivers influence socialization by their cultural ideologies. These ideologies affect caregivers' language and social interaction with children. Caregivers at child-care centers serving clientele of different socioeconomic statuses were found to have different expectations of children, which in turn affected the socialization practices and outcomes at the centers.

Caregivers or teachers who implement developmentally appropriate practices must know about child development and how to teach curriculum accordingly. To provide a beneficial caregiving environment for children, it is critical for professionals who care for infants and children to collaborate with families regarding socialization goals, including their position along the spectrum of individualism versus collectivism. Collaborative caregiving refers to the support provided to parents based on knowledge and experience.

Political ideology in the United States regarding children is that they should be protected. Caregivers and educators are mandated by law to report child maltreatment, including physical abuse, neglect, sexual abuse and exploitation, and emotional abuse or deprivation.

Activity

PURPOSE To assess the socialization that occurs in the child-care facilities in your community.

1. Look in the phone book and choose two child-care facilities in your community to visit. Note whether they are half- or full-day facilities and whether they serve infants/toddlers, preschoolers, and/or school-agers.
2. Describe each facility—physical setting, teacher–child ratio, ages of children, hours, fees, equipment (outdoor and indoor), toys, and creative materials.
3. Observe the interaction between the adults and the children. Describe.
4. Observe the interaction between the children. Describe.
5. What kind of curriculum is implemented? Describe.
6. Is there parent involvement and/or education in the program? Describe.
7. Are there support services (health, nutrition, counseling, referrals) for families of the enrolled children? Describe.

Related Readings

Baker, A. C., & Manfred-Petitt, L. A. (1998). *Circle of love: Relationships between parents, providers, and children in family child care*. St Paul, MN: Redleaf Press.

Bender, J., Flatter, C. H., & Sorrentino, J. (1998). *Half a childhood: Quality programs for out-of-school hours*. Nashville, TN: School Age Notes.

Besharov, D. J. (1990). *Recognizing child abuse*. New York: Free Press.

Brooks-Gunn, J., Fuligni, A. S., & Berlin, L. J. (Eds.). *Early child development in the 21st century*. New York: Teachers College Press.

Clarke-Stewart, K. A. (1993). *Daycare* (rev. ed.). Cambridge, MA: Harvard University Press.

Cochran, M., & Larner, M. (1990). *Extending families*. Cambridge, MA: Cambridge University Press.

Elkind, D. (1987). *Miseducation: Preschoolers at risk*. New York: Knopf.

Forward, S., & Buck, C. (1988). *Betrayal of innocence* (rev. ed.). New York: Penguin.

Helfer, M. E., Kempe, R. S., & Krugman, R. D. (Eds.). (1999). *The battered child* (5th ed.). Chicago: University of Chicago Press.

Isenberg, J. P., & Jalongo, M. R. (2003). *Major trends and issues in early childhood education* (2nd ed.). New York: Teachers College Press.

Kontos, S. (1992). *Family day care: Out of the shadows and into the limelight*. Washington, DC: National Association for the Education of Young Children.

U.S. Department of Education & U.S. Department of Health and Human Services. (2002). *Teaching our youngest: A guide for preschool teachers and child care and family providers*. Washington, DC: U.S. Government Printing Office.

Chapter 6

Creatas Images/Jupiterimages

Ecology of the School

The direction in which education starts a man will determine his future life.

— **PLATO**

Does learning occur in response to instinct or instruction? Is it a process or a product?

Do children learn best when they pursue their interests and the teacher guides them? Or when the teacher constructs a curriculum and motivates them with rewards (praise, points, grades)?

Plato's quote states the gist of this chapter, and also the next, which is that the school and teacher set the learner on a path of searching for knowledge. Will that path be straightforward, as in assimilating information that can be repeated; or will it branch out, as in accommodating information to solve new problems? The following classic French tale, *Emile*, by Jean Jacques Rousseau (1762), tells of a child's education from infancy to adulthood.

Once Upon a Time   A boy named Emile lived on a country estate. His education was delegated to a tutor who would nurture his natural abilities. Emile was to be exposed to natural things by direct experience, rather than through such societal influences as books and other people's words that might cause him to develop bad habits. His education was to be child-centered and individualistic; the tutor had to be sensitive to Emile's abilities, challenging him to learn more as he was able but not discouraging him with activities beyond his capacity.

Emile would first learn about the world through his senses. According to Rousseau, the senses are the first teachers and, therefore, are more efficient and desirable than formal learning in a schoolroom with a teacher and a curriculum. By observing his environment, Emile would acquire knowledge of nature, geography, and science. Learning would occur because Emile's curiosity would motivate him to find out, for example, how to grow food, where certain places in the world were located, and about the stars and planets.

Emile was encouraged to follow his instinctive curiosity and to express himself as he desired; he was not required to conform to society's morals or the usual formal ways of teaching subjects. Morality would be acquired by experiencing consequences for actions. Rousseau believed that formal education was based on symbols (words, numbers, maps). A child could learn the names of countries and cities but not know how to navigate his way to town without getting lost. Emile would learn by doing—his eyes would be his compass, adding information to his repertoire as he became capable of understanding and as the information became necessary. By the time Emile was 13 years old, he would have enough practical experience to be ready for formal schooling. He would also be able to deal with the "corrupt" influences of government, economics, business, and the arts because, at this age, he would be capable of evaluating information based on real experiences.

The "deschooling" philosophy described in *Emile* is ongoing today. Many children like Emile are being educated at home, because it is legal for parents to take charge of their child's education from kindergarten to college. A primary reason for home schooling is to protect children from the "corrupt" influences of school—drugs, alcohol, sex, and violence. A second reason is to teach values and morals, especially religious ones, that are synonymous with those of the family. Public schools must offer a nonsectarian education. A third reason is to maintain children's natural curiosity to learn. Home schooling enables children's learning to be more individualistic and spontaneous according to their interests. For example, if a child is fascinated with dinosaurs, a trip to the museum is easier to arrange than it would be in a school setting where approval and planning for a class field trip are required.

- **Is learning due to the student or the teacher?**

- **What and how should children learn?**

- **Should content or curiosity drive the curriculum?**

- **Should schools teach society's accumulated knowledge (a "core" curriculum) or stress skills to learn how to learn?**

- **Should individualism or collectivism be fostered?**

The School's Function as a Socializing Agent

What is the purpose of the school from the perspectives of society and the individual?

The school is society's formal institution where learning takes place. This chapter examines the school as a microsystem in which children develop. To better understand the socialization function of the school, macrosystem influences (political ideology, economics, culture/ethnicity, religion, and science/technology) and their changes over time (chronosystem influences) are discussed. Also relevant to understanding the school's function as a socialization agent are the linkages, or mesosystems, between school and family, school and peer group, school and media, and school and community. Figure 6.1 shows an ecological model of the systems involved in the process.

The school's function as a socializing agent is that it provides the intellectual and social experiences from which children develop the skills, knowledge, interests, and attitudes that characterize them as individuals and that shape their abilities to perform adult roles. Schools exert influence on children (1) by their educational policies leading to achievement; (2) by their formal organization, introducing students to authority; and (3) by the social relationships that evolve in the classroom. Some of these influences are intentional, such as instruction in a specific subject; and some are unintentional—for example, competitive grading, possibly leading to low motivation.

Figure 6.1

An Ecological Model of Human Development

The school is a significant influence on the child's development.

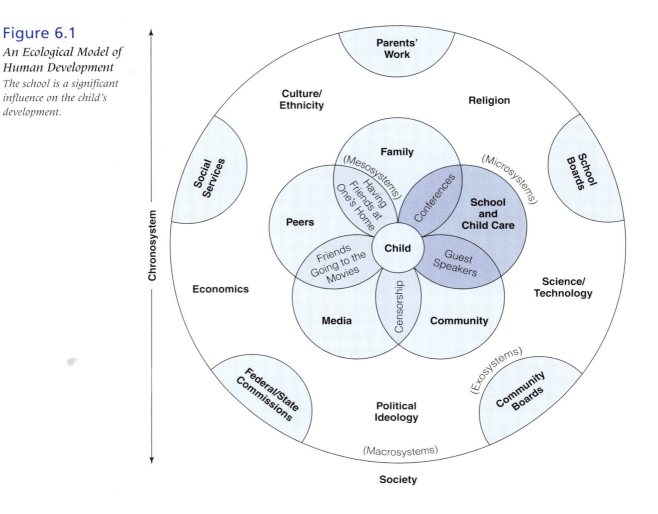

The primary purpose of education, from *society's* perspective, is the transmission of the cultural heritage: the accumulated knowledge, values, beliefs, and customs of the society. To transmit culture and maintain it, society needs trained people who can assume specialized roles as well as develop new knowledge and technology. The purpose of education from the *individual's* perspective is to acquire the necessary skills and knowledge to become self-sufficient and to participate effectively in society.

The school's function in the United States can be described as *universal* in that it is open to all, *formal* in that it is methodical, and *prescriptive* in that it provides directions based on custom. Society's expectations are expressed in goals—academic, vocational, social, civic, cultural, and personal—described more specifically in Table 6.1. These goals emerged from a detailed study of schooling led by John Goodlad (1984) in a sample of communities across the United States representing urban, suburban, and rural areas as well as different socioeconomic statuses. Elementary, junior high, and high schools were included in the observations. Questionnaires were given to teachers, parents, students, and administrators regarding their goals for education.

Table 6.1

Goals for Schooling in the United States

A. Academic Goals
  1. Mastery of basic skills (reading, writing, arithmetic) and fundamental processes (communicating ideas, using information resources)
  2. Intellectual development (accumulate general knowledge; think rationally, independently, and critically; solve problems; be curious)

B. Vocational Goals
  3. Career/vocational education (select a suitable occupation based on interest and abilities, develop appropriate work attitudes and habits, become economically independent and productive)

C. Social, Civic, and Cultural Goals
  4. Interpersonal understanding (various values, relationships, cultures)
  5. Citizenship participation (understand history and representational government, make informed choices, contribute to the welfare of others and the environment)
  6. Enculturation (awareness of values, behavioral norms, traditions, achievements of one's culture and other cultures)
  7. Moral and ethical character (evaluate choices, conduct, develop integrity)

D. Personal Goals
  8. Emotional and physical well-being (develop self-awareness, coping skills, time-management skills, healthy habits, physical fitness)
  9. Creativity and aesthetic expression (develop originality in problem solving, be tolerant of new ideas, appreciate various forms of creativity)
  10. Self-realization (evaluate abilities and limitations, set goals, accept responsibility for decisions made)

Sources: Goodlad, 1984; Johnson, Musial, Hall, Gollnick, & Dupuis, 2004

You and School

What was the *most* significant thing you learned or experienced in school and why?

What was the *least* significant you learned or experienced in school and why?

Macrosystem Influences on Schools

What societal factors play a significant role in how the school functions?

The school reflects macrosystem influences of society—specifically, its traditional values and future goals. The citizens of the society implement these values and goals. In a democratic society, the role of the school is continually debated by its citizens until a consensus is reached regarding funding, curricula, teacher education, class size, attendance requirements, assessment, and so on. Influential macrosystem factors in educational decisions are political ideology, economics, culture/ethnicity, religion, and science/technology.

EDUCATIONAL DECISIONS

On what bases are educational decisions made?

Political Ideology. The basic political ideology for which the United States of America stands is democracy—as Abraham Lincoln put it, "government *of* the people, *by* the people, and *for* the people." A democratic society presumes freedom from government oppression. Citizens in a democratic society, although diverse, are presumed to have equal rights and equal opportunities. As Thomas Jefferson wrote in the Declaration of Independence, "We hold these truths to be self-evident, that all men are created equal, that they are endowed by their Creator with certain unalienable Rights, that among these are Life, Liberty, and the Pursuit of Happiness."

For a democracy to function, its citizens must be educated to discuss and compromise on issues pertaining to them as individuals and as a group. They must be able to select competent leaders to rule by the will of the majority. And they must be able to evaluate the equity of the rules as well as the leaders' implementation of them. Exercising one's right to vote, thereby participating in decision making, is how this occurs. It wasn't until after the Civil War, however, that schooling became public, thereby offering all children, regardless of socioeconomic status, an equal opportunity to be educated and exercise their voice in government. The concept of equality has been expanded since the days of the writing of the Constitution to include race, creed, color, gender, age, national origin, and disability, implemented in various laws discussed in following pertinent sections.

Economics. How much society is willing to pay for the education of its citizens is influenced by values of equality of opportunity, concepts of knowledge and skills required for the future, and affordability of programs and curricula funded by taxes or other public or private resources. Educational policies are generally under the jurisdiction of the states, rather than the federal government; as a result, expenditures per pupil vary widely throughout the country, among and even within states. For example, in 2001–2002, New Jersey, ranked first among the states in per pupil spending for public education, spent about $11,700; Utah, ranked last, spent about $4,900 per pupil (National Center for Education Statistics, 2004). A major cause of school funding inequalities is that most states rely heavily on local property taxes for financing education. Thus, property taxes in wealthier districts usually generate adequate monies, while property taxes in poorer districts do not. Another cause of funding inequalities is a state's policy on school accountability for student learning. Some states, such as California, give "bonus" financial rewards to schools that have boosted students' scores on state achievement tests. To address the achievement gap between disadvantaged students and their peers, Congress passed the "No Child Left Behind Act" in 2001. A main principle of educational reform made schools accountable for student achievement by tying federal funding to standardized test scores.

Culture/Ethnicity. The school serves to impart traditional cultural values through the curriculum as well as via classroom management (Ballantine & Spade, 2004). A challenge facing educators is how to balance equity and assimilation into a common culture with diversity and maintenance of a distinctive heritage or identity. This challenge is exemplified by what information is included in textbooks—for example, including the perspective on Thanksgiving of Native Americans as well as of the colonists who came to America from Europe.

Scientific knowledge is one of the National Education Goals.

Religion. The first amendment to the Constitution guarantees freedom of religion and requires separation of church and state. This means that public schools cannot promote a particular religion, nor can they inhibit religious beliefs. This line has been debated throughout the country's history, as exemplified by such issues as school prayer, appropriate science curriculum, extracurricular activities in public school facilities, and school vouchers (tax rebates to families who choose a private, possibly religious, education instead of a public one).

Science/Technology. Advances in science and technology have affected not only school curricula but the methods of teaching (Oppenheimer, 2003). Technological aids for teaching include television, video or DVD recorders and players, computers, and modems. Children learn how to use such equipment to enhance learning and develop skills. Scientific research on how children process information has broadened teaching methods to include active participation and discovery in addition to passive recitation and rote learning.

SCHOOL CHOICE

What options do parents have regarding the education of their children?

Macrosystem influences can be seen in society's policies regarding school choice. Generally, students are assigned to a public school in the local district where they live. Educational decisions—hiring teachers and staff, curriculum, amount of attendance time required, textbooks, assessment procedures, class size and composition, extracurricular activities, school expenditures, rules and regulations—are made bureaucratically by the school district in compliance with state requirements. The rationale for allowing families to choose among schools include such beliefs as (1) school choice is consistent with a democratic form of government that promotes freedom; (2) choice will foster competition among schools to better educate students; and (3) individual students will be more empowered to succeed in some schools than in others (Olsen & Fuller, 2003).

In the 1970s, as schools accommodated to the federal requirement to desegregate, the concept of magnet schools emerged as one solution to the unpopularity of forced busing of children from their neighborhoods to distant schools to create racial balance. A **magnet school** is a public school that offers special educational programs, such as science, music, or performing arts, and draws students from different neighborhoods by choice.

Many people believe that private schools have more successful educational outcomes than do public schools, because of less bureaucracy, more family involvement, smaller classes, and students' backgrounds (Levine & Levine, 1996). Families who send their children to private school must pay tuition as well as school taxes for public schools. Since the 1970s, there has been much political pressure in various states to give public financial support to private schools. One mechanism is the *tax voucher*—a kind of coupon in the amount the school district would normally spend on that child's education—to be "spent" at whatever school the family chooses, public or private. Supporters claim that in a free market system, private schools should have as much right as public schools to be supported by the government. They argue that the best schools will attract the most students, thereby thriving and multiplying, and the worst schools will be eliminated or will improve to attract "customers" (Tozer et al., 2002).

The voucher system came under legal scrutiny in a court case in Cleveland, Ohio, in 1997, where the system was declared unconstitutional because it violated church–state separation. Most of the vouchers (public money) were being used for religious schools. However, the concept of vouchers as a school choice option is still viable, as evidenced by the No Child Left Behind Act of 2001, which tries to balance flexibility with accountability in schools receiving federal funds under Title I of the Elementary and Secondary Education Act (ESEA). The act gives parents certain rights, such as to inspect instructional material and assessments; it provides guidelines for school choice and vouchers as well as school prayer; and it sets out requirements for funding school improvement, teacher qualifications, and testing. Faith-based and community organizations are now eligible to apply for federal funds.

In response to the controversial nature of vouchers, many states have recently passed legislation to enable families to choose schools for their children—hence the creation of charter schools. A **charter school** is a school that is formed by a group of parents, teachers, or other community members with a shared educational philosophy and that is authorized and funded by a public school district. The charter that is granted states educational goals, methods, and outcomes. Like any other public school, the charter school must meet state educational standards. Charter schools provide entrepreneurial opportunities for those who design the curricula. The school has explicit responsibility for improved achievement, as measured by standardized tests.

Some families, who believe any mechanism involving public school improvement will not benefit their child, choose to provide home-based education. Although specific requirements vary from state to state, generally, home schools must have credentialed teachers and follow a prescribed curriculum. Some home-based education is combined with charter schools. Many families who choose home schooling do so because they believe it is the parents' right to control their children's education and to teach morals and values (usually religious) as they see fit (Kantrowitz & Wingert, 1998).

magnet school
a public school that offers special educational programs, such as science, music, or performing arts, and draws students from different neighborhoods by choice

charter school
a school formed by a group of parents, teachers, or other community members with a shared educational philosophy, that is authorized and funded by a public school district

DIVERSITY AND EQUITY

**How can the school meet the diverse needs of individuals
while also providing everyone with equal opportunities?**

All the macrosystem influences previously discussed relate to how diverse groups
in society, such as those characterized by gender, ethnicity, religion, or disability, are
enabled to have equitable opportunities to achieve. Here we examine the effects of
those macrosystem influences; in the next chapter, we examine how such diverse
groups are treated as part of the student population in the classroom.

Gender

Until 1972 when Title IX of the Education Amendments Act was passed, gender
inequities were common in schools. These inequities included different curriculum
opportunities for males and females (boys took "shop" and girls took "home
economics"), different academic and career advising, different amounts of money
allocated to athletic and extracurricular activities, and different portrayals in textbooks. The opening section of Title IX states:

> No person in the United States shall, on the basis of sex, be excluded from participation
> in, be denied the benefits of, or be subjected to discrimination under any education
> program or activity receiving federal financial assistance.

Every public school and most colleges and universities in the United States are
covered by Title IX, which prohibits discrimination in school admissions, in counseling and guidance, in competitive athletics, in student rules and regulations, and
in access to programs and courses, including vocational education and physical
education. Title IX also applies to sex discrimination in employment practices,
including interviewing and recruitment, hiring and promotion, compensation, job
assignments, and fringe benefits.

Ethnicity

The macrosystem ideology that the school is responsible for socializing ethnically
diverse groups is wedded to American immigration policy; those who live and work
here must learn good citizenship. They must accept democratic values as well as
adhere to the laws and principles of the Constitution.

Macrosystem philosophies regarding how diverse ethnic groups should be socialized, especially by the school, are *cultural assimilation* (microcultures assume attributes
of the macroculture), *melting pot* (all cultures blend into one), and *cultural pluralism*
(micro- and macroculture coexist).

Cultural assimilation is the process whereby a minority cultural group takes on
the characteristics of the dominant cultural group. The school has traditionally served
the socialization needs of the majority culture. For a long time it was felt that in order
for diverse ethnic groups to be assimilated into society, they had to adapt to the majority culture's ways. Examples of assimilation are English as the official language on
public documents, English immersion programs in schools, and celebrating American
holidays. An important influence in this attitude was Elwood P. Cubberley (1919),
a historian of U.S. education and an educational leader. Cubberley advocated an
intensive effort to Americanize the children of immigrants. He held that it was the
obligation of public schools in areas of great immigrant concentrations to assimilate
the children of newcomers into the superior "American race." His view was generally
accepted by school administrators and teachers.

cultural assimilation
the process whereby
a minority cultural
group takes on the
characteristics of the
dominant cultural
group

Later, the idea of America as a **melting pot**—that society should socialize diverse groups to blend into a common culture—became a popular approach to socializing immigrants and ethnic minorities. The melting-pot concept was first expressed by Hector Saint-John de Crevecoeur, who wrote in 1756, "Here in America individuals of all nations are melted into a new race of men" (cited in Krug, 1976). Advocates of the melting-pot theory deplored the hatreds and feuds that the immigrants brought with them from Europe and perpetuated in the United States, but they acknowledged that there was much good in their respective ethnic groups. They believed that the new emerging U.S. culture must be built not on the destruction of the ethnic values and mores of the various immigrant groups, but on their fusion with existing U.S. civilization, which itself was never purely Anglo-Saxon but a product of the interaction of Anglo-Saxon elements with French, Spanish, Dutch, Native American, and African American components.

The melting-pot concept presupposes respect for the ethnic heritage of the immigrants because it accepts their intrinsic values and their potential contribution to the cultural melting process that was—and is—taking place in the United States of America. This process envisions the emergence of a new American people. The melting-pot theorists rejected the idea of Anglo-Saxon superiority expressed by Cubberley and others. In the melting pot, all ethnic groups are equal, all to be reshaped into a new entity.

An example of the melting-pot philosophy is *Esperanto*, a language invented in 1887 for international use. It is based on word roots common to the main European languages. Currently, there is an Esperanto League of Cyberspace. Another example is intermarriage between people of different races or religions.

Today, the socialization of ethnically diverse groups has become associated with **cultural pluralism**, which involves a mutual appreciation and understanding of various cultures and the coexistence in society of different languages, religions, and lifestyles. Kallen (1956) maintained that the dominant culture benefits from coexistence and constant interaction with the cultures of other ethnic groups—in other words, "unity in diversity." The various ethnic groups, or microcultures, should accept and cherish the common elements of U.S. cultural, political, and social mores as represented by the public schools, but they should by their own efforts support supplemental education for their young to preserve their ethnic awareness and values:

> [This philosophy] embraces the ideals of mutual appreciation and understanding of various cultures in society; cooperation of diverse groups; coexistence of different languages, religious beliefs and life styles; and autonomy for each group to work out its own social purposes and future without interfering with the rights of other groups. (Ornstein & Levine, 1982, p. 245)

An example of the socialization philosophy of cultural pluralism is the concept of **bilingual/multicultural education**—education in the student's native language as well as English, respect for the student's culture and ethnicity, and enhancement of the student's self-concept—which will be discussed later.

What is the ideological background for socialization of diverse ethnic groups?

In general, children from ethnically diverse or minority families are much more likely to be poor, and therefore at risk for negative developmental outcomes, than are other children (Coll & Szalacha, 2004). "Minority" refers to an *ascribed*, or given social status, not necessarily a *statistical*, or actual one. Sometimes the label

melting pot the idea that society should socialize diverse groups to blend into a common culture

cultural pluralism mutual appreciation and understanding of various cultures and coexistence in society of different languages, religious beliefs, and lifestyles

bilingual/multicultural education education in the student's native language as well as English, respect for the student's culture and ethnicity, and enhancement of the student's self-concept

"minority" can be a self-fulfilling prophecy (Garcia, 1998). For example, workers from some ethnic minority families find it hard to get work when the economy slows down, and they are usually paid less for the work they do than are Euro-Americans (Levine & Levine, 1996). In addition, the educational level of certain ethnic groups, in general, is lower than that of Euro-Americans (Ballantine & Spade, 2004; Coleman, 1966).

Because education has become a more and more important requisite for success via employability, children from some ethnic minority families are disadvantaged in their quest for the "American dream," equal opportunity to achieve one's inborn potential. In other words, their capacity for achievement is handicapped because of their ascribed social status as minorities in U.S. society. A long history of prejudicial attitudes has been difficult to change. Attitudes will be discussed in Chapter 11.

Until recently, the general philosophy in the United States of socializing ethnic minorities was cultural assimilation. Those who did not learn the English language or "American" ways failed to become effective members of the larger society because they could not achieve in school—which meant that their knowledge of the world about them remained limited, as did the opportunities available to them as adults. Thus, their status remained low.

Various societal responses have attempted to address the unique socialization needs of ethnically diverse groups to enable resiliency and success. Laws have been passed, such as the Civil Rights Act of 1964, that prohibit discrimination on the basis of race, gender, or national origin in public accommodations, federally assisted programs, and private employment. Financial assistance has been allocated to schools and to community programs providing services to ethnic minorities, such as bilingual educational programs. And parents have been required to become involved with the school in the socialization of their children.

Historically, it has been very difficult to break the cycle of inequality of opportunity. Because ethnic minority parents were denied equal political rights, they were not involved in community affairs. They were neither elected to school boards or city councils nor appointed to committees or commissions, which were usually dominated by Euro-Americans. Ethnic minority representation on higher education faculties was rare. Thus, until recently, ethnically diverse groups had no place in decision-making bodies, or in advisory capacities, in government or education. Not only could they not be advocates for themselves, they could not provide leadership role models for their young.

To try to break the cycle of inequality, and as part of President Lyndon Johnson's War on Poverty, the U.S. Office of Education commissioned a study on the equality of educational opportunity. This concern with educational opportunities illustrated society's view in the 1960s regarding its obligation to meet the special socialization needs of ethnic minorities—that diverse groups should have educational opportunities in accordance with their talents and abilities.

James Coleman (1966), a sociologist at Johns Hopkins University, was given prime responsibility for surveying nearly 1 million pupils in 6,000 different schools across the nation to determine whether students were succeeding in accordance with their ability and, if not, why they were not. It was the first study to examine what attributes children bring to school that affect learning, rather than what educational methods the school employs to affect learning (Tozer et al., 2002). This famous survey, known as the Coleman Report, found that nonwhite and white students usually attended different schools. Nonwhites did less well than whites in verbal and nonverbal skills, reading comprehension, arithmetic skills, and general information. The difference became greater as they progressed through school. Coleman found that the school's social composition had the most influence on individual achievement. In other words, children were influenced by their classmates' social class backgrounds and aspirations. African Americans of low socioeconomic status attending school with European Americans of low socioeconomic status did not achieve as well as African Americans of low socioeconomic status attending school with European Americans of middle-class socioeconomic status.

Some interpreted the report as concluding that integration of schools and communities would eventually resolve the problem of unequal achievement. They reasoned that if poor African American children interacted with middle-class European American children, their achievement would improve. Others, who believed that integration was unattainable or would take too long, advocated compensatory education. They reasoned that poor African American children's achievement would improve if they were given more educational and related services, such as tutoring, reading specialists, preschool, and parental participation. As was discussed in Chapter 5, various types of compensatory educational programs appeared in the 1960s, with varying results.

The Coleman Report found a strong association between children's achievement levels and their attitudes, which came from family background, regarding their personal sense of control over their own destiny. Thus, it was felt that parental participation in schools and parental control over educational decision making might make a critical difference in children's achievement. Research (Lazar, 1977; Schorr, 1997; Schorr & Schorr, 1988) has shown that early intervention programs that include parents (participation and education) do result in improved test scores, but these improvements peter out in elementary school unless intervention is continued (Bronfenbrenner, 1977; Levine & Levine, 1996).

Students of ethnically diverse backgrounds who perform poorly in school do so for a number of possible reasons, some linked to ethnicity and others linked to social class (Bennett, 2003; Ornstein & Levine, 1989; Sadker & Sadker, 2003). These reasons include:

1. Inappropriate curricula and instruction. The lessons teachers plan and the kinds of materials teachers have been trained to use are often inappropriate for some children from ethnically diverse groups. Often the children are unfamiliar with the terminology and concepts, and many are unfamiliar with the language.

2. Differences between parental and school norms. The parents of children from ethnically diverse groups are likely to be unfamiliar with school norms and learning experiences. As a result, they are unlikely to reinforce such behaviors as creative thinking, reasoning, and self-direction.

3. Lack of previous success in school. Failure to achieve in the early grades leads to low self-esteem and a lack of feeling of control over what happens in school. Consequently, the motivation to try harder and achieve is diminished. The result may be learned helplessness, or simply giving up. (Motives and attributions will be discussed in Chapter 11.)

4. Teaching difficulties. Teachers of children from ethnically diverse groups often become frustrated by lack of success in the classroom. The students who do not succeed in school can exhibit behavioral problems. This becomes an additional burden for the teacher, especially because most teachers are not adequately trained in dealing with behavioral problems.

5. Teacher perceptions and standards. Because of published data and because of what they may have experienced, teachers of children from ethnically diverse groups are likely to have low expectations. These perceptions often result in a self-fulfilling prophecy; standards are lowered and students' low performance levels are reinforced. In other words, teachers who believe their students cannot learn are less likely to motivate them beyond their current performance level; therefore, the students do not succeed. Teachers who believe that their students can learn are more likely to design appropriate learning experiences that stimulate them to succeed.

6. Segregation. Children from ethnically diverse groups are more likely to attend school with their ethnic minority peers; or if they attend an integrated school, they are more likely to be placed in special classes than are Euro-American children. Consequently, they are reinforced by peers who have similar backgrounds as well as similar educational needs. These peer groups similarly lag in school performance levels. Thus, there is no motivation to succeed among the peer group because high performance by an individual would make that individual different from his or her friends, and the price to be paid for nonconformity—ostracism—is too great for many children to handle.

7. Differences in teacher/student backgrounds. Teachers with middle-class backgrounds may experience particular difficulties in understanding and motivating their students with lower-class backgrounds. Problems may also occur when teachers are from one ethnic group and students are from another. Schools reflect the communities from which they draw their students, as well as those from which they draw their teachers (Garcia, 1998). Sometimes a wide range of socioeconomic statuses is represented in the classroom. Though ethnic minority groups are represented in greater numbers than Euro-Americans in the lower socioeconomic classes, the disparity between oppression and privilege affects all.

The differential treatment of groups of people because of their class background, and the reinforcement of those differences through values and practices of societal institutions such as schools, is known as **classism**. Socioeconomic class, as was discussed in Chapter 3, is based on income, educational attainment, occupation, and power. Where a family falls on the continuum from poor to rich affects the manner in which its members live, how they think and act, and the way that others react to them (Gollnick & Chinn, 2005).

We are all socializing children in "a world of contradictions." On the one hand, children learn that everyone is "created equal" and that each individual has the right to "pursue happiness" (the Declaration of Independence); and that we as a nation are united to provide for the "common good" (the Constitution). On the other hand, in the community, children observe that certain groups of people are exploited while others compete for resources and power. Despite its egalitarian principles, the United States has generally been moving in a direction away from, rather than toward, a more equitable distribution of wealth (Ramsey, 2004).

Dealing with life's inevitable inconveniences is dependent on class. For example, if your car breaks down, do you bring it to a service station for repairs, rent a car, and go about your business? Or do you ask a relative or friend to help you fix it while you depend on others and public transportation to take you where you need to go? When you get sick, do you go to a doctor knowing that whatever the treatment, it will be covered by your insurance? Or do you go to bed and try to heal yourself? Likewise, in the classroom children who have access to books, computers, and trips can navigate more successfully through school projects than those who have few resources at home.

The consequences of classism in school are subtle, but significant. One consequence is that students of lower socioeconomic status are more likely to be assigned

classism the differential treatment of people because of their class background and the reinforcing of those differences through values and practices of societal institutions

to low ability groups in their early years, setting them on a track that is difficult to alter (Gollnick & Chinn, 2005; Levine & Levine, 1996). Another consequence is segregation of peer groups along socioeconomic lines, especially in middle or junior high school (Davidson & Schniedewind, 1992). What possessions students have, what neighborhoods they live in, what clothing they wear, the language and vocabulary they use can all interfere with positive social interaction, thereby reinforcing inequality in society.

How is bilingual/multicultural education an equitable response to diversity?

An increasing number of children from ethnically diverse groups with limited English proficiency (LEP) are attending U.S. schools and are at risk for failure. Research shows that disproportionately high numbers of ethnic minority students enter school unprepared for academic work (Haskins & Rouse, 2005) and do not finish school, and disproportionately high numbers of those who do remain in school are achieving far below their potential (Bennett, 2003). Through legislation, the federal government has tried to equalize opportunities for diverse groups. The basis for a variety of legislative acts and court decisions is Title VI of the Civil Rights Act of 1964, which states that "No person in the United States shall, on the grounds of race, color, or national origin, be excluded from participation in, be denied the benefits of, or be subjected to discrimination under any program or activity receiving federal financial assistance."

In 1974, Congress passed the Equal Educational Opportunity Act requiring schools to take "appropriate action" to overcome the language barriers of students who cannot communicate in English. The Supreme Court decision of 1974 in *Lau* v. *Nichols* held that schools receiving federal funds could not discriminate against children of limited or no English-speaking ability by denying them language training. It ruled that the civil rights of the students involved in the suit had been violated because the school had not provided an equal educational opportunity for them. The court gave school districts a choice of providing instruction in the child's native tongue while learning English (bilingual education), English as a second language (ESL) instruction, or other specialized services. The purpose of bilingual education is to help students achieve both communicative and academic competence (Garcia, 1998).

Many schools have added a multicultural component to bilingual education. A major goal is to prepare culturally literate citizens who can function effectively in their own microculture, other microcultures, and the macroculture (Banks, 2002). We live in a world that is becoming increasingly interdependent with other cultures about which most of us are culturally illiterate. Thus, it is both desirable and necessary that we understand diversity as well as impart this understanding to our children. Multicultural education should meet the needs of all children so that they can progress to their fullest potential in this ever-changing world.

Do bilingual/multicultural programs meet the unique socialization needs of children from ethnically diverse groups? There are still some issues that need to be resolved before this question can be answered. At one end of the continuum are those who believe the language and culture of diverse ethnic groups must be preserved to develop and maintain positive individual and group identity in an equitable society. At the other end of the continuum are those who believe that ethnic minority children will be better prepared to compete in society if they are immersed as soon as possible in English-language instruction. In between are a variety of approaches to enable the LEP student to make the transition from native language to English.

The research on the effects of bilingual/multicultural education is inconclusive. Some studies show that learning in one's native language facilitates achievement in English; others suggest that the earlier a student learns English, the more likely it is that achievement will occur in that language (Sadker & Sadker, 2003). Many factors in addition to language proficiency contribute to a child's success in school—individual learning ability, socioeconomic status, family involvement, and effective teaching, to name a few. The No Child Left Behind Act, with its emphasis on standardized achievement tests, has added to the challenge of teaching LEP students. A response to the lack of clear results from bilingual/multicultural education is the emergence of "English-only" movements across the United States, promoting the passage of state or local laws stating that English is the official language and must be used in public institutions and on public documents.

Students from different ethnic groups have notably different experiences in school. For example, Chinese, Japanese, and some Southeast Asian children have succeeded in American schools, whereas some other Asian, Pacific, and Native American children are less successful (Tharp, 1989). Because teachers are generally from the majority culture and invoke the ways of the majority culture, educational under-achievement by minority groups is usually blamed on incompatibilities between the child's culture and that of the school (Gollnick & Chinn, 2005; Levine & Levine, 1996).

Research indicates that individual learning styles vary; children's learning styles may be related to their ethnic socialization, and teachers should respond accordingly (Banks, 2002). However, teachers often communicate in the style of their own culture. For example, the time a teacher waits for a child to respond to a question and the time the teacher waits before talking again were compared between a Euro-American and a Navajo teacher of the same group of third-grade Navajo students (White & Tharp, 1988). The Navajo teacher waited considerably longer than the Euro-American teacher after the children responded before talking again. What was perceived by the Euro-American teacher as a completed response was often intended by the child as a pause, which the Euro-American teacher had interrupted. In contrast to Navajo students, who preferred long wait times between responses, Native Hawaiian students preferred "negative" wait times; that is, the listener speaks without waiting for the speaker to finish (White & Tharp, 1988). This is often interpreted by teachers from other ethnic groups as rude interruption, but in Hawaiian society it demonstrates involvement and relationship (Tharp, 1989).

Another variation related to ethnic socialization is behavior. For example, European American children are usually taught to look directly at an adult when being spoken to; African American, Mexican American, and Asian American children are often taught to lower their eyes. This behavior may be interpreted as disrespect. Teachers must develop an awareness of how ethnic background affects actions. The next chapter will explore the ecology of teaching a diverse student population.

Religion

As was discussed in Chapter 3, religion is a significant socializing mechanism in the transmission of values and behavior. Traditions, rituals, and religious institutions reinforce the values taught in families.

Religious pluralism flourishes in the United States. There are about 2,000 different religious groups, and with the influx of immigrants from Asia, Africa, and the Middle East, non-Western religions such as Islam, Hinduism, and Buddhism are joining the ranks of Protestantism, Catholicism, and Judaism (Gollnick & Chinn, 2005).

Although political ideology in the United States advocates separation of church and state (including public school), the two often intersect. For example, the phrase "One nation, under God" is now in the Pledge of Allegiance, and the phrase "In God we trust" appears on U.S. currency. The degree to which religious ideologies intersect with public school curricula and policies is significant in the socialization of all children who attend public school. Issues that have been controversial are school prayer, the curriculum (teaching evolution, sex education), censorship of certain books, and the celebration of certain holidays. Teachers need to be sensitive to the values of the families in the community in the context of a diverse society, while at the same time implementing the educational goals of the school district.

Sometimes the line between secular and nonsecular education is a fine one and must be determined by the courts. Legally, schools may teach the Bible as part of the history of literature (as a story), but they may not teach it as religion (as a holy document). Reading of scriptures and reciting prayers is a violation. Public schools may teach the scientific theory of evolution, but not biblical creationism. Dismissing children an hour early from public school for religious instruction is permitted.

How are secular and nonsecular distinguished? Secular deals with worldly experiences, nonsecular with spiritual ones. How can the Bible represent both, yet only be allowed to be taught as literature? Perhaps a quote from the late author Chaim Potok defining literature provides an apt explanation:

> Literature presents you with alternative mappings of the human experience. You see that the experiences of other people and other cultures are as rich, coherent and troubled as your own experiences. They are beset with suffering as yours. Literature is a kind of legitimate voyeurism through the keyhole of language, where you really come to know other people's lives—their anguish, their loves, their passions. (Johnson, 2002, p. B13)

Disability

As a result of changes in the law that reflect public attitudes—that education is a *right*, not a *privilege*—the school has become a designated agent for identifying children with special needs, such as disabilities, and including them in educational activities that are available to all children. Therefore, the attitudes, history, and laws regarding individuals with disabilities are discussed here.

A **disability** refers to the reduction of function or the absence of a particular body part or organ. An **impairment** refers to physical damage or deterioration. A **handicap** is defined as something that hampers a person—a disadvantage or hindrance.

Children with disabilities are those who have been evaluated as having mental retardation, a hearing impairment, deafness, a speech impairment, a visual impairment, a serious emotional disturbance, autism, an orthopedic impairment, another health impairment, deaf–blindness, multiple disabilities, a traumatic brain injury, or specific learning disabilities and who, because of those impairments, need a special education and related services.

The terms *disability* and/or *impairment* are used today instead of *handicap* in order to dispel negative stereotypes. People in wheelchairs are disabled. They are handicapped only when they try to enter a building with steps. A person may be handicapped in one situation but not in another. For example, Ray Charles was handicapped in *reading* music because he was blind. He certainly was not handicapped, however, in *playing* music. Thus, for children with disabilities, the main aim of socialization should be to minimize the effects of their disabilities and to maximize the effects of their abilities.

disability reduction in the functioning of a particular body part or organ, or its absence

impairment physical damage or deterioration

handicap something that hampers a person; a disadvantage, a hindrance

Some common assumptions about individuals with disabilities can affect interaction with them. Assuming that individuals with disabilities are helpless can lead to solicitude or overprotectiveness. The assumption that individuals with disabilities are incapable can lead to ostracism or neglect.

Assumptions and practices that promote the deferential and unequal treatment of people because they are different physically, mentally, or behaviorally is called **handicapism**. The word *handicap* is thought to be derived from the practice of beggars who held "cap in hand" to solicit charity, thereby indicating a dependent position (Biklen & Bogdan, 1977). The media have contributed to certain attitudes associated with disabilities. For example, children's stories tell of evil trolls, hunchbacks, or witches (who are old and deformed in some way), thus promoting an attitude of fear. Though handicapism has a long history, the media today are trying to include people with disabilities in TV shows and advertisements. Teachers need to be sensitive to handicapism and view children as individuals with abilities and disabilities, as applicable.

What is the ideological background for socialization of individuals with disabilities?

Historically, we can delineate four stages of attitudes toward people with disabilities that have affected their socialization (Hallahan & Kauffman, 2002; Kirk, Gallagher, & Anastasiow, 2000):

1. During the pre-Christian era, people with disabilities tended to be banished, neglected, and/or mistreated.
2. During the spread of Christianity, they were protected and pitied.
3. In the 18th and 19th centuries, institutions were established to provide separate education.
4. In the latter part of the 20th century, there was a movement toward accepting people with disabilities and integrating them into the mainstream of society to the fullest extent possible ("full inclusion"). Currently, laws enable individuals with disabilities to receive a free and equal education and to compete for jobs without discrimination.

In the early years of U.S. history, there was no concept of classification according to type of disability. The concept of individual differences, as we know it today, was not understood or appreciated. In those early years, there were no public provisions for people with disabilities. Such individuals were "stored away" in charitable houses or remained at home without educational opportunities.

In the early 1800s, residential schools were established in some states for people with disabilities. Those institutions offered training in a protective environment, often spanning the life of the individual. As the population of the United States increased and as large numbers of people congregated in the growing cities, the population of children with disabilities in any one place also increased. Parents and educators sought ways of keeping children with disabilities in their home communities because residential schools were far away, making it difficult for parents to visit their children. Therefore, in the latter part of the 19th century, special classes were introduced in the public schools.

The most significant influence on the history of special education has been the advocacy of the parents of children with disabilities. They raised money for treatment centers and research. They petitioned government organizations for new legislation that would provide funds for research, professional training, treatment, transportation, financial assistance, community health, and many other related needs.

handicapism
assumptions and practices that promote the deferential and unequal treatment of people because they are different physically, mentally, or behaviorally

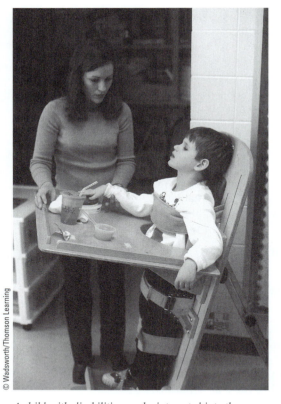

© Wadsworth/Thomson Learning

A child with disabilities can be integrated into the classroom with the support of special equipment and assistance from the teacher.

As the special-class movement grew, so did the research on the effectiveness of special-class placement. Some research indicated that special-class placement provided a more supportive and sheltered social environment for exceptional children, but other researchers found that special-class placement did little to increase children's learning and achievement (Dunlop, 1977).

In 1968, Lloyd Dunn wrote a classic article in the field of special education that drew serious widespread attention to the issue of special-class placement. The article questioned the appropriateness of special classes for many children labeled "educable mentally retarded." Dunn estimated that 60% to 80% of the pupils enrolled in classes for the mildly retarded were from low-socioeconomic-status backgrounds, "including Afro-Americans, American Indians, Mexicans, and Puerto Rican Americans, those from nonstandard English-speaking, broken, disorganized and inadequate homes, and children from other non-middle-class environments" (p. 5). In 1973, Jane Mercer found that among children labeled as retarded by the public schools, there were twice as many African Americans and 4.5 times as many Mexican Americans as might be expected from their proportions in the general population. Conversely, only half as many Euro-American children were labeled as retarded. Were the public schools using the special classes as a dumping ground for children who were not successful in the regular classroom, regardless of the reason?

Studies done during the late 1960s and early 1970s (Avery, 1971; Beez, 1968) indicated that teacher expectations were lower for labeled children than for others. Lowered expectations tend to reduce the chances of reaching optimal developmental capacity. A strong impetus for inclusion of students with disabilities in regular classes came from parents who claimed their children were not developing their full potential in special classes because not much was expected of them—they were receiving a "watered-down" curriculum.

The prevailing attitude up until the mid-1970s was that the school's role was to educate the majority. Thus, any students who might interfere with that role should be isolated if possible, or else not served. Those who were served were put in special classes to be trained by experts. Those who were not served by the public schools generally received no education at all, unless their families could afford a private tutor.

In 1975, Congress passed the Education for All Handicapped Children Act, which required that children with disabilities be educated in a regular public classroom whenever possible. It applied to children ages 3 to 21. In 1986, an amendment was passed to serve children from birth to age 3 in order to minimize the risks of developmental delays because of lack of appropriate services early on. In 1990, the name of the Education for All Handicapped Children Act was changed to the Individuals with Disabilities Education Act. In 1991, the Americans with

Disabilities Act was passed to ensure nondiscriminatory treatment of people with disabilities in areas of their lives such as employment, use of public facilities, transportation, and telecommunications.

How is the Individuals with Disabilities Education Act (IDEA) an equitable response to diversity?

The Individuals with Disabilities Education Act (IDEA), passed in 1990, provides federal money to states and local agencies to educate children with disabilities ages 3 to 21. In 2004, it was modified to conform to applicable requirements of the No Child Left Behind Act and to add requirements for transition services to promote postschool employment or education. Because of the possible effects of early categorization, IDEA allows states to use the category "developmental delay" for preschool children with special needs. Each state has specific criteria and evaluation procedures for determining children's eligibility for early intervention and special services, including what constitutes developmental delay (Wolery & Wilbers, 1994).

Many children are diagnosed early by physicians as having specific conditions, such as cerebral palsy or spina bifida. However, many other children are at risk for developmental delays or disabilities as a result of environmental variables such as abuse, exposure to toxins or disease, or poverty (Wolery & Wilbers, 1994). Such children are often not identified prior to their contact with social workers or teachers. Thus, early childhood professionals are significant identifiers of children with special needs. This identification can occur through informal observations of children, screening with developmental scales, and vision and hearing screening (Meisels & Wasik, 1990).

IDEA requires *nondiscriminatory evaluations*, appropriate to a child's cultural and linguistic background, of whether a child has a disability and, if so, the nature of the disability. A reevaluation must occur every three years. Parental approval is required.

The main purpose of the act is to guarantee that all children with disabilities have available to them a free and appropriate public education. The principal method of guaranteeing the fulfillment of that purpose is the **individualized education program (IEP)**. The IEP is basically a form of communication between the school and the family. It is developed by the group of people responsible for the child's education—the parents, the teacher, and other involved school personnel. Any child receiving special education services must have an IEP, which is generally written at the beginning of each year and reviewed at the end, but can be extended for up to three years in certain cases in which long-term planning is deemed more appropriate. The exact format varies, depending on the particular school district; however, all IEPs must include the following:

1. A statement of the child's present levels of educational performance.
2. A statement of annual goals, including short-term objectives.
3. A statement of the specific special education and related services to be provided to the child, and of the extent of the child's participation in regular education environments, including initiation dates and anticipated duration of services.
4. Required transition services from school to work or continued education (usually by age 14 to 16).
5. Objective criteria, evaluation procedures, and schedules for determining whether instructional objectives are being met.

individualized education program (IEP) a form of communication between school and family, developed by the group of people (teacher, parent, and other involved personnel) responsible for the education of a child with special needs

What is meant by "inclusion"?

Inclusion is the educational philosophy of being part of the whole—that children are entitled to participate fully in their school and community. The IDEA requires that students with disabilities be placed in the *least restrictive environment* (LRE). This means that they should be included in school programs with students who are not disabled to the maximum extent appropriate. Supplementary services such as attendants, tutors, interpreters, transportation, speech pathology and audiology, psychological services, physical and occupational therapy, recreation, and medical and counseling services enable inclusion. Supplementary aids such as wheelchairs, crutches, standing tables, hearing aids, embossed globes, braille dictionaries, and books with enlarged print also enable inclusion. Inclusion can be for the entire day or appropriate portions of the day.

Is the concept of inclusion appropriate for *all* children with disabilities? Some believe in *full inclusion* (Stainback, Stainback, East, & Sapon-Shevin, 1994), advocating appropriate support services as needed by all children. Others believe in *partial inclusion*, providing a continuum of services as well as integration in regular classrooms and regular activities whenever possible. They acknowledge the need for special, supplementary services or even separate schooling, if necessary (Smith & Bassett, 1991). The rationale for the availability of comprehensive special services is that students with disabilities may need more intensive, individualized instruction, and it helps ensure that students without disabilities in the regular classroom get appropriate education (Kaufman, 1989). The debate regarding optimal socialization environments for children with disabilities goes on. Many schools all over the country serving children ages 3 to 21 are experimenting with various educational reforms, especially using peers as socialization agents in an integrated classroom (Fulton, 1994).

Chronosystem Influences on Schools

What societal changes have affected schools?

Chronosystem influences on the school include its adaptation to societal change in general and to specific developments such as new technology, violence, and substance use/abuse. What aspects of past knowledge must be taught for survival in the present, and what coping skills must be taught for survival in the future? With new knowledge being discovered every day, choices have to be made. For example, most jobs being created today require workers who can (1) read, write, and compute at high levels; (2) analyze and interpret data, draw conclusions, and make decisions; and (3) function as part of a team.

From its inception, the public school system was intended to be a vehicle for social change. Schools, however, do not execute their functions in a vacuum. As we discussed, they are affected by macrosystems such as political ideology, economics, culture/ethnicity, religion, and science/technology, and are linked to other microsystems such as the family and community. They must teach children from diverse backgrounds with diverse skills. Therefore, in order to equalize opportunities, schools must implement a variety of programs in addition to basic reading, writing, and arithmetic (Levine & Levine, 1996). "The school has become a potential intervention site for almost every social problem affecting children" (Linney & Seidman, 1989, p. 336).

Schools today are supposed to have preventive programs such as sex education to help students avoid unplanned pregnancies, as well as the spread of AIDS and

inclusion
the educational philosophy that all children are entitled to participate fully in their school and community

other sexually transmitted diseases; health classes that discuss the danger of substance abuse; and conflict resolution to prevent violence. Schools are also supposed to keep up with technology, such as requiring computer literacy.

ADAPTATIONS TO SOCIETAL CHANGE

What changes have occurred in schools?

Elementary schools traditionally taught academic skills and good citizenship. Gradually, development of critical thinking skills, individuality and self-concept, and interpersonal relationship skills crept into the curriculum. The reasons for the gradual changes were many. The classic writings of John Dewey (*Democracy and Education*, 1944), Jean Piaget (*To Understand Is to Invent*, 1976), B. F. Skinner (*The Technology of Teaching*, 1968), and Carl Rogers (*Freedom to Learn*, 1969), to name a few, influenced educational practices. More recently, the work of Lev Vygotsky (*Mind and Society*, 1978) has been adapted for the classroom.

The political climate from the late 1950s to early 1970s was also supportive of change, as evidenced by the passage of legislation providing federal money for new programs. For example, the Economic Opportunity Act of 1964 provided federal money for preschool programs for disadvantaged children, and the Elementary and Secondary Education Acts of 1965 (Title I) provided federal aid to education. As discussed previously, federal funds for bilingual/multicultural education and the education of individuals with disabilities became available. Thus, government support allowed schools to benefit more children by individualizing programs to meet individual needs. During the 1980s, however, federal aid to education was reduced; public education was felt to be the responsibility of the states. That movement, away from what appeared to be a lack of "national purpose" in education, has now turned toward more federal contributions based on school achievement standards (the No Child Left Behind Act of 2001).

A 1983 report, titled *A Nation at Risk: The Imperative for Educational Reform*, by the National Commission on Excellence in Education (NCEE), helped create a public demand for change in the public schools. The report charged that U.S. citizens "have lost sight of the basics of schooling" and that "the educational foundations of our society are presently being eroded by a rising tide of mediocrity that threatens our very future as a nation and a people" (NCEE, 1983). The following were some of the report's recommendations:

- Raise high school graduation requirements for English, math, science, social studies, and computer science.
- Upgrade elementary curriculum.
- Adopt more rigorous academic standards for all educational institutions, using standardized tests to evaluate achievement.

As the 21st century approached, debates regarding the function of school had not changed very much. To address the charges made by the report, government, business, and educational leaders developed six national education goals, announced in 1990 and reconfirmed in 1999 in the Educational Excellence for All Children Act (National Educational Goals Panel, 1999). They stated that by the year 2000:

1. All children in America will start school ready to learn.
2. The high school graduation rate will increase to at least 90%.
3. American students will leave grades 4, 8, and 12 having demonstrated competency in challenging subject matter including English, mathematics, science, history, and

geography; and every school in America will ensure that all students learn to use their minds well, so they may be prepared for responsible citizenship, further learning, and productive employment in our modern economy.

4. American students will be first in the world in science and mathematics achievement.

5. Every adult American will be literate and will possess the knowledge and skills necessary to compete in a global economy and to exercise the rights and responsibilities of citizenship.

6. Every school in America will be free of drugs and violence and will offer a disciplined environment conducive to learning.

The passage of The No Child left Behind Act was intended to motivate schools and students to fulfill the expectations and standards set for them.

In order for any education strategy to be implemented and school socialization to be effective, children must come to school ready to learn. To assess what exactly was involved in "school readiness," the Carnegie Foundation for Advancement in Teaching took on the task of examining the influences of birth, family, child-care arrangements, and workplace and community supports (Boyer, 1991; Shonkoff & Phillips, 2000). Children's readiness to learn is discussed later in the chapter.

Reaching the goals requires significant improvements in a wide range of services for children, including health care, child care, parent education, and family support (Comer, 2004). It also requires many changes in schools, teacher education, and testing. Finally, it requires the involvement of businesses, communities, politicians, colleges, and universities. For example, to address the transition from school to work, especially for high school graduates who don't go to college or those who drop out, some states have established funding for apprenticeship programs in business areas such as health, machine tooling, and entrepreneurship.

TECHNOLOGY

Schooling for the future includes being prepared for the world of work and technological change. Learning to use computers is now essential to successful functioning in society. This is a good example of the impact of a macrosystem (technology) and a chronosystem (change) on a microsystem. Your bank statement is computerized, thereby requiring fewer people to provide you with information in less time. Your doctor may use a computer to assist with a diagnosis. Along with television and telephones, computers have revolutionized communication. Computers enable users who have access to the Internet to get information from anywhere in the world. In response to technological change, most schools (high, middle, elementary, and even preschools) have purchased computers to serve as educational tools.

The computer is an interactive tool that can enhance learning in a variety of subjects. It can present and store information, motivate and reward learners, diagnose and prescribe, provide drill and practice, and individualize instruction (Oppenheimer, 2003). It can support a wide range of learning styles because it enables children to construct their own knowledge (Haugland & Wright, 1997; Papert, 1993). The computer's effectiveness as a tool for learning depends on how it is used by teachers and students, as well as the software selected.

Computers are not really new to education. In the past, computers were used mainly for programmed instruction, which involves reading information and answering questions. Depending on one's responses, one branches into different program areas or goes back for more information and practice. The learning that occurs is determined by reacting to the program rather than discovery by the learner, although sometimes children discover different ways to get the same result by experimenting with different commands. Today, educational software includes interactive games, websites to visit, and discussion groups via e-mail.

How does computer education affect children? Does the computer foster independence at the expense of developing social skills? Does the computer enhance certain skills at the expense of creativity? Computers deal with facts. They do not convey or receive emotions. If computers become a primary medium of communication, especially in school, what happens to the socializing impact of the teacher through attachment and modeling? What happens to other mechanisms of socialization such as reasoning and group pressure?

According to Jane Healy (1991, 1998), the computer provides visual and sometimes auditory stimulation. However, optimal learning occurs, especially for preschoolers, when several senses are involved. The young child needs to manipulate things, as well as see them, in order to construct an understanding of the world.

Computers can be used as an adjunct to regular classroom activities, rather than a replacement. For example, computers can facilitate children's creative writing by using word processing to help simplify the physical aspects of writing, as well as manipulate writing structure (Daiute, 1983). When students don't get stuck on handwriting, spelling, and grammar, they are freer to express thoughts. However, some children exhibit *parallel* thinking (like hypertext) rather than *sequential* thinking (Oppenheimer, 2003). They don't connect their thoughts in a logical way; they just list things without understanding the relationship (Healy, 1991, 1998).

Creating software programs can encourage problem-solving skills and logic. For example, Seymour Papert (1999) developed a system using a computer language called LOGO, in which children learn mathematics by *being* mathematicians. LOGO is programmable, as opposed to direct-manipulation software. By controlling the movements of the "Turtle," the children (as young as age 3) learn about numbers, shapes, velocities, and rates of change, as well as problem solving. Various LOGO programs are used today in school for biology, physics, and driver's education, to name a few (Papert, 1993). Designing computer programs requires the child to think hypothetically. ("If I choose this command, then this will happen.") Programmable software, such as LOGO, enables the user to construct knowledge.

Computers can be used for collaboration and research. Students can network with each other in the classroom on projects. With a telephone hookup, they can access information from libraries, universities, government databases, and any online service subscribed to by their school. With computer-interactive multimedia capabilities, such as graphics, sound, and compact disks, students can "visit" museums, planetariums, and other countries, or go back in history. New software is being developed for learning via computer simulation. For example, the standard biology laboratory experiment of dissecting a dead frog can now be simulated. Some driver education programs start students on computers.

In sum, computers contribute to schooling for the future in that they can individualize instruction to accommodate

© Wadsworth/Thomson Learning

Technological advances affect what and how children learn.

different learning styles; they can be used for routine tasks, thereby freeing teachers to provide more creative ones; they can help develop self-directed learners, logical or hypothetical thinkers, and problem solvers; and they can provide access to infinite information. Parents and teachers must enable children to develop critical thinking skills to evaluate appropriate software, as well as the plethora of information on the Internet. In doing research on the Internet, students must learn to distinguish facts from opinions and reliable resources from unreliable ones.

Finally, computer technology has been used to link home and school or hospital and school for ill children, school to school for specialized instruction, and business to school for "virtual field trips." Such utilization is known as "distance education."

VIOLENCE

The National Academy of Sciences defines **violence** as "behaviors by individuals that intentionally threaten, attempt, or inflict harm on others" (Elders, 1994). Parents, teachers, students, and communities are very concerned about the rise in school violence in recent years. The shootings of 12 students and a teacher in 1999 at Columbine High School in Colorado alerted society to the negative outcomes of being rejected by peers, of being victims of bullying, and most important, of being disengaged from family, school, and community.

To have an optimal environment for learning, schools must be safe. Violence transcends all socioeconomic levels of schools and communities. Its roots are found in a family's dysfunctional way of solving problems, as well as in a community's racism, sexism, classism, and high unemployment. Children who grow up in families that practice spousal or child abuse or neglect are more likely to exhibit aggressive behavior in school. They may also model the violent behavior they see in their neighborhood (Coie & Dodge, 1998; Verdugo, Kuttner, Seidel, Wallace, Sosa, & Faber, 1990). Many believe that the pervasiveness of violence in society and in the media, as along with its portrayal as the normal means of conflict resolution, gives children the message that violence is acceptable and is an effective way to solve problems (Elders, 1994).

The incidence of hate-motivated violence is rising (National Education Association, 2001). The National Association of Education (NEA) defines hate crimes as "offenses motivated by hatred against a victim based on his or her beliefs or mental or physical characteristics, including race, ethnicity, and sexual orientation." Not only has there been an increase in hate incidents in school, but websites targeted to promote intolerance have proliferated. The NEA believes that preventing hate-motivated violence requires a comprehensive, coordinated educational effort in schools and communities, along with federal legislation.

The availability of guns and knives enables anger to be vented physically. Children have turned to gangs and weapons for the protection they believe they have not received from parents, teachers, or community members (Children's Defense Fund, 2004).

Children who grow up in violent communities are at risk for emotional and psychological problems, because growing up in a constant state of fear makes it difficult to establish trust, autonomy, and social competence (Wallach, 1993).

Growing up in an impoverished neighborhood lacking recreational and employment opportunities, as well as successful adult role models, leads to alienation of children. Children do not develop feelings of safety and nurturance; instead, they often develop feelings of hopelessness (National Research Council, 1993), leading to "learned helplessness," a motive to be discussed in more detail in Chapter 11.

violence behaviors that intentionally threaten, attempt, or inflict harm on others

In addition, poverty appears to inhibit the capacity of families to parent and hence to achieve social control over adolescents (Sampson & Laub, 1994). Although violence does occur in suburban and rural communities, it is more prevalent in urban communities (Verdugo et al., 1990).

What is being done? Some schools have hired security guards, installed metal detectors, installed camera surveillance, required students to carry photo identification, and/or given teachers cellular phones, but these are reactive measures to a problem the roots of which lie in a "socially toxic environment." To be proactive and cut those roots, all of a child's ecological systems have to participate.

How can macro-, exo-, meso-, and microsystems work to combat violence?

The *macrosystem*, or government, can implement laws, such as stricter policies on gun control and the portrayal of violence in the media (both of which are objectionable to a significant number of people). It can increase law enforcement in communities. It can provide funding for preventive programs in schools and families. Violence prevention in schools may involve having more counselors available to students and training teachers to intervene with children who are social isolates, bullies, or victims. Violence prevention in families may involve parent education and/or counseling.

The *exosystem*, such as business, can provide jobs, financial assistance to rebuild impoverished communities, and role models for youth. Businesses can support schools by giving time and money, offering opportunities for field trips, providing guest speakers, and funding after-school activities.

The *mesosystem*, exemplified by the link between schools and families, can empower families to share the responsibility for creating a safe school environment (Stomfay-Stitz, 1994). This means accompanying children to and from school and being involved in school activities. The mesosystem, exemplified by the link between communities and families, can provide services to support families (examples will be discussed in Chapter 10), thereby proactively contributing to the prevention of violence.

The *microsystem*, referring here to the school itself, can implement a curricular priority at all grade levels of anger management (learning cues to when angry feelings get out of control and how to deal with them appropriately) and conflict resolution (learning positive strategies to resolve differences). Consistent behavior standards and consequences, as well as academic expectations, must be established. Classes for parents in parenting methods, as well as violence prevention, should be available. Teacher in-service training should include methods for dealing with disruptive or uncooperative behavior before it escalates. Teachers need to be more responsive to bullies, victims, and social outcasts at all school levels. Teacher training should also include working with diverse groups and knowledge of how to connect with appropriate community resources (medical, psychological, and economic). Children should learn to respect differences and be empathetic to others (Verdugo et al., 1990). A two-year study of more than 11,000 first- to sixth-grade students in New York City public schools demonstrated that children whose teachers implemented a conflict resolution curriculum

© Michael Newman/PhotoEdit

School violence has become a national concern. These students must subject to being searched before they can enter the school.

exhibited positive changes in social emotional development. Specifically, these students used negotiation rather than hostile strategies in hypothetical provocative situations (Aber, Brown, & Jones, 2003).

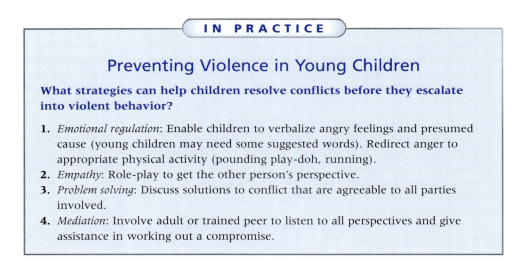

SUBSTANCE USE/ABUSE

Substance use and abuse remain major problems among high schoolers and are increasing among middle schoolers (American Academy of Pediatrics [AAP], 1995). Substances include tobacco, alcohol, and various drugs as well as performance-enhancing supplements. The use of mind- and physical-altering chemicals has dangerous effects on development and deleterious effects on school performance. Students under the influence of such substances are not in a state of readiness to learn, and there may be long-term impairment of cognitive ability and memory. Substance abuse is frequently associated with lack of motivation and self-discipline as well as reduced school attendance (National Commission on Drug-Free Schools, 1990). Substance abuse is also correlated with antisocial and violent behavior. Furthermore, studies indicate that users are more likely to engage in risk-taking behavior and sexual experimentation when under the influence of various substances (AAP, 1995).

The use of substances in school by some students impairs the educational environment for others. Along with the family and community, schools must be involved in dealing with the substance use and abuse problem. The U.S. Department of Health and Human Services (1991) and the U.S. Department of Education (1989) have identified ways for schools to participate in promoting the health of children and preventing substance abuse:

- The school must provide factual information about the harmful effects of drugs.
- Collaboration with parents and community members must occur to support and strengthen students' resistance to substances.
- The school should provide such services as confidential identification, assessment, and referral to appropriate treatment programs for users and abusers.
- Substance use should be monitored within the school, establishing clear guidelines and penalties for usage.

Can schools require students to submit to random drug tests in order to participate in extracurricular activities (such as sports, drama, band, or Academic

Decathlon)? Random drug tests typically involve selecting students at random, calling them out of class, and directing them to a bathroom where they must provide a urine sample in a container. A teacher usually waits outside the bathroom stall and seals the container for transport to the testing lab. The Supreme Court (*Earl v. Board of Education of Tecumseh, Oklahoma, Public School District*, 2002) held that drug testing did not violate students' rights under the Fourth Amendment to be free from warrantless searches. The rationale in the decision was that students in public school are under the temporary custody of the state and, therefore, have limited privacy rights, especially when a search is deemed necessary for their protection.

IN SUMMARY

Macrosystem/Chronosystem Influences on the School

In a changing society, the challenge continually facing educators is, How do you transmit the society's diverse cultural heritage and also prepare individuals for the future?

Political Ideology

Laws mandating equitable funding and programs for diverse groups

Value of equal opportunity, leading to intervention programs for social problems, compensatory programs, financial aid, and scholarships

Achievement and competitiveness issues, resulting in more early academics, an increase in advanced classes in high school, and more work/study programs

Economics

Cost-effectiveness, affecting programs, curricula, class size, and school improvements

Accountability (testing), enhancing preparation of students for future employability

Gender, Ethnicity, Religion, and Disability

Diverse student population, resulting in more individualized approaches to learning

Inclusion, leading to adaptation

Science/Technology

Scientific advances, leading to increased knowledge and new approaches to learning

Computers, resulting in increased access to information and more opportunities for skill development

Violence and Substance Use/Abuse

Safety/security issues vying with privacy rights

Mesosystem Influences on Schools

What linkages are influential in the school's ability to socialize?

Mesosystem influences on the school include its linkages with other ecosystems. Because children in the United States spend approximately 180 days per year for approximately 12 years in school (and more, if they attend preschool), the schools they attend and the teachers they encounter play significant roles in their socialization. The school, in designating programs and curricula, selects which experiences a child will have. In other words, the school determines which aspects of culture are to be transmitted.

By exposing children to different experiences, direct and vicarious, the school opens new avenues to them with which they would not otherwise have come into contact. A direct experience may be having a part in a play, for example. A vicarious experience may be seeing a movie about another country. The effect of these experiences on a child's development is often influenced by the child him- or herself, as well as the child's family, peer group, media experiences, and the community. Whereas the school is the *formal* system in which children learn, children learn *informally* in these other contexts. To optimize the socializing influence of the school, supportive linkages, or mesosystems, must be developed with these other ecosystems.

In *theory*, public education in the United States enables any child, according to his or her abilities, to acquire the skills necessary to fulfill virtually any role in the society. In *reality*, however, today's students are so diverse that educational opportunities are not equal. For example, factors such as family income, family structure, and parents' education have been correlated with grade repetition, special services, and dropping out of school (Haskins & Rouse, 2005). Also, because schools have different resources, different philosophies of education, and different teachers, children's learning abilities are affected accordingly.

SCHOOL–CHILD LINKAGES

Certain psychological characteristics of a child, such as learning style, may determine which type of learning environment is optimal for that child's development (Bennett, 2003; Levine & Levine, 1996). **Learning style** is defined as

> that consistent pattern of behavior and performance by which an individual approaches educational experiences. It is the composite of characteristic cognitive, affective, and physiological behaviors that serve as relatively stable indicators of how a learner perceives, interacts with, and responds to the learning environment. It is formed in the deep structure of neural organization and personality that molds and is molded by human development and the cultural experiences of home, school, and society. (Bennett, 2003, p. 186)

Learning style, then, is an aspect of socialization. How schools and teachers respond to the child's learning style affects the child's educational experience. Learning styles can be observed in children by various criteria. For example, does the child learn best by watching? by listening? by moving his or her body? Does the child achieve more alone or in a group? Is the child better at breaking down a whole task into components (analysis) or relating the components to each other to form a new whole (synthesis)? Is the child motivated by pleasing the teacher? by concrete rewards? by internalized interest? Does the child need much or little structure to carry out a task?

Some schools have given attention to psychologist Howard Gardner's theory of multiple intelligences. Gardner (1999) delineates a variety of intelligences: linguistic, logical/mathematical, spatial, musical, bodily/kinesthetic, interpersonal, intrapersonal, existential, and naturalist. Historically, the schools have focused primarily on linguistic and logical/mathematical. Gardner's theory has significant implications for meeting the individualized needs of various children. For example, different ethnic

learning style
a consistent pattern of behavior and performance by which an individual approaches educational experiences

groups tend to value and develop different areas of intelligence by the way they solve problems. Thus, by assessing children's learning styles and by developing individual learning profiles describing their strengths and weaknesses according to Gardner's categories of intelligences, teachers can empower all children to succeed.

SCHOOL–FAMILY LINKAGES

Socialization of the child begins in the family; the school extends the process by formal education. The outcome of this joint effort depends to a considerable extent on the relationship between family and school. Many research studies, from preschool to elementary school to high school (Cochran & Henderson, 1986; Epstein, 2001; Henderson & Berla, 1994), have provided evidence showing that when schools work together with families to support learning, children tend to succeed in school and afterward. These studies point to family involvement in learning as a more accurate predictor of school achievement than socioeconomic status. Specifically, when families (1) create a home environment that encourages learning, (2) express high (but not unrealistic) expectations for their children's achievement and future careers, and (3) become involved in their children's education at school and in the community, children from low-socioeconomic-status and ethnically diverse families fare comparably to middle-class children.

The effectiveness of the school as a socializing agency depends to a major degree on the kinds of families from which its children come (Coleman, 1966; Jencks, 1979; Levine & Levine, 1996; Sadker & Sadker, 2003). As discussed, the school has been less effective in educating children from low-socioeconomic-status families. Such children, in addition to being poor, are often from ethnic minority groups. The reasons

This parent supervises her child's homework, emphasizing the importance of effort and hard work.

Stock Connection/Jupiterimages

generally attributed for the school's lessened effectiveness are the fewer resources available for education in poor communities, the expectations of the teachers (most teachers are middle class), and the lack of certain preschool experiences expected of children their age by public schools. For example, sitting still at the table when working or eating is generally expected of school-age children. But some children do not have a table at home large enough to accommodate all the family members at one time, so there are no formal sit-down meals; instead, family members eat "on the run." Consequently, these children will have trouble in school until they learn to conform to sitting still and other school-expected behaviors.

It has been demonstrated that the effectiveness of school as a socializing agent depends on the degree of consistency, or supportive linkages, between children's home environment and their educational environment (Haskins & Rouse, 2005; Minuchin & Shapiro, 1983). This may explain why schools are generally less effective in educating children from lower socioeconomic levels. Beginning in the 1960s, the federal government attempted to remedy some of the inequalities in educational opportunities by providing intervention programs for children from lower socioeconomic levels. The rationale behind intervention programs was to provide learning experiences and skills disadvantaged children lacked because of their environments. Most federally funded programs require that schools and families work together.

The school's influence in the socialization process differs according to the value placed on the school by the family (Schaefer, 1991). In other words, if a family believes the school is very important in imparting cultural heritage (accumulated knowledge, values, and so forth) to their children, the family will support the school. The family will tell children that school is important, that school will help them achieve in life, that the teacher knows best. Parents will see that children do their homework and will respond to teachers' requests for behavioral change. Studies have consistently shown that parental involvement is related to the child's school performance and that the parents' education plays a significant role in their desire to be involved (Berger, 2003; Levine & Levine, 1996).

If, however, the family does *not* believe the school is a very significant socializing agent, parents will not take much interest in the work the child brings home. They may ignore the teacher's requests for help to change the child's behavior, and may even relate negative experiences they had at school to the child. Besides a lack of consensus on goals, another problem that may discourage the family from being involved in school is a mismatch in cognitive skills (Hess & Holloway, 1984; Levine & Levine, 1996). For example, the different ways language is used in the community and in school can result in learning problems for the child. A child who communicates in Black English dialect will have difficulty in a classroom where standard English is the norm (Banks, 2002; Heath, 1983).

What are the ways families can become involved in school?

There are three major types of family involvement: (1) decision making—determining school programs and policies; (2) participation—working in the classroom as paid or volunteer instructional assistants; and (3) partnership—providing home guidance to their children to support learning and extend school goals. Yale University psychiatrist Dr. James Comer (2004) found that involving parents of minority children in these three areas overcame parent distrust of the school. Students were viewed as having unmet needs rather than as having behavioral

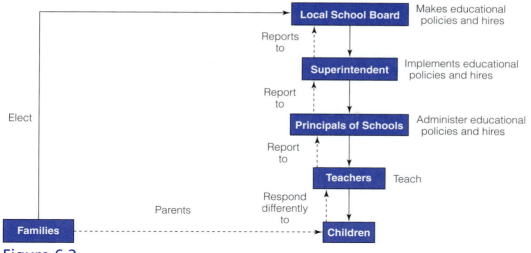

Figure 6.2
Child–Family–School Linkages

problems. The children were served by a mental health team as well as by resource teachers. There was a Crisis Room, where counselors provided positive alternatives to antisocial behavior. There was a Discovery Room, where teachers motivated learning based on children's interests and curiosity. The program thus joined social and intellectual skills. Parents' help was enlisted, and the school became a source of self-esteem and community pride.

Families also become involved in school and education when they vote. They elect people to serve on the local school board to make decisions about educational goals, school facilities, budget allocations, personnel, student standards of achievement and conduct, and evaluation methods. This interaction is indirect, but nonetheless influential (see Figure 6.2). Direct interaction occurs when families go to the school their children attend and talk to the administrators and teachers. For example, schools that have turned around truancy rates dramatically let the students know they care. In some cases, schools use a system in which every student is assigned one teacher to be sure that the student gets to school. The teacher makes wake-up calls and occasionally drops by the child's home on Saturdays to keep up school interest. If there is any sign of reluctance about going to school, the teacher will explore why and, if necessary, refer the student to appropriate social services. Successful schools, then, really work on human connectedness (Epstein, 2001; Steinberg, 1996).

Why is family involvement in schools so important to the school's ability to socialize?

When families are involved, children benefit by having more positive attitudes toward learning, better attendance, fewer placements in special education, better grades, and a greater likelihood of graduating from high school and going to work or continuing their education. When families are involved, they gain confidence in the school, the teacher, and themselves. Often they are motivated to continue their education. The school benefits by having community support, higher teacher morale, and better student achievement.

Thus, the school needs to interact with the family so that socialization goals for the child are complementary rather than contradictory. For example, in several studies of students in the early grades (Darling & Westberg, 2004; Tizard, Schofield, & Hewison, 1982), those children (of all reading levels) who were asked to read to their parents gained in reading skills (a school goal), whereas the control group of children did not.

How can families become involved in school?

The key to forming complementary goals for the child is communication. The school and the family need to talk to each other about their attitudes regarding education and parenting. What are the parents' expectations for the child's achievement and behavior at school? What are the school's expectations for the child's activities at home?

Studies report that parents of young children with some college background and middle to upper socioeconomic status have the most involvement in school (Berger, 2003; Epstein, 1995, 2001). As children progress from elementary school to upper grades, parental contact with school diminishes. Inner-city parents, single parents, dual-earner parents, and parents of secondary school children express the desire to be more involved and frustration with the school and teachers for not being more accessible.

To collaborate with parents and empower them, Indianapolis schools implemented weekly tutoring sessions, assignment monitoring, and workshops that enable parents to learn how to help their underachieving students. The program demonstrated that the school cared about the parents and the success of their children (Hyde, 1992).

However, not all parents are interested in becoming involved in their child's school. Why? Perhaps some disliked school as children, and their attitude prevents them from wanting to communicate with their child's teacher. Some may feel that parents are called to the school only when there is a problem. Perhaps some are so involved with working that they are too tired to make the effort. Or perhaps some parents do not speak English fluently enough to feel comfortable talking to the teacher.

What can the teacher do to break through these barriers? Probably the most effective way to break a barrier to communication is to allay the fears that built up that barrier. If parents will not come to school because they are afraid to hear bad things about their child, make it a habit to send positive notes home and call parents to let them know their child is doing well. If parents are very involved in their work, perhaps they could share their work with the class—visit the class, arrange a trip for the children to visit their workplace, or share information with their child so the child can share it with the class. If the parents' English is limited, invite them to visit the class to see their child's work—let them know that you would like to meet them because you care about their child. Their language facility is unimportant. Provide a translator, if possible.

Basically, parents need confidence, support, and praise. Parenting is work—hard work. In the business world, hard work is recognized by praise from supervisors, salary raises, or commissions, but in the home, the hard work of child rearing often goes unrecognized by the child. A teacher who is able to communicate to parents the positive results of their jobs as parents is, in effect, building their self-esteem and breaking down their doubts about their competence as parents. A teacher who can communicate respect for parents has taken the first step toward motivating the parents to become involved. Sustaining that involvement then depends on the teacher's genuine and constant interest. Workshops for teachers to enhance school–family partnerships are often provided by school districts as in-service training.

What Is Involved in Children's Readiness to Learn?

Illustrating the significance of child, family, and school linkages, the nation's primary educational goal is that all children will come to school "ready to learn." The challenge of reaching this goal for macrosystems, microsystems, and mesosystems is to employ the following strategies (Boyer, 1991, pp. 136–143):

1. *A healthy start.* Good health and good schooling are inextricably interlocked. Every child, to be ready to learn, must have a healthy birth, be well nourished, and be well protected in the early years of life.
2. *Empowered parents.* The home is the first classroom. Parents are the first and most essential teachers. All children, as a readiness requirement, should live in a secure environment where empowered parents encourage language development.
    a. Parents must speak frequently to children and listen to them.
    b. Parents must read to children.
    c. Parents must build a bridge between home and school.
3. *Quality preschool.* Many young children are cared for outside the home. These children need high-quality programs that not only provide good care but also address all dimensions of school readiness.
4. *A responsible workplace.* If each child in America is to come to school ready to learn, we must have workplace policies that are family friendly, offering child-care services and giving parents time to be with their young children.
    a. Provide available leave time.
    b. Have flexible scheduling.
    c. Enable job sharing.
    d. Link with community child-care services.
5. *Television as a teacher.* Next to parents, television is the child's most influential teacher. School readiness requires television programming that is both educational and enriching.
    a. Commercial companies selling children's products should help underwrite quality programs.
    b. Establish a Ready-to-Learn cable channel.
6. *Neighborhoods for learning.* All children need spaces and places for growth and exploration. They need safe and friendly neighborhoods that contribute richly to a child's readiness to learn.
    a. Have well-designed indoor and outdoor parks.
    b. Provide readiness programs in libraries, museums, and zoos.
    c. Establish ready-to-learn centers in malls where college students can volunteer their services.
7. *Connections across the generations.* Connections across the generations will give children a sense of security and continuity, contributing to their school readiness in the fullest sense.
    a. Build bridges between child care and senior citizen centers.
    b. Build bridges between child care and community schools and teachers.

In conclusion, children who are ready to succeed in school are healthy, immunized against disease, well nourished, and well rested. Their early experiences have given them a start in learning to cooperate, exercise self-control, articulate their thoughts and feelings, and follow rules. They are trusting and have a feeling of self-worth. They explore their environment actively and approach tasks with enthusiasm (U.S. Department of Education, 1991).

SCHOOL–PEER GROUP LINKAGES

Children's attitudes about learning can be influenced by the peer group to which they belong. The peer group can thus help or hinder the school's role in socialization.

Brian is not too sure of his status with his peers in class. The high school he attends has a strong tradition of academic excellence and has many intramural scholastic competitions. Brian's peers expect best efforts, which are rewarded by social recognition. Those who lag are put down. Brian works very hard academically to meet the standards of his peer group.

Todd, on the other hand, has a group of friends who believe it is not "cool" to carry books, give evidence of having done homework, or work hard academically. Todd, in choosing a group of friends whose value it is to "keep cool," probably is not working up to his full potential academically.

That peers influence the educational process was demonstrated by Coleman (1961) in his classic study on adolescents in schools. He found that in most high schools, boys value athletic ability and girls value popularity. That this is still true today is evidenced by the labeling of peer groups in junior high school and high school (Kinney, 1993): "brains," "nerds," "jocks," "populars," "normals," "unpopulars." Thus, students who depend on their peers for approval are less likely to endorse school and family values of academic success.

Research has established that under certain circumstances, such as attaining a superordinate goal (a group grade), the use of peers in a cooperative learning setting (students share responsibility for solving academic tasks and preparing reports) increases student achievement more than a teacher-directed setting. In addition, working together in a cooperative learning setting improves student self-esteem, social relations (particularly in the area of ethnic relations), and acceptance of students with disabilities who have been included (Johnson & Johnson, 1999; Slavin, 1991).

SCHOOL–MEDIA LINKAGES

Schools are linked to media through their use in the classroom as well as by media-related experiences outside the classroom that may influence student learning.

Many schools and teachers use the Public Broadcasting System (PBS) to complement their lessons. PBS offers a service called "Teacher Source" that provides educational support for prekindergarten through 12th grade. Schedules of local broadcasting of PBS shows are available online, as are related lesson plans and activities. PBS videos on arts and literature, health and fitness, math, science and technology, social studies, history, and early childhood can be purchased.

An example of media material that can be used with preschoolers is *Barney & Friends*. *Barney & Friends* was developed to address the interests and needs of young children ages 2 to 5. The programs are designed to enhance the cognitive, emotional, social, and physical development of the young child. Music, stories, examples, repetition, and positive reinforcement are some of the techniques used to teach social interaction, cooperation, sharing, language development, and coping with new experiences (such as going to the dentist, moving, and going to school).

An example of media material that can be used with high schoolers is the opera adaptation of Shakespeare's *Romeo and Juliet*. Some activity ideas are to have students research the Shakespearean era, write an opera that addresses a problem, and compare Shakespeare's *Romeo and Juliet* with modern film adaptations.

Many schools and teachers subscribe to Channel One, a for-profit TV news program, including commercials, beamed directly into U.S. schools. Schools participating in Channel One receive satellite dishes, wiring, VCRs, DVDs, and television monitors for each classroom. The programs must be shown in class. They consist of news sprinkled with ads aimed at children (Gatorade, Phisoderm, bubblegum).

SCHOOL–COMMUNITY LINKAGES

Communities allocate resources for schools. They may use tax money to fund school construction or services. They may pass laws requiring builders to include a school in a new housing development. They set school boundaries (districts), thereby influencing the economic and/or ethnic composition of schools.

Generally, large schools are found in large communities, and small schools are found in small communities. Communities with ample budgets can afford to have more schools per capita, hence smaller schools and classes. Studies relating the size of a school to socialization (Barker & Gump, 1964; Lee, 2004; Linney & Seidman, 1989) have found that students in small schools (fewer than 400 students) engage in a greater variety of activities than students in large schools (more than 760 students). Students in small schools also hold more leadership positions than those in large schools. Although there may be more choices of activities in large schools, students have to compete for acceptance to teams and extracurricular activities, such as the newspaper. Consequently, many students don't "try out." Thus, the size of the school influences the kind of socializing experiences students have, because participation in extracurricular activities contributes to leadership skills, responsibility, cognitive and social competence, and personality development. Raywid (1999) found that students attending small schools had higher achievement, better discipline, better attendance, and higher graduation rates than did students attending

© AP/Wide World Photos

Business and media, along with famous entertainers, often link with schools by advertising products, such as Jell-O, and sponsoring activities, such as reading contests.

large schools. Students and families reported more satisfaction with smaller schools. As a result of these studies, some communities have begun to offer schools within schools as a way of reorganizing the administration of existing large schools.

The size of the classes within a school also influences socialization. Classes are considered "large" if they have more than 25 students, "small" if they have fewer than 20 students, and "regular" if they are in between. In large classes, as the size of the group increases, participation in discussion by each child decreases; interaction with the teacher also decreases (Barker & Gump, 1964; Linney & Seidman, 1989; Mosteller, 1995). In small classes, more learning activities take place and the greater interaction among students enables them to understand one another, resulting in an increase in cooperative behavior. Teachers have more time to monitor students' "on-task" behavior and can provide quicker and more thorough feedback to students. Also, potential disciplinary problems can be identified and resolved more quickly (Pate-Bain, Achilles, Boyd-Zaharias, & McKenna, 1992).

That the size of the learning environment affects socialization was demonstrated in a large-scale experiment (Finn & Achilles, 1990) in which kindergarten students and teachers were assigned randomly to small and large classes within each participating school. Students remained in these classes for two years. At the end of each grade, they were given standardized tests in reading and mathematics. The results showed that students in reduced-size classes outperformed students in the regular-size classes in both subject areas. The study showed that minority students in particular benefited from the smaller class environment. As a result of the studies on class size, the federal government has mandated a maximum number of students per teacher depending on the grade.

The businesses in a community can support schools by donating resources and time ("Adopt-a-School"). A business can donate equipment, offer expert guest speakers, provide field trips, and/or offer apprenticeship training to students. Such

Communities provide many learning experiences for children and their families, such as the activities both inside and outside this museum.

© Davis Barber/PhotoEdit

supportive linkages enable children to understand the connection between school learning and the world of work, as well as discover new role models to emulate (Swick, 1997).

Communities may also have certain traditions that are reflected in its schools. For example, San Juan Capistrano, California, celebrates the return of the swallows every spring. There is a parade in which local schools participate; students decorate floats, bands play, and drill teams perform.

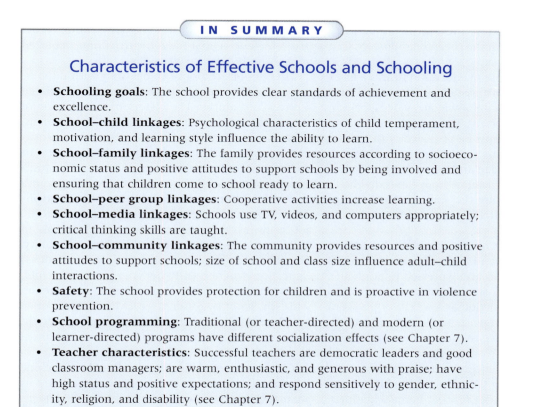

IN SUMMARY

Characteristics of Effective Schools and Schooling

- **Schooling goals**: The school provides clear standards of achievement and excellence.
- **School–child linkages**: Psychological characteristics of child temperament, motivation, and learning style influence the ability to learn.
- **School–family linkages**: The family provides resources according to socioeconomic status and positive attitudes to support schools by being involved and ensuring that children come to school ready to learn.
- **School–peer group linkages**: Cooperative activities increase learning.
- **School–media linkages**: Schools use TV, videos, and computers appropriately; critical thinking skills are taught.
- **School–community linkages**: The community provides resources and positive attitudes to support schools; size of school and class size influence adult–child interactions.
- **Safety**: The school provides protection for children and is proactive in violence prevention.
- **School programming**: Traditional (or teacher-directed) and modern (or learner-directed) programs have different socialization effects (see Chapter 7).
- **Teacher characteristics**: Successful teachers are democratic leaders and good classroom managers; are warm, enthusiastic, and generous with praise; have high status and positive expectations; and respond sensitively to gender, ethnicity, religion, and disability (see Chapter 7).

Epilogue

The school's basic function in society is to develop future contributing citizens. What is important to impart to children varies as societies change. Philosophies on teaching and learning also vary regarding the best way to accomplish this. Rousseau's philosophy was learner-directed (let the child's natural curiosity determine what is learned); formal traditional schooling is teacher-directed (the teacher determines what the child learns); home schooling can be either or both.

For the school to be an effective socializer, the family and community must be involved in the child's education.

Summary

The school is an agent of socialization. It is a setting for intellectual and social experiences from which children develop the skills, knowledge, interest, and attitudes that characterize them as individuals and that shape their abilities to perform adult roles.

Schools influence children through their educational policies, leading to achievement; through their formal organization, introducing students to authority; and through the social relationships that evolve in the classroom.

The primary purpose of education from society's perspective is the transmission of the cultural heritage—the accumulated knowledge, values, beliefs, and customs of the society. To transmit culture and maintain it, society must be provided with trained people who can assume specialized roles as well as develop new knowledge and technology.

The function of education from the individual's perspective is to acquire the skills and knowledge needed to become self-sufficient and to participate effectively in society.

The school's function in the United States is universal, formal, and prescriptive. Society's expectations of schools are expressed in academic, vocational, social, civic, cultural, and personal goals. The school's function as a socialization agent is affected by the larger macrosystem context—political ideology, economics, culture/ethnicity, religion, and science/technology.

Macrosystem influences are evidenced by society's policies regarding school choice (public/private schools, vouchers, charter schools, home schooling). Macrosystem influences are also demonstrated by society's policies concerning diversity and equity with regard to gender, ethnicity, religion, and disability.

The school's response to gender equity involves implementation of Title IX of the Education Amendments Act, which prohibits sex discrimination.

The school's response to ethnic diversity is that it has traditionally served the needs of the majority culture. For a long time the attitude toward the socialization of ethnic minorities was cultural assimilation—teaching them to adapt to the ways of the majority culture. Later, the idea of a cultural blending (the melting pot) became popular. Today, the socialization approach has become associated with the theory of cultural pluralism—that the majority culture should coexist and interact with the various cultural minorities for the benefit of all. Bilingual/multicultural education is an example. However, "English-only" programs are gaining popularity.

The school's response to religious pluralism involves sensitivity regarding which religious values intersect with educational goals. Controversial issues include school prayer, curriculum, required books, and holiday celebrations.

The school's response to children with disabilities is to provide special education and related services as required. The history of socialization of individuals with disabilities spans banishment, neglect, pity, protection, segregation, and education. Currently, the trend is toward integration or inclusion into the mainstream of society. The Individuals with Disabilities Education Act guarantees that all children with disabilities will have available to them a free and appropriate education. The act requires nondiscriminatory evaluations to determine whether or not a child has a disability. The act also requires that an Individualized Education Program (IEP) be written for each child; it is developed by school personnel in conjunction with the parents. Students with disabilities must be placed in the least restrictive environment (LRE), and supplementary aids and services must be provided as necessary.

Chronosystem influences on the school include its adaptation to societal change in general and its adaptation to specific developments such as technology, violence, and substance use/abuse.

In a changing society, the challenge continually facing educators is how to transmit the cultural heritage as well as prepare individuals for the future. Educators have approached this dilemma differently. Some believe only academic skills, cultural heritage, and good citizenship should be taught; others believe that critical thinking skills, self-concept, and interpersonal relationship skills should be part of the mix.

Schooling for the future involves being prepared for the world of work and technological change. Knowing how to use computers and software as tools is essential to successful functioning in our society. The effectiveness of the computer as a learning tool depends on how it is used by teachers and students, as well as the software selected.

To maintain an effective environment for learning, schools must be safe. Violence is rooted in families and communities. Children model parents' behavior. They see violence in the media and in the community as a way to solve conflicts, have access to guns and knives, and turn to gangs for protection. Children who are rejected by their peers are at risk for violent behavior, as are children who are disengaged from caring adults. Conflict resolution training in schools is effective in deflecting aggression.

Substance use/abuse remains a problem in schools. Issues of health and safety, learning environment, and privacy are involved.

Mesosystem influences on the school include its links with other ecosystems: school–child, school–family, school–peer group, school–media, and school–community. Linkages supportive of education will have beneficial socialization outcomes for the child.

Family involvement in the school is the most important influence on children's educational success because the family is the primary socializer of children. Some of the benefits for children of family involvement in the school are positive attitudes toward learning, higher academic achievement, and higher aspirations. Some of the benefits for the family members involved are higher self-esteem and more interaction with their children.

Family involvement can occur in decision making, participation, and/or partnership. Families need encouragement and support from teachers. Teachers need good communication skills to work collaboratively.

Activity

PURPOSE To understand the school's role in influencing the socialization of children.

1. Attend a school board meeting where a controversial issue (school rules, dress code, curriculum, extracurricular activities, use of federal funds) is discussed. Agendas can be obtained in advance by contacting the school district office.
2. Describe the issue in at least a paragraph, giving background information if possible.
3. Explain the views of (a) the board, (b) the school administration, (c) the teachers, and (d) the parents and/or students.
4. What was the outcome of the discussion?
5. What was your opinion of the experience?

Related Readings

Berger, E. H. (2003). *Parents as partners in education: Families and schools working together* (6th ed.). Englewood Cliffs, NJ: Prentice-Hall.

Darling-Hammond, L. (2001). *The right to learn: A blueprint for creating schools that work*. San Francisco: Jossey-Bass.

Dewey, J. (1944). *Democracy and education*. New York: Free Press.

Epstein, J. L. (2001). *School, family, and community partnerships: Preparing educators and improving schools*. Boulder, CO: Westview Press.

Farnham-Diggory, S. (1990). *Schooling*. Cambridge, MA: Harvard University Press.

Gardner, H. (1999). *Intelligence reframed: Multiple intelligences for the 21st century*. New York: Basic Books.

Gollnick, D. M., & Chinn, P. C. (2005). *Multicultural education in a pluralistic society* (7th ed.). Upper Saddle River, NJ: Prentice Hall.

Goodlad, J. I. (1984). *A place called school: Prospects for the future*. New York: McGraw-Hill.

Hallahan, D., & Kauffman, J. (2002). *Exceptional learners: Introduction to special education* (8th ed.). Boston: Allyn and Bacon.

Healy, J. (1991). *Endangered minds: Why children don't think and what we can do about it*. New York: Touchstone.

Holt, J. (1970). *How children learn*. New York: Dell.

Kozol, J. (1991). *Savage inequalities: Children in America's schools*. New York: Crown.

Lareau, A. (2000). *Home advantage*. Lanham, MD: Rowman & Littlefield.

Moss, W. L. (2004). *Children don't come with an instruction manual: A teacher's guide to problems that affect learners*. New York: Teachers College Press.

Papert, S. (1999). *The children's machine: Rethinking school in the age of the computer* (2nd ed.). New York: Basic Books.

Rothenberg, P. S. (1998). *Race, class, and gender in the United States: An integrated study* (4th ed.). New York: St. Martin's Press.

Stewart, E. C., & Bennet, M. J. (1991). *American cultural patterns: A cross-cultural perspective* (rev. ed.). Yarmouth, ME: Intercultural Press.

Chapter 7

Blend Images/Jupiterimages

Ecology of Teaching

The ideal condition would be, I admit, that men should be right by instinct;
But since we are all likely to go astray,
The reasonable thing is to learn from those who can teach.

— SOPHOCLES

What is effective teaching? What characteristics do students bring to the learning situation?

The following East African folktale, *Men of Different Colors* (Heady, 1968), is an example of how history is effectively taught through stories. In rural Africa, the people turn to the village storyteller for explanations of things they do not understand. This teacher plays a significant role in preserving the culture and in socializing the children. Here the teacher tells of how diversity came to be and why the unique characteristics of individuals should be valued.

Once Upon a Time A very long time ago, a stranger carrying large sheets of paper came to the village. He looked different from anyone the villagers had ever seen. Some said his skin was white; others said it was the color of cream. His hair was different, too. It didn't stay curled neatly to his scalp, but stuck up like dry grass straw, straight and spiky. It was nearly the color of straw, too.

Even though the stranger was nice, drawing pictures on his paper to amuse the children and giving them sweets, the villagers were frightened. They went to Mama Semamingi, the old storyteller, to ask about the white stranger.

"You want to know why he is so different," she said.

"Yes; please tell us," they replied.

"He was made that way, just as you were made as you are," answered the grandmother. "Did you know that people like Hamed, the Indian, are different, too?"

None of the children had been to Hamed's shop; they had only heard of him. "No, is he red?" asked one of the children.

"He is not red, nor white, nor black. He is a brown man," replied Mama Semamingi. "My story tells about him, too; do you want to hear it?"

"Yes, yes; please tell us," cried the children.

Way back in time, our great god Mungu lived in a white ice palace on the top of the high mountain. He became tired of his sparkling castle. He was lonely and wanted someone to help him make thunder and lightning. So, he set off downhill to look for some clay.

In a little open place among the trees, he found a spring of bubbling water that sparkled off down the hillside in a little stream. On either side, there was thick, dark, shiny black clay.

"Just the thing for my man," said Mungu. He worked for many hours. When at last he had finished, he clapped his hands and the clay statue of a man opened his eyes and said, "You are the great Mungu."

Mungu replied, "You shall be my helper and live with me in my white palace. I will call you Mutunyeusi, the black man."

For many weeks Mungu and Mutunyeusi lived in the ice palace, but the black man, made from clay, began to get stiff from the cold. He begged Mungu to allow him to go down the mountain to the streams and green forests where it was warmer. "If you will, I can guard the lower valleys while you guard the heavens."

Mungu agreed. So, Mutunyeusi went down the mountain to hunt and pick fresh berries and fruit. In time, however, he became lonely. He asked Mungu to make him a companion.

Mungu and Mutunyeusi then went to the stream to fashion another man from the black clay. "Why not make another man? Three will be less lonely than two, and perhaps one can visit me in my palace," said Mungu.

After the men were created, Mungu pondered his work. The great mountain god was troubled. "How could he tell the clay men apart?" He thought and thought about a way to make his three black men different.

One day when Mungu was out walking, he came upon a little pool of pure white water that stood in a hollow below the great river of ice. He thought of a plan. He called his three black sons and said to them, "See that pool? I want each of you in turn to wash in it. Something wonderful will happen if you do."

"Very well, master," said Mutunyeusi, the first man. "Let my younger brothers wash before me." He then pushed one black brother into the white liquid pool. When he emerged, he had lost his black color and was a shining, pinkish white!

"Oh, let me try!" cried the next brother, and ran into the shallow pool. Alas, there wasn't much water left and he was barely dampened. His color, when he came out, was a light brown. At last came Mutunyeusi's turn, but there was so little of the water left in the pool that all he could wet was the palms of his hands and the soles of his feet, which turned a pinkish color.

Mungu was very pleased, "Now I shall always know my children apart," he said. "You, Mutunyeusi, shall remain black and be the father of a family of black children. You shall live in the plains and forests surrounding my mountain. Then, turning to the son who bathed first, Mungu said, "You shall be known as Muzungu, the white man, and to you and your children I give all the lands to the north." Finally, turning to the third son, Mungu said, "You will be the father of the brown people and your name will be Muhindi. To you I give all the lands to the east."

The brothers went their separate ways, happy with the blessings their father had given them. And that is why, to this very day, men are so different from one another and have learned to prosper in such different ways.

The children thanked the storyteller for explaining why people are different . . . and they were no longer frightened.

While storytelling is one way of teaching, this chapter explores other techniques. Think about the following questions:

- **Does effective teaching involve eliciting what a student already knows and enabling the student to accommodate that knowledge to form new concepts?**

- **Does effective teaching involve choosing from all available information and shaping that knowledge so that it can be assimilated by the student?**

- **Does effective teaching involve knowing one's students individually, so one can combine various methods?**

The Teacher's Role as a Socializing Agent

Who was your best teacher and who was your worst?

> My best teacher was Mr. Brown* in seventh grade. He was very handsome; you could easily look at him all day and absorb whatever he was saying. I loved him because he was genuinely interested in us, his students. He would ask us what we planned to do with our lives; you just wanted to succeed to have his approval. I continued to return to my old junior high school, even when I was in college, just to tell him of my accomplishments.
>
> My worst teacher was Mr. Kane* in high school. He taught chemistry, the first class in which I failed an exam. It seemed like he enjoyed yelling at us, as a class and individually, more than he liked teaching. He especially chose the girls in the class to belittle for achievement efforts or behavior. Once, he made me do time in detention because I turned around to lend the person seated behind me a pencil. I was too intimidated to choose physics to meet my science requirement the next year.
>
> * The names were changed to preserve their anonymity.

For the past 25 years or so, I have been asking my students to think back over their education in elementary, middle, and high school and remember the characteristics of their best teacher and those of their worst. Though the exact wording differs, without fail "best" teachers are interesting, competent, caring, encouraging, and flexible, yet have demanding standards; "worst" teachers are boring, incompetent, distant, demeaning, and rigid with inflexible standards, or inconsistent with lax standards. After exploring reasons for students' choices, the message becomes quite clear: "best" teachers make students want to learn and reinforce their efforts, while "worst" teachers turn students off.

It is most interesting that the results of my informal surveys correspond to the formal research on effective role models. According to Albert Bandura (1986, 1989), models whom children imitate are perceived as being warm and as having prestige, control over resources, and the potential to reinforce or punish behavior. Recent research confirms this. Primary-grade students reported good teachers to be caring, responsive, and stimulating (Daniels, Kalkman, & McCombs, 2001).

This chapter examines the teacher's role as a socializing agent along with his/her bidirectional relationship with the student and its impact on learning. The student comes to school with a unique combination of family background, learning style,

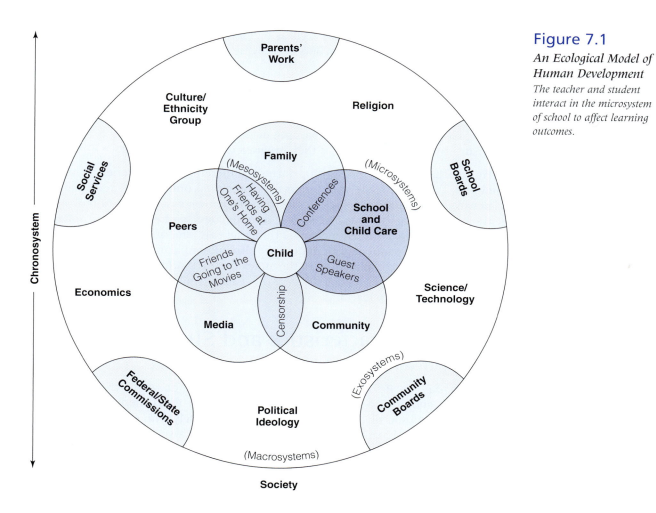

Figure 7.1

An Ecological Model of Human Development
The teacher and student interact in the microsystem of school to affect learning outcomes.

abilities, motives, and interests. The teacher comes to school with certain abilities and characteristics, such as teaching style, ways of management, and expectations. Student–teacher interactions take place in a classroom environment that may enhance or detract from learning. Other students, personal problems, or difficulty performing well on standardized tests may compete for student interest in learning the prescribed curriculum. Students at risk for negative developmental outcomes will be discussed in this chapter, as will some suggestions for empowering student success.

The most powerful socializing influence of the school lies in those who translate program goals into action—the teachers (Brophy, 1992). Teachers provide the environment for children's learning. They understand children's needs, interests, and abilities and can feel empathy for children's fears of failure. Teachers can encourage children to explore, to satisfy their natural curiosity, and to love learning—to love it so much that it becomes part of their lives forever. Teachers also play a major role in helping children learn to deal with positions of authority, to cooperate with others, to cope with problems, and to achieve competence.

The teacher is responsible for selecting materials relevant to the learner, for managing the group dynamics in the classroom, and for interacting individually with each child. When teachers interact with their students, they communicate attitudes about learning and behavior, as well as feelings about individuals. Following are some of the things effective teachers do (Levine & Levine, 1996):

- Provide time and opportunity to learn; pace instruction accordingly
- Communicate high expectations for student success
- Involve all students in learning activities by engaging them in discussion and providing motivating work
- Adapt levels of instruction to learning needs and abilities of students
- Ensure success for students as they progress through curriculum

The teacher–student relationship forms a different social experience for each child and, therefore, leads to different developmental outcomes. One explanation relates to **perception**, a biological construct that involves interpretation of stimuli by the brain. Factors such as maturation, attentiveness, past experiences, and emotions influence how a student perceives things, events, and interactions. A teacher's perception and consequent presentation are also influential in student learning. Can you recall a teacher's explanation of the attack on the World Trade Center in 2001?

We will first examine characteristics of the teacher, and then characteristics of the student, that influence learning.

Teacher Characteristics and Student Learning

What characteristics of teachers foster student learning?

For me, it was Mr. Brown's knowledge of who did well at what, who was friends with whom, and how to implement those facts to make everyone want to improve academically and socially. Teachers who try to work closely with each child and who understand group dynamics are more likely to provide a successful and rewarding learning environment. For example, studies (Agne, 1992; Brophy & Good, 1986; Daniels et al., 2001) have found that successful, or effective, teachers are those who are warm, enthusiastic, and generous with praise, and have high status. Also, successful teachers communicate well and are responsive to students. Conversely, unsuccessful, or ineffective, teachers are aloof, critical, and negative. They tend to communicate in ways that are difficult for students to understand and are unresponsive to students' needs. Teachers who are warm and friendly in their relationships with children are likely to encourage favorable rather than aggressive behavior and constructive, conscientious attitudes toward schoolwork.

When teachers communicate with children, learning is influenced; when teachers ask questions, verbalization is elicited from the child. For example, teachers' verbal styles have been found to have an impact on the development of language skills in preschool children (Schickedanz, 1990). Teachers who use expansive verbal descriptions and who encourage the children to converse with each other effect an increase in their students' verbal skills. It was also found that teachers who use reinforcement (verbal praise, smile, touch) can foster the learning of certain tasks. Preschool children who were observed in the presence of a friendly, approving adult behaved in a more exploratory, inquisitive manner than when a critical, aloof adult was present (Moore & Bulbulian, 1976).

The relationship of teachers' characteristics to their degree of success and their impact on socialization can be explained by the classic research of Bandura and Walters (1963) on modeling, mentioned earlier. They point out that "models who are rewarding, prestigeful or competent, who possess high status, and who have control over rewarding resources are more readily imitated than are models who lack these qualities" (p. 107).

perception
a biological construct that involves interpretation of stimuli from the brain

Stock Image/Jupiterimages

This teacher is a powerful influence on learning through her ability to stimulate the children's interest and engage their involvement.

Students who model their teachers pick up subtle behaviors and attitudes about learning. It follows, then, that the most important influence on students' achievement is the competent teacher. More specifically, a competent teacher is one who is committed to work, is an effective classroom manager, is a positive role model with whom students can identify, is enthusiastic and warm, continues efforts for self-improvement in teaching, possesses skill in human relationships, and can adapt his or her skills to a specific context (Good & Brophy, 2003; Linney & Seidman, 1989).

TEACHERS AS LEADERS

How does the person in charge use his or her authority to enable learning?

Mr. Brown was a model (in more than one sense), able to engage a diverse classroom of students. Mr. Kane was authoritarian; it was his way, or no way. Teachers are leaders in that they direct, guide, and set an example. Teachers use different styles of leadership to accomplish their goals. To illustrate, a classic study done by Lewin, Lippitt, and White (1939) compared the effects of three leadership styles—authoritarian, democratic, and **laissez-faire** (a policy of letting people do as they please; permissive)—on three groups of 10-year-old boys. The boys were assigned randomly to one of three after-school recreational groups engaged in craft activities. The groups were led by three adults who behaved in different ways. In the *authoritarian* situation, the leader determined the group's policy, gave step-by-step directions, dictated each boy's particular task, assigned children to work with one another, was subjective in his praise of the children's work, and stayed aloof from group participation. In the *democratic* situation, the leader allowed the boys to participate in setting group policy, gave the boys a general idea of the steps involved in the project, suggested alternative procedures, allowed them to work with whomever they wished, evaluated them in a fair and objective manner, and tried to be a member of the group. In the *laissez-faire* situation, the leader gave the group

laissez-faire a policy of letting people do as they please; permissive

complete freedom to do as they wished, supplied material or information only when asked, and refrained almost completely from commenting on the boys' work.

The style of leadership was shown to have a definite effect on the interactions within each group. The boys in the authoritarian situation showed significantly more aggression toward one another and were far more discontented than the boys in the democratic condition. They also produced more work than the other two groups. The boys in the democratic group showed less hostility, more enjoyment, and continued to work even when the leader left the room, which was not true of the other two groups. Finally, the laissez-faire group accomplished relatively little; the boys were frequently bored and spent much time "fooling around." (See Figure 7.2.)

Do teachers' leadership styles influence the learning environment in the classroom? In several studies, Good and Brophy (1986) report that a teacher who is clearly the leader and authority and who directs the class toward specific goals (*direct instruction*) promotes achievement. In this learning environment, little emphasis is placed on discussion, student ideas, discovery learning, or other types of *indirect instruction*. Jonathon Kozol, in *Savage Inequalities* (1991), disagrees. He describes the plight of poor inner-city children trying to learn from teachers who can't relate to their students' experiences in overcrowded schools with dilapidated equipment. Herbert Kohl, in his classic book *36 Children* (1967), describes the remarkable progress in language and thinking abilities made by the children in his class when he brought books, art, and play materials to class and allowed the children to explore them freely and make discoveries. Kohl acted as a facilitator, a helper in the acquisition of knowledge, and in so doing, allowed the children to participate in their own learning. Kohl (1984) believes children learn best from teachers who are role models, who love learning.

Still another way of viewing the teacher's role as a leader is that of a mentor who guides participation (Rogoff, 1990). For example, when a teacher shows a child how to be more successful at doing math problems (addition, subtraction) by putting the numbers in boxes on graph paper, the teacher is not only guiding the

Figure 7.2

Teachers and Leadership Styles

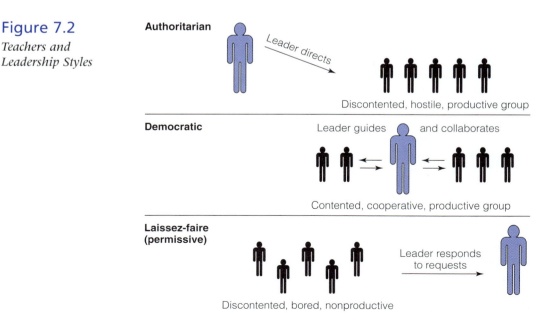

Authoritarian

Leader directs

Discontented, hostile, productive group

Democratic

Leader guides and collaborates

Contented, cooperative, productive group

Laissez-faire (permissive)

Leader responds to requests

Discontented, bored, nonproductive

child's participation but also providing support for success from one level to the next. Thus, teachers facilitate children's capacities to reach their full potential. Lev Vygotsky (1978) called the space between what a learner can do independently and what he or she can do while participating with more capable others the **zone of proximal development (ZPD)**. The effective teacher is one who is sensitive to the student's zone of development and provides appropriate independent, as well as collaborative, activities to enhance learning.

> My mother wanted to learn how to use the word-processing program on my computer. I demonstrated a few commands and let her practice, telling her to call me if she got stuck. When she felt she had mastered the basics, I showed her how to do more complicated things. With my assistance, my mother was able to learn more quickly than she would have on her own.

TEACHERS AS MANAGERS

What does a teacher's managing ability have to do with a student's learning ability?

Mr. Brown's teaching style motivated me—he actually was the person who encouraged me to write. In contrast, Mr. Kane squashed my desire to continue learning science. Kounin (1970) studied classroom management techniques and consequent student learning. His classic research showed that the key to successful management lay in preventive, rather than, consequential measures. The differences between successful and unsuccessful classroom managers lay in the planning and preparation of instruction, so that inattention and boredom were prevented.

Kounin found that student inattentiveness and misbehavior were often linked to problems of discontinuity in a lesson, which in turn were linked to inadequate preparation by the teacher. For example, a teacher who is giving instructions on how to do a book report and stops to find some appropriate books in the closet is likely to have lost the students' attention by the time the books are located. On the other hand, if a teacher has the exemplary books displayed on a table while the book report instructions are being given, it is likely that inattentiveness will be prevented.

Did you ever have teachers who had "eyes in the back of their heads"? Such teachers seem to know what their students are doing without looking and therefore are quick to react to potential problems. Kounin refers to this type of teacher behavior as "with-it-ness." Teachers who are "with it" respond immediately to incidents rather than waiting, quash minor problems before they turn into major ones, do not overreact to incidents, and focus accurately on the individuals involved in the incident rather than blaming someone wrongly. When students realize that the teacher knows what is going on, they are less likely to become involved in unproductive behavior.

Well-managed classrooms appear to run by themselves, with the teacher spending most of the time teaching rather than dealing with behavior problems. During a review of videotapes of their classes, teachers who were effective managers often referred to the preventive and anticipatory measures they had taken to avoid classroom problems—for example, encouraging student self-regulation (Emmer & Stough, 2001).

Another characteristic of successful classroom managers is the ability to "overlap"—that is, to deal with more than one activity at the same time (Good & Brophy, 2003).

zone of proximal development (ZPD) Vygotsky's term for the space between what a learner can do independently and what he or she can do while participating with more capable others

For example, while working with a group of students in one corner of the room, a teacher provides an appropriate motivating statement to a child who is wandering about, not involved in an activity ("Nadia, I'd like to read the paragraph you wrote, so we can think of another one"). Also, transitions from one activity to the next are smooth, not disruptive. "When you complete the chapter, you may work on the computer"; rather than "All books away; it is time for your test now."

In sum, then, teachers who succeed in producing substantial achievement gains in their students prevent most potential problems from occurring and are able to move activities along or give presentations without confusion or loss of focus because they are effective classroom managers. They also provide activities that are at the appropriate developmental level for their students and are interesting enough to hold their attention; they monitor the entire class continuously and can do two or more things simultaneously without breaking up the flow of learning (Brophy & Good, 1986; Good & Brophy, 2003).

TEACHERS' EXPECTATIONS

Do teachers' expectations affect the achievement and behavior of students?

Mr. Kane believed science was for boys, homemaking for girls. This was a powerful "downer" for me, who thought I might be a doctor. Because achievement was not expected from the girls in Mr. Kane's class, it did not occur. To document the significance of expectations, Rosenthal and Jacobson, in their book *Pygmalion in the Classroom* (1968), described a classic experiment in which they had all the teachers in an elementary school give a test to their students that was designed to identify intellectual "bloomers" (those who would show an academic spurt during the year). Actually, the test was a nonverbal IQ test and, unknown to the teachers, did not predict future intellectual spurts. After the test, however, the researchers provided the teachers with a list of bloomers. The bloomer list was not based on the test; instead, it was a random list of names from the teachers' rolls. Eight months later, all the children were retested with the same IQ test. The designated bloomers did, in fact, demonstrate significant intellectual growth; those in the first and second grades showed the most growth. This study raised the question, Are teachers trapped by their self-fulfilling prophecies for their students?

Rosenthal and Jacobson's study generated a lot of controversy because of methodological weaknesses and the inability of others to replicate the original results. Brophy and Good (1986) pointed out that attempting to induce teacher expectations by providing phony information generally has not shown results. However, studies observing actual teacher behavior in the classroom have shown the effects of expectancy (Sadker & Sadker, 2003). For example, in a longitudinal study of more than 1,500 middle school students whose teachers predicted their performance in math, there was a greater impact on future math achievement for low achievers, whose performance was overestimated, than for high achievers, whose performance was underestimated (Madon, Jussim, & Eccles, 1997). These findings demonstrate the power of "living up to expectation."

Brophy and Good explain the real-world effect of teacher expectations as follows: Teachers usually receive data about students at the beginning of the school year (test scores, past grades, family and health information, comments by previous teachers), which influence their expectations of students for achievement and behavior. Because of these expectations, the teacher tends to treat students differently. Students then react to the teacher differently. The students' behavior and achievement reinforce the teacher's expectations. Gradually, the students' self-concepts, motivation, and levels of aspiration reflect these expectations. If continued throughout the year, the students' performances will match or fulfill what the teacher expected or prophesied at the beginning of the year.

In addition to students' past records of achievement and behavior, teachers' expectations can be influenced by certain student characteristics, such as socioeconomic class, ethnicity, gender, personality, physical attractiveness, speech characteristics, and handwriting (Brophy & Good, 1986; Good & Brophy, 2003; Proctor, 1984).

Mrs. Levins has a child named Roy in her third-grade class who has moved several times and has below-normal achievement scores recorded in his cumulative folder. As Mrs. Levins reviews the folders belonging to the other children in her class, she finds three children (Sarah, Andrew, and Cary) who have consistently scored well above normal on achievement tests and whose folders also contain notes from previous teachers about what a joy each one was to teach. Upon observing Mrs. Levins midyear, we find that she waits less time for Roy to answer her questions than she does for Sarah, Andrew, or Cary. We also find that she is more critical of Roy than she is of the others and demands less of him in terms of work.

Of course, not all teachers translate their expectations into the type of behavior described in the example. Some teachers do not form expectations that continue throughout the year; rather, they change their expectations on the basis of the students' performance. Teacher expectations about students do not have a direct impact on student behavior; it is only when these expectations are communicated to the students, and selective reinforcement results in shaping their behavior, that teacher expectations have an impact. By becoming aware of possible biases in their behavior caused by their expectations, teachers can make a conscious effort to interact objectively with each child.

Student Characteristics and Teacher Interaction

Which students turn teachers on to teaching? Which ones turn them off?

Students who are engaged, interested in what I have to say, and willing to participate in class turn me on; I feel myself becoming more animated and willing to delve into topics of interest. Students who doze, who come in late or leave early, who won't participate no matter what, turn me off; I find myself struggling to make the material more interesting and becoming exhausted in the process.

Teacher–student interaction is bidirectional, with teachers eliciting responses in students and students, through their behavioral, cognitive, and affective qualities, eliciting responses in teachers (Bloom, 1982). According to Lillian Katz (1984), teacher–student interaction is specific and limited in that it relates to school matters. The intensity of affect between teacher and student is supposed to be low and somewhat detached, because teachers cannot get too emotionally involved with their students; otherwise they would lose objectivity (in their ability to evaluate, for example). Teachers must maintain rationality and intentionality in their curriculum goals. They must exhibit impartiality toward individual students, as their scope of responsibility is toward the whole group. Teaching a group of students from diverse backgrounds is a big challenge, especially when the group is large. The bidirectional relationship of teacher and student, which in turn affects socialization, is a complex dynamic reflecting factors such as gender, ethnicity, socioeconomic status, learning styles, and disability.

GENDER

Do teachers treat boys and girls differently?

Research shows that teacher–student interaction differs according to the gender of the student (the gender of the teacher does not seem to matter), though even when confronted with documentation (such as video recording), most teachers are unaware of inequities (Sadker & Sadker, 2003). Studies consistently show that boys have more interactions with teachers than do girls (Streitmatter, 1994). For example, it has been found (Serbin, O'Leary, Kent, & Tonick, 1973) that teachers are more responsive to the disruptive behavior of boys than of girls and are more likely to reprimand boys. When children request attention, teachers generally respond to boys with instructions and to girls with nurture. In addition, girls receive more attention when they are close to the teacher, whereas boys are given attention from a distance.

It has also been found that the feedback received by boys and girls on the intellectual quality of their work differs. Boys receive considerable criticism for failing to obey the rules, whereas girls receive criticism related to their performance. Boys attribute their failure to do well to lack of effort; girls attribute their failure to do well to lack of ability (Dweck, Davidson, Nelson, & Enna, 1978). Do some girls, then, give up trying to be successful when they reach high school because of the responses their elementary teachers have given them?

Why do girls perform better academically than boys in elementary school, but falter in high school? For example, girls do not do as well as boys in science and math by the time they reach adolescence (American Association of University Women [AAUW], 1991; Maccoby & Jacklin, 1974). There is evidence that girls generally take fewer advanced math classes than do boys in high school and college (AAUW, 1991; Sadker & Sadker, 1994, 2003).

Even though Title IX of the Educational Amendment Act of 1972 obliged schools to provide equal treatment for males and females, schools are still shortchanging girls (AAUW, 1991). Although more girls are involved in athletics (Eisenberg, Martin, & Fabes, 1996), the contributions and experiences of girls and women are not as visible in textbooks as are those of boys and men. The change is slow in gender-segregated enrollment patterns in vocational education (girls are primarily enrolled in office and business-training programs, whereas boys are in programs leading to higher-paying trade jobs). Sexuality and the realities of sexual activity (pregnancy, disease, rape) are rarely discussed in schools, although sexual harassment is required to be defined and consequences delineated (Chmielewski, 1997).

Teachers must be trained to foster assertive and affiliative skills in both girls and boys. School curricula and textbooks should be monitored for gender stereotypes and should provide positive role models for both girls and boys. Gender-role socialization will be discussed in more detail in Chapter 12.

ETHNICITY

Do teachers engage in ethnic stereotyping?

Ethnicity is a factor in teacher–student interaction in that both teacher and student come to the relationship with certain socialization experiences influencing their values, morals, attitudes, motives, behaviors, and roles. Diverse socialization yields diverse perspectives on what to learn, how to learn it, and how to show it has been learned. The role of teacher and school is to implement the values and traditions of society and so take on the responsibility of acculturation.

The United States is composed of many diverse ethnic groups. According to the U.S. Bureau of the Census (2003), the majority of individuals in the United States classify themselves as non-Hispanic White, but numerous minority groups include those of Hispanic origin, Asian–Pacific Island origin, African American origin, Native American origin, and others. Americans speak many languages. More than 32 million speak a language other than English at home; the largest language groups are Spanish, French, German, Chinese, and Italian (U.S. Bureau of the Census, 2003). Projections of population growth to the year 2050, based on life expectancies, fertility rates, and immigration, suggest that the gap between majority and minority ethnic groups is narrowing. This trend, plus the movement toward a global economy, points to the importance of understanding ethnic diversity. Examples of possible misunderstandings follow.

As the preschool teacher was helping the children settle down on their mats for naptime, she noticed red marks on Jenny Truong's neck and forehead. She asked Jenny how she got them and Jenny replied that her father put them there. The teacher, suspecting child abuse, reported it to the police. People from various Asian countries believe that internal winds cause illness. However, by bringing the wind to the surface, the illness can leave and that person will be healed. The way this is done is by "scratching the wind away," or "coining." A coin dipped in oil or menthol is vigorously rubbed against the head, neck, chest, back, or wherever the symptoms are exhibited. The skin is rubbed until it turns red. (Dresser, 1996)

One day a fifth-grade teacher noticed that Juanita, normally a tidy youngster, had a brown smear of dirt on one arm. That day and the next, the teacher said nothing. However, when Juanita came to class with the mark on her arm the third day, the teacher told her to go wash her dirty arm. When Juanita said it was not dirty, the teacher told her not to argue and to do as she was told. Juanita complied. Several days later, Juanita was taken out of school by her parents to attend the funeral of her sister. Two weeks had passed and Juanita had still not returned to school, so the principal went to her home to find out why. Juanita's mother told the principal that when someone is ill, each family member places a spot of oil and soil somewhere on the body. "We are one with nature. When someone is ill, that person is out of balance with nature. We use the oil and soil of our Mother, the earth, to show her we wish our sick one to be back in balance with nature. When Juanita's teacher made her wash her arm, our oneness with nature was broken. That is why her sister died. The teacher caused her death; Juanita can never return to her class." (Garcia, 1998)

Respect for cultural and ethnic differences requires teachers to be sensitive to a variety of customs. Asking appropriate questions and listening carefully can help avoid misunderstandings. The National Association for the Education of Young Children (NAEYC) has taken the following position:

> For optimal developmental and learning of all children, educators must accept the legitimacy of children's home language, respect (hold in high regard) and value (esteem, appreciate) the home culture and promote and encourage the active involvement and support of all families, including extended and nontraditional family units. (NAEYC, 1996a, p. 5)

Teacher sensitivity can be used to enable children to be tolerant and respectful of differences. When a kindergarten boy from India was called "garbage head" by his classmates because his hair smelled of coconut oil, the teacher planned a series of activities in which she and the children compared coconut oil to a variety of shampoos, conditioners, mousses, and gels. After much discussion about all the different things people put on their hair, the children came to realize that everyone's hair has a particular smell and coconut was simply one of a vast array (Ramsey, 2004).

Understanding diversity in *microcultures*, or minorities, involves examining the *macroculture*, or majority. Historically, political and social institutions in the United States developed from a Western European tradition. The English language came from England, and the American legal system is derived from English common law. The American political system of democratic elections comes from England and France (Gollnick & Chinn, 2005). American formal institutions (representing the macroculture), such as government, schools, business, and health and welfare agencies, reflect white Anglo-Saxon Protestant influences often referred to as the *Protestant ethic*.

What are some generalized values of the macroculture?

Although the macroculture includes people who are not white, Anglo-Saxon, or Protestant, certain basic values are shared to some degree by all members of the macroculture. Generally, the American macroculture is characterized by the following (Arensberg & Niehoff, 1975; Stewart & Bennett, 1991; Williams, 1960):

- **Emphasis on active mastery** rather than passive acceptance—individuals are responsible for what happens to them.
- **Valuation of the work ethic**—industriousness, ambition, competitiveness, individualism, independence. Status is based on occupation, education, and financial worth.
- **Stress on assertiveness and achievement**—achievement is valued above inheritance.
- **Valuation of fairness**—equal opportunities in social, political, and economic institutions.
- **More interest in the external world of things and events** than the internal world of meaning and feeling—achievement and success are measured by the quality of material goods purchased.
- **Emphasis on change, flow, movement**—new and modern are better than old and traditional; emphasis is on future rather than past or present.
- **Belief in rationalism** rather than traditionalism—not accepting things just because they have been done before; there has to be a logical reason for doing something.
- **Emphasis on peer relationships** rather than superordinate–subordinate; advocates equality, or horizontal relationships, rather than hierarchy, or vertical relationships.
- **Focus on individual personality** (individualism, independence) rather than group identity and responsibility (collectivism, interdependence)—idealizes an adaptive and outgoing personality rather than a conventional, introverted one.
- **Relationships to others** are impersonal or objective; communication is direct or confrontational.
- **Personal life and community affairs** are based on principles of right and wrong rather than on shame, dishonor, or ridicule.

How are these values exemplified in young children's behavior? Most children in the United States learn that nature is something you conquer and exploit. In the sandbox they often "build roads" or "dig to the other side of the world" (Ramsey, 2004).

Children are also encouraged to be actively engaged rather than "bored," as evidenced by the quantity of toys parents bring on long car rides.

What are some generalized values of the microculture?

The degree to which individual U.S. citizens subscribe to the general values of the macroculture depends, in part, on the values of the microculture, or ethnic group, to which they belong. The degree may also depend on how much an individual must interact with formal societal institutions for support (Gollnick & Chinn, 2005). For example, one who receives a government loan to further his or her education must comply with regulations by proving attendance at a college or university and following the prescribed schedule for repayment. To better understand possible areas of differences between macroculture (individualistic) and microculture (collectivistic) values in school, some generalities about microcultures follow:

- **Orientation toward the extended family**. The child is considered an important member of the family group; the family provides a psychological support system throughout the individual's life. Cousins are considered as close as brothers. Emphasis is placed on cooperation, helping those in need, and respect for elders. Family matters may take precedence over school attendance.
- **Fostering of sharing and group ownership**. To a child who has not been socialized to understand individual ownership ("These are *your* crayons"), *your* may mean belonging to the group. Thus, if Lee cannot find his pencil, he borrows Steve's without asking because whatever belongs to the group the child regards as his or hers, too.

These children are learning by observing and modeling their father and by working cooperatively on the task.

ImageState/Jupiterimages

- **Teaching children not to "show up" (demonstrate individual superiority over) their peers**. Children from collectivistic cultures may not exhibit competitive behaviors in classroom settings, such as responding to "Who has the best work?" However, when performance is socially defined as benefiting the peer society ("Which group has read the most books?"), children from collectivistic cultures compete well.
- **Learning by observation and being patient**. At home, children from collectivistic cultures may not be rewarded for curiosity and for asking questions; parents may even use legends and fables to discourage curiosity.
- **Teaching children to drop their heads as a sign of respect and compliance** rather than look directly at an adult, as is expected in the macroculture.
- **Status** in collectivistic cultures is based more on who you are (family name) than what you have.
- **Time orientation** is generally more present-oriented than future-oriented. Time is viewed as a continuum, with no beginning and no end. Ceremonies, for example, begin when the participants are ready, rather then punctually at the scheduled time.

How do individualistic and collectivistic orientations affect socialization?

Until recently, most of the research on child development has been carried out in the context of the dominant macroculture, which has an individualistic orientation. Consequently, the development of children from European American, middle-class families has come to be considered the norm for all children regardless of the ethnic, cultural, or economic context they inhabit (Bennett, 2003). Thus, to get a broad perspective on child development and to foster understanding of ethnically diverse children, the socialization backgrounds of collectivistic cultures will be compared to those of individualistic cultures. The following discussion comprises generalizations from research.

> The continuum of individualism/collectivism represents the degree to which a culture emphasizes individual fulfillment and choice versus interdependent relations, social responsibility, and the well-being of the group. Individualism makes the former a priority, collectivism, the latter. (Trumbull et al., 2001, p. 4)

Generally, the school is oriented toward the European American value and tradition of individualism, whereas most minority ethnic groups are oriented toward that of collectivism. To enable teachers to meet the challenges of education in a pluralistic society, Trumbull and colleagues (2001) describe how the individualistic–collectivistic continuum approach to different cultures can be applied in the classroom. They give the following example of an individualistic and a collectivistic response to the same situation (p. 6):

> At the end of the school day, when it is time to clean up, Salvador isn't feeling well. He asks his friend, Emanuel, to help him do his assigned job for the day, cleaning the blackboard. Emanuel isn't sure he'll have time to do his job and help Salvador.
> *Individualistic response*: The teacher gets a third person to do Salvador's job, as Emanuel has his own responsibility.
> *Collectivistic response*: The teacher tells Emanuel to help Salvador with his job.

What contrasts between individualism and collectivism affect teaching?

Objects/People. Children socialized in individualistic cultures generally learn about physical objects as a means toward independence. Parents give children toys and teach them how to use various materials so they can amuse and help themselves.

Parents use direct oral language to communicate instructions. Children socialized in collectivistic cultures generally are amused and helped by other people. Holding, touching, and modeling how to carry out a task tend to be the dominant form of communication. In school, where verbal instructions are often given, children who are not accustomed to that manner of learning may have difficulty. Demonstrating and working alongside the student may be more helpful.

Possessions. In collectivistic cultures, the emphasis on social relationships and getting along extends to possessions. Personal items, such as clothing, books, and toys, are often considered family property and are readily shared. In individualistic cultures, emphasis generally is on having and taking care of your own things—"that's mine!" is often heard. In school, where much emphasis is placed on producing one's own work and keeping one's things tidy in one's desk, children who are used to communal tasks and property may have difficulty adjusting. Teachers might incorporate cooperative activities in the classroom to allow such children an opportunity to contribute.

Achievement. Individualistic cultures tend to stress individual achievement and competition: "Who read the most books?" Related is the sense of self-expression and personal choice: "Who knows the answer?" "Which club do you want to join?" Collectivistic cultures tend to stress group affiliation and cooperation: "How is your friend feeling today?" "Let's let him hold your teddy bear." Related is the belief in the need for group harmony and saving face: "We need to help Maria with her math so she won't be embarrassed in class." Teachers might be cognizant of their use of praise for a child in front of the group. Although this is thought to reinforce desired achievement and competition and to foster self-esteem, it may have the opposite effect on children who interpret it as upsetting group harmony and causing embarrassment.

Social Roles. Children socialized in collectivistic cultures are generally taught to respect a hierarchy of authority roles, with grandparents, parents, teachers, and other adults possessing knowledge and being worthy of respect. Thus, they may not be very responsive if a teacher asks their opinion (their status in the age hierarchy implies they do not know enough to have one) or inquires whether they have questions (indicating that the material the teacher taught was not understood may be considered disrespectful). Children socialized in individualistic cultures are generally taught egalitarian principles in social roles; everyone has certain rights that must be respected, such as the right to voice an opinion. Collectivistic cultures usually have more rigid gender roles than do individualistic cultures. When I taught preschool, some little girls would always arrive clothed in pretty dresses, in spite of the suggestion to all parents that their children wear clothes suitable for climbing on the outdoor equipment and easily washable. Teachers might structure some learning activities using group structures and group leaders. Children in the group help each other and ask pertinent questions via the group leader, who serves as mediator between the group and the teacher. As the children become more competent with various school subjects, they can experience being a group leader.

SOCIOECONOMIC STATUS

Do all children have an equal opportunity to succeed in school?

It has been well documented that family socioeconomic status affects school readiness and later academic achievement (Duncan & Magnuson, 2005; McLoyd, 1998). "Since the term 'socioeconomic status' (SES) refers to one's social position as well

This child is learning how to play checkers as he is coached by a more expert peer.

© Dick Luria/Getty Images

as to the privileges and prestige that derive from access to economic and social resources, . . . it may be difficult to measure directly a family's access to resources or its position in a social hierarchy" (Duncan & Magnuson, 2005, p. 2). Therefore, researchers typically use one SES indicator, such as occupation, or combine several indicators, such as occupation, income, and parental education, into scales that reflect families' relative positions in a social hierarchy.

To understand the relationship between families' disparate socioeconomic circumstances and children's achievement, Duncan and Magnuson (2005) examined four components of SES: income, education, family structure, and neighborhood.

- **Income**. Children from birth to age 5 whose families' incomes were below the poverty line were found to score lower on a standardized test than children from families with average incomes. This is most likely due to the more stimulating learning environment of books, newspapers, educational games, and activities available in families able to afford such things.
- **Education**. Children whose parents finished high school and had some college education routinely score higher on cognitive and academic tests than do children of parents with less education.
- **Family structure**. Single-parent families are likely to have fewer resources than dual-parent families. Young children living with single mothers are more likely to be poor (Children's Defense Fund, 2004). Financial and time constraints may limit a single parent's ability to supervise and discipline children and to provide a supportive and stimulating environment. On average, children raised by single parents have lower social and academic well-being than do children of intact marriages (McLanahan & Sandefur, 1994). Part of the explanation is economic insecurity in young or single-parent families. Another part is parental conflict and strain in divorcing families. Finally, the many transitions experienced by children in young and single-parent families may result in feelings of instability.

- **Neighborhood**. Children growing up in high-poverty urban communities plagued by violence, gangs, drug activity, old housing, and vacant buildings may experience stress, a lack of positive role models, a lack of institutional resources (school, protective services), and negative peer influences (Duncan & Magnuson, 2005).

In sum, the lack of preparedness for school of low-SES children affects the teacher–student relationship. Low-SES families tend not to have physical or emotional resources for educational support. Many home experiences taken for granted in middle-class families, such as books, computers, and trips, are unavailable in poor families. Because low SES can be a self-perpetuating cycle, poor parents themselves may not have received an adequate education growing up and, therefore, may lack knowledge of readiness and supportive educational activities to provide for their child, such as language stimulation, reading, and games. For example, a study comparing home language environments of 3-year-olds from professional and poor families revealed that more than three times the number of words were used in interactions between parents and children in professional families than in poor families (Hart & Risley, 1995). Despite the heterogeneity of children in all social classes, teachers often stereotype children's potential based on their socioeconomic status and base expectations for achievement accordingly (Ramsey, 2004).

LEARNING STYLES

How do you learn best?

Children have different ways they learn best, and teachers have different ways they teach best. When I was in school, I liked listening to interesting lectures. I liked organization and analysis. When I had difficulty, I appreciated help from a neighboring student. I disliked being put into groups and given a task. I hated laboratory assignments. My daughter, on the other hand, loved working in groups and hated analytical tasks. She also liked writing creative stories. She was not too fond of lab work, either. I liked teachers who were structured and followed a plan; my daughter liked teachers who were innovative in their approaches to curriculum. Student learning style and teacher teaching style can be viewed as bidirectional, with one influencing the other. Learning styles have been studied along cultural lines, and teachers have been urged to accommodate their style to match the student's to facilitate academic success (Marshall, 2002). However, given the broad spectrum of human characteristics, in reality this is difficult.

Some children learn more effectively by observation, modeling, and apprenticeship rather than through verbal instruction, the teaching method most commonly used in American schools. To illustrate, Joan tells how she learned to prepare salmon as a child. After watching her mother, she was allowed to gradually take on portions of the task and to ask questions only if they were important. Once she told her mother that she didn't understand how to do "the backbone part." So her mother took an entire fish and repeated the deboning because, according to her, it is not possible to understand "the backbone part" except in the context of the whole fish.

Researchers (Hilliard, 1992; Ramirez & Castaneda, 1974; Tharp, 1989) suggest that children develop learning or cognitive styles based on the socialization they receive in their families and peer groups—although there are still many unanswered questions about cognitive styles. Children who live in families that are structured—members have defined roles, specific times are set aside for eating and sleeping, the family uses formal styles of group organization (relating to a leader, pursuing goals, receiving feedback)—have been observed to have an *analytical cognitive style*. Children who live in families that are less structured—roles are shared, individuals eat when hungry and sleep when tired—are more likely to exhibit a *relational cognitive style*.

With regard to other socialization outcomes, studies (Bennett, 2003; Hale-Benson, 1986) have shown that some children tend to be more oriented toward feelings and personal interaction, and are more proficient at nonverbal communication, than other children. For example, some African American children, as well as children from other ethnic groups, get a lot of experience interacting with people (Hale-Benson, 1986). Communication in these interactions may differ from that experienced by Euro-American children; talking may jump from topic to topic rather than following a linear sequence from the beginning of the story to the end (Ramsey, 2004). Euro-American children tend to be oriented toward objects; they usually have numerous opportunities to manipulate objects and discover properties and relationships. These experiences with objects help prepare them for school, which is also object-oriented, using books, computers, learning centers, and so on.

Some children exhibit a holistic, concrete, social approach to learning (Bennett, 2003; Ramirez & Castaneda, 1974). This style of learning, referred to as *field-dependent*, usually implies that the person works well in groups and perceives things in terms of the whole context. A *field-independent* learning style, on the other hand, describes an analytic and logical approach to tasks and usually implies that the person relates well to impersonal, abstract information, independent of the context. For example, Hispanic American children tend to be more field-dependent than Euro-American children because they tend to be socialized to be open, warm, committed to mutual dependence, cooperative, sensitive to the feelings of others, and respectful of adults and social convention (Escobedo & Huggans, 1983; Greenfield & Suzuki, 1998; Ramirez & Castaneda, 1974; Soldier, 1985). In general, Native American children also prefer holistic over analytic learning. In community storytelling, for example, Navajo children are not asked to recite details of a story or to dissect it; instead, they are expected to listen quietly to the long telling of stories (Tharp, 1989).

Another illustration of learning styles comes from studies of Native American children, who demonstrate the importance of visualization in learning (Bennett, 2003). These children generally learn through careful observation, noticing, for example, the behavior and expressions of adults, the changing weather conditions, the terrain, and so on. After observing an adult do a task, the child takes over small portions of the task under the guidance of the adult; the child becomes an apprentice. When the child feels ready to do the whole task, he or she practices it in private. Thus, failures are not seen and don't cause embarrassment, but success is demonstrated for the adult with pride (Vasquez, 1990).

Compared to the research on learning styles of other American ethnic groups, there is a scarcity of information on Asian American learners. Children who come from a country where many do not get a formal education (for example, the Hmong) have different ways of approaching cognitive tasks required in school than those who come from countries where formal education is necessary for success (Bennett, 2003; Thuy, 1983). Japanese Americans, for example, have the highest literacy rate of any ethnic group in the United States, tend to do well financially, and have been assimilated into the macroculture (Bennett, 2003). Similarities between the Buddhist–Confucian ethic of hard work and the Protestant ethic may be part of the explanation.

Japanese students are consistently top performers on achievement tests in both math and science (Stevenson & Lee, 1990; Stevenson, Stigler, Lee, Kitamura, & Kato, 1986). One possible influence is the time spent on homework. Japanese children are expected to practice all their lessons at home, and the mother is present to supervise and help. Another possible influence is the emphasis Japanese parents place on effort and hard work.

Japanese and American families tend to provide different socialization experiences to prepare children for work in the classroom (Hess, 1986). For example, Japanese mothers are likely to interact with their children in such a way as to promote internalization of adult norms and standards; American mothers are likely to rely more on external authority and direction. Japanese mothers tend to demonstrate how to perform a task correctly, expecting the child to eventually master it internally; guidance is gentle and supportive. American mothers tend to rely more on verbal instructions, external rewards, and punishment.

Some Asian children, though they do very well on tests and on homework assignments, may be less inclined to participate in class discussions or share ideas, and may be reluctant to work with other students on group projects. Such children have generally been socialized to view the teacher as the complete source of knowledge. The student's job is to listen, take notes, memorize, follow directions, and recite. Children's ideas are not requested, nor are they valued. Such students are taught not to ask questions, argue, or challenge the teacher (Dresser, 1996).

Because all children learn differently, Howard Gardner (1999) recommends that teachers adapt the curriculum to the multiple intelligences he believes encompass human capability (see Figure 7.3):

1. **Logical-mathematical**: skills related to solving logical problems and performing mathematical calculations (generally qualities of scientists, mathematicians)
2. **Linguistic**: skills related to the meaning, sound, and rhythm of words as well as the use of language (generally qualities of authors, journalists, poets)
3. **Bodily-kinesthetic**: ability to coordinate parts of the body and manipulate objects skillfully (generally qualities of athletes, dancers, surgeons)
4. **Musical**: ability to produce pitch and rhythm and appreciate musical expression (generally qualities of musicians, composers, singers)

Number smart
(Logical-mathematical)

Word smart
(Linguistic)

Body smart
(Body-kinesthetic)

Music smart
(Musical)

Figure 7.3
Gardner's Multiple Intelligences

Picture smart
(Spatial)

People smart
(Interpersonal)

Self smart
(Intrapersonal)

Nature smart
(Naturalist)

5. **Spatial**: ability to form a mental model of concrete objects and manipulate parts in relation to each other (generally qualities of architects, engineers, artists)
6. **Interpersonal**: ability to analyze and respond to behavior, feelings, and motives of other people (generally qualities of psychologists, teachers, salespeople)
7. **Intrapersonal**: ability to understand one's feelings and motives, using such knowledge to adapt one's behavior accordingly (generally qualities of actors, lawyers)
8. **Naturalist**: ability to discriminate among living things and be sensitive to the natural environment (generally qualities of botanists, zoologists, ecologists)

DISABILITY

Did you know that 30 years ago, children with disabilities could not attend public school in most states?

Today, thanks to legislation discussed in Chapter 6, all children have the right to a free and equitable education. Here we examine the teacher–student interaction as it is affected by the presence of a disability. Not only have laws been passed to give individuals with disabilities equal access rights, but educators have modified the teaching environment to include the following (Hallahan & Kauffman, 2002):

1. *Individualized instruction*, in which the child's abilities rather than prescribed academic content provide the basis for teaching techniques
2. *Adaptation of the curriculum to various learning styles*, whereby visual, auditory, and tactile learners are motivated to succeed
3. *Collaboration with various professionals*, so that services such as medical, physical therapy, speech therapy, and counseling are provided
4. *Peer tutoring*, in which children with greater abilities help those who are in need

Some examples of how the educational environment and teaching strategies can be modified to include children with disabilities are available on the *Child, Family, School, Community* companion website at http://www.thomsonedu.com/author/berns.

The Individuals with Disabilities Education Act (IDEA), discussed in Chapter 6, requires that children with disabilities be placed in the "least restrictive environment." This means inclusion with nondisabled peers whenever appropriate. In order to determine and maintain optimal placement, IDEA requires that an individualized education program (IEP) be written annually (IDEA 2004 allows for IEP long-term planning for up to three years in certain cases) and reviewed by (1) the child, (2) the parent, (3) the teacher, (4) the professional who has evaluated the child most recently, and (5) the principal or school district special resource person. The IEP must specify educational goals, methods for achieving those goals, special educational/resource services to be provided to meet the child's needs, and appropriate assessment measures.

Since the IEP is a vehicle that enables children with disabilities to interact with peers who do not have disabilities, teachers must provide appropriate interactive activities. An example of an appropriate interactive activity is cooperative learning. *Cooperative learning* as an educational goal structure was discussed in Chapter 6. It involves a set of strategies that organizes students into small groups of five or six and gives them a task to solve cooperatively. Students are enabled to learn problem-solving techniques and how to work constructively with others. The child with disabilities can be part of the group, making a contribution according to ability

(Kirk et al., 2000). Cooperative learning structures also provide opportunities for reinforcement and instruction through tutoring; such socialization methods were discussed in Chapter 2.

Reinforcement increases the chance of a behavior's being repeated. Thus, children without disabilities can reinforce certain behaviors in children with disabilities (for example, sharing tends to be repeated when it is appreciated), and children with disabilities can do likewise (for example, helping tends to be repeated when it results in a positive outcome).

While helping children to learn, *tutoring*, or *direct instruction*, also provides an opportunity for close social interaction. The learner gets instruction, and the tutor gains sensitivity to others, communication skills, and an opportunity to nurture. While the learner gains individual attention and an opportunity for cognitive growth, the tutor gains self-confidence and self-esteem.

Identification and Assessment of Children with Disabilities
How do families of children with disabilities find out what public services are available to them?

In 1986, Congress passed PL 99–457, which addressed the needs of infants, toddlers, and preschoolers with disabilities. It also recognized that families play a large role in the socialization of children with disabilities. Consequently, PL 99–457 provides that, whenever appropriate, the preschooler's IEP will include instruction for parents; it then becomes an individualized family service plan (IFSP). A variety of programs are available to meet the needs of preschool children with disabilities. These can be home-based or center-based and can be full- or part-time.

PL 99–457 authorized an early intervention program, establishing a state grant program for infants and toddlers with disabilities from birth to age 2 who are at risk for special needs. In this context, children *at risk* are those who are not currently identified as impaired or disabled but who are considered to have a greater than usual chance of developing a disability because of conditions surrounding their birth or home environment (Heward & Orlansky, 1994). Examples of at-risk conditions will be discussed in the next section.

PL 99–457 is supported by evidence that providing early educational and therapeutic programs for children with disabilities and their families reduces the number of children who will need intensive or long-term help (Lerner, Mardell-Czudnowski, & Goldberg, 1987). Therefore, it is crucial to diagnose and assess a child who has special socialization needs as soon as possible.

For children with certain kinds of disabling conditions, identification can occur at birth—for example, Down's syndrome and various physical deformities. Behaviors not usually exhibited by normal infants can be identified shortly after birth—for example, extreme lethargy, continual crying, convulsions, and paralysis. However, many disabling conditions, such as learning disabilities, are not readily apparent and may not be suspected until later.

Because more and more children are attending various types of preschool programs, teachers and others who work on a daily basis in such programs are in a unique position to assess young children. By observing and recording specific child behaviors that occur excessively, or that occur instead of appropriate behaviors, the teacher can identify children who may have potential disabilities.

Teachers and parents can observe behavior using a variety of techniques: anecdotal records, checklists and rating scales, time samples, and measurements of behavior.

- *Anecdotal records* report a child's adaptive behavior in various situations.
- *Checklists and rating scales* are used to compare a child's development against norms or averages.
- *Time samples* record everything a child does for a certain period of time each day (for example, from nine to ten o'clock for five consecutive days).
- *Measurements of behavior* record the frequency of a behavior, the duration of the behavior, the antecedents of the behavior, and the consequences of the behavior.

The teacher observation form (an assessment of general development for preschool children) provides a model that may be used to indicate the necessity for referral to other professionals—a pediatrician for health problems; an otologist for auditory problems; an ophthalmologist for visual problems; a neurologist for neurological problems; an orthopedist for bone, joint, or muscle problems; a psychologist or psychiatrist for emotional problems; and so on. To view an example of a teacher observation form, go to the *Child, Family, School, Community* companion website at http://thomsonedu.com/author/berns.

Many other assessment devices are available in addition to the teacher observation example provided on the companion website. Some are designed for a particular population; others assess specific areas of development. For example, a *medical assessment* consists of a medical history and a physical examination. A *psychological assessment* includes a psychological evaluation, such as one based on the American Psychiatric Association's Diagnostic and Statistical Manual, and a measurement of intelligence, such as one based on the Stanford-Binet Intelligence Quotient or the Weschler Scale.

Assessment, of course, is meaningless unless adequate follow-up and services are provided for children who need them. Services may involve corrective or supportive medical services and/or special educational programs. Corrective or supportive medical services may involve prosthetic devices and/or medication, plus physical and/or psychological therapy. Special educational programs can involve services at home (a professional works with the parent and child; the parent carries on the program between visits by the professional); services in a center (the child attends a center for several hours a day for education and therapy); or supportive services enabling the child to be mainstreamed (such as transportation, tutoring, or interpreting).

Services may also involve social work or counseling. For example, certain prescribed medical treatment that is to be carried out at home may necessitate training the parent (dialysis, diet therapy, physical therapy, for example). Social or counseling services may include advocacy for the child—informing the family of the services to which the child is legally entitled. Thus, the professional serves as an educator, a supporter, and a resource.

Assessment must be an ongoing process; hence, the IEP or IFSP, previously discussed, is used. When children are continually assessed, their performance can indicate the need to modify the special program.

Any program designed to meet the special needs of children with disabilities must involve the family, for several reasons (Hauser-Cram, Warfield, Shonkoff, & Krauss, 2001; Heward, 2002):

- Because parents of a child with disabilities will often be responsible for implementing the educational program at home, they need additional training.
- Parents can contribute much valuable information to the program staff regarding the behavior and performance of their child.

A child with disabilities can be included in school activities through special transportation services.

- In order for professionals to work with parents for the optimal development of the child, the particular dynamics of the family with a child with disabilities must be understood—the feelings (hopes, disappointments, frustrations, joys) and interactions.

Recognizing that parents are family members with myriad responsibilities and individual needs and preferences has a profound influence on parent–professional relationships in special education settings. The same concept of individuation embraced by the field of special education as pertinent to children and youth also applies to parents and other family members.

Inclusion
How can individuals with disabilities be integrated into the community and become contributing members?

The community, through legislation, has facilitated integration of individuals with disabilities into society. Not only do people with disabilities have a right to receive an appropriate education; they also have the right to equal employment opportunities and the right to enjoy the services provided by the community. The macrosystem behind such legislation is rooted in the principles of equal opportunity, independence, and economic self-sufficiency (Hardman, Drew, & Egan, 1999). The school and its teachers must help prepare students for inclusion in the community.

The Vocational Rehabilitation Act of 1973 (PL 93–112), amended in 1992, serves as a "bill of rights" for individuals with disabilities in order to guarantee equal opportunity. It requires that federal agencies and all organizations holding contracts or receiving funds from the U.S. government have affirmative action programs to hire and promote qualified persons with disabilities. It enforces an earlier law requiring that all buildings constructed with federal funds and buildings owned or leased by federal agencies have ramps, elevators, handrails, wide aisles, or other barrier-free access for persons who are disabled. It also prohibits discrimination against qualified persons with disabilities—students, employees, and receivers of health and other services—in all public and private institutions receiving federal assistance. For example, employers can ask about a person's ability to perform a job, but cannot inquire if she or he has a disability. The Americans with Disabilities Act (ADA), passed in 1990, bars discrimination in employment, transportation, public accommodations, and telecommunications. This law guarantees access to all aspects of life—not just those that are federally funded—for people with disabilities. The law specifies that "reasonable accommodations" be made according to the disability a person has. For example, telephone companies must provide services so that individuals with hearing or voice impairments can use ordinary telephones; all new construction and renovations of facilities must be accessible to those with disabilities; employers must restructure jobs and modify equipment as reasonably required.

Since the community has opened up opportunities for the livelihood and employment of individuals with disabilities, schools and support professionals must be involved in enabling those persons to make the transition from home to community. This means inclusion in leisure and social functions as well. The community must not only make physical accommodations, such as providing designated parking spaces and ramps, but also open leadership and/or advisory positions on boards, provide sensitivity training to businesses, and be more welcoming to individuals with disabilities in the neighborhood. For example, in one community, the Performing Arts Center installed special headphones in every seat for anyone who might be (or might become) hearing impaired.

RISK AND RESILIENCE

Why are some children at risk for psychological, social, or academic problems, whereas other children with similar characteristics are resilient?

Risk refers to endangerment. Children at risk are vulnerable to negative developmental outcomes, such as dropping out of school, substance abuse, violence, teenage pregnancy, unemployment, and suicide. Risk factors affecting infants and children can be classified as *genetic* (such as mental retardation), *prenatal* (such as drug exposure), *perinatal* (such as health care), and *environmental* (such as poverty) (Rickel & Becker, 1997). Children considered to be at risk tend to come from families that lack social support networks, experience unemployment, exhibit depression, engage in substance abuse, have poor marital relations, and/or practice domestic abuse (Children's Defense Fund, 2004; Rogosch et al., 1995).

Resilience refers to the ability to recover from, or adjust easily to, misfortune or change. Studies of psychological resiliency have revealed factors that enable children to thrive despite difficult or traumatic environments (Garbarino, 1995a; Rickel & Becker, 1997). For example, psychologist Emmy Werner (1993) began studying infants at risk in Hawaii more than 40 years ago. The children came from families who were chronically poor, alcoholic, and abusive. Expecting negative developmental outcomes for the children, she was surprised to find that approximately one-third of those she followed grew into emotionally healthy, competent adults. They had close friends, were in supportive marriages, attained a high level of education, and mastered vocational skills.

What enabled these children to become resilient to a traumatic childhood? The resilient children had a sense of autonomy and personal responsibility; they related

risk endangerment; vulnerability to negative outcomes

resilience the ability to recover from, or adjust easily to, misfortune or change

to others positively; perhaps most significantly, they had established a bond with an adult caregiver or mentor. Apparently, the "substitute" parent and positive relationships and experiences act as buffers against negative developmental outcomes.

> These buffers make a more profound impact on the life course of children who grow up under adverse conditions than do specific risk factors or stressful life events. They appear to transcend ethnic, social class, geographical, and historical boundaries. Most of all, they offer us a more optimistic outlook than the perspective that can be gleaned from the literature on the negative consequences of perinatal trauma, caregiving deficits, and chronic poverty. They provide us with a corrective lens—an awareness of self-righting tendencies that move children toward normal adult development under all but the most persistent adverse circumstances. (Werner & Smith, 1992)

The implications of such research are profound. The findings mean that parents, schools, community services, and others can help children develop into healthy, contributing adults by working together to build a socially nourishing environment (Comer, 2004; Epstein & Sanders, 2002; Garbarino, 1995a). According to James Comer (2004, p. xiv), "it is in our social environment that constructive attitudes, values, and ways of living—work, family relationships, child rearing, citizen contribution are created and perpetuated . . . or they are not."

Schools have the potential to provide optimal socialization experiences and foster resiliency in children. In his book *Leave No Child Behind*, Comer (2004) describes the success of one model. The Comer model, implemented in hundreds of schools all over the United States, is based on the principle that good relationships promote healthy development, which is inextricably linked to learning. Schools using the Comer model are an extension of the family, and the family is a reflection of the learning environment fostered by the school. Others agree that the school must work with families as well as children, and this has been documented by much research (Connors & Epstein, 1995; Funkhouser & Gonzales, 1997). Specifically, when families get involved in school, their children:

- Get better grades and test scores
- Graduate from high school at higher rates
- Are more likely to go on to higher education
- Behave more positively
- Are more achievement-oriented

Children and Poverty
What aspects of poverty affect the student–teacher relationship?

According to the Children's Defense Fund (2004), one out of every six children is classified by federal income standards as "poor." Poor families face many challenges besides their standard of living. Some of these include having both parents working outside the home, reliance on child care, inadequate health care, malnutrition, lack of adequate housing, and unsafe communities. In his book *Savage Inequalities*, Jonathan Kozol (1991) describes many poor neighborhoods and schools as being near chemical plants or sewage dumps, in ill repair, and plagued by crime and drugs.

The community's failure to support the teacher—because of economics and values—affects the teacher–student relationship. As we discussed in Chapter 6, schools in poor communities often lack money for school improvements, resources, and smaller classes. Teachers also have to motivate students to achieve in the face of **learned helplessness**—the perception, acquired through negative experiences, that

learned helplessness the perception, acquired through negative experiences, that effort has no effect on outcomes

effort has no effect on outcomes (to be discussed in more detail in Chapter 11. The difficulty comes from the belief, common in poor families, that there is little connection between educational achievement and making a living (Levine & Levine, 1996). Thus, delinquency and dropping out present additional challenges to teachers.

Poverty is a societal problem that must be addressed by macrosystems (political ideology, economics), exosystems (business, community services), and mesosystems (linkages), as well as the microsystems of school and family. As discussed in Chapter 6, The No Child Left Behind Act of 2001 is an example of a macrosystem response—government support of education. Included are provisions for mental health and counseling of students, gifted and talented education, safe and drug-free schools, community learning centers, reading and literacy, math and science education, testing and accountability, discipline, hate crimes, and parental rights. An example of mesosystems supporting education comes from a study on what makes adolescents feel connected to schools (McNeely, Nonnemaker, & Blum, 2002). The researchers found students' connections with their schools to be associated with:

- **School size**. The smaller the school (down to 600 pupils), the more connected students felt.
- **Discipline policies**. Harsh discipline, such as zero tolerance, made students feel less connected, though safer.
- **Student friendships**. Adolescents are more connected to school when they have more friends there because they are less socially isolated.

Children and Substance Abuse
How does substance abuse in the family affect the child in school?

The teacher–student relationship is affected by the child's exposure to the use/abuse of substances by family members. Substance abuse has been consistently linked with poor parenting and poor family functioning; addicted parents' primary relationship is with drugs, not with their children (Thompson, 1998).

Prenatal Substance Exposure. One group of children from at-risk families are those prenatally exposed to drugs or alcohol. (Postnatal exposure poses risks, too, as exemplified in the next section on alcohol.) Commonly abused drugs include crack cocaine, heroin, marijuana, tranquilizers, and stimulants. Substance-exposed infants exhibit low birth weight, sleeping and eating disorders, and increased irritability (Hardman et al., 1999). They experience not only physical and health problems but psychological and behavioral ones as well. The following is an example (Green, 1990).

> Five-year-old Jeffrey's foster parents are at their wits' end. Jeffrey has just hit the neighbor's cat with a golf club. Fortunately, the cat was quick to move, so only its tail got the brunt of the blow. Jeffrey is in perpetual motion most of his waking hours. He even has a hard time sitting still while eating or in front of the TV. Suddenly, he may burst into tears, or laughter, or trance-like states that can last an hour or more.

Jeffrey is a victim of his mother's addiction to crack cocaine, which she smoked during her pregnancy. Why the concern with such children?

About 15% of women of childbearing age in the United States are substance abusers. A conservative estimate of the incidence of prenatal exposure to illicit drugs is 11% of live births (Hardman et al., 1999).

Implementing interventions for mothers and their babies who have been exposed to drugs is challenging and expensive. Many drug-exposed babies are placed in foster care, which is costly too. There is also the cost of special education and services, which can be two or three times the amount (depending on the disability) spent on a child in a regular program at a public school, which averages about $7,5000 per year nationally.

Because of his mother's addiction to drugs, Jeffrey was removed from her care shortly after birth and placed in foster care. Jeffrey's antisocial behavior is likely to be related to the effects the drugs had on his developing brain in utero; cocaine causes blood vessels to constrict, thereby reducing the vital flow of oxygen and other nutrients to the brain as well as to other organs. Because fetal cells multiply rapidly in the first few months of development, the fetus is deprived of an optimal blood supply for normal growth.

Prenatal cocaine exposure affects brain chemistry as well. The drug alters the action of neurotransmitters, the messengers that travel between nerve cells and help control a person's mood and responsiveness. Such changes may explain the unusual behavior, including impulsiveness and moodiness, seen in some prenatally cocaine-exposed children as they mature (Toufexis, 1991).

Caring for prenatally cocaine-exposed babies is frustrating because they respond differently to natural adult overtures such as cooing, tickling, and bouncing. Whereas normal babies gurgle and laugh, babies prenatally exposed to drugs stiffen or scream. The mothers feel rejected and end up avoiding trying to make further contact, unless they are given the opportunity to learn how not to overstimulate the infant (Toufexis, 1991; Tyler, 1992).

As these children reach preschool and school age, they don't relate appropriately to other children or adults. They tend to ignore rules, have temper outbursts, be aggressive, and be unable to concentrate (Green, 1990; Hardman et al., 1999). Thus they have special socialization needs, and their caregivers need to learn techniques to optimize their development.

Alcohol. Another group of children at risk for negative developmental outcomes are those whose parents abuse alcohol. According to the American Academy of Child and Adolescent Psychiatry (AACAP, 1997a), one in five adult Americans lived with an alcoholic while growing up. **Alcoholism** is a chronic, progressive, and potentially fatal disease. It is characterized by excessive tolerance for alcohol and by physical dependency and/or pathologic organ changes as direct or indirect consequences of the alcohol ingested.

Alcohol is so common in our society that we seldom think of it as a drug. Yet beer, wine, and liquor are all central nervous system depressants. They are similar to barbiturates and other sedative drugs in slowing down bodily functions such as heart rate and respiration.

Alcohol consumption during pregnancy can produce abnormalities in the developing fetus. Alcohol interferes with the delivery of nutrients to the fetus, impairs the supply of fetal oxygen, and interferes with protein synthesis.

A specific cluster of abnormalities appearing in babies exposed prenatally to alcohol abuse (heavy drinking) was described and named *fetal alcohol syndrome* (FAS) by Kenneth Jones and his colleagues (Jones, Smith, Ulleland, & Streissguth, 1973). Among the distinguishing features of this syndrome are prenatal and postnatal growth retardation; facial abnormalities, including small head circumference; widely spaced eyes; short eyelid openings; a small, upturned nose; and a thin upper lip. Most FAS children have mental retardation. FAS is the leading known preventable cause

alcoholism a chronic, progressive, and potentially fatal disease characterized by excessive tolerance for alcohol and by physical dependence and/or pathologic organ changes

of mental retardation. Now warnings of possible birth defects are required on alcoholic beverages and in establishments that serve alcohol.

Behavior problems appear in infancy and persist into childhood; the most common are irritability, hyperactivity, poor concentration, and poor social skills. Sometimes affected children display other physical problems such as defects of the eyes, ears, heart, urinary tract, or immune system (Aaronson & MacNee, 1989).

Children whose parents abuse alcohol are prone to a range of psychological difficulties, including learning disabilities, anxiety, attempted and completed suicides, eating disorders, and compulsive achieving. The problems of most of such children remain invisible because their coping behavior tends to be approval-seeking and socially acceptable. They do their work, do not rock the boat, and do not reveal their secret. Many are high achievers and eager to please. Yet their adaptation to the chaos and inconsistency of an alcohol-abusing family often results in developing an inability to trust, an extreme need to control, an excessive sense of responsibility, and denial of feelings, all of which result in low self-esteem, depression, isolation, guilt, and difficulty maintaining satisfying relationships. These and other problems often persist throughout adulthood (Leershen & Namuth, 1988; Tubman, 1993).

Janet Geringer Woititz, in her classic book *Adult Children of Alcoholics* (1990), and Claudia Black in another classic, *It Will Never Happen to Me* (1991), discuss some common traits exhibited by adult children of alcoholics, such as guessing what is normal behavior, having difficulty following a project from beginning to end, lying instead of telling the truth, having difficulty having fun, constantly seeking approval, feeling they are different from other people, and tending to lock themselves into a course of action without giving consideration to consequences. As adults the wounded child within impairs emotional expressions (feelings are repressed) and relationships (trust) are difficult.

The child is often embarrassed by his or her parents. The ashamed child does not invite friends home and is afraid to ask anyone for help. The child also feels anger toward the alcoholic parent for drinking and may be angry with the nonalcoholic parent for lack of support and protection. The child may even feel guilty, perceiving himself or herself as the cause of the parent's drinking (AACAP, 1999).

Although the child tries to keep the parent's alcoholism a secret, teachers, friends, relatives, or other caring adults may sense that something is wrong. The following behaviors may signal a problem (AACAP, 1999):

- Failure in school; truancy
- Lack of friends; withdrawal from classmates
- Delinquent behavior, such as stealing or violence
- Frequent physical complaints, such as headaches or stomachaches
- Abuse of drugs or alcohol
- Aggression toward other children
- Risk-taking behaviors
- Depression or suicidal thoughts or behavior

Whether or not their parents are receiving treatment for alcoholism, these children can benefit from programs such as Al-Anon and Alateen. Therapists can help these children understand that they are not responsible for their parents' drinking problems. Therapists can also help the family, particularly when the alcoholic has stopped drinking, develop healthier ways of relating to one another. For example, a problem that emerges during recovery stems from the familial responsibilities undertaken by children during active parental alcoholism. When parents are drinking, children may run the household and care for younger siblings. The recovering alcoholic generally tries to reassume these responsibilities. Children are then asked to become children again instead of "little adults" or "parents." Because they are unaccustomed to behaving like children, the transition back to more traditional familial roles may cause conflict between parents and children (AACAP, 1999).

The consequences of living in an alcoholic family are particularly difficult for young children and adolescents because alcoholism affects the process of socialization of values, morals, attitudes, behavior, gender roles, self-control, and self-concept. The effects of alcoholism depend on the child's age, gender, relationship to the drinking and non-drinking parents, and relationship to other family members or other social networks.

Violence in Families
How does violence in families affect the child in school?

Violence in families includes child maltreatment and domestic abuse. Various types and observable signs of maltreatment were explained in Chapter 4; here the masked effects that interfere with development are discussed. Some of these less obvious developmental consequences for the child may result from the quality of parenting in a family that is dysfunctional. These include difficulty in regulating emotions, insecure attachments, difficulty achieving autonomy, aggressiveness with peers, noncompliance with adults, and impaired readiness to learn (Azar, 2002; Rogosch et al., 1995). It is important for teachers and caregivers to understand the interactive dynamics in at-risk families in order to provide support to enable them to be involved in their children's learning.

Children exposed to domestic violence are at risk for negative developmental outcomes. *Domestic violence* can be defined as "the systematic abuse by one person in an intimate relationship in order to control and dominate the partner" (Kearny, 1999, p. 290). Abusive behavior can be physical, emotional, mental, and/or sexual. Domestic violence is found in all socioeconomic classes and cultures (Greenfield, 1998). Most is experienced by women, although some men experience it too (Kearny, 1999). The government plays a significant role in preventing negative outcomes from domestic violence. It has passed laws making violence against women a crime and provided funding for shelters, counseling, and hot lines (National Coalition Against Domestic Violence, 1999).

Children who are exposed to domestic violence often experience the following feelings (Kearny, 1999, p. 291):

- **Anger**. They are angry at the abuser for perpetrating the violence, at the victim for tolerating it, or at themselves for not being able to stop it.
- **Fear/terror**. They are afraid that the mother or father will be seriously injured or killed, that they or their siblings will be hurt, that others will find out and then the parents will be "in trouble," or that they will be removed from the family.
- **Powerlessness**. Because they are unable to prevent the fights from happening, or to stop the violence when it occurs, they feel out of control.
- **Loneliness**. They feel unable or afraid to reach out to others, feeling "different" or isolated.
- **Confusion**. They are confused about why it happens, choosing sides, what they should do, what is "right" and "wrong." They are also confused about how the abuser can sometimes be caring and at other times, violent.
- **Shame**. They are ashamed about what is happening in their home.
- **Guilt**. They feel guilty that they may have caused the violence, or that they should have been able to stop it but couldn't.
- **Distrust**. They don't trust adults because experience tells them that adults are unpredictable, that they break promises, and/or that they don't mean well.

IN PRACTICE

What Supportive Strategies Can Teachers Use for Children Exposed to Domestic Violence?

Breaking the silence surrounding domestic violence and providing appropriate intervention can help. Specific preventive strategies include the following:

- **Identification**. Be alert to changes in emotional, social, and/or learning behaviors. Ask the child, "What is wrong?" (Does the child not want to go home? Is the child unusually attached to his or her teacher? Is the child withdrawn? Is the child aggressive or a bully?)
- **Support**. Be available to listen to the child and acknowledge his or her feelings without being judgmental. Help the child develop ways to release his or her feelings appropriately.
- **Modeling**. Exhibit nonviolent, cooperative ways of solving problems.

Children living in a violent environment often exhibit similar behavior with their peers, Chapter 6 listed some strategies to resolve conflicts before they escalate into violent behavior: emotional regulation, empathy, problem solving, and mediation.

Macrosystem Influences on Teaching

How is teaching in the classroom influenced by factors in the larger society?

Macrosystem influences on teaching include philosophical and theoretical foundations of teaching and learning that have undergone change over the years; classroom and curriculum contexts affected by school administration; and policies and procedures regarding accountability for achievement (standardization and individuation).

PHILOSOPHIES OF TEACHING AND LEARNING

Why do some teachers direct children whereas others let children find their our own direction in the learning environment?

Philosophies of teaching range from emphasis on the learner, with the goal of expanding an individual's knowledge, to emphasis on the teacher, with the goal of methodically presenting new knowledge to the student. One root of the learner-centered teaching philosophy comes from the Greek philosopher Socrates (469–399 B.C.E.), who believed "Knowledge is virtue." He developed the *Socratic method*, eliciting knowledge from individuals by questioning their statements until a satisfactory logical conclusion was reached. One root of the teacher-centered philosophy comes from the psychologist B. F. Skinner (1904–1990), who believed that any student can be conditioned to learn any subject, provided the tasks involved are divided into small, sequenced steps and the learner is reinforced appropriately for desired responses or behaviors (positive consequences for desirable behavior and negative consequences for undesirable behavior). This became known as the *behaviorist method*.

Table 7.1

Teacher- and Learner-Directed Classroom Contexts

TEACHER-DIRECTED (TRADITIONAL)	LEARNER-DIRECTED (MODERN)
STRUCTURE	
Day is organized by teacher and divided into time segments according to subject	Program is prepared by teacher based on student abilities and interest; time spent on activities depends on interest; activities not divided into specific subjects
MANAGEMENT	
There are many rules for appropriate behavior (being moral, having manners, following directions, paying attention, being quiet, sitting still, being neat)	Teacher encourages children to discuss standards of conduct and take responsibility for their behavior
CURRICULUM	
Predetermined by teacher and/or textbook Emphasis on reading, writing, arithmetic, science, social science Knowledge considered an end in itself; what is studied is preparation for life	Subjects determined by student ability and interest Activities and problem-solving experiences based on student interest Knowledge considered a means to an end, the process of living; subject matter grows out of experience
MOTIVATION	
Extrinsic (grades)—success mainly a function of how well the required tasks are mastered according to teacher's standards Advancement determined by subjects and tests passed, time spent in system Competitive	Intrinsic (child's interests)—success is mainly a function of self-evaluation (based on accomplishment of a self-chosen goal) Advancement according to activities chosen and skills developed Cooperative
METHOD	
Teacher teaches generally the same thing at the same time to all students or a group of students Teaching style is dominative Teaching of content Direct encouragement of children's participation	Learning is individualized and students are responsible for their own learning Teaching style is integrative Teaching of process Indirect encouragement of children's participation

Source: Adapted from George H. Morrison (1980). *Early childhood education today* (2nd ed.) (Columbus, OH: Merrill), pp. 146–149, 152–153. Reprinted by permission of the publisher.

There are many types of educational programs, based on various philosophies of teaching and learning. For the sake of simplicity, the programs discussed here are categorized according to their emphasis on who takes responsibility for the learning that takes place—the teacher or the learner (see Table 7.1). In reality, most programs emphasize both teacher and student responsibility for learning, but to different degrees. Because different programs provide different learning environments, experiences, and interactions, the school's program influences a child's development and socialization in a particular way.

Teacher-directed educational environments (sometimes referred to as *traditional*) usually subscribe to the philosophy that the functions of the school are to impart basic factual knowledge (reading, writing, arithmetic) and to preserve the American cultural heritage (Sadker & Sadker, 2003; Toch, 1996). Those who support this philosophy believe that education should include homework, tests, memorization, and strict discipline. They view the school as a place where hard work and obedience are expected. The teacher structures the curriculum. Subjects chosen are based on the teacher's, school's, or community's goals.

The roots of teacher-directed learning can be traced back to Plato's (427–347 B.C.E.) *Republic*. Plato's thesis stated that the mind is what it learns, so the content of the curriculum is vital for an educated society.

Learner-directed educational environments (sometimes referred to as *progressive* or *modern*) usually subscribe to the philosophy that the function of the school is to develop the whole child. Curriculum emerges from the child's interests and abilities, and knowledge is constructed as the child is capable of processing it (Toch, 1996). This process is called "constructivism." The teacher scaffolds, or supports, the child's initiated learning via appropriate curriculum.

The roots of learner-directed learning can be traced back to Rousseau's *Emile* (1762). Rousseau concentrated on the development of the child rather than the subjects to be taught. His thesis stated that *how* learning occurs is more important than *what* is taught.

John Dewey (1859–1952), influenced by Rousseau, was the first progressive educator. He believed that education should place emphasis on the children and their interests, rather than on subject matter. Dewey also believed that education was a *process* of living, not a *preparation* for living. Those who subscribe to this philosophy believe learning occurs spontaneously and occurs best when children can interact with materials and people in their environment. Learning materials may be grouped in various centers, which children explore. Children are given opportunities for inquiry and discovery. They become involved in their own learning by making choices about what they will learn. Subject matter is integrated into student activities.

To determine the extent to which a philosophy shapes teaching practices, Putnam (1983) observed the classroom interactions in six inner-city kindergartens—three of

This classroom is organized to provide many learner-centered activities.

BananaStock/Jupiterimages

which followed a traditional or teacher-directed approach to reading readiness and three of which followed an interactive or more learner-directed approach.

Teachers in traditional kindergartens assume that before trying to read, children should develop a set of foundational skills—visual and auditory discrimination, letter naming, beginning word sounds, and so on—that will allow them to be successful when they learn to read in first grade. The following is an example of this approach.

> Mrs. Hall's kindergartners have just listened to a song about Mr. D., who loves doughnuts, dogs, deer, and other things that begin with *d*. Mrs. Hall then asks the children to name other things that begin with the *d* sound. "Raise your hand; don't call out, speak in a sentence," she says. One child says, "I sit at a desk."
>
> "Very good, 'desk' begins with *d*," replies Mrs. Hall. After several responses the children are given worksheets on which they are to circle pictures of items beginning with a *d*.

In this teacher-directed environment, the children were expected to sit quietly, follow directions, listen attentively, and talk only when called upon to answer a question. Discussion with fellow classmates was frowned upon (Putnam, 1986).

In contrast, teachers in the interactive or learner-directed kindergartens created a reading environment in these ways:

- Giving children plentiful opportunities to listen to literature and nonfiction being read aloud
- Providing opportunities for children to act out and discuss the readings
- Allowing children to express their understanding of the readings through art
- Enabling the children to experiment with writing and reading their own "books"

There was some instruction in letter sounds, but most of the focus was on interpreting whole messages. The children were encouraged to collaborate with one another in talking, asking questions, and comprehending material. The children spent time each day "reading" a book (looking at pictures, reciting the story, and trying to decode the words) or "writing" a story (drawing, inventing spelling, and talking about ideas). The teacher moved around listening to pretend readings, asking the writers to "read" their stories, helping with invented spelling, answering questions, and praising efforts. In this learner-directed approach to reading readiness, the children had a greater degree of control, choice, and responsibility (Putnam, 1986).

SOCIALIZATION OUTCOMES OF DIFFERENT CLASSROOM CONTEXTS

What does research say about the effects of teacher-directed and learner-directed programs on socialization?

In a review of approximately 200 research studies on elementary school programs, Horwitz (1979) noted the different socializing effects of modern versus traditional settings. In general, he found that children in modern (learner-directed) settings tended to have a more positive attitude about school and their teachers than did children in traditional (teacher-directed) settings. They were more likely to find friends of both genders. They also tended to be involved in cooperative work more often and showed more autonomy, or self-reliant behavior. Why? Modern and traditional environments provide different opportunities for cooperative work. In traditional environments, teachers generally teach to the whole class and children work individually; sharing information is seen as cheating. In modern classrooms, there is considerable small-group effort and an emphasis on developing a cooperative work ethic (Atkinson & Green, 1990; Minuchin & Shapiro, 1983).

Horwitz did not find any significant differences in the academic achievement of children in modern versus traditional settings. However, later studies (Chall, 2000; Good & Brophy, 1986) indicated that students in traditional, teacher-directed classrooms tended to perform better academically than students in modern, learner-directed programs. Why? Most likely it was because standardized tests are based more on teacher-directed goals than on learner-directed ones.

We can conclude, then, that different patterns of competence emerge as a result of the different experiences that children have in various programs (Daniels et al., 2001; Toch, 1996). Social competence is enhanced in instructional settings where students interact with each other and the teacher to accomplish educational goals; academic competence is fostered in instructional settings where students are motivated and rewarded for accomplishing the teacher's educational goals.

To encourage certain socialization outcomes, instructional settings can be organized into "goal structures" (Johnson & Johnson, 1999). The three types of goal structures are **cooperative**, in which students work together to accomplish shared goals; **competitive**, in which students work against each other to achieve goals that only a few students can attain; and **individualized**, in which one student's achievement of a goal is unrelated to other students' achievement of that goal. Each type of goal structure, according to Johnson and Johnson, promotes a different pattern of interaction among students. A cooperative goal structure promotes positive interpersonal relationships, such as sharing, helping, trust, and acceptance. A competitive goal structure promotes comparisons and mistrust and for some, achievement motivation. An individualized goal structure promotes student–teacher interaction and responsibility for oneself. Table 7.2 describes the conditions under which each goal structure is most effective in promoting the desired learning.

An interesting application of the cooperative type of goal structure, as it relates to socialization, was described by Aronson and Patenoe (1996). The goal of the activity was to get students in a newly integrated classroom to interact positively with one another. The students were divided into small groups and given tasks in which they had to cooperate with each other in order to succeed. Each student was given a piece of information that the rest of the group needed in order to finish the task. All the members had to share their pieces of information with the others. Aronson called this "the jigsaw-puzzle method." The results were higher achievement, a decrease in social insults, higher self-esteem, and improved attitudes toward school. Several successful adaptations of cooperative goal structures have been developed to include children with disabilities and those who are ethnically diverse and to prepare students for an increasingly collaborative workforce (Slavin, 1991).

Thus, the way teachers manage the classroom environment, including arranging the room, planning the activities, observing behavior, and organizing groups, affects the socialization taking place in that classroom.

cooperative goal structure students working together to accomplish shared goals

competitive goal structure students working against each other to achieve goals that only a few students can attain

individualized goal structure one student's achievement of the goal is unrelated to other students' achievement of that goal

Table 7.2

Classroom Management: Goal Structures and Socialization

GOAL STRUCTURES	TYPE OF INSTRUCTIONAL ACTIVITY	IMPORTANCE OF GOAL FOR SOCIALIZATION	STUDENT EXPECTATIONS	EXPECTED SOURCE OF SUPPORT
COOPERATIVE	Problem-solving; divergent thinking or creative tasks; assignments can be more ambiguous with students doing the clarifying, decision making, and inquiring	Goal is perceived as important for each student, and students expect group to achieve the goal	Each student expects positive interaction with other students; sharing ideas and materials; support for risk taking; making contributions to the group effort; dividing the task among group members; capitalizing on diversity among group members	Other students
INDIVIDUALIZED	Specific skill or knowledge acquisition; assignment is clear and behavior specified to avoid confusion and need for extra help	Goal is perceived as important for each student, and each student expects eventually to achieve this goal	Each student expects to be left alone by other students; to take a major part of the responsibility for completing the task; to take a major part in evaluating his/her progress toward task completion and the quality of his/her effort	Teacher
COMPETITIVE	Skill practice; knowledge recall and review; assignment is clear with rules for completing specified skills or knowledge	Goal is *not* perceived to be of large importance to the students, and they can accept either winning or losing	Each student expects to have an equal chance of winning; to enjoy the activity (win or lose); to monitor the progress of his/her competitor to compare ability with peers	Teacher

Source: Adapted from David W. Johnson and Roger T. Johnson (1999). *Learning together and alone: Cooperative, competitive, and individualized learning* (5th ed.). Reprinted by permission of Allyn and Bacon, Needham Heights, MA.

ACCOUNTABILITY AND STANDARDIZATION

How do schools and teachers evaluate students' learning? Should they be accountable for achievement outcomes?

As applied to education, **accountability** refers to making schools and teachers responsible for student learning or achievement outcomes. It means that educational expenditures must be justified. Educational accountability is a result of rising costs,

accountability
making schools and teachers responsible for student learning or achievement outcomes

These children are enjoying learning by working cooperatively on an activity that permits collaboration.

© Wadsworth/Thomson Learning

poor student performance in the business world, the need to compete in global markets, and the desire to maintain leadership in the world in science and technology.

The first formal mandate from the federal government for educational accountability was the Elementary and Secondary Education Act of 1965. Schools had to produce documented results, in terms of educational attainment, in order to receive public funding. Since then, state and local school districts have tied funding to performance. To measure performance, schools must set goals or standards—for example, that all students completing first grade will be able to read and comprehend simple stories. The federal Educational Excellence for All Children Act of 1999 (discussed in Chapter 6) is a model of six national educational goals for states to implement. Assessment instruments must then be devised to measure achievement of the goals. Another federal law, the No Child Left Behind Act of 2001, which is a model for *standards-based education*, requires annual testing in all states. Although states and local school districts vary in specifics, generally, student achievement is tested in reading, writing, math, and science throughout elementary and middle school and on graduation from high school.

Although bureaucrats and taxpayers generally applaud standardization, teachers and those advocating for diverse groups call for more flexibility in assessments to accommodate individual teaching and learning styles. A practice used in some schools is **authentic assessment**, in which evaluations are based on real performance showing mastery of a task (such as building a model of house) rather than test performance (figuring out the square footage of a house in a math problem).

Mesosystem Influences on Teaching

What links to other microsystems foster student learning in the classroom?

Mesosystem influences on teaching include community support and family involvement. Community support can be financial, as in donations and grants; it can be service-oriented, as in mental health; it can be extensions of the learning

authentic assessment
evaluation based on real performance, rather than test performance, showing mastery of a task

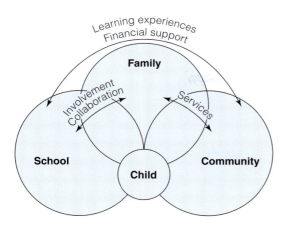

Figure 7.4

Mesosystem Influences on Teaching: Fostering Student Learning

environment, as in field trips and guest speakers. Family involvement and collaboration with teachers are important throughout school, but are especially important before the child enters formal school so that appropriate attitudes toward future learning are developed. (See Figure 7.4.)

FAMILY INVOLVEMENT IN LEARNING

How can families empower student success?

As noted previously, families and schools share a collaborative role in successful student learning. Families help ready children for school and support school goals.

IN PRACTICE

What Strategies Can Be Used to Encourage Learning?

What strategies can teachers implement to involve families in learning?

1. Recognize and show that parents are significant contributors to their child's development. Call on parents for advice, help, support, and critical evaluations.
2. Present a realistic picture of what the child's program is designed to accomplish.
3. Maintain ongoing communication with parents. Provide written information regarding due process procedures, parent organizations, and other relevant matters as well as oral and written information about the child's progress.
4. Show parents you care about their child. Call, write notes, spend time listening to parents' concerns.
5. Keep parents informed as to how they can help their child at home. Enable parents to enjoy their children.
6. Use parents' ideas, materials, and activities to work with the child.
7. Know community services and resources so you can refer parents when necessary.
8. Be yourself. Don't appear to know all the answers when you don't; don't be afraid to ask for advice or refer parents to others.

9. Recognize that diverse family structures and parenting styles will influence parent participation.

10. Help parents grow in confidence and in self-esteem. (Heward, 2002)

What strategies can families implement to prepare children to learn?

1. Express your love.
   - Spend time with your child.
   - Talk and listen.
   - Help child to be independent (let child do things of which he/she is capable).

2. Use everyday opportunities to teach about the world.
   - Talk about scenery, weather, news.
   - Figure things out together—how much time has passed, how to divide the pie, how to repair the toilet.
   - Enable the child to follow directions.
   - Plan together (activities, goals).

3. Encourage questions.
   - How does this work?
   - Why did this happen?

4. Give approval for trying new things.
   - Reward accomplishments.
   - Make it understood that mistakes happen—what can we learn?
   - Stimulate creativity.

5. Instill a love of books.
   - Model reading.
   - Read to your child.
   - Answer questions.
   - Visit the library.
   - Tell stories, and have child tell them too.

6. Get involved in school.
   - Talk about school positively.
   - Visit school.
   - Encourage attendance.
   - Support homework.

7. Limit TV viewing.
   - Select appropriate programs.
   - Encourage reading and imaginary and physical activities.
   - Discuss programs with child.

8. Encourage writing.
   - Have child write and/or draw thank-you notes, messages, stories.

9. Develop math concepts.
   - Cook together.
   - Play games.
   - Give allowance money to save and spend.

10. Develop science concepts.
    - Encourage collections.
    - Observe plants and animals.
    - Visit museums.

11. Develop social studies concepts.
    - Discuss current events.
    - Observe national holidays.
    - Demonstrate good citizenship by being well informed, discussing decision making, voting.
12. Get involved in the community (Hatcher & Beck, 1997).
    - Visit workplaces (post office, fire department, factory, office).
    - Visit historical sites.
    - Participate in community service.
13. Be a model of lifelong learning (Rich, 1992).
    - Confidence ("I can do it.")
    - Motivation ("I want to do it.")
    - Effort ("I'm willing to try hard.")
    - Responsibility ("I follow through on commitments.")
    - Initiative ("I am a self-starter.")
    - Perseverance ("I finish what I start.")
    - Caring ("I show concern for others.")
    - Teamwork ("I work cooperatively with others.")
    - Common sense ("I use good judgment.")
    - Problem solving ("I use my knowledge and experience effectively.")

DEVELOPMENTALLY APPROPRIATE LEARNING AND ASSESSMENT

How can schools empower student success?

Many schools have interpreted the concept of "readiness" to mean children's ability to succeed at school-related tasks and have used entrance testing to make this evaluation (Lewit & Baker, 1995). For example, **standardized tests**, in which an individual is compared to a norm on scientifically selected items, have been developed to assess kindergarten readiness. The National Association for the Education of Young Children (1988) asserts that such tests are inappropriate for young children because each child comes from a unique set of family experiences. What one family makes available for its children, another does not. Some children travel extensively; others seldom go outside their immediate community. Some children speak a language other than English. Some have had preschool experiences; others remained at home. Also, maturational differences influence children's ability to perform well on standardized tests—for example, the ability to listen and follow instructions, control a pencil, and sit still for a certain period of time.

If the concept of readiness were shared by the school, the school could do more to individualize school curricula and group children by developmental readiness instead of by age alone (Lewit & Baker, 1995). Thus, children who were of the legal age to attend school, but were not as "ready" to learn as their peers because of diverse family backgrounds, could be provided with developmentally appropriate activities. In addition, authentic assessments (for example, evaluating a portfolio of a child's writing or art) could be used, rather than relying solely on standardized paper-and-pencil tests.

In conclusion, the *school* should be ready for children to learn when they come to school, just as *children* should be ready to learn when they come to school.

standardized tests
tests in which an individual is compared to a norm on scientifically selected items

Epilogue

The teacher–student relationship is complicated. Both teacher and learner bring characteristics to a bidirectional relationship that is affected by the broader context of society, as well as the linkages within subcontexts. Different teaching methods may have specific socialization outcomes, but the real influence depends on whether the teacher is a model for the student to emulate, thus stimulating learning. The village storyteller was such a teacher.

Summary

The most powerful socializing influence of the school lies in those who translate program goals into action—the teachers. Effective teachers are warm, enthusiastic, and generous with praise, and have high status. These characteristics make them role models for children. Other characteristics of successful teachers are the ability to communicate well and responsiveness to students.

The teacher plays a major leadership role in helping children learn to deal with positions of authority, to cooperate with others, to cope with problems, and to achieve competence. Types of leaders include authoritarian, democratic, and laissez-faire (permissive).

The teacher is responsible for selecting materials relevant to the learner, for managing the group dynamics in the classroom, and for interacting individually with each child. Goal structures (cooperative, individualized, competitive) have different socialization effects.

Teachers' expectations of children often influence their interactions with them and, consequently, the children's performance. Teachers need to be aware of the effects of the self-fulfilling prophecy. Teachers also need to be aware of their responses to gender—generally teachers give more attention to boys for their work and girls for appropriate behavior—as well as to children from diverse ethnic groups (individualistic and collectivistic orientations), social classes, and religions; to children with disabilities; and to those at risk for negative developmental outcomes because of poverty, substance abuse, or violence in the family. Children's backgrounds may affect the teacher–student relationship, which is bidirectional.

Gender equity remains an issue in schools. Teachers must be aware of differential treatment of males and females in areas such as attention, curricular issues, role models in books, career counseling, and extracurricular activities.

Ethnic diversity needs to be understood because the United States is composed of many diverse ethnic groups, speaking a variety of languages, and the world is moving toward a global economy.

The U.S. macroculture—usually defined as white Anglo-Saxon Protestant—generally shares certain values. The degree to which individual Americans subscribe to the general values depends, in part, on the microculture or ethnic group of which the individual is a member. It may also depend on how much an individual must interact with the formal institutions of U.S. society (school, government, health and welfare agencies) for support. Diverse ethnic groups can be classified according to where they best fit along a continuum of individualistic versus collectivistic orientations.

Learning, or cognitive, styles are aspects of socialization that have implications for education. Analysis, deductive reasoning, accuracy, individual and competitive work, and verbal communication are associated with an analytical and field-independent cognitive style. Viewing things in their entirety, using approximations, focusing on people, preferring simultaneous involvement in activities, and being proficient in nonverbal communication are characteristic of a relational, field-dependent cognitive style.

To enable children with disabilities to have positive developmental outcomes, society, schools, and teachers have provided support. Laws have been passed requiring individuals with disabilities to be included in the mainstream of society. Educational methods have been modified to include children with specific disabilities to optimize their socialization.

The Individuals with Disabilities Act (IDEA) requires that an individualized education program (IEP) be written annually specifying educational goals, methods, and resources/services required to meet the child's needs. PL 99–457 provides for a variety of programs for infants, toddlers, and preschoolers with disabilities, and includes instruction for parents in the socialization of their child via an individualized family service plan (IFSP).

The community, via legislation, has aided integration of individuals with disabilities. The Vocational Rehabilitation Act of 1973 and, more recently, the Americans with Disabilities Act of 1990 guarantee certain rights to individuals with disabilities, such as affirmative action and access. Thus, schools and support professionals must be involved in the transition from home to community.

Children at risk for negative developmental outcomes, such as children from families experiencing poverty, substance abuse, and/or domestic violence, need special support from teachers and other adults to enable resiliency and achievement motivation.

Macrosystem influences on teaching include curriculum philosophies, as well as policies on accountability and standardization. Philosophies of teaching and learning range from teacher-directed programs to learner-directed ones.

Teacher-directed (traditional) educational environments usually subscribe to the philosophy that the functions of the school are to impart basic factual knowledge and preserve the cultural heritage. Traditional education includes homework, tests, memorization, and strict discipline. Learner-directed (modern) educational environments subscribe to the philosophy that the function of the school is to develop the whole child, physically, socially, and emotionally as well as cognitively. Curriculum emerges from the child's interests and abilities and is constructed accordingly.

Socialization outcomes differ according to the setting. Children in traditional settings perform better on academic tasks and are "on-task" more often than children in modern settings. Children in modern settings tend to have a more positive attitude toward school, are involved in more cooperative work, and show more autonomy than children in traditional settings.

Schools and teachers must now be accountable for student learning. In order to receive public funding, schools administer achievement tests and students are compared to a standard for their grade.

Linkages between the child, family, school, and community are necessary to optimize socialization and empower success. The significance of these mesosystems is demonstrated in the nation's number-one education goal, that all children will come to school "ready to learn." "Readiness" encompasses health, nutrition, and social/emotional factors. Families can enable children to be ready by nurturing, communicating, encouraging learning, and getting involved in school. Schools can enable "readiness" by individualizing the curriculum, providing activities that are developmentally appropriate, and using authentic assessments rather than relying on standardized tests.

Activity

PURPOSE To understand the teacher's influence on socialization.

1. Choose two elementary school classrooms (same grade) to observe. One should be primarily teacher-directed, or traditional; the other should be primarily learner-directed, or modern. (You may have to go to two different schools.)
2. Describe the physical arrangement of each classroom environment.
3. Describe the activity going on during the time of your observation in each classroom. How are simultaneous activities (computer work and reading group, for example) handled? What about transitions from one activity to another?
4. Describe the social interaction (for example, warm/hostile, flexible/inflexible, caring/uncaring) between the teacher and children in each classroom. Note teachers' responses to gender and ethnic diversity (and disability, if included).
5. Can you draw any conclusions regarding the socialization of the children in each classroom?

Related Readings

Bennett, C. E. (2003). *Comprehensive multicultural education: Theory and practice* (5th ed.). Boston: Allyn and Bacon.

Black, C. (1991). *It will never happen to me* (rev. ed.). New York: Ballantine Books.

Byrnes, D. A., & Kigler, G. (Eds.). (1996). *Common bonds: Anti-bias teaching in a diverse society*. Wheaton, MD: Association for Childhood Education International.

Chall, J. (2000). *The academic achievement challenge: What really works in the classroom?* New York: Guilford.

Comer, J. P. (2004). *Leave no child behind: Preparing today's youth for tomorrow's world*. New Haven, CT: Yale University Press.

Farnham-Diggory, S. (1992). *The learning-disabled child*. Cambridge, MA: Harvard University Press.

Geffner, R. A., & Jouriles, E. N. (1998). *Children exposed to marital violence: Theory, research, and applied issues*. Washington, DC: American Psychological Association.

Ginott, H. (1972). *Teacher and child*. New York: Avon Books.

Gordon, T. (1974). *T.E.T.: Teacher effectiveness training*. New York: Wyden.

Heck, S. F., & Williams, C. R. (1984). *The complex roles of the teacher: An ecological perspective*. New York: Teachers College Press.

Marshall, P. L. (2002). *Cultural diversity in our schools*. Belmont, CA: Wadsworth.

Ramsey, P. G. (2004). *Teaching and learning in a diverse world: Multicultural education for young children* (3rd ed.). New York: Teachers College Press.

Schank, R. L. (2004). *Making minds less well educated than our own*. Mahwah, NJ: Lawrence Erlbaum.

Wolery, M., & Wilbers, J. S. (Eds.). (1994). *Including children with special needs in early childhood programs*. Washington, DC: National Association for the Education of Young Children.

York, S. (1991). *Roots and wings: Affirming culture in early childhood programs*. St. Paul, MN: Toys 'n Things Press.

Chapter 8

HIRB/Index Stock Imagery

Ecology of the Peer Group

Without friends no one would choose to live, though he had all other goods.
— ARISTOTLE

What makes a good friend? Why is it important to have at least one?

A Nigerian folktale reminds us that friends remain true even though they may view things differently.

Once Upon a Time A long time ago, there were two boys who

were great friends, and they were determined to remain that way forever. When they grew up and got married, they built their houses facing one another. There was a small path that formed a border between their farms.

One day, a trickster from the village decided to play a trick on them. He dressed himself in a two-color coat that was divided down the middle. So, one side of the coat was red, and the other side was blue.

The trickster wore this coat and walked along the narrow path between the houses of the two friends, who were working opposite each other in their fields. The trickster made enough noise as he passed them to make sure that each of them would look up and see him passing.

At the end of the day, one friend said to the other, "Wasn't that a beautiful red coat that man was wearing today?"

"No," the other replied. "It was a blue coat."

"I saw the man clearly as he walked between us!" said the first. "His coat was red."

"You are wrong!" said the other man. "I saw it too, and it was blue."

"I know what I saw!" insisted the first man. "The coat was red!"

"You don't know anything," the second man replied angrily. "It was blue!"

They kept arguing about this over and over, insulted each other, and eventually began to beat each other and roll around on the ground.

Just then, the trickster returned and faced the two men, who were punching and kicking each other and shouting, "Our friendship is OVER!"

The trickster walked directly in front of them, and showed them his coat. He laughed at their silly fight. The two friends saw that his coat was red on one side and blue on the other.

The two friends stopped fighting and screamed at the trickster saying, "We have lived side by side like brothers all our lives, and it is all your fault that we are fighting. You have started a war between us."

"Don't blame me for the battle," replied the trickster. "I did not make you fight. Both of you are wrong, and both of you are right. Yes, what each one saw was true. You are fighting because you only looked at my coat from your own point of view."

Source: MotherlandNigeria.com (© 1998–2002). The Red and Blue Coat.

- **What is the value of friendship?**

- **How do friends work through conflicts?**

- **What are some issues that arise in a group that affect friendship?**

- **What are some strategies that friends engage in to maintain the relationship?**

The Peer Group as a Socializing Agent

Why is the peer group considered to be a socializing agent?

The peer group is a microsystem in that it comprises relationships, roles, and activities. **Peers** are equals, individuals who are usually of the same gender, age, and social status and who share interests. Although *outwardly* the peer group appears to comprise equals, *inwardly* the dynamics of the peer group reveal that some members are more equal than others (Adler & Adler, 1998; Steinberg, 1996). Interactions, dynamics, and social hierarchies in the peer group will be discussed later.

Experiences with peers enable children to acquire a wide range of skills, attitudes, and roles that influence their adaptation throughout life (Rubin et al., 1998). Peer groups are significant socializers, contributing beyond the influence of family and school because:

- They satisfy certain belonging needs (Adler & Adler, 1998).
- They are often preferred to other socializing agents (Harris, 1998).
- They influence not only social development, but cognitive and psychological development as well (Ladd, 1999).

Today, as more mothers are being employed outside the home, more and more children are being cared for in group settings. Consequently, children are experiencing social interaction with peers today earlier and for longer periods of time than they were a generation ago. Also, school-age children and adolescents who are not supervised by adults after school are more likely to turn to their peers for support. In this chapter, we examine various peer group influences; Figure 8.1 shows an ecological model of the systems involved in the process.

THE SIGNIFICANCE OF PEERS TO DEVELOPMENT

How do peers contribute to normal development?

Peer groups are significant because they satisfy certain basic human needs: the need to belong to a group and interact socially, and the need to develop a sense of self (a personal identity). Belonging to a peer group enables one to have social interactions with others and have experiences independent of parents or other adults. By interacting socially with others, we derive an opinion of ourselves. We referred to this concept in Chapter 2 as the "looking-glass self" (Cooley, 1909/1964) and the "generalized other" (Mead, 1934). We think of ourselves as having pretty hair, cute freckles, or a large nose because others tell us so. We think of ourselves as clever, as fast runners, or as good at drawing by comparing our skills to those of others.

peers individuals who are of approximately the same gender, age, and social status and who share interests

Figure 8.1

An Ecological Model of Human Development

Peers are a significant influence on the child's development.

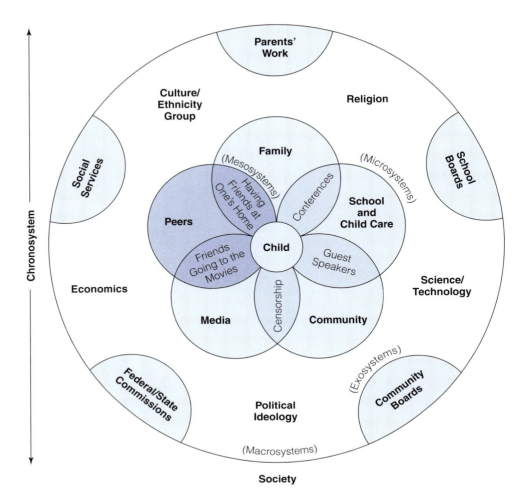

What Were Some of the Things You Did Growing Up to Be Accepted by Peers?

When I was 13 years old, I sneaked out of the house to go to a party in my neighborhood when I was supposed to be babysitting for my brother. I was so scared my parents would come home while I was gone, or my brother would wake up and not find me, that I had a horrible time. I ended up telling my friends my parents would be home early, so they would not be mad at me for leaving.

Belonging Needs and Social Interaction

Although the need to belong to groups and to interact with others is characteristic of humans, individual differences in intensity and amount exist. Some differences are due to *nature*, or temperament, and some are due to *nurture*, or socialization experiences. Child–peer relationships are bidirectional. For example, individual temperamental characteristics, such as shyness or sociability, may influence a child's ability to make friends. These temperamental traits affect parent responses in that parents of shy children may have to provide more encouragement to have peer experiences than do parents of sociable children (Rubin et al., 1998). Also, parents who provide opportunities for their children to have contact with peers may coach their children to interact positively and may intervene when negative behavior occurs (Pettit & Mize, 1993). Parent–child relationships from infancy to middle childhood will be examined to better understand how they influence peer relationships.

Infancy/Toddlerhood (Birth to Age 1$\frac{1}{2}$ or 2). The sense of belonging develops first within the family. A baby gets the feeling he or she "belongs" to his or her mother when the mother holds, soothes, and meets the baby's needs. Babies whose mothers or caregivers are sensitive and responsive to their needs—for example, feeding them when they are hungry and comforting them when they are frightened—are *securely attached* (Ainsworth, 1979; Rubin et al., 1998). The importance of attachment in socialization was discussed in Chapter 2. Attachment theory suggests that the child who enjoys a secure attachment relationship with his or her caregiver is likely to possess a model to imitate for responsiveness to others (Rubin et al., 1998; Schneider, Atkinson, & Tardif, 2001). In addition, it is believed that a secure attachment provides a secure base for exploratory behavior (Ainsworth, 1973, 1979, 1982). Infants and toddlers who are secure in their relationship with their caregivers feel confident in leaving them to explore their environment (including objects and people) because they know their caregiver will be available should the need arise. On the other hand, babies who are *insecurely attached*, those who have experienced parental rejection or inconsistency of care, tend to avoid peer relationships (Troy & Sroufe, 1987).

Babies who form secure attachments during their first year are described at age 3$\frac{1}{2}$ as socially involved with their peers. Children who are securely attached tend to approach others with positive expectations more readily than do children who are insecurely attached (Ainsworth, 1979; Jacobson & Wille, 1986; Rubin et al., 1998). They are often leaders proactively engaged in activities (Park & Waters, 1989). In contrast, a child who has experienced insecure attachments in which

These babies are already interested in each other as distinct human beings.

his or her needs were met insensitively or inconsistently may have negative expectations toward peers, acting as if peers will be rejecting (Howes, Matheson, & Hamilton, 1994). Such children may exhibit withdrawal or aggressive behavior (Rubin et al., 1998).

After toddlerhood, a gradual shift occurs in the relative importance of adults and peers in children's lives. Children who attend preschool increasingly look to their peers for attention and decreasingly seek proximity to the caregivers (Hartup, 1983). This was demonstrated by Corsaro (1981) in a field study done in a preschool with children ranging in age from 2 years 11 months to 4 years 10 months. Field notes and videotapes showed that the children rarely engaged in solitary play and that when they found themselves alone, they consistently tried to gain entry into ongoing peer activities: "Can I play? I'll be your friend." Also, children who were involved in peer activities often protected the interaction by resisting children who attempted to gain access: "You can't play; you're not our friend." Thus, the more important peers become to the child, the more expansive are his or her social experiences.

Early Childhood (Ages 2 to 5 or 6). Preschool children's social interactions are affected not only by how secure they feel in their attachment to their mothers but also by the willingness of adults to provide opportunities for social interaction (Ladd & LeSieur, 1995). For instance, where the family resides determines the number of same-age children living nearby. The willingness of parents to invite other children to their home or to take their child to another's home, and whether or not a child attends a preschool program, affect the amount of social interaction that can take place.

Parenting styles (discussed in Chapter 4) have been found to influence children's competence in interacting with peers. *Authoritative* (democratic) parenting has been associated with children's social-behavioral competence and confidence (Baumrind, 1973). *Authoritarian* (adult-directed), *permissive* (child-directed), and *indifferent/ uninvolved* parenting styles, in contrast, have been linked to low competence in social interaction (Ladd & LeSieur, 1995; Ladd & Pettit, 2002). It is likely that children model parental interactions with their friends.

Middle Childhood (Ages 6 to 12 or 13). By school age, opportunities for social interaction increase. Children spend most of the day with other children—in class, on the school bus, and in the neighborhood. Children no longer need adults to structure their social interactions. In the middle years, children become more and more dependent on the recognition and approval of their peers, rather than of adults. Their sense of belonging extends and expands. Interestingly, however, it was found that children whose parents took an active role in arranging and organizing their peer relations (inviting specific children to the home, encouraging the child to participate in a school or community group, and discussing the child's friends and interactions) tended to develop closer, more harmonious ties with peers (Ladd & LeSieur, 1995).

Adolescence (Ages 12 or 13 to ~18). Adolescents generally delineate their belonging needs and consequent social interactions according to the closeness of the relationship. The closest relationships and most intimate social interactions, such as sharing feelings, occur with one or two "best" friends; next are relationships with about 6 to 10 peers who are friends who do things together (the "clique"); finally, there are relationships with the larger, more loosely organized peer group (or the "crowd") with which the adolescent identifies (Steinberg, 1996).

Sense of Self

Throughout development, peer relationships contribute to the self-concept, including one's perception of his or her personal identity (Who am I?) and self-esteem (How do I feel about myself?).

Infancy/Toddlerhood. Infants as young as 6 months look at, vocalize to, smile at, and touch other infants, thereby distinguishing themselves from others (Hay, 1985). As babies develop, relations with peers change, becoming more reciprocal. For example, at about a year, their smiles, vocalizations, and playful activities are often imitated or reacted to (Howes & Matheson, 1992). During the second year, toddlers use words to communicate and can coordinate their behavior with that of a playmate (Rubin et al., 1998).

Early Childhood. When children begin to play in groups, generally after age 2 or 3, they have a chance to play a variety of roles that were not available to them in the family context. Now they have to grapple with and work through issues of power, compliance, cooperation, and conflict (Kemple, 1991). Such issues contribute to the development of a sense of self and personal identity, giving children the opportunity to be assertive regarding ownership and to negotiate regarding desires: "That's my puzzle; you can't play with it." "If you let me ride the bike, I'll let you hold my doll."

Middle Childhood. For the middle-years child (ages 6 to 12 or 13), the peer group is attractive because it provides opportunities for greater independence than does the family, thereby enhancing the sense of self. Did you ever build a fort or a tree house when you were a child? The underlying idea, of course, was for the group to have a place of its own, where it could be independent of adult supervision and where unwanted children could be excluded.

In the peer group, children can say what they feel without being told "You should not say things like that." Or they can make suggestions without being told "You're too young to do that." Or they can do things without being told "It will never work" (as an adult might say).

Middle-years children, especially toward preadolescence (age 11 to 13), long to find others like themselves; to know that others share their doubts, their fears, their wishes, and their perceptions. The peer group is an important source of self-confirmation in that children learn, by comparing their thoughts and feelings with those of others, that they are not really different or "weird." Thus, belonging to a group clarifies personal identity and enhances self-esteem. The concern about acceptance in the peer group is often exhibited by gossip. Teasley and Parker (1995) found that much gossip among middle-years children is negative, involving defamation of third parties. "Did you hear that Jane actually bribed Sam to go to the party with her?" Children like to discuss who their friends are and who their enemies are. "Don't you just hate Brian; he's such a dork!"

Peers also provide empathy and support for one another when children's desires for independent action conflict with adults' demands: "My father won't let me touch his CD player. He's so mean!" "Can you believe Mrs. Millard made me clean the whole floor after school just because I shot one spit-wad? It's not fair!"

The peer group, in addition to clarifying and supporting one's identity, also provides models for what one can become. Peers show what is worth doing and how to do it. It was probably your friends who taught you how to dance and to like popular music, as well as influencing what style of clothes you wore.

Achieving personal identity is a slow and difficult process during which children turn to their peers instead of their parents for certain kinds of support. However, entrance into the peer group creates some difficulties of its own (Grusec & Lytton, 1988). First, there is the change from protected to unprotected competition. At home, squabbles between children can be settled by adults; in the peer group one has to learn to protect oneself, whether it be getting to the swing first or not letting someone tease you. Second, the responses expected and rewarded at home and school are different from those in the peer group. At home and at school the child is encouraged to be obedient and submissive; in the peer group, self-assertion and domination are the virtues that are rewarded.

Adolescence. Adolescence (about age 13 to 18) is a time in our society when peer group activities escalate. One reason is that adolescents are not fully included in the adult world of responsibility and recognition for contributions. Therefore, they turn to peers. Adolescents often experience differences in the values of the family and those of the peer group. For example, academic achievement is an important value in some families, whereas among some groups of adolescents, athletic performance seems to be more important (Steinberg, 1996). Normally, which values are adolescents more likely to adopt, their family's or their friends'? According to Hans Sebald (1989, 1992), adolescents turn to their parents with regard to scholastic or occupational goals—in general, *future-oriented decisions*. They turn to their friends with regard to clothing, social activities, dating, and recreation—in general, *present-oriented decisions*. On *moral issues*, parental values dominate; on *appearance*, such as grooming, peer values dominate (Niles, 1981).

Parenting styles have been found to be associated with adult versus peer influence (Mounts, 2002). Parents, as was discussed, do influence with whom their children interact. The following findings link child–parent relationships to child–peer relationships.

- *Authoritative* parents—those who are warm, accepting, neither too controlling nor too lax, and consistent in their child-rearing management—generally have children who are attached and who internalize their values. These children have little need to rebel or to desperately seek acceptance from peers (Fuligni & Eccles, 1993). They usually associate with friends who share their values, so they are not faced with negative peer influences (Fletcher, Darling, Steinberg, & Dornsbusch, 1995).
- *Authoritarian* parents—those who are very strict, cold, and do not adjust to their adolescent's need for greater autonomy—typically have children who alienate themselves from parental values and are attracted to the peer group to gain understanding and acceptance (Fuligni & Eccles, 1993). These adolescents are at risk for negative peer influences.
- *Permissive* parents—those who indulge their children by not providing standards, rules, or behavioral consequences and/or who ignore their children's activities—typically risk having adolescents who are attracted to antisocial peer groups (Dishion, Patterson, Stoolmiller, & Skinner, 1991).

Do such generalizations relating parenting styles to peer group attraction apply to diverse ethnic groups?

This is a question still being researched. It is known that authoritarian parenting is more common among ethnic minority families than among Euro-American families (Chen & Rubin, 1994), and also that some adverse effects of authoritarian parenting found among Euro-American youngsters may not be as common among youth of other ethnicities (Chao, 1994). In addition, it is known that some ethnic groups place more emphasis on *interdependence* and social support networks than do European Americans, who tend to emphasize *independence* and individuality (Greenfield & Suzuki, 1998). Social support networks include extended family members as well as friends. This was documented in a field observation study by Hutchison (1987), conducted in public parks in Chicago, that included 18,000 groups engaged in various leisure activities. In general, European Americans engaged in more individualized activities, Hispanics engaged in the most family–peer combined activities, and African Americans engaged in the most peer-oriented activities.

Thus, the significance of peer group attraction may differ according to ethnic origin. Regardless of parenting style, the peer group may provide one with a desired connection to the community and positive social support. Because of the peer group's attractiveness to the individual, it may become a negative influence on values and behavior.

In sum, the process of achieving a sense of self involves the major task of balancing group identification with personal autonomy while simultaneously forging an individual role within the group. To participate in group activities, one must develop the required skills to engage in its games, as well as master the rules and agreements that govern its activities. In reaching a balance between group identification and personal autonomy, children must weigh loyalty to group norms against individual norms and parental norms. They need to develop their roles in the group structure (leading or following, for example) and cope with feelings of being accepted, popular, unpopular, or rejected (Grusec & Lytton, 1988; Minuchin, 1977; Rubin et al., 1998).

PSYCHOLOGICAL DEVELOPMENT: EMOTIONS

How do peer relations predict adult life course development?

Individuals who do not have normal peer relations are affected in their later psychological development. Studies (Asher & Coie, 1990; Hartup, 1983; Ladd, 1999; Rubin et al., 1998) have indicated that poor peer relations in childhood are linked to the later development of neurotic and psychotic behavior and to a greater tendency to drop out of school. Psychologists actually find that sociometric measures (measures of patterns of attraction and rejection among members of a group, discussed later in the chapter) taken in the elementary grades predict adjustment in later life better than other educational or personality tests: The child's peer group seems to serve as a barometer, showing current and predicting future adjustment problems (Asher, 1982; Hymel, Bowker, & Woody, 1993; Parker & Asher, 1987). Why is this so? One's ability to deal with the social world depends on communicative skills, a repertoire for coordinating one's actions with those of others, reciprocity, cooperation, and competition. These competencies develop through interactions and experiences in the peer group. In addition, peer groups have certain norms for behavior, sometimes positive (cooperation, for example) and sometimes negative (exclusion of some children or rebelliousness, for example). Children learn to compete for status in the peer group by *compliance* with group norms ("*followership*") and *creation* of group norms (*leadership*) at appropriate times. Sometimes I have to go along with the group; sometimes I come up with the idea of what to do. Even though one might have occasions to lead and to follow, generally statuses, or social hierarchies, remain fairly stable in the group, with those who don't fit in being cast out or leaving on their own (American Academy of Pediatrics, 2002).

Figure 8.2

Conformity Peaks

Prosocial conformity peaks at sixth grade, whereas antisocial conformity peaks at ninth grade.

Source: T. J. Berndt (1979). Developmental changes in conformity to peers and parents. *Developmental Psychology, 15,* 608–616. Copyright © 1979 by the American Psychological Association. Reprinted by permission.

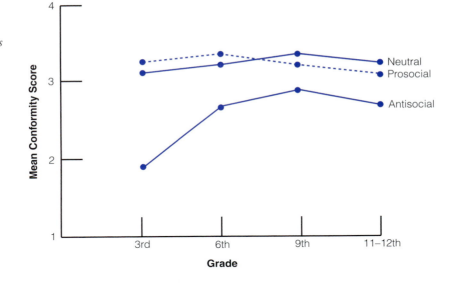

How do children negotiate their status?

According to Harris (1998), children not only learn the importance of conforming to be accepted by the peer group; they also learn through experience such aspects of social competence as the dynamics of power, manipulation, and popularity as well as how to negotiate these attributes.

SOCIAL DEVELOPMENT: SOCIAL COMPETENCE

Does being socially competent mean conforming?

Social competence involves behavior informed by an understanding of others' feelings and intentions, the ability to respond appropriately, and knowledge of the consequences of one's actions. Being part of a social group involves conforming to group norms. The degree of social conformity that individuals exhibit depends on their age and stage of cognitive development, the situation, and such psychological factors as temperament, values, morals, motives, and self-esteem.

Age and Stage of Cognitive Development. Studies (Berndt, 1979; Brown, Clasen, & Eicher, 1986; Foster-Clark & Blyth, 1991) have shown that children become most susceptible to the influence of peers in middle childhood and become less conforming in adolescence (see Figure 8.2). Even when it is known to be wrong, middle-years children still go along with the majority opinion of the group (Berenda, 1950). In a classic study, 90 children ages 7 to 13 were asked to compare the lengths of lines on 12 pairs of cards. They had already taken this same test in school. This time, however, the children participating in the experiment were tested in a room with the eight brightest children in their class. Answers were given aloud. These eight children had been instructed beforehand to give 7 wrong answers out of 12. The results pointed to the power of group influence. Whereas almost all the subjects had given correct answers to the seven critical questions in the original test taken in school, only 43% of the 7- to 10-year-olds, and only 54% of the 10- to 13-year-olds, gave correct answers on the second test in the group setting. The rest changed their former answers to match the group's, which were intentionally incorrect.

social competence
behavior informed by an understanding of others' feelings and intentions, the ability to respond appropriately, and knowledge of the consequences of one's actions

Situation. Such conformity is even more apparent in ambiguous situations where children are unsure about what they should do or are supposed to do (Cohen, Bornstein, & Sherman, 1973; Hartup, 1983; Steinberg, 1996). For example, Thomas Berndt (1979; Berndt & Ladd, 1989) gave a questionnaire to students ranging from 3rd to 12th grade, asking how they would respond to various hypothetical situations (*prosocial, neutral, antisocial*). A question exemplifying a *prosocial* situation asked the students whether they would help a classmate with a report if asked by their peers, instead of doing what they wanted to do, which was helping another classmate operate the film projector. A question exemplifying a *neutral* situation asked the students whether they would go to a movie if asked by their peers, even if they were not particularly interested in that movie. A question exemplifying an *antisocial* situation asked the students whether they would steal some candy if a peer wanted help in doing it.

Psychological Factors. One of Berndt's (1979) findings was that conformity to antisocial behavior and neutral situations peaked in the ninth grade and then dropped off to previous levels. Another finding was that conformity to prosocial behavior peaked in the sixth grade and then dropped. In general, the sixth- to ninth-graders exhibited the most conforming behavior. The results are plotted in Figure 8.2. Berndt also found that whether or not people conformed to the group depended on their feelings about the particular situation—how "good" or "bad" they felt about it. Students were more likely to conform to situations they did not feel very "bad" about. Thus, personal values do affect one's likelihood of conforming to the peer group.

COGNITIVE DEVELOPMENT: SOCIAL COGNITION

Why are preadolescent children (age 11 to 13) more susceptible to peer group influences than children of other ages?

Even though children interact with one another increasingly from infancy on, the ability to cope with complex social messages increases with age. For example, children under age 7 do not have the cognitive ability even to be aware of peer pressure to conform or the consequences for deviance. They have difficulty taking another's point of view and cannot, therefore, project what the peer group thinks of them. Much documentation has been accumulating regarding the connection between social development and cognitive development (Ladd, 1999). This connection is referred to as **social cognition**—conceptions and reasoning about people, the self, relations between people, social groups' roles and rules, and the relation of such conceptions to social behavior (Shantz, 1983). Collaboration with peers through language and play enables the child to construct thoughts (Berk & Winsler, 1995). The social interactions with peers also contribute to the child's cognitive understanding of his or her culture.

Young children ages 7–11 are in the stage of cognitive development that Jean Piaget (1952) termed *concrete operations*. The concrete operational stage is characterized by the ability to apply logical, systematic principles to help interpret specific or tangible experiences, but also by the inability to distinguish between intangible assumptions, or hypotheses, and facts, or reality.

According to David Elkind (1981a), concrete-operational children make theories about reality (situations and people) assumed to be true without examining or evaluating contradictory data (**assumptive realities**), no matter how illogical they are. For example, U.S. children of this age who have seen a globe at school might try to dig a hole in the ground to get to China, because China is on the other side of the globe (I used to do this at the beach). No amount of adult logic in terms of distances can dissuade them. Concrete-operational children also assume they are clever. David Elkind

social cognition
conceptions and reasoning about people, the self, relations between people, social group's roles and rules, and the relation of such conceptions to social behavior

assumptive reality
a theory about reality assumed to be true without examining or evaluating contradictory data

calls this **cognitive conceit**, the exhibition of too much faith in one's reasoning ability and cleverness. The concept of cognitive conceit is illustrated in some favorite stories of children of this age—for example, *Peter Pan* (a child who outwits Captain Hook, an adult) or *Alice in Wonderland* (a young girl who makes the queen look like a fool).

Because children under age 11 often think they know it all, they sometimes feel they do not have to pay attention to the opinions of others, be they adults or other children. "I don't have to" (a common remark at this age), then, is not really defiance but a statement of concrete-operational children's beliefs about their abilities (Piaget, 1952).

About age 11, children become capable of logical thought. Piaget called this the stage of *formal operations* because the child now understands the *form* behind a concept and can add ideas to or subtract them from it. The stage of formal operations is characterized by the ability to think logically about abstract ideas and hypotheses, as well as concrete facts; one can now construct all the possibilities of a proposition—the ones related to fact and the ones contrary to fact. Preadolescent children, then, can conceptualize their own thoughts and discover the arbitrariness of their assumptions. They also discover rules for testing assumptions against facts (**reality testing**). This leads to diminished confidence in their ability, especially their cleverness. Preadolescent children are aware of the reactions of others and the need to conform to their expectations. This new awareness exhibits itself in the **imaginary audience**—the belief that others are as concerned with one's behavior and appearance as one is oneself. Thus, preadolescent children believe they are the focus of attention, and they strive extra hard to be like their peers so that they will not stand out.

As children approach adolescence (ages 13 to 15), the imaginary audience comes to be regarded as an assumption to be tested against reality. As a consequence of this testing, adolescents gradually come to recognize the difference between their own preoccupations and the interests and concerns of others. Therefore, conformity decreases because adolescents realize that they are expected to conform to some situations but can be independent in others. Adolescents have also developed better social skills and a greater reliance on their own judgment.

One reason preadolescent children are more conforming than other age groups is that their level of cognitive development is capable of logical thought; that is, they can project how others react and evaluate their assumptions. However, they have not yet had the experience of testing their assumptions on reality, for example:

cognitive conceit
Elkind's term for children in Piaget's stage of concrete operations who put too much faith in their reasoning ability and cleverness

reality testing testing assumptions against facts

imaginary audience the beliefs that others are as concerned with one's behavior and appearance as one is oneself

> When my daughter began junior high school, she refused to take the backpack I had bought her for her books. She said, "All the kids will laugh at me; only kids in elementary school use backpacks." I asked her what the junior high kids used to carry their books. Exhibiting pre-adolescent assumptions, she did not know exactly (she had not been there yet), but she thought they used satchels. For the first week of school, she carried her books loosely in her arms. When the second week of school came, she grudgingly put her books in the backpack, saying she was tired of dropping books and that her arms ached. One day after school had been in session for about a month, I picked up my daughter at school. I noticed that a lot of kids had backpacks. I said nothing, but I thought to myself, "She assumed all the other kids would have satchels and she didn't want to be different. She had to make sure that enough other kids had backpacks before she would take hers to school." Can you remember being reluctant to do something before you saw others do it? What were your concerns?

Another reason preadolescent children are more conforming than other age groups is that they are entering Erikson's (1963) fifth psychosocial stage of development—*identity versus identity (role) confusion* (Who am I, and what is my role in life?). Erikson's stages were discussed in Chapter 2. In the process of finding an identity, preadolescent children repeat the crises of the earlier stages—*basic trust versus basic mistrust* (Do I generally trust people, or distrust them?); *autonomy versus shame and doubt* (Am I confident I can be independent, or am I doubtful about my ability to be independent?); *initiative versus guilt* (Do I feel good about starting new things or meeting new people, or do I feel guilty?); and *industry versus inferiority* (Do I feel competent about my abilities, or inferior?).

"The growing and developing youths, faced with this psychological revolution within them, and with tangible adult tasks ahead of them, are now primarily concerned with what they appear to be in the eyes of others as compared with what they feel they are" (Erikson, 1963, p. 261). They are trying out roles and using the reactions of others to judge how well the roles fit their self-concept. Thus, in the process of wondering "Who am I?" children beginning this psychosocial stage of development tend to "temporarily overidentify to the point of apparent complete loss of identity, with heroes of cliques and crowds" (p. 262).

Erikson explains the clannishness and cruelty of excluding those who are different from the group as a defense against a sense of identity confusion. Preadolescent children who are on the brink of entering the identity-versus-role-confusion stage look to the peer group for their identity. The group's symbols and rituals (ways of dressing, ways of behaving, attitudes, opinions), as well as its approval and support, help define what is good and what is bad, thereby contributing to the development of ego identity. Identifying with a group and excluding those who are not like the members of the group helps children identify *who they are* by affirming *who they are not*. As preadolescence gives way to adolescence, young people begin to derive an identity from the accumulation of their experiences, their abilities, and their goals. They begin to look within themselves rather than to others for who they are. The peer group, then, serves to mediate between the individual and society, playing a powerful role in shaping the individual's identity (Adler & Adler, 1998).

PEER GROUP SOCIALIZING MECHANISMS

What socializing mechanisms does the peer group employ to influence behavior?

Typical socializing methods include reinforcement (approval and acceptance), modeling (imitation), punishment (rejection and exclusion), and apprenticeship (when a novice learns from an expert).

Reinforcement

One important way in which children influence each other is through reinforcement, or giving attention. Approving another's behavior (smiling, laughing, patting, hugging, verbalizing praise) increases the likelihood of that behavior's recurring (Kindermann, 1998). The behavior could be sharing, or it could be aggression against another (Martin & Pear, 2003). Reinforcement also involves acceptance into the group. Criteria for acceptance will be discussed later.

That reinforcement, rather than degree of friendship, increases behavior was demonstrated in a study in which young children ages 4 and 5 performed better at simple tasks when a child they disliked praised their performance than when a child they liked did so (Hartup, 1964, 1983).

Sometimes reinforcement is unintentional, but it is still effective. To illustrate, one study (Patterson, Littman, & Bricker, 1976) showed that preschool children reacted to physical aggression (bullying) by becoming passive, assuming a defensive posture, crying, telling the teacher, retrieving their property, or retaliating with aggression. When a child responded with reinforcers, such as passiveness, defensiveness, or crying, the aggression tended to be repeated on the same victim. When the child responded with proactive behavior, such as telling the teacher, retrieving property, or counteraggression, the aggressor or bully tended to behave differently toward the former victim. Thus, passivity unintentionally reinforces aggression toward the victim; action serves to redirect the aggression away from the victim.

To determine whether certain social stimuli functioned as reinforcers, Furman and Masters (1980) observed and recorded rates of laughter and praise (*positive* reinforcers); crying, physical attack, and disapproval (*negative* reinforcers); and other expressions (*neutral* reinforcers) in preschool children. They found that behaviors classified as positive reinforcements were twice as likely to be followed by similar affective behaviors, whereas punitive acts were more than five times as likely to be succeeded by negative behaviors. Parents and teachers need to be alert to patterns of peer reinforcement so that peers can be used effectively to help change negative or disruptive behavior.

Modeling

Children also influence each other through modeling, or imitation (Kindermann, 1998). Modeling is related to conformity. Observing a child behave in a certain manner can affect another's consequent behavior in three different ways (Bandura, 1989):

This child is intent on modeling her friend.

© Elizabeth Crews

- The observing child may learn how to do something new that he or she could not do previously (such as drawing a picture of a dog) or would probably not have thought of (such as riding a bike with "no hands").
- The child may learn the consequences of behavior by observing someone else. For example, pinching another results in being punished by the teacher, or getting to the swings first results in getting the longest turn.
- A model may suggest how a child can behave in a new situation. For example, when the children lined up at the edge of the pool for their first dive, Maureen was first. She said, "I can do it. I've watched my brother hundreds of times." As the instructor was showing her how to hold her arms and keep her head down, the others watched nervously. In a second, she hit the water, and in another few seconds she popped up smiling. The others relaxed.

In a classic study by Bandura, Ross, and Ross (1963), children who were shown a film in which a model struck a doll, sat on it, and screamed at it later copied the model's aggressive behavior when given a similar doll to play with. Other researchers (Hartup, 1983; Hartup & Coates, 1967) studied a group of 4- and 5-year-old children who were asked to watch one of their classmates work out problems. The classmate, the model, received some trinkets for doing the task. This model put aside some of the trinkets for a mythical child. The children who watched were then asked to do the problems, and the model left the room. They were also given trinkets and were also given the opportunity to save some trinkets for "the other child." Another group of 4- and 5-year-olds, who did not watch a model do the problems and exhibit altruistic behavior, were asked to do the same problems, were given trinkets, and were given the opportunity to save some for "the other child." The children who observed altruistic behavior gave more trinkets than those who did not.

The extent to which modeling influences behavior depends on the following factors:

- **Situation**. Active behavior is more likely to be imitated than passive behavior.
- **Model**. A model who is perceived to be similar to the observer and has desirable or admirable traits is more likely to be imitated than one who does not seem similar or who has traits not particularly desirable to the observer.
- **Observer**. The observer's cognitive and physical ability to reproduce the observed behavior also influences modeling. The observer must understand and remember the behavior and must be able to perform the verbal and/or motor functions involved. (Bandura, 1989)

Studying children in preschool classes has shown that a great deal of imitation, some positive and some negative, of both verbal and motor acts occurs in day-by-day interactions (Abramovitch & Grusec, 1978). Imitation seems to decrease from preschool to age 10, perhaps because deferred, rather than immediate, imitation and other subtle forms of observational learning become more favored as children get older. Dominant children in a group are imitated more often by others, but they imitate others as well (Grusec & Lytton, 1988).

As a socializing method, modeling has broader effects than reinforcement. A large number of children can be influenced by one carefully selected model, whereas direct reinforcement requires one-to-one interaction between the teacher and the learner. Modeling can provide a means of inducing behavior that otherwise might not occur. It may give the child an idea for doing something never done before, or it may remind the child of something done before and induce the child to repeat it (Bandura, 1989). Using reinforcement as a behavior modification technique requires waiting for the behavior to appear and then reinforcing it (Martin & Pear, 2003).

Punishment

Still another way in which children influence each other is through punishment—teasing, physical aggression, or rejection by the group. Criteria for rejection will be discussed later. An extreme of such punishment is being a victim of bullying. *Victims* are usually withdrawn, passive, shy, insecure, and have difficulty asserting themselves in a group. *Bullies* are usually dominant, aggressive, impulsive, angry, and have a low frustration tolerance. Bullying and victimization require adult intervention strategies, to be discussed later (Crick, Casas, & Ku, 1999; Olweus, 1993).

Sometimes children are rejected or punished by peers because of physical characteristics (being overweight, for example) or behavioral characteristics (bragging, dominating, or criticizing, for example) (Adler & Adler, 1998; Coie, Dodge, & Kupersmidt, 1990; Parkhurst & Asher, 1992). The consequence of being punished by exclusion and teasing by the peer group are described in the box "Peers, Power, Pecking Order, and Punishment." The social dynamics of inclusion, exclusion, and social hierarchies are discussed later.

IN PRACTICE

Peers, Power, Pecking Order, and Punishment

Peer groups in schools are manifested in the formation of **cliques**—friends who view themselves as mutually connected and doing things together—and **crowds**—loosely organized reference groups of cliques. Cliques and crowds are significant contributors to children's and adolescents' quests for identity.

In elementary school, cliques are hierarchical friendship groups based on popularity and prestige. By the time children reach high school, the clique social hierarchy is stratified. Typically, one finds "jocks," "preppies," or "populars"; "brains," or "nerds"; and "unpopulars" (Eder, 1995). High school social life was popularized in the media by the TV show *Beverly Hills 90210*. By interacting within and between friendship groups, children learn what kind of social competence they possess. The high-status clique is the "populars"; below them are the "wannabes" (the group that hangs around hoping for inclusion); next are smaller, independent groups; and at the bottom of the social hierarchy are the "social isolates" (those who only occasionally find playmates) (Adler & Adler, 1998).

Cliques are dominated by leaders. They are exclusive in nature, so that not all individuals who desire membership are accepted. The critical way that cliques maintain exclusivity is through careful membership screening. Acceptance or rejection of potential new members is linked to the power of the leaders. Leaders derive their power through popularity and use it to make decisions and influence social stratification (pecking order) within the group (Adler & Adler, 1998).

In their observations of preadolescents in school, Adler and Adler (1998, p. 76) found that the popular clique "set the tone for, and in many ways influenced, the behavior of the entire grade." Maintaining membership takes a concerted effort of conforming to desires of the leaders. The exclusivity of membership is a reward for those who are "in" and a punishment for those who are "out." The "wannabes" try to be "cool" by imitating the "populars"—wearing the same clothing and hairstyles, buying the same music, and using the same vocabulary (Eder, 1995). Their conforming behavior is reinforced because, occasionally, they are invited to participate in clique activities even though they are not fully accepted into the group.

cliques friends who view themselves as mutually connected and do things together

crowds loosely organized reference groups of cliques

Those who are "out," the "social isolates" (the "loners," "drifters," "dweebs," "nerds"), are excluded because they are different in some way—appearance, behavior, and/or language. Those who are "in" or the "wannabes" treat them poorly by teasing and laughing at them. It is as though everyone in the pecking order offsets his or her own insecurities by humiliating the individuals who are lower in status (Thorne, 1993). The exclusion of the "social isolates" from nearly all of the cliques' social activities, coupled with the extreme degradation they suffer, takes a heavy toll on their feelings of self-worth.

The significance of these findings from peer group studies was manifested in 1999 at Columbine High School in Littleton, Colorado, where two social isolates, Harris and Klebold, shot and killed 12 students and a teacher, as well as themselves. Interviews with students and community members pointed to the injustice and harassment done to Harris and Klebold by the "jocks," combined with their disengagement from caring adults (Wilson & Mishra, 1999). That such rage was acted out, when cliques and cruelty have been around for years in children's groups, poses a disturbing question. In 1961, James Coleman studied 11 high schools of varied socioeconomic statuses and found similar peer group stratification, similar values (athletes having the highest prestige; brains and unpopulars, the lowest), and similar behavior. The adolescents in his study seemed to accept things as "normal" for high school life; so why did the Columbine tragedy occur?

According to Greenfield and Juvonen (1999), Harris and Klebold acquired knowledge from the broader society (macrosystem) beyond home and school: (1) They had *role models* (media showing heroes engaged in violence to accomplish goals); (2) they had *tools* (guns and assault weapons available for purchase along with Internet instructions on how to construct a bomb); (3) they had *social validation* from Internet groups; and (4) they had opportunities to practice their objectives (via violent video games). Thus, peers are influenced by other ecosystems.

Apprenticeship

This chapter contains numerous references to the influence of peers, as in having introduced you to hip-hop music, having taught you to dance, or having "educated" you about sex. The concept intended by such references was of someone with more expertise (the expert) helping someone with less (the novice), as in an apprenticeship. The concept of apprenticeship as a method of socialization was discussed in Chapter 2. Traditionally, the word *apprenticeship* has been used in the world of work—a beginner becomes an apprentice under a master until he or she learns a trade well enough to succeed alone.

Lev Vygotsky (1978) postulated that a more knowledgeable person, such as a teacher or an expert peer, initially guides the learner's, or novice's, activity. Gradually, the two begin to share problem-solving functions, with the novice taking the initiative and the expert peer correcting and guiding when the novice falters. Finally, the expert peer cedes control and acts as a supportive audience.

An illustration of Vygotsky's hypothesis might be your learning how to ride a two-wheel bike from a friend who has mastered the skill. Your friend shows you how to get on the bike, how to balance, how to pedal, and how to stop. You get on the bike while your friend supports it. Your friend holds on while you pedal. After many falls, you can finally balance and pedal at the same time, so your friend lets go (but runs after you yelling instructions on how to stop).

Vygotsky believed that engaging in such apprenticeship activities advances the novice's level of development. Vygotsky suggested that the boundaries for a novice's learning abilities lie between (1) his or her *actual* development, or what he or she can do independently, and (2) his or her *potential* development, or what he or she can do while participating with more capable others. He called this space the *zone of proximal development (ZPD)*, discussed in Chapter 7. Examples of how schools implement ZPD are peer collaboration on projects, peer tutoring, and peer counseling.

A personal example of ZPD is my husband, who has a talent for drawing. I persuaded him to take an art class to develop his ability further. The students in the class submitted their drawings every week for peer review and suggestions for improvement, while the instructor served as a moderator. At the end of the course, my husband's drawings were significantly more elaborate and sophisticated than when he began the class. Peer review is a technique also used in other classes, such as writing and speech.

Macrosystem Influences on the Peer Group: Developmental Tasks

What jobs does society expect the peer group to perform?

Developmental tasks, discussed in Chapter 2, are midway between an individual need and a societal demand. Macrosystem influences on the peer group involve reinforcing the values and traditions of society. The peer group, in turn, provides the setting and the means for children to achieve some of the expected developmental tasks of early and middle childhood (Havighurst, 1972; Zarbatany, Hartmann, & Rankin, 1990), especially social competence. This means children must learn to get along with others, develop morals and values, learn appropriate social and cultural roles, and achieve personal independence while formulating an identity (Rubin et al., 1998).

GETTING ALONG WITH OTHERS

How do children learn the give-and-take of relationships?

Playing with children of the same age is a vehicle for socializing the capacity to "get along" by learning to give and take. Getting along involves recognition of the rights of others. The peer group provides children with opportunities for understanding the limitations that group life places on the individual: "At my house I can play with my Legos all I want, but at preschool I have to share." "When I'm with my friends, I can't always have my way. We talk about what we're going to do on Sunday, trying to please everyone. If Barbara, Joan, and Carol want to go shopping and I don't, the group tells me if I come with them, they'll stop by my favorite ice-cream place on the way home. Even though I don't get my way, I get the feeling I'm wanted and that the group is trying to please me. I agree to go shopping."

The ability to get along is developmentally progressive in that it involves both seeing things from another's perspective and verbal communication (Grusec & Lytton, 1988). It depends, then, on increasing cognitive abilities as well as social experiences. Some studies (Clarke-Stewart, 1992; Lamb, 1998) have shown that young children who are in child-care centers are more socially competent than those who are cared for at home, but are also more aggressive. It is likely that these children learn early how to "stick up" for themselves and compete for toys.

DEVELOPING MORALS AND VALUES

How does the peer group contribute to children's concepts of right and wrong, worthy and unworthy?

The development of *morals* (distinguishing right from wrong) and *values* (determining what is worthwhile) occurs in a social setting. By interacting with others, the child comes to know what is and what is not acceptable behavior. Children learn morals and values from parents and other adults through instruction, reasoning, modeling, reinforcement, and punishment; they learn morals and values from peers through real experiences (learning by doing).

Most studies of the development of morals and values involve school-age children and adolescents who are capable of articulating judgments about hypothetical dilemmas, as will be discussed in Chapter 11. However, research by Judy Dunn (1988) on the beginnings of social understanding, which is the cornerstone of moral development, has shown that from 18 months on, children understand how to hurt, comfort, or exacerbate another's pain. They understand the consequences of their hurtful actions toward others in their own environment and can anticipate the responses of adults to their own and others' misdeeds. Preschoolers enter the peer group setting with a rudimentary understanding of social rules influenced by their family context. As children develop, peer group experiences expand this understanding (Rubin et al., 1998).

Understanding rules is part of moral development in that both involve rule formulation, rule following, cooperation, limit setting, division of roles, and territoriality: "Consciousness of rules cannot be isolated from the moral life of the child as a whole" (Piaget, 1965, p. 50). Rules are related to morals in that both have to do with established guides for conduct. In the peer group, common rules based on common experience begin to develop. These rules may be devised to meet a specific situation; they may be copied from adults' rules or those of older children. Between the ages of 3 and 7, children sometimes observe the rules of the group and sometimes not. Even when playing together, children of this age play "each one on his own" (Piaget, 1965, p. 27)—everyone has his or her own views of the way the game is played—without any real regard for the codification of the rules.

Around the age of 7 or 8, children "begin to concern themselves with the question of mutual control and of unification of the rules" (Piaget, 1965, p. 27), even though their understanding of the rules may be rather vague. At 11 or 12, children fix the rules in their groups; everyone in the group understands and observes them. For example, in the game of Four Square, whoever misses the ball is out. Everyone knows that rule. However, some groups will make rules regarding how the ball is returned, like "no babies." A "baby" is a ball bounced so lightly that it barely comes off the ground and, therefore, is almost impossible to get. Thus, if a child wants to belong to the group, the rules must be respected and obeyed. If "babies" are not allowed, one cannot use them if one wants to continue to play with the group. Learning the conditions attached to belonging to the group, then, is the way children are socialized as to the requirements for participation. It is also a way in which children develop morality.

Piaget (1965) contrasts two types of morality. One type, *heteronomous morality* or **morality of constraint**, consists of behavior based on respect for persons in authority. It is imposed by a prestigeful and powerful source, usually the parent or another adult. This type of morality fosters the ideal that to obey the will of the authority is good; to obey one's own will is bad. Such morality is fostered in the

morality of constraint behavior based on respect for persons in authority

In game playing, children's moral development is influenced by practicing such activities as rule following, cooperation, and limit setting.

HIRB/Index Stock Imagery

family and in school. The other type, *autonomous morality* or **morality of cooperation**, consists of behavior based on mutual understanding between equals. It involves the acceptance of rules because they are necessary for the continuance of group life. If one wants to participate in the group, one freely accepts the rules; the rules are imposed on oneself by oneself. This type of morality emerges from the mutual respect of the children in the group. Thus, peer group participation—participation among equals—helps foster *morality of cooperation*, whereas *morality of constraint* is more likely to be fostered in authoritarian, adult-dominated situations, such as the family or school.

In our society, we must obey certain rules because they were imposed by an authority, whether or not we agree (draft registration, for example). We also impose certain rules on ourselves for the benefit of group life (compromise with a neighbor regarding the property line, for example). To participate effectively in society, then, children need both types of morality training. To exemplify, studies (Devereaux, 1970; Ladd & LeSieur, 1995; Ladd & Pettit, 2002) have shown that children who come from homes with moderate to high levels of discipline and control (authoritative parenting) and who have had a great deal of peer group experience tend to be autonomous, socially competent, and have strong moral character. In contrast, children who come from homes characterized by low levels of discipline and control (permissive parenting) or high levels of punitiveness (authoritarian parenting), and who have had a great deal of peer group experience, tend to be "peer conformists" or "chameleons."

morality of cooperation behavior based on mutual understanding between equals

It would seem, then, that the peer group helps children in the *process* of developing morals, whereas the *level* of moral development is greatly influenced by parenting styles. Contemporary research (Bogenschneider, Wu, Raffaelli, & Tsay, 1998; Kerns, Contreras, & Neal-Barnett, 2000) documents the importance of contingent linkages between parents and peers in moral behavior.

LEARNING APPROPRIATE SOCIOCULTURAL ROLES

How do peer experiences contribute to children's understanding of how to behave in group situations?

Although the family imparts sociocultural roles, such as *independence* and *interdependence*, the peer group gives the child opportunities to try out roles learned at home (Greenfield & Suzuki, 1998). The child gains an understanding of the individual's responsibility in a group situation. For example, does one exercise *autonomy* and respect peers' right to free choice ("I want to play Scrabble; what game do you want to play?"); or does one exercise *empathy*, anticipating the desires of peers ("I know you like to play chess, so let's play that")? Does one communicate in a *direct, assertive* manner ("I want to try your new bike") or in an *indirect, passive* manner ("That's a nice new bike you got")? Does one *compete* with peers for *individual* recognition or *cooperate* with peers for *group* recognition? Does one *confront* conflict or *avoid* it?

An example of how appropriate sociocultural roles are learned can be seen when children who have never had to share things at home or who have never had to take turns learn to do so in the peer group or else be excluded. From the peer group, children receive feedback about their behavior and skills. Your peers will not hesitate to tell you when you are acting dumb. Children not only learn the sociocultural roles of cooperation and appropriate behavior from each other, they also learn how to compete. They evaluate their skills in terms of whether they can do better than, as well as, or worse than others in the group. They also learn methods of conflict resolution. An example of cultural conflicts is when children who have been socialized by their families to emphasize cooperation in the group are on a team with children who have been socialized to emphasize competition. "Two immigrant Latina players talk about wanting the team to work as a unit. They complain that the Euro-American girls just want themselves to look good, sometimes even at the expense of the team's performance" (Greenfield & Sukuki, 1998, p. 1091).

The box "How Three Cultures Shape Sociocultural Role Development via the Peer Group" illustrates how societal values influence what are considered appropriate sociocultural roles for young children.

IN PRACTICE

How Three Cultures Shape Sociocultural Role Development via the Peer Group

The peer group can provide a mechanism whereby the socialization goals of the macrosystem are implemented. How three countries shape their children was studied by observing and comparing 4-year-olds in Chinese, Japanese, and American preschools. It was found that these countries viewed preschools as agents that preserve certain traditional cultural values even in times of social change (Tobin, Wu, & Davidson, 1989).

In China, a collective society valuing interdependence, population pressure has caused the government to mandate that only one child be born to a nuclear family. Therefore, Chinese preschools are expected to provide experiences with peers that will counter the undivided attention that the only child gets from parents and grandparents.

In Japan, a society that values fitting in and working cooperatively with others, parents believe that preschools enable their children to learn this traditional value by functioning in a large group. Social change in Japan has resulted in shrinking birthrates and movement of young people away from their extended families. When families were large and many relatives lived close by, Japanese children could learn social skills in their families and identify with members of a group; now the preschool has become the vehicle.

In the United States, a society valuing independence and individuality, social change has resulted in increased family mobility, employment of mothers, and the growth of single-parent families. Parents have turned to preschools to provide stability, enrichment, and guidance for children.

Based on interviews with teachers, administrators, parents, and child development specialists, the researchers found that preschools in all three cultures stressed the importance of learning to cooperate and be a member of a group. In addition, Chinese preschools especially valued learning citizenship, discipline, and perseverance; Japanese preschools especially valued learning sympathy, empathy, and concern for others; American preschools especially valued learning self-reliance and self-confidence.

Chinese children are taught citizenship through regimentation and orderly conduct. The role of the preschool is to instill values of self-control, discipline, cooperation, and responsibility. Children do the same activities at the same time under the direction of the teacher, whether it be calisthenics, singing, or building with blocks. The children copy what the teacher does; no talking is permitted. The children line up to go to the bathroom at a specified time. Children are taught to regulate bodily functions to synchronize with the group. Sociocultural roles of interdependence, order, and conformity are thereby reinforced.

Whereas Chinese preschools maintain order by direct adult control, Japanese preschools seek to maintain order by relying on the peer group to deal with disputes and misbehavior. The children arrive at school and play with their friends until the "clean-up" song. The teacher leads them in group exercises. Once seated at their tables, the children begin a workbook project. The teacher makes no attempt to stop the talking, laughing, or even playful fighting that occurs. After their work, there is free play and then lunch. A little girl tells the teacher about a particularly raucous boy, but the teacher just encourages her to go deal with the problem herself. Eventually, the fighting ceases, and the children listen to a song before settling down to rest. Thus, the Japanese child's preschool experience involves learning to enjoy ties to peers, to transfer the warmth of the parent–child relations to other relationships, and to balance informality with formality, emotion with control, and family with society. Sociocultural roles of interdependence and harmony are thereby reinforced.

American children generally experience much freedom of choice and expression at preschool. The preschool is expected to make young children more independent and self-reliant. Its function is to promote individuality, autonomy, problem solving, cognitive development, and friendship. Whereas Chinese preschools instill discipline primarily by regimentation, modeling appropriate behavior, criticism, and praise, and Japanese preschools instill it by fostering a sense of concern for the group, American preschools instill discipline by fostering a sense of individual rights.

The American children observed began their day with free play until all the children arrived. The teacher then gathered everyone together for "show and tell," thereby encouraging individual expression. After a flannel-board story and a song, the children were told they could choose to go to any of the several learning centers set up for that day. The learning centers consisted of an art project, the housekeeping corner, blocks, books, manipulative toys, a cooking center, and water play. The children moved about freely. The teachers assisted the children in the learning activities. A disruptive child was told by the teacher that his actions may have caused another child to get hurt and was told to sit in the "timeout" chair to think about what he had done. Sociocultural roles of independence and individual rights are thereby reinforced.

Thus, the peer group in preschool settings serves as a vehicle by which children learn certain cultural values. In China, children learn to conform to the group through the teacher's structuring the activities accordingly, criticizing those who don't conform, and praising those who do. In Japan, children learn to get along in the peer group through the teacher's encouragement and noninterference. In the United States, children learn to respect other children's rights through the teacher's interceding in conflicts, explaining why they are hurtful or unsafe, and providing a consequence (Tobin et al., 1989).

How do children acquire sociocultural concepts of sex?

Sex is a broad term encompassing an individual's biological characteristics, psychological construct of appropriate male/female behavior (gender role), sex education, and sexual activity.

Gender Role. Gender role is sociocultural in that children learn from their peers what is culturally acceptable and admirable for boys and girls (Best, 1983; Pitcher & Schultz, 1983; Thorne, 1993). For example, Jerry, age 4, wanted to join a group of girls who were playing with their dolls. Jerry had a doll at home that he bathed and dressed while his mother or father bathed his baby sister. When Jerry approached the girls, they said, "Boys don't play with dolls!" Peer pressure for *appropriate* gender-type play has been observed to begin as early as age 2 (Fagot, 1985; Maccoby 1990, 2000; Serbin, Powlishta, & Gulko, 1993).

Peer groups generally segregate boys and girls beginning in preschool (Maccoby, 1990, 2000; Ruble & Martin, 1998). In the preschool years, girls become interested in small group games in small spaces, games that allow them to practice and refine social rules and roles (for example, playing in the house corner). Boys engage in larger group games that are more physically active and wide-ranging. These games tend to have a more extensive set of explicit rules that involve reaching a defined goal. The games tend to be competitive (for example, the "good guys against the bad guys," in the form of Batman or Darth Vader, with the goal being "to save the world"). Thus, segregated peer group play leads to different outcomes for boys and girls in achievement motivation, personal relationships, and self-concept (Dweck, 1981). Gender roles will be discussed in more detail in Chapter 12.

Sex Education. The peer group is often the imparter of information about sexuality. Children and adolescents share their knowledge with each other—knowledge they may have gained from their families, from the media, from school, or from friends. With their limited cognitive ability, they often have an incomplete understanding of normal sexual development, which, combined with their friends' incomplete understanding, distorts the total picture of sexuality.

In the United States, adolescents receive information on sex and sexuality from parents, school, media, and peers (Katchadourian, 1990; Thornburg, 1981). Topics such as love, contraception, ejaculation, homosexuality, intercourse, masturbation, petting, and prostitution are discussed with peers. Schools provide information on topics such as abstinence, sexually transmitted diseases, menstruation, semen production, and pregnancy. Parents transmit their attitudes about sex, love, and marriage. The media present the excitement of sex without the consequences. Thus, knowledge about the *mechanics of reproduction* apparently comes from parents and school, but knowledge about sexual *behavior* apparently comes from peers and the media.

Regarding the danger of sexually transmitted diseases and the consequences of teen pregnancy, adults need to be "tuned in" to the role that peers and other socializing agents play in sex education. They need to talk to children before puberty about love, marriage, sex, and reproduction and continue to communicate throughout adolescence, being "askable," available, and willing to answer questions.

Observations of elementary school children in the United States demonstrate that girls and boys are very aware of the opposite sex and what is expected of heterosexual behavior (Best, 1983; Thorne, 1993). Children continually talk about who "loves" whom and who is "cute." As preparation for later heterosexual relations, children play chase-and-kiss games. Usually, the girls try to catch the boys and kiss them, pronouncing they have "cooties." The others who watch will engage in laughing and teasing.

In the United States, the onset of sexual activity is influenced by peers, gender, and ethnic orientation (Brooks-Gunn & Furstenberg, 1989). One's peers establish the norm for initiating sex. Assumptions (rather than actual knowledge) about what one's peers are doing has been found to be associated with sexual behavior (actual behavior is difficult to research because of disclosure reluctance). In teens 15 to 19, studies have found early dating to be associated with early intercourse (Brooks-Gunn & Furstenberg, 1989). Historically, boys have been much more likely to engage in sexual intercourse earlier than girls. This may have been due to peer pressure "to become a man" as well as not having to bear the consequences of becoming pregnant. However, the gender gap in the onset of sexual activity has narrowed (Miller, Christopherson, & King, 1993). This may be due to media influence portraying females as sexual seductresses as well as easier access to contraception. Parental influence on sexual behavior is believed to outweigh peers and the media if there is a feeling of connectedness and support as well as open communication (Brooks-Gunn & Furstenberg, 1989; Small & Luster, 1994).

Onset of sexual behavior in teens differs according to ethnic orientation, especially as indicated by out-of-wedlock births. For example, according to the National Center for Health Statistics (2004), African American, Hispanic American, and Native American children ages 10–14 have higher birthrates than do Euro-Americans or Asian Americans (though births to teens have generally been on the decline for several years). However, ethnicity may not be the sole influence (Adams, Gullotta, & Markstrom-Adams, 1994). As socioeconomic status decreases, sexual activity has been found to increase. Teens from single-parent families report a higher incidence of sexual activity; those who attend church, do well in school, and are on academic rather than vocational tracks report lower activity. Thus, other factors often linked with ethnic orientation, in addition to possibly greater peer affiliation, could explain the ethnic differences found in the onset of sexual activity.

ACHIEVING PERSONAL INDEPENDENCE AND IDENTITY

How does the peer group contribute to individuality?

As was discussed earlier, peer groups enable children to become increasingly independent of adults. "Individuals juggle different and often conflicting images of self between the childish self shown to their families and the maturing self shown to their peers" (Adler & Adler, 1998, p. 198). In addition, as children get older, peers become increasingly important as social support (Belle, 1989). **Social support** refers to the resources (tangible, intellectual, social, emotional) provided by others in times of need. Tangible support includes sharing toys, clothes, and money. Intellectual support includes giving information or advice. Social support involves companionship. Emotional support involves listening and empathy.

Children develop their identities through meaningful interactions and accomplishments in the peer group. Children begin to view the peer group as a reference group beginning about age 7 or 8 and increasing through adolescence (Levine & Levine, 1996).

- Peers provide validation for the self: "Do you like my hair?" "C'mon, let's play ball." "I have a secret to tell you."
- Peers provide encouragement to try new things: "I'll join Girl Scouts if you will too." "Do you want to go camping with me 'n' my dad?"
- Peers provide opportunities for comparison: "I beat Sam in the race." "Sally made the team, but I didn't."
- Peers enable self-disclosure. Children are more likely to disclose their innermost feelings to trusted friends than to adults (Parker & Gottman, 1989): "I'm in love with Brad; I let him French kiss me."
- Peers provide identity: "I want to be a *popular* when I go to high school next year."

According to Ungar (2000), in a study of high-risk adolescents, the participating youths indicated that adopting the behavior and appearance of peers was a conscious strategy to enhance personal and social power. Identification with the peer group enabled the young person to avoid feelings of alienation, especially if there were family problems, in that peers served as a source of support. Participants described peer groups as a means to assert both individual and collective identities. In other words, peer influence was bidirectional: the members shaped the group, and the group, in turn, shaped the members.

Chronosystem Influences on the Peer Group: Play/Activities

How does children's play change throughout development?

Chronosystem influences on the peer group refer here to changes in structure, activities, and relationships as peers grow and develop psychologically, socially, and cognitively. Because child-initiated play is the main activity that occurs in peer groups, it is discussed first; adult-initiated play is discussed later.

social support
resources (tangible, intellectual, social, emotional) provided by others in times of need

A place secluded from adults allows children to experiment with different roles, behaviors, and interactions.

Creatas Images/Jupiterimages

THE SIGNIFICANCE AND DEVELOPMENT OF PLAY

How does play contribute to developmental outcomes?

"**Play** is behavior that is enjoyed for its own sake" (Evans & McCandless, 1978, p. 110). It is significant to development for many reasons. Play, according to Jean Piaget (1962), is the way the child learns about his or her environment because its interactive nature allows for construction of knowledge. Vygotsky (1978) and Berk and Winsler (1995) believed play to be an imaginary situation governed by social rules. Play contributes to development in that it enables the child to separate thought from actions and objects. It also enables the child to move from impulsive activity to planned goals and self-regulation (instead of taking a desired toy, the child asks permission to play with it). Anna Freud (1968) viewed play as an acceptable way to express emotions and impulses. Groos (1901) described play as a way for children to practice skills necessary for adult life. These various functions of play enable therapists and educators to learn what the child feels and understands by observing his or her play activities.

Years ago, in a classic study based on observations of nursery school children at "free play," Mildred Parten (1932) examined developmental changes in their social play according to type of social interaction: solitary, onlooker, parallel, associative, and cooperative.

- **Solitary**. The child plays alone and independently. The child seems to concentrate on the activity rather than on other children who may be nearby. Solitary play is typical of infant/toddlers.
- **Onlooker**. The child watches other children playing. Conversations with the others may be initiated. Though there is no actual engagement in the play being observed, the child is definitely involved as a spectator. Two-year-olds engage in a considerable amount of onlooker play.

play behavior enjoyed for its own sake

These children are engaged in parallel play; they enjoy playing next to each other while engaged in similar activities, but true interaction doesn't take place.

- **Parallel**. The child plays alone, but with toys like those that other children are using, or plays in a manner that mimics the behavior of playing children. Parallel play is common among 2- and 3-year-olds, but diminishes as the child gets older.
- **Associative**. Social interaction and communication are involved in associative play, but with little or no organization. Children engage in play activities similar to those of other children; however, they appear to be more interested in being associated with each other than in the tasks at hand. Associative play is common among 3- and particularly among 4-year-olds.
- **Cooperative**. Social interaction in a group characterizes cooperative play. The activity is organized, and the group has a purpose—for example, a group building a fort together, a group playing "store," or a game of baseball. Cooperative play is the prototype for the games of middle childhood. Cooperative play begins to be exhibited by 4- to 5-year-olds.

Contemporary research shows that these play forms emerge in the order suggested by Parten, but earlier forms may coexist with later forms, rather than being replaced by them (Howes & Matheson, 1992). However, the complexity of the form does change with age (Rubin & Coplan, 1992). Children will combine *type of activity* with *type of social interaction* (what Parten classified as "stage of play"). For example, when children engage in the activity of pretending, they may do it solitarily or cooperatively (Hughes, 1999).

Brian Sutton-Smith (1971) categorized play by type of activity: imitative, exploratory, testing, and model building.

- **Imitative Play**. During the first year of life, the baby imitates the parent. During the second year of life, the child can put together parts of acts already imitated or observed in new combinations. In the third year, children imitate whole roles, such as mother or father. Most of this early imitative play consists of imitation of the important and powerful people in children's lives. Between 4 and 6, imitative social play tends to be governed by one player acting as a central person and the others acting in satellite roles, by players taking turns and alternating the roles, or by all the players doing much the same thing at the same time.

- **Exploratory Play**. In the first year, the child explores—touches, tastes, and manipulates. In the second year, the child also empties, fills, inserts, puts in and out, pulls, stacks, and rolls. In the third year, the child arranges, heaps, combines, transfers, sorts, and spreads. Novel manipulations are a delight to the child and can be manipulations of objects or of words.
- **Testing Play**. In many types of play, what children are actually doing is testing themselves. During the second year, children test their motor skills. They pull wagons, lift objects, climb, run, and jump. As children get older, they test themselves in games. They compete with others to measure their skills, both physical and intellectual. They also test their emotions, such as fear and anger.
- **Model-Building Play.** About age 4, model-building play becomes explicit, when blocks are organized into buildings, trucks into highway traffic, dishes into tea parties. Children begin to put elements of their experiences together in unique ways.

As can be seen, children's play becomes more complex and interactive with age. The increasingly social nature of play requires a combination of physical/motor skills, interpersonal skills, and cognitive skills. Through play, children discover their capacities. They explore and test their physical and mental abilities against their own standards and in comparison to others. Children often issue a challenge just to see if they can make their bodies and minds do what they want them to: "I bet I can climb to the top of that tree"; "I can figure out that puzzle in five minutes!"

Young children often engage in rough-and-tumble play. This type of play involves fighting, wrestling, and/or chasing. It is viewed more as "mock" aggression than "real" aggression (Hughes, 1999). Children in many cultures exhibit it, as do young animals. Thus, it may have evolutionary survival roots to develop protective skills in the young.

A very common type of *pretend play* among young children is "superhero/heroine play" (Kostelnik, Whiren, & Stein, 1986). Superheroes and heroines emerged in radio, comics, movies, and television. Some examples are Buck Rogers (1920s), Superman and Batman (1930s), Wonder Woman (1940s), Captain Video (1950s), Captain Kirk (1960s), Luke Skywalker and Princess Leia (1970s), He-Man (1980s), Ninja Turtles and Power Rangers (1990s), and Spiderman and Catwoman (2000s). What super characters have in common is that they possess powers children wish they themselves had: they are good, strong, can fly, swim under water, change the shape of their bodies, and overcome all obstacles they may encounter. In other words, they are in control—no one tells them what to do, they know what is right, and they have respect and approval from others. Unfortunately, in this kind of play, some children exploit being in control by intimidating others and, therefore, cause hostile and hurt feelings.

Superhero/heroine play allows children to experience power and prestige unavailable to them in their daily lives. It also provides them with concrete models whose behavior is easy to emulate, unlike real-life models, whose behavior is often too ambiguous or complex for children to figure out. Finally, it gives children a chance to experience concretely abstract values such as honor, justice, courage, honesty, and mercy. Some preschools ban superhero/heroine play because it usually involves aggression, but others use it to enable children to be creative rather than imitative, such as "How would Spiderman fix that broken chair?" (Levin, 1998).

INFANT/TODDLER PEER ACTIVITIES

Do babies play?

Peer groups emerge early in the child's life, the time varying according to the family situation, including attachment and play patterns, the availability of age-mates, and the temperament and social competence of the child (Ladd, 1999; Parke, 1990). Research suggests that peer sociability is influenced by the relationship with the caregiver. When caregiving is sensitive and responsive, babies learn how to send and interpret emotional cues, and these skills carry over to peer relationships (Mize & Pettit, 1997; Vandell & Mueller, 1995).

Observations of babies in institutions have shown that even at 2 months babies are oriented toward the movements of a baby in an adjoining crib (Bridges, 1933). Between 6 and 8 months, babies look at each other and sometimes touch each other; between 9 and 13 months, they sometimes fight, mainly over toys (Hay, 1985; Vincze, 1971). During the second year, toddlers interact positively with peers, once conflicts over toys have been resolved (Hughes, 1999; Rubenstein & Howes, 1976). They imitate each other (Asendorpf & Baudoniere, 1993) and show responsiveness (Howes, 1988).

Children become increasingly able to empathize with others—first on an emotional level, then on a behavioral level. For example, it has been found that by the end of the first year, babies often cry when they observe another baby crying; by the middle of the second year, they pat or hug the crying baby; by the end of the second year, they offer specific kinds of help, like a toy or a Band-Aid (Saani, Mumme, & Campos, 1998). Then they also begin to empathize cognitively. For example, the studies of Zahn-Waxler and colleagues (Zahn-Waxler & Radke-Yarrow, 1990; Zahn-Waxler, Radke-Yarrow, Wagner, & Chapman, 1992; Zahn-Waxler, Robinson, & Emde, 1992) showed that during the second year, children's responses to the distress of others become increasingly differentiated and their ability to comfort increasingly effective. They were more likely to empathize with family and friends than they were with strangers. They were also more likely to verbalize their empathy and respond sensitively: "Please don't cry; I'll let you play with my doll."

EARLY CHILDHOOD PEER ACTIVITIES

Do preschoolers have friends?

From age 2 to age 5, peer interaction increases in frequency and becomes more complex (Rubin et al., 1998). Sometime about age 3 or 4, children begin to enjoy playing in groups—at first usually on an informal and transitory basis (Howes, 1988). Young children, however, are limited in their friends. Playmates come from the immediate neighborhood—or from school, if parents are willing to chauffeur or have friends over.

Successful social relationships depend on the ability of one person to take the point of view of another, the ability to empathize, and the ability to communicate. Generally, children under 3 not only cannot take another's point of view or empathize, they also lack the skills for effective two-way communication. Even though some children under age 3 do exhibit some prosocial behaviors, such as empathy, they also exhibit some antisocial behaviors, such as selfishness and aggressiveness. According to Dunn (1988), children begin to exhibit social understanding in the family setting by 18 months; then they must have experiences with peers to implement their understanding of social situations effectively.

Developmental advances in cognition and language enable preschoolers to engage in increasingly complex social interactions. They participate in more cooperative ventures, but they also exhibit more aggression. They direct more speech to their peers as well (Rubin et al., 1998).

MIDDLE CHILDHOOD/PREADOLESCENT PEER ACTIVITIES

What do school-agers do with their "free" time?

The middle years represent a change in the proportion of social interaction involving peers; approximately 10% of the social interaction for 2-year-olds involves peers, whereas for 6- to 12-year olds it is more than 30%. The remainder is spent with siblings, parents, and other adults (Rubin et al., 1998). The settings of peer interaction also change during the middle years, from supervised (home and preschool) to more unsupervised (neighborhood).

As children reach school age, they spend some of their time hanging around informally, talking, teasing, "roughhousing," and bike riding, but they often move spontaneously into group games. Such games involve the development of skill, understanding, and acceptance of rules, and the ability to cooperate as well as compete.

As children's physical and mental capacities and interests mature, the quality of their games changes; they tend to reflect the culture, and they are apt to be more gender-specific (Best, 1983; Hughes, 1999; Sutton-Smith, 1972). For girls, there are jump rope, hopscotch, jacks, dolls, and playing house or school. Boys play baseball, football, cars, trains, cops and robbers, or spacemen. According to Sutton-Smith (1972), games involving verbal and rhythmic content, such as guessing games, have traditionally been played predominantly by girls, whereas physically active games and organized sports have traditionally been played mostly by boys. Chasing and teasing games have been played by both genders. Title IX of the Education Code,

In this soccer game, it appears that some girls are deriving more enjoyment from the game than are others.

© John Neubauer/PhotoEdit

passed in 1972, which prohibited sex discrimination in school activities, has enabled girls to have more opportunities to play organized sports.

Game patterns change with cognitive development, as children become more capable of handling complex rules and strategies. According to Sutton-Smith (1972), children ages 6 to 9 enjoy simple games with dramatic content (cops and robbers). Older children like games requiring strategy, such as checkers or chess, as well as organized team sports.

Games also change with children's psychological development. For example, their self-concepts change. Sutton-Smith (1972) points out that in younger children's games, such as Simon Says or Giant Steps, the person who is "It," operating from a home base, is safe and has power to control the moves of the others. The structure of these games provides a nonthreatening opportunity for children to venture into a leadership role. From about age 10 on, the games enjoyed involve a central figure who is vulnerable to attack by others who seek the leadership role (King of the Castle). Older children also enjoy competitive games, in which one wins and one is defeated, because these types of games offer the experience of competence.

Children's games reflect the culture in which they live. For example, according to Parker (1984), competitive games, such as soccer, basketball, or football, offer practice in territorial invasion. Card games offer practice in bluffing and calculating odds. All games involve memory, manipulation, and strategizing. Thus, games offer opportunities for children to practice skills they will need in adult life (Hughes, 1999).

Today, children generally spend less time in spontaneously organized play (stickball, hide-and-seek, marbles, jacks) than they did a generation ago because children can buy many prepared board games with printed instructions and rules, as well as computer and video games. The sandlot neighborhood versions of baseball and football have given way, for many children, to organized sports supervised by adults, such as Little League and AYSO, that come with rule books and procedures. One reason is safety; parents fear letting their children play unsupervised because of traffic, crime, and kidnapping issues. Another reason is to provide structured time after school, especially when both parents are employed. Adult–peer group linkages are discussed later in more detail. Although children gain many physical, cognitive, and social skills from adult-organized play, they are not getting many opportunities to experience making and revising their own rules and enforcing them with their peers.

Media technology enables many preadolescents to spend time text messaging and file sharing with friends on their computers. Cell phones also are commonly used to stay connected with peers.

ADOLESCENT PEER ACTIVITIES

How do adolescents "hang out"?

Adolescents like to "hang out"—talk, watch TV, listen to music, play video games, be seen, see who else is "hanging" with whom, wait for something to happen (Jaffe, 1998). In early adolescence, most activities occur with same-sex peers, whereas in later adolescence, activities that attract and include the opposite sex are favored, such as parties, sporting events, and concerts. Adolescents, when not engaged in organized school, sports, or community activities, spend a lot of time on their appearance—clothing, makeup, jewelry, body art—and connecting with friends via pagers, cell phones, e-mail, chat rooms, and text messaging. According to Roberts and Foehr (2004), the average 11- to 14-year-old spends more time with media than in any other waking activity. Media influences will be discussed in greater detail in Chapter 9.

Peer Group Interaction

Why is peer group interaction easy for some children and difficult for others?

The relationships children form when interacting with peers, as well as why some children are successful in making friends, vary based on a variety of factors, such as ability to make friends and acceptance, neglect, or rejection by the group.

DEVELOPMENT OF FRIENDSHIP

How do children make friends?

Like the activities children engage in as they develop, their social relationships and friendships also become more complex and interactive with age.

Howes (1988) studied the social interaction and friendship formations of young children in a child-care setting. Although young children's social competence is limited by their cognitive development, apparently early experience with peers enhances interaction skills. She found that 13- to 24-month-old toddlers differentiated friends among available playmates at their child-care center. These friendships were marked by emotional responsiveness (happiness in seeing each other or comforting in times of stress). Children 25 to 36 months were able to distinguish between the emotional and play components of friendship by approaching different peers when in need of comfort and when wanting to run or wrestle.

Selman and Selman (1979) interviewed more than 250 individuals between the ages of 3 and 45 to get a developmental perspective on friendship patterns. They delineated the following five stages:

1. Momentary playmateship (early childhood, to 4 years)
2. One-way assistance (early to middle childhood, 4–9 years)
3. Two-way, fair-weather cooperation (middle childhood, 6–12 years)
4. Intimate, mutually shared relationships (middle childhood to adolescence, 9–15 years)
5. Autonomous interdependent friendships (adolescence to adulthood, 12 years on)

Early Childhood. Most children under age 4 and some older ones are in the first stage—*momentary playmateship*. They are unable to consider the viewpoint of another person and can think only about what they want from the friendship. Friends are defined by how close they live ("He's my friend; he lives next door") or by their material possessions ("She's my friend; she has a dollhouse and a swing set").

Early to Middle Childhood. The second stage is *one-way assistance*. From about age 4 until about age 9, children are more capable of telling the difference between their own perspectives and those of others. However, friendship is based on whether or not someone does what the child wants that person to do ("He's not my friend anymore; he didn't want to play cars"). Youniss and Volpe (1978), in a study of the friendships of children between 6 and 14, found that the 6- and 7-year-olds thought of friendship in terms of playing together and sharing material goods ("She plays dress-up with me"; "She always shares her candy with me").

Middle Childhood. In the third stage—*two-way, fair-weather cooperation*—children 6 to 12 acknowledge that friendship involves give-and-take. However, they see friendship as mutually serving individual interests rather than mutually cooperating toward a common interest. ("We are friends; we do things for each other"). Youniss and Volpe found that 9- and 10-year-olds regard friends as those who share with one another ("Someone who plays with you when you don't have anyone else to play with"). At this age, children emphasize similarities between friends, as well as equalities and reciprocities ("We all like to collect baseball cards. We trade them and give doubles to our friends who are missing those. No one brags."). Children of this age are beginning to recognize that friendship is based on getting along—sharing interests, ideas, and feelings.

Middle Childhood to Adolescence. The fourth stage is one of *intimate, mutually shared relationships*. Children between 9 and 15 can view a friendship as an entity in itself. It is an ongoing, committed relationship that incorporates more than just doing things for each other; it tends to be treasured for its own sake and may involve possessiveness and jealousy ("She is my best friend. How can she go to the movies with Susan?"). Youniss and Volpe report that the 12- and 13-year-olds in their study carried the earlier principles of equality and reciprocity further ("If someone picks on me, my friend helps me. My friend does not leave me to go off with some other kids.").

These preschool girls are enjoying each other while they share a meal.

Photo courtesy of Michael Berns

Adolescence to Adulthood. Finally, there is the stage of *autonomous interdependent friendships*. About age 12, children are capable of respecting their friends' needs for both dependency and autonomy ("We like to do most things together and we talk about our problems, but sometimes Jason just likes to be by himself. I don't mind.").

Are there gender differences in friendships? Generally, girls refer to a best friend as someone you can have an intimate conversation with and who is "faithful" more than do boys; boys refer more to the companionship nature of best friends and the sharing of activities (Lever, 1976; Maccoby, 1990, 2000).

Is there a connection between the ability to have friends and emotional adjustment in adulthood? Reviews of the literature on peer relationships verify a link between problematic childhood peer interactions and adjustment difficulties in adolescence and adulthood (Bagwell, Newcomb, & Bukowski, 2000; Kupersmidt, Coie, & Dodge, 1990). In the next section, we look at some reasons for peer acceptance and rejection, as well as how to help children be more successful in making friends. Generally, having friends and being accepted by the peer group are related; children who are well liked by peers have many opportunities to make friends. However, it is not always the case that children who are rejected by the peer group do not have friends. Children who are rejected by the group but have at least one friend have fewer problems later in life than those who are rejected and also have no friends (Howes, 1988; Rubin et al., 1998).

ACCEPTANCE/NEGLECT/REJECTION BY PEERS

Who is accepted by the group and why?

The significance of being accepted, neglected, or rejected by peers came to the attention of the media in 1999 when two rejected adolescents shot 12 students and a teacher at the school they attended in Colorado. Apparently the athletes who repeatedly teased them were the targets for retaliation. Which children are readily accepted by the group? According to several studies (Asher, Gottman, & Oden, 1977; Dodge, 1983; Hartup, 1983; Rubin et al., 1998), a child's acceptance by peers and successful interactions with them depend on a willingness to cooperate and interact positively with other children. Children who are popular with their peers tend to be healthy and vigorous, capable of initiative, and well poised. They are also adaptable and conforming, as well as dependable, affectionate, and considerate.

Being yourself, being happy, showing enthusiasm and concern for others, and showing self-confidence but not conceit are among the characteristics that lead to popularity (Hartup, 1983; Rubin et al., 1998). Certain physical and intellectual factors can also affect a child's popularity. Studies have shown that, on average, children who are physically attractive are more popular than those who are not (Adams & Crane, 1980; Adler & Adler, 1998; Ritts, Patterson, & Tubbs, 1992). A study of 6- to 10-year-old boys (Hartup, 1983) revealed that those with muscular physiques were more popular than those who were skinny or plump; this is consistent with findings that athletic ability is related to popularity (Adler & Alder, 1998; Coleman, 1961). Children who are more intelligent have been found to be more popular than those who are less intelligent (Berndt, 1983; Rubin et al., 1998). Other studies have shown that the ability to use language and communicate ideas effectively helps in peer acceptance (Gottman, Gonso, & Rasmussen, 1975; Kemple, 1991). In general, popular children approach others in a friendly manner, respond appropriately to communications, interpret emotional states correctly, and are generous with praise and approval. See Table 8.1 for a summary of characteristics of children who are accepted, versus those who are neglected or rejected, by their peers.

ACCEPTED	NEGLECTED/REJECTED
Cooperative	Shy
Positive in interactions	Withdrawn
Capable of initiating interaction	Dishonest
Adaptable and conforming	Unsporting attitude when losing
Understands emotional expressions	Incapable of initiating interaction
Shows concern for others	Socially unskilled
Able to communicate effectively	Unable to interpret others' emotional states
Happy	Unable to communicate easily
Dependable	Whiny
Affectionate	Disruptive
Considerate	Miserly with praise
Well-poised	Bossy
Generous with praise	Aggressive
Intelligent	"Different" physically, behaviorally, academically
Friendly	Negative social reputation
Self-confident (not conceited)	
Physically attractive	
Athletic ability	
Prosocial behavior	
Positive social reputation	

Table 8.1

Summary of Characteristics of Children Accepted/ Neglected/Rejected by Peers

Prosocial behavior (being empathetic, cooperative, helpful) is the most consistent correlate of peer group acceptance (Wentzel & Erdley, 1993). Socialization of pro- and antisocial behavior will be discussed more thoroughly in Chapter 12.

Family interaction patterns play a role in children's successful integration into the group (Hartup, 1989, 1996). In the family, children learn to express and interpret various emotions such as pleasure, displeasure, attachment, and distancing. Children also learn to respond to such emotional expressions and to regulate their behavior according to family requirements. Thus social competence, which leads to peer acceptance, begins in the family.

Which children are neglected or rejected by the group? The rise and fall of children's likes and dislikes causes almost every school-age child to feel neglected or rejected at some point by other children. The child not asked to play, not chosen to be on the team, not invited to the party, or excluded from the club feels that a crucial part of his or her world has been shattered. The reason a child is neglected or rejected may be shyness or lack of social skills. Children who do not know how to initiate a friendship, who are withdrawn, who misinterpret others' emotional states, who have difficulty communicating, who are bossy, who are disruptive in class, and/or who rarely praise their peers are not readily accepted by the group.

Also, children who are poor losers, who cheat or whine, and who are aggressive are not welcome in most children's groups. Antisocial behavior is the most consistent correlate of peer rejection (Coie & Cillesen, 1993; Coie et al., 1990).

Sometimes children are rejected for reasons they cannot change or even understand. For example, *Blubber*, by Judy Blume (1974), is about an overweight girl who is the brunt of her fifth-grade classmates' teasing and scapegoating: "She won't need a coat this winter; she's got her blubber to keep her warm." Sometimes children are teased and ostracized from the group because they are different physically (weight, height, skin color); behaviorally (accent, speech impediment, style of dress, religious preference); academically (learning disabled, gifted); or even in their names (Hartup, 1983; Langlois, 1986; Sandstrom & Coie, 1999). The following story appeared in the *Los Angeles Times* in 1982.

> A 9-year-old boy named Alfonse wrote a letter to Senator Alfonse D'Amato (R-N.Y.), asking him how he got his name. The boy couldn't ask his father why he was named Alfonse, because his father had died. He wrote that he hated his name because the kids at school joked about it. D'Amato wrote back that the name Alfonse means "prepared for battle," and when you're young, "you'd better be." D'Amato also wrote that when he asked his father why he was named Alfonse, his father replied, "Son, your Uncle Alfonse was a very wealthy man, and that's how we got the down payment on the house." The senator recommended that young Alfonse tell his friends to call him Al.

Family problems can have damaging effects on children's peer relations (Baker, Barthelemy, & Kurdek, 1993; Burton, 1985; Ladd, 1999). For example, children whose parents are getting a divorce may act out feelings of anger and fear at school, eliciting rejection from peers in the process. Children who have a parent who is an alcoholic may be reluctant to bring friends home and may avoid making close friends out of embarrassment. Likewise, children who are abused, children of homosexual parents, or children whose parents have a disability or health impairment may isolate themselves from others to avoid judgment by others.

Many studies suggest that children's behaviors and characteristics contribute to how well liked they are by peers, but Kemple (1991) suggests it is also important to consider the role that peers play in maintaining a child's level of social acceptance. Once a child has established a reputation as someone who is nice and fun to play with, acceptance is easy; whereas for a child who has a reputation of being unpleasant, acceptance is difficult.

In sum, factors linked to acceptance (initiating and maintaining a relationship) enable group belonging; whereas factors linked to neglect and rejection (unsociable, disruptive, aggressive) make it difficult to belong to a group. Dodge and others (Coie & Dodge, 1998; Dodge, 1986) propose that these factors are influenced by how children cognitively process social information, including their ability to interpret stimuli, remember, and respond.

PEER SOCIOTHERAPY

How can children who are neglected or rejected by peers be helped?

sociometry
techniques used to measure patterns of acceptance, neglect, and rejection among members of a group

Techniques known collectively as **sociometry** have been developed to measure patterns of acceptance, neglect, and rejection among members of a group. Sociometry was originally used in school classrooms but is now widely used in other settings, such as recreational, work, and prison environments. Contemporary researchers typically use sociometry to identify the extent to which children prefer to be with certain peers (Cillesen & Bukowski, 2000; Parkhurst & Asher, 1992).

A sociometric rating is easy to conduct; it involves asking children questions anonymously about each other and tabulating the results. For example: Who is your best friend? With whom would you prefer and not prefer to work on a project? With whom would you share a secret? Preschoolers can be shown photographs of classmates and asked with whom they like and dislike playing. Children with the most "liked" votes are popular; those with the most "disliked" responses are neglected or rejected.

Sociometric results can help adults facilitate the inclusion of neglected or rejected children into the group. By careful observations, adults can assess where the neglected or rejected child needs intervention (Kemple, 1991)—*social* (Does the child cooperate? share? boast?); *emotional* (Does the child interpret others' emotions correctly? empathize?); *language* (Does the child make relevant responses to peers' communications? communicate desires clearly?); or *physical* (Does the child resort to aggression to resolve conflicts?). Adults can then choose appropriate intervention strategies or sociotherapy.

Selman and Selman's (1979) developmental stages of friendship have been used in peer **sociotherapy**, an intervention to help children who have trouble making and keeping friends learn to relate to others. By assessing their levels of social relationships with others, a therapist or teacher can sometimes help children to move on to the next developmental level.

Children who have difficulty making friends can be helped by giving them a chance to play with younger children. Some researchers (Bullock, 1992; Howes, 1988) have found that socially withdrawn preschoolers become more sociable after they have had a chance to play, one on one, with children one to two years younger than themselves during play sessions. The researchers conclude that being with younger children gives socially withdrawn children a chance to be assertive in initiating and directing activity. Once they experience success with younger children, they are better able to interact with children their own age.

Children who have difficulty reading other children's social cues may benefit by watching others who interact successfully. This can be done in real situations with an adult coach, watched on videotape, or performed by puppets (Bullock, 1992).

Also, having a friend in a new situation, such as school, or in a stressful situation, such as divorce, helps the child cope and better adjust to what is going on (Ladd, 1990, 1999). This is another reason why it is important to enable children to make friends.

In order to help children who are not readily accepted by their peers get along better, Oden and Asher (1977) identified four categories of social skills, based on the research on popularity: *participation* (playing with others, paying attention); *communication* (talking and listening); *cooperation* (taking turns, sharing); and *validation/ support* (offering encouragement or help).

A group of unpopular school-age children were coached on these specific skills. The coaching sessions involved demonstration (instruction and role modeling), discussion (explanation and feedback), and shaping by reinforcing desired behavior (behavior modification). A year later, the group of unpopular children who were coached showed more sociability and acceptance by peers than the control group of unpopular children who were not coached. Coaching strategies have been used successfully with preschool as well as school-age children (Mize & Ladd, 1990).

Another study (Sandstrom & Coie, 1999) found that elementary school children who were initially rejected could improve their status with peers by participating in extracurricular activities and by having their parents monitor their social interactions (arranging for play with cooperative peers, intervening in conflicts). See the box for suggestions on how to improve children's social skills.

sociotherapy an intervention to help children who have trouble making and keeping friends learn to relate to others

---

IN PRACTICE

Improving Children's Social Skills

The following are some guidelines that teachers and parents can use in monitoring children's interactions to improve their social skills (Asher, 1982; Bullock, 1992).

Model

- Observe how others interact positively.
- Imitate behaviors and communications that were successful in promoting friendship.

Participate

- Get involved with others.
- Get started on an activity, a project, or a game.
- Pay attention to the activity.
- Try to do your best.
- Help someone who is younger.

Cooperate

- Take turns.
- Share the game, materials, or props.
- Make suggestions if there's a problem.
- If there is disagreement about the rules, work out a mutually agreeable alternative.

Communicate

- Talk with others.
- Say things about the activity or about yourself.
- Ask a question about the activity.
- Ask a question about the other person.
- Listen when the other person talks.
- Look at the other person to see how he or she is doing.

Validate and Support

- Give some attention to the other person.
- Say something nice when the other person does well.
- Smile.
- Have fun.
- Offer help or suggestions when needed.

Peer Group Dynamics and Social Hierarchies

What social mechanisms establish order and control within the peer group?

The peer group is a microsystem with dynamic roles and relationships affecting its participants. Unlike the microsystems of family, school, and community, the peer group is generally unencumbered by adult guidance. The peer group uses informal social mechanisms to develop norms, statuses, alliances, consequences, and feelings about self (Thompson, Cohen, & Grace 2002). These social mechanisms are illustrated in the box "Peers, Prestige, Power, and Persuasion."

IN PRACTICE

Peers, Prestige, Power, and Persuasion

William Golding's classic novel *Lord of the Flies* (1954) is about a group of English schoolboys, ranging in age from 6 to 12, who are marooned on a desert island when their plane crashes. The adults are killed, and the youngsters, despairing of rescue, set out to build their own society. At first, the older boys try to draw on their memory of English society, but they do not remember enough, and there are no elders they can turn to for guidance. They establish their own system of socialization, first by investing authority in a leader chosen on the basis of appearance and perceived power (he possesses a conch shell) and then by setting up rituals to provide order amid the chaos. In the beginning, the boys try to cooperate, making shelters, gathering food, and keeping signal fires going. Ralph takes on the leadership role, trying to impose order by delegating responsibilities for survival chores. Piggy, Ralph's spectacled, chubby friend, dispenses logic and rationale to the necessary decisions. His thick spectacles come in handy for lighting fires. However, disagreements and conflict soon give way to savagery. The other boys would rather play, swim, or hunt the island's wild pig population than plan for survival. Soon they begin to ignore Ralph's rules, and Jack challenges them outright. Jack, the leader of his subgroup of savages, starts luring Ralph and Piggy's followers to join him. Ralph and Piggy now become the hunted, instead of the hunters, as emotion overtakes reason. Piggy, the continual reminder of adult standards of behavior, is brutally killed before the rescuers arrive. The children have forgotten how they were socialized to resolve differences appropriately, such as by negotiation, and resort to competition for status and power, using aggressive means to get them.

A parallel example of peer group dynamics is the "reality" TV series *Survivor*. A group of adult contestants are castaways on a deserted island. Each week, the survivors compete in grueling physical competitions in games as well as for resources to survive. The prize for which they are competing is to be the last one left on the island and, hence, the winner of a million dollars. What begins as fun turns into manipulation and maliciousness. Every week, the group meets with its leaders in a Tribal Council to vote one contestant off the island. Everyone must explain the rationale behind his or her vote. The ejected member must give a farewell speech, describing his or her experiences and feelings. Unlike the children in *Lord of the Flies*, *Survivor* adults do remember how to negotiate differences, but like the children, they engage in competition for status and power, using manipulative means to get them.

INCLUSION AND EXCLUSION

How does one become part of the "in" group?

According to Adler and Adler (1998), who studied groups of children ages 8 to 12 in a predominantly white, middle-class community for eight years, dynamics in peer cliques include techniques of *inclusion* (recruitment of new members, treatment of

This child is being teased by the group leader.

"wannabes," friendship realignment, ingratiation) and *exclusion* (out-group subjugation, in-group subjugation, compliance, stigmatization, expulsion).

Inclusionary Techniques. Recruitment of a new member into a clique was usually by invitation; if a member met and liked someone, that individual was afforded "probationary" status until the other members agreed to include him or her. "Wannabes" sometimes gained entry by doing nice things for members of the clique or by doing something to gain their respect, such as helping the school team win. The hierarchical structure within the clique, with shifts in status and power, caused friendship loyalties to be compromised.

Higher-status members often co-opted lower-status members to maintain their popularity. Lower-status members might abandon their lower-status friends in order to gain favor with a higher-status member, thereby moving up the social hierarchy. Ingratiation, or currying favors with clique members, was directed both upward, toward peers of higher status (for example, adulation), and downward, toward peers of lower status (for example, domination).

Exclusionary Techniques. Out-group subjugation, such as teasing, picking on, and being mean to those outside the clique, served to solidify the cohesiveness of the group and assure the strength of the group's position with other groups. In-group subjugation occurred when high-level insiders harassed or ridiculed low-level insiders for dominance. Lower-status members complied with leaders' or high-status members' wishes in order to gain favor. Stigmatization, such as branding a member as a tattletale, a cheat, or a crybaby, was used to disempower a clique member who fell into disfavor. Expulsion, or being cast out of the group permanently, occurred when a member engaged in a serious infraction of the group's rules or stood up for his or her rights against the dominant leaders.

BULLIES/VICTIMS

Who gets" picked on," by whom, and why?

An extreme example of the dynamics and social hierarchies in peer groups is bullying. Dan Olweus (1993) has extensively studied bullies and their victims at school. He defines *bullying*, or victimization, as being "exposed, repeatedly and over time, to negative actions on the part of one or more other students." Negative actions, or harassment, include threats, taunts, teasing, name-calling, and making faces or dirty gestures, as well as hitting, kicking, pinching, and physically restraining another.

Bullies tend to have the following characteristics:

- Domination needs—need to feel powerful, superior
- Impulsive, low frustration tolerance, easily angered
- Usually physically stronger than peers
- Difficulty adhering to rules
- Generally oppositional, defiant, aggressive
- Show little empathy

- A relatively positive self-concept
- Engage in antisocial behavior

Victims tend to have the following characteristics:

- Usually physically weaker than peers
- Poor physical coordination
- Exhibit fear of being hurt or hurting themselves
- Cautious, sensitive, quiet, passive, submissive, shy
- Anxious, insecure, unhappy
- A relatively negative self-concept
- Difficulty asserting themselves
- Often relate better to adults than peers

What can be done about bullies and their victims?

- Awareness, supervision, and involvement by adults
- Interventions with bullies by parents, teachers, and peers that do not reinforce harassment
- Class rules with consequences, training in alternative behaviors, role playing, cooperative learning
- Interventions with victims to alter their negative self-concept, training to be assertive and respond in nonreinforcing ways to threats (ignoring, humor)

GANGS

Why do peer groups sometimes engage in negative behavior?

Sometimes peer group dynamics can result in negative or antisocial behaviors. Peers (or, more specifically, "hanging around with the wrong crowd") are often blamed for delinquency and substance abuse, but in reality the single most consistent characteristic of delinquents is lack of support and socialization by their families (Jackson & McBride, 1985; Rutter, Giller, & Hagell, 1998). Antagonistic relationships between parents are often found in families with antisocial children (Patterson, Reid, & Dishion, 1992; Rutter, 1971). When children do not have their needs met in their families, they often turn to their peers. There is also a relationship between peer rejection and delinquency (Bagwell, Coie, Terry, & Lochman, 2000). Delinquent behavior is often socialized by peers (Dishion, McCord, & Poulin, 1999; Goldstein, 1991).

Poor neighborhoods with poor-quality schools, limited recreational and employment opportunities, and adult criminal subcultures tend to be predictive of juvenile gang activity (Farrington & Loeber, 2000).

Social change, microsystems (family, school, community) under stress, and consequent lack of support for children tend to be associated with an increase in delinquency rates (National Research Council, 1993). Many young people lack positive adult role models. The gap between the consumerism perpetuated by the media and reality may entice young people to turn to delinquency. Personality factors may contribute to the reasons some adolescents become delinquents. It is known that those who become delinquent are more likely to be defiant, ambivalent to authority, resentful, hostile, impulsive, and lacking in self-control (Goldstein, 1991; Thompson & Dodder, 1986). Those who get poor grades in school, have been reported for classroom misconduct, and have trouble getting along with other children and teachers show a greater tendency to become delinquents (Ladd & LeSieur, 1995; Landre, Miller, & Porter, 1997). Thus, the peer group may be the setting in which preexisting antisocial behavior due to family factors, social change, personality characteristics, or being out of synch with the school is reinforced (Goldstein, 1991; Rubin et al., 1998).

"A **gang** is a group of people who form an allegiance for a common purpose and engage in unlawful or criminal activity" (Jackson & McBride, 1985, p. 20). Gangs are of concern not only because of their antisocial activities, but also because of their increase (Goldstein, 1991). Gangs usually consist of males, although there are female gangs. Gang members identify themselves through names, clothes, tattoos, slang, sign language, and graffiti. The problem of gangs is spreading throughout our society like a plague. They are present in neighborhoods and schools, affecting businesses, recreation, and education (Landre et al., 1997). Gang violence has tragic consequences; gangs deal drugs, steal, hurt, and kill. Innocent bystanders are often victims (U.S. Department of Justice, 2000).

What is the appeal of gangs?

Gangs give members companionship, guidance, excitement, and identity (Goldstein, 1991). When a member needs something, the others come to the rescue and provide protection (Landre et al., 1997). Gang members have experienced failure and alienation in their lives. They tend to live in depressed or deprived environments, which their families may be helpless to change. Because they feel they can't accomplish anything individually, gang members band together to exercise influence over their lives (Jackson & McBride, 1985).

The homes of gang-oriented children are characterized by either high permissiveness or high punitiveness (Devereaux, 1970). The parents of such peer-oriented children also show less concern and affection; by such passive neglect, rather than active maltreatment, they push their children to look to peers for support (Condry & Simon, 1974; Ladd & LeSieur, 1995). Youngsters living with both biological parents are less susceptible to pressure from peers to engage in deviant behavior than youngsters living in single-parent homes or with stepfamilies. Thus, the stability of the home is an important protector against pressure toward deviant behavior (Steinberg, 1987).

Gang members have significantly lower levels of self-esteem compared to their nongang peers. They also could name fewer adult role models in their families and communities than did their nongang peers (Wang, 1994).

In sum, sociological forces in the formation of gangs include the following (Jackson & McBride, 1985):

- **Racism**. Gangs are usually made up of one race, thereby being a source of identity and support.
- **Socioeconomics**. Gang members usually come from poor families in densely populated areas where there is competition for resources, although recently there are increasing numbers of gangs in middle-class neighborhoods.
- **Family structure**. Gang members usually come from families with minimal adult supervision; a mother-headed family; a two-adult family in which the father, stepfather, or boyfriend is a negative role model; or a family that has a gang lineage.
- **Belief system**. Gang members believe they are victims and blame society for their problems. They also feel that because society hasn't helped them, they are justified in protecting themselves outside of society's rules.

PEER COLLABORATION, TUTORING, AND COUNSELING

What positive outcomes can result from peer dynamics?

gang a group of people who form an alliance for a common purpose and engage in unlawful or criminal activity

Peer group dynamics, often with the help of adults, can have positive outcomes for participants. Collaboration, tutoring, and counseling are methods encouraged by adults to enable peers to be supportive of one another. Peers who *collaborate* learn to solve problems through consensus. Peers who *tutor* learn how to analyze and synthesize information for others. Peers who *counsel* learn how to care, help, and give support to others.

Peer collaborations with different outcomes are discussed by Piaget and Vygotsky. According to Piaget (1965), when children interact, they discover that others have opinions and perspectives different from theirs. As a result, they reorganize their cognitive structures (accommodate) to fit discrepant information. Thus, Piaget believed that cognitive development was more likely to result from *conflict* with same-age peers than from interaction with older children and adults (Berk & Winsler, 1995). Vygotsky (1978), on the other hand, believed that cognitive development resulted from *collaboration* with peers. Peer conflict could only contribute to heightened understanding if the disagreement was compromised or resolved. Vygotsky emphasized the importance of mixed-age groups that provide each child opportunities to interact with more knowledgeable companions and give each child a chance to serve as a resource for others. Expert peers can serve as mentors, models, or tutors, whereas novice peers can be apprentices. Adults must guide collaborative activities, teaching social and problem-solving skills, intervening when necessary (Berk & Winsler, 1995).

Peer tutoring is exemplified by inclusion programs in which a child with a disability is assisted, academically and/or socially, by a classmate (Vaughn, Bos, & Schumm, 1997). Peer tutoring provides a zone of proximal development (ZPD), discussed earlier, in which what one is capable of learning independently is potentially increased by participating with more capable others.

An example of peer counseling is "positive peer culture," or PPC (Vorrath & Brendtro, 1985). PPC involves a group of peers with an adult leader. It is designed to "turn around" negative youth subculture and mobilize the power of the peer group to foster positive behavior. A person is asked not whether he or she wants to *receive* help, but whether he or she is willing to *give* help. As the person becomes of value to others, his or her feelings of self-worth are enhanced (Vorrath & Brendtro, 1985). PPC is predicated on the belief that delinquent youth, who are often rebellious and strong-willed, have much to contribute when redirected. Those who have encountered difficulties in their lives are often in the best position to help others. PPC provides students with what they do not get from other socializing agents: care and a sense of responsibility—for themselves and others.

> A group home for troubled girls had severe drug-abuse problems. The result of the many attempts to suppress this activity was a cold war between staff and youth. Suspicion, searches, and restriction became commonplace. That was a year ago. Now staff members no longer police students for drugs, and the climate of intrigue is gone. As a new girl enters, her peers confiscate any drugs she may have and tell her, "We don't have to use dope around here." Drug problems are dealt with openly in a helpful, matter-of-fact way. Group members state with strong conviction that when a person has good feelings about herself, she no longer needs to get high on drugs.

Mesosystem Influences on the Peer Group

How do links with groups in the community affect peer group outcomes?

Adults play a significant role in "setting the stage" for peer group experiences. Earlier, the adult role was discussed in terms of secure attachment and arranging for friends to get together in the home. According to Steinberg (1996), the neighborhood in which a child lives influences whether the peer group has positive or negative effects.

Neighborhoods that include parents who are involved in schools, who participate in organized activities for children (sports, arts, scouts), and who monitor their children tend to have children who provide positive peer influences for one another. On the other hand, neighborhoods that include parents who are disengaged from school and community activities tend to have children who provide negative peer influences for one another. Thus, parents can influence whether a child's peer group experiences are positive or negative by knowing who their child's friends are and by being involved in their child's activities.

Peer groups linked to and structured by adults include team sports, clubs, Scouts, and church groups. They differ, because of their organization, from the informal peer groups (neighborhood or school groups of friends) that have been discussed so far, which are formed and maintained by the children themselves. Whereas child-structured groups are casual and informal, adult-structured groups are purposeful and formal.

Adult-structured and child-structured groups differ in their socializing influences on children. When adults organize groups, there are rules, guidelines, or suggestions about appropriate or expected behavior in an activity. Adults supply the structure through verbal instructions, praise, criticism, feedback about the activity or the child's performance, and modeling ways to perform the activity. The structuring of a setting influences the behavior that goes on within it. For example, formal groups organized by adults encourage children to play according to established rules, to be compliant, and to seek guidance as well as recognition from adults; groups organized by the children themselves encourage children to be active and assertive with peers, to take initiative, and to behave independently (Huston, Carpenter, Atwater, & Johnson, 1986). Studies of preschool children have found that girls prefer more adult-structured groups (Carpenter, Huston, & Hart, 1986; Powlishta, Serbin, & Moller, 1993). A similar pattern of gender differences has been shown to exist for school-age children (Carpenter, 1983; Huston, 1983; Maccoby, 1990, 2000).

Groups structured by adults are also characterized by the different values that are imparted to children. Clubs may be formed at church, at school, or in the community. A church club may serve the purpose of fellowship—getting to know children of similar religious backgrounds. A school club may provide extracurricular activities for interested children—for example, computer club, chorus, or drama club. A community club may be for recreation (the Y) or for character building (Scouts). For example, the ideology of the Boy and Girl Scouts of America is to foster patriotism, reverence, leadership, and emotional development. Children are encouraged to develop self-reliance by accomplishing certain tasks to earn badges—for example, water safety or cooking.

ADULT-MEDIATED GROUP INTERACTION

How do adults affect peer group interaction?

How adults mediate, or structure, the social interaction within a peer group—specifically, whether it is *competitive* or *cooperative*—influences children's behavior. To illustrate, psychologist Mustaf Sherif (1956) and his colleagues (Sherif, Harvey, White, Hood, & Sherif, 1961) conducted a classic series of naturalistic experiments in which middle-class, white, Protestant boys, 11 years old, were recruited and sent to a camp during the summer. Within a few weeks, adult mediation brought about two sharply contrasting patterns of behavior in this sample of normal boys. The sample was divided into two separate groups (the Rattlers and the Eagles) who did not know each other. The counselors/observers were able to transform each group into a hostile, destructive, antisocial gang through various strategies, such as competitive sports in which winning was all-important and letting each group know the other group was "the enemy." Then, within a few days, the counselors/observers were able to change these groups into cooperative, constructive workers and friends who were concerned about the other members of the community. Various problems at the camp were set up to foster a cooperative spirit. For example, a water line was deliberately broken so that the two groups of boys would have to work together to fix it. Another time, the camp truck broke down on the way to town for food. The boys had to help get the engine started.

Several findings emerged from Sherif's (1956) and his colleagues' (Sherif et al., 1961) naturalistic experiments regarding peer group behavior:

- Groups tend to *stratify*, with some individuals assuming more dominant roles and others more submissive ones.
- Groups develop *norms*—standards that serve to guide and regulate individuals' actions as members of a group.
- Frustration and competition contribute to hostility between groups.
- Competition *between* groups fosters cohesiveness *within* groups.
- Intergroup hostility can often be reduced by setting up a *superordinate*, or common, goal that requires the mutual efforts of both groups. When overriding goals that are real and important for all concerned need to be achieved, then hostility between groups diminishes.

The significance of these studies of peer group dynamics is that they suggest strategies for enabling children to work together. The findings on cooperation and competition were implemented by a team of researchers at Johns Hopkins University (Johnson & Johnson, 1999; Slavin, Devries, & Hutten, 1975). A Team Games Tournament (TGT) was developed to see if cooperation in a competitive setting would increase academic achievement. In TGT, four or five children of varying academic ability, gender, and race are put on each team. Teams are equated on average ability level. Individuals *compete* with individuals who are members of other teams. Each person's game score is added to those of the others on the team to form a team score. Team members *cooperate* by studying as a group and helping each other prepare for the tournament. TGT has had positive effects on mathematics achievement in the junior high school, language arts achievement in elementary school, and, in general, on attitudes toward subject matter and classroom procedures. Increases have occurred in class solidarity, fostering friendships among girls and boys as well as among children of differing ethnic backgrounds. A sample sociometric test—a measure of acceptance or rejection by the group, discussed earlier—revealed that children who succeeded as team members were liked more than when they succeeded as individuals.

ADULT LEADERSHIP STYLES

What effect does adult leadership style have on group dynamics?

Groups led by adults can differ markedly according to the kind of leadership provided, as was exemplified by teachers' leadership styles in Chapter 7. Leadership style influences socialization, as illustrated by a classic series of studies (Lewin et al., 1939; Lippitt & White, 1943) that distinguished three kinds of adult leadership and measured their effects on groups of 10-year-old boys. The boys were organized into clubs and worked on such activities as soap carving, mask making, and mural painting. The three kinds of leadership were categorized as follows:

- **Authoritarian**. Policies, activities, techniques, and delegation of tasks were dictated by the leader. Praise and criticism of the group members' work was subjective. ("You are good at that.") The leader did not participate actively in the group's activities.
- **Democratic (Authoritative)**. Policies and activities were determined by group discussion. The leader presented techniques and delegation of tasks in terms of alternatives from which the group members could choose. Praise and criticism were objective. ("Your soap carving has a lot of detailed work; it must have taken you a lot of time to do that.") The leader participated in the activities.
- **Laissez-faire (Permissive)**. Policies, activities, techniques, and delegation of tasks were left up to the group members. The leader supplied materials for the projects and was available for information, if requested. Comments about the group members' work were very infrequent. The leader did not participate in the group's activities.

Because each adult in the studies rotated through the three leadership styles, differences in the group's behavior were determined to be a function of the style of leadership, rather than the leader's personality. Children in the groups with *authoritarian* leaders became either submissive or aggressive. The boys were discontented with the activities and worked less constructively when the leader left the room. They tended to be competitive with one another. Children in the groups with *democratic* leaders had high morale. The boys were involved in their group goals and were cooperative. They sustained their level of activity even when the leader left the room. Children in the groups with *laissez-faire* leaders were disorganized and frustrated. The boys made efforts to mobilize themselves as a group, but were unable to sustain their efforts.

In all three situations, the behavior of the adult set the tone for group effort (see Table 8.2). Within each situation, children got different messages about how to make decisions and work with others toward a goal.

TEAM SPORTS

What role do sports play in socialization?

Sports are "organized interactions of children in competitive and/or cooperative team or individual enjoyable physical activities" (Humphrey, 1993, p. 3). In the United States, sports are not only a major form of recreation, but are also considered a means of achieving physical health. Sports are also regarded as a way for children to learn leadership skills, loyalty, and other desirable traits, and as valuable training in competitiveness and give-and-take relationships. Organized sports are also a vehicle for promoting the development of talent.

Sports are a pervasive part of American culture. Sports lingo—competition, teamwork, winning the game—is widely used in the corporate world (Murphy, 1999). The American attitude toward sports is revealed by the statistics: more than 20 million U.S. children, age 6 and older, play on organized sports teams; more than 2.5 million play Little League baseball, more than 1 million play organized football, and the rest are involved in such sports as hockey, soccer, swimming, track, and gymnastics (Poinsett, 1997). Most local youth sports organizations belong to national associations, which set guidelines for the games and the coaches.

ADULT	CHILDREN
AUTHORITARIAN	Aggressive Submissive Discontented Competitive
DEMOCRATIC	High morale Cooperative Self-supporting, cohesive
LAISSEZ-FAIRE	Disorganized Frustrated Nonsupporting, fragmented

Table 8.2

Socialization Effects of Leadership Styles

Do all children benefit from the experience of playing sports? According to Murphy (1999), many do not. Some children do learn a lot about themselves and their capabilities, about their potential for improvement (however modest), about the value of teamwork, about the fun of sports, and about the lifelong importance of physical fitness (Poinsett, 1997). Other children, however, are humiliated by their experience in organized sports. Perhaps they are being pushed to succeed by their parents; not being able to live up to their parents' expectations, they become discouraged and end up hating the sport or themselves. I remember watching many Little League games while my son was involved. It was not uncommon to hear a father yell to his son from the stands, "You dummy, how could you miss that ball? Wake up!"

> When I was 11 years old, I was on a softball team. I desperately wanted to be the pitcher, but I wasn't chosen. My throwing was accurate, but it wasn't fast enough. The coach put me in centerfield because I was also a good fielder. I was so crushed that I almost quit. What I didn't understand then was that the team already had a good pitcher, but the shortstop made a lot of errors and the right- and leftfielders were daydreamers. The coach's logic was to put me in centerfield because I could catch and throw, and because I could also run fast, I could get the balls missed by the others. It took me quite a few games to understand that teamwork makes everyone play better because teamwork coordinates all the individual abilities. No matter how good one person on the team is, if the others are not playing well, the team can't win. I wanted to be the pitcher because I wanted to be the star. I learned that stars don't succeed without the support of the cast.

In some cases, the coach of a team may place more emphasis on winning than on playing. Winning can mean several things. It can mean self-improvement and a sense of accomplishment when a player's performance improves, or it can mean beating the other team. When winning is narrowed down to beating the other team, undue pressures are put on children (Galton, 1980; Humphrey, 1993). If children are ridiculed, belittled, or threatened when they fumble, or if the coach gives attention only to the better players, then some children are not benefiting from participating on that team. On the other hand, if the coach gives extra support to those lacking in confidence, they will benefit in more ways than just improving their athletic skills. Thus, sports training can be of benefit in developing an attitude of positive thinking and setting goals that go beyond what one thinks one can presently do. A significant factor is that coaches consider the developmental needs of children and foster an environment based on respect for effort, rather than just for winning (Murphy, 1999).

> At a gymnastics competition I saw a girl fall off the bar. She was not hurt, but her confidence was shaken. Her coach told her the mistake and made her do the routine again correctly even though it would not count for points. The girl took a deep breath, focused, and completed her flip on the bar. Everyone applauded. The girl learned not to give up if perfection is not achieved on the first attempt and that effort can be as appreciated by the audience as much as the performance.

Epilogue

Relations with friends influences adaptation across the life span. Like the friends in the Nigerian folktale, children learn by experience the challenges of maintaining a friendship. Peers are significant socializers. Being accepted by peers influences one's self-concept, behavior, and values. Being rejected by the group can have damaging developmental and real consequences. A desire to be part of the group and to have status within it helps explain why children conform.

Summary

The peer group is a microsystem in that it comprises relationships, roles, and activities. Peers are a group of equals, usually of the same age, gender, and socioeconomic status, who share the same interests. Experiences with peers enable children to acquire a wide range of skills, attitudes, and behaviors that influence their social adaptation throughout life.

Peer groups are significant because having a group of friends meets the human needs of belonging and social interaction as well as promoting a sense of self and personal identity.

The need to belong is first established in the family through attachment. Infants and toddlers who are securely attached are more likely to interact socially with others. Opportunities for social interaction are influenced by parents.

The peer group influences the sense of self by providing opportunities for comparisons with others. It also influences personal identity by providing opportunities for independence from adults and allows children to "learn by doing." Children work through issues of power, compliance, cooperation, and conflict.

As children enter the middle years of childhood (ages 6 to 12 or 13), the peer group becomes increasingly important. Experiments show that children become more susceptible to the influence of peers in middle childhood (especially around preadolescence, ages 11 to 13) and become less conforming in adolescence. The reasons for this have to do with the child's cognitive level (transition from Piaget's stage of concrete operations to formal operations) and stage of personality development (entrance into Erikson's psychosocial stage of identity versus identity confusion). Also, the child's social cognitive abilities are becoming more complex.

The relative importance of adult and peer influence depends on parenting style, particular values, and ethnicity. Children of authoritative parents are less likely to be influenced by peers than are children of authoritarian or permissive parents.

Parents, in general, are more likely to influence future decisions and values; peers, present ones. Ethnic groups valuing interdependence are more group-oriented than ethnic groups valuing independence.

In achieving a personal identity, a major task for the child is to balance group identification with personal autonomy while forging an individual role within the group. The socializing influence of peer groups has outcomes on psychological (emotions), social (social competence), and cognitive (social cognition) development.

The socializing mechanisms that peers employ to influence one another's behavior are reinforcement (approval and acceptance), modeling, punishment (rejection and exclusion), and apprenticeship (novice learns from expert).

Macrosystem influences on the peer group enable children to accomplish certain developmental tasks: getting along with others, developing morals and values, learning appropriate sociocultural roles (including gender roles, sex education, and sexual activity), and achieving personal independence and identity.

Chronosystem influences on the peer group involve changes in structure, activities, and relationships as children develop and have new experiences. When children get together in informal groups, they play. Play has cognitive, social, psychological, and adaptive functions for adult life.

Parten identified categories of play based on social interactions: solitary, onlooker, parallel, associative, and cooperative. Sutton-Smith identified four types of play based on activities: imitative, exploratory, testing, and model building.

As children develop, their play and their social relationships become more complicated. Selman and Selman delineated five stages of friendship: momentary playmateship; one-way assistance; two-way, fair-weather cooperation; intimate, mutually shared relationships; and autonomous, interdependent friendships.

Children who are readily accepted by the peer group tend to be healthy, vigorous, initiating, well-poised, adaptable, conforming, dependable, affectionate, considerate, happy, enthusiastic, concerned for others, and self-confident. Family interaction patterns play a role in children's successful integration into the group.

Children who are neglected or rejected by the peer group tend to have difficulty initiating a friendship, have difficulty communicating, rarely praise their peers, and are shy, poor losers, cheaters, whiners, or aggressive. Sometimes children are rejected because they are different physically, behaviorally, in style of dress, academically, or in their names. Family problems can have damaging effects on children's peer relations. Rejected children tend to be attracted to deviant peer groups.

Sociometry is a set of techniques to measure acceptance, neglect, and rejection among members of a group. Selman and Selman have applied their developmental stages of friendship in peer sociotherapy. Children who have trouble making and keeping friends can sometimes be helped to move on to the next developmental level.

Ways to help children improve their social skills and be more acceptable to their peers are modeling, participation, communication, cooperation, and validation/support. Children who were coached in these categories were more sociable and acceptable to their peers than those who were not coached.

Peer group dynamics and social hierarchies involve norms, statuses, alliances, consequences, and outcomes that are related to self-esteem.

Peer groups can have negative effects on children. Bullies who victimize children can cause psychological as well as physical harm. Delinquency usually occurs in the peer groups whose members lack family support and live in poor, unsupportive neighborhoods. Gangs are allegiances that engage in unlawful activities.

The influence of peers can be positive, too. Peer groups can be used to solve problems, educate, and help others, with appropriate adult guidance. Examples are peer collaboration, tutoring, and counseling.

Mesosystem influences on peer groups emerge from links with adults. Groups structured by adults differ from those structured by children in that adults provide values, rules, and suggestions. Examples of adult-structured peer groups are clubs, Scouts, church groups, and sports teams. Team sports can be a positive influence for learning competitiveness and cooperation and gaining self-esteem.

Groups led by adults can differ markedly according to the kind of leadership provided by the adult. Children in groups with authoritarian leaders tend to become either submissive or aggressive. Children in groups with democratic (authoritative) leaders tend to cooperate and have high morale. Children in groups with laissez-faire (permissive) leaders tend to be disorganized and frustrated.

How adults mediate, or structure, the social interaction within a peer group (competitive or cooperative) influences children's behavior. For example, frustration and competition contribute to hostility between groups; competition between groups fosters cohesiveness within each group; and intergroup hostility can often be reduced by setting a superordinate, or common, goal that requires the mutual efforts of both groups.

Activity

PURPOSE To understand peer influences at different ages on attitudes, values, and behavior.

1. Choose at least six children (two preschoolers, age 4–5; two elementary school children, 7–9; and two middle school children, 11–13). Separately ask each one the following questions, marking parents (P) or peers (pr) in the appropriate column in the chart below.
2. Write a summary of about a page on which choices were most influenced by parents and which were most influenced by peers. Explain. Did you notice an age difference regarding peer influence? Explain. Did you notice a personality difference, such as being shy or outgoing, in those children who chose peers over parents or vice versa? Explain.

	Preschool	Elementary School	Middle School
1. Whom do you tell about what happened at school (your mom or dad or your friends)?			
2. Whom do you ask about which TV shows you should watch?			
3. Who has helped you decide what you want to be when you grow up?			
4. Who most often helps you decide whom your friends should be?			
5. Whom do you talk to most about games or sports you would like to play?			
6. If someone hurts your feelings, whom do you talk to about it?			
7. Who suggests books to you to read (or toys to play with)?			
8. Whom do you ask about what you should wear?			
9. If something exciting happened to you, whom would you tell first?			
10. Who tells you about snack foods to try?			

Related Readings

Adler, P. A., & Adler, P. (1998). *Peer power: Preadolescent culture and identity.* New Brunswick, NJ: Rutgers University Press.

Asher, S. R., & Gottman, J. M. (Eds.). (1981). *The development of children's friendships.* Cambridge, UK: Cambridge University Press.

Bukowski, M. W., Newcomb, A. F., & Hartup, W. W. (Eds.). (1996). *The company they keep: Friendship during childhood and adolescence.* New York: Cambridge University Press.

Dunn, J. (1988). *The beginnings of social understanding.* Cambridge, MA: Harvard University Press.

Garvey, C. (1990). *Play*. Cambridge, MA: Harvard University Press.

Goldstein, A. P. (1991). *Delinquent gangs: A psychological perspective*. Champaign, IL: Research Press.

Harris, J. R. (1998). *The nurture assumption*. New York: Free Press.

Herron, R. E., & Sutton-Smith, B. (1971). *Child's play*. New York: Wiley.

Kerns, K. A., Contreras, J. M., & Neal-Barnett, A. M. (2000). *Family and peers: Linking two social worlds*. Westport, CT: Praeger.

Landre, R., Miller, M., & Porter, D. (1997). *Gangs: A handbook for community awareness*. New York: Facts on File.

Olweus, D. (1993). *Bullying at school: What we know and what we can do about it*. Cambridge, MA: Blackwell.

Rubin, K. H., & Thompson, K. (2003). *The friendship factor*. New York: Penguin.

Simmons, R. (2002). *Odd girl out: The hidden culture of aggression in girls*. San Diego: Harcourt.

Thompson, M., Cohen, L., & Grace, C. O. (2002). *Best friends, worst enemies: Understanding the social lives of children*. New York: Ballantine Books.

Chapter 9

PhotoAlto/Index Stock Imagery

Ecology of the Mass Media

The medium is the message.

—MARSHALL McLUHAN

Long before people recorded events as history, the medium used to share group traditions and values was oral stories, which were passed from one generation to the next. The oral tradition was personal (face-to-face). A significant feature of this type of communication was that it could be adapted to the interest and understanding of the listener. When the printing press was invented and stories could be written, now it was the reader who had to adapt his or her understanding to the storyteller's message. When the electronic media revolution occurred and television became a medium for storytelling, business became linked to the viewing experience. Now stories are told not by elders, not by teachers, but by economic enterprises with something to sell (Gerbner, Gross, Morgan, & Signorielli, 2002).

The following modern English tale, *Charlie and the Chocolate Factory* by Roald Dahl (1964), tells of the idiosyncrasies of five children (one is a TV addict). Each child has different socialization outcomes, even though they all experienced growing up in a competitive culture characterized by consumerism and winning.

Once Upon a Time
Not so long ago, there was a chocolate factory owned by a man named Willy Wonka. Mr. Wonka offers a tour of his factory and a lifetime supply of Wonka Bars to the lucky five children who find a golden ticket in their chocolate bars. The winners are Augustus Gloop, a greedy boy; Veruca Salt, a spoiled girl; Violet Beauregarde, a girl who constantly chews gum; Mike Teavee, a boy who does nothing but watch television; and Charlie Bucket (the hero), a kind and caring boy (he tends for his ailing relatives).

On the appointed day, the children, accompanied by their parents, show up at the Chocolate Factory for a tour. As they visit each room, one by one all the children except Charlie get into trouble because of their bad habits. For every mischievous deed, the factory workers—the Oompa Loompas—sing a metaphor and mime the appropriate lesson to be learned. Mike Teavee, the TV buff, exemplifies such mischief. He is most fascinated by Willy Wonka's television chocolate room. Willy has invented a machine to send chocolate to people's homes in much the same way that TV sends images. The children are told not to disturb anything in the room, but while Willy is demonstrating the machine, Mike disobeys and steps in front of the camera. He is instantly zapped and reduced to tiny particles that disappear into the air, later to reappear on the TV screen as a miniature Mike Teavee. The Oompa Loompas then sing the following message (Dahl, 1964, pp. 145–147):

The most important thing we've learned,
So far as children are concerned,
Is never, Never, NEVER let

Them near your television set—
Or better still, just don't install
The idiot thing at all.
In almost every house we've been,
We've watched them gaping at the screen.
They loll and slop and lounge about,
And stare until their eyes pop out. . . .
But did you ever stop to think,
To wonder just exactly what
This does to your beloved tot?

IT ROTS THE SENSES IN THE HEAD!
IT KILLS IMAGINATION DEAD!
IT CLOGS AND CLUTTERS UP THE MIND!
IT MAKES A CHILD SO DULL AND BLIND
HE CAN NO LONGER UNDERSTAND
A FANTASY, A FAIRYLAND!
HIS BRAIN BECOMES AS SOFT AS CHEESE!
HIS POWERS OF THINKING RUST AND FREEZE!
HE CANNOT THINK—HE ONLY SEES! . . .

What used the darling ones to do?
How used they keep themselves contented
Before this monster was invented?
Have you forgotten? Don't you know?
We'll say it loud and slow:
THEY . . . USED . . . TO . . . READ! They'd READ, READ, AND READ.

From *Charlie and the Chocolate Factory* by Roald Dahl. Text and illustrations copyright © 1964, renewed 1992 by Roald Dahl Nominee Limited. Used by permission of Alfred A. Knopf, an imprint of Random House Children's Books, a division of Random House, Inc.

At the end of the factory tour, the only child left who has not gotten into trouble is Charlie. Willy Wonka bequeaths the Chocolate Factory to Charlie because he has proved himself to be trustworthy. The other children go home with their lifetime supplies of chocolate bars, the promised reward for having found the lucky tickets in their candy.

- **What messages are being received via various media and what are their effects on children?**

- **Do media stimulate critical thinking or inhibit it?**

- **Is media access to information a cultural equalizer or a cultural divider (segregating the information-rich and the information-poor)?**

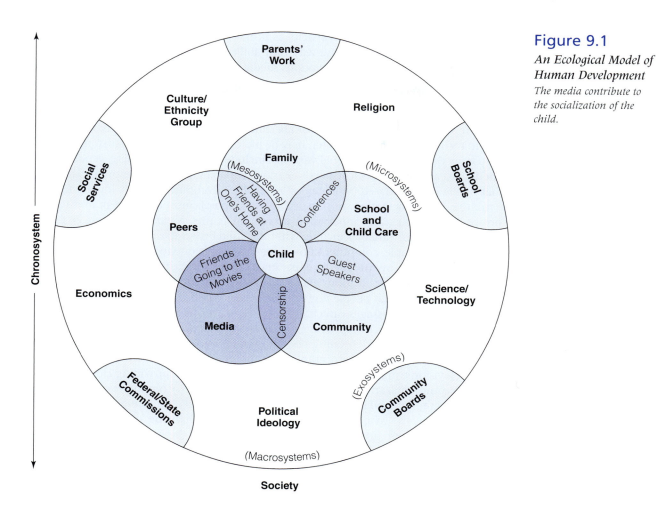

Figure 9.1
*An Ecological Model of
Human Development*
The media contribute to
the socialization of the
child.

Understanding Mass Media

What is meant by "mass media" and how do they affect socialization?

Media, the plural of *medium*, refers to a type of communication. A medium is an intervening means through which a force acts or an effect is produced. This chapter focuses on socialization and **mass media**, the form of communication in which large audiences quickly receive a given message via an impersonal medium between the sender and the receiver. Examples include newspapers, magazines, books, radio, television, movies, videos, popular music, computers, and various multimedia.

Communications theorist Marshall McLuhan's (1964) famous aphorism "The medium is the message" means that media are external extensions of the human being and "the 'message' of any medium is the change of scale or pace or pattern that it introduces into human affairs" (p. 8). New media create new environments, as well as new ways of looking at environments that already exist. Thus, the mass media are both shapers and spreaders of *culture* (defined in Chapter 2 as the knowledge, beliefs, art, morals, law, customs, skills, and traditions acquired by humans as members of society). The mass media are *shapers* of culture in that their form and content affect us in some way (the products we buy, for example). The mass media are *spreaders* of

mass media
newspapers,
magazines, books,
radio, television,
movies, videos, and
other means of
communication that
reach large audiences
via an impersonal
medium between the
sender and the receiver

culture in that they extend our capacity as human beings to process information and, in so doing, transform us in some way (our ability to multitask, for example).

What are the shared effects of various media on children in general? What are the diverse effects on children as individuals who experience media at different ages, with varying backgrounds and perceptions? What immediate and long-term effects have been cultivated by media exposure? The outcomes for children of mass media experiences are sometimes difficult to sort out because of the many variables involved—variables that change over time and that may be bidirectional (Anderson, Huston, Schmitt, Linebarger, & Wright, 2001). Child variables include age, cognitive ability, gender, social experience, and psychological needs. Family variables include economics, affecting what media are purchased (videotapes, books, CDs, computers); time, including what alternative leisure activities are pursued (games, sports, museums, trips); and mediation, or how much adult supervision accompanies media exposure (Dorr & Rabin, 1995). Bidirectional variables include what the child brings to the media experience to change it (for example, computer knowledge can enable one to program software such as Photoshop) and how the media experience changes the child (for example, surfing the Internet can provide vicarious experiences such as travel). "It is not what the media does to people but what people do with the media" (Lull, 1980, p. 198).

Media and their messages can change experience, enhance experience, or interfere with experience. Books or television can, for example, *change* the neutral experience of going to sleep into a frightening one for a child, by showing monsters coming out from under a bed. Movies can employ computer graphics and simulations to alter reality. Television can *enhance* the experience of a parade by providing close-up shots, supplying comments, and increasing the pace of the action. Computers equipped with multimedia graphics and sound can enable the user to make infinite combinations and projections with the available information, thereby enhancing the computer user's experience. Television and movies can also *interfere* with the experience of imagining what a storybook character looks like by choosing an actor with certain characteristics to play the role.

IN PRACTICE

What Does *TV Guide* Say About TV?

The socialization role played by television was accurately described more than 40 years ago in *TV Guide* and is still applicable:

What I think must be said is that television is not just a great force in modern life, but that it virtually is modern life. What, one might ask, doesn't it do? It gives us—be we rich, poor, snowbound, bedridden, or slow-witted—the time, the weather, the small news, sport news, now in spoken headlines, now in pictured narrative, now at the very scene of the crime or the coronation itself. It plays, sings, whistles and dances for us, takes us to movies and theaters, concerts and operas, prize fights and ball games, ski jumps and tennis tournaments. . . . It teaches you French, rope dancing, bird calls and first aid; provides debates and seminars and symposiums, quizzes and contests and it tells you jokes, gags, wheezes, wisecracks, jokes and jokes. (Krononberger, 1966, p. 15)

Extending our human capacity to process information changes the way we perceive reality. We can, via television, "see and hear things happening at the other end of the world" (Esslin, 1982). Satellite communications have transformed the world into a "global village" by compressing time and distance. According to McLuhan (1989), we now live in a global village that has become a global theater. Because of the electronic media revolution, we perceive ourselves differently than people did 50 years ago. Whereas learning about the world through reading is solitary, single-sensory, and gradual, learning about the world through television, videos, and computers is massive, multisensory, and immediate. For example, how many of you were "at" the World Trade Center in New York on September 11, 2001?

Chronosystem Influences on Mass Media

How has new technology affected media devices, content, and interactive use?

The media scene has changed drastically in the last few years as new devices, with the capability to combine different types of media in miniaturized forms for customized use, have emerged. One can be connected to someone or something via sound, text, and/or picture 24/7. The media environment affecting children today is characterized by availability, variety of choices, proliferation of portable devices, facility of use, and affordability (Roberts & Foehr, 2004). This means kids have access to multiple TV and radio channels, videotapes, computer discs, iPods, and cell phones. The technology enables individuals to choose what they will watch or listen to, and when and where they will do so. An impact of such flexibility is that while communication with others is facilitated, media usage for entertainment or learning becomes more personal than social. For example, games can be played on a computer, rather than with a friend; TV shows can be viewed alone rather than with family; information can be gleaned from the Internet rather than a teacher.

Media technology has been undergoing change over the past 100 years, from books to radio to movies to television to computer to multimedia. Now the widespread use of communications satellites has enabled almost instantaneous delivery of media content and has changed mass communication from a national to a global enterprise (Perse, 2001). Cable TV, satellite dishes, and wireless technology have multiplied the available programming. The VCR, DVD, TiVo, and computer have added to the choices. The decreasing cost of such technologies has afforded families the opportunity to own multiple TV sets and other devices. Technology that combines media, such as TiVo (TV, computer, and digital recorder), gives viewers the ability to choose and control available programming. Parents who own such devices can preselect what children watch based on what they consider appropriate.

Even though media technology has changed, concerns regarding its influence on children remain the same. "In general, proponents of media innovation argue that the new technology benefits children by opening up new worlds to them, while opponents argue that new media might be used to substitute for real life in learning ethical principles, undermining children's morality" (Wartella & Jennings, 2000, p. 32). Research on children and media has spanned such areas as which demographic groups of children are gaining access to new technologies, what their preferences are for different genres, how much time is being spent and what other activities are being displaced, and how the content of various media exposure may be affecting children (Anderson et al., 2001).

Over time, every new communication medium that has become available for popular use has elicited concern regarding its effects, especially on children and adolescents (Perse, 2001). For example, the introduction of broadcast radio in the 1920s, touting its educational and entertainment benefits, brought forth parental concerns about the decrease in family communication and the effect of violence in programming (Wartella & Jennings, 2000). Television emerged as a mass medium in 1948 and critics said:

> It brought the world to everyone's living room, but most particularly it gave children an earlier look at far places and adult behavior. It became the greatest and loudest sales- man of goods, and sent children clamoring to their parents for boxtops. It created heroes and villains, fads, fashions, and stereotypes, and nowhere so successfully, apparently, as with the pliable minds of children. (Schramm, Lyle, & Parker, 1961, pp. 11–12)

Dominating the media scene today are interactive media, such as computers, video games, and cell phones. While these offer the potential for expanded learn- ing and socialization of children, they also increase the risk of exposure to content and experiences that may be inappropriate for children (Wartella & Jennings, 2000). The influence on children's development of active participation in such media, compared to passive participation in radio and television, is of special con- cern. Research on interactive media is discussed later.

Chronosystem influences on media involve not only technological changes but content changes as well. As we will discuss, violence, sex, and advertising have increased over time. The media appeal to different ages and diverse populations has also changed. For example, more television shows and movies are geared toward children and adolescents. Shows are available in different languages. Shows are available with closed captions for people with hearing impairments. Nontraditional relationships are more visible. Reality-based, or unscripted, entertainment is becom- ing more and more popular, especially when viewers can participate by calling or e-mailing their opinions to the broadcaster. Advertising is changing from separate, timed commercials to placement of sponsors' products within shows (for example, a Coke can or bottle is placed on a table, as in *American Idol*). Advertisements have also infiltrated the movie theater as well as the Internet.

What Is the E-Generation and How Does It Function?

E-mail, e-commerce, e-books, e-entertainment, e-network, e-communication, e-banking, e-library, e-news, e-pals, e-forums, e-photos, e-courses, e-diplomas . . . Was Willy Wonka's invention of television chocolate so far off?

Macrosystem Influences on Mass Media

What influence do politics, economics, and technology have on the broadcasting media?

In order to understand the impact of the media on children, we must examine the broadcast system under which radio and television operate and the macrosystem influences on it (politics, economics, technology). Politics includes the laws under which the media operate. Economics include corporate sponsors for the shows. Technology includes the type of medium as well as its message, or content.

The mass communication system in the United States is generally characterized by private ownership and dedicated to corporate profits (this does not of course apply to public TV). The broadcast media are subject to control by the Federal Communications Commission (FCC). That is, the federal government controls the frequencies, transmitting power, and transmitting times of radio and TV. During the 1930s, Congress established the principle that the airwaves belong to the people. Therefore, the government, through an agency, could legally issue licenses and control transmitters in the interest of the people. In addition to federal regulations, there are also state and local laws pertaining to broadcasting. Cable channels, because they do not use the public airwaves, are not under the same obligation to serve the public interest as broadcast television.

The FCC can award a license to broadcast when such an action is "in the public interest, convenience, or necessity." However, there are no clear standards for what constitutes "serving the public interest." When frequencies are available, they are auctioned to the highest bidder. The FCC is thus supposed to encourage competition. It is also prohibited from censoring program content. However, broadcasters must refrain from using obscene material and, until recently, had to regulate the amount of time allocated to commercials. There are no comparable FCC rules for cable (pay) television or videocassettes. In 1984, the FCC lifted some of its restrictions when the Reagan administration moved to deregulate and to reduce government intervention. The FCC held that marketplace competition could best serve children's interests. Two trends resulted from this shift in policy: educational content declined, and advertising increased. These developments led Congress to enact legislation known as the Children's Television Act of 1990. This law imposed a limit of 10.5 minutes of commercials each hour for children's programming on weekdays and 12 minutes an hour on weekends. In 1996 the FCC expanded this act by ruling that all commercial stations must broadcast at least three hours of children's educational or informational programs per week.

In 1997, most of the television industry implemented a rating system intended to give parents advance information about the content of programs (see the box "Parental Guidelines"). Specifically, the guidelines address the level of violence, foul language, and sexually suggestive content. Television manufacturers are now installing V-chips—computer chips that can be programmed to block undesirable programs—in all new sets. They are also available as add-ons for existing TVs. These V-chips enable families to set their own viewing standards.

Radio and TV make their profits from advertising. The broadcaster sells the advertiser time. Advertisers choose the vehicle—the program—that will expose the demographic audience best suited for their commercials. Within this system, control over content really rests with the audience. If the audience is not interested in the content of a program, the program is dropped. Thus, the tastes and interests of viewers and listeners serve as indirect but powerful controls.

The main emphasis of mass communication in the United States is on entertainment (Huston, Zillman, & Bryant, 1994; Perse, 2001). Generally, the major media aim their content at the broadest spectrum of viewers in order to gain the attention of the largest number of consumers for the products advertised on their programs. A major result is that the broadcast media must continually produce a "mass culture" geared to popular or majority tastes. However, with the availability of new technologies such as cable, satellite, video, and computers, audiences have become more fractionated, so advertisers have to target their products to special interests. Audience fractionation increases as family income increases (Dorr & Rabin, 1995; Roberts & Foehr, 2004), because more TV sets and other technologies are available to those with higher socioeconomic status.

Yet, as long as the broadcast media in the United States are designed to attract audiences to sell products, they will convey messages that are likely to influence attitudes and behavior (Huston et al., 1994; Perse, 2001). Parents, then, must be cognizant of what is, and is not, appropriate for their children to watch, listen, and interact with. The website of the American Academy of Child and Adolescent Psychiatry (AACAP) has a section, "Kids and Popular Culture," that provides reviews and articles by experts on TV, movies, books, music, video games, and Internet sites to help parents and other caregivers make healthy media decisions.

IN PRACTICE

Parental Guidelines (TV and Movies)

Television

There are two categories of ratings, one for children's programs and one for programs not specifically designed for children.

The following categories apply to programs designed solely for children:

TV Y — All Children. *This program is designed to be appropriate for all children*. Whether animated or live action, the themes and elements in this program are specifically designed for a very young audience, including children ages 2–6. This program is not expected to frighten young children.

TV Y7 — Directed to Older Children. *This program is designed for children age 7 and above*. It may be more appropriate for children who have acquired the developmental skills needed to distinguish between make-believe and reality. Themes and elements in this program may include mild fantasy or comedic violence, or may frighten children under the age of 7. Therefore, parents may wish to consider the suitability of this program for their very young children. Programs containing fantasy violence that may be more intense or more combative than other programs in this category are designed as TV-Y7-FV.

The following categories apply to programs designed for the entire audience:

TV G — General Audience. *Most parents would find this program suitable for all ages*. Although this rating does not signify a program designed specifically for children, most parents may let younger children watch this program unattended. It contains little or no violence, no strong language, and little or no sexual dialogue or situations.

TV PG — Parental Guidance Suggested. *This program contains material that parents may find unsuitable for younger children*. Many parents may want to watch it with their younger children. The theme itself may call for parental guidance and/or the program contains one or more of the following: moderate violence (V), some sexual situations (S), infrequent coarse language (L), or some suggestive dialogue (D).

TV 14 — Parents Strongly Cautioned. *This program contains some material that many parents would find unsuitable for children under age 14*. Parents are strongly urged to exercise greater care in monitoring this program and are cautioned against letting children under the age of 14 watch unattended. This program contains one or more of the following: intense violence (V), intense sexual situations (S), strong coarse language (L), or intensely suggestive dialogue (D).

TV MA **Mature Audience Only**. *This program is specifically designed to be viewed by adults and therefore may be unsuitable for children under 17.* This program contains one or more of the following: graphic violence (V), explicit sexual activity (S), or crude, indecent language (L).

When a program is broadcast, the appropriate icon should appear in the upper left corner of the picture frame for the first 15 seconds. If the program is longer than one hour, the icon should be repeated at the beginning of the second hour. Guidelines are also displayed in TV listings in a number of newspapers and magazines.

Movies

G	General Audiences	All ages admitted.
PG	Parental Guidance Suggested	Some material may not be suitable for children.
PG-13	Parents Strongly Cautioned	Some material may be inappropriate for children under 13.
R	Restricted	Under 17 requires accompanying parent or adult guardian.
NC-17	No One 17 and Under Admitted	

Screen Media: Television and Movies (Videos, DVDs)

Why the special concern for children regarding TV and movies?

Television includes network and cable shows received on a TV set. Movies include productions made for the theater and for home viewing on a TV set in video or DVD format. According to national studies by the Kaiser Family Foundation (1999, 2003, 2005a), the American family remains strongly connected to television, even though other media are available and are used in addition to TV (multimedia use is discussed later). Families use TV for entertainment, education, news, and consumer information.

Television and movies have evoked many concerns, especially about their content, their socializing effects on children, and potential public response. Television has certain properties that distinguish it from other media, including its attention demands, the brevity of its sequences, the rapid succession of presented material, and its visual orientation (Singer, Singer, & Zuckerman, 1990).

Children are a special audience in regard to the medium of television (Strasburger & Wilson, 2002). Because of cognitive immaturity, they are generally assumed to be more vulnerable than adults to the amount of time spent watching TV and to believing that the images they see are real, that violence is the way to solve problems, that one should buy what is advertised, and that the values, stereotypes, and behavior portrayed on TV constitute the way one should be. "Television is a particularly appealing medium to young children in part because many of its images and modes of representation are readily understood;

it does not require the child to learn a complicated system of decoding as does reading, for example" (Huston et al., 1994, p. 5). As a result, television has important socializing potential.

CONCERNS ABOUT TELEVISION AND MOVIES

How have TV and movies affected our lives?

Advances in television broadcasting have created changes in the sleep habits, meal arrangements, use of leisure time, and conversation patterns of millions of U.S. families (Andreasen, 2001; Huston et al., 1994). Mass communications have also created changes in our culture. New products advertised via television, magazines, newspapers, and the Internet can be adopted in a very short time. The rapid spread of other cultural forms, such as fashion fads, hairstyles, and types of music or sports, can be stimulated by the media. All of these changes have understandably given rise to some concern.

> It has never been much of a secret . . . that movies influence manners, attitudes, and behavior. In the fifties, they told us how to dress for a rumble or a board meeting, how far to go on the first date, what to think about Martians or, closer to home, Jews, blacks, and homosexuals. They taught girls whether they should have husbands or careers, boys whether to pursue work or pleasure. They told us what was right and what was wrong, what was good and what was bad; they defined our problems and suggested solutions. (Biskind, 1983, p. 2)

What are the effects of TV and movie viewing on potential social and physical activities?

The statistics on TV viewing habits indicate that, on average, children spend three to five hours a day in front of the television set and often do it with little parental monitoring (Comstock & Sharrer, 2001; Kaiser Family Foundation, 2005a). Young children from economically and educationally disadvantaged backgrounds spend even more time watching TV than do children from more affluent, better-educated families (Huston & Wright, 1998; Roberts & Foehr, 2004).

It would seem likely that if children are spending that much time in front of the television set or VCR, activities that they might otherwise be engaged in, such as reading, hobbies, games, physical activity or sports, and family or peer interactions, are being neglected. As Urie Bronfenbrenner (1970b) said in an address to the National Association for Education of Young Children:

> Like the sorcerer of old, the television set casts its magic spell, freezing speech and action, turning the living into silent statues so long as the enchantment lasts. The primary danger of the television screen lies not so much in the behavior it produces—although there is danger there—as in the behavior it prevents: the talks, the games, the family festivities and arguments through which much of the child's learning takes place and through which his character is formed. Turning on the television set can turn off the process that transforms children into people.

Family Rituals and Interactions. *Rituals*, discussed in Chapter 2, are shared customs or ceremonies that give life meaning (Bria, 1998). Marie Winn (1977), in *The Plug-In Drug*, discusses what has happened to family life and rituals with the advent of television. She defines family rituals as "those regular, dependable recurrent happenings that gave members of a family a feeling of belonging to a home . . . those experiences that act as the adhesive of family unity" (p. 124).

> When I was a small child, my grandmother had weekly family dinners, at which we children got to tell all the adults about our achievements and then gloried in their praise. We also got to listen to adult gossip. When we got bored by the conversation, we'd explore my grandmother's house. She had drawers full of old clothes, pictures, and letters—she never threw away anything. Or we'd play cards, and if we lost, we could always hustle a game with one of the adults, who would see to it that we'd win. That was before my grandmother bought a TV.

Although television may have replaced extended family conversations around the dinner table, card games, or singing songs, it has become an integral part of family life in that viewing is an activity that often occurs with other family members, especially for young children. While parents and children are often in close proximity when watching TV, sometimes touching and hugging, they tend to talk less to one another when viewing TV than in other activities (Wright, St. Peters, & Huston, 1990). Parents and siblings provide a model of how to use television, and children are exposed to what their parents and siblings view simply because they are in the same household (Huston & Wright, 1998). A generation ago, when only about 50% of homes had more than one TV set, families assembled to watch shows together. Now, with the majority of households having multiple televisions, opportunities for shared experiences have decreased (Kaiser Family Foundation, 2005a).

Time spent watching TV affects family interactions—development of relationships, communication, and resolution of problems. Interpersonal relationships take work. To get along with someone, you must be able to communicate your feelings and wishes as well as receive that person's feelings and wishes. When these feelings and wishes are compatible, the two individuals are said to "get along"; when they are incompatible, the two must compromise in order to get along. The compromise may involve taking turns or modifying one's desires. Such problem solving contributes to children's language as well as social development. Children must use words to express feelings and wishes. They must receive a message and process it and respond to it. By having to listen to another's message, the child is also moving away from egocentrism (the inability to see things from another's point of view).

Physical Activity. Time spent watching TV is time that potentially could be used for physical activity. A study found that children who watched four or more hours of TV per day were significantly more likely to be obese than children who watched an hour or less (Crespo, Smit, Troiano, Bartlett, Macera, & Anderson, 2001). Another study of preschoolers (ages 1–4) found that a child's risk of being overweight increased by 6% for every hour of television watched per day. If that child had a TV in his or her bedroom, the odds of being overweight jumped an additional 31% for every hour watched. Preschool children who had TVs in their bedrooms watched 4.8 hours more of TV or videos per week than those who did not (Dennison, Erb, & Jenkins, 2002).

What are the effects of TV and movie viewing on the perception of reality?

According to Piaget (1962), young children think very differently from adults. They believe that everything that moves is alive, that the sun follows them when they go for a walk, and that dreams come in through the window at night when they sleep. Preschool children believe that the cartoon characters and actual people they see on television are all equally "real" and are inside the television set. This is because they have difficulty conceptualizing the distinction between a pictorial representation and the actual thing represented. They also have difficulty understanding pretense (Flavell, Miller, & Miller, 2001). Preschool children believe that if they turn off a program, the same program will be on when they turn the set on again (as if one were putting a marker inside a book). For the preschool child, reality (actual objects) and fantasy (images of objects) are likely to be interchangeable. Flavell (1986) demonstrated the difficulty that preschoolers have distinguishing appearance from reality. For example, 3-year-olds assert that a rock-shaped sponge not only looks like a rock but *is* a rock. However, children over age 5 can make the distinction.

Preschool children usually cannot distinguish the commercials from the program. This may be because they can only deal with one "script" at a time (Flavell et al., 2001). They also accept messags literally and uncritically. Because of their stage of cognitive development, preschool children are unable to understand that advertisements are intended to sell products rather than entertain them. The gullibility of preschool children can be dangerous. A number of children each month are brought to hospital emergency rooms with broken bones from leaping from tops of buildings or smashing objects with bare hands—a sad way to find out you are not Superman. One 4-year-old spent two days in intensive hospital care after swallowing 40 children's vitamins—the TV commercial said vitamins would make him "big and strong real fast" (Leibert, Neil, & Davidson, 1973). It is not until about age 7 that children realize ads are intended to be persuasive messages. And although the ability to evaluate advertising claims increases with age, even adolescents exhibit gullibility (Dorr & Rabin, 1995).

Because young children confuse reality and fantasy, many of their ideas about the world beyond their families and neighborhood come from television programs and movies (Cantor, 1998; Perse, 2001). The more limited the life experiences or economic circumstances of children, the more likely they are to believe what they see on television (Roberts & Foehr, 2004). Although some people believe that fantasy on television can lead to imaginative and creative expression, it also permits children (especially troubled ones) to retreat from real-life situations and can encourage them to seek immediate gratification of their impulses or instant solutions to problems (Comstock & Paik, 1991).

"Television substitutes its own image of reality (usually made to the specifications of adult media executives) for the image of reality the child is beginning to form as he develops his capacity for symbolic activity" (Gatz, 1975, p. 415). In effect, TV is saying, "This is the world the way it is." Because children have not experienced much of the real world, they accept what TV portrays as the truth and neglect to test it against reality. According to "cultivation theory," TV fosters the growth of preferences, attitudes, behaviors, and fears engendered by what is portrayed, especially among heavy viewers (Gerbner et al., 2002).

As children get older (between 5 and 7) and have more experience with different types of TV programming, as well as reality, they learn to recognize form and content cues denoting fact and fiction on TV (Wright, Huston, Reitz, & Piemymat, 1994). By about age 7 or 8, children come to distinguish between things that are real and those that are make-believe on television. At first, they judge according to format (cartoons are make-believe and live action shows are real). Then they come to realize that certain things portrayed on TV—whether animated or live—are physically impossible (people can't fly like Superman). They come to evaluate reality on TV based on whether things in the story match what exists in the real world (a police story is real because police are present in the community). By about age 10, children begin to understand that some programs are script-acted for the purpose of telling a story, while others show real events that actually happened, such as news and documentaries (Cantor, 1998).

What are the effects of TV and movie viewing on imagination?

Jean Piaget (1962) believed that the thinking process involves a balance between the demands the outside world makes on us (objectivity) and the demands we make on the outside world (subjectivity). When this balance is shifted in the direction of the data presented by the world, we *imitate*. When it is shifted in the direction of our interpretation, we *imagine*. "Imaginative play," writes Piaget, "is a symbolic transposition which subjects things to the child's activity without rules or limitations" (p. 87). When a child plays, the world bends itself to the child's wishes.

> Five-year-old Tammy went to her room after lunch, having come home from kindergarten. She didn't nap anymore, but her mother felt she needed some quiet time alone before going outside to play with her friends. Tammy got out her model horses and "galloped" them around her bed on the floor. The horses spoke to each other—they were arguing over space to graze. Tammy then got out her blocks and attempted to build a barn for one of the horses. She succeeded in building the sides but could not get the roof to stay on without tumbling on the horse. The play then abruptly changed to a rodeo, and the blocks used to build a barn became an obstacle course. The horses, no longer arguing, took turns jumping and turning corners, complete with sound effects. Forty-five minutes had passed, and Tammy emerged from her room cheerful and ready to play with her friends.

Does viewing inhibit or stimulate creative play? Some believe television makes imagination subservient to imitation. Further, TV's images become reality for the child, who is then unable to break through that mindset later when experiencing the real world. For example, studies by Singer and Singer (1990) found that children, ages 3 to 8, whose play themes reflected specific television references to cartoons, superheroes, and action-detective shows were more likely to be aggressive. The children's imagination was measured by an inkblot test. It was found that those with the least imagination who also watched television with large amounts of violence were most likely to imitate the aggression in school. They also found that the imaginative children were less likely to engage in impulsive acts or gross aggression.

Others say that although television does not ordinarily stimulate imaginative play and creativity, children do find ideas for make-believe play in everything around them, including television. In a review of the research, Valkenburg (2001) found that television's influence on imaginative play depended on the type of program. Benign, nonviolent programs did not directly affect imaginative play, whereas programs with high levels of violence reduced imaginative play. However, certain educational programs were exceptions in that they did enhance imaginative activities.

Scholastic Studio 10/Index Stock Imagery

These children are engaged in imaginative play.

Although imaginative play and creativity may be reduced by heavy viewing, if an adult watches TV with a child, the adult can stimulate the child's imagination by asking questions about the show, interpreting words and actions on the show, and suggesting various alternative solutions to what is happening.

What are the effects of viewing the prevalent violence on TV and in movies?

"Television and movies, by their very nature, have the ability to introduce children to frightening images, events, and ideas, many of which they would not encounter in their entire lives without the mass media" (Cantor, 1998, p. 3). An example is *violence*, defined as the "overt expression of physical force against others or self, or compelling action against one's will and pain of being hurt or killed or actually hurting or killing" (Gerbner, Gloss, Jackson-Beck, Jeffries-Fox, & Signorielli, 1978). Violence on TV is measured in terms of *prevalence, rate,* and *role.* Prevalence is the extent to which violence occurs in the program; rate is the frequency of violent episodes; and role is the number of characterizations of violence or victimization. Violence on television is a concern because, over the years, there has been an increase in violence on children's Saturday morning programs as well as on prime-time television (8 to 11 P.M.) (Center for Communication and Social Policy, 1998; Mediascope, 1997).

The National Television Violence Study (NTVS) (Center for Communication and Social Policy, 1998; Mediascope, 1997) has demonstrated that there is a great deal of violence on American television, and today there are more venues and channels available on which to find it. In addition, much of this violence is portrayed in formulaic ways that glamorize, sanitize, and trivialize aggression. Some programming with violent content, popular with children, are *Avatar, Digimon, Xialon Showdown,* and *Yu-Gi-Oh.* The NTVS concludes that not all violence portrayed on TV has similar effects on children. Characterization in which the perpetrator is attractive is more likely to influence the viewer's identification and modeling. When violence is justified, goes unpunished, or shows no harm or pain to the victim, it is also more likely to influence viewer behavior.

According to the Center for Media and Public Affairs (1999), scenes of serious violence (physical force) hammer TV viewers and moviegoers every 4 minutes. Of the 10 most violent television movies, a majority carried a PG-13 rating, and a majority of the 10 most violent television shows were rated TV-PG. The concern is not only with the prevalence of violence, but that it is portrayed as necessary and relatively harmless (Comstock & Sharrer, 1999).

Although it may be difficult to prove that excessive viewing of televised violence can or does provoke violent crime in any specific individual, it is clear that children who watch a great deal of televised violence are more prone to behave aggressively than are children who do not watch TV violence (Geen, 1994; Perse, 2001). The NTVS (Center for Communication and Social Policy, 1998; Mediascope, 1997) demonstrated that the context in which most violence is presented on TV poses the following risks for viewers: (1) learning to behave violently, (2) becoming desensitized to violence, and (3) becoming fearful of being attacked. Characteristics of the child, such as age, real experiences, temperament, and cognitive developmental level, influence the impact of viewing violence. Explanations from psychological research for these findings follow.

Observational Learning. Observational learning is based on Albert Bandura's (1974, 1989) social cognitive theory; we learn by observing and imitating behavior. This theory states that role models, especially attractive ones, act as stimuli to produce similar behavior in the observer of the role model. The behavior is learned by being imitated, rewarded, or reinforced in a variety of ways. Responses produced often enough and over a long enough period of time maintain the behavior. Bandura outlines four steps necessary for this process: (1) attention to the stimulus, (2) retention of the observed behavior and consequences, (3) ability to reproduce the behavior, and (4) motivation to perform the observationally learned behavior.

Are children likely to learn and remember new forms of aggressive behavior by watching them on TV? If children learn and remember, will they practice the behavior? Research shows that children do learn and remember novel forms of aggression seen on TV or in films. They are more likely to remember the behavior learned by observation if they have tried it at least once. Whether or not children will practice the behavior depends on the similarity of the observed setting to their real setting; that is, if they imitate an observed aggression and it "works" (is reinforced) in solving a problem or attaining a goal, it is likely to be repeated. For example, a young child who sees Superman punching a criminal to retrieve a bag of money and prevent innocent bystanders from getting shot might be likely to try the observed aggressive behavior to take a toy away from another child, not having comprehended the concept of the Superman scene—that aggression is justifiable for protection. If the child's aggressive behavior results in getting the toy, the child is likely to repeat the behavior. Thus, children may learn aggressive behavior from TV, but whether or not they perform it depends on factors within the child, such as anger, as well as the situation (Huston & Wright, 1998; Perse, 2001).

Attitudes. Does watching television influence people's attitudes? The more television children watch, the more accepting they are of aggressive behavior. It has been shown that persons who often watch television tend to be more suspicious and distrustful of others, and they also believe there is more violence in the world than do those who do not watch much television (Comstock & Paik, 1991; Perse, 2001).

In psychological theory, attitudes include attributions, rules, and explanations that people gradually learn from observations of behavior. Therefore, for individuals who watch a great deal of television, attitudes will be built on the basis of what they see, and the attitudes will, in turn, have an effect on their behavior.

Apparently, young children are more willing to accept the aggressive behavior of other children after viewing violent scenes (Paik & Comstock, 1994). However, studies have shown that children's attitudes are changed if adults discuss the program (Huston & Wright, 1998). In an experimental study (Huesmann, Eron, Klein, Brice, & Fisher, 1983), one group of children who regularly watched violent programs were shown excerpts from violent shows. They then took part in discussion sessions about the unreality of television violence, as well as alternative strategies to solve conflicts, and wrote essays. Another group, who also watched many violent programs, were shown nonviolent excerpts followed by a neutral discussion of content. The children who took part in the sessions on unreality and alternative strategies exhibited significantly less aggressive strategies in their essays than those in the control group.

Arousal. Arousal theories examine physiological changes in the body and subsequent emotions that occur when viewing violent episodes. One response might be *desensitization*.

Does viewing violence on TV decrease one's sensitivity to violence in real life? Research shows that repetition of violence in the media results in classical desensitization. **Desensitization**—the gradual reduction in response to a stimulus after repeated exposure—is used in behavior therapy to overcome fears. For example, the more one is exposed to riding in an airplane, the less one should fear flying. A news story several years ago depicted this very kind of desensitization. A masked burglar gagged and tied a woman to a chair while he robbed her home of valuables. He told her 5-year-old son to watch television and not to call the police until the show was over. Four hours later, the son phoned. Apparently, the boy's emotional sensitivity to the real event had been so reduced that he did not react immediately. Also, the boy may have been so accustomed to seeing similar events on TV that he did not realize the seriousness of the real event.

In yet another study, school-age boys who regularly viewed violent programs showed less physiological response when they looked at new violent programs (Pearl, 1982) than did boys who were not used to viewing much violence (Condry, 1989). If viewing violence desensitizes one to aggression, then the material will have to be more and more graphic in order to keep the audience attentive. Some TV critics believe this is exactly what has occurred.

Another response to viewing televised violence might be an increase in aggressive behavior resulting from the increase in general arousal that occurs because viewing televised violence releases socialized constraints on behavior. Thus, viewing televised aggression can have a disinhibiting effect, making subsequent aggression more likely, especially in certain situations (Condry, 1989; Perse, 2001).

A recent longitudinal study examined the relation between TV-violence viewing at ages 6 to 10 and adult aggressive behavior about 15 years later for a sample growing up in the 1970s and 1980s. Follow-up archival data and interview data revealed that childhood exposure to media violence predicts young adult aggressive behavior for both males and females. Identification with aggressive TV characters and perceived realism of TV violence also predicted later aggression. These relationships persisted even when the effects of socioeconomic status, intellectual ability, and a variety of parenting factors were controlled (Huesmann, Moise-Titus, Podolski, & Eron, 2003).

What are the effects of viewing TV and movie advertising?

Every hour of television is carefully planned to contain enough minutes for "commercial messages." By selling commercial messages to advertisers, TV stations are able to defray the costs of their programs and make a profit. Commercials are cost effective for the advertisers. Even though seconds cost thousands of dollars, mailings to individuals would cost much more. The federal agency responsible for regulating TV commercials is the Federal Trade Commission (FTC). The Better Business Bureau, to which most advertisers belong, has a self-regulatory Children's Advertising Review Unit.

Annually, on average, children between the ages of 2 and 11 are exposed to between 20,000 and 40,000 television commercials. The number of product commercials has increased steadily (Center for Media Education, 1997; Condry, Bence, & Scheibe, 1988; Kunkel, 2001). On a typical Saturday morning, the average young viewer may see more than 100 child-directed commercials. Including advertising directed specifically at them, children are exposed to toy, cereal, sugared snack, and beverage commercials.

Why advertise to children? Children and youth today have money—from allowances, gifts, doing chores. They also can be quite persuasive with parents. ("Please, please, pretty please buy me that Pokémon; I've been good.") Children have decades of buying power ahead of them and, unlike adults, have no preconceived

desensitization the gradual reduction in response to a stimulus after repeated exposure

product preferences. They are open to suggestion and are impulsive (Kunkel, 2001; Stabiner, 1993). Advertisers report that children start asking for brand names as early as 2 years old. One successful way to gain a child consumer is to give the child a sense of power or importance. For example, Kool-Aid was marketed as a product "just for kids." Also, it contained coupons that children could save and trade in for toys (Stabiner, 1993).

Gorn and Goldberg (1982) directly tested the effects of exposure to commercials for sugared snacks on children's actual food selections. The study was conducted in a summer camp setting with children who were between the ages of 4 and 8. During each of 14 consecutive days, the children viewed a different half-hour Saturday morning cartoon. Four experimental groups were devised according to the nature of the commercials: (1) sweetened snack foods, such as candy, Cracker Jacks, and Kool-Aid; (2) fruit, such as orange juice or grapes; (3) public service announcements that emphasized the value of eating a balanced, nutritious diet; and (4) no commercials. The commercials took up 4.5 minutes during a half-hour show. Snack choices were made available each day immediately after the television viewing. The snack choices consisted of orange juice, Kool-Aid, two fruits, and two candy bars. The children exposed to the sweetened snack food commercials selected Kool-Aid and candy more often than did the other groups. The children exposed to the fruit commercials selected the most orange juice and more fruit than the sweetened snack group.

Ray Stubblebine/Reuters/Landov

Marketing products to children has become common.

According to the American Psychological Association Task Force Report on Advertising and Children (Kunkel, Wilcox, Cantor, Palmer, Linn, & Dowrick, 2004), children under age 8 are easy targets for commercial persuasion. Children's health is of particular concern, because the products most commonly marketed to children are sugared cereals, sweets, sodas, and snack foods. Much research documents that children who watch a lot of TV are fatter than children who watch less (Kunkel, 2001; Huston & Wright, 1998). This is due partially to lack of physical activity and partially to the tendency to snack while watching TV.

Gullibility. Why are children easy targets for commercials? Young children take things literally, rather than figuratively, which makes them more vulnerable to advertising messages (Stabiner, 1993). Although most children by age 3 can distinguish program content from commercials, children below age 8 seldom understand that the purpose of the ad is to sell something. Research suggests that repeated exposure to ads turns children into mini-salespersons who make demands on their parents for what they see advertised on TV (Kunkel, 2001). Their parents, in turn, complain that advertising causes conflict in the parent–child relationship ("I want" versus "You can't have").

Whereas children below age 8 do not understand the persuasive intent of advertising and are, therefore, particularly vulnerable to its appeals, children over age 8, who are more aware of the purposes of advertising, are still apt to be persuaded by appeals that are subtly deceptive or misleading (Kunkel, 2001). For example, they don't understand product disclosures or disclaimers, comparative claims, the real meaning of endorsements by famous characters, or the use of premiums, promotions, and sweepstakes (Council of Better Business Bureaus, 2000).

To illustrate the fact that young children do not critically evaluate the commercials they see, one study (Atkin & Gibson, 1978) showed that children often take advertisements literally. Two cartoon characters, Fred Flintstone and Barney Rubble, said a cereal was "chocolatey enough to make you smile." When asked why they wanted the cereal, two-thirds of the children said because of the chocolate taste, three-fifths said because it would make them smile, and more than half said because Fred and Barney like it. Another study (Atkin & Gibson, 1978) reported that children who saw a cereal advertisement with a circus strongman lifting a heavy weight believed that eating the cereal would make them strong.

Despite increased awareness of the purpose of advertising, even older children find commercials convincing. In a study of 8- to 14-year-old boys, celebrity endorsement of a racing toy made the product more attractive; including live racetrack footage led to exaggerated estimates of the toy's features as well as decreased awareness that the ad was staged (Ross, Campbell, Wright, Huston, Rice, & Turk, 1984).

A growing development in children's television is programs that feature characters corresponding to toys (Levin, 1998), known as "toy tie-in" marketing. In essence, these are program-length commercials and constitute unfair soliciting of children, according to Action for Children's Television (Condry, 1989; Huston & Wright, 1998; Strasburger & Wilson, 2002). Product-related programming is of concern for reasons other than its commercial intent. Its content is "formulaic" and stereotyped (Huston & Wright, 1998). Children's play with program-featured toys was found to be more imitative and less imaginative than play with other toys (Greenfield, Yut, Chung, & Land, 1990). Another development causing concern is interactive TV programming. Children buy the required toy, such as a gun, aim it at the screen, and exchange fire with on-screen enemies (Tuchscherer, 1988). Recently, interactive toys (Teletubbies) have been developed for children as young as 1 year.

Adolescents are affected by TV commercials, too. By glamorizing smoking, cigarette advertising increases the likelihood that teenagers will experiment with cigarettes. The same holds true for alcohol (Strasburger, 2001).

If children are influenced by TV ads for toys and foods, what about all the medication commercials? Although ads for medicine are not intentionally directed at children, children are nevertheless exposed to them. Prescription drug ads can be now be seen during 14% of all prime-time episodes, and ads for over-the-counter medicines are common in 50% of all popular adult programs (Christenson, Henriksen, & Roberts, 2000). Do the ads give children the perception that drugs give quick relief for pain or stress? Does exposure to such advertising increase the likelihood that children will turn to drugs when they have problems? According to Neil Postman, New York University Professor of Communication Arts and Sciences:

> A commercial teaches a child three interesting things. The first is that all problems are resolvable. The second is that all problems are resolvable fast. And the third is that all problems are resolvable fast through the agency of some technology. It may be a drug. It may be a detergent. It may be an airplane or some piece of machinery, like an automobile or computer. (Postman, 1982, pp. 43–45)

The essential message of a commercial, then, is that people have problems—lack of confidence, lack of friends, lack of money, lack of health, and so on, and these problems are solvable through the product advertised.

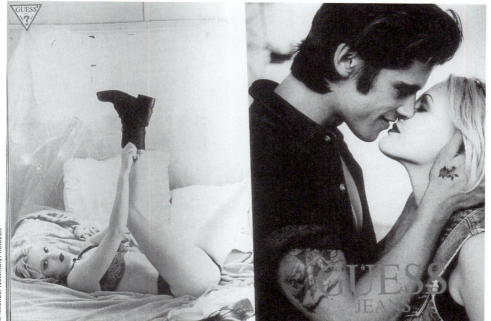

Advertising sells more than products; it sells a message. These ads exemplify equating sexual desirability with purchasing the product.

According to James McNeal, author of *Children As Consumers* (1987), advertisers are attuned to children's developmental stages and their needs for peer approval, status, and independence. The basic advertising message being communicated, then, is "things make the person."

Commercialism not only invades the home; it is present in the school as well. Chapter 6 discussed some advertising strategies implemented in school (Channel One, fundraisers, sponsorships of clubs and sports). Are the promotional messages and commercial influences undermining the integrity of children's education? Studies demonstrate that students in schools with Channel One show a greater consumer orientation and intent to purchase products than students not exposed to Channel One (Huston & Wright, 1998).

What is the effect of TV and movie viewing on the perpetuation of values?

Values, discussed in Chapter 2, refer to qualities or beliefs that are viewed as desirable or important. They influence attitudes, motives, and behavior. Of concern here are how behavioral, sexual, and stereotypical values portrayed on TV are interpreted by children.

As has been discussed, children not only watch "kid vid" (TV shows especially for children) but spend much of their viewing time watching "adult" programs (action/dramas, situation comedies, news). The problem is that an adult knows about certain aspects of life—its tragedies, its contradictions, its unfairness, its mysteries, its joys—that a child does not have the intellectual capability or life experience to comprehend. What television does is communicate the same information to everyone simultaneously, regardless of age, level of education, or experience. And, in the quest for new material to hold its audience, television has been increasingly exposing its audiences to life experiences previously considered forbidden: explicit sexuality, adultery, family violence, incest, corruption, extreme violence, pornography, and horror.

Consequently, "with TV's relentless revelation of all adult secrets, it is not inconceivable that in the near future we shall return to the thirteenth- and fourteenth-century situation in which no words were unfit for a youthful ear" (Postman, 1982). If so, what values are being perpetuated?

Behavior. According to Dr. Isidore Ziferstein, a fellow of the American Psychiatric Association, television has presented to children a set of "anti-values" regarding behavior (Larrick, 1975). Following are some examples.

- *Anti–interpersonal relations values*: A woman kills her husband in order to get his insurance.
- *Anti-cooperation values*: Life is presented on television as consisting of conflicts, strife, and war.
- *Anti-democratic values*: Television heroes succeed by operating outside the law.

But viewers get much less information on cooperation, peace, and obeying the laws. A television show often contains more excitement, adventure, power, and violence than the average person experiences in a lifetime. By comparison, everyday life seems boring (Huston & Wright, 1998).

Not all shows present negative values; some exhibit socially desirable behaviors that benefit others. Studies have shown that children who watch altruistic behavior (generosity, helping, and cooperation) on television become more altruistic themselves (Comstock & Paik, 1991; Perse, 2001). For example, children who watched a prosocial episode of *Lassie*, in which Lassie's master risked his life by hanging over the edge of a mineshaft to rescue Lassie's puppy, exhibited more prosocial behavior than did children who watched a neutral episode of *Lassie* (Sprafkin et al., 1975). Although many children's TV shows today are designed to illustrate prosocial behavior, there are few lasting effects unless an adult watches the show with the child, discusses the positive behavior, and encourages the child to model it. Unfortunately, research shows that not many adults do so (Dorr & Rabin, 1995).

According to Fred Rogers, host and producer of *Mister Rogers' Neighborhood*:

> So much of what we see on television is so terrifically limited. Just think of the problem solving on television that people are exposed to and how in so many instances, it is so uncreative. If somebody gets angry with somebody else, he just annihilates that other person. Children look to adults to discover how they solve problems. . . . It would be helpful for kids to see that there is a wide variety of ways to deal in a costructive fashion with what the world hands out. (Boyer, 1983, p. 1)

Sexuality. Presentation of behaviors, lifestyles, and attitudes that are felt to be harmful to children has led some parents to organize into groups to protest against what they consider to be invasions of family and religious values. For example, TV is bolder about sexual activity than it was several years ago (Kaiser Family Foundation, 2005b; Perse, 2001). The shows of the 1970s that caused a furor only talked about sex, whereas the shows in the late 1980s began to present sex acts visually. Men and women are now seen in bed together. Moreover, these presumably copulating couples are typically not married to each other. Finally, sex acts previously considered taboo, such as sexual abuse, incest, rape, and prostitution, are now openly discussed and depicted on TV (Greenberg, 1994; Strasburger & Wilson, 2002). According to *Sex on TV 4*, a biennial study by the Kaiser Family Foundation (2005b), the number of sexual scenes on TV has nearly doubled since 1998.

A significant portion of adolescents' sex education comes from prime-time TV programming. Watching shows depicting premarital, extramarital, or nonmarital sex affects the moral values of young teens in that they report such sexual behavior to be acceptable (Malamuth & Impett, 2001). However, family discussions of values can intervene (Bryant & Rockwell, 1994).

Young people today are exposed to an incessant flow of sexual images. Television and movies have increasingly included nudity, profanity, and sexually explicit activities. Sex appeal and sexual activity are glamorized. Unfortunately, much less attention is paid by the media to the potential consequences of casual sexual behavior (Kaiser Family Foundation, 2005b). It wasn't until 1995 that TV and radio carried ads for condoms (Jaffe, 1998).

Stereotypes. A **stereotype** is an oversimplified representation of members of a particular group. Stereotypes generally conform to a pattern of dress or behavior that is easily recognized and understood. Generally, stereotypes are less real, more perfect, or imperfect, and more predictable than their real-life counterparts. Some stereotyping on television may be unavoidable because of the format; 30- or 60-minute programs do not allow for full character development. Many minority groups—women, older people, African Americans, Italian Americans, Hispanic Americans, Asian Americans, Native Americans, and Middle Eastern Americans—claim that television and movies either ignore them or distort them. A study (Scheibe, 1989) of 2,135 commercials containing more than 6,000 characters found that men outnumbered women. However, females made up the majority of characters in commercials for cleaners, hygiene/beauty products, apparel, and toys, whereas males appeared in ads for alcohol, cars, leisure/travel, and financial services. TV commercials overrepresented young adults by 3:1. Most of the characters on TV commercials were white (94%); nearly all the rest were African American. Other ethnic groups were underrepresented relative to their true demographic distribution in the population. Finally, TV commercials overrepresented white-collar, managerial, and professional occupations while under representing blue-collar occupations.

In situation comedies or action dramas, ethnic minorities are most often associated with violence, servile occupations, or comic roles. Studies show that both African American and European American children accept television's stereotypes of ethnic minorities and their lifestyles as realistic. On the other hand, the portrayal of ethnic minorities on children's programs has become increasingly favorable. Research shows that prosocial programs reflecting ethnic variety tend to have a beneficial effect on children's perception of, and interactions with, members of minority groups (Comstock & Paik, 1991).

Gender stereotypes have decreased on TV but are still prevalent in behaviors, relationships, and occupational roles (Huston & Wright, 1998; Perse, 2001; Signorielli, 2001). Males outnumber females on children's TV, and males dominate in action roles. They exert authority, display bravado, and demonstrate competence or expertise. Females dominate in nurturing roles and dependent behavior. A meta-analysis of TV shows documents correlations between television viewing and gender-role stereotyping (Signorella, Bigler, & Liben, 1993). Although children who have stereotyped beliefs are likely to be attracted to stereotyped shows, it was demonstrated in a classic study that the television show *Freestyle*, with boys in nurturing roles and girls as mechanics, changed the perceptions of its sixth- to ninth-grade viewers (Johnston & Ettema, 1982). When school viewing was accompanied by class discussion, changes in stereotypes and attitudes endured in a nine-month follow-up (Huston & Wright, 1998).

stereotype an oversimplified representation of members of a particular group

Both the young and the old are represented differently from reality on TV (Condry, 1989). The typical female on television is young (under age 35), whereas men are generally older. Elderly women are portrayed on TV as victims of crime 30 times more often than is so in real life. Older men are portrayed as successful and powerful. The effect of these stereotypes is that children assume that the real world mirrors that of TV unless they have actual experiences to alter this perception (Signorielli, 2001).

How do children perceive ethnicity and class as represented by the media? A study of 1,200 children representing African American, Asian American, Latino American, and Euro-American ethnic groups (Children Now, 1998) found that children believe it is very important to see their own ethnic group on television. Euro-American children reported seeing people of their group most frequently, followed by African American children. Asian American and Latino American children see people of their groups much less frequently. All groups recognized the media's use of stereotypes, frequently attributing positive traits and roles to Euro-American characters, and negative traits and roles to minorities.

What are the effects of TV and movie viewing on children's cognitive development?

Reading and Communication Skills. In addition to watching TV, children learn about the world by reading and communicating. There is concern that time spent in front of the TV has been responsible for the general decline in reading levels and test scores on standardized tests, such as the Scholastic Aptitude Test (Healy, 1998; National Commission on Excellence in Education, 1983). TV viewing takes time away from other pursuits, such as reading, hobbies, attending concerts, and visiting museums—pursuits that enhance intellectual development as measured by college entrance exams.

According to research reviews (Comstock & Scharrer, 2001; Kaiser Family Foundation, 2003), there is no doubt that children read fewer books when television is available to them. This is probably because it is human nature to opt for the activity requiring less effort (entertainment) rather than the activity requiring more effort (reading). However, family values regarding what constitutes "useful" leisure activities can be very influential on what children choose to do (Neuman, 1991).

Television has the potential to motivate reading. For example, an award-winning show, *Reading Rainbow*, broadcast on public television, has proven to encourage reading. Once a book is spotlighted on the show, libraries and bookstores report an increase in demand (Trelease, 2001).

Information Processing. Information processing involves selecting content to attend to based on interest, past experiences, and cognitive development (Huston & Wright, 1998). Reading is an active process in that it involves creating images in the reader's mind through symbols: the printed words. Television viewing, on the other hand, does not involve decoding and transformation of symbols; the whole sensory message and experience are there all at once. Many educators report that children who watch a lot of television show a low tolerance for the frustration involved in learning. Watching television accustoms the child to being entertained. Programs such as *Sesame Street* and cartoons, all designed for children, "tend to give students unrealistic expectations of teachers. Kids are so used to being entertained by personalities on TV that they expect teachers to do the same" (Fiske, 1980, p. 55). Further, students accustomed to being entertained by "show biz" techniques become bored with schoolwork that requires complex thought or sustained concentration. Children may have attention and listening problems (Healy, 1998). Once again, adult involvement in viewing and discussion can be influential by stimulating children to think about what they have seen (Dorr & Rabin, 1995).

Until recently, there was little research on how the brain absorbs information from TV. TV primarily stimulates the right half of the brain, the part that specializes in emotional responses, rather than the left half, which specializes in analytical thinking. By connecting viewers to instruments that measure brain waves, one researcher found periods of right-brain activity outnumbering left-brain activity by a 2:1 ratio (Mann, 1982). Because reading demands complex mental manipulations, a reader is required to concentrate far more than a television viewer. In reading, the reader has control over the pace. If the material is not understood, the reader can reread, slow down, or go to other sources for elucidation before continuing. Similarly, if the material is familiar, or easily understood, the reader can skip over it, speed up, or skim it. Also, if the material evokes an emotional reaction, readers can stop and experience their feelings, then return to the printed material without having lost anything.

Television's pace cannot be controlled by the viewer (unless one has TiVo)—another reason it affects the viewer's ability to concentrate (Healy, 1998). The TV program continually moves forward; what is misunderstood by the viewer remains so, and what evokes delight cannot be slowed down. Television is essentially a visual medium. Pictures move very rapidly (the average length of a slot on network TV is about three seconds). Although words are spoken, it is the picture that contains the most important meaning. Because viewing the rapid succession of pictures doesn't allow time for the viewer's own reflections, some researchers have speculated that television viewing leads to an impulsive rather than reflective style of thought and to a lack of persistence in intellectual tasks. Evidence comes from studies in which television viewing was restricted and children were tested on intellectual impulsiveness and reflectivity, as well as on ability to wait (Greenfield, 1984; Healy, 1998).

Academic Achievement. A longitudinal study (Anderson et al., 2001) following more than 500 children from preschool to adolescence found that the content of television shows has a significant impact on academic achievement. Specifically, viewing educational programs as preschoolers was correlated with higher grades in school, reading more books, placing more value on achievement, greater creativity, and less aggression. These associations were more consistent for boys than for girls, with the exception of girls who watched violent programs as preschoolers. These findings held true even after taking into account family background. The importance of this study is that it underscores the potential positive influence of television and that educational TV works.

Children and adolescents actively choose media and assimilate their messages into their own meaning systems (Brown & Cantor, 2000). The aforementioned study raises the question of the potential socializing influence of television at different developmental periods as well as its potential to cultivate attitudes over time, thereby having cumulative effects.

Television has made significant contributions to children's realms of experience, their vocabulary, and their ability to communicate. The challenge for educators and parents, in regard to improving academic skills, is to capitalize on the useful aspects of children's viewing experiences.

MEDIATING INFLUENCES ON SOCIALIZATION OUTCOMES

Why is it so difficult to determine the causes and effects of media experiences?

In a comprehensive review of all evidence on the effects of television on children, Comstock and colleagues concluded that television is indeed a major socializer of children (Comstock & Paik, 1991; Comstock & Scharrer, 1999). However, it is difficult to pinpoint the exact effects of television on behavior because of other mediating or intervening influences, such as the viewer's cognitive developmental level, psychological needs, attitudes, motives, habits, interests, values, morals, beliefs, and experiences (Huston & Wright, 1998; Perse, 2001) (see Figure 9.2). For example, teens who need to feel part of the group are more influenced by ads touting the "in" clothes, perfume, or CDs than are adults whose need for belonging has been met. For another example, some of my college students who watch certain talk shows said they could not relate to some of the topics because what was being discussed was against their moral beliefs. These mediating influences determine what viewers will selectively attend to in their environments. Thus, media effects are bidirectional:

> Children are not just recipients of media messages; they choose the content to which they are exposed, and they interpret the content within their own frames of reference. They receive media messages in contexts of family, peers, and social institutions, all of which may modify or determine how children integrate messages into their existing store of information and beliefs. (Huston & Wright, 1998, p. 1027)

Figure 9.2

Mediating Influences Affecting the Outcomes of Media Messages on the Viewer

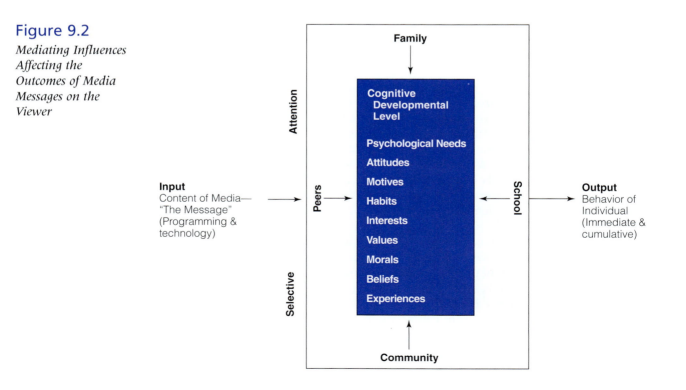

Selective Attention

Selective attention involves choosing stimuli from one's environment to notice, observe, and consider. Our senses (sight, hearing, touch, taste, and smell) are equipped to respond to stimuli in the environment. However, it is impossible to pay attention to everything going on about us; thus we select, or consciously attend to, only some of the available stimuli. Research has been done on infants and children in order to understand what parts of their environment they attend to. Selective attention is crucial to learning because children's perceptions and concepts of the world depend on which aspects of it get their attention. The following are examples of classic research findings that illustrate the role of selective attention in learning.

Babies respond to movement. A 5-day-old who is sucking on a pacifier will stop sucking if a light moves across its visual field (Haith, 1966). Babies also respond to novelty. One-day-old babies will look longer at a patterned surface than at a plain one (Fantz, 1965). Children between 2 and 3 years tend to pay more attention to the color of the object than to the form, whereas children between 4 and 6 tend to prefer form to color (Stevenson, 1972).

As children grow, their attention tends to focus on what they judge to be the important aspects of a situation. Eight-year-olds are more capable than 4- to 6-year-olds of deliberately ignoring irrelevant information when confronted with a problem (Bjorklund, 2005; Osler & Kofsky, 1965). Although children become increasingly better at selective attention as they get older, developing attentional strategies, it is not until about age 7 that they can purposely ignore "attention-grabbers" (Bjorklund, 2005), such as colors or songs used in advertisements.

As children approach adulthood, they selectively attend to those messages that are related to their individual interests, are consistent with their attitudes, are congruent with their beliefs, and are supportive of their values. For example, children will spend more time watching families on television that are similar to theirs in regard to ethnicity or single- or stepparenthood (Dorr & Rabin, 1995; Huston & Wright, 1998).

In his book *The Psychology of Television*, Condry (1989) summarized the specific aspects of television that children attend to. Starting in infancy, the amount of time children spend looking at a TV set while it is on increases steadily with age. The largest increase comes between the ages of 2 and 3. Preschool children show elevated attention to women, puppets, animation, strange voices, lively music, auditory changes, and rhyming, repetition, and alliteration. Children of this age pay less attention to men, animals, inactivity, and still pictures. Commercials capitalize on these findings.

Older children pay attention to more complexities as they gain in cognitive development. They are now able to understand story plots and characters. They are attracted to action, adventure, and family situation comedies. School-agers need to attend to visual techniques more than adolescents do to understand the story line (Comstock & Paik, 1991). In general, media cues that attract attention are "outstandingness," novelty, contrast, and how closely the cue is related to the viewer's frame of reference. This partially explains the finding that variations in media experiences are related to age, race and ethnicity, gender, socioeconomic status, and various indicators of social and psychological adjustment, such as happiness or anger (Roberts & Foehr, 2004).

Adult Involvement

Although television programmers may be able to attract the audience's attention by manipulating the level of "outstandingness," novelty, or contrast, it is ultimately up to the viewer to decide whether that message belongs in his or her frame of reference.

selective attention
choosing stimuli from one's environment to notice, observe, and consider

By viewing TV with their children, these parents can mediate the messages that are broadcast.

Parents, especially, can mediate the amount and level of attention given to TV by their children by being the primary socializers in their children's frames of reference. Children are more likely to attend to messages on TV that conform to their family's interests, attitudes, beliefs, and values. Parents, teachers, and older siblings are probably most important in determining television programming effects on children (Comstock & Paik, 1991; Roberts & Foehr, 2004). Early evidence of this importance was found in a first-year evaluation of *Sesame Street*. It was shown that those children who watched the show with their mothers and talked to them about the show learned more than did other children (Ball & Bogatz, 1970). This finding was supported by later research on the vocabulary development of preschoolers (Rice, Huston, Truglio, & Wright, 1990).

Parents can mediate television viewing (1) by controlling the number of hours of television exposure, (2) by checking ratings and evaluating what kinds of programs may be viewed, (3) by viewing television with their children and discussing the programs, and (4) by arranging family activities other than television viewing.

Several studies (Dorr & Rabin, 1995; Huston & Wright, 1998; Perse, 2001) support the value of significant others' involvement in children's television viewing. For example, one study (Wilson & Weiss, 1993) showed that co-viewing a show with older siblings increased preschoolers' enjoyment of and decreased their arousal to a scary program. Another study (Haefner & Wartella, 1987) showed that co-viewing changed 6- and 7-year olds' evaluations of certain characters in two programs.

Why is significant other or adult mediation important? One reason is that children do not "see" television in the same way adults do; according to Marieli Rowe, executive director of the American Council for Better Broadcasts, "The impact television has on a viewer depends to a great extent on what the viewer brings to TV" (Condry, 1989; Perse, 2001). Adult viewers can analyze and evaluate content. They can tune out irrelevancies, absorb complicated plots, and understand underlying messages. For the most part, children cannot.

A second reason, mentioned previously, is that young children cannot distinguish fantasy and reality; their understanding is based on appearances. They do not know what is fact and what is opinion. They have neither the experiences nor the knowledge to enable them to comprehend the basis of many events that occur in the world. Yet they are exposed to the whole world through the television screen before they have even developed an understanding of their own immediate world. We do not expect children to read a book before they can recognize letters. Adults, then, must develop strategies to mediate children's television viewing according to their values and their children's cognitive developmental level.

Mesosystem Influences

What role do links with other microsystems play in media socialization?

Mesosystem influences on television and movies consist of linkages with the community, the school, the peer group, and the family. These linkages affect the pervasiveness of media exposure, types of media and messages experienced, adult mediation, and the impact of socialization outcomes.

COMMUNITY–MEDIA LINKAGES

How has the community responded to concerns about broadcast (free) TV?

The community's response to commercial programs transmitted over the airwaves has been to develop alternatives—such as the Public Broadcasting Service (PBS), cable and satellite TV, and recording devices (VCRs, DVDs, TiVo) to record particular shows and view selected movies—and to form public interest groups.

The Public Broadcasting Service. PBS is an alliance of local community and educational stations financially supported by the Corporation for Public Broadcasting and by annual membership fees of licensees as well as by selling time to advertisers. Supplemental funds come from grants from the National Endowment for the Humanities, from universities, and from big corporations, with the aim of providing more specialized, diversified, and high-quality programs to reach specific age, social, and cultural groups.

Some examples of children's programs broadcast on PBS are *Sesame Street*—designed for preschoolers (programs are creative and educational); *Wishbone*—designed for school-agers (adaptations of excellent children's literature to promote reading), and *Scientific American Frontiers*—designed for young adolescents (about stimulating scientific discoveries).

Cable and Satellite Television. Families that pay for cable television or have purchased satellite dishes can view certain channels that show movies, sports, and educational programs. One such channel, available only through cable TV, is Nickelodeon—a television channel for children. Every day there are shows for children ages 2 to 15. For example, there are songs for young children, adventures for middle-years children, and talk shows for teenagers. Cable TV also provides music television (MTV) in which rock stars "act out" rock music.

Recording Devices. The business community has provided expanded uses of television. In many homes, television sets are currently used as display terminals for videotapes or discs and video games. Families that have home recorders or TiVo can play a more active role in selecting and managing their leisure time. A home recorder enables you to rent or purchase VHS tapes or DVDs of selected movies or instruction to show at home. It also enables you to record shows you don't want to miss, as does TiVo. Teachers, too, can record television shows and play them back in their classrooms. The advantage of such a medium is that the tape or disc can be stopped at any point for a discussion. Sometimes videos or discs are used to illustrate literature. Viewing Zeffirelli's *Romeo and Juliet* aided my son's understanding of Shakespeare's play.

The proliferation of videos and discs makes movies produced for the big screen accessible and affordable. Unless adults mediate the selection, young people can be exposed to violence, sexuality, and "anti-values," as was discussed in regard to TV.

Public Interest Groups. Public interest groups, such as Action for Children's Television (ACT) and the Center for Media Education (CME), have been formed to pressure broadcasters for change, to lobby the government for regulations, and to educate the public to monitor its own viewing habits and those of its children. They have been influential in reducing violence on children's TV, reducing the number of commercials on children's shows, and preventing program hosts or celebrities from advertising on their shows, as well as developing the rating system for television and movies.

Other advocate organizations, such as the national Parents and Teachers Association (PTA), were influential in pressuring the Federal Communications Commission in 1996 to strengthen the Children's Television Act of 1990 by mandating that commercial television stations broadcast at least three hours of educational/informational (E/I) programming per week for children. These programs must be labeled and advertised in a TV schedule. There are also mechanisms for public accountability wherein parents can rate the shows.

The PTA has become involved in educating parents and teachers on how they can help children develop critical viewing skills (see the box "Strategies for Children's Television Viewing and Development of Critical Viewing Skills").

SCHOOL–MEDIA LINKAGES

How does the school influence media use?

PBS airs a variety of programs specifically developed for the classroom, referred to as Educational Television (ETV). Many teachers nationwide use ETV as part of their curriculum, and millions of school-age children receive a portion of their regular instruction through television. Supporters of television in the classroom suggest that ETV provides memorability, concreteness, and emotional involvement, and also stimulates reading, encourages class discussion, and promotes student interactions (Greenfield, 1984). However, ETV has been criticized because many programs are financed by corporations that advertise their products on the show. It is felt that the classroom should not be a marketplace.

Schools have tried various tactics to control children's viewing habits. Some schools ask parents to keep children away from the tube entirely. Some recommend setting limits of a certain number of hours per day or specifying only certain shows. Other schools have taken steps to educate parents on the effects of TV on academic performance, rather than making across-the-board rules. Parents are then encouraged to develop their own family policies. Still other schools give parents ideas for alternative activities to TV viewing. Obviously, the success of school efforts to ban, limit, provide alternatives, or develop critical viewing skills for television depends on the cooperation of the family.

PEER–MEDIA LINKAGES

How does the peer group use media to foster its influence?

Young people who have digital devices can keep connected. Cell phones with instant text messaging, cameras, music players, organizers, and Internet connections enable users to interact "24/7." The ability to connect with friends is a significant factor in being part of a peer group (Roberts & Foehr, 2004). "If you don't talk online with people, you might miss something that happened, and then when you see the kids at school, you won't know what they're talking about."

Online chat rooms, instant messaging (IM), and e-mail enable kids to connect with groups of people. In addition to being a source of social engagement, it can be a way for youth to experiment with different "personas." An adolescent may be a "brain" in high school math, but becomes "Darth Vader 69" online. Chat rooms, IM, and e-mail can also be sources of gossip. A rumor about someone can be spread in seconds, too short a time to check the rumor's validity.

Special interest websites, such as for sports or a certain music genre, as well as MySpace and Friendster, are sources of peer connection. File sharing among peers who have similar interests can further such connections.

FAMILY–MEDIA LINKAGES

How can families optimize the media experience for children?

There can be no doubt that television as a medium of communication and information is of great potential value. Shows such as *The American Experience, Nova,* and *National Geographic* enrich viewers by exposing them to history, culture, geography, science, and travel—perspectives on life that they may never have experienced. Shows such as *Barney, Sesame Street,* and *Mister Rogers' Neighborhood* can provide children with models of cooperation, altruism, self-control, and empathy. Research shows that exposure to television programs that provide models of prosocial behavior enhances children's prosocial tendencies (Friedrich & Stein, 1973; Leibert & Sprafkin, 1988). Parental co-viewing and discussion of the prosocial program are even more enhancing (Huston & Wright, 1998; Perse, 2001; Roberts & Foehr, 2004).

Parents must exercise their primary responsibility in regulating and monitoring their children's viewing habits. In a democratic society, it is ultimately the viewer who bears responsibility for the effects of television; families must accept that responsibility by not viewing what is offensive and/or by supporting public interest groups.

Unfortunately, several studies (Huston & Wright, 1998; Perse, 2001; Roberts & Foehr, 2004) indicate that parental involvement in children's viewing is infrequent. Some children are allowed to watch what and when they want. Other children are restricted to how early and how late they may watch. Still others have restrictions on their total viewing time per day. And some children are restricted to viewing certain approved shows. Although many shows are viewed with other family members, especially siblings, two intensive, longitudinal studies of young children and their families concluded that parents do not use the time to mediate the shows (St. Peters, Marguerite, Huston, Wright, & Eakins, 1991; Desmond, Singer, & Singer, 1990).

Parental involvement is difficult for many families, because the parents may both work. In some families, the child comes home after school to an empty house and turns on the television for companionship. In other families, the television unintentionally becomes an "electronic babysitter" while the parent is busy with chores, caring for other children, or engaged in some activity. In still other families, the child has his or her own personal media devices. In these families, then, adult mediation is lacking and television becomes a powerful socializing agent. If parents do not take the time to regularly view with their children, at least they should teach their children how to watch TV and use the Internet selectively and critically.

IN PRACTICE

Strategies for Children's Television Viewing and Development of Critical Viewing Skills

1. Know what your children watch and when.

- A log of how much time they spend in front of the tube will often speak for itself about whether TV is playing too large a role in their lives.
- Be alert to the content of the program as well as the commercials. Notice ways in which viewing affects your children's behavior. Do they become transfixed after watching for a while? Or does viewing make them tense and lead to fighting? What effects does it have on family communication when you all watch together?

- How are ethnic groups, gender roles, and age groups presented? How are conflicts resolved?

2. **Know the ratings and choose what to watch.**
   - Don't leave watching to chance—you wouldn't put a refrigerator in your children's room and allow them to eat what they wanted on the chance they would eventually meet their nutritional requirements. Learn to turn off the set when your choice is over.

3. **Set limits.**
   - Talking over a set of guidelines with family members, agreeing on them, and sticking to them is effective in establishing a new routine for viewing TV. For example, your family may choose to ban TV during dinner, to allow viewing only after other responsibilities (homework, chores) have been done, or to allow each family member to have a choice of selecting a program each week.
   - Help children choose activities to do when the TV is off (read a book, draw a picture, play a game).

4. **Whenever possible, view with children.**
   - When watching with young children, point out what is real and what is fantasy.
   - When values presented on TV conflict with your family values, say so! When values agree, say so too!
   - Discuss the differences between fantasy and reality.
   - Discuss conflict situations and how problems could be solved without violence.
   - Discuss situations involving cooperation, and note behaviors your child might imitate.
   - Point out characters who represent a variety of ethnic groups.
   - Point out men/women who represent a variety of occupations.
   - Discuss food advertisements in terms of what is healthy and nutritious.
   - Discuss toy advertisements in terms of play potential, safety, and age appropriateness.

5. **Use the time in front of the TV to benefit the child.**
   - Television can be a rich source of vocabulary development. Explain new words to children.
   - Television can expand a child's horizons. Talk about other places in the world, other cultures, new experiences.
   - Television programs can stimulate reading of related material if the child is encouraged.
   - Television can stimulate discussion on sensitive topics by older children—such as drugs, rape, and teenage pregnancy—and thus may provide the opportunity for parents to discuss such topics.

Source: Action for Children's Television, n/d.

Print Media: Books and Magazines

Why is it harder to study the socialization effects of print than screen media?

Compared to screen media, such as television, print media are more difficult to investigate scientifically because they are often long, have complex structures and provoke more individual imagery than does television. Thus, it is difficult to separate the socializing effects of the *content* of the book or magazine from the socializing effects of the *interpretation* of the reader.

Unlike the screen media, where the visual image is provided, the print media describe in words the images of the writer. These words must then be translated into visual images by the reader. Obviously, reading is much more personal than is television viewing because the visual images readers conjure up from printed words depend on their vocabulary, reading ability, and real-life experiences.

Also, it is difficult to compare the socialization effects of books and TV because, until children gain a fair amount of reading skill, adults usually read books to them. This means adults are present to explain, answer questions, and adjust the tempo of the book to the child's level of understanding and interest. In addition, adults choose most of the books young children read. Parents and relatives buy them. Teachers assign certain books, and librarians choose which books will fill the library shelves. Thus, adults play a large role in determining the influence books will have on children, whereas this has not been the case with television viewing.

What do we know about the socialization potential of the print media?

According to Roberts and Foehr (2004), children's and adolescents' exposure to print media is influenced by the socioeconomic status of the family and the educational level of the parents—more income means more resources for printed material; greater education means a higher value placed on books and reading. I am astounded by the number of homes I have been in that have no bookcases, but do have entertainment units, in their living rooms.

The role that print media are known to play in socialization is that of passing on culture to the next generation, as illustrated by the prologues to each chapter in this book. The print media teach history, values, morals, ideals, and attitudes. Print-based culture is still the primary basis for information about education, religion, and government (Gerbner et al., 2002). The core of an educated person is **literacy**, being able to communicate through reading and writing. According to Postman (1986, p. 2), "the written word endures, the spoken word disappears." That print media make a powerful contribution to literacy may seem obvious, but why?

Different media elicit different thinking skills (Healy, 1990). Meringoff (1980) and colleagues (Char & Meringoff, 1981) compared young children's abilities to comprehend and reproduce narratives presented in different media (stories in print versus stories on television and radio). They found that even when the same soundtracks were used, television focused children's attention on the actions of characters, whereas radio or book format directed attention to the quality of the language. Children were more likely to consider television as an experience apart from themselves when answering questions about the program, whereas they were more likely to include their own personal experiences when answering questions about stories in books. Thus, print and screen media require different ways to process information.

The development of literacy is a social process, embedded in social relationships, particularly in children's relationships with parents, siblings, grandparents, friends, caretakers, and teachers. These people serve as models, provide materials, establish expectations, and offer help, instruction, and encouragement. (McLane & McNamee, 1990, p. 7)

literacy the ability to communicate through reading and writing

HOW BOOKS AND MAGAZINES SOCIALIZE CHILDREN

What impact does language have on socialization?

Books are written language. Language, as was discussed in Chapter 2, enables socialization to take place. Language makes ideas and communication of these ideas possible; language also makes it possible to replace action with thoughts. Language is a vehicle by which individuals can express emotions (Rovenger, 2000). Language enables humans to internalize attitudes of others. Language is the means of passing on the cultural heritage from one generation to the next.

Magazines are written language, too; but they are infused with pictures and advertisements, sometimes in greater proportion than their articles. Thus, a socializing effect of magazines is consumerism. Magazines usually cater to special interests, such as fashion, sports, celebrities, music, computers, science, or pets, thereby contributing to the knowledge base of their readers. Teenagers often turn to magazines for advice on such things as relationships, appearance, and "cool" things to have (Kaiser Family Foundation, 2004).

Jim Trelease (2001), in *The Read-Aloud Handbook*, cites evidence stressing the importance of reading for building knowledge. Reading aloud improves children's *listening comprehension*, a skill that must occur before *reading comprehension*. It is the activity of reading aloud to children that enables them to become successful readers. Reading aloud is so important because it enhances attachment, and socialization begins with personal attachment. Reading aloud also provides a model for children to imitate. As Gail E. Haley said in the 1971 Caldecott Medal acceptance speech (the **Caldecott Medal** is an award given yearly for the most distinguished American picture book for children):

> Children who are not spoken to by live and responsive adults will not learn to speak properly. Children who are not answered will stop asking questions. They will become incurious. And children who are not told stories and who are not read to will have few reasons for wanting to learn to read.

Ellen Spitz, in *Inside Picture Books* (1999), analyzes books that adults have read to children for generations like *Goodnight Moon* (Brown, 1947) and *Where the Wild Things Are* (Sendak, 1963). She discusses how well-known picture books transmit psychological wisdom, convey moral lessons, and shape tastes. Hidden in these familiar stories are the anxieties of childhood, such as fear of separation and loss, or threat of aggression. Reading to children builds a special bond between the reader and listener.

How do print media influence children's development?

Cognitive Development. The way children use their brains causes physical changes in their neural wiring. Children who are stimulated and are actively engaged in experiences such as reading have more neural connections than children who have fewer experiences (Begley, 1997). These neural connections allow for different functions, so the child with more connections not only can master more skills but also is more adaptable in learning them. Analogously, one can get to a destination more successfully if one knows alternative routes to use in case of road work or traffic. Print media involve hierarchal cognitive skills, because readers must follow a sequence of ideas from beginning to middle to end to grasp the meaning (Desmond, 2001). Hierarchal skills are a component of logic and are used, for example, by crime scene investigators.

Caldecott Medal
award given yearly for the most distinguished picture book for children

Language and Reading Development. Books enhance language development. The relationship of children's language to the amount of reading they do and the amount of reading aloud to them was examined. It was found that children who are read to often and who read a lot on their own are more advanced in their language development than children who are rarely read to and do not read very much on their own (Chomsky, 1972; McLane & McNamee, 1990).

By reading aloud to children, adults can enhance children's language development as well as the desire to read on their own.

Part of the explanation for the effect on language development of reading, compared to talking and/or other media, is that literary language is more structured and more complex. The language in children's books is more complex and richer in syntactic patterns than the language used in children's television programs (Healy, 1990; Postman, 1992). Television engages the child with language in a passive way, whereas reading books and telling stories engage the child in an active way. Active use of language has more impact on language development than does passive listening (Barclay, Benelli, & Curtis, 1995).

Not surprisingly, books also enhance reading development (Desmond, 2001). Research indicates that children who are read to learn to read earlier and more easily than children who are not read to. It has been shown that children who learned to read early had been read to and had had someone to answer their questions (Barclay et al., 1995; Schickedanz, 1986; Teale, 1984). Although most children learn to read at school, preschool children who are read to develop emergent literary skills, such as understanding that words tell stories and words are made up of different letters (Whitehurst & Lonigan, 1998). Letter recognition has been found to correlate with future reading achievement scores (Lonigan, Burgess, & Anthony, 2000).

Cognitive Development. Books nourish cognitive development. Not only do they provide information and concepts, they also provide vicarious experiences and stimulate the child's imagination. For example, *The Very Hungry Caterpillar* (for preschoolers) by Eric Carle (1986) helps teach a child the days of the week, how to count to five, and how a caterpillar becomes a butterfly, all in bright pictures.

Books can be used to help children gain an understanding of themselves and others across time and space (Norton & Norton, 2002). For example, *The Three Pigs* (for preschoolers) by David Wiesner (2001), was the 2002 winner of the Caldecott Medal. The book is an adaptation of the classic folktale. The pigs are huffed and puffed off the page into a new world. Transformations occur as the pigs boldly enter new stories, make new friends, and ultimately control their own fate.

Psychosocial Development. Books provide models for children—models of behavior, models of gender roles, and models of occupational roles (Rovenger, 2000). For example, *Mothers Can Do Anything* (for preschoolers) by Joe Lasker (1972) demonstrates the variety of jobs mothers can hold, including scientist, linesman, artist, and lion tamer.

Books can also be used to impart a desired value system (Bennett, 1993). For example, Linda Sue Park's (2001) *A Single Shard* (for school-agers) was the 2002 winner of the **Newbery Medal**, an award presented yearly for the most distinguished

Newbery Medal
award given yearly for the most distinguished contribution to American literature for children

contribution to American literature for children. The book is about dedication to one's dreams. The story takes place in 12th-century Korea where Tree-ear, an orphan, becomes fascinated by the artistry and craft of some potters who live nearby. Despite great odds, Tree-ear's courage, honor, and perseverance enable him to become an apprentice to the master potter, Min. He achieves great happiness by fulfilling his dream of becoming an artist.

Literature can be of value in helping children cope with and master problems of importance in their lives (Bettelheim, 1976; Cashdan, 1999; Rovenger, 2000). For example, some fairy tales and folk stories deal with aggressive and negative traits of human beings and indicate ways of coping with them. Folk and fairy tales lie at the root of every culture and, despite geographical differences, have many similarities in theme (Campbell, 1968; Norton & Norton, 2002): tribal history, local history, myth, legend, trickster, and entertainment. Folk and fairy tales are appealing to children because they explain things in terms to which children can relate.

Books offer children the opportunity to explore and understand their own feelings and the feelings of others (Rovenger, 2000). For example, in *The Hundred Dresses* (for school-agers), a classic by Eleanor Estes (1944), a group of schoolchildren realize too late that their cruelty has destroyed the happiness of a poor girl, Wanda Petronski, and her family, who immigrated to the United States from Poland. Wanda attempts to win a place in the group by telling of the hundred dresses she owns. However, she wears the same faded dress to school every day and is teased by the other girls because of it and because she has a funny name. The ostracism that the Petronski family experiences compels them to move away. Soon afterward, Wanda's hundred dresses—that is, her drawings of 100 dresses—are presented in an art contest. The girls finally understand Wanda's feelings, but it is too late to undo that cruelty. This book helps children understand what values are truly important and also that mistakes cannot always be rectified.

Literature, then, can help children understand the realities of life. It can provide them with models of behavior that are useful in dealing with problems; it can also help children understand the consequences of certain behaviors.

CONCERNS ABOUT BOOKS AND MAGAZINES

What concerns are associated with print media?

Books can elicit some of the concerns that were described earlier in this chapter regarding television, such as fantasy being confused with reality, violence, the perpetuation of certain values and stereotypes, and even commercialism (toy tie-ins, clothing, or movies). The degree to which books should reflect reality leads to controversy regarding how the characters solve problems and how they are portrayed (Norton & Norton, 2002).

Fantasy and Reality

Some books have young characters who overcome obstacles, apparently caused by adults, through real problem-solving or through fantasy (Norton & Norton, 2002). For example, Maurice Sendak's *Where the Wild Things Are* (1963) illustrates Max's imagination when, because of his misbehavior, his mother sends him to his room without supper. This book was banned in some schools because its illustrations were regarded as "frightening" to young children and because of its message. Others highly recommend the book because readers can identify with Max and his strong feelings expressed through fantasy.

The Goosebumps books, a series of monster mysteries by R. L. Stine, were introduced to school-agers through school book clubs. There are five basic plots written in a clipped style thick with thumps and gasps. They are advertised on TV and have games and toys for children to act out the plots, thereby blurring the boundaries of fantasy and reality (Gellene, 1996). Critics say they don't promote literacy but do promote commercialism.

A popular series for older school-agers is *Harry Potter* by J. K. Rowlings. Apparently these best-sellers are stimulating children's imaginations through their blend of fantasy, magic, mystery, and reality. Attendance at the movies and video purchases, as well as book sales, attest to *Harry Potter's* popularity. Harry is an 11-year-old English boy who became an orphan when his "good wizard" parents died saving him from an evil wizard. The action surrounds Harry's dual life among the "muggles" (ordinary human beings, including his cruel foster parents) and his teachers at the Hogwarts School of Witchcraft and Wizardry, and his progress toward initiation as a sorcerer/magician. The classic theme of the power of magic still attracts readers.

Some classic juvenile book series, such as *Nancy Drew* and *The Hardy Boys* books by Edward Stratemyer, have been criticized for being formulaic. The themes are danger, mystery, and excitement. Stratemyer's formula consisted of capturing the reader's interest on the first page, providing a dramatic highpoint in the middle of every chapter, and ending each chapter with a "cliff-hanging event." Romances, westerns, and mysteries usually contain a great deal of action; the characters are ideal types, and the ending is happy. Such books convey an unrealistic view of life, based on the following questionable assumptions (Carlsen, 1980, pp. 52–53):

1. Children and adolescents are more perceptive than adults; if they could switch places with adults, they could do a better job at everything adults generally do.
2. Dramatic changes, as in personality or personal appearance, can occur in a short period of time.
3. Premonitions turn out to be accurate.
4. There is a solution for every problem, and it is usually a simple one.
5. One's physical appearance indicates one's character.
6. People are either good or bad. Good always wins over bad, and bad people are punished.
7. It is OK for the good people to use deceptive or illegal techniques because they have the right goals—"The end justifies the means."
8. Heroes and heroines are the culture's male and female stereotypes (handsome, brave males and pretty, dainty females). They also tend to have anglicized names (Nancy Drew).
9. Villains are different from the cultural ideal stereotypes. They may be fat, hairy, or dark. They also tend to have foreign-sounding names (Fu Manchu).
10. The wealthy tend to be corrupt, whereas the lower and middle classes tend to be good.

Books, as has been said, are agents of socialization. Psychologist Bruno Bettelheim (1976) wrote, "The acquisition of skills . . . becomes devalued when what one has learned to read adds nothing of importance to one's life." Books should help a child examine values, sort them out, and make decisions. Reading stereotyped and formula fiction is unlikely to achieve such ends. Research shows that children's attitudes and achievements are affected by certain biases in books (Norton & Norton, 2002). As a response, Bennett (1993) compiled his book of moral stories and poems to influence children's values.

Violence

Children were exposed to violence in stories and fairy tales long before there was television, and it has been shown that children imitate aggression from storybooks, just as they do from television (Neuman, 1991). Bettelheim (1976) and Cashdan (1999) believe that fairy tales help children cope with their strong emotions on an unconscious level: "It seems particularly appropriate to a child that exactly what the evildoer wishes to inflict on the hero should be the bad person's fate—as the witch in "Hansel and Gretel" who wants to cook children in the oven is pushed into it and burned to death" (Bettelheim, 1976, p. 144).

In *The Witch Must Die*, Cashdan (1999) explores how fairy tales help children project their own inner struggles with good and evil onto battles enacted by characters in the stories. Thus, the violence we, as adults, see in literature for young children, especially in fairy tales, is really a catharsis, a mechanism for release of strong feelings. According to Huck and Helper (1996), however, a well-written book enables the reader to empathize with the human suffering of people's inhumane acts, whereas television or films are more apt to concentrate on the act itself.

A well-written book can provide a perspective on people's pain and suffering because the author has time to develop the characters, which is not true of television. In a book, the reader gets to know the motives and pressures of each individual and can understand and empathize with the characters (Norton & Norton, 2002).

Stereotyping

Stereotypes continue to appear in children's books, textbooks, and magazines as they do on TV. Males, European Americans, and middle-class families tend to be overrepresented. Men and boys are more likely to be active and presented in adventuresome or exciting roles; females are more likely to be passive or dependent and presented in inconspicuous or immobile roles. Fairy tales, especially those made into Disney movies, are good examples (*Cinderella, Snow White and the Seven Dwarfs, Beauty and the Beast*). Minority groups are underrepresented; when they are shown, they are usually portrayed as conventional and middle class (Dougherty & Engle, 1987; Gollnick & Chinn, 2005; Sadker, Sadker, & Klein, 1991).

Recently, however, children's literature has made progress. Specifically, award-winning books have begun to present more equitable portrayals of gender and cultural diversity (Dellman-Jenkins, Florjancic, & Swadener, 1993; MacLeod, 1994). A study by Dougherty and Engle (1987) assessed the gender-role distribution of characters in a sample of Caldecott Medal books from 1981 to 1985. They compared their assessment to a similar study done 14 years earlier by Weitzman (1972) of Caldecott Medal books from 1967 to 1971. The earlier study found that males in the titles of picture books outnumbered females 8:1. The later study found males still outnumbering females, but in a ratio of 2:1. Whereas the earlier study found males portrayed as active and females as passive, the later study found instances of females being portrayed as active and independent; in these instances, the females occupied central roles in the story. Similar findings were reported in an analysis of sexism in Newbery Medal–award books from 1977 to 1984 (Kinman & Henderson, 1985).

Similar changes have generally occurred in elementary school textbook gender-role stereotyping. Since 1972, when Scott, Foresman and Company was the first publisher to issue guidelines for improving the image of women in textbooks, all major publishers have issued recommendations for reducing inequities in instructional materials (Levine & Levine, 1996). However, Myra and David Sadker (1994), in their research on sexism in schools, found twice as many boys and men as girls and women pictured in language arts textbooks; and in a 631-page history text, only 7 pages were related to women.

Although basal reader books have tried to become more equitable in their inclusion of previously underrepresented groups, reality is still misrepresented (Sadker & Sadker, 2003). For example, in an attempt to correct previous imbalances, ethnic minority males are overrepresented in working roles, as compared to the actual makeup of the labor force. Individuals with disabilities, on the other hand, are underrepresented in basal reader series. People over age 55 not only are underrepresented, but are often shown walking in parks, rocking in chairs, and being cranky. Finally, relatively few of the families portrayed in basal readers have single parents, even though about half the children reading these books are likely to spend at least part of their childhood with only one parent.

A problem with depending solely on a textbook for classroom instruction is that sometimes the validity of its content is not questioned. Sadker and Sadker (2003) recommend critically examining textbooks for the following biases:

1. *Invisibility*: the underrepresentation of certain groups
2. *Stereotyping*: the attribution of rigid roles to certain groups
3. *Selectivity and imbalance*: the interpretation of issues and situations from only one perspective
4. *Unreality*: the exclusion of sensitive and controversial topics
5. *Fragmentation and isolation*: separating issues, information, and contributions of certain groups from main instructional materials rather than integrating them
6. *Linguistic bias*: the omission of feminine and ethnic group references, pronouns, and names
7. *Cosmetic bias*: the superficial appearance of a well-balanced curriculum, giving the illusion of equity

Concern about the effects of school textbooks on gender-role stereotyping, attitudes about ethnic minorities and people with disabilities, and acquisition of values has caused some state boards of education to adopt guidelines for purchase.

IN PRACTICE

Ten Quick Ways to Analyze Children's Books for Ethnic and Gender Stereotypes

1. Check the illustrations. Look for stereotypes, tokenism (presentation as a symbol with no real significance), and who is doing what.
2. Check the story line. What is the standard for success? How are problems presented, conceived, and resolved in the story? What is the role of women?
3. Look at the lifestyles.
4. Weigh the relationships between people.
5. Note the heroes.
6. Consider the effects on a child's self-image.
7. Consider the author's or illustrator's background.
8. Check out the author's perspective. Is the perspective patriarchal or feminist? Is it Eurocentric, or do minority ethnic perspectives also receive attention?

> 9. Watch for loaded words (those that ridicule or have insulting overtones).
> 10. Look at the copyright date. Books on minority themes began appearing in the mid-1960s, but they were usually written by white authors. Not until the 1970s did children's books begin to reflect the realities of a multiethnic society, as well as exhibit more gender equity.
>
> *Source:* Council on Interracial Books for Children, n/d.

Magazines for teenagers have been around for decades; for example, *Seventeen*, a magazine for teenage girls, was first published in 1944 and still dominates sales (Palladino, 1996). It has articles on fashion, cosmetics, celebrities, and relationships. Teenage boys prefer to read magazines about sports, cars, or computers (Jaffe, 1998). Some magazines have websites that solicit reader feedback, providing forums and chat rooms where teens can "blog" to other teens. Some magazines use the web to recruit "cool hunters" to stay informed about emerging trends in the youth culture (Kaiser Family Foundation, 2004).

One study (Evans, Rutberg, Sather, & Turner, 1991) sampled 10 issues each of three widely circulated female-oriented magazines (*Seventeen*, *Sassy*, and *YM*) to identify messages directed at teenage girls and how they related to female identity. The conclusion was that the road to happiness for girls is to attract males by physical beautification (presumably by purchasing the products advertised in the magazine). Many articles implied that female self-esteem should be related to body image, physical attractiveness, and satisfaction with one's weight. Relatively few articles discussed personal enhancement through professional development or leadership. Few articles promoted intellectual pursuits, sports, or the social issues most women face.

BOOKS, SOCIALIZATION, AND DEVELOPMENTAL LEVELS OF CHILDREN

The developmental level, or cognitive stage, of a child influences the socializing effect of books on that child, illustrating the concept of bidirectionality. How children selectively attend to their environment, perceive information, process it in their brains, remember it, and use it are influential factors. Several authors (Huck & Helper, 1996; Norton & Norton, 2002) believe that children's favorite stories (usually the ones that endure from one generation to the next) correspond to their stages of cognitive development described by Piaget.

Preoperational Stage (About Ages 2 to 7)

Children in the preoperational stage are unable to deal with more than one aspect at a time, nor can they deal with complex relationships or abstractions. Thus, for example, folktales that repeat each event from the beginning—such as "The Gingerbread Boy"—are very appealing to preoperational children, especially 2- to 4-year-olds. Such folktales are cumulative; that is, they bring all previous events into the present to build a visible scene for the reader. Examples of classic books that appeal to older preoperational children are *Blueberries for Sal* by Robert McCloskey (1948) and *Harry the Dirty Dog* by Gene Zion (1956).

As preoperational children begin to understand seriation (arranging things in a sequence), they become interested in stories that have characters of increasing size, such as "The Three Bears," or stories that denote growth, such as the classic *Peter's Chair* by Ezra Jack Keats (1967). Books can extend and reinforce children's developing concepts—the sequence of time, for example.

Concrete Operational Stage (About Ages 7 to 11 or 12)

As children move from the preoperational to the concrete operational level of thought, their ability to understand literature expands. At this level, thought is more flexible and reversible, so they can understand such classic stories as Leo Lionni's (1968) *The Biggest House in the World*. They can also project themselves into the past and future, and so understand flashbacks and shifts in time periods. Finally, concrete operational children can more easily identify with other points of view and are able to understand a wide variety of books. Informational books can expand their interests and experiences. Biographies can provide them with models with whom to identify.

Formal Operational Stage (About Age 11 or 12 and Up)

The stage of formal operations is characterized by abstract, logical thought. Children in this stage can reason from hypotheses to conclusions. They can hold several plots or subplots in their minds simultaneously and see interrelations among them. They can also interpret abstract symbols and different meanings in literature. They can analyze and evaluate what they read. They are able to understand the values presented in books and can examine various issues presented from different viewpoints. For example, in Marjorie Rawlings' (1938) classic *The Yearling*, Jody's parents reluctantly consent to his adopting an orphan fawn because he is so lonely. The two become great friends, but when the fawn destroys the family's meager crops, Jody realizes he must sacrifice the fawn. In giving up what he loves, he leaves behind his own yearling days. Books can provide role models, morals, and attitudes for children to explore. Books play an important role in socialization at this time because formal operational children are beginning to develop a sense of self, including a gender-role identity, a moral code, and a set of values.

Audio Media: Popular Music

What makes popular music different from other media?

Music expresses aspects of the culture as it changes through history; for example, popular music through the years has ranged from patriotic "Yankee Doodle" to jazz to rock (Sklaroff, 2002). What sets today's popular music apart from television and books is that it is an expression of the subculture of youth and also that it effectively alienates many adults (Elkind, 1994; Jaffe, 1998). "Pop" music usually refers to rock, but other types of music, such as hip-hop, R&B, and alternative, which may go in and out of vogue, also have a socializing effect.

According to reviews of the research on popular music (Christenson & Roberts, 1998; Roberts & Foehr, 2004), children's interest in rock music accelerates at about the third and fourth grades, and by early adolescence, teens listen to music (radio, CDs, tapes, music videos) from 2 to 5 hours each day. Girls listen more than boys. African Americans and Hispanics watch music videos more than European Americans.

Music preferences become more specific as children get older. Boys generally prefer the louder forms of rock; girls generally prefer softer, more romantic forms. Ethnicity and socioeconomic status also play a role in music choice. African Americans report

Teens at this rock concert are enjoying each other's company as well as the music.

a preference for soul, rap, and rhythm and blues; Hispanics lean toward salsa; European Americans say they like all types of rock (Roberts & Foehr, 2004).

The medium of vocal music is a socializing influence in that it engages one's attention and emotions with the sound while espousing certain values with the lyrics (American Academy of Child and Adolescent Psychiatry, 1997b; Jaffe, 1998). However, motivation, experience, knowledge, and self-concept are factors in the interpretation of the lyrics. For example, some studies (Prinsky & Rosenbaum, 1987; Thompson, 1993) have discovered that preadolescents and adolescents often don't understand or attend to the underlying themes in the lyrics. Other studies (Larson, 1995) report music listening as a fantasy experience to explore possible selves (images of power and conquest, rescue by an idealized lover). This effect is magnified by music videos with their visual, as well as audio, components (for example, MTV) (Strouse, Buerkel-Rothfuss, & Long, 1995) and is reduced by the presence of family members who disapprove (Thompson & Larson, 1995). Christenson and Roberts (1998) found that teenagers who report watching music videos or music television shows do so to find out what is "cool," rather than learning any social values.

Throughout time and across cultures, people have always created and listened to music. It is a form of communication, emotional expression, art, celebration, tradition, and enjoyment. The media of records, radio, television, videos, and CDs provide the ways and means for popular music today.

Teenagers in the 1950s were attracted to a form of popular music known as "rock 'n' roll." The term was coined by Alan Freed (1922–1956) on his radio show in 1951. Teens liked the dance beats and rhythms, the wailing instruments, and the emotional vocal tones of the singers (Gay, 1998). The music and dance often celebrated sexuality and other freedoms beyond what most adults considered to be acceptable boundaries (Gay, 1998). The general themes of the lyrics were alienation, romantic longing for an ideal partner, and frustrated sexuality (Jaffe, 1998). As teenagers demanded more rock music on the radio and purchased more records, the genre spread to other media (TV, movies, audiotapes, and later, videotapes and compact discs). By the 1960s, rock music was featured in movies about gangs and juvenile delinquents, reinforcing an association between teenage music and alienation (Jaffe, 1998).

> With its origins in the music of slaves and other downtrodden groups, rock music has always spoken to values and points of view outside the mainstream, values frequently divergent from or in opposition to adult culture. . . . Rock music offers an antidote to and an escape from the unrelenting socialization pressures that emanate daily from family and school. Popular music does not tell its listeners to delay gratification and prepare for adulthood. Rather, it tells young people that the concerns they have today are of importance, that they merit expression in music, and that one ought to value one's youth and not worry so much about the future. (Larson, Kubey, & Colletti, 1989, pp. 584, 596–597)

Does listening to music about sensual gratification or reckless behavior influence teenagers' behavior, or are troubled teens attracted to such music because it reflects their state of confusion? Consistent with the hypothesis that solitary music listening allows adolescents to explore their possible selves, one study (Took & Weiss, 1994) concluded that heavy metal and rap music empower male teenagers and provide them with an identity "complete with clothes and hairstyle." Such music also offers a peer group with only similar music taste as a requirement for entry.

Some (Arnett, 1991; Roberts & Christenson, 2001) suggest that adolescents' fascination with the despairing lyrics of heavy metal music is a *symptom* of alienation, not its *cause*. For some teens, drug use and careless behavior provide an escape from a chaotic family environment. Acting on the lyric suggestions reflects an absence of parental supervision. For most fans, heavy metal music serves not as a source of anger and frustration, but as a release.

Popular music provides many adolescents with a means of identifying with a particular group or performer (American Academy of Child and Adolescent Psychiatry, 1997b; Larson, 1995), especially when real positive role models are lacking in the young person's life. Going to concerts, collecting rock stars' music, wearing certain clothing, adopting certain hairstyles, and getting tattooed or body pierced can all be part of an adolescent's search for identity—it's a style to "try on," a group of which to be a part. Performers are powerful image makers; their effect on children depends on the role of other significant socializing agents, such as family and friends.

The question that remains is whether the songs *reflect* the values of a particular generation or *influence* that generation's values. Concern centers on the issue of contagion. **Contagion** is the phenomenon in which an individual exposed to a suggestion will act on it. For example, there is a concern regarding the language and the social criticism set to rhyme (rap) in the music genre hip-hop. Also of concern to adults is the potential for alienation of the youth who listen, because the lyrics generally are self-assertive expressions of disgust with the establishment. However, rap and hip-hop remain popular and have been commercialized. The artists themselves, their style of dress, or the genre's lyrics and beat are used to sell products (Rice & Dolgin, 2002). Adults fear the contagious effect such role models may have on their children regarding language, violence, sexuality, substance abuse, and anti-establishment messages.

A highly controversial provider of entertainment, because of its ability to captivate young audiences, is MTV, or Music Television, first introduced in 1983. MTV is a 24-hour rock music, cable television channel that promotes new songs by accompanying them with visual dramatization. These videos have been criticized for their violence, sexism, substance abuse, and sexual content (American Academy of Pediatrics, 1996), as well as stereotyping of ethnic groups (Rich, Woods, Goodman, Emans, & DuRant, 1998). A concern about the marriage of music to television is that many adolescents in the United States view MTV, or other music video channels, at least once a week (Roberts & Foehr, 2004). Mental images once formed by rhythm, beat, and perceived lyrics are now created by special effects on video. Another concern is the commercialism. Music videos show images that sell the product (Gay, 1998); therefore, what messages are really being promoted must be questioned. For example, many preadolescents and adolescents are influenced by the clothing, jewelry, hairstyles, and body art adorning rock stars.

Some rock stars try to contribute positively to the community by agreeing to be role models for anti-drug campaigns, or by donating their time for rock concerts to raise money for Third World countries. For example, in 2005, free worldwide concerts ("Live 8") were held to redirect activism from the streets to politics with the goal of making poverty history. Their message was broadcast in more than 140 countries on the radio and the Internet.

contagion the phenomenon in which an individual exposed to a suggestion will act on it

IN PRACTICE

Is Hip-Hop a Reflector or a Shaper of the Culture?

My aerobics teacher plays hip-hop music for our step class. Initially, I didn't relate because I was used to dancing to a rock beat. Recently, however, I found myself in "the zone" while doing the moves. "The zone" is an experience familiar to athletes, but anyone can encounter it. Being in "the zone" is losing oneself in an activity—being so completely absorbed that the sense of time, thoughts, and problems seem to disappear (Csikszentmihalyli, 1991). For me, it was as though the hip-hop beat was the engine firing up my muscles to dance. The energy generated was accompanied by a transcendence of body, mind, and soul. It was addictive. Perhaps herein lies the attraction to hip-hop. Who doesn't want to go beyond the limits of self-consciousness and effortlessly experience a sense of mastery?

The seeds of hip-hop were sown on the streets of the Bronx during the 1970s, when unemployment of inexperienced youth ranged from 60% to 70% and kids spent their free time creating graffiti and break dancing. Hip-hop, including rap, was influenced by jazz, disco, gospel, work songs, and R&B music, as well as Jamaican and African American culture. The block was where kids would exhibit innovative acrobatic dance moves, often to the beat of music. The dancing was called "break," or "beat," because it was done in rhythm to the percussion sounds of a song. To increase the time of the beat segment, records were forwarded and reversed on a turntable hooked up to loudspeakers. Later, the percussive and scratching sounds could be generated by a computer. Sometimes, rhyming lyrics were synchronized to the rhythm. This was known as "rap." Rapping became a means of vocal self-expression, whereas the break dancing was more physical. Along with the rapping and hip-hop came a style of life, including language, dress, substance use by some, and attitude.

The propagation of hip-hop within mainstream culture is credited first to DJs Kool Herc, Hollywood, and Afrika Bamaata, who popularized the genre in disco clubs, radio, and recordings. In the early days, rapping was slang set to rhyme. It was used at parties to acknowledge and interact with who was there. For example, "Yo this is Kool Herc in the joint-ski saying my mellow-ski Marky D is in the house." The recognized individual could then reply with a rhyme created for the occasion (Ogg & Upshal, 1999).

Rap caught on with urban New Yorkers and spread elsewhere because it provided a new opportunity for self-expression. It also offered challenges to be creative and get affirmation from one's peers. As rapping became more popular, personal problems as well as reflections on political, social, and economic conditions were included in the rhymes. Some lyrics were meant to be shocking, as in "gangsta rap." For example, aggressive, socially conscious lyrics by Ice T captured the underside of life as a black man in white America. Gangsta rap tells of street and prison life as it seeks to shock and challenge the perceived obstructions to racial inequality—the white rulers. Other lyrics were meant to be motivating, as in "political rap," such as Eminem's lyrics about the Iraqi conflict. For another example, many rap artists performed in the 2004 Rock the Vote Campaign, hosting events across the country. The purpose of these shows were to get the message out that young people's opinions matter and count. Democracy gives you a say in your future.

The mass media have cultivated hip-hop culture, commodifying the music, dancing, graffiti art, language, and style of dress (Watkins, 2005). Today, many advertisements aimed at the youth generation are set to hip-hop music or rap rhyme. Russell Simmons and Sean "P. Diddy" Combs are examples of rappers who capitalized on hip-hop's business appeal, having recognized that hip-hop is about aspiration and creating a better life. Many hip-hop artists have become prominent in screen media as well as audio. Many have used hip-hop as a means of political activism to call attention to urban blight, poverty, gang violence, racism, drugs, authoritarianism, and global issues. The catchy beat beckons attention.

According to Gerbner and colleagues (2002), mass media cultivate attitudes and values already present in a culture; the media propagate these values among members of a culture, thus binding it together. Hip-hop has demonstrated just that. As author Luis J. Rodriguez said, hip-hop "draws from the fire, verve, rage, injustices, pains, victories, and creativity of a whole generation of marginalized, forgotten, pissed-on, and pissed-off youth" (Chang, 2005, back cover).

Interactive and Multimedia

What is the impact of new media technology that enhances interaction and multi-usage?

Interactive and multimedia are technologies that enable the user to participate actively, such as computers, video games, and cell phones. According to the Kaiser Family Foundation (2005a), the total amount of media content young people (ages 8–18) are exposed to each day has increased more than an hour since 2000 (from about 7 to 8 hours), excluding schoolwork, with most of the increase coming from video games and computers. Much of the media exposure is multidimensional, meaning that more than one medium is used at a time (for example, going online while watching TV). Even children ages 0–6 spend as much time with TV, computers, and video games as playing outside (Kaiser Family Foundation, 2003). While it is difficult to generalize about the impact on children of this flexibility of use, most psychologists and educators agree that it is empowering. Children's sense of self-efficacy is enhanced by being able to easily access information, entertainment, and communication.

According to Piaget's theory of cognitive development (1952), school-age and some adolescent children fail to differentiate between perceptions (based on objective facts or reality) and beliefs (based on subjective feelings or attitudes). This results in an *assumptive reality*, defined in Chapter 8 as a theory about reality assumed to be true without examining or evaluating contradictory data. Children make assumptions about reality based on limited information because they do not yet have the capability to critically evaluate their assumptions against contradictory information. Elkind (1981a) used the term *cognitive conceit* to describe the assumptive reality whereby children believe that because they know *some* things, they know *all*. Some children may assume that because they know how to use multimedia, they are wiser than their parents or teachers and may look to the media, rather than a significant adult, to learn the ways of the world. The media provide numerous examples that reinforce this misconception by portraying children as wiser than adults—for example, *Home Alone* and *Harry Potter*.

COMPUTERS AND THE INTERNET

The Internet, formerly known as the Arapnet by the U.S. Department of Defense, was first constructed to form a network that would always be operable under any form of attack because there was no central distribution point. This network soon came to be used by universities to share information with each other and was later adopted by the private sector and individuals. The Internet created public space and removed barriers to communication, such as time and space. This public network is neither owned nor controlled by any individual or institution; free speech prevails. As an international network, the Internet encompasses many different cultures. Websites, e-mail, instant messaging, chat rooms, and newsgroups create what McLuhan called a "global village."

The Internet is a pool of information. Whatever may be of interest to you, no matter how major or minor, is potentially there. Information is typically stored on the web pages posted by individuals and content producers. Because websites are not categorized, search engines have emerged as a means to sort and index the sites. Websites sometimes provide means for feedback from visitors, and forums can be created wherein collaboration can take place. It can be a challenge to distinguish objectivity from subjectivity (Alexander & Tate, 1999).

Information on the Internet is multidimensional rather than linear. Topics can expand in various directions through hyperlinks among websites. One has to take care not to get distracted.

Some of the problems with Internet technology are (1) piracy issues over illegal transferring of copyright material, (2) privacy issues regarding the ability to track online usage patterns and gain access to personal data, (3) the capacity to hack into unauthorized information, (4) viruses and worms that can destroy data on computers, and (5) unsolicited junk mail, or "spam."

More than two-thirds of U.S. children have access to computers at home, and virtually all have access at school. There is concern regarding the disparities of opportunities for children of different socioeconomic statuses to learn to use computers effectively as tools in their lives and to experience enriched learning in the classroom (Shields & Behrman, 2000). Thus, some children may lag behind in the very skills needed to succeed in our increasingly computer-dependent society. Are we creating a gap between the information-rich and information-poor?

As noted previously, computers can present information, enable students to practice skills, foster creativity (an essay, for example) because time doesn't have to be spent on mechanics (spelling, for example), and allow for assessment. The interactive capabilities of computers with CD-ROMs and modems allow for practically unlimited access to information. Children need to learn how to do an appropriate search without getting "sidetracked." They have to learn to evaluate sources of information and distinguish facts from opinions.

What about the socializing effects of computers outside the educational domain? What are the influences on a child's development of playing computer games? How do children cope with access to all kinds of information on the Internet without having developed critical thinking skills? What about access to information negating family values, such as pornography? How can children distinguish commercial interests from educational ones?

Video games actively engage children in media technology.

© Holos/Getty Images

One concern is that children who have home computers will be social isolates and choose solitary activities over interactive ones. So far, this has not been widely proven. One study (Sleek, 1998) over a two-year time span of people who regularly log on to the Internet, found that as use of the Internet increased, the number of social activities engaged in and social support experiences decreased. On the other hand, children often *use* a computer to attract playmates, as by sharing software and games. They also use it to communicate with friends. In the classroom, it serves as a means for children to engage in collaborative activities (Crook, 1992; Haugland & Wright, 1997; Weinstein, 1991).

Another concern is that children will access information that negates their family's values. Pornography, for example, is common in pop-up ads and junk e-mails. Individuals can easily connect to banks, businesses, government, stores, libraries, universities, people with certain interests, and so on. How does such access affect children? Most likely it will depend, like the influence of all the other media discussed, on the involvement of parents. Parents will have to help children develop critical thinking skills to evaluate the information and services accessible on the Internet. Parents can now, with certain software, block out parts of the Internet (pornography, for example) to which they don't want their children exposed. The problem with such software filters is that they block access to websites via certain banned words; thus, it may block "breast" links not only to pornography but also to cancer. Recently, the Federal Trade Commission (FTC) set privacy rules to protect children from data gathering by online marketers, requiring parental permission prior to obtaining information. Some states have laws banning sending spam to children. Parents can register their e-mail address to block inappropriate messages online.

As Postman (1992) eloquently argues in his book *Technopoly: The Surrender of Culture to Technology*, we must take charge of the technology that is running our lives and place it within the larger context of human goals and social values.

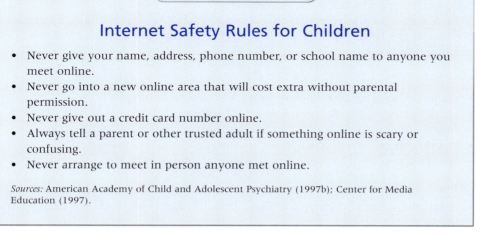

IN PRACTICE

Internet Safety Rules for Children

- Never give your name, address, phone number, or school name to anyone you meet online.
- Never go into a new online area that will cost extra without parental permission.
- Never give out a credit card number online.
- Always tell a parent or other trusted adult if something online is scary or confusing.
- Never arrange to meet in person anyone met online.

Sources: American Academy of Child and Adolescent Psychiatry (1997b); Center for Media Education (1997).

COMPUTERIZED VIDEO/CD GAMES

Playing video games at home on the TV screen or computer monitor is an alternative to watching television. Some games can be educational in that they reinforce certain skills, such as math, spelling, and reading, or require players to use certain strategies. "Video games are the first medium to combine visual dynamism with an active participatory role for the child" (Greenfield, 1984, p. 101). According to the Kaiser Family Foundation (2002), 92% of children and adolescents ages 2–17 play video games and, on average, spend 20–33 minutes doing so. It is estimated that 67% of households with children own a video game system (Subrahmanyam, Kraut, Greenfield, & Gross, 2001). Video games represent a fusion of media technology: television and computer. The major forces in the current entertainment video game market are Nintendo, Xbox, and Pokémon, although many other interactive systems are available, some in videotape format and others in compact disk format. Pokémon is an example of a multimedia phenomenon (Solomon, 1999). It ranked first in popularity among TV shows for children ages 2 to 11. It is also a video game, a card game, and a toy. The most popular categories of video games are fantasy violence, sports, general entertainment, human violence, and educational games (Cesarone, 1994).

The main concern with these popular interactive games is the prevalence of aggression, sex, and gender-role stereotyping, as well as their rule-bound logic designed by the programmers (Dietz, 1998; National Institute on Media and the Family, 2001; Provenzo, 1991). Congress recently called for an investigation by the Federal Trade Commission of games such as *Grand Theft Auto* for content inappropriate to their rating.

Males play video games more than females (Cesarone, 1994). TV producers and video game manufacturers may produce violent games for this audience. The demand for such aggressive games may arise from a need to have strong role models, rather than from male hormones.

Also of concern regarding electronic games, computers, and the Internet are the increasing opportunities for extension of real experiences to virtual ones. Multimedia technology enables children to interact with simulated characters, assume multiple identities, and chat with strangers who may also have simulated identities (Subrahmanyam et al., 2001). How do children shift from reality to simulation and back to reality, and what is the outcome?

In a review of the research on video game playing, the National Institute on Media and the Family (2001) summarized the positive and negative influences on children as follows:

Positive

- Games provide an introduction to information technology.
- Games can give practice in following directions.
- Some games provide practice in problem solving and logic.
- Games can provide practice in use of fine motor and spatial skills.
- Games can provide an opportunity for adult and child to play together.

Negative

- Practicing violent acts may contribute more to aggressive behavior than passive viewing of violence.
- Games are often based on plots of aggression, competition, and stereotyping.
- More often games do not present opportunities for independent thought or creativity.
- Games can confuse reality and fantasy.
- Academic achievement may be negatively related to overall time spent playing video or computer games.

Multimedia technology in cell phones enables users not only to communicate with other people but also to communicate with the Internet and play purchased games for entertainment. Future research is needed on the impact of mobile connections.

In sum, adults should become cognizant of available technology, software, and games. They should use video game ratings to determine developmental appropriateness for their child. They should also limit the time spent playing games, with homework and chores being done first. In addition, they should discuss the game content with the child, explaining discrepancies between reality and fantasy.

Epilogue

Media transmit cultural values, whether via oral tradition, pictures, print, sound, or computer. For example, Charlie Bucket learned the value of being truthful. Media users must cultivate critical thinking skills to evaluate how media messages compare to personal and family values. Adults must be involved in children's media use, just as adults were involved in socializing Charlie Bucket. Willy Wonka taught Charlie a lesson by bequeathing him the chocolate factory for being kind and caring.

Summary

Mass media discussed in this chapter include television, movies (including videos and DVDs), books, magazines, popular music, computers, video games, and multimedia.

Media are intervening means through which forces act or effects are produced. They are shapers, spreaders, and transformers of culture.

Chronosystem influences on the media are mainly related to new technology. Children's changing interests and abilities as they develop affect the media they select as well as the media's outcomes for the child (bidirectional effects).

Macrosystem influences on mass media include politics (laws), economics (corporate sponsors), and technology (medium and message). Whatever is broadcast on the airwaves in the United States must be in the public interest. The responsibility of determining what constitutes public interest rests with the broadcasters, who must find sponsors to make their programming cost effective. Some government regulations exist regarding children's television, which is monitored by the Federal Communication Commission, the agency that grants licenses to broadcasters. Recently, a rating system has been developed for TV programs.

Television in the United States is mostly perceived as a form of entertainment. Television's multisensory experience forces its audience to employ selective attention. Selective attention depends on one's frame of reference—one's psychological needs, attitudes, motives, habits, interests, values, morals, beliefs, and experiences. These mediating or intervening effects of selective attention make research on television's direct effects on children confusing. It is difficult to separate the content of a show from the viewing experience. Parental or older sibling involvement has also been shown to have a mediating effect.

Concerns regarding pictorial media include time spent watching TV and movies, changes in family life rituals, confusion between reality and fantasy, the effect on imagination, the prevalence of violence, the effect of advertising, the perpetuation of certain values (sexuality, stereotyping), the effect on reading and communication skills, and the effect on academic achievement.

Mesosystem influences on media include linkages with the community, school, and family.

The community's linkage to media (broadcast television) has been to develop alternatives, such as the Public Broadcasting System, cable and satellite television, video recorders, and computerized video games. Another response has been the formation of public interest groups to pressure broadcasters to change programming, to lobby the government for regulations, and to educate the public regarding the importance of monitoring its television-viewing habits, especially those of its children.

The school's linkage to media is to teach critical viewing skills as well as to use educational television programs in the classroom.

The family's linkage to the media is to mediate television viewing and help develop critical viewing skills by knowing the ratings, knowing what your children watch and when, choosing what to watch, setting limits, viewing with your children whenever possible, and using the time in front of the TV to benefit the child.

Print media (books and magazines) are more difficult to investigate experimentally than are pictorial media (television and movies). Unlike the pictorial media, where the visual image is provided, the print media describe in words the images of the writer. These words must then be translated into visual images by the reader. The visual image one is able to conjure up from printed words depends on one's vocabulary, one's reading ability, and one's real-life experiences. The print and pictorial media require different ways to process information.

It is difficult to compare the socializing effects of print and pictorial media because adults are more likely to mediate books than television. Until children gain a fair amount of reading skill, adults usually choose their books and read to them.

Reading is important for building knowledge. Reading aloud to children enables them to become successful readers. Reading aloud enhances personal attachment, which is a basic ingredient of socialization. It also improves listening skills, which are necessary for reading comprehension. And it provides a model for children to imitate.

Print plays a role in socialization in that it passes on culture to the next generation. It teaches history, values, morals, ideals, and attitudes.

Books also socialize children by influencing language and reading development, cognitive development, and psychosocial development. One of the criteria influencing the effect of books on a child's socialization is the developmental level, or cognitive stage, of the child.

Some concerns regarding the influence of print media on children revolve around certain themes and values perpetuated in comic books, juvenile series books, romances, westerns, mysteries, and magazines. Other concerns involve unrealistic life views, violence, consumerism, and stereotyping.

Popular music is a socializing influence in that it engages one's attention and emotions with the sound while espousing certain values with the lyrics. Whether children's values and behavior are influenced by the lyrics is open to question because other mediating factors, such as relationships and self-concept, are involved. Popular music provides many adolescents with a means of identifying with a particular group or performer. Such identification may affect dress, behavior, friends, and self-concept.

Interactive and multimedia—computers, video games, and cell phones—have provoked many questions regarding their socializing effects. Their use in the classroom to assist instruction generally expands the nature of learning, but the effects of their use at home are under debate. Current concerns focus on diminished social interaction; reduced time spent on other activities; aggressive, sexual, and stereotypical games; the prevalence of rule-bound logic at the expense of creative thought; the confusion of reality with fantasy; and access to information without the necessary critical skills, as well as to information negating family values.

Activity

PURPOSE To increase your awareness of television's impact.

1. Monitor a child's (or your own) television viewing behavior for a week, using the chart that follows as a model.

2. Note the total viewing hours for the week.

3. Keep track of the time spent in other leisure activities for a week.

4. Analyze your findings to determine what types of shows are viewed and the potential impact of their content and commercial messages on viewers.

DATE, DAY, TIME	NAME AND TYPE* OF SHOW	DESCRIPTION OF ACTION (CONFLICTS/ COOPERATION)	DESCRIPTION OF ROLE PORTRAYAL (ETHNIC, GENDER, OR OCCUPATION)	NUMBER AND KIND† OF ADVERTISEMENTS

* Comedy, sports, news, drama, cartoon, musical, mystery, and so on.
† Food, toy, beverage, medicine, public service, and so on.

Related Readings

Bryant, J., & Bryant, A. J. (Eds.). (2001). *Television and the American family* (2nd ed.). Mahwah, NJ: Lawrence Erlbaum.

Cantor, J. (1998). *"Mommy, I'm scared": How TV and movies frighten children and what we can do to protect them*. San Diego: Harcourt Brace.

Carlsen, G. R. (1980). *Books and the teenage reader*. New York: Harper & Row.

Cashdan, S. (1999). *The witch must die: How fairy tales shape our lives*. New York: Basic Books.

Cassell, J., & Jenkins, H. (Eds.). (1999). *From* Barbie *to* Mortal Kombat: *Gender and computer games*. Cambridge, MA: MIT Press.

Chang, J. (2005). *Can't stop won't stop: A history of the hip-hop generation*. New York: St. Martin's Press.

Comstock, G., & Scharrer, E. (1999). *Television: What's on, who's watching, and what it means*. San Diego: Academic Press.

Haugland, S. W., & Wright, J. L. (1997). *Young children and technology: A world of discovery*. Needham Heights, MA: Allyn and Bacon.

Healy, J. (1998). *Failure to connect: How computers affect our children's minds—for better and worse*. New York: Touchstone Books.

Levin, D. E. (1998). *Remote control childhood? Combating the hazards of media culture*. Washington, DC: National Association for Education of Young Children.

Levine, M. (1996). *Viewing violence: How media violence affects your child's and adolescent's development*. New York: Doubleday.

Lull, J. (Ed.). (1987). *Popular music and communication*. Newbury Park, CA: Sage.

Norton, D. E., & Norton, S.E. (2002). *Through the eyes of a child: An introduction to children's literature* (6th ed.). Upper Saddle River, NJ: Prentice-Hall.

Perse, E. M. (2001). *Media effects and society*. Mahwah, NJ: Lawrence Erlbaum.

Postman, N. (1992). *Technopoly: The surrender of culture to technology*. New York: Vintage Books.

Provenzo, E. F., Jr. (1991). *Video kids: Making sense of Nintendo*. Cambridge, MA: Harvard University Press.

Ravitch, D., & Vitterriti, J. P. (Eds.). (2003). *Kid stuff: Marketing sex and violence to America's children*. Baltimore: Johns Hopkins University Press.

Roberts, D. F., & Foehr, U. G. (2004). *Kids and media in America*. New York: Cambridge University Press.

Spitz, E. H. (1999). *Inside picture books*. New Haven, CT: Yale University Press.

Trelease, J. (2001). *The read-aloud handbook* (5th ed.). New York: Viking.

Chapter 10

FoodPix/Jupiterimages

Ecology of the Community

No man is wise enough by himself.

— TITUS MACCIUS PLAUTUS

How did communities evolve?

The following Russian folktale, *The Clever Judge* (Deutsch, 1952), provides an example of how a community oversees the rights and obligations of its citizens. The people in the story lived on vast plains raising animals to sell for food and clothing. Business was conducted in the villages.

Once Upon a Time A long time ago, in the prairies of southwestern Asia known as the "steppes," lived a man who was famous for his justice and wisdom. At that time, if a man had a reputation of being fair, people came from far and wide to ask him to settle their disputes. And so one day, two villagers appeared before this wise man and asked him to resolve their quarrel.

"Tell me your story," the judge said to the plaintiff.

"I had to leave my village," said the plaintiff, "for I had business elsewhere. And all my wealth was a hundred gold coins. I did not come by them easily. I had to work hard for them and I did not want them to be stolen while I was away. Nor did I care to carry so much money with me on my journey. So, I entrusted these gold coins for safekeeping to this man here. When I got back from my journey, he denied that he had ever received the money from me."

"And who saw you give these hundred gold coins?" asked the judge.

"No one saw it. We went together to the heart of the forest and there I handed him the coins."

"What have you to say to this?" the judge asked, turning to the defendant.

The defendant shrugged his shoulders.

"I don't know what he is talking about," said the man. "I never went to the forest with him. I never saw his gold coins."

"Do you remember the place where you handed over the money?" the judge asked the plaintiff.

"Of course; it was under a tall oak tree. I remember it well. I can point it out for you."

So you do have a witness, after all, said the judge. "Here, take my signet ring, go to the tall tree under which you stood when you handed over the money. Set the seal of my signet ring against the trunk, and bid the tree appear before me to bear out the truth of your story."

The plaintiff went off to carry out the judge's demand while the defendant remained behind to wait for his return.

After some time had passed, the judge turned to the defendant and asked, "Do you think he has reached the oak by now?"

"No, not yet," was the reply.

After more time had gone by, the judge asked again, "Do you think he has reached the tree by now?"

"Yes," was the answer; "by this time he must have reached it."

Not long thereafter, the plaintiff returned. "I did as you said; I walked into the forest until I came to the tall oak tree under which I stood when I handed over my gold coins to this man for safekeeping. I then set the seal of your signet ring against the trunk and bade the tree to appear before you as a witness, but the tree did not reply and did not budge."

"Never mind," said the judge. "The oak has appeared before me and it has borne witness in your favor."

At that the defendant exclaimed, "How can you say such a thing! I have been here all this while and no tree has stalked into this place."

"But," replied the judge, "you said that you had not been in the forest at all. And yet when I asked you whether the plaintiff had reached the oak, first you answered, 'Not yet.' Then, when I asked you a second time, you said, 'By now, he must surely have reached it.' Therefore, you had to have been in the forest to remember where the oak tree stood in order to know how long it took to get to it. You were there to receive the plaintiff's gold coins, which he entrusted to you for safekeeping. Now, you must not only return to him the hundred gold pieces, but you must also pay a fine for having tried to cheat him."

And so the tree was a witness without budging, and justice was done.

A community is a group of people who share something in common. The commonality of the people in the story was their livelihood. They herded cattle, sheep, and goats for a living. They relied on each other for help when in need and turned to a respected leader for judgment when disagreements arose. A community is created because no individual is self-sufficing. As John Donne (1572–1631) wrote, "No man is an island entire of itself; every man is a piece of continent; a part of the main." For the parts of the community to work, rules, or common policies, for group behavior and consequences for deviations must be established. Common social rules regarding safety, theft, and truth-telling are examples of how the community protects its citizens. This chapter will explore what communities do for individuals and what individuals do for communities.

- **Does the individual shape the community, or does the community shape the individual?**

- **How can we know what rules are fair to all, and who is qualified to decide?**

Community: Structure and Functions

What constitutes a "community," and what does it do?

The word *community* derives from the Latin *communis*, which means "shared." The concept of sharing can refer to space, norms, values, customs, beliefs, rules, or obligations. The spatial aspect of community may be small and nearby, as when one refers to one's neighborhood; or it may be large and far-reaching, as when one

Figure 10.1

An Ecological Model of Human Development

The community in which the child grows up is a significant influence on his or her development.

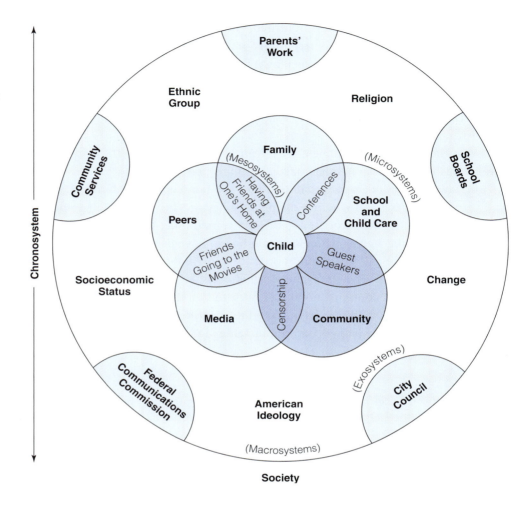

community ecology
the psychological and practical relationships between humans and their social, as well as physical, environment

refers to one's country or to society in general. Thus, a *community*, as introduced in Chapter 2, is a group of people living in the same geographic area (neighborhood, town, or city) under common laws; it is also a group of people sharing fellowship, a friendly association, and common interests. **Community ecology** comprises the psychological and practical relationships between people and their social, as well as physical, environment. Thus, the crucial component of a community is the relationship of people to one another and the sense of belonging and of obligation to the group.

The community is a microsystem in which much socialization and development take place. It also represents an expansion of family and friendship ties, commonly described as a "sense of community." The sense of community was graphically exhibited in New York when the twin towers of the World Trade Center and the people within and around them were horrifically destroyed. My cousin was one of those who perished. While people were crazed with shock, they did not hesitate to help one another. Strangers risked their lives to try to save those who were buried in the rubble. Doctors, firefighters, and police donated their time. People from all over the country came to look for bodies so that families could identify their loved ones. Others came to clean up the debris. And even after the last embers died out and the foul air left the city, people stayed connected. This terrible tragedy was felt all around the globe. It made people realize the importance of community—that people need people to survive.

The sense of community was again challenged when Hurricane Katrina hit New Orleans and other areas of the Gulf Coast. People from all over the country came to assist those who were stranded without shelter or food. The American Red Cross coordinated a fundraising drive with the help of technology. Internet websites donated space for Red Cross ads, as did TV and radio stations and bank ATMs. Donations poured in.

Will this profound sense of community persist, or will it dissipate through time or succumb to feelings of helplessness? Before these disasters, reviews of the research (Schorr, 1997) concluded that community ties had eroded almost everywhere, for several reasons:

- Fear of violence deters people from gathering informally in public spaces.
- Advances in transportation and communication enable people to move far from family, friends, and neighbors in order to work.
- Technological advances make it less necessary to leave home for entertainment.
- The larger scale of most institutions and businesses makes it harder to connect with others.

The need for community is both psychological and practical, or economic. *Psychologically*, humans need companionship and the emotional security that comes from belonging to a social group whose members share the same ideas and patterns of behavior. *Practically*, humans need to cooperate with others in order to share in the necessities of life—food, shelter, and security. Therefore, a community is structured to have five functions (Warren, 1983):

1. **Production, distribution, consumption**. The community provides its members with the means to make a living. This may be agriculture, industry, or services.
2. **Socialization**. The community has means by which it instills its norms and values in its members. This may be tradition, modeling, and/or formal education.
3. **Social control**. The community has the means to enforce adherence to community values. This may be group pressure to conform and/or formal laws.
4. **Social participation**. The community fulfills the need for companionship. This may occur in a neighborhood, church, business, or other group.
5. **Mutual support**. The community enables its members to cooperate to accomplish tasks too large or too urgent to be handled by a single person. Supporting a community hospital with tax dollars and donations is an example of people cooperating to accomplish the task of health care.

Communities, small or large, perform these functions in many different ways. The ways in which a particular community performs these functions influence the socialization of children growing up there. We will examine how different factors—physical, economic, social, and personal—characterizing a community might influence socialization.

The Community's Influence on Socialization

How did the neighborhood(s) in which you grew help shape you?

How Did You Get to Know Your Neighbors?

When I was growing up, the kids played in the street. Houses faced each other in rows, and the street was the commons. We played stickball, hopscotch, jump rope, and hide-and-seek. We biked and roller-skated in the street. The only traffic was from the residents, who knew to watch out for the children. We knew who our neighbors were because at dinnertime, one or another's mother would open the front door and call. If someone got hurt, we would have to knock on that person's door to get adult help.

When I was married and living in the university housing development, the apartments faced each other in attached rows along a long sidewalk. The children would play there and on play equipment at the end of the walkway. Several times a year, someone would organize a potluck supper for the block, so everyone could meet each other and welcome newcomers.

When I started a family, we lived in a suburb where the homes were on large lots. It was in the Midwest where it was cold in the winter and hot in the summer. People did not "hang out" outside. My son took the school bus to school and played with the neighbor kids in someone's backyard. For the first time in my life, I felt isolated in my neighborhood.

When my second child was born and my husband got another job, we moved. We chose a neighborhood where the houses faced each other and the street ended in a cul-de-sac. The kids played in the street, easily supervised by any adult looking out the window of their home. Potlucks were regular holiday events, set up in the street or at the neighborhood pool. Neighbors worked together on school and community issues. They helped when someone was ill or had serious problems.

Looking back at the neighborhoods in which I lived, I realize that what mattered most was the relationship with neighbors, not the house or the socioeconomic status of the community. What was your experience?

The neighborhood or neighborhoods (nearby geographic areas) in which we grew up conjure up rich imagery of what constitutes a sense of community. We may picture a small town with a mini-mall consisting of several stores, the gas station, and the movie theater; the outlying streets with a church or two, the school, and homes separated by bushes or fences. We may picture apartment houses grouped closely together on the street, with the bus stop on the corner and the park and school several blocks away. We may picture acres of farmland and the town, miles away, with a large mall that we visited only once a week. We may picture a large housing tract with lawns, cars, bicycles, and no sidewalks.

Part of the imagery of the neighborhood in which we grew up involves the people who lived there. How did they earn a living? We may picture farmers, shopkeepers, laborers working in factories or mines, or people rushing to and from work dressed in business suits.

How did the people in our community instill in us their norms and values? We may visualize the schools we attended or the clubs we belonged to. We may remember some community traditions like the Fourth of July picnic when everyone brought food to share, or the annual school music festival when every class had certain songs to sing, or we may remember the razzing from the boys on the street when we wore our new shoes.

How did our community enforce its rules? We may picture everyone watching over everyone else and knowing that if we did something wrong, Mrs. Nader would be sure to tell Mother. We may picture the police officer on the corner or the sheriff's car patrolling the streets. We may picture the neighborhood bully beating up someone for being a "rat fink."

How did the people in our neighborhood community socialize with one another? We may visualize our mothers gathered in someone's kitchen or on the street in front of someone's house, a group of men entering a bar after work, a group of adults dancing in the church social hall. Or we may remember our homes filled with company on various occasions.

How did the people in our neighborhood community help one another? We may recall the flurry of activity after the Masons' house burned down. Everyone contributed clothing, food, or household items. We may think of the Garcias' house after their 2-year-old was killed by a car—people crowded inside, talking quietly and crying. We may picture the hospital room where our father spent several weeks—filled with plants, flowers, and cards from friends. We may picture the waiting room of a medical clinic and the cries of sick children, or people waiting in line to fill out forms at a government office.

The community is a socializing agent because it is where children learn the role expectations for adults as well as for themselves. It is in the community that children get to observe, model, and become apprentices to adults; it is in the community that children get to "try themselves out." Socialization requires active involvement:

> For the things we have to learn before we can do them, we learn by doing them. We become just by doing just acts, temperate by doing temperate acts, brave by doing brave acts . . . states of character are formed by doing the corresponding acts. (Aristotle, *Methaphysics*, Book 1, Ch. 1)

According to a survey of leaders from 90 cities and towns across the United States by the National League of Cities (Meyers & Kyle, 1998), there are five main characteristics that make a community "family-friendly": education (quality academic programs and safe schools); recreation (facilities and opportunities); community safety; citizen involvement; and physical environment (clean, safe, attractive, well cared for). Other important factors are employment opportunities (good jobs, economic growth) and neighborhood quality (housing affordability, good government, cultural opportunities, specific supports for children and families).

PHYSICAL FACTORS

What physical characteristics of the community affect how people behave?

Research has shown that certain characteristics of the physical environment of the community influence behavior (Bell, Greene, Fisher, & Baum, 2001). These are population density and characteristics, noise, arrangement and types of houses, and play settings.

Population Density and Characteristics

Population density refers to the number of people occupying a certain area of space. High population density can have positive effects on social relationships in that

The community in which the child grows up is a significant influence on his or her development.

ThinkStock LLC/Index Stock Imagery

people have many opportunities to mingle, provided there are spaces (places to sit or play) to do so (Etzioni, 1993).

High population density can also have negative effects, such as excessive social contact, reduced behavioral freedom, scarcity of resources, personal space violations, and inability to maintain desired privacy (Bell et al., 2001). People who report excessive, unwanted social interactions and insufficient privacy have been observed to withdraw socially. The consequence of social withdrawal is a breakdown in socially supportive relationships (Evans, Palsane, Lepore, & Martin, 1989).

Studies (Bell et al., 2001; Rodin, 1976) have demonstrated a relationship between residential density and susceptibility to learned helplessness. *Learned helplessness*, introduced in Chapter 7 and discussed further in Chapter 11, is a sense of apathy that develops when people perceive that they have no control over events, that their actions no longer influence outcomes. (Did you ever get low grades no matter how hard you studied in a class and, consequently, didn't put forth your best effort on the final because you figured "What's the point?") Rodin (1976) found that children who lived in high-density areas were less likely than those in low-density areas to try to control the amount of rewards they would get if they performed certain tasks. She also found that when initially given a frustrating task that was not related to getting rewards, the children who lived in high-density areas did worse on a later task that was related to getting rewards than those who lived in low-density areas.

Density thus appears to influence learned helplessness. The density of an environment tends to affect people's perception of control over that environment—the higher the density, the less control one feels one has. For example, fires, floods, earthquakes, hurricanes, and tornadoes are much more damaging in high-density than in low-density environments. In addition, they serve as reminders of how vulnerable one is to natural forces one cannot control, no matter how technologically advanced society becomes. When people continually experience loss of control, which apparently occurs more often in high-density areas, they are likely to lose the motivation to act; they become helpless.

Additionally, communities characterized by high density tend to be associated with more violence and higher crime rates than low-density communities (Limber & Nation, 1998). For example, Sampson (1983) found that rates of victimization were three times greater in high-density than low-density neighborhoods, even after holding other demographic variables constant. The study also found a relationship between multi-family housing units and crime rates. This continual exposure to violence and crime most likely contributes to feelings of helplessness.

The rate of population turnover in a neighborhood influences the interactions with newcomers, as well as the degree of community involvement (Bell et al., 2001; Garbarino, 1992). The degree of transience in a neighborhood affects both those who remain and those who move. When people do not plan to remain in a neighborhood more than a few years, they tend not to get involved in community activities. Those who do remain in the neighborhood make fewer efforts to establish close personal ties with newcomers whom they expect to depart.

Neighborhoods differ in the extent to which they include people of differing ages, income levels, religions, ethnicities, and educational backgrounds (Garbarino, 1992). *Homogeneous* neighborhoods include people of similar backgrounds; *heterogeneous* neighborhoods include people of differing backgrounds.

Children who grow up in homogeneous neighborhoods—for example, many suburban neighborhoods—have few opportunities to interact with children or adults who differ in their backgrounds and values. Children whose neighborhoods are accessible to a larger town only by car have little opportunity even to observe the work world of adults. Children who grow up in heterogeneous neighborhoods—for example, some urban neighborhoods—are more likely to have opportunities to interact with children of differing backgrounds at school or on the playground. Because stores and businesses are more accessible, children have more opportunities to interact with adults in their work roles.

Noise

Noise is "unwanted sound" (Bell et al., 2001). High levels can lead to hearing loss, increases in arousal levels, and stress. It can interfere with attention.

Cohen, Glass, and Singer (1973) studied children living in a large high-rise apartment complex situated over a noisy highway in New York City. They found that exposure to noise was more severe on the lower floors of the complex than on the upper floors. When the researchers controlled for other factors, such as social class and air pollution, they found that the children on the noisier lower floors had poorer hearing discrimination than the children on the upper floors. Moreover, the hearing problems of children on the lower floors may have influenced their poorer reading performance in school.

A study conducted by the California Department of Health Services linked freeway noise to poorer school test scores (Savage, 1983). The study compared third- and sixth-graders in two comparable sets of nine schools, one set located near freeways and the other farther away. The children in the noisy schools generally did less well academically in reading and mathematics than their counterparts in quieter schools. One sixth-grader said, "We can't hear the teacher, and she gets mad because we don't hear what she says." Another child said, "You can't concentrate when the trucks are passing." Noise interferes with verbal communication and may affect productivity (Bell et al., 2001).

Another study (Evans, Hygges, & Bullinger, 1993) found that third- and fourth-grade children who lived near the Munich International Airport and were chronically exposed to airport noise had higher stress levels (measured by blood pressure, heart rate, and blood levels of stress hormones) when performing cognitive tasks than did children who lived in quieter neighborhoods.

In sum, the effect of noise on performance depends on the type of noise, the complexity of the task, and individual factors such as personality and adaptation level (Bell et al., 2001).

Arrangement and Types of Houses

The way houses and streets are arranged affects the interactions among people living in a neighborhood (Bell et al., 2001; Garbarino, 1992). When houses face the street or a courtyard, people have a common place of contact. Children living in such a setting usually play on the court or sidewalk or in the street, provided there is not much traffic. This direct access to the outside maximizes the potential for parental supervision (Taishido Study Group, 1984/1985). In other words, children can be watched from inside simply by looking out. On the other hand, houses that have no common area, such as apartments, minimize the potential for parental supervision. When children in such houses leave to play, their actions cannot be supervised unless the children are accompanied by a parent or other adult.

Play Settings

Play settings influence socialization by the types of activities that occur in them and by whether or not adults are present to supervise. Some neighborhoods provide playgrounds for children, and the type of equipment available appears to affect their use (Rivkin, 1995). A study (Hayward, Rothenberg, & Beasley, 1974) comparing different playground settings (traditional, modern, adventure) found that the availability of play materials clearly influenced the play activity. The *traditional* playground setting had swings, a slide, a teeter-totter, and a sandbox. The *modern* playground had various sculptures on which children could climb, crawl, and slide. The *adventure* playground had old lumber, tires, crates, bricks, and rocks.

Children were interviewed and observed in each of the settings. Preschool children, often accompanied by adults, used the traditional and modern playground more often; school-age children and teenagers used the adventure playground more often. The children in the traditional and modern playgrounds were involved in using the equipment, whereas children in the adventure playground were involved in expressing ideas and fantasies.

ECONOMIC FACTORS

How do economic characteristics of the community affect people's lives?

Economic factors in a community play a central role in shaping the daily lives of families who live and work there. Local economic systems vary depending on the jobs, goods, and services provided by the business sector of the community. When a local plant closes, the employees are forced to find work elsewhere, often at lower wages. Often they have to bridge the income gap by working more hours. Thus, wage earners have fewer hours to spend with their families.

Community economics have affected the costs of housing, transportation, education, and health care, all of which have risen steadily since the 1970s and today consume substantially more of a typical family's income than they did then. In recent decades, the average working family's tax burden has also risen.

To accommodate family lifestyle to economic changes in the community, more than two-thirds of mothers with young children are working in the labor force

(U.S. Bureau of the Census, 2003). When mothers work, adjustments have to be made in the workplace and in communities. As will be discussed later, the main adjustments involve businesses becoming more responsive to families and, as was discussed in Chapter 5, communities providing quality child care.

Children's economic well-being is directly related to that of their families. When families have an adequate income, they are better able to meet their children's material, intellectual, and emotional needs and help them become healthy, productive adults. Yet today, children, especially those in single-parent families, are the poorest Americans (Children's Defense Fund [CDF], 2004; McLoyd, 1998). Failure to address the economic needs of families, especially the threat of poverty, leads to social consequences affecting individuals, families, and the whole community. Examples of such ills are more crime and delinquency, more substance abuse, more school failure, more child abuse and neglect, more teenage childbearing, more unhealthy children, and lower productivity by tomorrow's labor force. These problems impose enormous costs on the community, including expenditures for treatment of illnesses and chronic health conditions, special education, foster care, prisons, and welfare (CDF, 2004; Evans & English, 2002). Social problems related to poverty and their costs are discussed in more detail later.

Community economics, specifically unemployment, is related to how children in families are socialized. There is evidence that economic hardship threatens the psychological well-being of parents and undermines their capacity for supportive child rearing. When parents have difficulty coping financially and share their problems with their children, children experience increased psychological distress (McLoyd, 1998; McLoyd & Wilson, 1990).

Many inner-city neighborhoods are plagued by the highest level of joblessness since the Depression (Wilson, 1995). Unemployment, as experienced in different neighborhood settings, has different connotations and hence effects on children. A jobless family that lives in an area of relatively low unemployment and poverty differs from a jobless family that lives in a predominately poor neighborhood. Neighborhoods plagued with high levels of joblessness tend to have high levels of crime, gang violence, and drug trafficking. The decline of legitimate employment opportunities increases the incentive to sell drugs (Fagan, 1993). Children see drug dealers with cars, fancy clothes, and money, things they don't see at home. They also have trouble connecting education with postschool employment because most of the adults in their community don't work in spite of having gone to school (Wilson, 1995).

Surprisingly, the effect of unemployment on children has not always been negative. A classic longitudinal study by Glen Elder (1974), discussed in Chapter 1, found that adolescents whose fathers lost their jobs had to assume certain responsibilities in the family to keep it functioning. This contribution to family welfare enabled the adolescents to adjust successfully to adult life. They did well in school, were satisfied with their marriages, and had successful careers. However, such positive outcomes were not true of children under age 14 whose fathers lost their jobs. They were resentful, lost respect for their fathers, and did not

Much interaction with a variety of people is possible in this highly populated neighborhood; however, some people may experience a feeling of being crowded.

Hoa Qui/Index Stock Imagery

generally adjust well to adult life. They were vulnerable to impaired development because at the time economic crisis hit their families, they were most dependent and in need of a role model.

The different findings in present studies and those of the Depression may be due to the type of supportive relationships the child or adolescent had with relatives and nonrelatives during the earlier period of widespread economic hardship (Coleman, 1990). These social supports included common values of neighborhood residents to maintain effective social control (supervise children's activities, monitor children's behavior, and motivate children to be productive).

SOCIAL AND PERSONAL FACTORS

What perceived social and personal characteristics of the community affect people's relationships?

In addition to the physical and economic characteristics of a community, certain other factors, less tangible and more individualistic, influence socialization. These factors include the neighborhood setting and the patterns of community interaction.

The Neighborhood Setting

The neighborhood, referring to people and places nearby, is the geographic setting in which children generally spend their unstructured time (Garbarino, 1992). The neighborhood is where children explore, interact with other children, observe adults engaged in work or other activities, and have various experiences themselves.

Neighborhood settings differ not only in the physical environments (streets, parks, facilities) available for children, but also in the social environments (who is available to interact with whom). Since children are minimally mobile, they play close to home and interact with those who live close by. Medrich and his colleagues (Medrich, Roizen, Rukin, & Buckley, 1981) studied how children in different neighborhoods spent their time after school. Five neighborhoods (their names were changed for publication) exemplify how different settings affect children's daily experiences and hence their socialization. Were any of these similar to neighborhoods you grew up in?

Mountainside

Mountainside has no sidewalks, and its streets are hilly. The houses are set back from the road, and you get a feeling of isolation. The shops, library, school, park, and recreation center are clustered in "the village" at the base of the hill, several miles from most of the houses. Children spend most of their free time close to home because it's not easy to get around in this neighborhood—the hills are too steep for bicycles. They play baseball and soccer in diamonds they have painted on the streets. They build tree houses and rope swings and share them with other neighborhood children. The children interact with few adults other than their parents, and that doesn't seem to bother them. They have to rely on their parents to drive them to lessons or recreational facilities.

Rosewood

Rosewood is a neighborhood with sidewalks and connecting streets on which the children ride their bicycles and play softball. There are few boundaries between the houses. The neighborhood is centered on the school. Anyone can get there within a seven-minute walk, and many children use the playground as a meeting place. Rosewood is heterogeneous in character and dense with children. The majority of children are European American, but a large proportion are African American. Friends are chosen on the basis of similarities in age and race.

Bancroft

Bancroft is a neighborhood with no sidewalks or street lamps. The roads are narrow and patched with asphalt. Most houses cannot be seen from the street. Yards are separated by fences. In Bancroft both parents are apt to work, and children are frequently left on their own when not at school; children are expected to stay close to home after school so parents know where they are. Children's time is often spent in the company of brothers and sisters. Children rarely leave their block except to go to school, run an errand, or keep an appointment. This may be because the school and park both front on streets heavy with traffic.

Glenn

Glenn begins where the trucking companies and shipping warehouses along a freeway exit end. The houses look like fortresses. There are a lot of apartments. Neighbors sit on banisters, and children hang around the streets. Although buses and large trucks run through continually, there are no stop signs. Shops and churches are located mostly in one area; all have locked gates because vandalism rates are high. There is a park with a recreation center that many people frequent. Glenn is a neighborhood with strong ethnic ties—most families are African American, a lot are Hispanic, and few are European American. Friendships seem to be formed along ethnic lines, and tightly knit adolescent gangs are common.

Eastside

Eastside is a neighborhood with stark streets and debris collecting at the curbs. Yards are fenced, and most lack trees. Despite its physical appearance, the neighborhood is vibrant with street life. Many Eastside families migrated from the South and talk with one another about relatives back there or recent visits. The children congregate on the street. Many go to the community center, where they are eligible for free lunch. Friendships are formed easily according to whoever is nearby. Not only are peers considered to be friends to children, but so are neighbors and shopkeepers. Children have a lot of comfortable relations with different adults. The schoolyard can be reached in five minutes, and children often gather there to play. Age doesn't seem to matter regarding playmates, but skills count. It is not uncommon to find a broad age range of children getting together to play ball.

These examples illustrate how the neighborhood setting affects children's mobility, exposure to adults, friendship patterns, and types of play (Berg & Medrich, 1980; Medrich et al., 1981).

Patterns of Community Interaction

Community interaction is an important factor in development because, according to Bronfenbrenner (1979, 1989), the developmental potential of a setting—in this case, the community—is enhanced as a function of the number of its supportive links with other settings the child might be in, such as the family or school. Patterns of interaction vary considerably with the size of a community. In a small town, one person may interact directly with almost every other person in a given week or month. In contrast, a resident of a large city might conceivably roam the streets without ever seeing a familiar face.

The social density, or the degree to which an environment contains a diversity of roles and experiences for children to learn from and for parents to draw upon, affects families and children. A dense setting contains a variety of businesspeople as

The designs of some neighborhoods foster interpersonal interaction.

Carl and Ann Purcell/Index Stock Imagery

well as a variety of ages and ethnic groups. Such a setting provides many opportunities for children to learn what community relations are all about. Such a setting also affords families a choice of social networks on which they can rely for support (Garbarino, 1992; Hareven, 1989).

Interaction in a small town involves close contact with relatives, friends, and acquaintances. Because of this, people in a small community tend to be involved in each other's lives—their marriages, their children, their illnesses, and their employment are subjects of discussion, concern, and gossip. Interaction in a large city, on the other hand, involves less personal contact, but more impersonal interactions. For example, interactions with co-workers, bankers, clerks, and bus drivers may occur daily, but only in the context of the specific roles they perform. For personal interactions, residents of large cities must rely on immediate family members and voluntary associations (church, PTA, lodge, club).

The norms of a small town are more homogeneous than those of a large city, and are also more widely understood and accepted (Garbarino, 1992). Because of this consensus, socialization of children tends to proceed more smoothly in a small town than in a large city. In a small town, shared convictions about what is right or wrong, proper or improper, tend to be passed on from generation to generation and become institutionalized. In other words, the unwritten local customs become the common law. The community, then, becomes the medium through which the basic values, norms, and customs of society are interpreted and reinforced through repeated interaction of community members.

As an example of an institutionalized *value* mediated by the community, "Honor thy father and mother" may mean that community members ask children if their parents know where they are before inviting them into their homes. An example of a *norm* mediated by the community might be the appropriate ways of dressing—it may not be appropriate to wear shorts certain places in town. An example of a *custom* mediated by the community might be how people greet one another—"Hello, how are you?" or "Hi, y'all, what's happening?" or shaking hands or bowing.

Table 10.1

*Basic Social
Relationships*

GEMEINSCHAFT	GESELLSCHAFT
Mutually dependent	Independent
Caring	Contractual
Informal	Formal
Intimate	Associative
Trusting	Mistrusting
Kin	Employers/managers
Friends	Employees
Neighbors	Business associates
Special-interest groups	Achievement objectives
Collectively oriented	Individually oriented

Unlike a small town, a large city brings together people from a wide variety of ethnic, religious, regional, educational, and occupational groups, all of whom are products of their own socialization. The majority of the population may have similar values, but their norms and ways have not been institutionalized. Therefore, large cities must rely more on formal rules and regulations than on informal methods for influencing behavior. For example, in a small town it is highly unlikely that you would play your stereo loudly at 11 P.M. Your behavior is regulated by courtesy to your neighbor. In a large city, however, where neighbors often do not know each other, behavior might have to be regulated by rules restricting noise to certain hours.

Mechanisms of social control differ in small towns and large cities. In a small town, residents know they are under constant surveillance and that any misconduct will become a matter of community concern. Social control is achieved through fear of social rejection and gossip. In large cities, the police and courts are more often relied upon to provide social control through formal sanctions.

Industrialization and urban growth have been accompanied by increasingly impersonal forms of interaction, according to Ferdinand Tonnies (1957/1987). His book *Gemeinschaft und Gesellschaft*, considered to be a classic, defines two basic types of social relationships. *Gemeinschaft* relationships are mutually dependent and caring. People relate to each other because they are kin, because they live in a particular locality, or because they are likeminded and wish to pursue a common goal. **Gemeinschaft** interpersonal relationships are communal, cooperative, close, intimate, and informal. There is mutual trust and concern, as well as willing cooperation. *Gesellschaft* relationships, on the other hand, are independent and contractual. People relate to each other because it is a practical way of achieving an objective, like paying for services rendered. **Gesellschaft** interpersonal relationships are associative, practical, objective, and formal. They are characterized by individualism and mutual distrust. Typically, interactions are for a particular purpose. Children who primarily experience gemeinschaft relationships have socialization experiences that are very different from those of children who primarily experience gesellschaft relationships (see Table 10.1).

The decline of contemporary morality has been blamed on too much gesellschaft, or individualism, in communities and not enough gemeinschaft, or communalism (Etzioni, 1993; Hayes & Lipset, 1993/1994). Those who favor communalism do so

gemeinschaft communal, cooperative, close, intimate, and informal interpersonal relationships

gesellschaft associative, practical, objective, and formal interpersonal relationships

because they believe the norms of responsibility common to gemeinschaft communities should be emphasized to counterbalance the selfishness of individualism. Those who favor individualism do so because it is embedded in the American culture and because they believe that Americans should use the tools with which their individualistic culture provides them (efficiency, specificity, and practicality, for example) to fix the social problems, such as crime and substance abuse, common in gesellschaft communities. What kind of social relationships did you primarily have in the community or culture in which you grew up, and how did they influence you?

The Community as a Learning Environment

How can the community contribute to people's learning experiences?

The community is a setting that provides much potential for learning (Decker & Decker, 2001). Libraries, museums, zoos, farms, businesses, people's experiences, and collectibles (family heirlooms, antiques, photographs, and so on) are all rich sources for involving children (Hatcher & Beck, 1997).

To illustrate the community's potential for learning, an experiment was initiated in Philadelphia to try a "school without walls" (Brenner & Von Moschzisker, 1971). Students in grades 9–12 were chosen by lottery from eight school districts; neither economic nor academic background was a factor. There was no school building; each of the eight areas had a headquarters with office space for staff and lockers for students. All teaching took place within the community. Art was studied at the art museum; biology was studied at the zoo; vocational education took place at various business locations. A higher than average percentage of students who attended went on to college.

Many school districts have *alternative schools* that follow this model. The philosophy of alternative education is that "the child, like the adult, learns the art and technique of citizenship, not through admonitions or through lectures on civics, but from involvement in real issues" (Hatcher & Beck, 1997; Ward, 1978, p. 184). Some high schools and colleges have combined work–study programs, in which students can apply theoretical knowledge learned in school to practical experience at work. Existing schools can find many ways of using the community as an educational resource—inviting guest speakers to class, going on field trips, and working on a community project (such as planting trees, participating in a parade, or raising money for individuals in need).

Today, many high schools around the country require students to perform community service in order to graduate. The National and Community Service Act, passed in 1990, gives grants to schools to develop and implement student involvement projects (Levine & Levine, 1996). Projects can include environmental conservation, hospitals, child-care facilities, law enforcement, and social service agencies, to name a few.

Part of the National School Goals 2000, reform strategies discussed in Chapter 6, is the commitment of communities to learning. The business community can facilitate child socialization by fostering school and related educational work or recreational projects in several ways. Members of the business community can provide specific schools with materials, financial aid, human resources, and professional support. (Some communities refer to such a project as "Adopt-a-School.") They can serve on school advisory councils or on school boards. They can offer schools the use of business settings for job placement or offer field sites for work experience programs. A specific example of a cooperative business–school venture to facilitate child socialization is one operated by the Boston Private Industry Council Partnerships. John Hancock, an insurance company, collaborates with various schools in Boston to motivate disadvantaged minority children toward academic and career achievement. Classes of 11th and 12th graders are transported twice a week to the company, where they learn business skills to give them a head start for permanent positions at John Hancock or another company. In addition, employees at the company volunteer at the schools, and the company sponsors workshops for parents on "partnering" as well as for students to find summer jobs.

In conclusion, the community becomes a place and a resource for learning when citizens (parents, educators, businesspeople, religious groups, service providers, legislators) are committed to mutually beneficial goals that focus on the positive growth and development of children (Decker & Decker, 2001; Pagano, 1997).

The Community as a Support System

How can the community service families?

The community can provide *informal support* to families, as when neighbors watch each other's children or share resources (gemeinschaft), or it can provide *formal support* through its publicly or privately funded community services (gesellschaft). Community services are necessary for several reasons:

- **Increasing population**. As more people compete for available resources, more people need supportive services to survive—job assistance, housing assistance, financial support, food subsidies, and medical care. As people live longer, the number of years that they are likely to depend on Social Security payments for support in their retirement years, as well as on Medicare for their health insurance, increases. As advances in science occur, more people's lives are prolonged. These people may have diseases or disabilities that prevent them from working; they, too, will need financial assistance as well as other services to survive.
- **Changing nature of the family**. More births to teenagers, more divorces, more single-parent families, and more employed mothers mean an increasing need for such services as financial assistance, social services, and child care. The mobility of families has caused separation from relatives. When relatives are unavailable, families turn to the community for support.
- **Increasing urbanization of communities**. The centralization of industries in certain areas, with the consequent migration—from rural to urban areas—of people seeking employment, has increased the number of people living in a smaller amount of space. People living in cities must turn to the community for various kinds of services. Because of the high density of people living in a small area, for example, the community is expected to provide open-space areas for recreation. Rural areas, because they are less populated, have fewer public services than urban areas.

CHRONOSYSTEM AND MACROSYSTEM INFLUENCES ON COMMUNITY SERVICES

How have changes in the macrosystem over time (the chronosystem) affected community services?

An aspect of the macrosystem, political ideology, might relate to what services government leaders believe to be worthy of support; for example, the Head Start preschool program was launched under President Lyndon Johnson. Political ideology also refers to legislation. For example, in 1975, the Education of All Handicapped Children's Act was passed ensuring that all children, regardless of disability, had a right to a free and appropriate education.

Another aspect of the macrosystem, economics, relates to various sources of funding for a community service. Agencies providing services may be public, private, or a combination.

Public agencies are financed by taxation. They are administered within the legal framework of the local, state, or federal government. For example, an outcome of the 1910 White House Conference on the Care of Dependent Children was the establishment of the U.S. Children's Bureau, the oldest federal agency for children, for the purpose of protecting children from harm. Since then the role of government in the protection of children has expanded in scope, as well as in the economic resources allocated to programs from tax monies. The Children's Bureau is now administered by the U.S. Administration for Children and Families in the Department of Health and Human Services. The Children's Bureau works with state and local agencies to develop a number of programs that focus on preventing the maltreatment of children, protecting them from abuse, and providing permanent placement if their home is not safe.

Private agencies may be financed by donations, membership dues, corporate contributions, consultation fees, investment income, foundation grants, publication sales, or conference fees. They are established by individuals or philanthropic, religious, fraternal, or humanitarian groups; their management is the responsibility of a board of directors. An example of the nation's oldest and largest membership-based child welfare organization is the Child Welfare League of America (CWLA, 2002), founded in 1920. CWLA's member agencies directly provide at-risk children and families with services in the areas of child abuse prevention and treatment, kinship care, juvenile justice, family foster care, adoption, positive youth development, residential group care, child day care, family-centered practice, and adolescent parenting and pregnancy prevention. CWLA's trained staff address such issues as behavioral health care, substance abuse, housing and homelessness, and HIV/AIDS.

Combination agencies, those using both public and private sources of money, may get government grants to implement research or innovations and private donations to provide services over and above what is funded by the grant. For example, the Office of Community Services, administered by the Administration for Youth and Families, was set up by the federal government to work in partnership with states, communities, and other agencies to provide a wide range of human and community development services and activities that ameliorate the causes and characteristics of poverty and otherwise assist persons in need. Various agencies, public or private, can submit applications for competitive funding of grants.

PREVENTIVE, SUPPORTIVE, AND REHABILITATIVE SERVICES

What are the categories of community services?

preventive services
programs that seek to lessen the stresses and strains of life resulting from social and technological changes and to avert problems

Community services, whether publicly or privately funded, can be categorized according to their primary function as preventive, supportive, or rehabilitative.

- **Preventive services** attempt to lessen the stresses and strains of life resulting from social and technological changes and to avert problems. For example, parks and recreation programs set up in rapidly developing urban areas are meant to be used by children in their free time to keep them from engaging in delinquent behavior.

- **Supportive services** include educational programs, counseling services, health services, policies related to demographic changes, employment training, and community development projects. These services maintain the health, education, and welfare of the community.
- **Rehabilitative services** enable or restore people's ability to participate in the community effectively.

Preventive Services: Parks, Recreation, and Education

The purpose of preventive services is to provide for people's needs for space, socializing, physical activity, and mental stimulation. Children need room to play and explore. Families need places to go to relax and enjoy each other's company. Everyone needs space to exercise and be physically fit. Many community members enjoy taking classes to learn new skills or to broaden their perspectives on life (cultural, historical, technological, linguistic).

Open spaces have been set aside for public enjoyment as far back in history as early Greek and Roman civilization. As Western European cities grew, parks or plazas were established. The first parkland in America designated for the public was purchased in 1660. As the colonies grew, so did the number of parks. One of the best-known parks, established in about 1853, is Central Park in New York City. The 843 acres of land were reserved for the purpose of recreation and relief from urban conditions. Other large cities followed New York's example (Rivkin, 1995).

In the 1890s and early 1900s, the public began to pressure government to assume responsibility for community recreation. This pressure was probably due to the growth of large cities and resultant lack of play space for children. Local governments responded by setting up agencies and organizations to provide recreation for children. By 1900, some 14 cities had made provision for supervised play, and in 1906, the Playground and Recreation Association of America (now called the National Recreation Association) was set up. Its purpose was to promote community recreational facilities and programs.

supportive services programs that maintain the health, education, and welfare of the community

rehabilitative services programs that enable or restore people's ability to participate in the community

A park in the middle of the city allows all residents to enjoy outdoor activities.

Omni Photo Communications Inc./Index Stock Imagery

Some of the services that community parks and recreation programs supply are providing and maintaining natural or designed environments, promoting physical fitness, and offering classes to enable people to develop interests and skills for use of their leisure time or to enhance their employability.

The environments provided and maintained by parks and recreation departments may include parks with play equipment, marked trails in which flora are labeled or historical events recorded on signs, museums with varying exhibits, zoos, botanical gardens, planetariums, and aquariums.

Some of the programs promoting physical fitness and interest and skill development include organized team sports and classes in tennis, fishing, sailing, photography, and arts and crafts. Opportunities for camping and other trips may be provided. Special events, such as hobby shows, pet shows, and camping demonstrations, may be sponsored by parks and recreational programs. Some communities have classes in computers, languages, parenting, art, and astronomy, to name a few.

Many federal as well as state and local agencies are responsible for administering recreational programs. Federal agencies performing this service include the National Park Service and the Cooperative Extension Service. The National Park Service, created in 1916 under the U.S. Department of the Interior, is the federal agency responsible for managing the country's 29 national parks. This service attempts to keep national park resources as natural as possible. For example, dead trees are allowed to stand or fall in order to provide homes and food for wildlife. Historical sites are sometimes reconstructed to provide visitors with a feeling of "what it was like then."

The Cooperative Extension Service, under the Department of Agriculture, was originally designed to improve the rural economy by providing educational services and information to farmers. It works through state agricultural colleges and county agricultural agents to provide direct community services. One of its services is the establishment and maintenance of 4-H clubs. Many children participate in these clubs, learning farm and home skills, science, and camping, and participating in various recreational activities. The mission of 4-H (head, heart, hands, and health) is to enable young people to become self-directing, productive, and contributing members of society through learn-by-doing experiences.

Many state agencies responsible for park and recreational services have functions similar to their federal counterparts. However, some functions vary greatly from state to state—such as the actual services provided to local communities, the laws regarding protection and conservation of wildlife and natural resources, and the maintenance of lands and waters for public use.

Some of the private and voluntary groups providing recreational services to children in the community are the Boy Scouts of America, Girl Scouts of America, Boys' and Girls' Clubs of America, American Red Cross, Young Men's Christian Association (YMCA), and Young Women's Christian Association (YWCA). These agencies promote certain values, emphasize learning by doing, and are concerned with personal development; their leaders come from the community and serve as role models. For example, the Boy Scouts of America promotes the ability of young people to do things for themselves and others. Leaders train the boys in self-reliance, courage, and good citizenship. In addition, patriotism is emphasized. For another example, the Boys' and Girls' Clubs of America, which includes boys and girls ages 6 to 18 who are at risk for behavioral, social, or academic problems, provide programs and services to enhance children's lives and enable youth to develop skills to become employable. The clubs also build knowledge to engage in positive behaviors and safe health practices, as well as to become responsible citizens.

Supportive Services: Family and Child

The purpose of family services is to preserve a healthy family life by helping family members achieve harmonious relationships. In helping families, family services consider the influence on the family of ethnicity, religion, and pattern of organization (Feldman & Scherz, 1987; Schorr, Both, & Copple, 1991).

Referrals. Problems that threaten the stability of family life include discord between husband and wife, discord between parent and child, illness, accidents, economic problems, desertion, delinquency, teen pregnancy, and alcohol or drug abuse. Family service agencies provide referrals to specific agencies dealing with these specific problems. They also give counseling, which may include advice on budgeting and home management, vocational opportunities, and family relationships.

Economic Assistance. Both public and private social agencies offer family services. Generally, public agencies offer services based on the family's economic need (families must meet legal eligibility requirements to qualify for assistance)—for example, in arranging financial assistance, finding a job, and locating affordable and suitable housing. Assistance may also include the distribution of food and medicine, as well as child-care services. Private family service agencies are concerned primarily with personal problems and emotional maladjustment of family members rather than with economic problems. Private agencies do, however, provide financial help in emergencies (especially when the family is waiting to see if it qualifies for public assistance or when the family has recently immigrated to the United States and does not qualify for public assistance). Family agencies may deal with personal problems involving an economic commitment such as placement of children in special schools or camps, or placement of adults in mental institutions or homes for the aged.

Counseling. Family services include marriage counseling, prenatal and family planning, family life education, homemaker services, and senior citizen services. Counseling services help marriage partners meet their marital responsibilities and resolve marital conflicts. They may also help in emotional maladjustment problems such as lack of communication between parents and teenagers, in premarital counseling, or in problems involved in adjusting to divorce. Prenatal care and family planning services promote the mental and physical health of children (and mothers) from the prenatal stage onward. Family planning includes birth control education. Child guidance services include family therapy and parenting training.

Family Preservation. The federal Family Preservation and Support Services Program was officially enacted in 1993. States receive money to develop family preservation and support services, thereby providing incentives to change the way services have traditionally been delivered to families (see Table 10.2).

The purpose of family preservation services is (1) to keep the family safe, (2) to avoid unnecessary placement of children in substitute care and the consequent high human and financial cost, and (3) to improve family functioning so that the behavior that led to the crisis will be less likely to reoccur (CDF, 2004; Cole & Duva, 1990). Family preservation services offer a mix of counseling, education, referrals, concrete assistance, and advocacy. An example is family life education, which includes education in home economics and management, parenting, and family relationships. Homemaker services send a trained person to the home when the mother is temporarily unable to care for the family. The services enable the family to stay together and carry on in crises such as hospitalization, chronic illness, and impairment due to a disabling condition.

Table 10.2

How Are Services to Families Delivered?

FAMILY PRESERVATION SUPPORT SERVICES	TRADITIONAL FAMILY SUPPORT SERVICES
• Build on family strengths	• Emphasize family deficits
• Focus on families	• Focus on individuals
• Respond flexibly to family needs	• Program and funding source dictate services
• Reach out to families	• Have strict eligibility requirements
• Treat families as partners in goal setting	• Workers set goals and solutions
• Offer services in home or homelike setting	• Services are office-based
• Respond quickly to needs	• Often have waiting lists

Keeping families together involves protecting children's safety in the home and strengthening families' abilities to deal with their problems. Family preservation programs may include intensive family-based crisis intervention services. For example, when a child is at risk for abuse, rather than remove the child from the family, a trained professional goes to the home to give practical assistance on immediate problems and parenting training, and helps to link the family with other support services in the community.

A fatherhood training curriculum has recently been implemented to help support personnel engage and involve fathers in their children's lives.

Senior Citizens. Senior citizen services may include economic assistance, in-home care, day care, institutionalization, recreation, Meals on Wheels (a program that delivers meals to the homes of the housebound), friendly visiting, and arranging for other community services to "adopt a grandparent" (for example, a child-care center might welcome the experience and extra help a senior citizen could provide for the children).

Child Health and Welfare. The term *child welfare* encompasses care for individuals who may be indigent, neglected, abused, deserted, sick, disabled, maladjusted, or delinquent. The purpose of child welfare agencies is to protect the physical, intellectual, and emotional well-being of children (Zaslow, Tout, Smith, & Moore, 1998). Child welfare services provide (1) economic and personal aid to children living in their own homes, (2) foster care for children who have no home or cannot remain with their own families, and (3) institutional care when children cannot be placed in a foster home or cannot remain with their own families (CWLA, 2002).

Traditionally, children whose families could not care for them, because of death, illness, or poverty, were placed in institutions. Private agencies and charitable organizations took the major responsibility for child welfare. Today, however, children are enabled to remain with their families; they are removed only as an emergency measure—for example, in cases of abuse.

The need for financial assistance to mothers in order to preserve the family was first emphasized at the White House Conference on the Care of Dependent Children in 1910. The first national welfare legislation was passed as part of the Social Security Act of 1935 (Zaslow et al., 1998). Public funds are available under the Temporary Aid to Needy Families (TANF) Program, enabling families to provide a minimum of shelter, food, clothing, and medical care for their children.

In 1996, the Family Support Act (amended in 2001) implemented the Job Opportunities and Basic Skills Training (JOBS) Program, which provided education and job training, as well as child care, for mothers with young children to enable them to make the transition from government assistance to independence. Today, the Personal Responsibility and Work Opportunity Reconciliation Act of 1996 sets time limits for the transition from government aid to the achievement of financial independence resulting from being trained for the workforce.

The states carry out maternal and child health programs with the financial support of the federal government. These programs include family planning services, prenatal clinics, well-baby clinics for regular medical examinations of young children, hearing and vision screening, birthing, nursing, dental services, and mental health services.

The state governments also administer programs that provide services for children with disabilities, partially financed by matching funds from the federal government. Services include locating children with disabilities (physicians, nurses, and teachers do the referrals); providing medical, surgical, and corrective services for them; providing facilities for diagnosis, hospitalization, and rehabilitative care; and providing aids and prosthetic appliances, physiotherapy, and medical social services.

Protective. There is a need for services that provide protection for children against abuse and neglect. Protective services are usually invoked upon a report from a teacher, doctor, or neighbor. An investigation of the family takes place and, depending on the circumstances, the child may be removed from the home and temporarily placed in foster or institutional care until the parents can prove they can care for the child appropriately. Often the parents must receive counseling and take classes in child development and parenting.

Children's services also include the care and protection of children born to unmarried mothers. Typical services for unmarried mothers include financial assistance, prenatal care, hospitalization, and counseling. Educational programs (child development, parenting, health and nutrition, vocational, and academic education) are often included.

Child Care. Child-care centers serve preschool children whose parents are employed. Most care is for children age 2 to 5, but more and more centers are serving infants and toddlers. Some centers include health and educational services as part of their programs. Extended day-care programs serve school-age children whose parents are employed. Children come to the center before and after school, as necessitated by their parents' work schedules. Extended day-care programs are sometimes located in elementary schools and sometimes in community centers. When necessary, the extended day-care program provides transportation between school and center.

Foster Care. Foster care services are provided for children who are neglected or abused and, therefore, need protection, as well as for children whose parents are temporarily unable to care for them. Foster homes are carefully selected by the community social service agency. Children placed in these homes are closely supervised by the agency, which provides money for room and board, clothing, medical and dental care, and often an allowance for the children. Counseling services are provided for the foster parents.

Adoption. In contrast to foster care, adoption is a social and legal process by which a child becomes a permanent member of the adopting family, with legal rights, including that of inheritance. The social process of adoption seeks to provide children of incapacitated or deceased natural parents with a healthy home environment. The legal process seeks to ensure that separation from natural parents is resorted to only when absolutely necessary and only with consent, if the parents are alive. Social agencies arranging for adoption conduct investigations to match the child and the adoptive family. Character, motivation, age, finances, and sometimes ethnic and religious background of the family are examined.

Rehabilitative Services: Correction, Mental Health, Special Needs

The purpose of rehabilitative agencies is to enable or restore an individual's capacity to participate effectively in the community by correcting behavior, addressing mental health, and/or providing needed services to those who have recently immigrated to this country as well as to those who have a disability.

Correction. Correctional services are provided for children, youths, and adults who have difficulties abiding by the legal rules of community life. What constitutes deviant behavior varies among different social groups. Some children may be encouraged by their friends and neighbors to behave delinquently; for example, stealing may be a prerequisite to being accepted by the neighborhood gang. Another child in another neighborhood who behaves similarly may be brought to a social agency, such as a child guidance clinic. Still another child may be arrested and cited before the juvenile court.

Since human behavior is influenced in part by the customs of the society in which we live, some deviant behavior may stem from conflicting values within and between ethnic groups in society (Garbarino, 1992). For example, different ethnic groups may have different attitudes toward fighting. Societal mores, as expressed by the U.S. legal system, punish aggressive acts, especially if the aggression harms someone or someone's property. A particular ethnic group may feel that aggression is the only acceptable way to avenge an insult. One explanation for "machismo" behavior, or male dominance including physical power, in Hispanic culture is that it evolved from a survival response during the time of the Spanish Invasion to defend the honor of victimized females (Vigil, 1980). Another explanation for variations in attitudes toward aggression is a reactive strategy to neighborhood dangers, disrespect, a social cognitive awareness of stereotypes, a lack of social supports, and/or a distorted personal orientation (feeling of "superiority") (Spencer, 2001).

Children under age 18 who are deemed neglected or delinquent are under the jurisdiction of the juvenile court. The juvenile court is not a criminal court; it does not file charges against the child. Therefore, there is no jury to determine guilt or innocence. Rather, the court attempts to understand the causes for the particular maladjustment and determines which steps must be taken for rehabilitation. In order to understand the causes for the maladjusted or deviant behavior, the child and his or her family background are examined. Also, the physical, socioeconomic, and cultural conditions under which the child is living are explored.

Sometimes, to join a gang, middle and high school students will get tattoos, even though it is illegal for anyone under age 18 to get one. If these kids want to leave the gang, they have to either move out of town or get the tattoo removed so they won't be identified by rivals and possibly even killed.

A juvenile officer in Monrovia, California, has established a corrective program in which, using funds from private donations, he will help a remorseful gang member get the tattoo removed in a medical facility with a ruby laser. The youth must write an essay on the reasons he/she got the tattoo, problems regarding it, and why he/she wants it removed. The officer then interviews the youth and tells him/her the requirements of the program: parental involvement, periodic contact for three years, and acceptable grades.

Juvenile court judges may place children under the supervision of their parents in their home, with the stipulation that the family receive counseling. Or children may be removed from their homes and placed in foster care or institutions. Judges may also require children (or their parents) to pay for damages caused by the delinquent behavior.

Mental Health. Children are usually referred to local child guidance clinics by teachers, medical personnel, or the court. Behavioral problems indicating the need for referral include truancy, running away, lying, stealing, vandalism, setting fires, and extreme aggressiveness. Other behaviors may include excessive shyness, apathy, daydreaming, withdrawal, excessive fearfulness, enuresis, eating disorders, and nightmares. Child guidance clinics provide medical and psychological examinations for the child. The parents and often the siblings, as well as the child, may come for treatment. Services are coordinated with the school.

Special Needs. Services for recent immigrants to the United States encompass education (English language, American history, government, and culture), financial assistance, housing assistance, and vocational counseling, as well as referrals to other agencies providing specific services.

Services for people with disabilities emphasize inclusion. Self-help and productive work are the goals of rehabilitation. These services encompass evaluation, special education, financial assistance, counseling, vocational training, recreation, and referrals for treatment (Epps & Jackson, 2000).

Table 10.3 summarizes the main categories of community services.

PREVENTIVE AGENCIES	SUPPORTIVE AGENCIES	REHABILITATIVE AGENCIES
Parks	Family and child services	Correction
Recreation	Referrals	Mental health
Education	Economic assistance	Special needs
	Counseling	
	Family preservation	
	Senior citizens	
	Child health and welfare	
	Protective care	
	Child care	
	Foster care	
	Adoption	

Table 10.3

Categories of Community Services

Creating Caring Communities

How can communities be enabled to meet the needs of families and children?

Even though different communities can provide a variety of services, some of which were described earlier, many do not provide enough to adequately meet the needs of children and families. Sensitizing individuals, especially those on decision-making bodies, to the unmet needs of children and to society's obligation to respond to those needs is known as *child advocacy*. In general, *advocacy*, introduced in Chapter 2, refers to the process of supporting a person, group, or cause. *Society* can mean public agencies, such as the government or the school; private agencies, such as religious groups or businesses; or concerned members of the community.

The National Commission on Children (NCC) was created by Congress and the president "to serve as a forum on behalf of children of the Nation." The commission, comprised of parents, grandparents, teachers, health and child development experts, business leaders, professionals, elected officials, and others, became official in 1989. Its mandated task was to assess the status of children and families in the United States and to propose new directions for policy and program development in order to improve the opportunities for every young person, regardless of circumstances, to become a healthy, secure, educated, economically self-sufficient, and productive adult. The commission's final report, *Beyond Rhetoric: A New American Agenda for Children and Families* (NCC, 1991), made recommendations in nine general areas:

1. Ensuring income security
2. Improving health
3. Increasing educational achievement
4. Preparing adolescents for adulthood
5. Strengthening and supporting families
6. Protecting vulnerable children and their families
7. Making policies and programs work
8. Creating a moral climate for children
9. Providing financing for programs

Specific issues addressed were a yearly refundable tax credit for children; a government-guaranteed minimum child support payment, as well as tough enforcement; continuation of the job training program, as well as child care and health insurance, to help low-income families make the transition from welfare to work; and community responsibility for health care and education programs. Recommendations included development of a universal system of health insurance, expansion of Head Start to all income-eligible children, and improvement of the quality of education and accountability. The commission also recommended that public support for family services should be continued; that businesses should have family-oriented policies; that the quality, availability, and affordability of child-care services should be improved; that community-based family support programs should be developed and expanded; and that salaries and training opportunities in early childhood and welfare fields should be increased. Finally, the commission recommended that greater diligence be exercised in both public and private sectors in terms of giving children and adolescents clear, consistent messages about personal conduct and responsibility to others, and that the allocation of financial resources be shared by the private and public sectors.

When George W. Bush became president of the United States, one of his first official acts was to create the White House Office of Faith-Based and Community Initiatives in 2001. This office was tasked with leading "a determined attack on need" by strengthening and expanding the role of faith-based and community organizations in addressing the nation's social problems. The president's goal was to allow faith-based organizations to compete equally with other, nonsectarian groups for government or private funds.

President Bush also created Centers for Faith-Based and Community Initiatives in the U.S. Departments of Justice, Agriculture, Labor, Health and Human Services, Housing and Urban Development, and Education, as well as the Agency for International Development. The mission of the White House office and these centers is to empower faith-based and other community organizations to apply for federal social service grants. The White House office and the centers strive to support organizations that serve people in need, particularly those that serve the following populations:

- At-risk youth
- Ex-offenders
- Homeless and hungry
- Substance abusers
- Those with HIV/AIDS
- Welfare-to-work families

ECONOMIC ASSISTANCE

What is being done to alleviate poverty?

One in six children in the United States lives in poverty—in families with incomes below the federally designated poverty line ($18,660 for a family of four in 2003). The poverty rate for African Americans is about 34%, for Hispanic Americans about 29.9%, for Asian Americans and Pacific Islanders about 12.5%, and for Euro-Americans about 9.8% (CDF, 2004; U.S. Bureau of the Census, 2003).

Many families are poor even though one or both parents are employed. Such families are often large and represent various ethnic minority groups, although the largest recent increase in families that are poor has been among European Americans under age 30 (U.S. Bureau of the Census, 2003). Both family structure and the labor market affect the duration of childhood poverty (Corcoran & Chandry, 1997). A common feature of poor families that the head of the household is less educated than heads of households in families that are not poor. A large proportion of families that are poor are headed by single women. Families headed by single mothers are more likely to be poor because of the cost of child care and the lower average wage paid to women than to men (CDF, 2004).

Rafael Gomez works as a gardener for a landscape company. He earns $350 per week. He and his wife have five children, ranging in age from 6 months to 12 years. Mrs. Gomez stays home to care for the family. The rent for a three-bedroom apartment in a dilapidated building is $425 per month. The Gomez children wear hand-me-down clothes from each other and from relatives. The family does not own a car, or have medical insurance.

Joan Thomas is age 20; she has three children, ages 1 month, 2, and 4. She gets government assistance for welfare, food, and medical services. Her husband recently deserted her. Because she first became pregnant while in high school, she never completed her education. Her lack of education limits her job opportunities. She would like to work, but she knows that the job would be low paying because of her lack of skills, and she worries about the cost of child care and her ability to juggle all the responsibilities.

Federal programs that attempt to alleviate some of the conditions of poverty include the following:

- **Temporary Assistance for Needy Families (TANF)** is a federal and state matching program that provides temporary financial support for families with children. Eligibility, work requirements, and time limits for benefits are established by individual states. This welfare reform program replaced Aid to Families with Dependent Children (AFDC).
- **Unemployment compensation** covers all workers in the labor force. Financed by employers' contributions, it is intended to maintain about 50% of a worker's income for a temporary period of involuntary unemployment. The program is administered by federal and state governments.
- **Social Security survivor or disability benefits** are administered by the federal government; payments come from the Social Security Trust Fund, through taxes on employer and employee. Social Security benefits earned by those who die or become disabled are paid to their survivors or dependents.
- **Supplemental Security Income (SSI)** provides a guaranteed minimum income for the aged and disabled.
- **Veterans' benefits** are paid by the federal government to survivors or dependents of veterans who die or are disabled in the service.
- **Child nutrition services** are federally funded programs administered by the states. They are intended to improve the nutritional standards of low-income families. Included are the Food Stamp Program, in which participants buy food stamps, according to a formula based on income and family size, at a subsidized cost and then use the stamps to buy food; the National School Lunch Program; the Special Supplemental Food Program for Women, Infants, and Children (WIC); and the National School Breakfast Program.
- **Other services** include a variety of social services funded through state grants under Title IV and Title XX of the Social Security Act. Large proportions of these funds provide day care for children of employed mothers and other child welfare services. Title I of the Elementary and Secondary Education Act and Head Start provide educational and related services to low-income children. Child health programs and Medicaid also provide services to poor families.

Why have the federal programs not succeeded in alleviating poverty? According to the Children's Defense Fund (2004), five major factors have been pushing more and more children and families into poverty. These factors exemplify how exosystems and macrosystems affect children:

1. The persistently high rate of unemployment among parents
2. The inability of parents to earn high enough wages to escape poverty
3. The growth in the number of female-headed households because of divorce and out-of-wedlock births
4. Inadequate education and job training
5. The reduction of budgets in government programs

Unemployment and low-wage employment have outcomes beyond poverty, including loss of self-worth, increased family tensions, alcoholism, abuse, and lower academic achievement of children. Often, when a family's economic support system of breaks down, so does its ability to provide emotional support (Behrman, 2002; Huston, McLoyd, & Coll, 1994).

Economists Ross and Sawhill (1975) as well as others (Huston et al., 1994; Wilson, 1995) reported that family disintegration increased in families whose head was unemployed for a long period of time, compared to similar families not experiencing long-term unemployment. For example, at a congressional hearing, the former president of the United Automobile Workers testified that as unemployment increased, so did the number of people seeking assistance because of alcoholism and child abuse (Marcossen & Fleming, 1978).

Which public policies are designed to overcome the effects of economic problems, especially unemployment? In addition to unemployment compensation, the federal government creates certain jobs and provides certain tax exemptions. To create jobs, local units of government (cities, towns, counties) can submit applications for federal money to pay for local public construction—for example, road and street improvements or building additions. The local community thus both relieves unemployment and gets some funds for public works. The federal government also creates certain jobs by giving money to local units of government to hire unemployed individuals. Thus, needed public services are provided (clerks, park attendants), and jobs are created for those in need.

Tax exemptions are provided for those receiving unemployment compensation; they are granted to businesses hiring certain individuals, such as those with disabilities or those in government work-training programs; and they are granted for child care required by the mother's employment.

Although welfare reform has contributed to declining poverty rates, problems regarding government support for poor families with children remain. Among the ongoing issues are the income level at which the government considers a family poor enough to receive assistance, the funding levels for welfare-to-work programs, implementation of job training, employment prospects, child care, housing, and adequate health care coverage (Behrman, 1997a, 1997b, 2002).

The ramifications of poverty are numerous and significant. For example, poor children are at least twice as likely as nonpoor children to suffer stunted growth or lead poisoning, or to be kept back in school. Poor children score significantly lower on reading, math, and vocabulary tests when compared with otherwise similar nonpoor children. More than half of poor Americans experience serious deprivations during the year (defined as lack of food, utility shutoffs, crowded or substandard housing, or lack of a stove or refrigerator) (CDF, 2004).

What is being done to address the needs of families who are homeless?

Related to poverty is the ability of a family to provide shelter. Families with children are the fastest-growing segment of Americans who are homeless. Families with children make up more than one-third of the nation's homeless population (CDF, 2004).

The threat of homelessness is even graver than the statistics suggest because millions of families are just one crisis away from losing their homes. A crisis could be an unexpected expense, illness, disability, or job loss. Other families are at risk for homelessness because they spend most of their income on housing and have no financial cushion if their rent goes up or their income falls even slightly (CDF, 2004).

The incidence of families that are homeless has increased greatly.

© Tony Freeman/PhotoEdit

Homelessness is the result of many simultaneous trends: shrinking incomes for many young families, rising housing costs, a decreasing supply of low-cost housing, a decline in government housing assistance, and deinstitutionalization of those with mental disorders (CDF, 2004). A significant number of youths who are homeless have run away or been kicked out of their homes (Levine & Levine, 1996). An alarming trend is the number of homeless youths who were formerly children in foster care (Balk, 1995). Nearly all state child protective services stop foster care payments when children reach age 18; few young people have the skills at this age to be self-supporting.

Other problems associated with those who are homeless are poverty, poor health, inadequate education, poor employment prospects, and social isolation (CDF, 2004). Children who are homeless suffer psychological, as well as behavioral and educational, consequences (McCormick & Holden, 1992).

Thomas Green, age 6, took his stuffed dog and lay down on the mattress with his sister, Eva, age 3, who was already asleep. The mattress was a piece of foam rubber donated to the church that was to be Thomas's home for the next few months (the town had no public shelter for the homeless). Thomas's mother, Vicki, had been living in motel rooms with the children and whoever was her current boyfriend until he left or was arrested. Vicki took odd jobs in between boyfriends to support herself and the children, but being a high school dropout, she had limited skills and, consequently, limited work opportunities.

In the morning, Vicki took Thomas to the nearby school to enroll him in kindergarten. He had to repeat kindergarten because he had moved so many times the previous year that his school attendance hadn't enabled him to be ready for first grade. Eva was invited to go to the church preschool while Vicki spent the day looking for work.

Local governments have often been unable or unwilling to deal effectively with the problems of families and children who are homeless, and the federal government has provided only limited assistance (CDF, 2004). The federal government gives funds to states for temporary shelters and money to schools to assure that children who are homeless have access to free public education.

Teachers need to be sensitive to characteristics that may be observed in children who are homeless, including depression, anxiety, severe separation problems, poor-quality relationships, shyness, aggressiveness, sleep disorders, temper tantrums, and short attention spans (McCormick & Holden, 1992). Many parents who are homeless have substance abuse problems, are victims of domestic violence, and have fragmented social support networks (McCormick & Holden, 1992).

HEALTH CARE

What is being done regarding preventing disease and increasing public access to health care?

As a nation, we spend enormous amounts of money on health care. For insured persons, we have an excellent health care system that covers crises and serious illnesses, but we have inadequate preventive and public health care (CDF, 2004). There are serious inequities in health standards for families with low incomes and for those from ethnic minorities, as well as too few medical resources in rural and inner-city communities, too little prenatal care for many women, and not enough regular immunizations against disease (CDF, 2004; NCC, 1991). To address these inadequacies, the Children's Health Insurance Program (CHIP) was enacted in 1997. Federal funds are granted to states to design and implement programs.

> Thu Truong, 7 years old, developed a high fever and a cough one Saturday night. His mother gave him aspirin and some cough syrup, but by Sunday the fever was still high and the cough was worse. Mrs. Truong decided to take him to the emergency room, because she has no regular doctor (she relies on health clinics for medical care). It took her an hour and a half by bus to reach the hospital. Because Thu was not "critical" (bleeding profusely, unable to breathe, for instance), he had to wait an hour before a doctor was available to examine him.
>
> Lara Michaels had her third baby several weeks prematurely. The baby remained in intensive care for two months. Al Michaels' insurance policy did not cover newborn health care, so the Michaels face an enormous hospital bill that will keep them in debt for years.

The most important factors influencing child health occur before birth. A baby is likely to grow into a healthy child when the mother had good nutrition during childhood and during pregnancy, received prenatal care early in pregnancy, is between the ages of 20 and 35, is in good health, has not been pregnant recently, and does not abuse drugs or alcohol. A baby is more likely to have a low birth weight (under 5.5 lb.) and/or birth defects, or die, when its mother is poorly nourished, has no prenatal care, is under 18, is in poor health (has a sexually transmitted disease, for example), has just been pregnant, smokes, or abuses drugs or alcohol. The infant mortality rate in the United States remains high compared to other industrialized nations (CDF, 2004). Thus, girls and women need to be educated *before* they get pregnant about their future child's health.

Early and continuous health care for children after birth saves lives and helps minimize long-term health problems. High-quality preventive, primary, and remedial pediatric health care can ensure that problems that can develop during infancy, such as respiratory, neurologic, or orthopedic impairments, are detected and treated.

Health professionals working with schoolchildren from low-income families have found that they are twice as likely as children from middle- and upper-income families to be suffering from one or more untreated medical conditions. Untreated problems such as vision, hearing, and dental, as well as anemia, mental health, and developmental conditions, can impair a child's ability to benefit from school, thereby affecting that child's later life (CDF, 2004; NCC, 1991).

Children born exposed to drugs or alcohol are especially vulnerable to serious physical and mental disabilities, as well as behavior problems and learning impairments. Acquired immune deficiency syndrome (AIDS) threatens a growing number of children each year, primarily through transmission from their mothers before or at birth. The risk of human immunodeficiency virus (HIV), which can develop into AIDS, is also growing among adolescents who are intravenous drug users or sexually active (NCC, 1991).

Human-made environmental hazards increasingly threaten the health of all children. For example, absorption or inhalation of lead causes damage to the central nervous system, mental retardation, and blood and urinary tract infection. Thus, technological advances must continually be monitored for their environmental impact on health and safety.

Government programs promoting children's health include the following:

- **Medicaid** provides matching money to the states to pay for medical services for the indigent and medically needy. Children who are eligible for Medicaid receive early and periodic screening, diagnosis, and treatment.
- **Maternal and child health services** provide federal money to states for projects to reduce infant mortality and improve the health of low-income mothers and children; to provide comprehensive health care to low-income children up to age 21; to provide dental care for low-income children; and to provide outreach, diagnosis, and medical and related services for low-income and medically indigent children with physically disabilities. Also included are neighborhood health centers, migrant health centers, and Native American health services.
- **Centers for Disease Control** provide federal funds to the states for the purchase of vaccines.
- **Child nutrition programs** include school lunch programs, school breakfast programs, and special food programs for low-income children and children with disabilities in day care or other nonresidential settings. Also included is the Women, Infants and Children Program (WIC), which provides nutritious food to low-income pregnant and lactating women and children under age 4 who are at nutritional risk.

SUPPORT FOR FAMILIES

What financial assistance exists for families in need?

Traditionally, many U.S. family services have been provided by private voluntary organizations on a charitable basis. In recent years, more and more public agencies have begun to play a part in services to families. The combination of public and private social services is often fragmented and uncoordinated, but there are successful collaborative examples across the country (Schorr, 1997).

Government programs providing some support to families include the following:

- **Child welfare services** fund state efforts to preserve families by strengthening their ability to address their problems and avoid unnecessary foster care, and to reunite with their parents children who have been placed in foster care.

- **Social services block grants (Title XX)** provide various preventive, counseling, and other support services for low-income children and families as well as for vulnerable, abused, and neglected children and their families.
- **Child and adolescent service system program** helps ensure that youths with serious emotional problems receive needed mental health services by improving coordination among the numerous agencies responsible for them.

> Jill Sanger, age 15, lives in a suburban town. Her father is an engineer for an aerospace company and often works late. Her mother is not employed but is involved in school and community activities, as well as caring for her 10-year-old twin brothers and 6-year-old sister. Jill has been reported truant from school on several occasions. She refuses to communicate with her parents and has become involved with drugs. Her parents want to get help.
>
> Helen Black, recently divorced, has two young children. Her ex-husband is lax in sending child support payments. Helen wants to become a computer programmer and feels confident she can get a job. Someday, she would like to buy a computer and work at home. Meanwhile, however, she must go to school, and needs child care.
>
> Jack (age 13) and Sally (age 12) Baker have been cared for and supported by their mother since their father deserted them when Sally was a year old. When Jack was 6 and Sally was 5, however, their mother became very ill. She had to be hospitalized for three months and then recuperate for six months. Having no relatives, the children were placed in foster care. When their mother could again care for them, they were returned to her. A year later, however, their mother had a relapse and the children were placed in another foster home. This time they were separated because a home was not available that would take both of them.

Two changes in family structure have accelerated tremendously in the past few years—the increase in the number of women employed, especially mothers of young children under age 6, and the growth in the number of children living in families headed by one parent, usually the mother. Among the family supports that can respond to the needs of mothers who are poor, employed, and/or single, as well as to the needs of the children, is a system of quality child-care services, in home or center settings.

As was discussed in Chapter 5, families seeking child care for their children can choose (where available) child-care centers, family day-care homes, or home care by a relative, neighbor, or paid person. Even though some centers and some day-care homes are licensed, this is no guarantee of quality because enforcement of licensing standards may be minimal. Some children have to care for themselves (see the box "Is This Child Ready for Self-Care?").

What problems are associated with self-care by children?

Mothers who are employed outside the home and have school-age children often do not or cannot make provision for after-school care. These children are sometimes referred to as "latchkey children" because they have to let themselves into their homes with a key. Unsupervised by adults, children who care for themselves tend to be vulnerable to delinquency, vandalism, injury, rape, and drug use (Collins, Harris, & Susman, 1995).

There are other problems, as well, for children in self-care. Studies comparing self-care children, ranging in age from 5 to 12, with their supervised counterparts have found that children who are left alone to care for themselves and/or siblings often feel afraid regardless of their age, capabilities, or parents' assurances (Behrman, 1999; Belle, 1999; Long & Long, 1982). Their fearfulness may stem from warnings and cautions about people coming to the door, about cooking, and about various household problems that might occur.

Self-care children are usually restricted to their homes until their parents return. They are generally prohibited from having friends over. Sometimes older children are given the responsibility for caring for younger siblings.

It took a tragedy to bring national attention to the problems surrounding self-care children. A little boy, 5 years old, left alone in his house while his mother worked, was accidentally shot and killed by a police officer who mistook the background noise of the television and the shadow on the wall of the toy gun as threats to his life. He didn't see the little boy until it was too late.

Government programs assisting families experiencing such changes include the following:

- **Income tax deductions** are provided for child-care expenses of employed mothers.
- **Subsidized day care** (such as Head Start and Title XX) is among the social services supported by federal and state matching funds.

Although some children flounder when forced to be responsible for themselves, others (especially children over 10) flourish. They enjoy the independence and have learned what to do if various situations arise, such as a stranger coming to the door, the electricity going out, or not feeling well (Belle, 1999). Apparently, developmental outcomes from self-care depend on characteristics of the child, family circumstances (Is someone available by phone?), and neighborhood features (Is it safe?) (Vandell & Su, 1999).

IN PRACTICE

Is This Child Ready for Self-Care?

- Is the child mature enough to care for him- or herself?
- Has the child indicated that he or she would be willing to try self-care?
- Is the child able to solve problems?
- Is the child able to communicate with adults?
- Is the child able to complete daily tasks?
- Is the child generally unafraid to be alone?
- Is the child generally unafraid to enter the house alone?
- Can the child unlock and lock the doors to the home unassisted?
- Is there an adult living or working nearby whom their child knows and can rely on in case of an emergency?
- Is there adequate household security?
- Is the neighborhood safe?

If the answer to any of the above questions is "no," then plans to leave the child in self-care should be delayed or abandoned (Long & Long, 1983).

SPECIAL CHILD-CARE SERVICES

What is being done to support children with disabilities or who have been maltreated?

Some children have special needs—they have disabilities, are maltreated, or have been abandoned by their families; they are orphans, or have run away from desperate situations.

Julie was born prematurely and required special care when her mother brought her home from the hospital one month after she was born. After a week at home, Julie had lost a significant amount of weight and was listless. She was diagnosed as suffering from "failure to thrive" resulting from neglect and was placed in foster care. Her mother, just 18 years old, had a history of drug abuse. She had trouble keeping track of medical appointments, filling prescriptions, and meeting Julie's needs. In one year, Julie was shifted three times from her mother's care to foster care. Julie's current foster mother wants to adopt her, but the biological mother will not sign the papers.

Kenny, age 13, is the oldest of four children. Both his parents are alcoholics. Kenny has been involved in some stealing incidents in the neighborhood, but he was never reported to the police because the shopkeepers felt sorry for him. Kenny stole when his father spent his paycheck on booze and there was no food in the house. Recently, however, Kenny has been hanging around with some older kids who deal in drugs. Kenny sees this as an easy way to make money and get out of the house. The first time he tries to make a sale, though, he gets caught.

Mike was born without hip sockets. In order for him to use his legs and walk normally, he needs several surgeries. In addition to the surgeries, he will need special equipment such as a walker to keep mobile until he heals. He will also need daily physical therapy to strengthen his muscles. Mike's father deserted the family after Mike's birth; he couldn't deal with having a disabled son. Mike's mother has to work to support Mike and his two older sisters. She has no medical insurance, nor does she have the time or energy to give Mike the special care he needs.

Children who are abused and neglected have recently received more national attention, due in part to the establishment in 1974 of a National Center on Child Abuse and Neglect. Children who are abused, neglected, or abandoned, as well as those who are orphaned and sometimes those who run away, are often placed in foster homes. Foster care is funded by federal, state, and local sources. Foster care provides temporary care when children cannot be cared for in their own homes for any of the following reasons: death or illness of a parent, divorce or desertion, inadequate financial support, abuse or neglect, and behavioral problems with which the parent cannot cope. The problems with foster care placement are several. Relatively few foster parents have training in dealing with maltreated children; some children placed in foster care drift from one home to another, never returning to their own homes; some children may even be abused by their foster parents.

In spite of the fact that many children placed in foster care are eligible for adoption, it seldom happens. Present legislation results in the loss of federal support for foster children if they are adopted by the family with which they reside. Support is not only financial—it includes medical, dental, and clothing allowances. Many private insurance companies will not cover preexisting medical conditions that some

Table 10.4

Key Federal Assistance Programs for Children and Families

POVERTY	CHILD HEALTH	SUPPORT FOR FAMILIES	SPECIAL CHILD-CARE NEEDS
Temporary Assistance for Needy Families	Medicaid	Child welfare services	Foster care
Unemployment compensation	Maternal and child health services	Social services block grant (Title XX)	Adoption assistance program
Social Security survivor or disability benefits	Children's health insurance programs	Child and adolescent service system program	Child abuse prevention and treatment
Supplemental Security Income	Centers for Disease Control	Income tax deduction for child-care expenses	Family violence prevention and services
Veteran's benefits			
Child nutrition services programs	Child nutrition		
Other services: child care, educational, health	Head Start	Subsidized child care	Head Start
Homeless assistance			

of these children have. However, a government Adoption Assistance Program provides financial grants to families adopting "hard to place" children, including those with health problems (physical or emotional) or disabling conditions and children from ethnic minority backgrounds.

In many states, terminating parental custody is very difficult; therefore, the child cannot be legally adopted. Often, this is damaging to the child's emotional health because the child does not know to whom he or she really belongs (Nazario, 1988).

In addition to foster care funding and adoption assistance, other government programs for children with special needs include the following (see also Table 10.4):

- **The Child Abuse Prevention and Treatment Act** authorizes grants to states to assist them in developing and strengthening programs designed to prevent child abuse and neglect while providing treatment for its victims.
- **The Family Violence Prevention and Services Program** supports local programs that provide immediate shelter and related services to victims of family violence and their children.

Mesosystem Influences: Linking Community Services to Families and Schools

How can mesosystems collaborate to support children's development?

To be effective in supporting children's development, community child-care services should be comprehensive in that they link with health, nutrition, social services, and education for children and their parents (CDF, 2004; Decker & Decker, 2001). Such collaboration strengthens the immediate environment of vulnerable children, making them more resilient to stress (Hurd, Lerner, & Barton, 1999).

IN PRACTICE

What Typifies Effective Characteristics of Community Services?

- The earlier intervention is undertaken in a child's life, the better the outcome.
- Comprehensive approaches are more effective than limited interventions.
- Services must be easily accessible to individuals; in some cases, aggressive outreach may be required.
- Staff involvement in, and knowledge of, the situation are critical.
- Stable, caring adults, including mentors, are important role models.
- Parental involvement is crucial to success with children.
- Involvement in the school system is a key element of successful intervention.
- Highly structured programs are the most successful.

Source: Rickel & Becker, 1997, pp. 7–8.

Examples of comprehensive service linkages between children, families, and schools are the Head Start preschool program (discussed in Chapter 5) and the Brookline Early Education Program (BEEP) for prekindergarten children in the public schools. Head Start addresses the physical, emotional, cognitive, and family support needs of the child. BEEP focuses on family involvement and empowerment in children's education.

Examples of service linkages between children, families, and communities are child-care resource and referral agencies providing information to parents regarding child-care arrangements; health and social services; parent education; family-friendly businesses; and university programs providing model schools, teacher training, and collaboration with schools in the community (Decker & Decker, 2001; Hurd et al., 1999).

IN PRACTICE

How Can Communities Help to Optimize Children's Development?

1. **Establish a local commission for children and families**. This commission should find out what is being done in the community and what needs to be done for children and families. More specifically, it should examine the adequacy of existing programs, such as maternal and child health services, social services, day-care facilities, and recreational opportunities. The commission should include representatives of the major institutions dealing with children and families, as well as business, industry, and labor representatives. Older children, who can speak from their own experience, should also be included.
2. **Establish a neighborhood family center**. A place that provides a focal point for leisure, learning, sharing, and problem solving should be established in a school, church, or community building. To eliminate the fragmentation of human services, the center should be the place where community members

A neighborhood family center provides social and recreational services.

receive information on family health, social services, child care, legal aid, and welfare. The center should emphasize cross-age rather than age-segregated activities.

3. **Foster community projects**. Projects involving cleaning up the environment; caring for the aged, sick, or lonely; and planning parades, fairs, and picnics are excellent ways for community members of all ages to learn to work together and appreciate each other's talents and skills. These projects should provide an opportunity for young people to act as collaborators rather than subordinates.

4. **Combat alcohol, drugs, and violence**. Provide successful community role models for children. Work with families and schools to give children skills to solve problems without having to resort to substance abuse or violence. Work with families and schools on strong sanctions against substance abuse and violence.

5. **Foster youth participation in local policy bodies**. Every community organization affecting children and youth should include teenagers and older children as voting members. These would include such organizations as school boards, recreation commissions, health boards, and welfare commissions.

6. **Plan communities to consider the children who will be growing up in them**. When planning and designing new communities, some of the factors that should be considered are the location of shops and businesses where children can have contact with adults at work, recreational and day-care facilities that are readily accessible to parents as well as children, provision for a family neighborhood center and family-oriented facilities and services, availability of public transportation, and "places to walk, sit, and talk in common company" (Bronfenbrenner, 1980; Garbarino, 1995a; U.S. Department of Education, 1994).

Involvement and Advocacy

How can you become involved in the community to support services for families and children?

To support services for families and children, one must be aware of what needs to be done and be willing to do it. According to anthropologist Margaret Mead: "Never doubt that a small group of thoughtful, committed citizens can change the world; indeed, it is the only thing that ever has" (quoted by Schorr, 1997). There are numerous examples of community services (family, educational, and welfare) throughout the country that have succeeded by injecting flexibility and creativity into bureaucratic policies that govern their existence.

TYPES OF ADVOCACY GROUPS

Advocacy groups can form to solve and monitor a particular problem (for example, Action for Children's Television); they can be a source of ongoing support for children's problems in general (such as raising money); or they can be an official government lobby (pressuring members of Congress to pass appropriate legislation). An example of an ongoing children's advocacy group, mentioned earlier, is the Children's Defense Fund (CDF), developed in 1973 to provide a strong and effective voice for all the children in America who cannot vote, lobby, or speak for themselves. Particular attention is paid to the needs of poor and minority children and those with disabilities (CDF, 2004).

The CDF's goal is to educate the nation about the needs of children and encourage preventive investment in children before they become ill, drop out of school, suffer family breakdown, or get into trouble. CDF monitors the development and implementation of federal and state policies (CDF, 2004).

Being an effective advocate requires knowledge of both the facts and the law. Careful research into various situations must occur before advocacy efforts at reforms are undertaken. Advocacy involves not only research and pressure for legislative reform but also following up on implementation of the reform. CDF staff include specialists in health, education, child welfare, mental health, child development, adolescent pregnancy prevention, family income, and youth employment.

The work of another ongoing children's advocacy group, the Child Welfare League of America (CWLA), also discussed earlier, is grounded in knowledge and understanding of the needs of children and their families. The league takes the position that advocacy is an important aspect of the total responsibility of contemporary child welfare agencies. According to the league's philosophy, a contemporary social agency cannot merely be a provider of services; it must also be concerned with the general welfare policies of the community. It must take into account the external forces and conditions that affect people's ability to function. Child welfare agencies are expected to help change unfavorable community conditions that affect children and their families adversely (Goffin & Lombardi, 1988). In this respect, CWLA employs an ecological approach to human development.

Agencies that belong to the CWLA must be committed to securing the fullest measure of services and rights to which children are entitled, halting processes and procedures that are adverse to children's interests, promoting humane and rational responses by government and others to the needs of children and families, discovering gaps in services and proposing ways to fill them, and focusing public attention on the nature and extent of problems and on possible solutions (Whittaker, 1983).

Many children's advocacy groups exist on a local level as well as on the national level. In some cases, local groups join together to form a national coalition in order to influence national public policy. A familiar example is the National Congress of Parents and Teachers Associations (PTA), which is devoted to improving relations between home and school on behalf of children.

In addition to the unmet needs of children examined earlier, there are still many others, such as child maltreatment, a more humane system of juvenile justice, and transition programs for young people leaving protective community services to become independent functioning adults. If these things bother you and you want to do something about them, you need to know how to become an advocate (NAEYC, 1996b; Phillips, 1981).

IN PRACTICE

How Can You Become an Advocate?

1. **Make a personal commitment**. Speak out, write, and be heard regarding a certain problem or need.
2. **Keep informed**. Do research and get facts. For example, if the problem in your neighborhood is lack of after-school care for children, find out how many families could benefit from such a service, what facilities would be available, what licensing requirements exist, what the cost would be, and so on. Find out what is currently being done to alleviate the problems or meet the need (publicly and privately). For example, do any public schools in your areas remain open after regular hours?
3. **Know the process**. Determine what must be done. Set priorities, and have a plan of action for how to use the information most effectively.
4. **Express your views**. Write letters, send e-mails, make telephone calls, talk in person to those in decision-making roles.
5. **Get support**. Seek allies both outside the system and inside the system (people or organizations that have the power to make changes).
6. **Be visible**. Be physically present at hearings, at meetings in the community, in legislators' offices.
7. **Show appreciation**. When those in power respond positively to your request by taking action or speaking publicly, send a "thank-you" message immediately.
8. **Monitor implementation**. Legislation often outlines intent and directions, as it is a result of compromise; continue to watch the specifics in order to correct misinterpretations or problems; analyze budgets.
9. **Build rapport and trust**. Be a reliable source of information to those in power so you will be trusted; volunteer to help your elected official; influence legislation.
10. **Educate your legislators**. Meet new decision makers, keep them informed by sending them articles, invite them to speak at meetings and visit targeted programs, influence appointments to advisory boards.

ADVOCATING FOR CHILD PROTECTION

What can you do to help protect children?

Inappropriate parenting practices resulting in child abuse or neglect were discussed in Chapter 4, and the role of the caregiver in protecting children who might be maltreated was discussed in Chapter 5. Here, advocacy for children is exemplified in the law (macrosystem influence) and in the community services provided to help families in need of emotional support and parenting skills, as well as children who have been maltreated (mesosystem influence of linkages between the community and families). According to the National Clearinghouse on Child Abuse and Neglect (2002):

1. Know your state's child abuse/neglect laws. All states require that suspected child abuse be reported, but each state defines abuse differently and has different reporting procedures. You can get a copy of your state's law from a department of social services; a law enforcement agency; a state, district, city, or county attorney's office; or a regional office of child development.

2. Know who must report abuse and neglect. Injury, sexual molestation, death, abuse, or physical neglect that is suspected of having been inflicted upon any child under age 18 by other than accidental means *must* be reported by the following persons:

- physician
- surgeon
- teacher
- child caregiver
- dental hygienist
- ophthalmologist
- pharmacist
- commercial film and photographic print processor
- dentist
- chiropractor
- osteopath
- podiatrist
- nurse
- hospital intern or resident
- foster parent
- group home personnel
- marriage, family, child counselor
- school personnel
- social worker
- county medical examiner
- psychologist
- law enforcement officer
- audiologist
- clinical laboratory technician
- speech pathologist
- others having responsibility for child care

3. Know how to report abuse and neglect according to the law. Table 5.4 in Chapter 5, titled "Indications of Possible Maltreatment," describes physical and behavioral indicators of possible abuse. If you consistently notice several of the indicators over a period of time, you have a valid reason to report your observations.

Every state requires that a report of suspected child abuse be made "immediately" or "promptly." This means that as soon as you suspect abuse, you must inform the appropriate agency. The person taking the call is trained to determine whether it is an emergency situation and an immediate response is required or whether it can wait a few days. The response depends on the age of the child, the severity of the abuse, and how accessible the child is to the perpetrator. In a typical protective service investigation of alleged maltreatment, the professional must decide not "Has this child been maltreated?" but rather "Is this maltreatment extreme enough to justify community intervention?"

Once an investigation is made by a social worker and a police officer, it is determined whether or not to remove the child into protective custody. If the child is removed, he or she is placed in an institution until the court decides on final placement. The court hearing must take place within a specified time (usually 72 hours) after the child has been taken into protective custody. The child and the accused abusers are assigned different lawyers. The court can require a family preservation program, such as counseling or parent education, along with supervision by a social worker. The court can rule that the child be placed in an institution or in foster care for a specified time while the accused become rehabilitated. Then another hearing takes place to determine whether the family is ready for reunification.

Individuals who report abuse or neglect do have legal protection. That is, those people who report abuse in good faith are granted immunity from civil and criminal court action, such as lawsuits, even if the report, when investigated, turns out to be erroneous. Family members who have been wrongly accused of child abuse or neglect can suffer emotional turmoil, so it is important to observe and take notes to document observations before reporting the suspected abuse. A national organization for victims of child abuse laws, called VOCAL, exists to address their concerns.

What treatment or intervention programs are available for child maltreatment?

Beyond identifying and assessing maltreatment, agencies and practitioners confront the challenge of providing effective treatment or intervention programs. In order to protect children, *legal intervention* is the first requirement (Goodman et al., 1998).

Once suspected abuse or neglect is reported to the appropriate authorities, a social worker and/or a police officer is sent to the home or school to investigate. If it is determined that the child is endangered, the child is placed in protective custody—which usually means the child is taken away from the parents or guardians and is brought to a state, county, or city institution until the case is heard in court (usually within 72 hours). Some communities assign a child advocate to the child, usually a trained volunteer with an interest in helping children. The child advocate supports the child through interviews with police and lawyers as well as going to court with the child, if necessary.

If, on the other hand, it is legally determined that the child is not in immediate danger but there may be some risk of future abuse or neglect, the social services agency, as directed by the court, may provide a variety of support services to the family. Such services may also be required if and when the child is returned home after being in protective custody.

The following are various types of *therapeutic intervention* or *treatment* used with families that are abusive, depending on the particular case (Goodman et al., 1998; Wolfe, 1994). The individual child, the family, and the community context (what is available and/or ethnically amenable) must be considered in deciding the most effective treatment (Garbarino et al., 1986).

- **Family preservation**. The child remains at home under the supervision of the protective agency. The child protective worker visits the home on a scheduled basis. The worker can teach child development and child management to the parents.
- **Homemaker services**. A person employed by the appropriate community agency helps the family with home management and child care.
- **Parent education**. The parents take a formal course given in their community.
- **Child care**. The child is cared for during the day at a center or in a family day-care home.
- **Family therapy**. A therapist addresses the whole family's interaction patterns.
- **Kinship care**. The child is temporarily (or permanently) placed in the care of grandparents or other close relatives.
- **Foster care**. The child is temporarily placed in another home until his or her family can provide adequate care.

- **Parent groups**. The parents are required to join a support group, such as Parents Anonymous (a voluntary organization of child abusers), and/or become involved in their child's school.
- **Institutionalization**. The child is temporarily placed in an institution for abused/neglected children until his or her family can provide adequate care.
- **Residential family care**. The whole family moves into a supervised environment.
- **Adoption**. When returning the child to his or her home is unwise or impossible, the child is put up for adoption. This avoids interminable foster care.

Support. The goals of treating the family that is abusive are to help the parents with their problems, help the children with their problems, and improve the relationship between parents and children in order to prevent further abuse (Cole & Duva, 1990).

Before any changes can be made in the abusive adults' behavior, it must be realized that they may have unmet needs and may need to be "parented" themselves before they can become adequate parents to their children. This support can come from therapy, a parent aide, or a group such as Parents Anonymous. Also, the parents have to want to make changes in their behavior. They have to understand their own self-destructive pattern and its consequences.

Parents Anonymous, founded in 1970, now has chapters all over the country. Parents can join on their own or can be ordered to join by the court. When parents join Parents Anonymous, they are taught how to handle anger or frustration— for example, going into a room alone and then screaming, kicking, or pounding. The point is to get the aggression out on objects so that no one gets hurt. Members share their difficulties and try to work them out at meetings, with the help of other members. They try to develop solutions to their problems and to learn to feel better about themselves. The members maintain a network of telephone numbers so that they can call one another for support when they feel a crisis coming on.

Parents are children's primary role models, the most important people in their lives. Much of what children learn about dealing with stress and conflict is patterned on their parents' behavior (Iverson & Segal, 1990). Children's Village, a treatment facility for children who have been abused and their families, and other programs like it reflect the current attitude among social service professionals that treatment for abuse should include reeducating the parents and strengthening the family wherever possible, while making sure that the child who is victimized is protected.

Parents who are abusive need to alter their behavior in these ways:

- *They need to learn to deal appropriately with emotions and stress*. They need to increase their repertoire of coping mechanisms in dealing with frustration. They need to become less isolated and learn to turn to others when in need of help or support. They should be able to develop an improved self-esteem and be increasingly able to enjoy life.
- *They need to develop more realistic expectations of themselves and of others*. They also must work on breaking potentially self-destructive patterns of interpersonal relationships. For example, a mother must learn not to continually become involved with passive–aggressive men. A passive–aggressive person tends to resist the demands of others in an indirect way—procrastination, inefficiency, forgetfulness, complaining.

- *They need to learn what is age- and developmentally appropriate behavior for children*. They must also learn to tolerate and understand children's negative behavior. They need to view the child as an individual, rather than a personal need–satisfying object. To do this, they must learn empathy and respect for the child's individuality. Finally, the parents must learn to express affection toward the child, both verbally and physically.

Prevention. Social agencies have begun to develop various programs to help families with problems. With the passage of the Child Abuse Prevention Act in 1974, government funds became available for research on effective preventive programs. Some programs are based on parent effectiveness training, which concentrates on developing good communication between parents and their children. These programs theorize that abuse often occurs because parents do not understand or know how to react to their children's expressions of need and affection. Other programs teach behavior modification techniques. The aim of these programs is to provide alternatives to physical punishment when disciplining children. Parents are trained to notice their children behaving appropriately and to reward them accordingly. In some communities, hotlines provide counseling advice, available any time of the day.

Still other programs concentrate on preventing abuse, even before birth. For example, Johns Hopkins University has such a preventive program for high-risk mothers. These women are sought out while pregnant. They are counseled and may choose abortion. Those who choose to have their children are given classes in parenting, health, and nutrition. They are also assisted in planning their future education and career, as well as in learning how to use the community services available to them.

Epilogue

A community serves both the individual and the group. The judge in the Russian folktale, while protecting the plaintiff's rights to his money, also protected the security of the people in the village. By sentencing the defendant to pay for lying and cheating, the judge preserved the law and order of the group.

If children are to grow up to be contributing members of adult society, they need positive role models, mentors, and leaders. They need to experience democracy in action—involvement, discussion, collaboration, and compromise.

Summary

The community comprises a group of people living in the same district under common laws who have a sense of fellowship among themselves. Community ecology comprises the relationship between those people and their environment. The need for community is both psychological and practical.

The community is structured to have five functions: production/distribution/consumption, socialization, social control, social participation, and mutual support. These functions are performed in many different ways by different communities, thereby affecting the socialization of the children growing up in them.

The community influences socialization through the role models it provides for adults, such as earning a living, socializing with one another, and helping one another. The community influences socialization by the way the people in it instill their norms and values in children. And the community also influences socialization by the way it enforces its rules. Finally, the community is where children can "try themselves out" and learn the consequences of their behavior.

Physical factors in the community that have an impact on socialization are population density and characteristics, noise, arrangement and types of houses, and play settings.

Economic factors in a community play a central role in shaping the daily lives of families who live and work there. Economics affects unemployment rates, whether mothers seek employment, the ability of young adults to afford homes of their own, and the cost of living.

Certain social and personal factors, such as the neighborhood setting and patterns of community interaction, influence socialization. The neighborhood setting affects children's mobility, exposure to adults, friendship patterns, and types of play. Community interaction is important because of its supportive links to the family or school. Community relationships can be classified as informal, mutually dependent, and caring (gemeinschaft) or formal, independent, and contractual (gesellschaft).

Children can be involved in the community in order to learn. Libraries, museums, zoos, farms, businesses, and people's experiences are all rich sources of involvement. Children can make better use of the community if the school treats the community as an educational resource and if the community itself—the business community, for example—opens itself to children.

The community represents a formal support system through its community services. Community services are necessary because of population increase, the changing nature of the family, and increasing urbanization.

Chronosystem influences on community services involve changes in the macrosystem, such as political ideology and economics. Community agencies may be public, private, or a combination. Some community services are preventive, such as parks, recreation, and education agencies; some are supportive, such as family and child services; and some are rehabilitative, such as correction, mental health, and special needs agencies.

Mesosystem influences—linking community services to families and schools—can be fostered by establishing a local commission for children and families, establishing a neighborhood family center, fostering community projects, fostering youth participation in local policy bodies, and planning communities so as to consider the children who will be growing up in them.

Community services have attempted to meet the needs of children and families, but many needs are still unmet, such as economic, health, support, and special child care needs.

Child advocacy is the process of sensitizing individuals and groups to the unmet needs of children and to society's obligation to provide a positive response to those needs. To be an advocate, one must make a personal commitment, keep informed, know the process, express one's views, get support, be visible, show appreciation, build rapport and trust, and educate one's legislators.

Child maltreatment must be reported to police or social agencies. Professionals and persons responsible for child care are required by each state to report suspected cases of child abuse or neglect immediately. In turn, they are granted immunity from being sued if the investigation proves false.

Treatments for abusive parents include therapy, training in child development and child management, parent education, support groups, and supervision by a child protective agency. Various programs for the child include hospitalization when necessary, residential care, child care, foster care, adoption, and therapy. The choice, as well as the effectiveness, of such intervention programs depends on the individual child, the family, and the community context. The main goal in treating the family that is abusive is to improve the relationship between the parents and children in order to prevent further maltreatment.

Activity

PURPOSE   To learn about the services in your community.

Following are 10 hypothetical case studies involving families and children in a community. Read each of these case studies and select one family (or make up your own hypothetical one*) that you would like to help. Then complete the following steps:

1. Provide the family with a list of three agencies that may be helpful to them in their particular situation. Your list should include the following information about each agency (share with your class):
   a. Name of agency
   b. Address
   c. Telephone
   d. Hours
   e. Services provided
   f. Eligibility
   g. Fees
   h. Area served
2. Choose one of the three agencies on the list, call to make an appointment to visit the agency, and interview one person employed there (for example, director, counselor, teacher, therapist, or case worker). In this section of your report, be sure to include the following information:
   a. What steps would the agency take to help this hypothetical family (person)? Explain the services provided by this agency.
   b. For the person interviewed, describe job requirements, educational background, previous experience, job satisfactions/dissatisfactions, and other pertinent information.
   c. For the agency, give the number of employees, physical layout, number of people served, and other information regarding its scope and mission.

* Ideas: at-risk infant (premature, drug- or alcohol-exposed); relative with a terminal disease; transition programs for 18-year-olds no longer eligible for special or protective services; disaster (tornado, fire, hurricane, earthquake) assistance.

CASE STUDY 1: THE WILSON FAMILY

Matt Wilson is 67 years old. His wife has recently died. His daughter and her family, who live in another state, have persuaded Matt to sell his home and move close to them. After he finds an apartment and gets somewhat settled, Matt's family notices that he is having a difficult time adjusting. He seems continually depressed and sometimes confused. He does not leave his apartment often (although he has a car and drives), spends his days watching television, and doesn't seem to seek out other people. He is also not eating properly, and his family is afraid that his physical, as well as mental, health will begin to decline rapidly.

Is there help available for Matt in your community? What would you recommend to Matt's family in order to help him?

CASE STUDY 2: THE JOHNSON FAMILY

You are a first-grade teacher at an elementary school. You are especially worried about one of the students in your class, Michael Johnson. He always seems to arrive at school extra early (usually about 30 minutes). He is never dressed appropriately for the weather, and his general appearance is sloppy. His schoolwork is on grade level. However, at times his behavior is aggressive and hostile (especially toward classmates). On several occasions you have noticed bruises on Michael, and when you ask him about these, he is really evasive. During your first parent/teacher conference, you share your concerns with Mrs. Johnson. She breaks down and tells you that her husband, Michael's stepfather, is very hard on him. He is sarcastic, always belittling Michael, and at times gets physically violent with him. Mrs. Johnson asks you for help. What is your role as a teacher? What assistance is available to Michael and to his family in your community?

CASE STUDY 3: THE PETERSON FAMILY

Mary Peterson is a single parent living in your community. She has three children, Pam (16), Brian (14), and Lynn (12). Mary works full-time, and the three children all attend school. Mary's oldest daughter, Pam, has always been a good student and has had a nice group of friends. Pam has rarely had any problems that could not be worked out easily. Recently, however, Pam has been very withdrawn and moody. She spends a lot of time in her room, and Mary suspects that she is crying a lot. When confronted, Pam gets emotional and shouts at Mary, "Mind your own business and leave me alone!" Mary questions her other children about Pam's behavior. Finally, Lynn tells her Mom that Pam thinks she is pregnant. Where would you suggest that Pam and Mary Peterson go for help in this situation? What kind of assistance is available to them in your community? Who can help Pam explore her options and make a decision about this pregnancy?

CASE STUDY 4:
THE MEYERS FAMILY

Paula and Larry Meyers live in your community with their two children, Kelly (4) and Lisa (18 months). Lisa is not showing the normal development that Kelly did at this age, and Paula is very concerned. Lisa is not yet standing or walking. She does not respond to the family with love and affection and often seems to be in her own little world. Their pediatrician has suggested that the Meyers take Lisa to a neurologist for some testing. After extensive tests, it is determined that Lisa has cerebral palsy. Paula and Larry want to provide Lisa with every possible opportunity for a normal life. What services are available to Lisa and her family in your community? Where would you recommend the Meyers go to get assistance?

CASE STUDY 5:
THE SIMMONS FAMILY

Martin Simmons lives in your community with his wife, Sue, and their 14-year-old son, Steve. Martin has worked for a large engineering firm in the area for the past 12 years. Recently, due to cutbacks, Martin lost his job. He has been unemployed for the past eight months, and his family is really feeling the pressure of his job loss. Martin was actively looking for a job for the first month of his unemployment. Lately, however, he has begun drinking more and more and looking for work less and less. Since he began drinking, his relationship with his wife, and especially with his son, has suffered a tremendous strain. Sue is convinced that Martin is becoming

addicted to alcohol and feels he is settling deeper and deeper into a depressed state. Steve is angry with his dad, and they are continually fighting with one another. Sue has asked you to help her find assistance for herself and her family. What agencies would you suggest the Simmons family contact for assistance?

CASE STUDY 6:
THE HERNANDEZ FAMILY

During lunch break on the junior high school playground, you notice a group of boys in a small circle intently examining something. As you approach the group, Roberto hastily shoves something in his pocket. In the haste, a joint drops on the ground. You pick it up and escort the group to the principal's office. You learn that Roberto got the marijuana from his older brother, who is in a gang, and brought it to show his friends. Mr. and Mrs. Hernandez are called, and a conference is scheduled. After explaining the situation to the parents, where do you refer this family for help?

CASE STUDY 7:
THE LAMBERT FAMILY

Mrs. Lambert waits to speak to you after picking up her daughter at the day-care center. She tells you that her husband has been laid off and his unemployment checks will stop next week. She can't pay the tuition at the center, and she has no other place to leave her daughter while she works. She must work to pay the rent and buy food. She hopes her husband will find work soon (he spends all day looking), because unpaid bills are piling up. The family no longer has medical insurance since the father lost his job. They have several doctor bills to pay for a severe ear infection their daughter had last month. The family car's tire treads are so worn that driving is unsafe, yet the car is the family's only means of transportation to work, the day-care center, and the store. Mrs. Lambert is terrified of having her family become homeless. Where would you refer Mrs. Lambert for help?

CASE STUDY 8:
THE SULLIVAN FAMILY

You are a prekindergarten teacher at a local preschool. Brian is a student who turned 5 in November.

Brian's behavior in class is causing problems for you and for the other students. He has difficulty sitting still, attending long enough to a story, completing any activities, and keeping his hands to himself. Brian is easily frustrated and is prone to temper tantrums and outbursts of aggression. Mrs. Sullivan, a single parent, has experienced the same problems with Brian at home. What could be the cause of Brian's behavior, and where would you refer this family for help?

CASE STUDY 9: THE NGUYEN FAMILY

A child enters your public school preschool class the first day and speaks no English. You wait for his mother to pick him up so you can get some information about the child. The mother's English is very limited. You resort to communicating in simple words combined with gestures. You even draw pictures in order to communicate. You learn that the family has recently arrived from Vietnam and is staying with relatives who were sponsored to come to the United States the previous year. The father works in a local electronics factory, and the mother is expecting another child in three months.

The mother is most anxious that her son, as well as she and her husband, learn English and the "American way" as quickly as possible. Where do you refer this family for help with American culture?

CASE STUDY 10: THE HORVATH FAMILY

For the past two years, Mr. Horvath has brought and picked up two of his children, now $4\frac{1}{2}$ and $5\frac{1}{2}$, to the children's center. You have never met the mother. One day a woman comes to the center claiming she is the Horvath children's mother. She asks to have them released to her. You refuse because her name is not on their information form. She produces a court document stating she has legal custody of the children and demands they be released to her. You assign someone to watch the children while you call the police and the father (immediate attention is required by the legal authorities). The father admits the mother was granted legal custody, but she was continually drunk, so he took them. He has had them for two years, and she has never even visited them once. What do you advise him to do?

Related Readings

Belle, D. (1999). *The after-school lives of children: Alone and with others while parents work*. Mahwah, NJ: Lawrence Erlbaum.

Decker, L. E., & Decker, V. A. (2001). *Engaging families and communities: Pathways to educational success* (2nd ed.). Fairfax, VA: National Community Education Association.

Etzioni, A. (1993). *The spirit of the community: The reinvention of American society*. New York: Touchstone.

Garbarino, J. (1995). *Building a socially nourishing environment with children*. San Francisco: Jossey-Bass.

Goffin, S. G., & Lombardi, J. (1988). *Speaking out: Early childhood advocacy*. Washington, DC: National Association for Education of Young Children.

Nazario, T. A. (1988). *In defense of children: Understanding the rights, needs, and interests of the child*. New York: Charles Scribner's.

Putnam, R. D. (2000). *Bowling alone: The collapse and revival of American community*. New York: Simon & Schuster.

Rickel, A. U., & Becker, E. (1997). *Keeping children from harm's way: How national policy affects psychological development*. Washington, DC: American Psychological Association.

Rivkin, M. S. (1995). *The great outdoors: Restoring children's rights to play outside*. Washington, DC: National Association for the Education of Young Children.

Robinson, A., & Stark, D. (2005). *Advocates in action: Making a difference for young children* (2nd ed.). Washington, DC: National Association for Young Children.

Schorr, L. B. (1997). *Common purpose: Strengthening families and neighborhoods to rebuild America*. New York: Anchor Books.

Warren, R. L., & Lyon, L. (1983). *New perspectives on the American community*. Homewood, IL: Dorsey Press.

Whittaker, J. K., & Garbarino, J. (1983). *Social support networks: Informal helping in the human services*. New York: Aldine.

Chapter 11

Brand X Pictures/Jupiterimages

Emotional and Cognitive Socialization Outcomes

What gives life its value you can find—and lose. But never possess. This holds good above all for "the truth about life."

— DAG HAMMARSKJÖLD

What influences have contributed to how you have come to feel and think about things?

The following Burmese folktale, *The Four Puppets*, illustrates the chapter's introductory quote. The story tells of a young man seeking his fortune and getting different advice from four talking puppets. He learns by experience that one's actions lead to certain outcomes, thereby gaining a sense of "personal agency" as well as what values are important in life.

Once Upon a Time A long time ago, there lived a puppet maker who had a son named Aung. The father hoped his son would become a puppet maker like himself, but Aung wanted to leave home to seek his fortune. His father sadly agreed and said, "Let me give you some companions for your journey."

He showed his son four wooden puppets that he had carved. "Each puppet has its own virtue and value," said the father. The first puppet was the king of the gods. "The god's virtue is wisdom," said the puppet maker. The second was a green-faced ogre. "The ogre's virtue is strength." The third was a mystic sorcerer. "The sorcerer's virtue is knowledge." The fourth was a holy hermit. "The hermit's virtue is goodness."

The father told his son, "Each of these virtues can help you on your way; but remember, strength and knowledge must always serve wisdom and goodness."

Aung started out on his journey the next day, carrying a bamboo pole with food and clothing on one end and the puppets hanging from the other.

When night fell, Aung found himself deep in the jungle. He set his things down under a banyan tree and thought, "I wonder if this is a safe place to sleep. I'll just ask one of the puppets."

Aung looked at the king of the gods and said, "Tell me, is it safe here?"

To his amazement, the puppet came alive, got down from the pole, and grew to life size. The god told Aung, "Open your eyes and look around you. That is the first step to wisdom. If you fail to see what is right before you, how easy it will be for others to misguide you!" In a moment, the puppet was hanging from the pole.

When Aung had gotten over his shock, he looked around. There, in the soft dirt, were the tracks of a tiger! Aung climbed the tree and slept in the branches.

The next day, Aung reached the mountains. He camped a little way off the side of the road that night. In the morning, when he awoke, he saw a caravan coming. "That looks like it might belong to some rich merchants; I wish I had wealth like that," Aung mused. He then turned to the green-faced ogre puppet, "Tell me, how can I gain such riches?"

Aung watched the puppet leave the pole, grow to life size, and shout, "If you have strength, you can take whatever you like. Watch this!" The ogre stamped his foot and the earth shook. Dirt and rocks broke loose and rushed down the mountain blocking the road. The terrified merchants jumped off their carts and ran off.

Aung hurried down from his campsite to the carts full of rich fabrics and precious metals. "All of this is mine now!" he cried. Just then, he heard a sob. Hiding in one of the carts was a young woman of the same age as Aung. "Don't worry; I won't hurt you," said Aung gently. "Who are you?"

"My name is Mala," she said in a small voice. "My father is the owner of this caravan. We were on our way to meet him." Aung fell immediately in love. He wanted to be with Mala forever, so he said, "I'll take you with me and care for you."

Mala replied angrily, "Go ahead! Take me; you took everything else, you thief! But I'll never speak to you!"

Aung was shocked; he didn't know what to say or do. The ogre came up beside him saying, "Don't listen to her. She'll change her mind—and anyway, you did get what you wanted. Now, let's go."

The ogre cleared the road, then helped Aung lead the caravan. When they came out of the mountains and neared the capital city, Aung asked the ogre, "What should I do with these riches?"

"Don't ask me," said the ogre. "Ask the sorcerer."

Aung turned to the mystic sorcerer. "Can you tell me what to do?"

The puppet came to life, floating before him, as Mala gaped. "If you want your wealth to grow," said the sorcerer, "you must learn the secrets of nature."

He tapped Aung with his red wand, and together they rose high in the air. Looking down, Aung saw everything in a new way. He could tell what land was best for farming, and which mountains held gold and silver.

"This is wonderful! Just think how I could help people with what I know," said Aung.

"Certainly you could," said the sorcerer. "But knowledge is power. Why not keep it to yourself; isn't that what others do?"

"I suppose so," replied Aung as he entered the city. Aung became a merchant, and with the help of the ogre and the sorcerer, he grew many times richer than at first. He bought a palace for himself, Mala, and the puppets. But Mala still would not speak to him.

Aung was not happy. He gave Maal beautiful clothes and magnificent jewels, but still she turned away. Aung went to the puppets' room and spoke to the ogre and the sorcerer. "I have more wealth than I need and Mala's father must be very poor. I'll help Mala find him, so I can return what I took, then maybe she'll speak to me and even, perhaps, love me."

"What a terrible idea!" said the ogre. "You should never give up what is yours; you're just being weak!"

"It doesn't matter anyway because Mala ran away last night," said the sorcerer.

Aung looked all over the palace, but Mala was nowhere to be found. He rushed to the puppet's room and despairingly cried, "What good is all my wealth if I've lost what I care for most?" The ogre and sorcerer were silent.

Then Aung remembered there was one puppet he had never called on. He turned to the holy hermit. "Tell me, why has everything gone wrong?"

The puppet came to life and said, "You imagined that wealth brings happiness. But true happiness comes only from goodness. What is important is not what you have but what you do with it."

The king of the gods then came to life and stood beside the hermit. "You forgot what your father told you, Aung. Strength and knowledge are useful, but they must always serve wisdom and goodness."

"I won't forget again," said Aung. From then on, he used his wealth to build a holy pagoda, offering food and shelter to those who visited the shrine.

One day, among the visitors, Aung saw a familiar face. It was Mala! She was walking with an old man. Aung rushed over to them and knelt. "Sir, I have done you great wrong. I beg your forgiveness. All I have is yours and I give it up gladly. I will be content to return to my village and make puppets."

"Father, this is Aung; but he has changed!" said Mala.

"So it seems," said Mala's father. "If so, it would be a shame to let go of a young man with such talent. Perhaps he would like to work for me, and live with us in the palace."

And so, Aung became the old merchant's assistant, and before long, his partner, and in time, when Mala's heart was won, his son-in-law.

Aung continued to call on the puppets as needed, and even though he was helped by strength and knowledge, he always was guided by wisdom and goodness.

Source: "The Four Puppets," retold by Khin Myo Chit, in *Folk Tales from Asia for Children Everywhere,* Book 3, UNESCO, 1976.

The four puppets in the story represent various outcomes of socialization. When Aung leaves home, he totally relies on the puppets' advice, becoming helpless. When the outcome of that advice becomes contrary to his upbringing, he realizes that he, too, can produce outcomes by taking charge. When he takes responsibility for using what he has learned to help others, he gains a feeling of high self-esteem.

The outcomes of socialization that are examined in this chapter and the next can be categorized as primarily emotional and cognitive (such as values, attitudes, motives, attributions, and self-esteem) or primarily social and behavioral (such as self-regulation, morals, and gender roles). These outcomes are the result of child, family, school, peer, and community interaction (mesosystems). Also influencing the development of these outcomes are exosystems (such as parents' work or school board policies), factors in individuals' macrosystems (such as religion, ethnicity, or economics), and the chronosystem (changes in society or in individuals themselves, such as today's sexual norms compared to those of one's grandparents). Figure 11.1 provides an ecological model of the systems involved in the process.

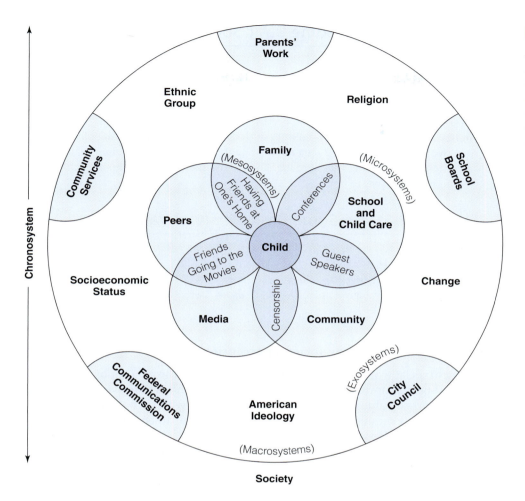

Figure 11.1

An Ecological Model of Human Development

The child's values, attitudes, motives, attributions, and self-esteem are outcomes of his or her socialization.

- **How can socializing agents enable children to develop humanitarian values and attitudes, rather than stereotypical ones?**

- **How can socializing agents work together to foster achievement motives and a sense of personal responsibility in children?**

- **How can young people's self-esteem be supported?**

Values

What is important to you in life?

Values, as introduced in Chapter 2, are qualities or beliefs that are viewed as desirable or important. They can include such related characteristics as attitudes or morals, which affect our behavior. Values are outcomes of socialization. Some of our values reflect the values of our parents, our teachers, our religion, our culture, our profession, or our friends. Some reflect what we have read, or seen on TV or film, as well as what we have directly experienced. Values, whether societal or personal, can change over time.

What Are Some Basic Societal Values?

Equal justice for all. "Do unto others as you would have them do unto you."
    —The Golden Rule
Compassion for those in need. "With malice toward none, with charity for all."
    —Abraham Lincoln
Equality of opportunity. "We hold these truths to be self-evident: that all men
    are created equal, that they are endowed by their Creator with certain inalien-
    able rights; that among these are life, liberty, and the pursuit of happiness."
    —Thomas Jefferson

What Are Some Basic Personal Values?

Truth. "The truth shall make you free." —John
Love. "to love and be loved." —Edgar Allan Poe
Knowledge. "Knowledge is power." —*Meditationes Sacrae*

How are values affected by societal perceptions?

According to social work professor Sophie Freud (1999), the concept of "normality" is based on societal norms at a given time, as well as who is perceived as deviating from those norms. Values also affect how society deals with such deviations. In the United States, it is common for deviations from "normal" to be referred to psychologists or social workers who believe their professional support can alleviate the "problem," or they may be referred to psychiatrists who believe medication is what is needed. However, in other times and in other cultures, individuals with problems would rarely divulge confidences and personal feelings to a stranger. Rather, common practice for those experiencing problems is to keep them private because divulging deviance would be shameful. Sometimes, though, individuals do turn to family and/or religion for help.

It is common in the United States to label deviations from normal in order to provide formal and appropriate help (diagnosis and treatment). Labels, however, are really value judgments influenced by chronosystem factors such as politics, economics, and technology. For example, the American Psychiatric Association's Diagnostic and Statistical Manual no longer lists homosexuality as a disorder. Recent additions to the list of pathologies are attention deficit hyperactivity disorder (ADHD) and posttraumatic stress disorder (PTSD).

How are values affected by personal perceptions?

Factors such as age, experience, cognitive development, and moral reasoning affect values. The following story illustrates diverse personal perceptions, reflecting the perspectives of different generations.

Jessy wanted to have a party for her graduation from high school. The neighborhood where she lived with her family had a recreation room, which was rented out for a nominal fee to various groups for meetings, club functions, and parties. Jessy's parents, Tom and

Cheryl, agreed to let Jessy have the party provided the rules for rental were followed. One rule was that parties for minors had to be chaperoned; another was that there could be no more than fifty people; another was that the room had to be cleaned after the party; and the last was that no alcohol could be served to minors. Jessy agreed to all but the last: "How can you have a graduation party without beer? C'mon, get real . . . no one will come!" "Sorry," said Tom, "you want a party, you have to abide by the rules." "OK, OK, but we better have great food," Jessy grumbled.

One week before the party, Cheryl got a phone call from a parent of a girl she did not know. The parent wanted to confirm that there was in fact a party, that beer would be served, and that the cost of a formal invitation was $10. Cheryl could hardly contain her shock and anger. Apparently, a flier had been distributed at school "advertising" the party. Cheryl thanked the parent and said there would be no such party.

Cheryl told Tom what happened and together they confronted Jessy. Jessy said it was one of her friends who had distributed the flier (Jessy would not tell who). Tom said he was extremely disappointed that she hadn't stopped her friend, as they had agreed to the rules for the party—especially no alcohol—in advance; as a result, there would be no party. Tom explained that advertising the party, especially one in which beer would be served, was setting up her parents for trouble—uninvited kids having to be denied entrance to the party and leaving, angry neighbors calling the police, and he and Cheryl being responsible for any alcohol-related accidents. Jessy listened and said she understood her father's position but that he and Cheryl were out of touch with reality: all graduation parties have booze; they didn't understand her position; she couldn't have a party and not do what was expected. "Well, then, I guess the party is off," said Tom, "because we had expectations, too."

The next evening several of Jessy's friends came over to beg Tom and Cheryl to reconsider. They claimed drinking was going to occur on graduation night whether or not Jessy had the party; Jessy's having the party would at least keep the kids from driving around drunk. The best way to prevent alcohol-related accidents was to let Jessy have the party, take everyone's car keys, and have all the kids spend the night.

Cheryl said, "That's an interesting argument, but first, I feel morally wrong serving kids alcohol; second, the recreation room belongs to the community, and the rules cannot be broken; and third, it is illegal for kids under 21 to drink in this state."

Tom shook his head and said to Cheryl, "The values of this generation are so different from those of ours. Why does booze have to be the essential ingredient for having a good time?"

Jessy placed more value on what her friends thought than what her parents thought. Her parents, on the other hand, placed more value on obeying the law and following the community policy in regard to minors drinking alcohol than on Jessy's saving face with her friends.

In the pop culture, as portrayed by the media, much value is placed on drinking alcohol as a means of having fun, whereas in certain religious and ethnic groups, drinking alcohol is considered sinful. Thus, some people might experience conflict in social situations.

As soon as children can understand language, they have access to their parents' and their culture's values (Damon, 1988). As children develop cognitively and can interpret the meaning of their social interactions and real experiences, they begin to construct their own values, which will change and be redefined as they get older.

VALUES CLARIFICATION

How do individuals come to know what is personally important?

One technique is known as **values clarification**—the process of discovering what is personally worthwhile or desirable in life. This process can help individuals understand their own moral codes, their attitudes and motives, their prosocial or antisocial behavior, their gender roles, and themselves. For example, in teaching about the founding of the United States, a *factual* discussion might explore dates and events; a *conceptual* discussion might discuss emigration and freedom of religion; a *values* discussion might address questions like these: What is so important to you that if it were taken away, you would leave your country? If you left, what would you take with you? A values clarification exercise can be found in the chapter activity.

Values clarification involves making decisions—choosing among alternatives. Sometimes the process is difficult because values may conflict. For example, Tom and Cheryl had to choose between their values of respect for the law and family harmony; Jessy had to weigh her value of preserving friendship against that of respecting the law.

How is personal values clarification influenced by human and societal values?

At times, the process of values clarification is less difficult because certain basic *human* values are enshrined in the laws of most civilized societies. The Ten Commandments are an example of basic human values, some of which ("Thou shalt not kill") are also found in laws. Other values are basic to a particular society. An example of a basic *societal* value is the Bill of Rights, which lists the rights and freedoms (freedom of speech, for instance) assumed to be essential to people in our society.

values clarification
the process of discovering what is personally worthwhile or desirable in life

Many adolescents in this culture equate alcohol with having a good time.

FogStock LLC/Index Stock Imagery

Human values and societal values are part of our cultural heritage. Many of the decisions we make are based on such learned values. Still other values are *personal*; they develop through experiences and relationships. Differences in social and personal interactions make for a wide divergence in human values. For example, some people value money over leisure time. They would rather spend most of their time working to earn money to afford a large house or an expensive car. Others would rather schedule their work so that they have some time for leisure—time to enjoy their families, their homes, or their environment—even if, by so doing, they earn less money.

Values influence parenting styles, as discussed in Chapter 4. Some parents believe the most effective way to raise a child is to be *authoritarian*; others believe an *authoritative* style is best; still others believe a *permissive* style is optimal. Values in adolescents, outcomes of diverse parenting styles, have been found to be related to delinquency, substance abuse, and sexual activity (Goff & Goddard, 1999). Teens valuing fun/enjoyment and security were strongly identified with delinquency and substance abuse, whereas those valuing self-respect, a sense of accomplishment, and a warm relationship with others exhibited a low frequency of delinquent behavior and substance abuse. Sexual activity was found to be related to wanting a warm relationship with others.

Values also influence government policies. For example, during the 1960s, many social programs were initiated as part of the War on Poverty; in the 1980s, many social programs were cut back or eliminated as a way to achieve the goal of a balanced budget. The 1990s bore the goal of building a nation of learners, which continues in the 2000s with the Leave No Child Behind Act.

Values of specific groups have an impact on government decisions and consequent policies, mentioned in the advocacy discussion in Chapter 10. A pertinent example of how group values influence public policy is the Human Capital Initiative, launched by professional associations in the behavioral sciences (National Science Foundation, 1994). Government funding for this NSF initiative supports research to better understand how human processes (intellectual, physical, and psychological) influence productive citizenship. Values of the NSF are reflected in these specific areas prioritized for funding:

1. Building strong neighborhoods
2. Educating for the future
3. Employing a productive workforce
4. Fostering successful families
5. Overcoming poverty and deprivation
6. Reducing disadvantages in a diverse society

Since the 1970s, many people have begun to question the role of the federal government in services to children and families (Children's Defense Fund, 2004; Schorr, 1997). Some believe that many of the country's expensive public health and public welfare programs, such as child abuse and neglect programs, residential and outpatient psychotherapy, and rehabilitation following avoidable accidents, might be greatly reduced if parents were more effective in nurturing and socializing their children. Whereas most people value the importance of the family to children, few supported the 1980 White House Conference on Families' proposal to implement universal parent education in the schools (Caldwell, 1986). Thus, although people may share a value, they may not agree as to how to implement it.

Attitudes

How are attitudes related to values as outcomes of socialization?

In 2005, the National Collegiate Athletic Association voted to ban the use of nicknames and mascots it considers "hostile or abusive" in terms of race, ethnicity, or national origin during its postseason college sports events. Most cited were Native American images or references. The rationale behind the decision is the belief that stereotypes and caricatures via logos or mascots are harmful to children. Some people argue that sports teams differ from street or city names because of the competition involved—a sports team creates a division because one team wins and one loses. Others disagree, saying that a school's use of a nickname and symbol shows honor and respect. For example, the Tribal Council of the Seminole Tribe of Florida supports Florida State University's use of Chief Osceola, who gallops onto the football field on horseback and plants a burning spear in the turf before home games. The new rules would "have us cover the Seminole name and symbol as if we were embarrassed," said the university president (Norwood, 2005, p. 20).

Recently, after many consultations with members of the community and experts in Aztec culture, San Diego State University replaced its Monty Montezuma mascot to make its depiction of Aztecs historically accurate and culturally appropriate. SDSU was successful in being excluded from the ban. Some people, often alumni, who have no ties to Indian heritage, develop strong identity ties to their school mascots. One Caucasian woman told a reporter, "I'm a third generation Redskin!"

Generally, colleges and universities may adopt any logo or mascot they wish, as that is an institutional decision. However, the NCAA is a national organization that must be sensitive to the attitudes of people in the communities where postseason games or championships are held.

An *attitude,* as introduced in Chapter 2, is a tendency to respond positively (favorably) or negatively (unfavorably) to certain persons, objects, or situations. The NCAA has a negative attitude toward the use of Native American mascots.

Prejudice is an attitude. The word means "prejudgment." It generally refers to the application of a previously formed judgment to some person, object, or situation. It can be favorable or unfavorable. Usually, prejudice comes from categorizing or stereotyping. The Seminole Tribal Council believes the NCAA is being prejudiced in deciding which mascots are inappropriate.

A *stereotype,* as introduced in Chapter 9, is an oversimplified, fixed attitude or set of beliefs that is held about members of a group. Stereotypical attitudes usually do not allow for individual exceptions. The reason for the NCAA ban is to minimize stereotyping of ethnic groups.

Attitudes are composed of beliefs, feelings, and behavior tendencies. Most psychologists agree that attitudes determine what we attend to in our environment, how we perceive the information about the object of our attention, and how we respond to that object. Thus, attitudes guide behavior. For example, someone with the attitude that intelligence is genetic will not support educational programs for children with learning problems in school, because he or she believes that environment cannot change biology.

prejudice an attitude involving prejudgment; the application of a previously formed judgment to some person, object, or situation

DEVELOPMENT OF ATTITUDES

How do attitudes develop?

The development of attitudes is influenced by age, cognitive development, and social experiences (Van Ausdale & Feagin, 2001). Researchers (Derman-Sparks,

1989; Van Ausdale & Feagin, 2001) suggest that attitudes about ethnic groups develop in the following sequence:

- Phase I—awareness of ethnic differences, beginning at about age $2\frac{1}{2}$ to 3
- Phase II—orientation toward specific ethnic-related words and concepts, beginning at about age 4
- Phase III—attitudes toward various ethnic groups, beginning at about age 7

This developmental sequence is probably due to the reaction of others to children's appearance—remarks about skin color, hair, and facial features alert children to the fact that people look different. Cognitive development and social experience are also factors.

As children develop cognitively, they begin to categorize (assimilate and accommodate) similarities and differences. Reviewing many studies of European American children's attitudes toward other groups, Aboud (1988) reported that 4- to 7-year-old European American children were already aware that "white" was the ethnic identity favored by their society. They referred to other groups as "bad" or with negative characteristics. ("He's lazy because he's colored.") Many African American children felt ambivalent about being African American and were envious of European American children. Hispanic children followed a similar pattern. After age 7, however, children of all ethnic groups were found to be less prejudiced toward other groups and had more positive attitudes toward their own group. Aboud explained young children's prejudicial attitudes as due to cognitive immaturity rather than malice.

Social experiences, including observation and interaction, provide children with a perspective of the macrosystem in which they live (Hirschfeld, 1997). Children come to know attitudes about ethnicity, religion, socioeconomic status, gender, disability, and age by watching TV, by hearing significant adults talk and seeing how they behave, and by noticing differences in neighborhood facilities (schools, theaters, sidewalks) and practices (employment, discrimination, violence). Exemplifying how color attitudes can be transmitted subtly, a 1993 Caldecott Honor Book (recognition given for pictures), *Seven Blind Mice*, by Ed Young (1992), is about seven blind mice, each a different and brilliant color, whose task is to identify an object. The white mouse solves the riddle and correctly identifies the object as an elephant. Many have criticized the book, complaining that the white mouse is portrayed as the "savior," thereby perpetuating prejudicial attitudes of "white supremacy" (Jacobs & Tunnell, 1996). Children will abstract attitudinal concepts from their social experiences and try them out. For example, in wanting to control the space in the sandbox, 4-year-old Carla says only people who speak Spanish are allowed; experimenting with a racial epitaph, Jimmy discovers he can be dominant by hurting others' feelings (Van Ausdale & Feagin, 2001).

Whether children act on messages from the media depends on their real-life experiences and interactions, especially with parents. Studies of young children show that those with the most prejudicial attitudes have parents who are authoritarian, who use strict disciplinary techniques, and who are inflexible in their attitudes toward right and wrong (Aboud, 1988; Boswell & Williams, 1975; Katz, 1975). Thus, rigid parental attitudes foster similar ones in their children.

Prejudicial attitudes are found in regard not only to ethnic differences but to disabilities as well. In a longitudinal study of children's attitudes toward those with mental *illness*, Weiss (1994) found that by the time children entered kindergarten, they already had stigmatizing attitudes, which remained stable when examined eight years later. However, perception of those with mental *disabilities* had changed from stigmatizing to more accepting. Perhaps the inclusion of children with mental disabilities in schools and their inclusion in the media and community have influenced the attitude change.

IN PRACTICE

How Does Prejudice Develop?

The following is a typical developmental sequence of how children become prejudiced:

- **Awareness**—being alert to, seeing, noticing, and understanding differences among people even though they may never have been described or talked about. Children model behavior they observe in adults they look up to.
- **Identification**—naming, labeling, and classifying people based on physical characteristics that children notice. Verbal identification relieves the stress that comes from being aware of or confused by something that you can't describe or no one else is talking about. Identification is the child's attempt to break the adult silence and make sense of the world. Children mimic what they see, hear, and read about.
- **Attitude**—having thoughts and feelings that become an inclination or opinion toward another person and their way of living in the world. Children may displace their feelings onto others who are less powerful.
- **Preference**—valuing, favoring, and giving priority to one physical attribute, person, or lifestyle over another, usually based on similarities and differences. Children understand the world from the perspective of their own experience.
- **Prejudice**—holding a preconceived hostile attitude, opinion, feeling, or action against a person, ethnic group, or their lifestyle without knowing them. Children generalize their personal experiences to the world.

Source: S. York (1991). *Roots and Wings: Affirming Culture in Early Childhood Programs.* St. Paul, MN: Toys 'n' Things Press, pp. 169–170.

INFLUENCES ON ATTITUDE DEVELOPMENT

What role do significant socializing agents play in influencing children's attitudes toward those who are similar and those who are different?

Family

Parents have a large impact on children's attitudes and values. Many studies have shown that the attitudes of children tend to resemble those of their parents; for example, 76% of a national sample of high school seniors favored the political party favored by both of their parents (McGuire, 1985). Ethnic prejudice also follows this general pattern. The ethnic prejudices of European American elementary school children tend to resemble those of their parents, as do the ethnic prejudices of African American elementary school children (Aboud, 1988).

Modeling. One explanation of the resemblance of children's and parents' ethnic attitudes is that children develop attitudes through role modeling. Children identify with models who are powerful and admirable. Through the process of identification, they begin to assume attitudes of the people they would like to emulate (parents, relatives, friends, fictional heroes or heroines, television and movie characters, rock stars).

Instruction. We often think of the ethnic majority as being prejudiced against ethnic minorities. However, prejudice is present in ethnic minorities, too. The following description illustrates how a Jewish boy's parents tried to socialize him to be prejudiced against Christians because they had been persecuted by prejudiced Christians.

My first impressions of Christianity came in the home, of course. My parents brought with them the burden of the Middle Ages from the blood-soaked continent of Europe. They had come from the villages of Eastern Europe where Christians were feared with legitimate reason.

When occasionally a Jewish drunk was seen in our neighborhood, our parents would say, "He's behaving like a Gentile."

For in truth, our parents had often witnessed the Polish, Romanian, Hungarian, and Russian peasants gather around a barrel of whiskey on Saturday night, drink themselves into oblivion, "and beat their wives." Once in a while the rumor would spread through the tenements that a fellow had struck his wife, and on all sides we heard the inevitable, "Just like a Gentile."

Oddly enough, too, our parents had us convinced that the Gentiles were noisy, boisterous, and loud—unlike the Jews. It is indeed strange how often stereotypes are exactly reversed.

If we raised our voices, we were told, "Jewish boys don't shout." And this admonition covered every activity in and out of the home: "Jewish boys don't fight." "Jewish boys don't get dirty." "Jewish boys study hard."

It wasn't until I was in school and was subjected to the influence of Gentile teachers and met Gentile social workers and classmates that I began to question these generalizations. Then I began to read and I found myself finally dismissing all prejudice from my mind. (Golden, 1962, p. 210)

The example illustrates one way children learn attitudes—by instruction. Young children accept as true the statements of their parents and others they admire because, with their limited experience, they are not apt to have heard anything different.

According to Ramsey (2004), children assimilate ethnically related attitudes, preferences, and social expectations at an early age. They understand the world in terms of absolutes and believe overgeneralizations. Therefore, because of their cognitive level of development, they are receptive to global stereotypical and prejudicial comments of adults. For example, in an experiment (Bigler, Brown, & Markell, 2001), 7- to 12-year-olds attending a summer school program were randomly assigned to groups denoted by yellow or blue T-shirts. The status of each group was artificially manipulated by the teachers; posters depicted members of the yellow group as having won more spelling and athletic competitions, giving their group higher status than the blue group. Teachers called attention to the different statuses, using them as a basis for seating arrangements, task assignments, and certain class privileges. When the children were asked to evaluate each other, those in the yellow group rated each other higher than the blue group, and the blue group rated each other lower. Those children not exposed to the artificial evaluative judgment of adults did not express prejudice toward each other.

Reinforcement and Punishment. The socializing techniques of reinforcement and punishment are also involved in the way children learn attitudes. For example, it has been demonstrated that attitudes toward ethnic groups can be influenced simply by associating them with positive words (reinforcement), such as *happy* or *successful,* or negative words (punishment), such as *ugly* or *failure* (Aboud, 1988; Lohr & Staats, 1973). For another example, negative attitudes about individuals with disabilities, such as they are vocationally limited or socially inept, are reinforced when such individuals are excluded from the mainstream of society (Gollnick & Chinn, 2005).

Peers

Peers influence attitudes and behavior. Children compare the acceptability of their beliefs with those of their friends. Children and adolescents whose peers are academically motivated are more likely to do well in school (Eccles, Wigfield, & Schiefele, 1998).

Coleman's (1966) classic study showed how prejudicial attitudes were molded among high school students. Another study (Margolis, 1971) found that the main factor affecting African Americans' association with European Americans was how they thought their African American friends would react.

Peers are also very influential in the development of gender-role attitudes, as was discussed in Chapter 8, as well as influencing who is accepted or rejected from the group based on similarities and/or differences. Because preadolescent children have a great need to identify with the peer group, someone who is ethnically different or who has a disability is often excluded (Gollnick & Chinn, 2005). Other attitudes influenced by peers involve dress, dating, personal problems, and sex (Sebald, 1986, 1989).

Because peer opinion is important to children, peers can be used to influence attitudes regarding achievement. Cooperative learning settings enable peers to help each other learn by sharing resources and modeling academic skills. Also, inclusion of diverse children in such cooperative learning groups reduces stereotypical and prejudicial attitudes (Eccles et al., 1998).

Mass Media

Television and Movies. Children and adolescents frequently cite television as a source of information that influences their attitudes about people and things (Comstock & Paik, 1991; Perse, 2001). "You see so much violence that it's meaningless. If I saw someone really get killed, it wouldn't be a big deal. I guess I'm turning into a hard rock," said an 11-year-old. "When I see a beautiful girl using shampoo or a cosmetic on TV, I buy them because I'll look like her. I have a ton of cosmetics," said a 13-year-old. Several studies have reported that middle and high school students rate the mass media as their most important source of information and opinions, even more important than their parents, teachers, and friends (Perse, 2001). Television, discussed in Chapter 9, is a source of social stereotypes. For example, although the occupational roles of African Americans have become more varied than the subservient roles shown in the past, other minority groups are often cast as villains or victims (Leibert & Sprafkin, 1988). To illustrate, Arab Americans have experienced negative stereotyping in movies. They are often portrayed as villains, criminals, or terrorists, as well as enacting taboos of American society such as polygamy (Bennett, 2003).

Although television and movies have generally had the reputation of perpetuating negative attitudes, they also have the potential for bringing people to new levels of empathetic understanding. TV documentaries and biographies of ethnically diverse historical and sports figures, such as *The Jackie Robinson Story*, have given viewers insight. Movies such as *Schindler's List* and *Life Is Beautiful* have brought awareness to the plight of Jews during World War II. *A Beautiful Mind* portrayed the life of a brilliant professor who had to cope with schizophrenia.

Merely being exposed to diversity, however, is not effective in changing attitudes over a long period of time; children have to be taught nonstereotypical attitudes directly (Bigler & Liben, 1990) through social experience. Similarly, although more programs on TV today portray women in traditionally male-dominated activities, to really influence children's gender-role attitudes, adults have to engage in discussion and provide nonstereotypical activities (Roberts & Foehr, 2004).

Books. Books are influential in attitude formation. Consider the controversy some books stir up, resulting in their removal from library shelves (Norton & Norton, 2002). For example, in the 1960s, Garth Williams' *The Rabbit's Wedding* (1982) was criticized because the illustrations showed the marriage of a black rabbit and a white rabbit. In the 1970s, Maurice Sendak's (1970) *In the Night Kitchen* was taken off some library shelves because the child in the story was nude. In the 1980s, Helen Bannerman's *The Story of Little Black Sambo*, which was first published in 1899 and had enjoyed much popularity over the years, was attacked for being offensive to African Americans because of the story line and crudely drawn figures of characters with stereotypical features. The major controversies in children's books include how attitudes regarding stereotypes (gender, ethnicity, disabilities), sexuality, violence, profanity, and family problems are portrayed (Feldstein, 1989).

Positive ways books can be used to influence attitudes is evident in *McGuffey's Reader*, popular in U.S. schools in the early part of the 20th century. The reader contained stories with moral messages. William Bennett (1993), former U.S. Secretary of Education, published *The Book of Virtues* for a similar purpose. Spitz (1999) claims that even when they are not intended to do so, "picture books provide children with some of their earliest takes on morality, taste, and basic cultural knowledge, including messages about gender, race, and class. They supply a stock of images for children's mental museums" (p. 14). A classic book defying gender stereotypes is *The Story of Ferdinand* by Munro Leaf (1936). Ferdinand is a bull who would rather smell the flowers than fight; the attitude portrayed is that it is OK to be yourself rather than conform to cultural role prescriptions.

Community

Community customs and traditions influence attitudes. For example, in certain countries only men are allowed into the teahouses to socialize; women stay home. Before the U.S. civil rights movement, signs designated racially segregated bathrooms in southern communities ("White," "Colored"). In many communities today, one finds signs that say "Adults Only." These examples illustrate attitudes of discrimination by gender, ethnicity, and age. Children thus acquire attitudes that represent the status quo in their environment.

Is the community population diverse? Does it include many ethnic groups? Or is it homogeneous? Do the people who live there have similar backgrounds? How do different people in the community interact? As has been discussed, research shows that positive interactions with people different from oneself foster positive attitudes toward them.

A community's attitudes are reflected most obviously in the ways it chooses to spend its tax money. This, in turn, affects the services it provides. Is money spent on educational programs, recreation, preventive services, support services, and compensatory services? By examining a community's budget, one can determine rather quickly, for example, the degree to which children and families are valued. Children are very likely to incorporate their community's attitudes into their own attitudes.

The attitudes of the community toward providing support for its families are likely to affect the level of stress and social pathology experienced by some families (Etzioni, 1993; Schorr, 1997). These families, then, may come to feel a loss in their ability to control what happens to them (Seligman, 1975). On the other hand, several studies have reported that social support received by children is one important resource that protects them against the negative effects of life stressors (Sandler, Miller, Short, & Wolchik, 1989).

Specific social pathologies involving families that have been related to the community's attitude of support (or lack thereof) are infant death and disease, teenage pregnancy, juvenile delinquency, and child abuse and neglect (Garbarino, 1992). Communities that provide prenatal and perinatal support to young, high-risk mothers have lower infant mortality rates (Children's Defense Fund, 2004; Schorr, 1997). One reason is that attitudes toward mothering and child health change for the positive. Community attitudes toward providing support and guidance to pregnant teenagers are influential in the teenagers' attitudes toward birth control, education, and occupational goals (Furstenberg, 1976). Community attitudes regarding law enforcement, recreation, youth employment, and curfews can affect the level of juvenile delinquency (Garbarino, 1992). Finally, the attitudes of the community members toward helping one another can affect the level of child abuse and neglect in community families by influencing parenting attitudes. Mothers in communities of high support reported that their children were significantly easier to care for than did mothers in communities of low support (Garbarino & Sherman, 1980).

School

Schools influence attitude formation. A review of various studies (Sadker & Sadker, 1994, 2003) illustrated how gender-role stereotyping is perpetuated in schools. Schools that separate male and female activities and encourage boys to play in the "block corner" or take science classes and girls to go to the "housekeeping" area or take English classes, for example, are teaching children which activities are gender appropriate. Teachers who project their gender-typed expectations on boys and girls reinforce traditional gender-role behavior. In other words, if a teacher *expects* boys to be more active and aggressive than girls, the teacher will tend to allow this behavior. Likewise, a teacher who *expects* girls to be passive and docile will likely encourage girls to conform to this pattern.

Although teachers are generally committed to the idea of ethnic and gender equality, biased attitudes in the form of certain classroom practices still emerge. An example is the "self-fulfilling prophecy," in which teacher expectations of performance influence actual performance (Good & Brophy, 1986, 2003). However, classroom organization can be very effective in influencing attitudes toward others. For example, researchers (Johnson & Johnson, 1999; Johnson, Johnson, & Maruyama, 1983) tried to identify conditions in schools that led to positive attitudes regarding ethnically diverse students as well as students with disabilities. They found that when members of both heterogeneous and homogeneous groups cooperated instead of competed to achieve a common goal, greater positive attitudes emerged among the group members. These positive attitudes included more realistic views of self and group members, greater expectations of success, and increased expectations of favorable future interactions with group members (regardless of how different the individuals were).

CHANGING ATTITUDES ABOUT DIVERSITY

Can prejudicial attitudes be changed?

Understanding the reasons behind children's attitudes about diversity as they develop can help parents and teachers enable change. Prejudicial attitudes toward various ethnic groups occur for different reasons in children according to age (Aboud, 1988). Prejudice in children under age 7 is due to perceived differences in appearance. Children this age are cognitively immature and lack much social experience. They may fear anyone who does not look like them. Older children often exhibit prejudice because they are frustrated with authority; in response, they turn on other groups perceived to have less power or status (Van Ausdale & Feagin, 2001).

Techniques used to counter the ethnically biased attitudes of European American second- and fifth-graders (as determined by a test) follow. All four methods were found to be effective on a short-term basis, and two were effective for a long time (Katz & Zalk, 1978).

1. *Increased positive interethnic contact*. Children worked in interethnic teams at an interesting puzzle and were all praised for their work.
2. *Vicarious interethnic contact*. Children heard an interesting story about a sympathetic and resourceful African American child.
3. *Reinforcement of the color black*. Children were given a marble (which could be traded in for a prize) every time they chose a picture of a black animal in response to a question such as "Which animal runs fastest?"
4. *Perceptual differentiation*. Children were shown slides of an African American woman whose appearance varied depending on whether or not she was wearing glasses, which of two different hairdos she was wearing, and whether she was smiling or frowning. Each different-appearing face had a name, and the children were tested to see how well they remembered the names.

After two weeks, the children's levels of prejudice were measured again. All the groups that had been exposed to any of the four techniques showed less prejudice than did children in the control groups. Four to six months after the experiment, a second posttest showed that the children who had learned to perceive differences in the African American faces and those who had heard the stories about African American children had more positive attitudes than those in the other two groups. Younger children showed more gains than older children.

Apparently, prejudicial attitudes can be changed by enabling children to have positive experiences (both real and vicarious) with ethnic minorities. When an adult mediates the experience by pointing out individual differences, it is especially effective. Thus, children learn to view people as individuals rather than as representatives of a certain group with certain fixed characteristics.

An experiment was carried out to help children feel what it is like to experience prejudice, to be discriminated against (Weiner & Wright, 1973). European American third-grade children were randomly divided into two groups: the Orange people and

The friendship among these children is more important than societal attitudes about race.

FogStock LLC/Index Stock Imagery

the Green people. On one day, the Orange children were "superior"; they were praised by the teacher and given preferential treatment in the day's activities. On this day, the Green children were discriminated against; they were criticized and denied privileges. On the second day, the positions were reversed: the Green children were favored, and the Orange children were discriminated against. On the third day, and again two weeks later, the children's ethnic beliefs were measured. Compared to children who had not had this experience, the experimental class expressed fewer prejudicial beliefs about African Americans and were significantly more likely to want to have a picnic with African American children. Thus, prejudiced attitudes can be changed by role taking—experiencing the feelings that discrimination brings.

A similar experiment was carried out in an Iowa third grade by teacher Jane Elliott, using blue and brown eyes as criteria for superiority and inferiority. After a specified time, she switched the criteria for inferiority and superiority so that both the "blues" and the "browns" could experience discrimination. The experiment was documented in the film *Eye of the Storm* (1971) and repeated with adult parole officers, documented in *A Class Divided* (1992). Both the children, who were interviewed as adults, and the parole officers reported a major change in their attitudes toward diversity as a result of the experiment.

One of the purposes of the Individuals with Disabilities Education Act of 1990 (amended in 2004) was to include children with disabilities in public school. Teachers had to revise prior stereotypical attitudes they might have had to emphasize *abilities* rather than *disabilities* (Heward, 2002)—for example, "Kevin is a third-grader who reads in a fourth-grade book and who needs assistance with physical tasks" rather than "Kevin is wheelchair-bound and requires an aide."

Changing attitudes about diversity includes gender as well as ethnicity and disability. Influences on the development of gender roles are discussed in

Chapter 12. An example of a macrosystem influence is Title IX of the Education Amendments of 1972, whose purpose was to provide equal opportunities and funding of activities for girls and boys. Enabling girls to take "shop" classes and boys to take "home economics" classes helped revise some perceptions about male and female abilities.

IN PRACTICE

How Do You Create an Antibias Classroom Environment?

An antibias classroom should include the following:

1. Images in abundance of all the children, families, and staff in your program. Photos and other pictures reflecting the varying backgrounds of the children and staff should be displayed attractively.

2. If the classroom population is racially/ethnically homogeneous, images of children and adults from the major racial/ethnic groups in your community and in U.S. society.

3. Images that reflect accurately people's current daily lives in the United States, working and with their families during recreational activities.

4. A numerical balance among different groups. Be sure that people of color are not represented as "tokens"—only one or two.

5. A fair balance of images of women and men, shown doing "jobs in the home" and "jobs outside the home." Show women and men doing blue-collar work (e.g., factory worker, repair person) and pink-collar work (e.g., beautician, salesperson), as well as white-collar work (e.g., teacher, doctor).

6. Images of elderly people from varying backgrounds performing different activities.

7. Images of people with disabilities from varying backgrounds shown doing work and with their families in recreational activities. Be careful not to use images that depict people with disabilities as dependent and passive.

8. Images of diversity in family styles: single mothers or fathers, extended families, gay or lesbian parents (families with two mothers or fathers), families in which one parent and a grandmother are the parents, inter-racial and multiethnic families, families of adoptive children, families with a member who is disabled (the person may be either a child or a parent).

9. Images of important individuals—past and present. These should reflect racial/ethnic, gender, and special need diversity, and should include people who participated in important struggles for social justice.

10. Artwork—prints, sculpture, and textiles by artists from varying backgrounds that reflect the aesthetic environment and the culture of the families represented in your classroom and of groups in your community and in the United States.

Source: L. Derman-Sparks, and the Antibias Task Force (1989). *Antibias curriculum: Tools for empowering young children.* Washington, DC: National Association for the Education of Young Children, pp. 11–12.

Participation of individuals with disabilities in athletic events has helped communicate positive attitudes regarding their abilities.

HIRB/Index Stock Imagery

Motives and Attributions

What drives you to act or achieve, and how do you explain it?

A *motive*, as introduced in Chapter 2, is a need or emotion that causes a person to act. To be *motivated* is to be *moved* to do something. An *attribution*, as introduced in Chapter 2, is an explanation for one's performance. "Do you *attribute* an Olympian's athletic ability to training, genetics, or both?"

According to Robert White (1959), people are motivated to act by the urge to be competent, or achieve. People of all ages strive to develop skills that will help them understand and control their environment, whether or not they receive external reinforcement. The inborn motive to explore, understand, and control one's environment is referred to as *mastery motivation*, as introduced in Chapter 2 (Mayes & Zigler, 1992). This is illustrated when infants and toddlers open cabinets, empty out drawers, drop things in the toilet. Whereas mastery motivation is believed to be inborn, *achievement motivation* is thought to be learned. Children learn via socialization what is considered acceptable and unacceptable performance standards in their culture, as well as how to evaluate their behavior accordingly. Introduced in Chapter 2, *achievement motivation*, the motivation to be competent, expresses itself in behavior aimed at approaching challenging tasks with the confidence of accomplishment (McClelland et al., 1953)—for example, the child who tries out for the choir saying, "Oh, I know I'll make it."

Ryan and Deci (2000) distinguish between achievement motivation that is *intrinsic* (doing an activity for inherent satisfaction or enjoyment) and *extrinsic* (doing an activity to attain some separable outcome, to get a reward or avoid punishment). As people act to pursue different goals, why are some driven primarily intrinsically and others, extrinsically? Explanations can be categorized as (1) within-person (intrinsic) changes resulting from cognitive or emotional

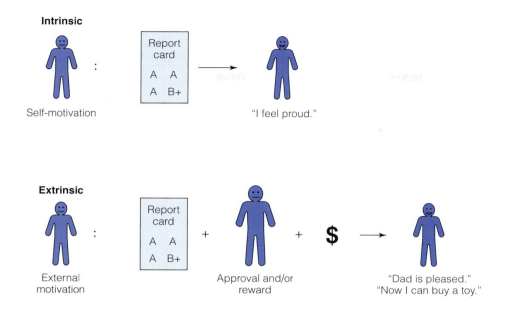

Figure 11.2

Intrinsic and Extrinsic Motivation

maturation, such as becoming more curious as one is able to learn more and becoming more competent as one is able to master more and (2) socially mediated (extrinsic) changes resulting from contexts children experience as they grow, such as family, school, or peer group, and the accompanying feelings of autonomy or control (Eccles et al., 1998).

According to Ryan and Deci (2000), home and classroom environments can "facilitate or forestall" intrinsic motivation by "supporting or thwarting" a child's needs for competence and autonomy. For example, in a study of parent–child relationships, home learning environment, and school readiness, researchers found that children whose parents understood and encouraged their learning through play exhibited independence, curiosity, and creativity in the classroom (Lamb, Parker, Boak, Griffin, & Peax, 1999). Children whose parents were strict and rule-bound over play time and activities exhibited distractibility and hostility in the classroom. Other studies (Ryan & Deci, 2000) have shown that tangible rewards (money, candy, toys), threats, deadlines, directives, and competition pressure related to task performance tend to diminish intrinsic motivation because they are experienced as controllers of behavior; whereas choice and the opportunity for self-direction appear to enhance intrinsic motivation because they enable a sense of autonomy. (See Figure 11.2.)

Attributions, or explanations for performance, are related to motives in that achievement motivation has been linked to **locus of control**—how one *attributes* his or her performance, or where one places responsibility for successes or failure. Locus of control is *internal* if one attributes responsibility inside the self; it is *external* if one attributes responsibility to forces outside the self. "Am I responsible for my grade, or is the teacher?" When individuals feel they have no control over events and, therefore, no responsibility, they are no longer motivated to achieve. *Learned helplessness*, as introduced in Chapter 7, is a phenomenon exhibited by people who no longer perform effectively in a number of situations; they have learned to be helpless as opposed to competent. The relationship of motives and attributions to actual performance is outlined in Figure 11.3.

locus of control
one's attribution of performance, or perception of responsibility for success or failure; may be internal or external

Figure 11.3

Relationship of Motives and Attributions to Actual Performance

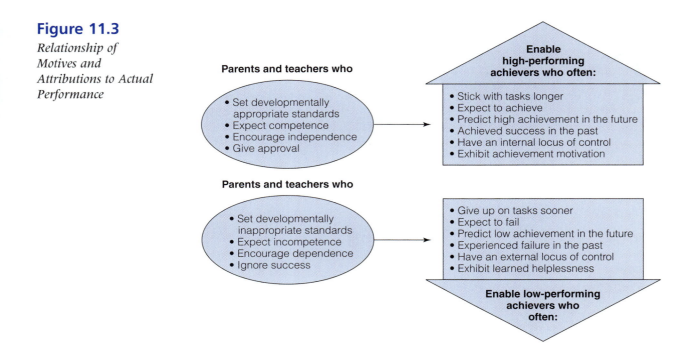

Parents and teachers who

- Set developmentally appropriate standards
- Expect competence
- Encourage independence
- Give approval

Enable high-performing achievers who often:

- Stick with tasks longer
- Expect to achieve
- Predict high achievement in the future
- Achieved success in the past
- Have an internal locus of control
- Exhibit achievement motivation

Parents and teachers who

- Set developmentally inappropriate standards
- Expect incompetence
- Encourage dependence
- Ignore success

- Give up on tasks sooner
- Expect to fail
- Predict low achievement in the future
- Experienced failure in the past
- Have an external locus of control
- Exhibit learned helplessness

Enable low-performing achievers who often:

ACHIEVEMENT MOTIVATION

How do people differ in their motivations to achieve?

In a classic study to assess the differences in strengths of people's achievement motives, David McClelland and his colleagues (1953) developed a projection technique using selected picture cards from the Thematic Apperception Test (TAT). The technique assumes that when asked to write stories about the pictures, people will project their feelings about themselves onto the characters in the pictures shown to them.

The pictures show such scenes as two men ("inventors") in a shop working on a machine, a young boy and a violin, or a boy sitting at a desk with an open book in front of him. Participants are asked to answer the following questions about the pictures:

1. What is happening? Who are the persons?
2. What were the circumstances leading up to the situation in the pictures?
3. What are the characters thinking? What do they want?
4. What will happen? What will be done?

The assessment of the stories involves noting references to achievement goals (concern over reaching a standard of excellence). Subjects who refer often to achievement goals are rated high in achievement motivation; subjects who rarely or never refer to achievement goals are rated low.

Achievement motivation is often correlated with actual achievement behavior (Bandura, 1997; Eccles et al., 1998). The motivation to achieve, however, may manifest itself only in behavior that the child values. For example, a child's high motivation to achieve may be exhibited in athletics, but not in schoolwork. Thus, different situations have different achievement-attaining values for children (Eccles et al., 1998; Harter & Connell, 1984).

How does the motivation to achieve develop?

In one study, 1- to 5-year-olds were observed doing objectively measured performance-based tasks, such as hammering pegs in a pegboard, putting puzzle pieces together, building a stack of blocks, and knocking down plastic pins with a bowling ball (Stipek, Recchia, & McClintic, 1992). Some of the tasks were individual, and some required competition with a peer. It was found that children go through three stages in learning to evaluate their personal achievement against performance standards (average attainment by peers) as evaluated by teachers.

- *Stage 1: Joy in mastery*. Children under age 2 approach the given task to master it. If they fail, they tend to move on to another task rather than get upset.
- *Stage 2: Approval-seeking*. As they approach age 2, toddlers seem to realize the significance of others' reactions to their performance. When they accomplish a task, they tend to smile or say "I did it" to the nearby adult. When they do not succeed, they tend to turn away.
- *Stage 3: Use of standards, or averages, for individual comparison*. Children age 3 and over seemed to show pride in accomplishments. Some praised themselves; some went on to a more challenging tasks. In most cases, performance was not dependent on others' evaluations. Children $3\frac{1}{2}$ to 5 showed happiness when they won a competitive task; losers slowed down or gave up, but did not appear to be upset.

Thus, there seems to be a general developmental progression among children who are learning the cultural value of achievement. What about individual differences?

The origins of individual differences in achievement motivation (also called "need achievement") have most often been linked to parenting practices. In a classic study by Rosen and D'Andrade (1959), two groups of 10-year-old boys with similar socioeconomic backgrounds and IQ scores but different levels of need achievement were observed in their homes with their parents watching them do a task. The task was rather difficult. It involved building a tower out of irregularly shaped blocks while blindfolded and restricted to the use of one hand. The parents were told to watch the boy do the task. The parents could say or do anything they pleased, but they could not touch the blocks. They were also told the height of the tower the "average boy" would erect and were asked to predict (confidentially to the researchers) how well their son would do. The parents of the high need-achievement boys predicted a better level of performance than did the parents of the low need-achievement boys.

While the boys were doing the task, the parents of sons with high need achievement were more encouraging and more likely to reward accomplishment with warm praise. Fathers of the high need-achievement boys were warm and friendly while their sons were working, but did not interfere with their sons' decisions regarding how to complete the task, other than giving a hint or two. (They allowed for independence.) The fathers of low need-achievement boys, on the other hand, were more domineering, in that they gave specific directions on how to complete the task and were more likely to show irritation when things went awry.

Apparently, the parents of the high need-achievement boys set high standards of excellence for them, but not so high as to discourage the boys. They also allowed the boys to solve problems independently and communicated approval. In contrast, the parents of the low need-achievement boys set standards that were either too high or not high enough, and they were less likely to permit independence in solving the problem. In short, parenting style is related to the development of need achievement when parents set standards of excellence, expect competence, allow independence, and communicate approval after success. These characteristics are components of the *authoritative* parenting style. Many more recent studies correlate authoritative parenting with achievement in children and adolescents (Baumrind, 1973; Eccles et al., 1998; Lamborn, Mounts, Steinberg, & Dornbusch, 1991; Steinberg et al., 1989).

When some investigators (Hermans, Terlaak, & Maes, 1972) questioned teachers, they learned that children with high achievement motivation were viewed as being more interested in striving toward goals, showing a higher degree of personal responsibility for their work, and being more persistent in following through on tasks they had begun. Research has demonstrated that achievement motivation is a relatively stable characteristic of personality. Longitudinal studies have demonstrated a consistent relationship between the level of achievement motivation in preschool, elementary school, and high school (Deci & Ryan, 1985; Eccles et al., 1998; Feld, 1967; Kagan & Moss, 1959).

What is the relationship between parenting practices/expectations and achievement motivation?

In a study of the antecedents of achievement motivation (McClelland and Pilon, 1983), mothers' reports of child-rearing practices when their children were 5 years old were compared to those children's achievement motivation scores when they were in their 30s. The mothers had been interviewed in 1951 in a study of child-rearing practices. Twenty-five years later, the children were interviewed to assess their achievement motivation.

McClelland and Pilon consistently found a relationship between child-rearing practices emphasizing scheduled feeding and conscientious toilet training (putting the child on the potty at regular times and watching for clues that the child needs to urinate or defecate) and achievement motivation for males and females from lower- and middle-class backgrounds. They concluded that the scheduled feeding and conscientious toilet training were examples of standards of excellence set by the parents. Parental expectations play a significant role in children's motivation to achieve (Ginsberg & Bronstein, 1993; Parsons, Adler, & Kaczala, 1982; Phillips, 1987).

McClelland and Pilon also found that child-rearing practices emphasizing early independence (by age 5) were *not* significantly related to adult achievement motivation. Perhaps parental expectations for independence by age 5 freed the parents of their role in continually communicating standards to the child. Or perhaps expecting the child to be independent by age 5 was too high a standard. There are indications that when the achievement standard is set at an unrealistic level, the effect is the opposite of what was intended. Thus, children who are expected to do well on tasks with which they are too young to cope exhibit a lower level of achievement motivation. These children, instead of learning to achieve, learn to give up. The desire to achieve, then, is created by optimally challenging the child—providing a task that can be done with effort (not too easy) so that the accomplishment is meaningful (Burhans & Dweck, 1995; McClelland, 1961). Such tasks are referred to today as *developmentally appropriate*.

In sum, the child-rearing environment of children who show high achievement motivation includes developmentally appropriate timing of achievement demands (early, but not too early, and continuing encouragement), high confidence in the child's abilities, a supportive affective family environment (orientation toward exploration and investigation as well as positive feedback), and highly motivated role models (Eccles et al., 1998).

What is the relationship between child performance/expectations and achievement motivation?

Individuals' actual achievement behavior depends not only on their motivation to achieve but also on whether or not they *expect* to achieve and whether or not they fear failure. People are more likely to work hard when they perceive a reasonable chance of success than when they perceive a goal to be out of reach (Atkinson, 1964). Children's expectations of success can be measured by asking them to predict a certain grade, indicate how sure they are that they can solve a particular problem, or select the hardest task they think they can do from a collection of tasks varying in difficulty (Phillips, 1987).

Children with high expectations for success on a task usually persist at it longer and perform better than children with low expectations. Studies have found that children with high IQs and high expectations of success in school did, in fact, get the highest grades; whereas children with high IQs and low expectations received lower grades than children with low IQs and high expectations (Eccles, 1983; Eccles et al., 1998). In addition to child-rearing practices, discussed previously, teaching styles and communication affect children's attributions. When teachers are caring, supportive, and emphasize the learning process over performance outcomes, as well as give feedback, children tend to be motivated to achieve and expect success (Daniels et al., 2001).

One's expectation of success is related to (1) one's history of success or failure, (2) one's perception of how difficult the task is, and (3) the attributions for one's performance. Generally, someone who has mostly been successful in the past expects to succeed in the present and future; someone who has mostly failed in the past expects to fail in the present and future.

FogStock LLC/Index Stock Imagery

This girl's achievement is influenced by her personal responsibility to perform and her confidence of success.

In some situations, however, people who usually succeed fail and people who usually fail succeed. A second possible factor, then, affecting an individual's expectation of success may be how difficult the person originally perceived the task to be. Failure on a task perceived to be very easy results in a different self-evaluation than failure on a task perceived to be very difficult.

A third possible factor affecting an individual's expectation of success is to what the individual's performance is attributed (Weiner, 1992). People may attribute performance (1) to themselves—their ability or their effort; (2) to others—a teacher's opinion of them, or the teacher's ability to teach; (3) to the situation—the test was too difficult or the room was too noisy; or (4) to luck—good or bad.

LOCUS OF CONTROL

Where do you attribute responsibility for the consequences of your actions—to your ability, your effort, others, task difficulty, fate, or luck?

Recall that *locus of control* relates to one's attribution of performance, or sense of personal responsibility. Locus of control refers to where people place responsibility for success or failure (inside or outside the self). Individuals who have strong beliefs that they are in control of their world, that they can cause things to happen if they choose, and that they can command their own rewards have an **internal locus of control**. These people attribute their success (or failure) to themselves. Individuals who perceive that others or outside forces have more control over them than they do over themselves have an **external locus of control**. These people attribute their success (or failure) to factors outside themselves.

What factors influence an individual's belief that control lies inside or outside the self?

One factor influencing one's control beliefs is the perceived relationship between a person's actions and his or her success or failure (Skinner, 1995). The more successful a person is at accomplishing tasks, the more likely it is that the person will feel "in control"; feeling "out of control" is more likely when failures outnumber successes. Achievement is related to whether the person believes he or she controls the outcome. Another factor related to control beliefs is age. As children get older, their understanding of causality and explanations for outcomes becomes more differentiated. Whereas 7- and 8-year-olds tend to consider all possible factors—luck, effort, ability, task difficulty—in explaining performance, 11- and 12-year-olds tend to put more emphasis on external factors, such as luck and task difficulty, than on internal factors, such as ability and effort, in attributing locus of control. (See Figure 11.4.) Moreover, 7- and 8- year-olds think that ability can change with effort, whereas 11- and 12-year-olds perceive ability as relatively stable (Skinner, 1995).

How is locus of control measured?

Julian Rotter (1966, 1971) developed a locus of control scale that is used to study the internal–external dimension of personal responsibility. The Internal–External Scale is constructed so that each item can be scored as *internal* or *external*. Some sample items are given in the box "Measuring Locus of Control." Subjects are to indicate, in each pair of statements, the more appropriate of the two.

internal locus of control perception that one is responsible for one's own fate

external locus of control perception that others or outside forces are responsible for one's fate

Internal locus of control

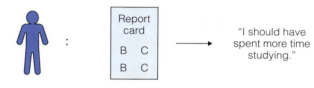

"I should have spent more time studying."

External locus of control

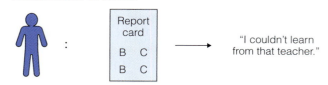

"I couldn't learn from that teacher."

Figure 11.4

Internal and External Locus of Control

IN PRACTICE

Measuring Locus of Control

I more strongly believe that:

1. a. Promotions are earned through hard work and persistence.
   b. Making a lot of money is largely a matter of getting the "right breaks."
2. a. There is usually a direct connection between how hard I study and the grades I get.
   b. Many times, the grades teachers give seem haphazard to me.
3. a. The number of divorces in our society indicates that more and more people are not trying to make their marriages work.
   b. Marriage is largely a gamble; it's no one's fault if it doesn't work.
4. a. When I am right, I can usually convince others that I am.
   b. It is silly to think that one can really change another person's basic attitudes.
5. a. In our society, earning power is dependent upon ability.
   b. Getting promoted is really a matter of being a little luckier than the next person.
6. a. If one knows how to deal with people, they are really quite easily led.
   b. I have little influence over the way other people behave.
7. a. People can change the course of world affairs if they make themselves heard.
   b. It is only wishful thinking to believe that one can really influence what happens in society at large.
8. a. I am the master of my fate.
   b. A great deal that happens to me is probably a matter of chance.
9. a. Getting along with people is a skill that must be practiced.
   b. It is impossible to figure out how to please some people.

Source: J. B. Rotter (1971). "Who Rules You? External Control and Internal Control," *Psychology Today, 5,* 37–42. Reprinted from *Psychology Today.* Copyright 1971 by the American Psychological Association.

Locus of control is an aspect of personality that interests educators because children with an *internal* locus of control generally do better academically and are more competent and effective than those with an *external* locus of control (Nowicki & Segal, 1974; Swick, 1986). For example, in an experiment that required subjects work on a verbal ability test, children with an internal locus of control budgeted the time allotted them in a way that related to the difficulty of each item, whereas children with an external locus of control did not (Gozali, Cleary, Walster, & Gozali, 1973). And in a review of more than 100 studies, Findley and Cooper (1983) found that internals earn higher grades and outperform externals on standardized achievement tests.

One explanation for the relationship between locus of control and academic achievement is that internals view outcomes as within their control. Therefore, if they succeed, they can figure out what they did correctly and do it again. If they fail, they believe they can change the outcome in the future by exerting more effort to correct their mistakes (for example, study harder or differently). They develop a *mastery-oriented attribution*. Externals, on the other hand, view outcomes as outside their control. Therefore, if they succeed, they attribute it to good luck, and if they fail, they attribute it to bad luck or lack of ability. Since they don't attribute the outcomes of their performance to their own efforts or strategies, they give up quickly. They develop a *helpless-oriented attribution* (Dweck & Leggett, 1988).

Reviews of the literature on locus of control (Eccles et al., 1998; Young & Shorr, 1986) confirmed that internal locus of control was significantly related to age (at about age 9, there is an increase in perceptions of internal control), gender (elementary school girls are more internal than boys), socioeconomic status (middle- and upper-class children are more internal than lower-class children), and achievement. In each case, the diverse socialization experiences of the group likely play a prominent part.

How does locus of control develop?

Piaget's observations of infants led him to conclude that it is not until about the age of 5 or 6 months that children show awareness that their own actions can bring about an effect. However, behavior does not become intentional or goal directed until about 8 to 12 months. A favorite game of infants this age is "drop and fetch." The infant drops a toy from the highchair or playpen, and the parent fetches. Therefore, it is at about age 1, according to Piaget, that children begin to distinguish between events caused by their own actions and those that are not (Flavell et al., 2001). Once children begin to understand that they have an impact on their environment, they begin to experiment with various autonomous behaviors—"No, me do it" is commonly heard in the second year.

© Brand X Pictures/Jupiterimages

This child is given the opportunity to correct a mistake, thereby gaining a feeling of autonomy. Such opportunities enable children to gain a sense of control and lead to self-confidence.

Children gradually develop a sense of control when things that happen to them are contingent upon their actions. As has been discussed in relation to Erik Erikson's (1963) theory of personality development, parental responsiveness to children's needs leads to attachment and a sense of trust (first year). When children are allowed to be autonomous, they gain a feeling of control; if not given opportunities to be autonomous, they feel self-doubt (ages 2–3). If children are allowed to initiate activities, they will feel a sense of control over their environment, rather than guilt over wanting to control it (ages 4–5). When children enter school, their experiences there will affect their feelings of industry or inferiority (ages 6–12). These are crucial years for development of self-esteem in that a sense of control and self-determination is related to the perception of self-competence (Beane, 1991).

Thus, locus of control develops through one's actions on the environment and one's interactions with others. The outcomes of these actions and interactions influence whether people attribute what happens to them to internal or external causes. Children growing up in lower-class families may demonstrate a less internal locus of control than children from middle-class backgrounds because of different parenting styles or the different environments experienced by lower- and middle-class children (Bain, Holliman, & McCallum, 1989; Stephens & Delys, 1973). Lower-class children have fewer opportunities to develop a sense of being in control or determining life outcomes. For example, financially, they have fewer choices.

IN PRACTICE

How Can Parents and Teachers Help Children Develop an Internal Locus of Control?

1. *Be responsive to children from the moment they are born.* Be affectionate, comforting, attentive. They need to know someone will respond to their actions, or else they will feel they have no control over their environment.
2. *Let children accept consequences for their actions.* If they spill milk, give them something with which to clean it up.
3. *Avoid performing tasks children can do for themselves.* Encourage effort, allow children to make mistakes, and don't expect adult performance.
4. *Give children developmentally appropriate responsibilities.* For example: age 3, put toys away; age 5, make bed; age 7, set and/or clear table.
5. *Give feedback.* Let children know when they have performed well and, if need be, how they can improve.
6. *Be an example of a person who makes things happen.* Don't wait for things to happen and then react.
7. *Encourage children's special interests.* Provide opportunities for children to initiate things themselves through questions and stimulating activities.
8. *Set standards and limits for behavior.* Explain the reasons for the rules ("You need to be home by 6 o'clock so we can all have dinner together").
9. *Show respect for children and for their accomplishments.* ("What an interesting painting; can you tell me about it?" rather than "What is that? It doesn't look like a kitty.")
10. *Allow children to make appropriate decisions that affect them.* ("You can have six children at your birthday party; whom would you like to invite?" "Do you want to play soccer this year?")

LEARNED HELPLESSNESS

Why do some individuals "give up" easily?

Martin Seligman presented evidence in his books, *Helplessness* (1975) and *Learned Optimism* (1990), that people become passive and lose motivation when placed in situations where outcomes are unaffected by their behavior. These people believe they are pawns of external circumstances; as a result, they have *learned helplessness*.

When does helplessness first appear? Research on infants shows that infants exposed to mobiles that spin independently of their actions do not learn to control new mobiles presented to them that can be activated by turning their heads. In contrast, infants exposed to stationary mobiles, and to mobiles that spin contingent upon their actions (head or arm moving), evidence no difficulty in learning to control the new mobiles. These differences in performance are still present after six weeks without any exposure to a mobile (Fincham & Cain, 1986). So, certain experiences involving the ability to control outcomes can affect even infants.

Gunnar (1980) demonstrated that the ability to control the onset of a potentially frightening toy reduces fear and increases positive approach responses in 12-month-old infants. Similar findings regarding control have been demonstrated in studies of infant attachment. When a baby cries and the mother responds to his or her needs, the baby experiences a "sense of control" even though he or she is not cognitively aware of it at first. Apparently, this sense of control, or trust that mother will meet baby's needs, enables the baby to develop a secure attachment to the mother (Ainsworth, 1982; Frankel & Bates, 1990).

As children get older and the number of their experiences with objects and people increases, their perceptions of being able to control outcomes and their ability to understand cause and effect influence when and if they manifest learned helplessness as opposed to motivation to achieve (Eccles et al., 1998; Fincham & Cain, 1986). Figure 11.3, earlier in this chapter, summarizes the factors involved in attributions for performance and their relation to actual performance.

By age 4, some children give up on even developmentally or age-appropriate tasks, such as building a tall tower out of blocks (Cain & Dweck, 1995). These children who are nonpersistent tend to believe they can't do the task and report feeling bad after failures. Children who are persistent, on the other hand, tend to believe they can succeed on challenging tasks if given more time and if they try harder. Children who are nonpersistent describe their parents as critical or punitive ("Daddy's going to get mad"). Children who are persistent describe their parents as supportive and encouraging ("Try it again, you'll do better next time").

Many economically deprived persons and some people from ethnic minorities have learned that they exert little control over their lives. As a result of their experiences, they believe that the external educational, economic, social, and political systems control them. For example, poverty makes higher education a luxury, but without it, people lack the skills and assurance to change their condition. Perhaps the lack of motivation attributed to those of lower socioeconomic status is really due to their lack of control over personal outcomes (National Commission on Children, 1991).

In a series of studies on learned helplessness, Dweck and colleagues found that when children believe their failures are due to uncontrollable factors in themselves, such as lack of ability ("I failed the math test because I'm dumb in math"), their subsequent task performance deteriorates after failure (Dweck, 1975; Dweck & Bush, 1976; Dweck & Gillard, 1975; Dweck & Reppucci, 1973; Elliot & Dweck, 1988). In a study of fourth- to sixth-grade children, those who had self-critical attributions, or learned helplessness, had little knowledge about effective study techniques to help them succeed at academic tasks (Pomeranz & Saxon, 2001). Thus, they were unable to connect effort or persistence with success. If, however, children are enabled to believe their failure was due to lack of effort, they tend to try harder on subsequent tasks and often show improved performance.

In several studies, Dweck and colleagues found that girls are more likely than boys to demonstrate learned helplessness that comes from attributing lack of ability to themselves. Boys more often tend to believe that when they do not do well, it is because they have not worked hard enough. Since the boys and girls scored similarly on achievement tests, it can be inferred that ability was similar but that the attributions for failure were different. Dweck and colleagues looked to the teachers to see if there was differential feedback to boys and girls relating to failure. They found that when boys submitted poor work, they were generally reprimanded for sloppiness, not paying attention, or lack of effort. Girls who submitted poor work were generally told, "You didn't do it right even though you tried."

In another study, Dweck and colleagues (1978) set up a classroom experiment. One group of boys and girls who were given an anagram test (rearrange the letters of given words to form new words) were told they had done poorly. The feedback implied lack of ability: "You didn't do very well that time; you didn't get it right." A second group of boys and girls were told they had not done very well *and* that they had not written the answers neatly enough. This feedback implied lack of effort. When the test was administered again, the boys and girls in the first group gave up more easily after the initial failure, but those in the second group tried harder.

In sum, if parents and teachers praise children for their effort when they succeed but question their ability when they fail, the children are less likely to persist at challenging tasks, thereby developing *learned helplessness*. If parents and teachers praise children's abilities when they succeed and emphasize lack of effort when they fail, the children are more likely to persist at challenging tasks, thereby developing *achievement motivation*. Thus, if adults treat children as if their mistakes can be remedied by their own actions, the children are likely to reflect this opinion of themselves and behave accordingly.

IN PRACTICE

How Can Parents and Teachers Help Children Who Have Learned Helplessness?

1. *Know the individual abilities (strengths and weaknesses) of the child, and set realistic goals for tasks.* Goals should be not too easy or too hard, challenging enough to make the child work, yet guaranteed to enable the child to succeed.
2. *Provide opportunities to learn by doing.* Experiencing consequences of one's actions leads to a sense of autonomy.
3. *Give feedback as soon as possible for the task performed.* Evaluation leads to insight into successes and failures. ("Maybe if you'd wash your brush after using each color, you wouldn't always end up with black.")
4. *Give encouragement for trying and for persistence.* "You worked really hard on cutting a straight line; I bet with just a little bit of practice you'll be able to do it."
5. *Let children know it is OK to make mistakes.* That is how we learn. Ask children how they can correct their mistake next time.

6. *Provide structured opportunities for decision making.* "Do you want to wear the red or the blue sweater?" rather than "Do you want to wear a sweater?" "Do you want to brush your teeth first or put on your pajamas before bed?" "You may do your math homework or spelling now."

7. *Explain to children that actions have consequences.* Desirable behavior leads to positive consequences, but undesirable behavior leads to negative consequences (finishing your work gets a star; not cleaning up when told to do so means you must clean up later when everyone else goes outside to play). Implementing positive and negative consequences enables children to learn to take responsibility for their actions.

8. *Teach children they have the power to make changes, and point to things they control.* "Remember when you couldn't pump yourself on the swing? Now look how high you can go!"

9. *Avoid high levels of competition.* Stress cooperation or activities in which every child can make a valued contribution.

10. *Model achievement motivation.* Show pride in accomplishments.

SELF-EFFICACY

What contributes to the feeling of being "in control"?

Self-efficacy, as introduced in Chapter 2, is the belief that one can master a situation and produce positive outcomes. It is related to *empowerment* (enabling individuals to have control over resources affecting them), as well as to concepts discussed earlier in this chapter, such as achievement motivation, internal locus of control, history of and attributions of success/failure, and learned helplessness. Whereas helplessness is the belief that "I can't," self-efficacy is the belief that "I can."

Albert Bandura, known for his social cognitive theory (involving learning via observation and modeling), has elaborated on these concepts (achievement motivation, locus of control, and learned helplessness) to formulate a performance-based valid predictor of students' learning—namely, their perceived capability on specific tasks (Bandura, 1997, 2000). Self-efficacy differs from the aforementioned concepts in that it can not only explain present performance but also predict future performance.

Self-efficacy can be assessed in terms of level, generality, and strength across activities and contexts (Bandura, 1997, 2000). The *level* of one's self-efficacy may vary depending on the difficulty of a particular task ("I can read fourth-grade books, but not fifth-grade books"). *Generality* refers to how one's self-efficacious beliefs transfer across tasks ("I can figure out a plane geometry problem, but not a solid geometry one"). The *strength* of one's perceived self-efficacy can be measured by the degree of certainty about performing a given task ("I am 25%, 50%, 75%, 100% sure I can accomplish this"). Thus, self-efficacy measures try to objectify one's perceived *performance capabilities* ("I usually get between 90% and 100% on a spelling test") rather than focusing on one's perceived *personal qualities* ("I am good at spelling"), which are considered to be a dimension of self-esteem, discussed later.

Self-efficacy beliefs provide students with a sense of **personal agency**—the realization that one's actions cause outcomes. Self-efficacy beliefs motivate learning because they enable students to use such self-regulatory processes as goal setting, self-monitoring, self-evaluation, and strategy use (Zimmerman, 2000). Efficacious

personal agency the realization that one's actions cause outcomes

students embrace challenging goals. They are better at monitoring their working time, more persistent, less likely to reject correct hypotheses prematurely, and better at solving conceptual problems than inefficacious students of equal ability. Self-efficacy beliefs affect the self-evaluation standards students use to judge outcomes of their self-monitoring. Self-efficacy beliefs also motivate students' use of learning strategies. Thus, a self-efficacious student might take an advanced placement class *and* an after-school job. This student might get tutoring to help get a better grade in math or practice basketball shots until they are automatic. He or she might do extensive research on a project citing different perspectives or enter a science fair with a complicated experiment.

What are some influences on self-efficacy beliefs? The most significant influence is actual experience—successfully performing tasks, solving problems, making things happen. Next is vicarious experience—observing others execute competent behavior. Also influential are verbal instruction, encouragement, and feedback on performance. Finally, physiological reactions, such as fatigue, stress, or anxiety, may distort an individual's perception of his or her capability at a particular time or while engaged in a certain activity; some examples are "writer's block," an athletic "slump," and math anxiety.

What can be done to support self-efficacious behavior? Self-efficacy measures can be used diagnostically to improve academic motivation (Zimmerman, 2000). Following are some teaching strategies to improve children's self-efficacy (Schunk, 2000; Stipek, 1996):

1. Provide instruction in specific learning strategies, such as highlighting, summarizing, and outlining, to enable students to focus on a task.
2. Help students make short-term, as well as long-term, goals, guiding them to evaluate their progress by regularly providing feedback.
3. Make reinforcement contingent on performance of specific tasks; reward students for mastery of a task, rather than mere engagement in one.
4. Give encouragement: "I know you can do this."
5. Provide positive adult and peer role models who demonstrate efficacious behavior—coping with challenging tasks, setting goals, using strategies, monitoring their effectiveness, and evaluating performance.

Self-Esteem

How do you feel about yourself?

A construct related to self-efficacy is self-concept, which incorporates many forms of self-knowledge and self-evaluative feelings (Zimmerman, 2000). To clarify terms, *self-concept*, introduced in Chapter 2, refers to one's idea of one's own identity as distinct from others. It includes physical, emotional, psychological, cognitive, social, and behavioral attributes. *Self-esteem*, introduced in Chapter 2, refers to the value one places on that identity (Harter, 1998, 1999). Self-esteem can be described as high or low. Some view self-esteem as a global perception of the self, whereas others

© Ryan McVay/Getty Images

This girl has a sense of self-efficacy, feeling that she can master any situation.

view it as multidimensional, consisting of (1) scholastic competence, (2) athletic competence, (3) social competence, (4) physical appearance, and (5) behavioral conduct, in addition to global self-worth (Harter, 1998, 1999). Occasionally, the terms *positive self-concept* or *negative self-concept* are used to describe self-esteem.

To exemplify these opposites, consider the following descriptions of two young girls, Alice and Zelda. Alice displays the characteristics of *competent* children (discussed in Chapter 4 in connection with parenting styles) (Baumrind, 1967; White, 1995). She uses adults as resources after first determining that a job is too difficult. She is capable of expressing affection and mild annoyance to peers as well as adults. She can lead and follow peers. She can compete with peers and shows pride in personal accomplishments. She is able to communicate well. She has the ability to anticipate consequences, can deal with abstractions, and can understand other points of view. She can plan and carry out complicated activities. Finally, she is aware of others, even while working on her own projects. Zelda, on the other hand, displays the characteristics of *incompetent* children; she is deficient in the aforementioned competencies.

> Alice is in kindergarten this year. You notice her immediately because she is so enthusiastic. She is almost always the first to raise her hand when the teacher asks a question. Sometimes she just calls out excitedly, "I know, I know." She doesn't always know, however. Sometimes she makes mistakes and answers incorrectly. When that happens, she shrugs her shoulders and giggles along with her classmates. She approaches her assignments with equal enthusiasm. When one approach fails, she tries another. If her persistence doesn't work, she asks the teacher for help. The other children like her. She is often the leader of the group, but also doesn't seem to mind following. At home she is responsible for dressing herself and keeping her room tidy. She is proud she can tie her shoelaces and make her bed.
>
> Zelda is in first grade this year. Her progress last year in kindergarten was below average. This year it's no better. Zelda's IQ is similar to Alice's, yet Zelda answers most questions with "I don't know." She never raises her hand or volunteers information. She approaches her assignments unenthusiastically and gives up at the first sign of difficulty. She never asks for help, and when the teacher approaches her, she says, "I can't do it." Zelda has few friends and rarely participates in group activities. At home, Zelda is more talkative. She has no responsibilities, and her mother still helps her to dress. She waits for others to do things for her because she "can't" do them for herself. (Chance, 1982, p. 54)

Alice and Zelda, even though alike in natural intelligence, are as far apart as A and Z in competence. Alice likes herself and feels comfortable in her environment. She takes control of her actions and takes responsibility for them. In other words, she decides what she is going to do, does it, and takes pride in doing it. If she makes a mistake, she owns up to it and tries again. Zelda, on the other hand, is full of self-doubt. She thinks her environment is harsh and unfriendly. She feels helpless in controlling what happens to her, so she does not even try. Alice has high self-esteem. She has a sense of trust, autonomy, and initiative. Zelda has low self-esteem. She has a sense of mistrust, self-doubt, and inferiority. The two represent opposite poles in Erikson's (1963) psychosocial stages of development, discussed in Chapter 2. Why have these two young children developed such differing levels of self-esteem?

When Alice was an infant, her mother most likely responded warmly and affectionately to her needs. When she fed Alice, her attention would be focused totally on her. After feeding, Alice's mother cuddled her and talked to her before putting her to bed. Zelda's mother probably was a bit cold and indifferent. She would use Zelda's feeding as a chance to catch up on her reading (she fed Zelda from a bottle). After feeding, Zelda's mother would bathe her and make sure her crib was immaculate, before putting her to bed.

By age 2, Alice was securely attached to her mother. She could be left with a babysitter without too much fuss, yet she was very happy when her mother returned. Zelda, at age 2, was insecurely attached. She would cling to her mother, screaming, when the babysitter came, yet when her mother returned, Zelda would ignore her.

When Alice entered school, she made friends easily. Her eager smile seemed to welcome other children. Even when she put her sweater on inside out and a few children laughed, she just laughed with them. When Zelda entered school, she approached no one. The only friends she made were the two children who sat on either side of her at her table. When Zelda had trouble using her scissors, she just gave up.

DEVELOPMENT OF SELF-ESTEEM

How do children's evaluations of themselves change through time?

As children grow, they accumulate a personal complex set of evaluations about themselves. They know how they look; they know what they are good at doing and what they are poor at doing. They also know what they would like to look like ("I hope I grow taller than my dad") and what they would like to be doing ("I'm going to be a dancer when I grow up"). As children grow, they begin to understand how they are viewed by others. During the process of socialization, people internalize the values and attitudes expressed by their significant others and, as a result, express them as their own. This holds true for values and attitudes about oneself as well as about other people, objects, and experiences. Thus, individuals come to respond to themselves in a way consistent with the way others have responded to them, thereby developing a concept of self. Self-esteem, or one's evaluation of sone's self-concept, emerges from success or failure at meeting one's internalized values and attitudes. As pointed out previously, George Mead (1934) viewed self-esteem as being derived from the reflected appraisal of others. Simplistically, according to Mead, if one has been treated with concern and approval, one will have high self-esteem; if one has been rejected and criticized, one will have low self-esteem. Thus, Alice's and Zelda's differing levels of self-esteem have emerged as a result of cumulative experiences in their young lives with other people, places, and things.

Coopersmith (1967), in a classic investigation, concluded that the following factors contribute to the development of self-esteem: "First and foremost is the amount of respectful, accepting, and concerned treatment that an individual receives from the significant others" (p. 37). Alice has a lot; Zelda has little. Second is the "history of successes and the status and position" an individual holds in the world. Alice has had many successes and is popular; Zelda has had few successes and few friends. Third is the individual's "manner of responding to devaluation." Alice is able to minimize or discount the teasing of others; Zelda is sensitive to others' judgments. She takes them as confirmation of her self-image of helplessness. Recent research concurs with Coopersmith's (1967) conclusions (Harter, 1998, 1999).

"Children value themselves to the degree that they have been valued," according to Dorothy Corkille Briggs, author of *Your Child's Self-Esteem* (1975, p. 14). "Words are less important than the judgments that accompany them . . . and a positive identity hinges on positive life experiences" (pp. 19–20). The differences in the experiences Alice and Zelda had growing up illustrate how self-esteem can be enhanced through messages of acceptance and understanding, as well as by providing opportunities for mastery in order to develop feelings of competence.

Coopersmith's classic study involved hundreds of fifth- and sixth-grade Euro-American, middle-class boys. He tested the level of self-esteem via an inventory, a sample of which is shown below (1967, pp. 265–266):

	Like me	Unlike me
I'm pretty sure of myself.	_____	_____
I often wish I were someone else.	_____	_____
I never worry about anything.	_____	_____
There are lots of things about myself I'd change if I could.	_____	_____
I can make up my mind without too much trouble.	_____	_____
I'm doing the best work that I can.	_____	_____
I give in very easily.	_____	_____
My parents expect too much of me.	_____	_____
Kids usually follow my ideas.	_____	_____

Coopersmith found the boys' self-esteem to be relatively constant, even after retesting them three years later. He also asked their teachers to rate them on such behaviors as reactions to failure, self-confidence in new situations, sociability with peers, and need for encouragement and reassurance. He then classified the children on the basis of their scores on the Self-Esteem Inventory and by teachers' ratings.

The children were further assessed through clinical tests and observations of their behavior in a variety of situations. For example, they were tested to determine how readily they would yield to group influence in a situation in which their own judgment was actually superior. The children were also given tasks that were either very difficult or very easy in order to determine whether their interest in working on a task was sharpened or weakened by success or failure. They were tested for creativity and asked how they usually behaved in real-life situations that called for assertiveness. Finally, their classmates were asked to choose the other children in the class whom they would like to have for friends, and a record was kept of how often each child was chosen.

On the basis of this extensive research, Coopersmith (1967) concluded that there are "significant differences in the experiential worlds and social behaviors of persons who differ in self-esteem."

Persons high in their own estimation approach tasks and persons with the expectation that they will be well received and successful. They have confidence in their perceptions and judgments and believe that they can bring their efforts to a favorable resolution. Their favorable self-attitudes lead them to accept their own opinions and place credence and trust in their reactions and conclusions. This permits them to follow their own judgments when there is a difference of opinion and also permits them to consider novel ideas. The trust in self that accompanies feelings of worthiness is likely to provide the conviction that one is correct and the courage to express those convictions. The attitudes and expectations that lead the individual with high self-esteem to greater social independence and creativity also lead him to more assertive and vigorous social actions. They are more likely to be participants than listeners in group discussions, they report less difficulty in forming friendships, and they will express opinions even when they know these opinions may meet with a hostile reception. Among the factors that underlie and contribute to the actions are their lack of preoccupation with personal problems. Lack of self-consciousness permits them to present their ideas in a full and forthright fashion; lack of self-preoccupation permits them to consider and examine external issues.

The picture of the individual with low self-esteem that emerges from these results is markedly different. These persons lack trust in themselves and are apprehensive about expressing unpopular or unusual ideas. They do not wish to expose themselves, anger others, or perform deeds that would attract attention. They are likely to live in the shadows of a social group, listening rather than participating, and preferring the solitude of withdrawal above the interchange of participation. Among the factors that contribute to the withdrawal of those low in self-esteem are their marked self-consciousness and preoccupation with inner problems. This great awareness of themselves distracts them from attending to other persons and issues and is likely to result in a morbid preoccupation with their difficulties. The effect is to limit their social intercourse and thus decrease the possibilities of friendly and supportive relationships. (Coopersmith, 1967, pp. 70–71; reproduced by special permission of the publisher, Consulting Psychologists Press, Inc., Palo Alto, CA 94306)

Coopersmith concluded that there are four criteria upon which self-esteem develops:

1. *Significance*—the way one perceives he or she is loved and cared about by significant others
2. *Competence*—the way one performs tasks one considers important
3. *Virtue*—how well one attains moral and ethical standards
4. *Power*—the extent to which one has control or influence over one's life and that of others

Whereas Coopersmith measured overall self-esteem, Susan Harter (1990, 1998, 1999) measured the five specific areas of competence listed earlier, as well as general feelings of self-worth ("I am happy with myself") in the Self-Perception Profile for Children. Harter found that self-esteem is well established by middle childhood. Children can make global judgments of their worth as well as distinguish their competencies. For example, a child may perceive himself or herself as a poor athlete but good scholastically. Finally, children's perceptions of themselves accurately reflect how others perceive them. Thus, Cooley's "looking-glass self" and Mead's "generalized other," described in Chapter 2, have found their way into contemporary conceptions of the self.

INFLUENCES ON THE DEVELOPMENT OF SELF-ESTEEM

How do significant socializing agents influence the development of self-esteem?

Family

"There is a growing body of empirical evidence revealing that parental approval is particularly critical in determining the self-esteem of children, supporting the looking-glass self formulation" (Harter, 1998, p. 583).

FogStock LLC/Index Stock Imagery

The self-esteem these boys feel is influenced by success in their performance.

Coopersmith (1967) investigated children's treatment by significant others—those whose attitudes matter most when children are forming their self-concepts. He did this by examining the parenting practices employed by his subjects' fathers and mothers. He administered a questionnaire to the mothers that required responses agreeing or disagreeing with statements having to do with parenting attitudes and practices. He also interviewed the mothers and the children. Coopersmith focused on acceptance of the child and affection exhibited, the kind and amount of punishment used, the level of achievement demands placed on the child, the strictness and consistency with which rules were enforced, the extent to which the child was allowed to participate in family decision making, the extent to which the child was listened to and consulted when rules were being set and enforced, and the extent to which the child was allowed independence. Interestingly, reviewing the many studies over the past 25 years that examined the relationship between parenting and child and adolescent outcomes, Holmbeck, Paikoff, and Brooks-Gunn (1995) concluded that those children exposed to authoritative parenting, the type described here by Coopersmith, are rated as more competent and higher in self-esteem, moral development, impulse control, and independence feelings than children from other types of parenting environments.

Coopersmith found some clear relationships between the parenting practices and self-esteem of sons. Parents of boys with high self-esteem were more often characterized as follows:

- *Warm* (accepting and affectionate). They frequently showed affection to their children, took an interest in their affairs, and became acquainted with their friends.
- *Strict*, but used noncoercive discipline. They enforced rules carefully and consistently. They believed it was important for children to meet high standards. They were firm and decisive in telling the child what he might or might not do. They disciplined their children by withdrawing privileges and by isolation. They tended to discuss the reasons behind the discipline with the children.
- *Democratic*. They allowed the children to participate in making family plans. The children were permitted to express their own opinions, even if it involved questioning the parents' point of view.

Baumrind (1967) found a similar relationship between parenting styles and competent children. The children who were happy, self-reliant, and able to directly meet challenging situations had parents who exercised a good deal of control over their children and demanded responsible, independent behavior from them. These parents also explained, listened, and provided emotional support. Baumrind's (1991) later research, investigating the relationship between authoritarian, authoritative, and permissive parenting styles and the behavior of children approaching adolescence, supported her original findings (1971b, 1973, 1977), as discussed in Chapter 4. Studies of competent adolescents found similar connections (Steinberg, 1993).

Why are parental warmth, strictness, and democracy associated with high self-esteem in children? If we view self-esteem in terms of Cooley's (1909/1964) "looking-glass self," then parents become the child's first mirror, so to speak. If parents are affectionate and accepting, then children will look upon themselves as worthy of affection and acceptance.

According to various investigators (Baumrind, 1971b; Coopersmith, 1967; Holmbeck et al., 1995), parental strictness helps the child develop firm inner controls. When parents give children a clear idea of how to behave, they are providing cues to maximize successful interaction and minimize conflict. Providing standards helps children judge their competence. When children experience a predictable, ordered social environment, it is easier for them to feel in control. Parental strictness combined with warmth demonstrates proof of parental concern for the child's welfare.

Democracy leads to confidence in the ability to express opinions and assert oneself. The opportunity to participate in family discussions enables children to better understand other people's views. Children whose parents respect their opinions and grant them concessions, if warranted, feel like contributing members of the family, and thus significant. It appears that the quality of the relationship with one's parents continues to influence self-esteem after the child becomes an adolescent (Harter, 1998, 1999; Walker & Greene, 1986).

School

Keeping in mind that the valued personality type in American culture is a responsible, self-reliant, autonomous, competent individual, the child who is reared to conform to these traits is likely to have high self-esteem. However, children who are raised in other cultures or in ethnic groups that are not dominant in American society do not necessarily have low self-esteem. Studies have shown that children from ethnic minorities generally enter American schools with strong, positive self-concepts, but that failure to conform to the majority group's expectations causes lower scores on measures of self-esteem (Phinney & Rotheram, 1987). More research is needed, especially on specific components of self-esteem such as Susan Harter's (1998, 1999) scale of global self-worth, scholastic competence, social acceptance, athletic competence, physical appearance, and behavioral conduct.

It probably could be predicted from the comparison of Alice and Zelda that Alice will go on to succeed in school while Zelda will continue to fail. It has been found that students with higher self-esteem are more likely to be successful in school and achieve more than children with low self-esteem (Cole, 1991; Harter, 1998, 1999). This relationship shows up as early as the primary grades and becomes even stronger as the student gets older.

Apparently, then, the more positively children feel about their ability to succeed, the more likely they are to exert effort and feel a sense of accomplishment when they finish a task. Likewise, the more negatively children evaluate their ability to succeed, the more likely they are to avoid tasks in which there is an uncertainty of success, the less likely they are to exert effort, and the less likely they are to attribute any success or lack of it to themselves ("Oh, it was just luck").

People with low self-esteem tend to have a high fear of failure. This causes them to set easy goals or unrealistically difficult goals in tasks where goal setting is required (Bednar, Wells, & Peterson, 1989). For example, in a ring-toss game in which students could toss the rings at the goal from any distance they desired, those with low self-esteem stood either right next to the peg or too far away (Covington & Beery, 1976). Those who stood next to the peg avoided feelings of failure by ensuring success. Those who stood far away ensured failure, but the distance provided an excuse. Students with positive self-esteem were more likely to set goals of intermediate difficulty. In the ring-toss game, they were more likely to choose a distance they thought reasonable for success. If they were given a chance to try the game again, they adjusted the distance according to how they performed on the first try. Those with low self-esteem did not make use of this information.

So far, the influence of self-esteem on achievement has been discussed, but what about the influence of achievement on self-esteem? According to Bloom (1973, p. 142):

> Successful experiences in school are no guarantee of a generally positive self-concept, but they increase the probabilities that such will be the case. In contrast, unsuccessful experiences guarantee that the individual will develop a negative academic self-concept and increase the probabilities that he will have a generally negative self-concept.

Bloom's observation has been supported by research (Bednar et al., 1989). One study, for example, found that preadolescents with high self-concepts were rated by teachers as being more popular, cooperative, and persistent in class, showed greater leadership, were lower in anxiety, had more supportive families, and had higher teacher expectations for their future success than students with lower self-concepts (Hay, Ashman, Vankraayenoord, 1998). Similarly, other studies of school-agers found that achievement in school influenced students' estimation of their own competence (Bandura, 2000; Harter, 1998, 1999; Harter & Connell, 1984). This estimation of competence, or self-efficacy, then, influenced their motivation to achieve.

IN PRACTICE

How Can Parents and Teachers Enhance Children's Self-Esteem?

1. *Enable children to feel accepted.* Understand and attend to their needs; be warm; accept their individuality; talk to them and listen to them.
2. *Enable children to be autonomous.* Provide opportunities for them to do things themselves; give them choices; encourage curiosity; encourage pride in achievement; provide challenges.
3. *Enable children to be successful.* Be an appropriate model; set clear limits; praise accomplishments and efforts; explain consequences and how to learn from mistakes.
4. *Enable children to interact with others positively.* Provide opportunities to cooperate with others; enable them to work out differences dealing with feelings and others' perspectives.
5. *Enable children to be responsible.* Encourage participation; provide opportunities for them to care for belongings, help with chores, and help others.

Peers

Children can be quite cruel to one another, as was discussed in Chapter 8. They tease and ostracize children who are different physically, intellectually, linguistically, or socially. Peer attitudes about "ideal" size, physique, and physical capabilities can influence children's self-esteem. Harter (1998, 1999) found that perceived physical appearance is consistently the domain most highly correlated with self-esteem from early childhood through adulthood, with no gender differences.

It is generally agreed that there are three basic human body types: *endomorphy* (short, heavy build), *mesomorphy* (medium, muscular build), and *ectomorphy* (tall, lean build). Of course, in reality, most people are variations of these basic body types. Body type plays a role in self-esteem in cultures that emphasize a certain ideal type. In the United States, the ideal type for females is slim, well proportioned, and well toned; for males, it is the muscular type. Thus, short, fat adolescent girls and boys as well as tall, skinny adolescent boys are unhappy with their bodies (O'Dea & Abraham, 1999; Phelps, Johnston, Jimenez, & Wilczenski, 1993).

Children discriminate among body types and know the cultural ideal quite early. One study (Johnson & Staffieri, 1971) demonstrated that by age 8, children distinguished among body types. Most of those children interviewed preferred the mesomorphic type over the other two. They rated endomorphy as socially unfavorable and associated ectomorphy with social submissiveness. It would follow, then, that children who do not conform to the ideal body type of their peers have lower self-esteem. This was found to be true in a study (Tucker, 1983) comparing the relationship between self-esteem and how close one's actual physical self conformed to one's ideal physical self. The larger the discrepancy, the greater tendency toward low self-esteem.

The rate at which one matures physically compared to one's peers affects self-concept. Studies have found that boys who mature early compared to their peers are more likely to have high self-esteem than boys who are late maturers (Alsaker, 1992; Apter, Galatzer, Beth-Halachmi, & Laron, 1981; Clausen, 1975). Early maturers are better able to excel in sports, are more likely to get attention from girls, and are chosen more often for leadership roles. Girls who mature early (in elementary school), however, are likely to have low self-esteem because they feel awkward and "out of sync" with their peers. By junior high school, though, girls who mature earlier than their friends have prestige. Junior high school and high school girls who mature late experience a more negative self-concept than do their physically developed peers (Rice & Dolgin, 2002). In general, it can be concluded that children who differ from their peers, especially in appearance, tend to have lower self-esteem than those who are like their peers and who conform to their peers' ideal.

Not only does one's appearance compared to the perceived ideal of one's peers affect self-esteem, so does one's perceived status in relation to the rest of the group. Studies have found children's and adolescents' self-esteem to be dependent on their perceived popularity among their friends (Cole, 1991; Harter, 1998, 1999; Walker & Greene, 1986). Another study found that the self-esteem of 7th- to 12th-graders was related to the status of the peer group to which they belonged at their school. Generally, those who belonged to the "in" crowd exhibited higher self-esteem than outsiders (Brown & Lohr, 1987).

Mass Media

Where do children get their attitudes about ideal body and personality types? Advertising strategies on television and in magazines portray ideal physical stereotypes—handsome, mesomorphic, well-dressed men; beautiful, trim, well-dressed women. Advertising techniques often lead the viewer or reader to believe that the product advertised will produce or perpetuate ideal characteristics. For men, the TV emphasis is on strength, performance, and skill; for women, it is on attractiveness and desirability (Basow, 1992; Crawford & Unger, 2000; Pipher, 1994; Wolf, 1991). Children's heroes and heroines in the media serve as models for the ideal type.

According to Naomi Wolf, author of *The Beauty Myth* (1991), the self-serving interests of advertisers make the ideal unattainable, thereby promoting low self-esteem in order to motivate purchase of their products.

Community

The community may contribute to the differences found in the self-esteem of males and females. In a longitudinal study of developmental changes in self-esteem in males and females from age 14 through age 23, Block and Robins (1993) found a tendency for self-esteem to increase in males and decrease in females. The investigators explain this differences as due to differences in gender-role socialization by society in general. Females are socialized to "get along," to connect and be mutually dependent; males are socialized to "get ahead," to achieve and be self-determinant (Block, 1973; Brown & Gilligan, 1990). As individuals enter adulthood, especially the career world, achievement is rewarded more than camaraderie. So, males, who are socialized accordingly, gain in self-esteem whereas females, who are not socialized to compete, lose in self-esteem. The discrepancy between the values people are socialized to accept as appropriate and those valued in the "real world" may influence self-esteem. The self-esteem level of previously confident females drops in early adolescence (Rosner & Rierdan, 1994). This may be due to the realization that their emphasis on relationships rather than competition is not highly valued in American society, or it may be due to lack of encouragement from the school, as was discussed earlier in the chapter, or both.

It may be that some adolescent girls must wrestle with what it means to be a woman in American society (Basow & Rubin, 1999). Evidence from research suggests that girls are more negatively affected by failure than are boys. This sensitivity tends to limit their willingness to take risks for more challenging opportunities. Also, many young women may still believe there is an inherent conflict between feminine goals of interdependence and support and cultural goals of independence and competition. Belief in this conflict creates ambivalence and anxiety when these young women find themselves in competitive achievement settings (Eccles, Barber, Jozefowicz, Malenchuk, & Vida, 1999). However, females in minority ethnic groups do not generally experience such ambivalence. In fact, African American adult women are respected in their community for being strong, outspoken, and achievement-oriented, as well as for being nurturant and caring, thereby influencing self-esteem. Asian American women subscribing to traditional gender roles were found to have lower self-esteem than those having nontraditional roles (Uba, 1999). For Hispanic American females, having a strong ethnic identity with group support contributed to high self-esteem (Phinney & Chavira, 1992).

The relation between an individual's social identity (ethnicity, religion, social class) and that of the majority of the people in the neighborhood affects one's self-esteem (Harter, 1998, 1999; Martinez & Dukes, 1991; Rosenberg, 1975). For example, Rosenberg (1975) found that the Jewish children raised in Jewish neighborhoods were likely to have higher self-esteem than Jewish children raised in Catholic neighborhoods. He and others (Martinez & Dukes, 1991) also found that African American students in integrated schools were likely to have lower self-esteem than those in all–African American schools. Children of lower status attending a school where the majority of children were of higher social status also had lower self-esteem than those attending a school where the majority of children were from lower-status environments. The same was true of children of upper status who were in the minority. Apparently, being socially different affects one's self-esteem, as has already been discussed in regard to appearance. Since we all cannot look like the ideal type of our peers, and since everyone is not part of the majority ethnic, racial, or religious group, how can self-esteem be enhanced in those who are different from the majority?

Individuals with disabilities are examples of those who differ from the majority in appearance. These individuals often have low self-esteem. One reason is that they do not conform to the ideal body type of society (Koff, Rierdan, & Stubbs, 1990). Another reason is that others often step in to do things for them that they may be capable of doing themselves, if allowed to try. Many individuals with disabilities have developed learned helplessness.

In a project I directed to train college students with disabilities to work as teacher assistants in various special-needs facilities (Berns, 1981), the students with disabilities were given the Tennessee Self-Concept Test upon entering the project (pretest) and a year after participation (posttest). This test measures identity (feelings about what I am); self-satisfaction (feelings about how I act); physical self (feelings about appearance, skills, sexuality); moral ethical self (feelings of being a good or bad person); personal self (sense of adequacy as a person); family self (sense of adequacy as a family member); and social self (sense of adequacy in relations with others).

The purpose of measuring the students' levels of self-esteem before and after participation was to find out whether helping others like themselves would contribute to a rise in their self-esteem. A typical example of participation in the project was one student with multiple sclerosis who relied on a wheelchair for mobility and chose to work in a school for children with orthopedic impairments and children with multiple disabilities.

On comparing pre- and posttest results, every project participant's total self-esteem score increased. Theoretically, the total self-esteem score reflects the overall level of self-esteem. Persons with high total scores tend to like themselves, feel they are persons of value and worth, have confidence in themselves, and act accordingly. When I asked the students, individually, for an explanation of the positive change in their self-concepts, the most frequent answer was "I realized I could do something worthwhile."

Thus, the community can play a significant role in enhancing self-esteem, especially among community members who feel they are different, by providing opportunities for members to do worthwhile and responsible things. Children and youth can help younger children in school or in recreational programs; they can be of service to older citizens; they can be allowed to serve on advisory boards; they can help with community projects. Older community members can contribute their skills and expertise to younger members. Senior citizens can help in day-care facilities, in schools, and in job-training programs. They, too, can serve on advisory boards and help with community projects. When many different people can have opportunities to work together, they learn that self-esteem comes from feeling proud of one's contribution, not from being like everyone else.

Epilogue

Parents hope that the outcome of their socialization efforts with children will be a contributing adult member of society. Many parents continue to give advice long after children have left home. In the story of "The Four Puppets," the puppet maker gives his son, Aung, puppets to advise him when needed. At first, Aung uses the puppets indiscriminately to get what he wants at whim. Eventually, he learns by experience that love and goodness are the most important things in life. Influencing this conclusion were the socialization messages gleaned from his father, the puppet maker, growing up. Aung realizes the puppets were given to him to support the values he learned as a child, and from then on he uses their advice discriminately.

Summary

Values are qualities or beliefs that are viewed as desirable or important. They are outcomes of socialization, and provide the framework in which we think, feel, and act. Children construct and redefine their values as they get older. Certain values are basic to all civilized societies; others are basic to a particular society; still others are personal.

An attitude is a tendency to respond positively or negatively to certain persons, objects, or situations. Attitudes are composed of beliefs, feelings, and action tendencies. Attitudes guide behavior.

The development of attitudes is influenced by age, cognitive development, and social experiences. Parents and peers have a large impact on children's attitudes through instruction, modeling, reinforcement, and punishment.

The media, the community, and the school have the potential to change prejudicial and stereotypical attitudes toward diversity.

A motive causes a person to act. An attribution is an explanation of one's performance when one does act.

Individuals are motivated to develop skills that help them understand and control their environment, whether or not they receive external enforcement. This motivation is exhibited in the need to achieve and the feeling of being in control of the outcomes of one's actions. When one is no longer motivated to master one's environment, overcome obstacles in solving problems, or do one's best, one is said to have learned helplessness.

The development of achievement motivation has been linked most often to parenting styles. In general, the child-rearing environment of children who show high achievement motivation includes warmth, developmentally appropriate timing of achievement demands, high confidence in the child's abilities, a supportive affective family environment, and highly motivated role models.

Achievement is also related to one's expectancy of success and one's fear of failure, as well as one's history of success and failure.

Locus of control relates to one's sense of personal responsibility. Individuals who believe they are in control of their world have an internal locus of control. Individuals who perceive that others or outside events have more control over them than they have over themselves have an external locus of control. External attribution factors include luck and powerful others; internal attribution factors include ability and effort.

Those who have an internal locus of control generally are more competent and effective than those with an external locus of control. Locus of control is related to age, gender, socioeconomic status, and performance attributes and outcomes.

When people are placed in situations in which outcomes are unaffected by their behaviors, they become passive and unmotivated. They have learned helplessness. Learned helplessness is influenced by experience and interaction with others, such as the kind of feedback one gets for performing a task.

Self-efficacy refers to the belief that one can master a situation and produce positive outcomes. It is a performance-based measure of perceived capability. It is related to achievement motivation, locus of control, and learned helplessness. It involves goal setting, self-monitoring, self-evaluation, and learning strategies.

Self-esteem, the value one places on one's self-concept, is derived from the reflected appraisal of others. Simplistically, if one has been treated with concern and approval, one will have high self-esteem; if one has been rejected and criticized, one will have low self-esteem. Specific dimensions of self-esteem include scholastic competence, athletic competence, social competence, physical appearance, and behavioral conduct, as well as global self-worth.

The factors contributing to self-esteem are the amount of respectful, accepting, and concerned treatment an individual receives from significant others; an individual's history of successes and failures; his or her status among peers; and his or her manner of responding to devaluation or failure.

Parenting practices contribute to the development of self-esteem. The parenting styles of children with high self-esteem are described as warm, strict, and democratic. However, these results apply to American society. Parenting styles in diverse ethnic groups and their effect on children's self-esteem may differ.

Children with high self-esteem are more likely to be successful in school and are likely to achieve more than children with low self-esteem.

Peers influence self-esteem by their reinforcement of "ideal" types. Children who differ from the ideal tend to have lower self-esteem. Peers get their attitudes about ideal types from the media.

The community can contribute to the enhancement of members' self-esteem by providing worthwhile, responsible activities in which to engage.

Activity

PURPOSE To gain insight into personal values.

1. The 18 values listed in the form "What Values Are Important to You?" are in alphabetical order. Select the value that is most important to you and write a 1 next to it in column I. Then choose your next most important value and write a 2 beside it in the same column. Continue until you have ranked all 18 values in column I.
2. Now rank the 18 values as you believe your parents, your spouse, or a very close friend would have ranked them. Put these numbers in column II.
3. Finally, rank the 18 values as you believe a person with whom you have not been able to get along would have ranked them. Put these numbers in column III.
4. Compare the rankings of the values in the three columns. How do your values compare to those of the person you are close to? How do they compare to those of the person who is your adversary? Compare your rankings with others'. What is your relationship with them? Is there any correlation between similarity in values and closeness of relationship?
5. What values are important to you? Because values and morals involve making choices, do the forced choice exercise that follows.

What Values Are Important to You?

	I	II	III
A COMFORTABLE LIFE a prosperous life			
EQUALITY brotherhood, equal opportunity for all			
AN EXCITING LIFE a stimulating, active life			
FAMILY SECURITY taking care of loved ones			
FREEDOM independence, free choice			
HAPPINESS contentedness			
INNER HARMONY freedom from inner conflict			

                                                    I   II   III

MATURE LOVE
   sexual and spiritual intimacy
NATIONAL SECURITY
   protection from attack
PLEASURE
   an enjoyable, leisurely life
SALVATION
   saved, eternal life
SELF-RESPECT
   self-esteem
A SENSE OF ACCOMPLISHMENT
   lasting contribution
SOCIAL RECOGNITION
   respect, admiration
TRUE FRIENDSHIP
   close companionship
WISDOM
   a mature understanding of life
A WORLD AT PEACE
   free of war and conflict
A WORLD OF BEAUTY
   beauty of nature and the arts

Source: Copyright 1967, 1982 by Milton Rokeach. Permission to reprint Halgren Tests, 873 Persimmon Avenue, Sunnyvale, California 94087.

Forced Choice Exercise

Instructions: Write your top 10 values from the list in any order. If you had to choose between #1 and #2, which would you choose. Circle your choice. #1 and #3? #1 and #4? and so on. If you had to choose between #2 and #3, which would you choose? #2 and #4, and so on. Continue making forced choices until you've completed (#9 or #10) the list. Now rank your values in order.

                                                    1 1 1 1 1 1 1 1
1. _____   2 3 4 5 6 7 8 9 10

                                                    2 2 2 2 2 2 2
2. _____   3 4 5 6 7 8 9 10

                                                    3 3 3 3 3 3 3
3. _____   4 5 6 7 8 9 10

                                                    4 4 4 4 4 4
4. _____   5 6 7 8 9 10

                                                    5 5 5 5 5
5. _____   6 7 8 9 10

                                                    6 6 6 6

6. _____   <u>7 8 9 10</u>

                                                               7 7 7

7. _____   <u>8 9 10</u>

                                                               8 8

8. _____   <u>9 10</u>

                                                               9

9. _____   10

10. _____

Related Readings

Aboud, F. (1988). *Children and prejudice.* Cambridge, MA: Basil Blackwell.

Bandura, A. (2000). *Self-efficacy: The exercise of control.* New York: Freeman.

Briggs, D. C. (1975). *Your child's self esteem.* New York: Dolphin.

Harter, S. (1999). *The construction of the self: A developmental perspective.* New York: Guilford.

Lawrence-Lightfoot, S. (1999). *Respect: An exploration.* Boulder, CO: Perseus.

Lewis, H. (1990). *A question of values.* San Francisco: Harper & Row.

McClelland, D. C. (1961). *The achieving society.* New York: Van Nostrand.

McInerney, P. K., & Rainbolt, G. W. (1994). *Ethics.* New York: HarperCollins.

Seligman, M. E. P. (1975). *Helplessness.* San Francisco: Freeman.

Seligman, M. E. P. (1990). *Learned optimism.* New York: Pocket Books.

Simon, S. B., Howe, L., & Kirschenbaum, H. (1972). *Values clarification: A practical handbook of strategies for teachers and students.* New York: Hart.

Van Ausdale, D., & Feagin, J. R. (2001). *The first R: How children learn race and racism.* Lanham, MD: Rowman & Littlefield.

Chapter 12

Rich Remsberg/Index Stock Imagery

Social and Behavioral Socialization Outcomes

All the world's a stage,
And all the men and women merely players:
They have their exits and their entrances;
And one man in his time plays many parts.

— WILLIAM SHAKESPEARE

The moral values constituting good and bad, right and wrong, form the foundation, or mores, of society because they encompass how people should treat one another. Such values have been immortalized and realized through religion, laws, history, and literature. Moral values are often found in stories read to children. The following Japanese folktale, "Momotaro: Boy of the Peach" (Uchida, 1949), is a story about kindness and its rewards.

Once Upon a Time A long time ago, in a small Japanese village, there lived a kind old man and a kind old woman. One day, they set out from their little cottage together. The old man went to the mountains to cut some firewood for their kitchen, and the old woman went to the river to wash their clothes.

As the old woman knelt down by a river rock to scrub the clothing, she saw something strange floating down the river. It was a big, giant peach! The old woman had never seen so fine a peach. "What a wonderful present it will make for the old man. I will take it home with me." But try as she would, she could not reach the peach. She looked around for a long stick, but all she could see were pebbles and sand. "Oh, dear! What shall I do?" she said to herself. After a moment, she had an idea. "I know, I'll sing to it.' In a sweet, clear voice, she sang:

"The deep waters are salty!

The shallow waters are sweet!

Stay away from the salty water,

And come where the water is sweet."

She sang this refrain over and over, clapping her hands in time to the song. Then, strangely enough, the big peach slowly began to bob along toward the shore where the water was shallow. Rumbley-bump, bumpety-bump it went until it finally came to a stop at the old woman's feet.

The old woman was so happy, she gently picked up the peach and quickly carried it home, cradling it in her arms. Impatiently, she waited for the old man to return. At day's end, she saw the old man coming toward the house carrying a big pack of wood on his back. She ran toward him shouting, "Come quickly, see what I have found!"

When the old man laid down his burden and entered the house, he exclaimed, "Well, well, what a fine present; I am so hungry, I will cut it up for our meal."

"Wait, old man! Don't cut me! " cried the peach. Before the surprised old man and woman could say a word, the beautiful big peach split in two, and a sweet little boy jumped out from inside.

"Oh, my goodness! Oh, my goodness!" they cried together over and over again. The old man and woman had wanted a child for the longest time, so they were happy beyond their wildest dreams. They decided to call the boy Momotaro, which means "Boy-of-the-Peach." They took very good care of this fine boy, loving him dearly.

When Momotaro was 15 years old, he came before the old man and woman saying, "You have both been good and kind to me, and I am grateful for all you have done, but now I think I am old enough to do some good for others, too. I have come to ask if I may leave you."

"You wish to leave us, my son? But why?" asked the old man sadly.

"I will not be gone long and I will return, but I wish to go to the Island of the Ogres to rid the land of those harmful creatures. They have killed many good people, and have stolen and robbed throughout the country. I wish to kill the ogres, so they can never kill again," replied Momotaro.

"That is a fine idea, my son. I wish you well," said the old man.

So, the old woman prepared some millet cakes for Momotaro's journey, and then she and the old man waved goodbye, saying "Be careful and come back soon."

"Yes, yes. Take care of yourselves while I am away," replied Momotaro, as he hurried away. He was anxious to get to the Island of the Ogres.

When Momotaro reached the forest, he sat down at the foot of a tall pine tree. He unwrapped the furoshiki that held the little millet cakes. But just then he heard a noise. A large dog as big as a calf came out of the grass. "Momotaro-san, Momotaro-san, what is it you have that smells so good?" asked the dog.

Momotaro was not frightened; he simply answered, "I am eating a delicious millet cake, which my good mother made for me this morning."

"Please," begged the dog, "Can I have one? I'm so hungry. If you give me one, I'll go with you on your journey. I can be of help to you."

"Very well then," said Momotaro. "I will take you with me to help kill the ogres." And he gave the dog one of his millet cakes to eat.

As they walked on, something jumped out of the branches of a tree, stopping in front of Momotaro. It was a monkey! "Greetings, Momotaro-san!" exclaimed the monkey. "I have heard of your journey to the Island of the Ogres and I wish to help you."

"Grr," growled the dog. "I am going with him to help; we do not need you!"

The monkey began to shriek, "How dare you speak to me like that?" And he leapt on the dog baring his claws. The dog barked and bit the monkey.

"Stop this fighting!" commanded Momotaro. "There is no reason why we three cannot go. I then shall have two helpers instead of one." He handed the monkey a millet cake from his furoshiki.

As the three went down the path to the edge of the woods, a large pheasant hopped out from the field in front of them. The dog growled and the monkey spit. Momotaro stopped the fight before it went any further, saying, "We are on our way to kill the ogres; would you like to come and help us?"

"Oh, I would indeed, for I want to rid this land of evil and danger," said the pheasant gratefully.

"Then, here, take this cake and join us," said Momotaro.

On the journey, the four became good friends. Before long, they came to the water's edge and found a boat big enough to carry them across the river. They climbed in and headed for the Island of the Ogres.

Soon they saw it in the distance wrapped in gray, foggy clouds. Dark stone walls rose up above towering cliffs and large iron gates that stood ready to keep out anyone who tried to enter.

Momotaro thought for a while and then turned to the pheasant. "You alone can wing your way over these high walls and gates. Fly into the ogres' fortress and do what you can to frighten them. We will follow as soon as we can."

So the pheasant flew far above the iron gates and stone walls and down onto the roof of the ogres' castle. "Momotaro-san has come to rid the land of you and your many evil deeds. Give up your stolen treasures now, and perhaps he will spare your lives!"

"Ho, Ho, Ho," laughed the ogres. "We are not afraid of a little bird like you and we surely are not afraid of Momotaro!"

Upon hearing this, the pheasant angrily flew down, pecking at the heads of the ogres with his sharp, pointed beak. While the pheasant was distracting the ogres, the dog and the monkey helped Momotaro tear down the iron gates, coming to the aid of the brave pheasant.

"Get away! Get away!" shouted the ogres, as the monkey clawed and scratched and the big dog growled and bit. With the continuous pecking and clawing and biting, the ogres began to run away. The pheasant, monkey, and dog kept this up until the ogres tumbled over the cliffs to the sea. Only the Chief of the Ogres remained. He threw up his hands, and bowed low to Momotaro, "Please spare me my life, and all our stolen treasures are yours. I promise never to rob or kill anyone again," he said.

Momotaro tied up the evil ogre, while the pheasant, the monkey, and the dog carried the boxes filled with jewels and treasures down to their boat. When the boat was laden with all it could hold, the four sailed homeward.

Upon arriving at his village, Momotaro went to everyone, returning many of the treasures that the ogres had stolen. "You will never again be troubled by the ogres of the Island!" he said triumphantly.

"You are a kind and brave lad, Momotaro. Thank you for making our land safe once again," the villagers said gratefully.

And then Momotaro went back to the home of the old man and woman, as he had promised. He had brought riches for them as well, so the three could live easily and happily for many, many years.

Momotaro's parents were role models for his moral behavior. They cared for him, being loving, kind, and generous. Momotaro wanted others to experience goodness. So, he embarked on a brave quest, sharing his kindness with a dog, a monkey, and a pheasant, who, in turn, learned how to cooperate and be helpful. Working together enabled them to be strong enough to conquer the evil forces in their land.

In real life, children are exposed to and socialized by many role models. This chapter explores the social and behavioral outcomes influenced by such interactions.

- **Do different cultures have varying concepts of "goodness"?**

- **Why do some people behave like ogres in that they lie, cheat, steal, or kill?**

- **Is the "hero role" just for boys, or can girls assume it too?**

Self-Regulation/Behavior

How do children learn to regulate their behavior appropriately?

Self-regulation (or *self-control*), as introduced in Chapter 2, refers to the ability to regulate or control one's impulses, behavior, and/or emotions until an appropriate time, place, or object is available for expression. Recall that self-regulation is one of the aims of socialization. Self-regulatory behavior involves the ability to delay gratification, the ability to sustain attention to a task, and the ability to plan and self-monitor a goal-directed activity, whether social or moral conduct or academic or athletic achievement (similar to self-efficacy). Self-regulatory skills are significantly related to inhibiting antisocial or aggressive behaviors and exhibiting prosocial or altruistic ones (Lengua, 2002). Self-regulatory difficulties may be symptomatic of conduct disorders, attention deficit hyperactivity disorder (ADHD), or depression (Winsler & Wallace, 2002). Figure 12.1 is an ecological model showing the relationships between microsystems and mesosystems, influenced by exosystems, and macrosystems, as they affect social and behavioral outcomes of socialization.

Self-regulation, or self-control, can be observed in children beginning about age 2 (Berk, 2003) and increasing with age (Logue, 1995). To behave appropriately, children have to have the cognitive maturity to understand that they are separate, autonomous beings with the ability to control their own actions. They also have to have the language development to understand directives, the memory capabilities to store and retrieve a caregiver's instructions, and the information-processing strategies to apply them to the particular situation. In addition, children need to have some concept of the future, which expands as they get older ("If I don't tease my brother, Mommy said she would take me skating").

According to Vygotsky (1978), children cannot control their behavior until they incorporate adult cultural standards expressed in communication into their own speech. This occurs when children transform adult standards (sanctions on behavior, stereotypical roles, and/or ideals for perfection), referred to as "social speech," into private, or "inner speech," to direct their own behavior. An example of an adult standard of behavior communicated to children is to resist temptation by delaying gratification. The ability to delay gratification involves waiting for an appropriate time to behave or achieve a desired result, instead of succumbing to temptation by reacting impulsively (acting without much thought to consequences). Mischel (1996) studied what preschool children say to themselves (inner speech) to promote delay of gratification when faced with tempting situations to gain immediate rewards. The children were given a choice of two rewards, a highly desirable one (such as a toy or candy) that they could have if they waited the prescribed amount

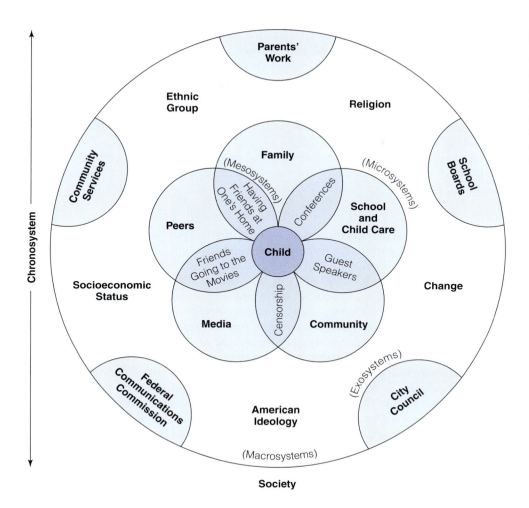

Figure 12.1

An Ecological Model of Human Development

The child's antisocial or prosocial behavior, gender role, and self-esteem are outcomes of his or her socialization.

of time, or a less desirable one (such as a sticker) that they could have anytime. The preschoolers who had the ability to delay gratification and resist the temptation of taking the immediate reward used strategies to divert their attention while waiting, such as covering their eyes, singing, and pretending to be asleep.

The development of such self-regulatory ability depends partly on biological factors, such as the child's temperament, and partly on contextual factors, such as parenting practices (Berk, 2003).

Temperament (easy, slow to warm up, difficult), discussed in Chapter 4, consists of genetically based characteristics that determine an individual's sensitivity to various experiences and responsiveness to patterns of social interaction. *Easy* children are more likely to comply with adult standards because, physiologically, they are more "relaxed." *Slow-to-warm-up* children may need time, reasoning, repetition, and patience to comply. *Difficult* children need even more of the same because they are more "tense" and, therefore, resistant to change.

Parenting practices influence the development of self-regulation in that the motive for children to internalize adult standards, as discussed in Chapter 2, is attachment. Children are willing to comply with parental demands because they want to please the individuals who love them; they try not to displease because they fear loss of that love. According to Damon (1988), this is the foundation of respect for authority and social order in society. Authoritative parenting practices, in which there is extensive verbal give and take, reasoning, and nonpunitive adult control, foster the development of self-control. Self-regulation, or control, is a continuous process, an outcome of affective, cognitive, and social forces. In the beginning, the child responds emotionally to situations instinctively. These biological reactions are responded to by adults and redefined through social experience. Through continuous instruction, observation, participation, feedback, and interpretation, various levels of self-control are established (Damon, 1988). Children who are maltreated by parents and exposed to domestic violence are less likely to develop self-control and emotional regulatory abilities (Maughan & Cicchetti, 2002).

What role do emotions play in self-regulatory behavior?

A component of self-regulation is emotional regulation, including the ability to control anger and exhibit empathy. In the next sections, we examine how these emotions are translated into antisocial behavior and prosocial behavior. **Antisocial behavior** includes any behavior that harms other people, such as aggression, violence, and crime. **Prosocial behavior** includes any behavior that benefits other people, such as altruism, sharing, and cooperation.

How do children learn behavior that is pro- rather than antisocial? Whereas antisocial behavior—aggression—has been studied for many years, it is only relatively recently that attention has been given to prosocial behavior—altruism. **Aggression** includes an unprovoked attack, fight, or quarrel. Types of aggression include *instrumental,* whose goal is to obtain an object, a privilege, or a space, and *hostile,* whose goal is to harm another person. (We focus on hostile aggression, because instrumental aggression usually declines as children develop language skills to express desires and self-regulatory skills to delay gratification.) **Altruism** encompasses voluntary actions that are intended to help or benefit another person or group of people without the actor's anticipation of external rewards. Such actions often entail some cost, self-sacrifice, or risk on the part of the actor (Eisenberg & Fabes, 1998).

antisocial behavior any behavior that harms other people, such as aggression, violence, and crime

prosocial behavior any behavior that benefits other people, such as altruism, sharing, and cooperation

aggression unprovoked attack, fight, or quarrel

altruism voluntary actions that are intended to help or benefit another person or group of people without the actor's anticipation of external rewards

---

IN PRACTICE

Does Zero Tolerance Inhibit or Enhance Self-Control?

In order to provide a safe environment for learning, schools across the nation are exerting their punitive power to suspend or expel students who violate the rules, which vary by state, and even by school district. Generally, school rules for appropriate conduct involve truancy, weapons, drugs, aggressive behavior, sexual misconduct, and insubordination.

- Is a "one-size-fits-all" policy best for dealing with misbehavior, or are there others?
- Does suspension or expulsion from school lead to increased alienation or dropout rates?
- How can children who are punished learn to improve their behavior?
- How can the families of children who are punished be engaged to collaborate with school rules for more optimal socialization outcomes?

ANTISOCIAL BEHAVIOR: AGGRESSION

How does aggressive behavior develop?

Researchers are interested in studying causes and correlates of aggressive behavior because childhood aggression, especially hostile aggression, often forecasts later maladaptive outcomes, such as delinquency and criminality (Coie & Dodge, 1998; Farrington, 1991). Antecedents of aggressive behavior in children may be noncompliance with adults, oppositional behavior, lying, stealing, and destruction of property.

What are the theories of aggressive behavior?

Existing theories explaining the causes of aggression fall into the following general categories: (1) it is biologically influenced; (2) it is learned; (3) it is an information-processing impulsive response to frustration; (4) it is a result of social cognitive factors such as peer group pressure or the reduction of restraining socialization forces; and (5) it is socialized by interacting ecological factors.

Biological

Biological influences on behavior include evolution and genetics. *Evolution* encompasses passing on the survival and adaptive characteristics of the species from one generation to the next; *genetics* refers to the individual characteristics of the parents that are passed on to their children.

Sigmund Freud (Freud, 1925; Hall, 1954) believed that humans are born with two opposing biological instincts: a life instinct (*Eros*), which causes the person to grow and survive, and a death instinct (*Thanatos*), which works toward the individual's self-destruction. According to him, the death instinct is often redirected outward against the external world in the form of aggression toward others. Freud believed that the energy for the death instinct is constantly generated and if it cannot be released in small amounts in socially acceptable ways, it will eventually be released in an extreme and socially unacceptable form, such as violence against others or violence against the self. Thus, if the aggressive instinct can be redirected (crying, punching a doll, hammering nails), then it can be defused.

Konrad Lorenz (1966) held that the aggressive instinct has made the major contribution to the evolution and survival of animals. Such vital functions as protecting one's territory against invasion, defending the young, and engaging in fights to eliminate the weak so they will not reproduce are basic to species survival. According to Lorenz, the expression of the aggressive instinct in most humans, especially in middle-class Western societies, has been inhibited; consequently, the drive will build up until it can be expressed, even if it is vicious.

However, the problem with Freud's and Lorenz's theories is that they do not explain the differences in levels of aggressiveness within a society and in various situations.

There is some evidence supporting a genetic basis for antisocial behavior. Behavioral tendencies that might be influenced genetically include impulse control, frustration tolerance, and activity level (Segal, 1997). Aggressive and antisocial behavior shows stability over the life course (Coie & Dodge, 1998). A large-scale study of adopted persons found that an individual was more likely to exhibit deviant criminal behavior if a biological parent was a criminal, regardless of the environment in the adoptive family (Mednick, Moffit, Gabrielli, & Hutchings, 1986). In addition, the level of certain hormones present in a person has been shown to be related to aggressive behavior (Olweus, 1986). Finally, males are more aggressive than females, not only physically but also verbally (Eley, Lichtenstein, & Stevenson, 1999; Maccoby & Jacklin, 1974, 1980).

Research analyses of the relationship of biological factors to aggressive behavior conclude that aggression occurs indirectly through the interaction of biological processes and environmental events (Coie & Dodge, 1998; Dodge & Pettit, 2003; Gifford-Smith & Rabiner, 2004).

Learning

According to Bandura (1973, 1991), children learn through a series of experiences when it is appropriate to act aggressively, what forms of aggression are permissible, and to whom they can express aggression without disapproval or punishment. For example, children cannot hit mothers when they take a toy away because severe socialization consequences ensue. However, children can hit peers when they take a toy away without experiencing such consequences.

Children identify with role models and imitate behavior. The role models can be peers. For example, a child who has been attending school for a while may come home and display some new behavior never displayed before (such as biting when angry). The role models can be parents. For example, parents sometimes respond to aggressive acts by spanking. Punishing aggression with aggression is providing model behavior for the child to imitate.

The role models can also be other adults. In one classic study by Bandura, Ross, and Ross (1963), a group of preschool children watched a film of woman hitting a Bobo doll (a 5-foot plastic inflated clown), while another group of children watched a model play with Tinkertoys. After watching the models, the children were left alone with a number of toys, including a Bobo doll and Tinkertoys, and were observed. The children who had watched the aggressive behavior on film acted more aggressively with the Bobo doll in the laboratory situation than did the other children. They punched, kicked, and hammered the doll. They even made the same aggressive comments the adult had.

Whether or not models will be imitated depends on their perceived status. Children have been found to imitate high-status dominant models (Bandura, 1989). Characteristics of the observer can also influence the incidence of imitation, such as

This parent's harsh and punitive child-rearing methods will likely influence this child to have an externally oriented conscience, behaving out of fear of punishment.

© Tony Freeman/PhotoEdit

motivation, ability to remember what is observed, and ability to perform the observed act (Bandura, 1989).

Whether or not aggressive acts will be imitated by the observer also depends on whether the aggressive model was rewarded or punished. In one experiment (Bandura, 1973), children were exposed to one of three conditions: they viewed a film showing a successful aggressive model enjoying a victory; they viewed a film showing an aggressive model being severely punished by the intended victim; or they did not see any film (the control condition). The children who saw the aggressive model rewarded for aggressive behavior exhibited more aggression on subsequent observation than did children who either saw the model punished or saw no model.

The explanation behind these results is that the consequences of the model's behavior may have served as cues to the kind of behavior that is permissible in a given social context. Responses that are rewarded tend to occur more frequently, because behavior that results in successful outcomes is likely to be repeated (Bandura, 1973, 1991). For example, if a child pushes another in order to get to the swing first and the other child acquiesces (does not resist or retaliate), it is likely that the aggressor will repeat the aggressive act the next time he or she pursues an activity that is being blocked by someone.

Responses that are rewarded intermittently resist extinction, or elimination. In other words, responses that are not rewarded every time they occur, but only sometimes, are very difficult to "unlearn." Aggressive acts are highly likely to be rewarded intermittently. For instance, they may be allowed to occur successfully by some children and not by others, and they may be punished by adults when noticed, which may not be every single occurrence.

That aggression can be learned through observation of an aggressive model causes attention to be turned to the content of television shows and their potential impact on children. As has been discussed, a number of studies (Comstock & Paik, 1991; Huston & Wright, 1998; Perse 2001) report that both children and adults are exposed to a lot of television violence. Many people believe that watching a lot of aggression on television increases the tendency of the viewers, especially children, to behave aggressively. By watching, children may learn that aggression is acceptable, and may even learn aggressive techniques. Others who believe that the aggressive instinct is present in all humans suggest that watching aggression acts as a catharsis, or a way of releasing pent-up aggressive feelings. If this is the case, then watching aggression on television reduces potential aggressive behavior. Still others hold that televised aggression has little effect on aggressive behavior, compared to direct rewards and models for aggression provided by parents, teachers, and friends.

Several factors have been found to moderate the effects of viewing television violence on aggressive behavior (Coie & Dodge, 1998). They include the child's repertoire of alternative behaviors; whether the child believes the violence on TV is real; whether the child identifies with the TV character; whether the parent watches and discusses the show with the child; and whether the aggressive acts viewed were punished, justified, or rewarded (the aggressor gets something or wins). An alternative behavior might be verbalization. Children who know how to verbalize their frustration ("I don't like it when you take my things"), as opposed to children who do not (when something is taken, the child just grabs it back, giving the transgressor a punch), are less likely to imitate aggressive behavior. Children who, due to cognitive immaturity, believe that what they see on TV is real, are more likely to imitate aggression, especially if they identify with the aggressor or if the aggressor is rewarded. Children whose parents mediate TV viewing are less likely to imitate aggression.

There is much documentation on the relationship between parenting practices and childhood aggression (Coie & Dodge, 1998; Kim, Hetherington, & Reiss, 1999; Patterson, 1982; Rubin, Stewart, & Chen, 1995). Coercive, hostile parenting is related to children's aggression. Thus, if parents want to discourage aggressive behavior in their children, they must not model it (spanking is aggressive behavior). They must also not reward it (let it succeed or go unnoticed). And they must teach alternative acceptable behaviors, such as talking about one's feelings.

Information Processing

Information processing refers to the way an individual attends to, perceives, interprets, remembers, and acts on events or situations. People who behave impulsively act without thinking ahead of the consequences. People who are frustrated view interfering factors as preventing them from achieving a goal. Some believe impulsivity is a genetic temperamental trait that affects behavior (Buss & Plomin, 1984; Coie & Dodge, 1998; Kagan, 1994). For example, some researchers have found a link between low impulsivity and self-control (Kochanska, DeVet, Goldman, Murray, & Putnam, 1994). Thus, aggressive behavior can be a response to frustrating experiences, especially in impulsive individuals (Staub, 1986). An example would be "road rage," in which people get involved in verbal or physical fights—or even shoot one another—when cut off in traffic. The strength of the frustrated motive, the degree of interference, and the number of goals blocked determine the intensity of the aggression exhibited (Grusec & Lytton, 1988). If a child's goal is to ride a tricycle during free play time, but the teacher calls everyone in before the child gets a turn, he or she might be frustrated. However, if the child had to wait an especially long time because the other children refused to give up their tricycles and, perhaps, even teased the waiting child, then the level of frustration is bound to escalate and may be expressed as aggression.

Others (Coie & Dodge, 1998; Dodge, 1986; Dodge & Pettit, 2003) believe that people's reactions to frustration depend not so much on the social cues (what *actually* happens) as on how they process the information (their *interpretation* of what happens). Dodge (1986) assumes that children enter each social situation with a memory of past experiences and a goal (making friends, for example). When an event occurs, such as being bumped into, the child must interpret its meaning. A child's past experiences with social interaction as well as his or her skills in processing information will influence whether the event will be interpreted as "accidental" or "purposeful." Aggressive children tend to interpret ambiguous events as hostile, whereas nonaggressive children tend to interpret such events as benign. Dodge's explanation of how such social information is processed cognitively will be discussed in more detail later.

Social Cognitive

People are influenced by the attitudes, values, and behavior patterns of those around them, particularly significant others. Aggression can be a result of peer group pressure. Studies (Coie & Dodge, 1998; Wall, Power, & Arbona, 1993) have shown that violence is much higher in some groups than in others. For example, in some parts of Italy violence is the acceptable reaction to personal affronts. If one wants to be part of the groups that subscribe to this norm, one must act as expected. For another example, adolescents of low socioeconomic status who had recently immigrated from Mexico were more susceptible to antisocial peer pressure than those who had been in the United States for a longer time.

information processing the way an individual attends to, perceives, interprets, remembers, and acts on events or situations

Peers are thought to supply the individual with the attitudes, motivations, and rationalizations to support antisocial behavior as well as providing opportunities to engage in specific delinquent acts (Coie & Dodge, 1998; Espeldge, Holt, & Henkel, 2003; Patterson et al., 1989). A study of children from first to sixth grade found the classroom context to be influential in increasing or reducing aggressive behavior (Kellam, Ling, Merisca, Brown, & Ialongo, 1999). Aggressive first-graders in class-rooms with aggressive peers showed an increase in aggressive behavior by sixth grade; whereas aggressive first-graders in classrooms using preventive intervention strategies showed a decrease in aggressive behavior by sixth grade. Whether or not individuals succumb to group pressure depends on their personalities, the situation, and also the number of reference groups to which they belong. If they belong to several groups that use aggression as an acceptable means of revenge, then the tendency to behave aggressively increases. On the other hand, if they belong to one group that subscribes to this norm but also to other groups that do not, the likelihood of conforming to the aggressive behavior of the one group decreases. Thus, if one's peer group sanctions aggression, one is more likely to exhibit aggressive behavior.

Some researchers believe that when restraining socialization forces are reduced, aggression is more likely. Restraining socialization forces can be external pressures, such as fear of consequences (punishment, criticism, opinion of others), or internal pressures (guilt, shame, moral development level).

Anonymity tends to reduce the restraining forces of external pressures. Thus, when people are anonymous, they are more likely to be aggressive than when their identity is known. Anonymity can result when a person is unknown to others (disguised, hidden by darkness) or is "lost in the crowd" (part of a uniformed group, or with too many people to be noticed). When people are anonymous, they cannot be identified by others and therefore cannot be evaluated, criticized, judged, or punished by them.

Experiments (Baron, 1970; Deax & Wrightsman, 1988) have shown that when individuals are made to feel anonymous, their levels of aggression increase in a laboratory situation. In a naturalistic study (Diener, Frasier, Beaman, & Kelem, 1976), 1,300 children were unobtrusively observed trick-or-treating on Halloween. They were given the opportunity to steal candy and money. When the children

When aggressive models are successful, they are likely to be imitated.

were anonymous (identities hidden by costumes), more stealing of extra candy and money was observed than when they had been previously asked to reveal their identities to the adult host.

"Sanctions for evil" (Sanford & Comstock, 1971) provided by a group may reduce internal restraining pressures such as guilt. For example, members of the group may feel that what they are doing is morally required (Duster, 1971). War exemplifies this: In war, loyalty to the group (the army, for instance) obliterates individuality. Soldiers are trained to do as they are ordered; the responsibility for decisions rests with their superiors, not them. Another example of sanctions for evil is the famous Milgram (1963) experiment, which focused on the conflict between obedience to authority and personal conscience. Subjects (in the role of teacher) were told to inflict electric shocks (even though shocks were not actually given) on other subjects (in the role of learner) when they gave a wrong answer. Some "teachers" refused immediately, and some "teachers" quit the experiment after they heard the other "learners" scream. However, 65% of the "teachers" obeyed orders to punish the "learners" and actually inflicted (or believed they inflicted) the maximum level of shock possible (450 volts!).

The community usually provides the restraining socialization forces for aggression through its members, its laws, and its police. Community members are a restraining force when they disapprove of aggression by another community member. The restraining force is the opinion of the group: "What will the neighbors say if I beat up Fred?" Anonymity or alienation reduces the force of that disapproval: "Why should I care what the neighbors think? They don't know me, so they'll never know who beat up Fred."

The laws of the community spell out what behavior is unacceptable and must be punished. The restraining force of the laws depends on how stringently they are enforced.

The police provide protection for community members. Parents and children living in neighborhoods characterized by high crime rates perceive their environments as unsafe (Fick, Osofsky, & Lewis, 1997). Adaptive behavior can result in fear, social isolation, and/or desensitization to violence.

Ecological

In reviews of the literature, Patterson and his colleagues (1989; Reid, Patterson, & Snyder, 2002) have synthesized the findings on aggression in the hypothesis that the route to chronic delinquency is marked by a reliable developmental sequence of ecological experiences: the first experience is ineffective parenting (influenced by such variables as the way the parents were parented, socioeconomic status, ethnicity, neighborhood, and education); the second is behavioral conduct disorders that lead to academic failure and peer rejection, which, in turn, lead to increased risk of involvement in a deviant peer group; and the third, occurring in early adolescence, is chronic delinquent behavior.

Thus, antisocial behavior appears to be a developmental trait that begins early in life (observable by age 4 to 5) and often continues into adolescence and adulthood. The socialization for aggression is bidirectional and interactional in several ecological contexts; it includes poor parenting skills, which affect child behavior, and child behavior, which affects not only parenting but school performance and peer relationships as well (Snyder & Patterson, 1995). The unintentional coercive training might begin with a parental demand that the child go to bed. The child refuses, and the parent yells. The child whines, complaining about always being picked on. The parent gives in, hence reinforcing in the child a coercive method of getting his or her way.

Patterson and his colleagues (1989; Reid et al., 2002) believe that prevention of antisocial behavior is feasible if young children who are both antisocial and unskilled in peer interactions can be identified, if they receive social skills training (as discussed in Chapter 8) as well as academic remediation, and if their parents receive parenting training.

How can children at risk for conduct disorders be identified? A study by Dodge, Pettit, and Bates (1994) identified some socialization mediators contributing to risky developmental outcomes. These were harsh parental discipline, lack of maternal warmth, exposure to aggressive adult models, maternal aggressive values, family life stressors, mother's lack of social support, peer group instability, and lack of cognitive stimulation. The children, who were from the lowest socio-economic status, were followed from preschool to grade three. The significance of these mediators as predictors of conduct disorders is that they often accompany socioeconomic stress found in families of low socioeconomic status or in those who were poor. Thus, it is not low socioeconomic status or poverty per se that influences aggressive behavior, but the *socialization mediators* that often accompany such socioeconomic stress (Coie & Dodge, 1998; Huston, McLoyd, & Coll, 1994). Socialization mediators have become the accepted way of studying aggression, as will be discussed next.

What approaches are used to study aggression?

Models that represent the factors involved in aggressive behavior can be categorized as social cognitive or ecological. These models delineate specific variables to research for further study.

Social Cognitive Model

A social cognitive model for studying aggression has been developed by researchers drawing on earlier studies. Basically, the social cognitive model attempts to identify mediating responses within the individual, such as an internal moral code and an ability to interpret social cues or behavioral responses from others. It also describes how these mediating responses may be predictive in various situations of an individual's aggressive behavior (Coie & Dodge, 1998; Dodge & Pettit, 2003; Parke & Slaby, 1983).

The social cognitive model assumes that the developing child makes social interpretations about which interactions with others constitute aggressive provocation and require retaliation. As was said earlier, according to Dodge (1986), children come to a particular social situation with a database (their memory store) and receive social cues as input from the interaction. Children's behavioral response to those cues is a function of certain cognitive processes: decoding the input, interpreting it, searching for potential responses, making a decision, and making a response.

For example, a child who is hit on the back by a peer must decode that action by searching for cues relevant to the peer's intention (was it on purpose or an accident?) and then focus on those cues. The child must also interpret those cues. (If the hit was intentional, was the peer trying to be friendly or mean?) The child's past experiences (memory store) aid in the interpretation. (If the peer runs away, then the action was intentionally mean; if the peer follows the hit with a comment such as "Let's go," then the action was intentionally friendly.) Once a situation is interpreted, the child has to search for possible behavioral responses (hit back, ignore, verbalize displeasure, and so on). The next step is to decide which response to execute. In choosing a response, the child must first assess the probable consequences of each response he or she has generated. ("If I hit back, I may get hit again.") Finally, the child must act out the chosen behavioral response. If the choice is made to respond verbally, the child must possess the necessary language skills to do so.

Dodge and his colleagues (1994) generally found that aggressive children were more likely to attribute hostile intentions to their peers than were nonaggressive children. This biased way of thinking, then, increased the likelihood that they would retaliate aggressively, with behavior they thought was justified (although their peers did not).

Other researchers (Gifford-Smith & Rabiner, 2004; Perry, Perry, & Rasmussen, 1986) found that not only do aggressive children often interpret provocation by others erroneously as hostility, they also respond aggressively because they expect their aggressiveness to be successful in eliminating their aversive state or to otherwise improve their plight. This supports Bandura's (1986) social cognitive theory: reinforced behavior, even behavior thought to be potentially reinforcing, will be repeated. The reinforcement, in this case, is the reduction of hostile (or perceived hostile) treatment by others.

Ecological Model

The development of aggression must also be viewed in an ecological context. The complex variables operating in aggressive behavior involve the *child* (personality, cognitive level, social skills), the *family* (parenting, interaction), the *school* (attitudes on handling aggressive behavior), the *peer group* (modeling, norms, acceptance/rejection), the *media* (modeling), and the *community* (socioeconomic stressors, attitudes on handling aggressive behavior, availability of support systems) (Beyers, Bates, Pettit, & Dodge, 2003; Coie & Dodge, 1998; Parke, 1982). Table 12.1 provides a summary of variables contributing to antisocial behavior.

The usefulness of the ecological model can be seen in the following example.

> Robert, age 8, was referred to the principal's office for the third time in two weeks for fighting in the playground. No consequence provided by the teacher seemed to be effective. The principal asked Robert's parents to come to school for a conference. Robert was very angry. He kept saying, "The other kids always start." He thought to himself, "I'll get them. I'll bring my brother's knife."

In order for the principal to deal with Robert's aggressiveness, she needs to know that Robert comes from a home where physical punishment is the means for dealing with misbehavior. Likewise, Robert resorts to physical means when he perceives others treating him badly. She also needs to understand that in Robert's neighborhood, gang fights are the primary means of settling disagreements; Robert's older brother belongs to a gang. Finally, she needs to be aware that Robert has been taught it is "unmanly" not to fight back when you have been challenged.

Once the principal becomes cognizant of Robert's ecological background, she will be better equipped to try an approach that might reduce his aggressive behavior in school. Robert might need some intensive individual attention from an adult whom he respects and will model. Referring him to a Big Brothers program might help. Robert also needs to learn social skills that will enable him to deal with ambiguous and/or confrontational situations without resorting to fighting. Robert needs help to discover an ability that other children might admire (art, music, drama, or athletics). If the principal can get Robert's parents to support the school's attempts to

Table 12.1

Summary of Variables Contributing to Antisocial Behavior

CHILD	FAMILY	SCHOOL	PEERS	MEDIA	COMMUNITY
Biological influences (evolution, genetics)	Parenting style (authoritarian, coercive)	Teaching style (authoritarian)	Peer group pressure	Modeling	Modeling
Gender	Interaction	Modeling	Situation	Reinforcement/ punishment of model	Acceptance of &/ or sanctions for violence
Hormones	Modeling Reinforcement/ punishment for behavior	Reinforcement/ punishment for behavior Expectations	Aggressive norms Modeling	Mediation by adults	Anonymity/ alienation Safety
Temperament (impulsivity, frustration tolerance, activity level)	Attitudes		Acceptance/ rejection		Socioeconomic stressors
Ability to delay gratification					Availability of informal/formal support systems
Information-processing ability					
Internally/externally oriented conscience (guilt vs. fear of punishment)					
Cognitive maturity					
Social skills					
Moral reasoning/ judgment					

help their son, there is a better chance the intervention will succeed in changing Robert's antisocial behavior.

The importance of early intervention in antisocial behavior is that aggression can be self-perpetuating. In a review of studies on children who were antisocial, Patterson and his colleagues (Patterson et al., 1989; Snyder & Patterson, 1995) conclude that coercive, or harsh, parenting contributes to the development of children's defiant, aggressive behaviors and hostile interpretations of others' behavior, which in turn can cause these children to be rejected by normal peers as well as to do poorly in school. Moreover, the rejection experienced by aggressive children in early childhood may contribute to their attraction in adolescence to deviant peers who devalue school and engage in antisocial or delinquent acts (Dishion et al., 1991).

IN PRACTICE

What Can Be Done to Inhibit Aggressiveness in Young Children?

1. Organize the environment to minimize conflicts. Minimize crowding. Have plenty of stimulating and engaging developmentally appropriate materials. Have enough so children can play together with similar materials (bicycles, paint, toys, and so on).
2. Set standards, stick to them, and provide consequences for noncompliance. Let children know aggression is not sanctioned: "You hit Bobby on the playground; you must sit on the bench now for 10 minutes." "You did not control your temper today. Since you disappointed me, I will have to disappoint you; you cannot stay up late, as you had wanted, to watch that program on television."
3. Stop aggression immediately. If possible, try not to let it carry to a successful completion. For example, if you see two children struggling over a toy, take the toy and ask both children to tell you their versions of the incident. Then ask them how you should resolve it. If they don't come up with a solution, say, "Well, you both think about it, and meanwhile I'll hold the toy."
4. Give children alternative ways of solving problems. Teach them how to verbalize their feelings and how to listen to others.
5. Anticipate possible situations in which aggressive behavior may occur, such as children playing together roughly or children complaining they have nothing to do, and redirect the children into an activity that interests them.
6. Provide opportunities for cooperative activities. Enable children to learn to listen to each other's ideas, to solve problems democratically, to compromise, and to respect each other.
7. Foster helpfulness and cooperation: "Could you help Daniel with that tower he's building?" "Could you help your sister put on her shoes while I make your lunch?"
8. Be a positive role model. Don't punish aggression with aggression; use alternative disciplinary methods.
9. Discuss rules and the reasons for them. Also discuss violence that children may be exposed to in the media or in their communities. Let children talk about their fears and feelings. Help children develop strategies for feeling protected by adults: "When you are scared, you can tell me." "Policeman Wilson is our friend."
10. Reward prosocial behavior. Give children attention when they share, are helpful or cooperative, or solve problems by discussion; don't allow them to get your attention only by being aggressive.

Sources: Caldwell & Crary, 1981; Slaby, Roedell, Arezzo, & Hendrix, 1995

PROSOCIAL BEHAVIOR: ALTRUISM

How does altruistic behavior develop?

One of the aims of socialization, as stated previously, is to teach developmental skills, which include getting along with others. To participate in a group, one must cooperate, share, and help others when needed. As we all know, some people

© Myrleen Ferguson Cate/PhotoEdit

This child is exhibiting prosocial behavior (altruism) by helping his friend tie his shoe.

exhibit more of these behaviors than others. What is it that motivates someone to rescue a total stranger from a fire, to send money to someone whose story has been told in the newspaper, or to volunteer to work in a senior citizen center?

Recall that altruism refers to behavior that is kind, considerate, generous, and helpful to others. Like aggression, it shows some consistency over time. Altruistic behavior begins to appear during the preschool years (in some children, it appears by age 2). Some researchers believe the brain may be "prewired" to be empathetic and to cooperate with others (Hoffman, 2000; Rilling, Gutman, Zeh, Pagnoni, Berns, & Kilts, 2002). Children's ability to take the perspective of others increases as they get older, so they become more aware that others' feelings may differ from theirs and, thus, are more capable of experiencing empathy (Eisenberg & Fabes, 1998). For example, Radke-Yarrow and Zahn-Waxler (1986) observed consistent patterns of sharing, helping, and comforting behaviors among 3- to 7-year-olds at play.

Zahn-Waxler and Radke-Yarrow (1990; Zahn-Waxler, Radke-Yarrow, et al., 1992) examined altruistic behaviors in children 10, 15, and 20 months over a nine-month period. They found that between 10 and 12 months of age, incidents of emotional distress brought no significant altruistic responses. Over the next six to eight months, however, the children began to exhibit concern (exhibited by facial expression or crying) and positive initiations (exhibited by patting or touching the other person) in response to the distress of others. Such responses, concerns, and positive interactions became increasingly differentiated and frequent by 18 and 24 months. For example, by age 2, children may bring objects to a person in distress, make suggestions about what to do, verbalize sympathy, bring someone else to help, aggressively protect the victim, and/or attempt to evoke a change in the feelings of the distressed person. Children age 2 may also avoid the encounter, cry, or even behave aggressively. Thus, by age 2, there are many individual differences in the exhibition of prosocial behaviors that can be classified as altruistic.

Prosocial responses, such as cooperating, sharing, giving comfort, and offering to help, become increasingly apparent throughout childhood as children develop cognitively and have more social interactions (Eisenberg & Fabes, 1998). For example, toddlers, ages 2 to 3, exhibit some sharing and demonstrations of sympathy. They often react to others' distress by becoming distressed themselves (Zahn-Waxler, Radke-Yarrow, et al., 1992). Preschoolers, age 3–6, begin to become less egocentric and exhibit altruistic acts if they also benefit the self ("I'll share so you'll be my friend"). School-agers, 6 to 12, who can take the role of others, better understand legitimate needs ("I'll help because he can't do it himself"). Adolescents, age 13 and over, understand prosocial behavior in terms of more abstract social responsibility and may feel guilty for not acting altruistically when it is needed ("I should partic- ipate in the jog-a-thon to raise money for children with cancer") (Eisenberg & Fabes, 1998).

Whether or not a child will behave prosocially may depend on the individuals involved, the specific situation, and how the child interprets it. Preschoolers, school- agers, and adolescents assist an individual more if that person has previously helped them (Eisenberg & Fabes, 1998). Children are more likely to help friends or those who are familiar, rather than those who are unfamiliar (Eisenberg & Fabes, 1998; Rose & Asher, 2004). And children's mood at the time of the incident affects their motivation to be helpful (Carlson, Charlin, & Miller, 1988).

What are the theories of altruistic behavior?

Existing theories explaining the causes of altruism can be categorized as follows: (1) biological (evolution and genetics), (2) learning (reinforcement, modeling, and instruction), (3) cognitive developmental, (4) social interactional, and (5) cultural.

Biological

Biological drives, such as reproduction (expressed in sexual desire) and survival (expressed in aggression), according to Freud (1938), are seated in the part of the personality that seeks self-gratification. Freud labeled that part the *id*. Children's experiences with reality cause them to assess the feasibility of satisfying their biological drives. Freud labeled the rational part of the personality the *ego*, which helps one to delay gratification. Children also experience pleasant feelings when they comply with parental standards and unpleasant feelings when they don't. Out of fear of parental hostility or loss of parental love, they develop a *superego*, or conscience, to regulate their impulses and behave accordingly to internalized parental standards. They may behave prosocially to avoid a feeling of guilt. Thus children's adoption of prosocial values, according to Freud, results from identifica- tion with parents.

Sociobiologists believe that evolution and genes account for certain complex human social behaviors. Children are believed to be genetically programmed to be kind and considerate as part of human nature. Altruism is regarded as behavior that promotes the genetic fitness of another at the expense of one's own fitness. Since altruism benefits the group's survival, natural selection favors those members of the species who have this characteristic (even though the altruistic member may die in performing the altruistic act). For example, protecting others is considered to be altruistic behavior. In the animal kingdom, the bee that protects the members of its species by stinging an intruder dies. Even though one member of the species dies, it is the altruistic action that enables the other members to live and reproduce. In the human species, the relationship of biology to sociology is explained by Richard Nalley (1973, p. 5) as follows:

> As early human beings bonded together in social groups, perhaps for the purpose of cooperative hunting, selection pressures began to build for those traits that allowed them to adapt to community life. Genes promoting flexibility and conformity, for example, were probably passed on. Aggression had to be harnessed, social structure improvised and forms of communication developed.

This acted as a kind of positive feedback loop: better communication led to reduced aggression, and vice versa.

The group, led by a dominant male, benefited each individual and his self-interested genes by providing protection, a ready supply of eligible mates and the ability to surround and bring down larger animals. From these cooperative dealings, sociobiologists say, culture arose: art, ethics, courtship rituals, and the rest. Humans came to reflect a mosaic of traits, each adaptive and not necessarily inherent in their old primate nature.

Martin Hoffman (1981, 1991, 2000) gives evidence supporting the idea that empathy—vicariously experiencing another's emotions—is part of human nature in that it is an inherited biological predisposition. Empathy, along with the internalization of society's moral norms and values, is the motive for altruism. One study (Martin & Clark, 1982) found that newborns became distressed by the cries of other newborns, thus indicating that humans are designed from birth to respond to the distress of their peers. Twin children (14 months old) were found to react similarly to simulation of distress in others at home and in the laboratory settings (Zahn-Waxler, Robinson, & Emde, 1992). Other studies (Eisenberg & Fabes, 1998; Rushton, Fulker, Neal, Nias, & Eysenck, 1986) found that identical twins (who have the same genes) were more similar to each other on questionnaires designed to assess altruism, empathy, and nurturance than were fraternal twins, who share about half of their genes. Thus, differences in genetic composition among people have a considerable influence on differences in their tendencies to behave both prosocially and antisocially.

Researchers have identified an area in the front of the brain's cerebral cortex, called the ventromedial area (located behind the bridge of the nose), that processes information regarding other people's suffering and one's own misdeeds. Apparently, the proper functioning of this area is vital to emotional responsiveness. Adults whose ventromedial areas were damaged did not react negatively to images of extreme human harm and showed less concern than others for not conforming to social norms for behavior (Damasio, 1994). Decety and Chaminade (2003) used neuroimaging techniques, such as positron emission tomography (PET scanning) to demonstrate that brain neural structures known to be involved in emotional responding, such as the amygdala, were activated when subjects listened to sad stories designed to elicit sympathy, whereas they were not active when subjects listened to neutral, or unemotional, stories.

Researchers used magnetic resonance imaging (MRI) while subjects played a strategic cooperative/competitive game based on the classic Prisoner's Dilemma: Two suspects are taken into custody by the police who do not have enough evidence to convict them. They are put in separate rooms to get them to confess. The one doing so first is promised freedom as a witness for the state. If both confess, both get sent to jail for a long time. If neither confesses, then the police can only jail them briefly for a minor offense. Thus, the motive for the prisoners to cooperate (remain silent) is a small consequence rather than a large one for competing to be the one to confess and losing. The researchers found that two areas of the brain significant in dopamine production (pleasure), the anteroventral stratum in the middle of the brain above the spinal cord and the orbitofrontal cortex in the region above the eyes, were activated when the subjects worked together to share a reward rather than compete with one getting a reward and the other getting nothing (Rilling et al., 2002). Apparently, the human brain is "wired" to cooperate and rewards itself for doing so with pleasurable feelings.

Learning

Despite the current uncertainty about how and when altruism begins, it is known that direct reinforcement or reward for an altruistic act or observing someone else engaging in the act (modeling) and getting reinforced encourages altruism (Eisenberg & Murphy, 1995). One investigator, for example, found that children age 4 were more likely to share marbles with other children if, after sharing, they were rewarded with bubble gum (Fischer, 1963). However, the effect of giving tangible rewards for prosocial behavior lasts only briefly. Social reinforcement, or praise, has been shown to increase altruism in children for longer periods. For example, after having been prompted to share and then praised for doing so, children were found to give more to others (Bar-Tal, Raviv, & Lesser, 1980; Gelfand, Hartman, Cromer, Smith, & Page, 1975).

Although concrete rewards may induce altruism in the given context, the long-term effect of concrete rewards may be negative because it undermines intrinsic motivation (Lepper, 1983; Zimmerman, 2000). Social rewards (praise) may induce altruism in the given context, but not in other contexts (Eisenberg & Fabes, 1998).

The peer group reinforces prosocial behavior, especially when it is directed at peers. Parkhurst and Asher (1992) found that among 12- to 14-year-olds, children who were actively rejected by peers were high in antisocial behavior, whereas children who were popular among peers were high in prosocial behavior. Peers exert pressure to behave in certain ways. The desire to maintain a friendship sometimes motivates a person to behave altruistically. For example, it was found that people are more willing to donate blood if they believe their peers support such an action (Foss, 1983).

Modeling. It has been shown repeatedly that observing a helpful model encourages observers to be helpful themselves (Bandura, 1986; Eisenberg & Murphy, 1995). This modeling effect is found whether the model is another child or an adult, and whether the model is live or on film. For example, children 10–11 who had observed an adult donating to a charity were more likely to donate than children who had not seen the altruistic model. When children observed the adult model keeping the money instead of donating it to charity, they also imitated that behavior (Harris, 1970). Media models, as shown on *Mister Rogers' Neighborhood* or *Sesame Street*, who exhibit prosocial behavior are likely to be imitated by their viewers, especially when an adult reinforces the show's message by discussion (Coates, Pusser, & Goodman, 1976; Huston & Wright, 1998; Perse, 2001; Roberts & Maccoby, 1985).

Modeling altruism has generalizable effects. It has been shown that children who are taught to act helpfully in one situation will also act helpfully in others (Elliot & Vasta, 1970; Radke-Yarrow & Zahn-Waxler, 1986). And after having observed an altruistic model, children were still acting generously four months later (Radke-Yarrow & Zahn-Waxler, 1986; Rice & Grusec, 1975).

Children learn from each other. They imitate behaviors of admired peers. For example, children who witness the charitable acts of an altruistic model are more likely to donate toys or money, even anonymously (Radke-Yarrow et al., 1983). Thus, if a child has a group of friends who consistently exhibit prosocial behavior, it is likely that child will exhibit it also (Eisenberg & Fabes, 1998). If parents know who their child's friends are, they can predict fairly well how their child will behave in various situations. As was seen in the discussion of aggression, those who belong to groups that condone aggressive behavior are likely to exhibit aggression. It can likewise be concluded that those who belong to groups that disapprove of aggressive behavior are less likely to exhibit it.

Instruction. Since a good altruistic example is so effective, what about just instructing children to be kind, considerate, and helpful? Generally, observing an adult sharing is more effective than just telling a child to share (Eisenberg & Murphy, 1995). However, one experiment (Rice & Grusec, 1975) found that if the child is initially undecided about whether or not to act altruistically, being told to help is as effective as actually observing the adult helping. But if the child is resistant about sharing, then being told to share is less effective than actual observation.

Teaching altruism can be as effective as modeling it, especially if the instructions are strongly stated and reasons are given for sharing (Grusec, Saas-Korlsaak, & Simutis, 1978).

Learning by Doing. The school can train children to be prosocial by using the technique of role playing (Eisenberg & Mussen, 1989). For example, Staub (1971) worked with pairs of kindergarten children, asking one child to act the part of someone who needed help (carrying something too heavy) and the other child to act the part of a helping person (to think of actions to help). The children were then asked to change roles. A week after training, helpfulness was tested by giving the children the chance to help a crying child in the next room and the chance to share candy with another child. The trained children were compared to those who had not received training. The children who had undergone the reciprocal role training were more likely to be helpful to another child than the children who had not received this training.

Schools can also assign children the responsibility of teaching others to be helpful or to share (Eisenberg & Murphy, 1995). For example, Staub (1970) explicitly assigned responsibility to kindergarten and first-grade children. When the children were told they were "in charge" by a departing adult, there was an increase in the probability, especially among the first-graders, that they would go to the aid of another child who was heard crying in the next room. As children get older, the assigned prosocial task is generalized to other situations (Peterson, 1983). For example, children (over age 7) who are induced to donate to needy others in one context are more likely to behave similarly in another context several days later (Eisenberg & Murphy, 1995).

Thus, prosocial behavior can be increased in children via real-life experiences. One way is to provide role-playing opportunities for them. When children take the place of a child who needs help, they know what it feels like to be in need; when they take the place of the helper, they learn what to do to be of assistance. Another way is to assign responsibility for a prosocial behavior. The child experiences what it is like to be helpful and gets adult and peer approval as well.

In sum, parents who instruct children in altruistic acts, practice (model) what they teach, and verbally reinforce children's helpful acts will foster prosocial behavior (Deax & Wrightsman, 1988; Eisenberg & Murphy, 1995).

Cognitive Developmental

Numerous theorists have hypothesized that as children develop cognitively, their ability to think about others increases. Their enhanced sociocognitive skills, particularly perspective taking and moral reasoning, foster prosocial behavior (Bengtsson, 2003; Eisenberg & Fabes, 1998). When individuals can put themselves in another's place, they are more likely to empathize and give comfort and help.

Lawrence Kohlberg (1976) believed prosocial behavior to be a component of moral reasoning, which is a function of cognitive development. Kohlberg emphasized the contributions of social interactions and cognitions regarding the ability to take others' perspectives and understand consequences of behavior. Whether an individual is self-oriented or other-oriented influences moral reasoning and consequent selfish or altruistic behavior. Emotions, such as empathy and guilt, may also play a role in moral judgment and behavior (Eisenberg & Fabes, 1998; Hoffman, 2000).

Social Interactional

The bidirectional interactions occurring in social groups influence prosocial behavior. The family provides such a context. A team of researchers (Zahn-Waxler, Radke-Yarrow, & King, 1979) studied young children's altruism by asking mothers of a group of 15-month-olds and mothers of a group of 20-month-olds for careful reports of incidents occurring during the children's daily lives. The mothers were trained as observers, and the study lasted for nine months. The mothers tape-recorded descriptions of every incident in which someone in the child's presence expressed painful feelings (anger, fear, sorrow, pain, and/or fatigue). The mothers also described events preceding and following the incident, as well as both the child's and their own reactions.

> Today Jerry was kind of cranky; he just started completely bawling and he wouldn't stop. John kept coming over and handing Jerry toys, trying to cheer him up, so to speak. He'd say things like, "Here, Jerry," and I said to John, "Jerry's sad; he doesn't feel good; he had a shot today." John would look at me with his eyebrows kind of wrinkled together like he really understood that Jerry was crying because he was unhappy, not that he was just being a crybaby. He went over and rubbed Jerry's arm and said, "Nice Jerry," and continued to give him toys. (pp. 321–322)

When the researchers found that the number of altruistic reactions varied greatly from child to child, they examined the individual mother's responses. They found that the way the mothers reprimanded their children was clearly related to the children's degree of altruism. The following exemplify the various responses.

- Moralizing: "Look, you made Susie cry; it's not nice to pull hair."
- Prohibition with explanation or statement of principle: "You must never poke anyone's eyes! He won't be able to see!"
- Withdrawal of love, physical or verbal: "I can't hug you when you've been mean."
- Neutral: "Russell is crying because you hurt him."
- Prohibitions without explanation: "Don't ever do that!"
- Physical restraint
- Physical punishment

The mother's use of moralizing and prohibitions (with explanations or statements of principle) when the child exhibited antisocial behavior was related to a high proportion of altruistic behaviors. Unexplained verbal prohibitions and physical punishment were associated with low degrees of altruism. Neutral explanations had little effect either way.

What other socializing techniques are related to prosocial behavior in children? A warm, nurturant, affectionate relationship between children and parents seems to contribute to the development of prosocial tendencies, in contrast to a cold, indifferent, distant relationship (Eisenberg & Murphy, 1995; Zhou et al., 2002).

The manner in which parents exert control—reasonable versus excessive or arbitrary—influences the development of prosocial behavior (Eisenberg & Fabes, 1998). *Control* refers to the setting of certain standards and rules by parents and their insistence on adherence to them when deemed necessary. There is strong evidence that frequent use of physical punishment by parents results in aggression, hostility, and resistance in children (Aronfreed, 1968; Coie & Dodge, 1998; Eron, Walder, & Lefkowitz, 1971; Patterson et al., 1989). On the other hand, nurturing persons who do not exert control seem to have no effect on prosocial behavior (Radke-Yarrow & Zahn-Waxler, 1986; Rosenhan & White, 1967; Weissbrod, 1976). Baumrind (1967, 1971a), as discussed in Chapter 4, found that firm enforcement of rules combined with reasoning and warmth (authoritative parenting) was associated with positive and effective social behavior. Thus, when parents are affectionate and have certain firm standards that they explain, the child is likely to display prosocial behavior.

Cultural

Anthropological and psychological studies in non-Western cultures show that societies vary greatly in the degree to which prosocial and cooperative behaviors are expected (Eisenberg & Fabes, 1998). How does the society one grows up in influence prosocial behavior? It has been documented that some societies provide more opportunities for learning to behave prosocially than do others, particularly by involving older children in the care of younger ones (Graves & Graves, 1983; Triandis, 1995; Whiting & Edwards, 1988). It has also been argued that the value

Brian Seed/Getty Images

Children from cultures that give them early responsibility in family functioning tend to exhibit spontaneous altruism.

a society puts on interdependence, cooperation, and social harmony (collectivistic orientation) versus independence, competition, and individual achievement (individualistic orientation) influences children accordingly (Bronfenbrenner, 1970b; Eisenberg & Fabes, 1998; Garbarino, 1992). For example, Hindu Indian culture emphasizes more duty-based social responsibility than American culture, which emphasizes moral justice-based social responsibility (Miller & Bersoff, 1993). In other words, Hindus are more likely to respond prosocially out of duty or obligation; whereas Americans are more likely to do so because "it's the right or fair thing to do."

Cultural variations in children's tendencies to cooperate or compete have been investigated in a classic study by Madsen and Shapira (1970), using various games that can be played cooperatively or competitively. One of these games is diagrammed in Figure 12.2.

The game board is 18 square inches and has an eyelet at each corner. A string passes through each of the eyelets and is attached to a metal weight that serves as a holder for a ball-point pen. A sheet of paper is placed on the game board for each trial so that the movement of the pen as the children pull their strings is recorded automatically.

In the *cooperative* condition, every time the pen crosses all four circles, all the players are rewarded. Thus, the more the children work together, the more they all win. In the *competitive* condition, each player is rewarded only when the pen crosses his or her circle. In this condition, if the children take turns helping one another, each child can win as often as any other. Some children never figure this out, however, and end up pulling the pen in their own direction, so no one wins.

Children reared in traditional rural subcultures and small, semi-agricultural communal settlements cooperated more readily than children reared in modern urban subcultures. For example, schoolchildren in Mexican villages and small towns were found to be more cooperative than their urban middle-class Mexican, Mexican American, African American, or European American peers (Madsen & Shapira, 1970). Similarly, Israeli children reared on a kibbutz and children from Arab villages were found to be more cooperative than Israeli urban children (Nadler, 1991; Shapira & Lomranz, 1972; Shapira & Madsen, 1974).

Figure 12.2

Cooperation Board Game

Source: M. C. Madsen & A. Shapira (1970). Cooperative and competitive behavior of urban Afro American, Anglo American, Mexican American, and Mexican village children. *Developmental Psychology 3*(1), p. 17. Copyright © 1970 by the American Psychological Association. Reprinted by permission of the publisher.

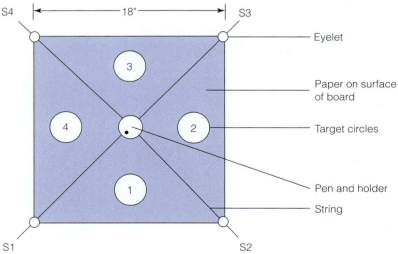

In these studies, if cooperation with others in the various test situations was rewarded directly (group rewards to be shared by all), children from all cultures cooperated. If, however, only individual rewards were given for performance, cultural differences showed up. The Mexican village children and those from Israeli kibbutzim continued to cooperate with each other, even in an individual reward (competitive) situation. "Let's help each other." "Let's take turns." "Start here—go there" were some comments. On the other hand, the urban African American, European American, Mexican American, middle-class, and Israeli children tended to compete ineffectively.

Apparently, children raised in traditional rural subcultures and small, semi-agricultural communal settlements (collectivistic orientation) have been socialized to have *gemeinschaft* relationships (close personal ties, concern with community members' welfare, reciprocity, readiness to lend a helping hand); children raised in urban subcultures (individualistic orientation) have been socialized to have *gesellschaft* relationships (impersonal ties, competitiveness, obligations based on contracts, behavior for personal advantage). These two types of relationships were discussed in Chapter 10.

Cross-cultural comparisons by Beatrice and John Whiting (1973, 1975) illustrate in natural settings some of the laboratory findings. Working in small communities in Kenya, India, the Philippines, Okinawa, Mexico, and the United States, they observed children between the ages of 3 and 6 and other children between the ages of 6 and 10. The children were rated for exhibiting altruistic behavior spontaneously—offering help, which included feeding and assisting in carrying out a task; offering support, which included giving comfort and reassurance; and offering helpful suggestions. They were also rated for exhibiting egoistic behavior—seeking help, seeking attention, or dominating another.

The Whitings found that the cultural variable most closely associated with altruistic behavior was the extent to which children in the various cultures were given the responsibility to perform household tasks or chores related to the family's economic security. Most of the children in Kenyan, Mexican, and Philippine cultures were high above the median of the total sample in altruism; whereas most of the children in the other three cultures (Okinawan, Indian, and American) scored low in altruism. Presumably, in

> simpler kin-oriented societies, with economies based upon subsistence gardening, altruistic behavior is highly valued and individual egoistic achievement frowned upon. Women must work in the fields, and the children must help in order for the family to subsist. To offer help, to support others, and to be responsible are taught both by precept and practice. Being helplessly dependent, showing off, boasting, and being egoistically dominant are incompatible with such a way of life.

> On the other hand, in the more complex societies, where no child knows what he is going to be when he grows up, individual achievement and success must be positively valued. To help a friend sitting next to you in an examination is defined as cheating. To ask for help from specialists such as mechanics, dressmakers, shopkeepers, psychotherapists, priests, or servants is expected and paid for in cash rather than in reciprocal services. (Whiting & Whiting, 1973, p. 64)

Thus, "children who . . . perform more domestic chores, help more with economic tasks and spend more time caring for their infant brothers, sisters, and cousins, score high on the altruistic versus egoistic dimension" (1973, p. 63).

Table 12.2 summarizes the variables contributing to prosocial behavior.

Table 12.2

Summary of Variables Contributing to Prosocial Behavior

CHILD	FAMILY	SCHOOL	PEERS	MEDIA	COMMUNITY
Genetics	Parenting style (authoritative, warm)	Instruction/set standards	Peer group pressure	Mediated discussion by adults	Simple social organization
Temperament	Communication of prosocial/ antisocial instructions	Positive/negative consequences	Learning by doing	Values of cooperation	Traditional, rural
Age	Reinforcement/ punishment	Reinforcement/ punishment	Collaborative activities	Modeling	Extended family ties
Cognitive maturity	Modeling	Modeling	Modeling		Early assignment of tasks and responsibility
Perspective and role-taking ability	Assignment of responsibility	Assignment of responsibility			Individualistic/ collectivistic orientation
Empathy	Opportunities for role playing	Opportunities for role playing			Justice-based/ duty-based social responsibility
Moral reasoning/ judgment	Discussion	Discussion			
Situation					

IN PRACTICE

How Can Prosocial Behavior Be Fostered in Young Children?

1. Be an example. Exhibit helping, cooperating, and sharing behavior.
2. Preach prosocial behavior, and give reasons. Take advantage of specific situations to instruct children how to share, how to be helpful, and how to cooperate.
3. Be warm and accepting.
4. Set firm standards of behavior that have consequences when not followed.
5. Provide role-playing opportunities in which children can experience others' perspectives.
6. Discuss how one's actions may affect another's feelings.
7. Provide activities that require cooperation, such as group projects.
8. Suggest specific ways in which children can be cooperative and helpful.
9. Provide meaningful responsibilities in which one's task helps another person or the group.
10. Praise prosocial behavior.

Sources: Eisenberg & Murphy, 1995; Eisenberg & Mussen, 1989

Morals

What is involved in a person's moral code?

Morals, as introduced in Chapter 2, encompass an individual's evaluation of what is right and wrong. They involve acceptance of rules and govern one's behavior toward others. Breaches of morals provoke consequences, as well as judgmental and emotional responses (Damon, 1988; Turiel, 1998, 2002).

Morality involves *feeling*, which includes empathy and guilt (Hoffman, 2000). Morality also involves *reasoning*, which includes the ability to understand rules, distinguish right from wrong, and take another person's perspective (Kohlberg, 1976; Piaget, 1965; Selman, 1980). Finally, morality involves *behaving*, which includes prosocial and antisocial acts (Eisenberg & Fabes, 1998), as well as self-regulation of impulses.

Children develop the ability to self-regulate impulses from familial and cultural socialization—for example, being reinforced for obedience and being sanctioned for wrongdoing. Children construct moral concepts according to their cognitive and emotional development from social interactions, which provide experience in collaboration and conflict (Turiel, 1998, 2002).

The issue of morality has been of concern since the beginning of civilization. In prescientific periods, philosophers and theologians debated the moral status of the newborn infant—was the infant inherently good, bad, or neutral? The outcome of these debates had important implications for child rearing. Those who believe a child is morally good tend to be more relaxed and more permissive in their parenting styles. Those who believe a child is morally bad tend to be stricter and more authoritarian in their parenting styles in order to socialize the child to be "good." Those who believe the child is morally neutral tend to place more emphasis on the interaction between parent and child because they believe morals develop from experiences of being good and bad, and observing right and wrong.

People differ not only in their beliefs about the inherent nature of children but also in their beliefs about what is and what is not acceptable behavior. In other words, people's moral codes differ. Sometimes one's moral code is guided by external rules, such as parental approval, convention, or the law; other times one's code is guided by internal rules, such as self-approval or self-condemnation. Moral variability does not stem solely from the influence of diverse groups such as family and culture; it reflects the flexible thinking of individuals interpreting aspects of their social worlds (Turiel, 1998).

MORAL DEVELOPMENT

How does one develop a moral code?

Standards of conduct and morality develop out of the necessity for people to get along with one another. Morality involves obeying society's rules for daily living, such as not stealing, not assaulting, not maligning another's character, and so on. It also involves one's conscience, or personal rules for interacting with others, such as being kind, cooperative, and helpful.

As children mature and develop, their morality changes. Infants and toddlers do not distinguish right from wrong. Thus, when they conform to parental demands it is usually because they are attached and fear loss of love. Preschoolers and school-agers consider right and wrong to be direct opposites, with nothing in between. They are not capable of factoring "on purpose" or "by mistake" into their judgments of wrongdoing. Adolescents begin to view right and wrong as a matter of degree. They take into account intention in judging an act.

Not only does children's maturation influence their moral codes, but so do intelligence, motivation, the need for approval, self-control, and the particular situation (Bandura, 1991). Most psychologists (Damon, 1988; Hoffman, 2000; Kohlberg, 1976; Piaget, 1965; Turiel, 1998) believe that one's moral code develops through social interaction in a societal context.

What are the major theories of moral development?

Piaget's Theory

Jean Piaget (1965) defined morality as "the understanding of and adherence to rules through one's own volition." Piaget analyzed morality from the perspective of how an individual's social experiences result in the formation of judgments about social relationships, rules, laws, and authority (Turiel, 1998). He approached the question of how one develops a moral code by observing and participating in children's games (games of marbles). He reasoned that games contain complex systems of rules that must be followed in order to play the game. These rules are handed down from one generation to another and are preserved solely by the respect that is felt for them by individuals. Because morality consists of a system of rules and the essence of all morality can be found in the respect an individual acquires for these rules, one can understand children's developing morality by studying their adherence to game rules.

Piaget worked with a group of Swiss schoolboys ranging in age from 4 to 13. He asked them questions about the rules of the game: What are the rules? Where did they come from? Could they be changed? Piaget found that for the youngest children (ages 4 and 5), the rules were poorly understood and were not binding. For the middle group of children (ages 6 to 9), rules were regarded as having been made by an authority ("morality of constraint") and were therefore sacred and unchangeable. Following rules is quite rigid; any bending of the rules results in "That isn't fair!" For the oldest group (ages 10 to 13), rules were regarded as law emanating from mutual consent ("morality of cooperation"); rules must be respected if you want to be loyal to the group, but rules can be changed if the majority of the group agrees.

Generally, children's moral reasoning shifts from the belief that one is subject to another's law, or *external control* (**heteronomous morality**—rules are moral absolutes that cannot be changed), to the belief that one is subject to one's own law, or *internal control* (**autonomous morality**—rules are arbitrary agreements that can be changed by those who have to follow them). As children develop, they begin to understand that things are not totally right or totally wrong. They can also gradually see things from other perspectives and, therefore, can consider the intentionality of an act when deciding whether the act is right or wrong.

Piaget examined the idea that younger children reason about the wrongness of an act in terms of the amount of damage done, rather than whether the act was done purposefully or accidentally. Reading pairs of stories like the following to children of varying ages, he asked which character in the stories was naughtier:

A little boy who is called John is in his room. He is called to dinner. He goes into the dining room. But behind the door there was a chair, and on the chair there was a tray with fifteen cups on it. John couldn't have known that there was all this behind the door. He goes in, the door knocks against the tray, bang go the fifteen cups, and they all get broken!

Once there was a little boy whose name was Henry. One day, waiting for a time when his mother was out, he tried to get some jam out of the cupboard. He climbed

heteronomous morality Piaget's stage of moral development in which children think of rules as moral absolutes that cannot be changed

autonomous morality Piaget's stage of moral development in which children realize that rules are arbitrary agreements that can be changed by those who have to follow them

up on a chair and stretched out his arm. But the jam was too high up and he couldn't reach it and have any. But while he was trying to get it, he knocked over a cup. The cup fell down and broke. (Piaget, 1965, p. 122)

Piaget found that for the younger children interviewed, the goodness or badness of the actors in the story was related solely to the extent of the consequences. They judged John to be naughtier than Henry because John had broken more cups. Older children, however, recognized the role of intention behind the acts. They judged Henry to be naughtier than John because Henry had been purposefully sneaking something whereas John had had an accident.

Contemporary researchers have corroborated Piaget's findings when his research methods are replicated (Jose, 1990; Lapsley, 1996; Smetana, 1981). For example, young children in various cultures emphasize consequences more than intent in judging the wrongness of an act.

Kohlberg's Theory

Lawrence Kohlberg (1976), influenced by Piaget's work, developed a theory of moral development after 20 years of interviewing children, adolescents, and adults in different cultures (see Table 12.3). He proposed that there was no consistent relationship between parental conditions of child rearing and various measures of conscience or internalized values because morality cannot be imposed; it has to be constructed as a consequence of social experiences (Turiel, 1998). Kohlberg presented his subjects with stories involving moral dilemmas and questioned them about the stories. Probably the best known is the following:

A woman in Europe was near death from cancer. One drug might save her, a form of radium that a druggist in the same town had recently discovered. The druggist was charging $2,000, ten times what the drug cost him to make. The sick woman's husband, Heinz, went to everyone he knew to borrow money, but could get together only about half of what it cost. He told the druggist that his wife was dying and asked him to sell it cheaper or let him pay later. But the druggist said "no." The husband was desperate and broke into the man's store to steal the drug for his wife. Should the husband have done that? Why or why not? (Kohlberg, 1969, p. 379)

Clearly, there is no "right" answer to this story (or the others Kohlberg used). On the one hand, there are the husband's feelings; on the other, there are the legal rights of the druggist.

Based on the *reasoning* behind the responses to the stories (see Table 12.4), Kohlberg concluded that there are six distinct stages, or perspectives, of moral development, which are associated with changes in the individual's intellectual development; each perspective is broader, taking into account more variables or aspects of a moral problem (Higgins, 1995). The stages begin at about age 6 and continue to adulthood. It is important to note that children and adults sometimes operate at several different stages simultaneously. Kohlberg's findings can be summarized as follows (Lickona, 1977):

1. The stages of moral reasoning are the same for all persons, regardless of culture.
2. Individuals progress from one stage to the next.
3. Changing from stage to stage is gradual. The change results from many social experiences.
4. Some individuals move more rapidly than others through the sequence of stages. Some advance further than others; for example, only 25% of U.S. adults were found to reason at stage 5 (principled morality).

Table 12.3

Stages of Moral Development

LEVEL AND STAGE	WHAT IS RIGHT	REASONS FOR DOING RIGHT	SOCIAL PERSPECTIVE OF STAGE
Level I. *Preconventional* **Stage 1:** Heteronomous morality	To avoid breaking rules backed by punishment, obedience for its own sake, and avoiding physical damage to persons and property.	Avoidance of punishment, and the superior power of authorities.	Egocentric point of view. Doesn't consider the interests of others or recognize that they differ from the actor's; doesn't relate two points of view. Actions are considered physically rather than in terms of psychological interests of others. Confusion of authority's perspective with one's own.
Stage 2: Individualism, instrumental purpose, and exchange	Following rules only when it is to someone's immediate interest; acting to meet one's own interests and needs and letting others do the same. Right is also what's fair, what's an equal exchange, a deal, an agreement.	To serve one's own needs or interests in a world where you have to recognize that other people have their interests, too.	Concrete individualistic perspective. Aware that everybody has his or her own exchange interest to pursue and that these interests conflict, so that right is relative (in the concrete individualistic sense).
Level II. *Conventional* **Stage 3:** Mutual interpersonal expectations, relationships, and interpersonal conformity	Living up to what is expected by people close to you or what people generally expect of your role as son, brother, friend, etc. "Being good" is important and means having good motives, showing concern about others. It also means keeping mutual relationships, such as trust, loyalty, respect, and gratitude.	The need to be a good person in your own eyes and those of others. Your caring for others. Belief in the Golden Rule. Desire to maintain rules and authority, which support stereotypical good behavior.	Individualistic perspective in relationships with other individuals. Aware of shared feelings, agreements, and expectations, which take primacy over individual interests. Relates points of view through the concrete Golden Rule, putting oneself in the other person's shoes. Does not yet consider generalized system perspective.
Stage 4: Social system and conscience	Fulfilling the actual duties to which you have agreed. Laws are to be upheld except in extreme cases where they conflict with other fixed social duties. Right is also contributing to society, the group, or institution.	To keep the institution going as a whole, to avoid the "if everyone did it," or the imperative of conscience to meet one's defined obligations (easily confused with stage 3 belief in rules and authority).	Differentiates societal point of view from interpersonal agreement or motives. Takes the point of view of the system that defines roles and rules. Considers individual relations in terms of place in the system.

LEVEL AND STAGE	WHAT IS RIGHT	REASONS FOR DOING RIGHT	SOCIAL PERSPECTIVE OF STAGE
Level III. **Postconventional** **Stage 5:** Social contract or utility and individual rights	Being aware that people hold a variety of values and opinions, that most values and rules are relative to your group. These relative rules should usually be upheld, however, in the interest of impartiality and because they are the social contract. Some nonrelative values and rights like *life* and *liberty*, however, must be upheld in any society and regardless of majority opinion.	A sense of obligation to law because of one's social contract to make and abide by laws for the welfare of all and for the protection of all people's rights. A feeling of contractual commitment, freely entered upon, to family, friendship, trust, and work obligations. Concern that laws and duties be based on rational calculation of overall utility, "the greatest good for the greatest number."	Perspective independent of formal rules. Perspective of a rational individual aware of values and rights (such as fairness) prior to social attachments and legal contracts. Integrates perspectives by formal mechanisms of agreement, legal contract, objective impartiality, and due process. Considers moral and legal points of view; recognizes that these sometimes conflict and finds it difficult to integrate them.
Stage 6: Universal ethical principles	Following self-chosen ethical principles. Particular laws or social agreements are usually valid because they rest upon such principles. When laws violate these principles, one acts in accordance with the principle. Principles are universal principles of justice: the equality of human rights and respect for the dignity of human beings as individual persons.	The belief as a rational person in the validity of universal moral principles, and a sense of personal commitment to them.	Perspective of a moral point of view from which social arrangements derive. Perspective is that of any rational individual recognizing the nature of morality or the fact that persons are ends in themselves and must be treated as such.

Source: "Moral Stages and Moralization," by Lawrence Kohlberg, from *Moral Development and Behavior*, edited by T. Lickona, copyright © 1976 by Holt, Rinehart and Winston, Inc., reprinted by permission of the publisher.

5. Although the particular stage of moral reasoning is not the only factor affecting people's moral conduct, the way they reason does influence how they actually behave in a moral situation.

6. Experiences that provide opportunities for role taking (assuming the viewpoints of others, putting oneself in another's place) foster progress through the stages. For example, children who participate in many peer relationships tend to be at more advanced moral stages than children whose peer interaction is low. Within the family, children whose parents encourage them to express their views and participate in family decisions reason at higher moral stages than children whose parents do not encourage these behaviors.

In summary, at the **preconventional level**, the individual considers and weighs the personal consequences of the behavior: "How will I be affected?" Preconventional moral reasoning focuses on individual results. At the **conventional level**, the individual can look beyond personal consequences and consider others' perspectives: "What will they think of me?" Conventional moral reasoning

preconventional level Kohlberg's stages of moral reasoning in which the individual considers and weighs the personal consequences of the behavior

conventional level Kohlberg's stages of moral reasoning in which the individual can look beyond personal consequences and consider others' perspectives

Table 12.4

Types of Moral Judgments Made in Heinz's Dilemma

	PRO	STAGE 1	CON
LEVEL I. PRECONVENTIONAL [WHAT WILL HAPPEN TO ME?]	If you let your wife die, you will get in trouble. You'll be blamed for not spending the money to save her, and there'll be an investigation of you and the druggist for your wife's death.	Action is motivated by avoidance of punishment, and "conscience" is irrational fear of punishment.	You shouldn't steal the drug: you'll be caught and sent to jail. If you do get away, your conscience will bother you, thinking how the police will catch up with you at any minute.
	PRO	**STAGE 2**	**CON**
	If you do happen to get caught, you could give the drug back, and wouldn't get much of a sentence. It wouldn't bother you much to serve a short jail term, if you have your wife when you get out.	Action motivated by desire for reward or benefit. Possible guilt reactions are ignored and punishment viewed in a pragmatic manner. (Differentiates own fear, pleasure, or pain from punishment—consequences.)	You may not get much of a jail term if you steal the drug, but your wife will probably die before you get out, so it won't do you much good. If your wife dies, you shouldn't blame yourself; it isn't your fault she has cancer.
	PRO	**STAGE 3**	**CON**
LEVEL II. CONVENTIONAL [WHAT WILL OTHERS THINK OF ME?]	No one will think you're bad if you steal the drug, but your family will think you're an inhuman husband if you don't. If you let your wife die, you'll never be able to look anybody in the face again.	Action motivated by anticipation of disapproval of others, actual or imagined– hypothetical (e.g., guilt). (Differentiation of disapproval from punishment, fear, and pain.)	It isn't just the druggist who will think you're a criminal; everyone else will, too. After you steal it, you'll feel bad thinking how you've brought dishonor on your family and yourself; you won't be able to face anyone again.
	PRO	**STAGE 4**	**CON**
	If you have any sense of honor, you won't let your wife die because you're afraid to do the only thing that will save her. You'll always feel guilty that you caused her death if you don't do your duty to her.	Action motivated by anticipation of dishonor— that is, institutionalized blame for failure of duty— and by guilt over concrete harm done to others. (Differentiates formal dishonor from informal disapproval. Differentiates guilt for bad consequences from disapproval.)	You're desperate, and you may not know you're doing wrong when you steal the drug. But you'll know you did wrong after you're punished and sent to jail. You'll always feel guilty for your dishonesty and lawbreaking.

LEVEL III. POSTCONVENTIONAL [WHAT WILL I THINK OF MYSELF?]	**PRO** You'd lose other people's respect, not gain it, if you don't steal. If you let your wife die, it would be out of fear, not out of reasoning. So you'd just lose self-respect and probably the respect of others, too.	**STAGE 5** Concern about maintaining respect of equals and of the community (assuming their respect is based on reason rather than emotions). Concern about own self-respect—that is, to avoid judging self as irrational, inconsistent, nonpurposive.	**CON** You'd lose your standing and respect in the community and violate the law. You'd lose respect for yourself if you're carried away by emotion and forget the long-range point of view.
	PRO If you didn't steal the drug and you let your wife die, you'd always condemn yourself for it afterward. You wouldn't be blamed and you would have lived up to the outside rule of the law, but you wouldn't have lived up to your own standards of conscience.	**STAGE 6** Concern about self-condemnation for violating one's own principles. (Differentiates between community respect and self-respect. Differentiates between self-respect for generally achieving rationality and self-respect for maintaining moral principles.)	**CON** If you stole the drug, you wouldn't be blamed by other people, but you'd condemn yourself because you wouldn't have lived up to your own conscience and standards of honesty.

Source: Nicholas J. Anastasiow. *Educational Psychology: A Contemporary View*, p. 131. Copyright © 1973 by Random House, Inc. Reprinted by permission of the publisher.

focuses on upholding the rules of society. At the **postconventional level**, the individual considers and weighs the values behind various consequences from various points of view: "How would I respect myself if I . . . ?" Postconventional moral reasoning considers principles that may be more important than upholding society's rules or laws.

For example, a current law in the United States is that all 18-year-old men must register with the Selective Service System. The rationale behind this rule is that if our country needed men for defense, these men could be called. A postconventional-level individual, who is generally a law-abiding citizen, may choose not to register because it violates his moral code, which says that only volunteers should be called for service; no one should be forced to fight.

Kohlberg (1976, 1986) believed that most children under age 9 are at the preconventional level of moral development (stages 1 and 2). Some preadolescents also score at this level. Most adolescents, and adults, reason at the conventional level (stages 3 and 4) when faced with moral dilemmas. A small percentage of older adolescents may reach the postconventional level (stages 5 and 6). Adults who are at the postconventional level are only a minority. Because of the idealistic nature of stage 6 reasoning, it was removed from the Kohlberg moral judgment scoring manual, but it is still considered to be theoretically important as a hypothetical construct (Colby & Kohlberg, 1987).

postconventional level Kohlberg's stages of moral reasoning in which the individual considers and weighs the values behind various consequences from various points of view

Kohlberg's stage theory has been criticized by some investigators even though his work has had significant influence on subsequent research (Turiel, 1998). One criticism is that the link between *moral reasoning* and *moral behavior* is not as strong as Kohlberg's theory would predict (Blas, 1990; Thoma, Rest, & Davidson, 1991). One's moral code consists of both moral reasoning (how one believes one should behave in a certain situation) and moral behavior (how one actually does behave in a certain situation). For some individuals, there is a difference between the two (Hartshorne & May, 1978; Kurtines & Gewirtz, 1991). When people think about real-life moral problems, they tend to rank at a lower stage than they do on hypothetical problems (Turiel, 1998).

Another criticism of Kohlberg's theory is his *cultural bias* toward a Western (individualistic) perspective on morality, involving justice or fairness to the individual. Studies comparing moral concepts in different cultures (Shweder, Mahapatra, & Miller, 1987) have demonstrated that culture defines morality for a child; in collectivistic cultures, what is best or "right" may be putting one's family obligations or honor above what might be fairer to the individual. For example, Hindu children believed it was more "wrong" to get a haircut on the day of one's father's funeral than for a husband to beat his wife for going to the movies without permission. Family honor is regarded as morally superior to a person's painful consequence for disobedience.

Still another criticism is *gender bias*; Kohlberg's original sample was all male. According to Gilligan (1982), the difference in the responses of females compared to the responses of the original male sample sheds some doubt on the applicability of Kohlberg's delineated stages of moral reasoning to all human development. Others disagree, citing that in real-life dilemmas, as opposed to hypothetical ones, the moral reasoning of males and females is similar, even though females do cite relationship and caring issues more often (Jaffee & Hyde, 2000; Turiel, 1998; Walker, 1991).

Carol Gilligan (1982, 1985) argues that Kohlberg's theory views morality only from a perspective of *justice*. The **justice moral perspective** (individualistic) emphasizes the rights of the individual. When individual rights conflict, equitable rules of justice must prevail. Cultures with an individualistic orientation exhibit just such a moral perspective. According to Gilligan, a perspective of morality that is not given significance by Kohlberg is that of *care*. The **care moral perspective** (collectivistic) views people in terms of their connectedness with others. In other words, others' welfare is intrinsically connected to one's own. People share in each other's fortunes and misfortunes and must accept responsibility for one another's care. Various cultures around the world that have a collectivistic orientation socialize children to have such a care moral perspective. For example, children and adolescents growing up in India give priority to interpersonal relationships in moral conflict situations, whereas most children and adolescents growing up in the United States give priority to individual rights (Miller & Bersoff, 1993).

Gilligan related examples of boys' and girls' reasoning regarding the Heinz dilemma, such as the following (Gilligan, 1982, pp. 26–28):

justice moral perspective emphasizes the rights of the individual; when individual rights conflict, equitable rules of justice must prevail

care moral perspective views people in terms of their connectedness with others; others' welfare is intrinsically connected to one's own

Jake: For one thing, human life is worth more than money, and if the druggist only makes $1,000 he is still going to live; but if Heinz doesn't steal the drug, his wife is going to die. (Why is life worth more than money?) Because the druggist can get $1,000 later from rich people with cancer, but Heinz can't get his wife again.

Amy: Well, I don't think so. I think there might be other ways besides stealing it, like if he could borrow the money or get a loan or something, but he really shouldn't steal the drug—but his wife shouldn't die either. (Why shouldn't he steal the drug?)

If he stole the drug, he might save his wife then, but if he did, he might have to go to jail, and then his wife might get sicker again, and he couldn't get more of the drug, and it might not be good. So, they should really just talk it out and find some other way to make the money.

In these examples, Jake's sense that people sometimes must act on their own, even in opposition to others, if they are to do the right thing is contrasted with Amy's assumption that people can work out their problems by "talking it out." Because Amy sees the social world as a network of relationships, she believes that the solution to the problem lies in making Heinz's wife's condition known to all concerned, especially the druggist. Surely, then, the people will work something out that will be responsive to the wife's needs. Jake, on the other hand, assumes no such consensus among those involved in the dilemma. So Jake believes Heinz may need to take the law into his own hands if he is to protect his rights. Jake concludes that Heinz's wife is a legitimate part of Heinz's rights by logically calculating the unique value of the wife's life as compared to the money the druggist can get for the drug from others (Damon, 1988).

Despite the criticisms, Kohlberg's model of moral development has stood the test of time. Most psychologists agree that morality, no matter which perspective you take, is developmental; that is, children universally progress through stages of understanding, and even though the timing of the progression and the highest stage reached are individual, the sequence of the stages is the same. "Debates now center on the roles of emotions and judgments, on the individual and the collectivity, on the contributions of constructions of moral understandings and culturally based meanings, and on how to distinguish between universally applicable and locally based moralities" (Turiel, 1998, p. 868).

INFLUENCES ON MORAL DEVELOPMENT

What significant factors influence moral development?

Contexts that have been shown to play a role in moral development are situational, individual, and socialization.

Situational Contexts

The situation an individual is in often influences actual moral behavior. Situational factors include the nature of the relationship between the individual and those involved in the problem, whether others are watching, previous experience in similar situations, and the value society places on various responses (Turiel, 1998, 2002). For example, killing in self-defense is condoned, whereas killing for revenge is not.

The relation between moral reasoning and moral behavior is not always clear. People may believe in honesty and think that individuals who cheat on tests should be punished, yet those same people may cheat on their income tax returns. One classic study (Krebs, 1967) found that in a sample of sixth-graders, the behavior of resisting temptation was related to children's stage of moral development, as delineated by Kohlberg. However, another study of a group of 7- to 11-year-olds found no relation between moral reasoning (based on intentionality and justice) and the individual child's behavior when resisting temptation in a laboratory situation (Grinder, 1964).

Turiel (1983, 1998, 2002) explains that the inconsistencies exhibited in individuals' moral reasoning are influenced by whether they judge the situation to be a "moral" or a "conventional" situation. According to Turiel, a *moral situation* involves other people's rights or welfare (you cannot hit other children), whereas a *conventional situation* involves rules for appropriate behavior in a social group (you must not interrupt when someone else is talking).

Judith Smetana (1981, 1985, 1989) found that even $2\frac{1}{2}$- to 3-year-olds distinguish between moral and conventional rules. Young children view moral transgressions, such as hitting, stealing, and refusing to share, as more serious and deserving of punishment than not saying "please" or forgetting to put away a toy. Thus, young children seem to have a greater understanding of rules in different situations than Piaget originally assumed.

Different cultures define moral and social conventional rules differently, depending on whether the culture has an individualistic or a collectivistic orientation (Rogoff, 2003; Shweder et al., 1987). According to Dien (1982), the Western system of morality—emphasizing individual autonomy and self-responsibility—is rooted in Judeo-Christian theology (humans were created with freedom of self-determination) and Greek philosophy (morality is based on rationality). In Western societies, morality emphasizes analytical thinking, individual choice, and responsibility. In contrast, Eastern systems of morality, based on the doctrine of Confucianism, believe the universe was designed to be just and moral. Humans have a duty to act accordingly, subordinating their own identity to the interest of the group to ensure a harmonious social order. In China, moral maturity involves the ability to make judgments based on conventional norms of reciprocity, rules of exchange, available resources, and sensitivity to complex relationship networks in a given situation. Means of resolving Western conflicts rely on laws that protect individual rights. The preference for resolving Chinese conflicts is through reconciliation.

Individual Contexts

Temperament. Moral development may be affected by an individual's *temperament*—those innate characteristics that determine sensitivity to various experiences and responsiveness to patterns of social interaction. Kochanska's (1993, 1995, 1997) studies on children's temperament (inhibited or shy, impulsive or aggressive) and conscience development conclude that children's temperaments can affect parenting methods. For example, maternal reasoning, polite requests, suggestions, and distractions predicted internalized conscience development in inhibited, but not in impulsive, 2- and 3-year-olds. Impulsive children were more likely to comply with directives when they had a secure attachment; power assertion resulted in anger and defiance. The way to internalize morals for such children is to maintain the affection of the parent.

Self-Control. Moral development may also be related to *self-control*—the ability to regulate impulses, behavior, and/or emotions. Some studies (Mischel, 1974; Mischel, Shoda, & Peake, 1988) have shown that preschool children who exhibit self-control, in that they are able to defer immediate gratification, are more successful than their more impulsive age-mates at resisting the temptation to cheat at experimental games. These self-controlled preschoolers were also rated as more self-competent and socially responsible 10 years later in adolescence. Children who can delay gratification have time to assess social cues and thus enable positive peer group functioning (Gronau & Waas, 1997).

Self-Esteem. Another influence on moral development may be *self-esteem*—specifically, the extent to which an individual needs approval from others (Hogan &

Emler, 1995). A longitudinal study (Dobkin, Tremblay, Masse, & Vitaro, 1995) showed that the need to receive approval from others was related negatively to the level of moral behavior. Specifically, the greater the dependency on others for esteem, the more likely individuals were to abuse substances and engage in antisocial acts. On the other hand, the need for approval from oneself was positively related to the level of moral behavior and consequent avoidance of drugs.

Age/Intelligence. Kohlberg and his colleagues (Colby, Kohlberg, Gibbs, & Lieberman, 1983) reported data from a 20-year longitudinal study of moral judgment in boys who were 10, 13, and 16 when first assessed. The data supported the theory that moral reasoning is significantly linked with age, IQ, education, and socioeconomic status. It also showed that stage 4 did not emerge in a majority of individuals until early adulthood (20s). In addition, the data indicated no distinction between individuals at the stages 5 and 6, using available assessment techniques.

Education. Advanced education, particularly the critical thinking and discussion common in college classes, promotes advanced moral reasoning, probably because it provides an opportunity to be exposed to diverse views (Mason & Gibbs, 1993).

Social Interaction. Several researchers (Walker & Taylor, 1991; Youniss, 1981) believe that one's moral code develops through social interaction—through discussion, debate, and emergence of consensus. This may explain why those growing up in democratic societies, whose existence depends on consensus among the majority, score at the higher levels (Bronfenbrenner & Garbarino, 1976; Miller, 1995).

Emotions. Jerome Kagan (1984) believes the morality of most persons to be directed more by emotions than by reasoning. Avoidance of unpleasant feelings and achievement of pleasant feelings are the major motivations for morality. Unpleasant feelings include fear of punishment, social disapproval, and failure, as well as guilt and uncertainty. Pleasant feelings include affection, pride, sense of belonging, and contribution.

Socialization Contexts

Family. The family is a social system and, therefore, has rules of conduct in order for its members to get along. Many of these rules are similar to those of society at large—for example, prohibitions against lying, stealing, aggression, and disorderly conduct. In both family and society, misbehavior is discouraged through sanctions such as disapproval and punishment; good behavior is encouraged through approval. The goal is for the child to develop a conscience. *Conscience* is a word that traditionally refers to the "cognitive and affective processes which constitute an internalized moral governor over an individual's conduct" (Aronfreed, 1968).

Although Kohlberg rejected the role of parents in a child's construction of morality, Damon (1988) believes that because parents first introduce the child to the laws and logic of a social system, they are a crucial ingredient in the child's moral development. The child-rearing methods that parents implement have an impact on the moral development of children. Several investigations have found that parents who discuss with their children issues such as the Heinz story, and the values behind such issues, tend to promote more advanced moral thought (Walker & Taylor, 1991).

Other researchers (Eisenberg & Murphy, 1995; Hoffman, 1983; Hoffman & Saltzstein, 1967) have found that children of parents who are punitive tend to have *externally focused consciences* (a description that generally corresponds to Kohlberg's stages 1–3). Children who have externally focused consciences are "good" in order to receive praise, avoid punishment, or please others. Children of parents who are warm and affectionate tend to have *internally focused consciences* (generally corresponding to Kohlberg's stages 4–6). Children who have internally focused consciences are "good" in order to fulfill their duty or conform to their own standards. Internally focused consciences can be conventional (tradition-oriented) and rigid, or humanistic (person-oriented) and flexible. A humanistic conscience develops when parents are not only affectionate but also use induction as a socializing technique—they explain the reasons for their demands and discuss the impact of the child's actions on others.

Hoffman and Saltzstein (1967), in a classic study, identified three kinds of parental discipline techniques that are related to conscience development: *power assertion, love withdrawal,* and *induction.* In one study, these researchers asked seventh-graders (matched for intelligence and social class) which method of discipline their parents ordinarily used. They also asked the parents which method of discipline they had used when their child was 5 years old. The children were rated for conscience development along several dimensions: severity of guilt, as expressed in story completions; acceptance of responsibility for wrongdoing, as judged by teachers; tendency to confess misdeeds, as reported by mothers; judgment of right and wrong independent of rewards and punishment; and consideration for other children, as judged by classmates. Results showed that discipline by power assertion was associated with low ratings on conscience development; discipline by induction was associated with high conscience ratings; and discipline by love withdrawal was not significantly associated with conscience development.

More recent studies have also demonstrated the relationship between parental socialization methods and moral development. For example, one study (Kochanska, 1991) found that mothers who deemphasized power strategies when trying to get their toddlers to comply with their rules had children who, when studied six years later, had a more internally focused conscience. Another study (Kuczynski, Kochanska, Radke-Yarrow, & Girnius-Brown, 1987) found that mothers who used strategies of direct control were associated with children who used strategies of direct defiance, whereas mothers who used negotiation had children who were more likely to use negotiation. Thus, children seem to model parental socialization methods.

It must be kept in mind, however, that moral reasoning is a complicated process involving perception, emotions, desires, and judgment. Even though children's earliest social interactions occur in the family, thus influencing moral development, these biologically influenced cognitive factors are also significant (Turiel, 1998).

Peers. Reciprocity is a fundamental ingredient of all human interchange: "Do unto others as you would have them do unto you." Reciprocity is learned by doing, through social interaction: I say something, you answer; I smile, you smile back; I grab your toy, you hit me; I share my cookies with you, you play with me.

Kohlberg (1976, 1985) and others (Damon, 1988; Saltzstein, 1976) believe that social interaction, especially the opportunity to take the role of another person and the opportunity to generate rules democratically, can enhance moral development. Children who have more opportunities for participation in the family, peer groups, and social settings may develop faster in moral thought and behavior than children who lack these supports. It was found that children who grew up on an Israeli kibbutz—with its intense peer group interaction, opportunities for shared decision making, and cooperative work responsibilities—typically reached stage 4 or 5 in adolescence. In contrast, children who were reared in situations where there was limited social exchange were often still at stage 1 or 2, even in late adolescence (Lickona, 1977; Kruger, 1992). Direct training in role taking may even induce people to advance in Kohlberg's developmental stages (Saltzstein, 1975).

Social conflicts between peers are a source of moral development (Killen & Nucci, 1995). Conflicts can stimulate children to take different points of view in order to restore balance in social situations, to consider the rights of others, and to coordinate others' needs with their own. Did you ever have to compromise in a disagreement with a friend in order to preserve the friendship?

School. Schools influence moral development through their programs and their staff (Kohlberg, 1985; Sadker & Sadker, 2003). Because, according to Piaget, moral development begins with the understanding and acceptance of rules, it will be useful to examine the relationship between the approach to classroom rules and moral development.

All programs have rules. The purpose of rules in a classroom is to ensure an optimal learning environment. If learning is to take place, students cannot interfere with one another or with the teacher. Students must respect and cooperate with one another when differences arise; they must learn how to compromise.

As has been discussed, traditional programs tend to emphasize rigid adherence to rules regarding behavior, interpersonal relationships, and manners. Teachers who implement traditional programs tend to be *authoritarian*, in that they make the rules and dole out the rewards and consequences. Modern programs also have rules, but they tend to be more flexible in their approach. Teachers who implement modern programs tend to be *authoritative*, in that they include students in the process of making rules. Damon (1988, 1999) believes that to enhance their moral development, children need guidance with reasoning, positive role models, and involvement in group discussions for decision making, social interaction, and perspective taking. For example, one four-year study (Higgins, 1995) demonstrated that students in a modern, or democratic, high school were more advanced in moral reasoning than students in a traditional, or autocratic, high school. A discussion of what authoritative teachers specifically do to enhance moral development follows.

Whether the rules emanate from external sources or internal sources, how the teacher communicates the rules, keeping in mind children's cognitive development, can have an impact on children's moral development. Consider the teacher who says, "You can't go out to recess until all your materials are put away," versus the teacher who says, "Here, let's put your materials away so that no one will step on them and get hurt." The first teacher is merely parroting a rule, whereas the second teacher is giving the child the reasoning behind the rule. The first teacher may get compliance, but will not be fostering moral development; the second teacher will.

Teachers create the atmosphere for modeling responses. Research has shown that modeling has a positive effect on moral development (Bandura, 1991, 2000). There is no comparable substitute for a teacher who models compassion, honesty, altruism, and justice. The teacher who encourages children to share, yet when asked for a certain book by another teacher says, "No, I'm sorry; we are going to use it later," and then does not, is not being an effective model. On the other hand, the teacher who says, "Let's see this film now (recess time), so Mr. Johnson's class will still have time to see it today, and I'll take you out to recess after the film," is being an effective model for cooperative behavior.

Certain activities incorporated into classroom programs have been found to foster moral development. For example, research (Higgins, 1995; Kohlberg, 1985; Lickona, 1991; Sadker & Sadker, 2003) has indicated that group discussions on moral issues can raise a person's level of moral reasoning. Group discussions can deal with various problems in the classroom, such as how certain transgressions (fighting, taking other people's things, tattling) should be handled. Or they can involve planning a group project. Such group projects tend to reduce egocentrism and foster cooperation because an opportunity is provided for everyone to listen to everyone else, and everyone can make a contribution. Many teachers use the team approach for group projects. For example, suppose a group of children on a team has to present an animal project to the class. One child records the information from books, another illustrates it, another writes a poem about it, and another organizes and narrates the information to the class. The children choose their jobs. They help each other, so the project represents their best team effort.

Still another group discussion technique that enhances moral development is the presentation of moral dilemmas to the class. The following is an example for middle-years children:

> Joe's father promised he could go to camp if he earned the $50 to pay for it, but he changed his mind and instead asked Joe to give him the money he had earned. Joe lied and said he had only earned $10 (which he gave to his father). He then went to camp using the other $40 he had made. Before he went, he told his younger brother, Alex, about lying to his father. Should Alex tell their father? Why or why not? (Good & Brophy, 1986, p. 121)

The significance for moral development is not in the answers but in the reasoning behind them. Dilemmas should be related to the student's level of cognitive development and interest. Discussions revolving around such dilemmas help students clarify their values, make choices, and understand the consequences of their choices. Hearing what others say also broadens their perspective and their alternatives.

As mentioned previously, perspective taking—giving children roles to play and discussing them—has been found to enhance moral development (Gibbs, 1995; Sadker & Sadker, 2003; Staub, 1971). Through role playing, children learn to view events from a variety of points of view. They learn what it feels like to be helpless, what it feels like to be helped, and what it feels like to be the helper. For example, how would you feel if you lost your dog? How would you feel if it were returned to you? How would you feel if you returned a lost dog to someone else?

Kohlberg suggests that teachers ask students questions about moral issues and listen to their explanations, in order to gain insight into their level of moral thought. He has found that discussions that are one stage above an individual's present level of moral reasoning are most effective in this regard. Finally, Kohlberg urges teachers to deal with situations posing broad problems and issues, rather than focus too much on discussions involving specific classroom rules and routines, because these specifics cannot be generalized (Kohlberg, 1980, 1985; Lickona, 1977, 1991).

IN PRACTICE

How Can Moral Growth Be Promoted in the Classroom?

1. Build a sense of community in the classroom where the students learn together in an atmosphere of respect and security.
2. Provide opportunities for the children to have a voice in establishing the rules of the classroom and the consequences for not following them.
3. Give reasons for consequences, stressing where possible the effect of the child's action on the group.
4. Discuss differences between rules for the good order of the school and rules affecting justice and human relations.
5. Provide opportunities for collaborative peer group work.
6. In stories and discussions of everyday experiences, help the children to consider the feelings of other persons, real or fictional.
7. Role-play experiences from daily life events that lead to disappointments, tensions, fights, and joys in order to provide opportunities for the students to see the events from perspectives other than their own.
8. Discuss concepts of fairness and unfairness.
9. Using stories, literature, history, current events, and/or films, stimulate discussions that will provoke higher-stage reasoning.
10. Be a role model and point out other role models as they occur in classroom activities.

Sources: Duska & Whelan, 1975; Higgins, 1995

Mass Media. As has been discussed, television is a significant socializing agent. Does it affect moral behavior? Some believe that TV and other popular media have helped create a large number of people who think it's perfectly OK to grab what they want and to do what they want, and the only bad thing is getting caught.

In a study of television and the moral judgment of young children, kindergartners who were heavy TV viewers (based on a television diary kept by their mothers) were found to exhibit less advanced moral reasoning when interviewed than those children who watched little TV (Rosenkoetter, Huston, & Wright, 1990).

Television may contribute to disruption of moral behavior. Specific programs have been followed by antisocial acts (Levin, 1998)—for example, various school shootings following news coverage of the Columbine High School massacre in Littleton, Colorado; or the 5-year-old boy who set fire to his home, killing his 2-year-old sister, following a similar episode on *Beavis and Butt-Head*; or the 13-year-old boy and his friend who were acting out the Russian roulette scene from the movie *The Deer Hunter* with a real gun (the boy died instantly).

The National Television Violence Study concluded that not only does violence pervade TV, it also involves repeated acts of aggression against a victim that go unpunished (Mediascope, 1997). Huesmann (1986) proposed that such repetition results in a cumulative learning process, having specific effects on short- and long-term behavior. One effect is that children learn new ways of aggressing by watching aggressive models. A second result is that socialized restraints over aggressive impulses are weakened because many violent acts are performed by heroes and are rationalized in the story context as "good triumphing over evil." The message portrayed, then, is that aggression is an appropriate tool for those who believe they are in the right (Coie & Dodge, 1998). A third effect of viewing violence is desensitization—emotional responsiveness is reduced. A fourth result is that the observer's sense of reality is altered. Frequent viewers, compared to infrequent ones, believe that real-world violence is more common, that the world is less safe, that group stereotypes are more valid, and that their chances of being victimized are greater (Coie & Dodge, 1998).

Because young children attend primarily to the consequences of acts and not intentions, they are unlikely to understand moral messages of programs, even when these are explicit. When children identify with televised models, they copy the observed behavior and accept the models' attitudes. It has been demonstrated that children's aggressiveness increases after being exposed to an aggressive model and children's altruism increases after being exposed to an altruistic model (Perse, 2001). Thus, the particular moral behavior children are exposed to on television is likely to influence their moral behavior. For example, what are the effects on children of observing rule breaking on television? The research literature reveals that observational learning can play a potent role in shaping responses to situations in which breaking an established rule will bring immediate gratification or benefits to the transgressor. It has been demonstrated that children exposed to a model who breaks an established rule will break rules more often in the absence of an adult than will those who have not been exposed to such an example. On the other hand, it has also been established that children who have been exposed to a model who adheres to established rules are more likely to adhere to rules, even when they are highly tempted and when their transgression will not be detected (Bandura, 1991; Leibert & Poulos, 1976).

Community.   As William Somerset Maugham said, "Conscience is the guardian in the individual of the rules which the community has evolved for its own preservation." Some psychologists (Damon, 1988; Miller & Bersoff, 1993; Shweder et al., 1987; Turiel, 1998) believe that moral development is influenced by the cultural ideology in one's community. For example, as discussed earlier, cultural ideology can be oriented toward individualism or collectivism. *Individualistic* cultures emphasize rights and justice, whereas *collectivistic* cultures emphasize duties and obligations. These different ideologies influence values and morals, in that community members judge behavior accordingly. Individualistic cultures value personal goals; collectivistic cultures value shared goals. Moral concepts in individualistic communities are interpreted in terms of independence, autonomy, self-reliance, and individual rights. Moral concepts in collectivistic communities are interpreted in terms of interdependence, conformity, duty, obedience toward authority, tradition, and social harmony. In moral dilemmas, individualistic communities judge whose rights have been violated, whereas collectivistic communities judge what obligations were not fulfilled (Rogoff, 2003; Turiel, 1998).

The interaction of the socializing agents in a culture with the individual's intellectual level of development and motivation determines the level of moral development. Bronfenbrenner and Garbarino (1976) describe three developmental levels of morality that are similar for individuals in all cultures:

- *Level 1: Amoral.* The individual's motivation at this level is basically to seek pleasure and avoid pain. The only moral judgment involved is self-interest. This level of morality is quite normal for very young children, but when it persists into adolescence or adulthood, it is considered to be deviant behavior for the individual and hazardous for the society in which he or she lives (corresponding to Kohlberg's stages 1 and 2).
- *Level 2: System of social agents.* The individual's motivation at this level comes from allegiance to others, either to certain individuals or to groups. The individual behaves in such a way as to gain approval (corresponding to Kohlberg's stages 3 and 4).
- *Level 3: Values and ideas.* The individual's motivation at this level is personal principles, his or her own system of beliefs. The individual does not depend on other socializing agents for direction (corresponding to Kohlberg's stages 5 and 6).

According to Bronfenbrenner and Garbarino, individuals who attain Level 3 have had experiences in which abstract thinking, speculation, and decision making were supported. In order for these experiences to take place, one needs to have some competitive allegiances that create enough tension within the individual to stimulate thought about loyalties and critical behavior. In other words, when people are exposed to a variety of settings and social agents representing different expectations and moral sanctions, conflict is produced. This conflict causes people to look within themselves for moral convictions with which they are comfortable. On the other hand, individuals who are exposed to a single setting are exposed to only one set of rules. Because they do not experience conflict, they need not look within themselves for resolution.

Support for Bronfenbrenner's (1970a) theory comes from his findings of differential moral judgments between Russian boarding school students and Russian day school students. The boarding school students, who were exposed to a single socializing agent (school), made moral judgments that were more authority-oriented than those made by the day school students, who were exposed to multiple socializing agents (school, parents, peers). The children were asked to respond to various moral dilemmas, such as the following:

> You and your friends accidentally find a sheet of paper the teacher lost. On this sheet are the questions and answers for a quiz that you are going to have tomorrow. Some of the kids suggest that you do not say anything to the teacher about it, so that all of you can get better marks. What would you really do? Suppose your friends decided to go ahead and keep the paper. Would you go along with them or refuse?

Other moral dilemmas included going to a movie recommended by friends but disapproved of by parents, neglecting homework to be with friends, and accidentally breaking a window and running away.

Bronfenbrenner and Garbarino (1976) used this moral dilemma test on groups of 12-year-old boys and girls in 13 different societies, to find out if being exposed to **pluralism** (the presence of more than one belief system) was related to the development of Level 3 moral judgment. The 13 participating countries were ranked on pluralism. Children growing up in the 1970s in countries that ranked high on pluralism, such as the United States and West Germany, were less authority-oriented and had more plural ideas about moral dilemmas than children growing up in the countries that ranked low on pluralism, such as Poland and Hungary. Children in cultures that allow individual freedom and in which diversity is common are likely to have had experiences that stimulate abstract thinking, speculation, and decision making. These experiences occur because of the existence of differing socializing

pluralism the presence of more than one belief system

agents competing for the individual's allegiance. The individual has to make some personal choices. The process of choosing (values clarification) leads to the development of moral judgment characteristic of Level 3.

Bronfenbrenner and Garbarino explain that experiences involving exposure to differing socializing agents do not occur in many cultures, which is why cross-cultural comparisons of levels of moral development show differences among same-age individuals. Pluralistic societies, those having many socializing agents with differing values, are more likely to produce individuals with Level 3 moral judgment, whereas monolithic societies, those whose socializing agents have a singular value system, are less likely to do so. Pluralism per se is no guarantee that individuals will be motivated to attain Level 3 moral judgment. There must be integration or a common goal linking the individual and the various socializing agents for the conflict over allegiance to occur. For example, a common goal of socializing agents in the United States is achievement. Parents urge children to work hard and do their best, teachers motivate achievement with grades, and friends cheer the kid who hits a home run for the team.

Occasionally, however, these socializing agents compete for one's loyalty as, for instance, when team practice conflicts with plans to study for a test. Which socializing agent gets one's loyalty then? When there is no common goal, conflict does not occur. For example, when Joan comes home from school, her mother asks her to empty the trash. Joan had already promised her friend she would go over to her house after school to work on a school project. There is no competition between socializing agents for Joan's loyalty because she can easily accomplish both activities.

Other research supports the theory that the more socializing agents one is exposed to that have a common goal yet sometimes compete for allegiance, the more likely one is to have Level 3 moral judgment. For example, studies of high school students have found that their stage of moral reasoning was positively related to the quantity and quality of their social participation (school clubs, friendship groups, leadership role), whether judged by teachers, peers, or themselves (Turiel, 1998). For another example, 14- and 17-year-old Finnish adolescents who experienced Western individualistic educational practices, compared to adolescents of the same age who grew up in Estonia during the period of Soviet socialism with collectivistic educational practices, exhibited more internal moral reasoning (Keltikangas-Järvinen, Terav, & Pakaslahti, 1999).

In conclusion, moral development is socially constructed (Davidson & Youniss, 1995). It represents an individual's scheme of personal and societal values that include a coordination of emotions, thoughts, and actions (Turiel, 1998). If one acts exclusively on personal values, one may too often overlook the rights and privileges of others in the social environment. To illustrate, in the example discussed in Chapter 11, Jessy overlooked her parents' liability if they break the law and allow her to have a party with alcohol because she is more concerned with her peers. On the other hand, if one acts on societal values or social convention, contract, or laws, one may fail to see how they can unjustly affect a given individual. For example, Jessy's parents did not fully understand her position in feeling she had to fulfill the expectations of her peers because they were more concerned with their responsibilities.

Thus, mature moral development—which is influenced by one's capacity to anticipate the future, to predict consequences, and to put oneself in another's place, along with one's level of self-esteem—is the ability to make rational decisions that balance one's own personal value system with the value system of society.

Gender Roles

How are gender differences perceived in society?

A *gender role*, or sex type, as discussed in Chapter 2, refers to the qualities an individual understands to characterize males and females in his or her culture. It is distinct from sex, which refers to the biological aspects of being male or female. Gender role is more of a psychological construct, whereas sex is more of a physical one.

The following English nursery rhyme from the early 1800s, illustrates how gender differences are perceived in society. Verses like these, in turn, influence how children are socialized to acquire their appropriate gender roles (Gould & Gould, 1962):

> What are little boys made of?
> Frogs and snails
> And puppy dogs' tails
> That's what little boys are made of.
> What are little girls made of?
> Sugar and spice
> And all things nice
> That's what little girls are made of.

DEVELOPMENT OF GENDER ROLES

How do boys and girls learn how to act like males and females?

Sex typing, or classification into gender roles based on biological sex, begins at birth (Maccoby, 1998, 2000; Ruble & Martin, 1998). The child is given what society considers to be a girl's name or a boy's name (those children whose names are ambiguous—for example, Jordan, which could be a girl's or boy's name—are possible targets for teasing). The child is then dressed according to that classification. Certain colors are generally worn by girls and certain ones by boys. Even though in the United States most children of both sexes wear shirts and pants, those worn by girls are usually decorated differently. And throughout childhood, the child is given certain toys for play, also usually classified by sex. Girls' toys are generally related to nurturing or home activities (dolls, stuffed animals, dishes); boys' toys are generally related to action or work activities (cars, trucks, tools).

Although various cultures provide a "gender curriculum," children play a role in their gender socialization, perhaps driven by biological programming within each sex, as well as between them (Lippa, 2005; Maccoby, 2000). For example, my eldest granddaughter, whose mother rarely wears jewelry or makeup, has been fascinated with adorning herself ever since she saw such items in the store. Because of her interest, I polished her nails for her 2nd birthday. Her sister, a year younger, has been attracted to climbing on everything and loves to take toys apart and throw and kick a ball. For her 2nd birthday, I gave her a riding car. When the eldest was 5, she chose to go to "art camp" for a week in the summer. The younger granddaughter, who was 4, chose to go to "bug camp."

What are the major theories of gender role development?

The following four main theories explain how children are socialized to assume the appropriate gender roles in their society (see Figure 12.3).

sex typing
classification into gender roles based on biological sex

Psychoanalytic

boy   loves   mother   and fears   father

Identification with father to gain mother's love and adopts male gender role

Social Learning, or Social Cognitive

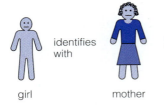

identifies with

and is reinforced for modeling mother's behavior

Adoption of female gender role

girl   mother

Cognitive Developmental

understands he is a male, therefore observes male behavior to model

Adoption of male gender role

boy

father and/or significant males

Gender Schema

observes female and male behavior

Adoption of female gender role

girl   mother and/or significant females   father and/or significant males

Figure 12.3
Theories of Gender Role Development

The boy playing with a truck and the girl choosing to play with a doll exemplifies stereotyped gender role behavior.

HIRB/Index Stock Imagery

Psychoanalytic Theory

Psychoanalytic theory deals with how one comes to *feel* like a male or female. According to Sigmund Freud (cited in Hall, 1954; Freud, 1925), children identify with the same-sex parent out of sexual love for the opposite-sex parent and fear of punishment from the same-sex parent for that love. In other words, a boy identifies with his father because he loves his mother (*Oedipus complex*) and is fearful that his father, who also loves his mother, will punish him for that love. A girl identifies with her mother because she loves her father (*Electra complex*) and is fearful that her mother, who also loves her father, will punish her for that love. In identifying with the same-sex parent, children unconsciously take on the characteristics of that parent. A boy becomes like his father so that his mother will love him as she loves his father; and a girl becomes like her mother so that her father will love her as he loves her mother. The process of gender identification occurs sometime between the ages of 3 and 5, the phallic stage in Freud's sequence of personality development (where focus is on the genitals). After age 5 or 6, children enter Freud's latency stage, in which they engage in normal play activities with same-sex peers and sexuality is dormant. At puberty, children enter Freud's genital stage, in which they normally begin to be sexually attracted to the opposite gender.

Social Learning, or Social Cognitive, Theory

This theory deals with how one comes to *behave* as a male or female. According to theorists Walter Mischel (1970) and Albert Bandura (1989), children behave in what are considered to be gender-appropriate ways because they are reinforced or rewarded when they do so and punished when they do not by the various agents of socialization. Boys identify with male models (usually their fathers) because they are rewarded for doing so: "You are strong, just like your daddy." Girls identify with female models (usually their mothers) for the same reason: "You look pretty, just like your mommy." Children choose models with whom to identify on the basis of whether the model is perceived to be like themselves, is warm and affectionate, and has prestige in their eyes. When children identify with the same-sex parent, they incorporate that parent's behavior into their own.

Cognitive Developmental Theory

This theory deals with how one comes to *think* of oneself as a male or female. According to Lawrence Kohlberg (1966), the assumption of gender role behavior is part of the child's total cognitive development. On the basis of their observations and interactions, children accommodate, or reconcile, the differences between the categories of male and female. Once children know and understand the concepts of maleness and femaleness (about age 5 or 6), they then assimilate the appropriate gender behavior that matches their biological sex. In other words, a boy thinks, "I am a boy; therefore, I do boy things," and a girl thinks, "I am a girl; therefore, I do girl things." What children consider to be appropriate gender behavior depends on their experiences in their family, peer group, school, and community, and what they observe in the media.

Gender Schema Theory

Gender schema theory, proposed by Sandra Bem (1981), as well as by Martin and Halverson (1981, 1987), deals with how one comes to *perceive* oneself as a male or female by processing gender-linked information. A *schema* (plural *schemata*) is a conceptual framework of one's experiences and understandings. It explains how children code new information in terms of gender. The basis for coding information is first the recognition of males and females as distinct gender categories. Labeling occurs about age $2\frac{1}{2}$. As children develop, they observe male and female behavior around them. Consequently, they form a schema for what males do in their society and another for what females do. These gender schemata influence how new information gets processed, guiding selective attention and imitation of same-sex models. For example, a girl observes her mother and her grandmother cooking. She also observes her father and other males doing repairs. About age 4 to 5, she can conceptualize that girls cook and boys fix things. Since she knows she is a girl, she chooses to engage in cooking activities rather than working with tools at preschool. Thus, she gains information about cooking and rejects information about building or doing repairs. By age 7 to 8, gender behavior is fairly rigid. Gender schema theory helps to explain why gender stereotypes are self-perpetuating and difficult to modify. It is as if one's earliest socialization experiences with gender set the path for later ones. This was demonstrated in a study of 5- to 10-year-olds, who were asked to predict feminine or masculine interests of target children with certain characteristics. For example, "I know a child who likes to play with tool kits. How much would this child want to wear a dress?" Older children's responses were more gender stereotypic ("No way!") than those of younger children (Martin, Wood, & Little, 1990).

Gender schema theory also proposes that self-concept is associated with the degree to which children perceive themselves as congruent with their schema of male or female. If their behavior matches what they interpret as appropriate to their gender, they feel positive about themselves; if they don't conform to the stereotype, they feel negative about themselves.

What does research say about gender roles?

Regardless of which theory or theories seem to best explain gender role socialization, the fact remains that males and females behave differently. There is a consensus that biological, cognitive, and social factors interactively contribute to sex-typed behavior (Liben & Bigler, 2002; Lippa, 2005; Ruble & Martin, 1998). Although genetics is a significant influence on sex-typed behavior, it is not wholly responsible, as documented by a large population study of 3- and 4-year-old twins and nontwin siblings (Iervolino, Hines, Golombok, Rust, & Plomin, 2005). Although large differences in gender role behavior are observed between the sexes, there is substantial variation within the sexes in typical male and female behavior. For example, in early childhood, boys generally prefer cars and trucks to dolls and jewelry and engage in more rough-and-tumble play than in caretaking role play. These sex-typed behaviors increase from early to middle childhood. However, twins who share the same environment, especially boys, exhibit more similar gender behavior than do nontwins who share the same environment (Iervolino et al., 2005).

In a classic review, researchers Eleanor Maccoby and Carol Jacklin (1974) analyzed more than 2,000 books and articles on possible psychological differences between males and females. They concluded that males are more aggressive than females, a difference that is apparent in infancy. They also concluded that girls have greater verbal ability than boys and that boys have greater visual–spatial ability than girls. These differences are more apparent in early adolescence. Maccoby and Jacklin discovered that some differences traditionally attributed to boys' and girls' behavior are myths. For example, girls are neither more "social" than boys, nor are they more suggestible. Boys do not have higher achievement motivation than girls, neither are they more "analytic." More recent reviews of research on gender differences have arrived at similar conclusions (Fagot, 1995; Ruble & Martin, 1998).

Maccoby and Jacklin's findings have implications for social and educational changes:

> We suggest that societies have the option of minimizing, rather than maximizing, sex differences through their socialization practices. . . . In our view, social institutions and social practices are not merely reflections of the biologically inevitable. A variety of social institutions are viable within the framework set by biology. It is up to human beings to select those that foster the lifestyles they most value. (Maccoby & Jacklin, 1974, p. 374)

Biology and socialization practices interact to produce the variety of sex-typed behaviors observed within and between males and females (Lippa, 2005). It is generally accepted that socialization maximizes genetically determined sex differences (Fagot, 1995; Ruble & Martin, 1998). For example, parents and significant others apply gender stereotypes to children as soon as they are born (or even in utero, if the sex is known). As a result, girls and boys are channeled into sex-typed behaviors that do not necessarily reflect the potential of their individual abilities (American Association of University Women [AAUW], 1991).

Jeanne Block (1984) reviewed the literature on psychological differences between the sexes in areas that included aggression, activity level, impulsivity, susceptibility to anxiety, achievement-related behaviors, self-concept, and social relationships. She concluded that differences in these areas arise from the different social contexts in which boys and girls grow up. In general, boys are given more opportunities for independent problem solving and exploration, whereas girls are more closely supervised and restricted in their experiences. According to Block, such differential socialization causes boys and girls to think differently about the world around them and to use different strategies in dealing with the world. For example, boys are more curious and competitive; girls seek approval more often and are more affiliated.

By the time children reach preschool, they know which type of behavior is expected of their sex. Several years ago, a little boy in my preschool class who was pretending to iron in the housekeeping corner was told by his friend, "Daddies don't iron!" As children enter elementary school, their gender roles become more restrictive (Ruble & Martin, 1998). They play with children of the same sex, thus learning "gender-appropriate" games (the boys tend to play games involving running or throwing a ball at recess; the girls tend to stay close to the teacher, talking or playing games such as jump rope or hopscotch). Because of their cognitive development, they are also becoming more aware of potential models of their sex with whom to identify. These models will be examined next to understand their influences on gender-role socialization.

INFLUENCES ON GENDER ROLE DEVELOPMENT

How do significant socializing agents (microsystems) influence gender-role development?

Family
Do mothers and fathers treat sons and daughters differently?

According to researchers, mothers and fathers do treat sons and daughters differently (Fagot, 1995; Leaper, 2000). Family dynamics and experiences are linked to individual differences in boys' and girls' gendered behavior (McHale et al., 2003). Studies show that parents describe their newborn sons as stronger, more coordinated, and more alert than daughters; and their newborn daughters as smaller, softer, and more fragile than sons (Huston, 1983; Rubin, Provenzano, & Luria, 1974). Fathers, in particular, engage in more rough-and-tumble play with sons and more cuddly play with daughters (Lamb, 1977; Lytton & Romney, 1991). Parents buy different toys for their sons and daughters (O'Brien & Huston, 1985; Rheingold & Cook, 1975; Ruble & Martin, 1998). For example, males are given trucks, war toys, and sports equipment; girls are given dolls, dollhouses, and books. Mothers and fathers even communicate differently to sons and daughters, using more directive and supportive language with girls than with boys (Ruble & Martin, 1998).

Throughout childhood, parents encourage males in active, gross motor, and manipulative play; females are encouraged in passive feminine role taking and fine motor play, with fathers being more stereotypical than mothers (Huston, 1983; Leaper, 2000). Males are also allowed to take risks (climb trees) and are left unsupervised more often and earlier than females (Basow, 1992; Huston, 1983). Finally, parents exert more achievement and independence demands on males while providing help more readily for females (Basow, 1992; Huston, 1983; Leaper, 2000).

Through observed interactions of fathers and mothers with sons and daughters, it has repeatedly been demonstrated that fathers are the more influential gender role socialization agent (Caldera, Huston, & O'Brien, 1989; Langlois & Downs, 1980; Ruble & Martin, 1998). For example, fathers' and mothers' reactions to preschool children's choice of toys were observed. Toys available were traditionally feminine (doll furniture, pots and pans) and masculine (cars, trucks, trains). Studies (Langlois & Downs, 1980; Lytton & Romney, 1991) found that fathers, more than mothers, chose different kinds of toys for boys and girls and encouraged play that they considered gender appropriate and discouraged play they considered gender inappropriate. More specifically, the fathers rewarded their children by approving, helping, and joining in the play more often for play with gender-appropriate toys than for play with gender-inappropriate toys, and they discouraged play with gender-inappropriate toys more than play with gender-appropriate toys. Mothers encouraged both boys and girls to play with toys traditionally considered appropriate for girls. Mothers also tended to discourage both boys and girls from playing with "masculine" toys. The degree of differences in parental treatment of boys and girls may be influenced by age, socioeconomic status, and ethnicity (Fagot, 1995; Lippa, 2005).

In addition, fathers engage in more physical play (tickling, chasing, playing ball) with both sons and daughters, whereas mothers spend more time in caretaking and nurturing activities (MacDonald & Parke, 1986). Apparently, this differential interaction with children enables mothers to become more, and fathers less, sensitive to individual needs of children (Lamb, 2004). Further, compared to mothers, fathers give more evaluative feedback of approval and disapproval (Fagot & Leinbach, 1987). Thus, fathers generally appear to be the more playful, less sensitive, more critical parent in terms of gender role socialization. Regarding relationships within the family, warm, positive father–son and mother–daughter relationships lead to the strongest gender role identification (Huston, 1983). Sons model their father's behavior, and daughters model their mother's. In this regard, too, studies have found that the father has more influence on gender role development of both boys and girls (Lamb, 2004).

When mothers are employed outside the home and fathers participate in child care, fathers' nontraditional activities influence their children's attitudes about gender role stereotypes (Ruble & Martin, 1998). Although mothers employed outside the home still perform most child care and housekeeping chores, husbands of employed wives participate more than husbands of nonemployed wives (Hoffman, 1989). Thus children whose mothers are employed have less stereotypical role models than those whose fathers are "breadwinners" and mothers are "breadbakers" (Gardner & LaBrecque, 1986). They also receive more independence training, have generally higher career goals, and have somewhat higher achievement motivation. These results are particularly true for daughters (Basow, 1992). The most likely explanation is that the mother employed outside the home presents a positive role model for achievement, especially when she is satisfied with her job and gets support for household chores and child care.

The sibling sex constellation—presence of sisters and brothers, and their birth order—influences children's gender role socialization, especially in traditional families (McHale et al., 1999; Rust, Golombok, Hines, Johnson, & Golding, 2000). Not only do sisters and brothers model and reinforce gender role behavior in their younger siblings, but their differential treatment according to sex by the parents has an impact on younger children's gender schemata.

In sum, individual differences in sex typing are influenced by biology, culture, paternal involvement, maternal work status, sex typing of parental roles within the home, and sibling sex constellation (Lippa, 2005; Serbin et al., 1993).

Peers
How greatly do peers influence stereotyped gender behavior?

Peers become progressively more influential as gender role socializing agents as children get older (Leaper, 1994: Lippa, 2005). Peers begin to exert influence during preschool and become increasingly important during elementary school and high school. For example, peers encourage both boys and girls to play with gender-appropriate toys and actively punish (ridicule and tease) play with toys considered appropriate for the opposite gender, especially among boys (Fagot, 1977, 1984; Martin, 1989). Children and adolescents try to do what they perceive to be "cool" to gain acceptance and status among their peers. Preadolescent boys gain status on the basis of athletic ability and toughness, whereas girls' status relates to physical appearance and social skills (Basow & Rubin, 1999; Pollack, 1999; Ruble & Martin, 1998)

Sex segregation begins in the preschool years and intensifies during the school years. This can be observed cross-culturally in both boys and girls (Maccoby & Jacklin, 1987; Rogoff, 2003; Whiting & Edwards, 1988). Sex-segregated play groups value different behaviors for girls and boys (Liben & Bigler, 2002; Maccoby, 1998). Girls tend to enjoy mutual play and use conflict mitigation strategies, whereas boys tend to play more roughly and use physical assertion to resolve conflicts.

One of the functions of the peer group, as discussed in Chapter 8, is to socialize children to learn appropriate sociocultural roles. Cognitively, since middle childhood is the age of concrete reasoning, it follows that children of this age have a rigid, rather than flexible, concept of gender roles. Because middle-years children are most susceptible to peer influence, it also follows that they will be likely to adopt, via modeling, reinforcement, and punishment, the gender roles expected by their peers. For example, boys will be socialized to be active and aggressive and not to show emotion; girls will be socialized to be passive, dependent, and compassionate. Children whose activities are regarded as gender appropriate by the peer group are rewarded by being included in the group. Children whose activities are regarded as gender inappropriate by the peer group are either teased or left to play alone (Thorne, 1993). "Sissy" and "tomboy" are familiar jeers heard in childhood.

The result of sex segregation is that boys and girls tend to grow up in different peer environments—in other words, different subcultures (Maccoby, 1998; Maccoby & Jacklin, 1987). Sociologists Janet Lever (1978) and Barrie Thorne (1993), in separate studies, found significant differences in the play of boys' and girls' peer groups. Lever observed fifth-grade children, mostly European American and middle class, in three schools. She discovered that boys' play was more complex than girls' play on all of the following dimensions and criteria:

- *Size of group.* Is it large or small?
- *Role differentiation.* Do the players have the same role, as in checkers, or different roles, as in baseball?
- *Player interdependence.* Does one player's move affect another's, as in chess or tennis, or not, as in darts or hopscotch?
- *Explicitness of goals.* Is playing merely a cooperative venture with no winners or end point, as in "playing house," or is the purpose playing for a goal, such as scoring the most points, or until a certain end point is reached (nine innings, for example)?
- *Number and specificity of rules.* Are there a few vague rules, as in tag, or many specific ones, as in baseball?
- *Team formation.* Does the play require teams?

Lever (1978) observed that boys typically engaged in team sports with 10–25 players; girls typically played tag, jump rope, or hopscotch, usually involving two to six participants. Boys' play often involved multiple roles, whereas girls' play rarely involved role differentiation. (Girls commonly engaged in activities in which they all played the same role, as in skating, or two roles, as in jump rope—the jumper and the turner.) Boys' play involved more interdependence, which required decision making in regard to strategies. Girls' play tended to require less interdependence, but when it did, play was of a cooperative nature. Boys' games were found to have more elaborate rules—often, interpretations and discussions ensued. Finally, boys were involved in team play more often.

Thorne (1993), who observed kindergarteners to sixth-graders, found that boys' play is generally characterized by larger groups, less proximity to adults, more public

FogStock LLC/Index Stock Imagery

Girls usually play in small groups involving turn taking.

play, more fighting and physical contact, more dominance attempts, and the estab-lishment of a hierarchical "pecking order." Girls' play is generally characterized by smaller, more intimate groups, closer proximity to adults, a strong convention of turn taking, and more mutuality in play and conversation. Such patterns have been observed among African American as well as European American children (Coates, 1987).

The significance of peer group play is that it socializes individuals for adult roles in society, according to the particular skills that are reinforced. According to Lever (1978), boys' play tends to reinforce the ability to deal with diverse actions simultaneously, coor-dinate actions in order to foster group cohesiveness and work for collective goals, engage in competition, cope with impersonal rules, and engage in strategic thinking. Girls' play, on the other hand, tends to reinforce cooperation, spontaneity, imagination, flexibility, and empathy. What socialization outcomes result from girls' participation in team sports? One study (Miller, Sabo, Farrell, Barnes, & Melnick, 1998) found that athletic participation influenced the status of girls and their relationships with boys. Specifically, athletic participation was associated with lower frequency of heterosexual intercourse, fewer partners, and later onset.

School
How does the school contribute to sex-typing?

When I attended public school in the 1950s, there were two entrance doors, one marked "Girls" and one marked "Boys." At recess, the girls played jump rope, and the boys either ran around chasing and hitting each other or played ball. When the teacher blew the whistle, everyone lined up, the girls in one line, the boys in another; each line then entered the school building through the appropriate door. Why differentiate? We all knew which sex we were. Surprisingly, many school activities are still sex-segregated.

Schools provide a number of gender-related messages to children, some intentional and some unintentional (Ruble & Martin, 1998; Sadker & Sadker, 2003). Schools have traditionally treated males and females differently—through portrayals of gender roles in textbooks, through different course requirements (for example, boys took shop and girls took home economics), through treatment by teachers and counselors, and even, subtly, through the uneven sex distribution on the staff.

> Men hold a disproportionate number of positions in higher administration, whereas women are more often teachers particularly in the "early" grades. Only in older grades are children likely to have many male teachers, and these are often in classes such as mathematics and science. (Ruble & Martin, 1998, p. 979)

The passage of federal legislation (Title IX Education Amendment) in 1972 outlawed discrimination on the basis of sex. As a result, textbooks are reviewed for sexual bias, courses are open to males and females, and teachers and counselors must channel students into higher educational programs or occupations on the basis of individual competencies rather than what was traditionally acceptable for the sexes.

One of the effects of Title IX has been the increased participation of girls in sports. A longitudinal study of sports participation in a sample of public and private American high schools (Women's Sports Foundation, 1989) found that both boys and girls who participated in sports had better images of themselves. They were healthier, more energetic, and had more self-confidence. After high school, they were more likely to be involved in community groups. This was true of African Americans, European Americans, and Hispanic Americans.

Despite Title IX and the greater awareness of how children develop gender role attitudes, it will be a while before teachers and school personnel can change any unconscious habitual behavior that interferes with children's developing to their full potential. An example of such unconscious behavior is the finding that teachers respond differently to boys and girls. Serbin and her colleagues (Serbin et al., 1973, 1993) found that teachers tend to respond negatively to the aggressive behavior of boys and positively to the proximity-seeking behavior of girls. Research in preschools (Fagot, 1984) confirmed that more teacher attention was given to boys for achievement-related behaviors and to girls for compliance.

Other studies (Sadker, Sadker, & Klein, 1991) revealed some differences in how elementary and high school teachers view male and female students. "Good" male students were described by the teachers as active, adventurous, aggressive, assertive, curious, energetic, enterprising, frank, independent, and inventive. "Good" female students were described as appreciative, calm, conscientious, considerate, cooperative, mannerly, poised, sensitive, dependable, efficient, mature, obliging, and thorough. Such attitudes may influence the way teachers interact with students and may even influence the way the students view their own gender roles. These stereotypical attitudes are similar to those found in Rosenthal and Jacobson's (1968) research on the effect of teachers' expectations on the achievement and behavior of their students (discussed in Chapter 7).

Sadker and Sadker (1994, 2003) report that from elementary to graduate school, boys are given more teacher attention and encouragement to learn. If a girl gave an incorrect answer when asked, the teacher called on someone else. If a boy gave an incorrect response, he was prompted to discover the right answer, then praised. When a girl gave a correct answer when asked, it was accepted with an "OK." If a girl called out a correct answer without being asked, she was likely to be reprimanded for talking out of turn; if a boy did the same, his answer was likely to be accepted. Thus, teachers tend to socialize boys to be active, assertive learners and girls to be quiet, passive learners. Also, boys were more likely to be encouraged to take math and science classes, thereby becoming advantaged in competing for higher-paying jobs; girls were more likely to be encouraged to take business classes, thereby becoming limited in their career options (AAUW, 1991).

Mass Media
How do the mass media contribute to sex typing?

Screen Media. The mass media affect gender role development. Television and movies portray distinct male and female roles; so do books, magazines, and newspapers. For example, not only do males appear with greater frequency on TV than females, they are also portrayed in a greater variety of occupations than are females and have higher-status jobs (Huston & Wright, 1998; Perse, 2001; Signorielli, 2001). Most of the lawyers, ministers, store owners, and doctors on television are men; women are usually secretaries, nurses, entertainers, teachers, and journalists (Signorielli, 1989, 1993). Even though women in commercials are increasingly being shown as having diverse occupations, they are still portrayed as experts for food products, laundry soap, and beauty aids (Signorielli, 2001).

In interactions between men and women on television, the men are ordinarily more dominant. Women are more passive and less involved in problem solving. For men, the emphasis is on strength, performance, and skill; for women, it is on attractiveness and desirability. That television has the potential for influencing gender role stereotyping was illustrated by several investigations (Condry, 1989) in which boys and girls were interviewed to determine how often they watched certain television programs and how they felt about males and females having certain occupational roles. Those who frequently watched programs in which women were portrayed in nontraditional female roles more often reported that they felt it was appropriate for women to have such occupations than did those who did not watch such programs very often.

Although TV's portrayals of male and female occupational roles are becoming less stereotypical, according to Signorielli (2001), those women most likely to be shown working outside the home are single or formerly married. The consistent image, then, is that the woman who is married cannot mix marriage, child rearing, and having a career. The situations in which women are portrayed as having nontraditional occupations still often show them reverting to traditional stereotypes regarding interpersonal relationships. For example, according to Susan Isaacs (1999), author of *Brave Dames and Wimpettes: What Women Are Really Doing on Page and Screen*, too many "heroines" today are being portrayed as weak or ineffectual (they are "wimpettes") because they give in to the stereotypes imposed on them by their gender. To illustrate, in the movie *Thelma and Louise* (1991), the women were dominated and oppressed by their men. They fought back weakly rather than bravely; they were overemotional and ineffectual, going on a shooting spree for revenge and killing themselves rather than face the consequences. Unlike "wimpettes," "brave dames" take responsibility and don't give up; they stand up to injustice and meet challenges. Examples of "brave dames" are Marge in *Fargo* (1996) and Erin in *Erin Brockovich* (2000). Marge is police chief in the town of Fargo. Though very pregnant, she does her job with dignity, respect, and a sense of humor. Erin is a single mother who, while working for a lawyer to support her family, uncovers serious violations of the Environmental Protection Act. She courageously fights business interests to win settlements for the families bearing the devastating consequences of the careless disposal of toxic wastes.

Although TV and movies have some influence on children's sex typing, children's prior attitudes about gender roles influence the impact of what they attend to. Children with highly stereotyped attitudes focus on traditional role portrayals, whereas children with more flexible attitudes attend equally well to both traditional and nontraditional role portrayals (List, Collins, & Westby, 1983; Signorielli, 1993).

That television affects gender attitudes was demonstrated in Canada, where television was introduced into several towns that had previously been unable to receive TV signals. Children in one town (Notel) had less traditional gender attitudes prior to TV introduction than children from a comparable town with access to multiple TV channels. After two years of television exposure, the children from Notel showed sharp increases in traditional gender attitudes (Kimball, 1986).

In conclusion, portrayals of male and female behavior in the screen media serve as role models for children. Whether the messages about gender will be cultivated in children as they develop depends on the total media experience as well as the attitudes acquired regarding appropriate gender behavior through socialization by significant agents.

Print Media. Gender role stereotypes also appear in the print media—in books and magazines. A research study by sociologist Janet Chafetz (1974) examined the Christmas toy catalogs of the two largest mail-order companies in the United States. Both of the catalogs had boys' and girls' sections. The boys' section featured athletic items and athletic hero dolls, building and technological toys (tractors, spaceships, cars), and war toys. The girls' section featured dolls, household items (dishes, appliances), and beauty aids. In my informal review of mail catalogs for toys from stores, I find this still generally holds true.

Studies of the Caldecott Medal picture books for preschool children, one from 1979 to 1982 (Collins, Ingoldsby, & Dellman, 1984) and another from 1989 to 1992 (Dellman-Jenkins et al., 1993), show an improvement in the representation of females as active, central characters. Males still dominate the world of picture books, however, and are generally presented in more independent, varied, and exciting roles, using productive items; females are generally presented in more dependent, helping, and pleasing roles, using household objects (Turner-Bowker, 1996).

Content analyses of many feature articles and advertisements in contemporary magazines, such as *Seventeen, Sports Illustrated, Teen, Time, Ebony, Newsweek,* and *Vogue,* have found that they contain sex-stereotyped messages (Strasburger & Wilson, 2002). For example, articles for females deal with depending on someone else to solve personal problems, attracting guys, and being appearance-conscious shoppers. Articles for males deal with sports, hobbies, business/finance, and sex.

Audio Media. Stereotypes about men's and women's behavior are visible in rock music videos (Strasburger & Wilson, 2002). Males are depicted as sexually aggressive, rational, demanding, and adventuresome. Females are portrayed as emotional, deceitful, illogical, frivolous, dependent, and passive. One of the most popular themes in popular music is still romantic love (Roberts & Christenson, 2001). However, rock music videos also show violence against women and women as sex objects (Huston & Wright, 1998; Strasburger & Wilson, 2002). In an interview for *Newsweek* (October 9, 2000), Rapper Ja Rule said, "What else can you rap about but money, sex, murder, or pimping? There isn't a whole lot else going on in our world."

Interactive and Multimedia. Most of the action-packed interactive media software is male-dominated and attractive to boys. One study (Dietz, 1998) found that nearly 80% of video games included aggression or violence as part of the strategy or object. In 28% of the games, women were portrayed as sex objects. Females are in stereotypical dependent roles and often are portrayed as sexual objects (Provenzo, 1991).

A critical issue regarding sex typing and the Internet is the pervasiveness of sexual content in ads, e-mail messages, pop-ups, and accessibility to pornographic websites (Strasburger & Wilson, 2002).

Community
What role does the community play in gender role development?

The community influences gender role development through its attitudes regarding what is appropriate behavior for males and females and the gender role models it provides with whom children can identify. The community's attitudes on gender roles affect what behaviors it reinforces and punishes in children. Comments like "That's unladylike" or "Go and stick up for yourself like a man" make a big impression on children. Sometimes community attitudes are expressed by the language used to describe males and females. Are females described by their appearance and men by their actions? Are occupational roles gender-free ("mail carrier," "salesperson")?

If the community has stereotypical attitudes—that women are nurturant and men are problem solvers, for example—the assignment of occupations to one or the other gender will be affected. One study (Arvey & Chapman, 1982) found that when identical applicants were compared, women received higher ratings for jobs as grocery clerks or telephone operators; whereas men were rated more favorably for auto or hardware clerk positions. Today, women still dominate occupations that involve service, nurturing, or teaching; men dominate such occupations as engineering, architecture, law, and medicine, which all involve problem solving (U.S. Bureau of the Census, 2003). Such attitudes, together with the social visibility of men and women in their jobs, affect children's perceptions of and expectations for themselves. The U.S. government has enforced equal opportunity laws, thereby opening up previously restricted fields to women; as a result, perhaps gender stereotypes in the world of work will gradually diminish.

Ethnicity influences children's perceptions and expectations for their gender, as does religion. For example, Asian American females are expected to marry, carry on domestic duties, and bear children even if they work (Sue, 1989). Mexican American women are traditionally subordinate to men. However, as women increasingly become employed outside the home, they generally have more equality in family decisions (Espin, 1993). Religious orientation was found to play an influential role in career choices of high school seniors; those attending religious schools indicated a greater preference for traditional gender occupations than those attending public schools (Rich & Golan, 1992).

Not all communities differentiate male and female roles as is commonly done in the United States. Anthropologists Beatrice Whiting and Carolyn Edwards (1988) studied the interaction patterns of 2- to 10-year-olds in 12 communities around the world to clarify how children were socialized for their respective gender roles. Although they found that, in most of the investigated societies, boys were dominant and aggressive and girls were dependent, compliant, and nurturant, there were cross-cultural differences in the tasks assigned to each gender. For example, in Nyansongo, an agricultural community in Kenya, as in many other East African communities, boys are categorized with girls and women until they reach puberty. Then the pubescent males are assigned "masculine" activities that, when accomplished, become part of the initiation rites into "manhood." Until that time, however, boys participate in caring for their younger siblings and help with domestic chores as needed. Girls, then, have some free time to play during those times when the boys assume their chores. Nyansongo men spend much of the day away from their

This adolescent boy exhibits nonstereotyped gender role behavior by reading to a group of preschool children.

© Michelle Bridwell/PhotoEdit

families. Consequently, fathers have little impact on their children's development. Compared to children from other cultures, Nyansongo children display less stereotypical gender roles.

In the United States, there are cultural variations in the gender role expectations and gender stereotypes of individuals from diverse racial, ethnic, socioeconomic, and sexual orientations (Basow & Rubin, 1999; Lippa, 2005). For example, one study of sex typing and gender role attitudes (Binion, 1990) found that African American women were twice as likely as European American women to describe themselves as androgynous—having both active/instrumental and nurturant/expressive traits. In another study (Vasquez-Nuttall, Romero-Garcia, & DeLeon, 1987), Hispanic American women were found to be more submissive and dependent than European American women. Similar findings also held true for Asian American women (Uba, 1999).

In conclusion, to the extent that a child grows up in a *restrictive* gendered world with strong pressures toward conformity, that child will likely place importance on behaving accordingly. In contrast, to the extent that a child grows up in a *flexible* gendered world emphasizing individual choice, that child is less likely to conform to stereotypical gender behavior (Eccles & Bryan, 1994; Lippa, 2005).

IN PRACTICE

How Do You Determine the Type of Gender Role Models Provided by the Community?

- In general, do mothers/fathers in the community stay home to raise their families, or are they employed outside the home?
- In what activities do most mothers/fathers in the community engage?
- Do children have an opportunity to observe people in their occupations?
- Do men and women who have various occupations come to school and talk to the children?

- Who occupies the positions of leadership in the community (government, church, service organizations, political organizations)?
- In what kinds of activities do boys and girls participate in the community outside of school?
- How are community jobs labeled?

Epilogue

Moral values are the cornerstone of society. Without concepts of "good" and "bad," people could not live with one another. In *Momotaro: Boy of the Peach*, the ogres are making life difficult for the villagers by killing and stealing. Momotaro, who has been treated kindly by his adoptive parents, decides to get rid of the ogres so people can once again live in harmony. He shares his goodness with others—the dog, the monkey, and the pheasant. They, in turn, help him to destroy the evil ogres. The villagers and his parents are most grateful for the law and order returned to their land. So, too, children must be socialized to regulate their behavior, develop moral codes, and exercise their gender roles to live together in society.

Summary

The ability to regulate one's impulses, behavior, and/or emotions until an appropriate time, place, or object is available for expression is referred to as self-regulation, or self-control. Self-regulatory behavior includes the ability to delay gratification, sustain attention to a task, and plan and self-monitor a goal-directed activity. Self-regulatory skills are significantly related to inhibiting antisocial behaviors and to acquiring prosocial ones. Antisocial behavior includes any behavior that harms other people, such as aggression, violence, and crime. Prosocial behavior includes any behavior that benefits other people, such as altruism, sharing, and cooperation.

The major theories explaining the causes of aggression are that it is biologically influenced; it is learned; it is an information-processing impulsive response to frustration; it is a result of social cognitive factors such as peer group pressure, or the reduction of restraining socialization forces; and it is socialized by interacting ecological factors.

Aggression can be studied from a social cognitive perspective (behavior is influenced by how one interprets social cues) and from an ecological perspective (behavior is influenced by the contexts of family, school, peer group, media, and community). Aggression can be inhibited by organizing the environment, establishing standards and consequences for behavior, providing alternative ways of solving problems, providing positive role models, and encouraging discussion and communication.

The theories explaining the causes of altruism are biological (evolution and genetics), learning (reinforcement, modeling, and instruction), cognitive developmental, social interactional, and cultural.

The family influences altruistic behavior. An authoritative parenting style (warmth, firm control, and reasoning) seems to encourage altruistic behavior, whereas an authoritarian parenting style (coldness with physical punishment) seems to foster aggressive behavior. Moralizing and prohibitions with explanations as to why antisocial behavior is unacceptable increase prosocial behavior, as do role-taking opportunities.

The media provide role models for behavior and can influence altruism. Schools can train children to be prosocial through role playing, discussion, and activities. Peer groups provide real experiences in prosocial behavior ("learning by doing") and reinforcement for behaving in certain ways.

The community influences prosocial behavior through cultural values of cooperation and social harmony. Children from traditional, rural cultures who are given the responsibility to perform various household tasks related to the family's economic security exhibit more altruism than children from modern, urban cultures that tend to be more competitive and achievement oriented.

Morals encompass an individual's evaluation of what is right and wrong. They involve acceptance of rules that govern one's behavior toward others. Morality involves feeling, reasoning, and behavior.

One's moral code develops through social interaction and reflects one's level of intellectual development, as well as one's attitudes. It involves awareness of alternatives, the ability to take another's perspective, and the ability to make judgments, as well as feelings about conformity and autonomy.

As children develop, their morality changes. Infants and toddlers do not distinguish right from wrong. Preschoolers and school-agers consider only the act, not the intent. Adolescents consider intent as well as situation. Important theories of moral development are Piaget's (heteronomous and autonomous morality), Kohlberg's (preconventional, conventional, postconventional morality), and Gilligan's (morality of care versus morality of justice). In general, at the lower moral development levels, people act out of concern for personal consequences; at the middle levels, they act out of concern for what others think; at the higher levels, they act to avoid self-condemnation.

Influences on moral development are categorized as situational, individual, and socialization contexts.

Cultural ideology influencing moral development involves the degree of pluralism in a society. Whether the culture stresses individualism or collectivism is also influential in internal or external moral orientations.

An individual's moral development is socially constructed and represents his or her scheme of personal and societal values that include a coordination of emotions, thoughts, and actions.

Gender roles, or sex types, are the qualities that an individual understands as characterizing males and females in his or her culture.

The four main theories of gender role development are psychoanalytic (feelings), social learning or social cognitive (behaving), cognitive developmental (thinking), and gender schema (information processing).

Males and females behave differently. Research confirms that males tend to be more aggressive and exhibit greater visual–spatial ability, and that females tend to exhibit greater verbal ability. Additional research indicates that socialization practices maximize gender differences. As a result, girls and boys are channeled into sex-typed behaviors valued by their culture.

Family dynamics and relationships influence the gender role development of both boys and girls. Parenting practices and sibling sex constellation are factors. Peers exert strong pressure to conform to traditionally stereotypical gender roles via modeling, reinforcement, punishment, and sex-segregated activities. The school, by its differential treatment of males and females, has maximized gender differences. This has occurred through teachers' responses to boys and girls as well as through gender role models in textbooks. The media still tend toward stereotypical portrayals of gender roles. The community's attitudes regarding gender roles and the models provided influence children's sex typing.

Activity

PURPOSE To analyze changes in children's social behavior over time.

1. Separately observe a group (more than two) of preschoolers (ages 3–5) and a group of school-agers (ages 6–12) in a "free play" activity.
2. Record and compare incidents of prosocial (at least one) and antisocial (at least one) activity for

the children in each group—antecedents, behavior, consequences.
   a. What event, item, or interaction preceded the prosocial or antisocial activity (antecedent)?

b. How did the children involved act (behavior)? Describe physical and verbal behavior.

c. What were the outcomes for all involved (consequences)?

3. Analyze similarities and differences in how preschoolers and school-agers interact with one another in a "free play" setting.

4. What factors, other than age, do you think were involved in influencing their behavior?

Related Readings

Bok, S. (1989). *Lying: Moral choice in public and private life.* New York: Vintage.

Damon, W. (1988). *The moral child: Nurturing children's natural moral growth.* New York: Free Press.

Dunn, J. (1988). *The beginnings of social understanding.* Cambridge, MA: Harvard University Press.

Ekman, P. (1989). *Why kids lie: How parents can encourage truthfulness.* New York: Penguin.

Gilligan, C. (1982). *In a different voice: Psychological theory and women's development.* Cambridge, MA: Harvard University Press.

Isaacs, S. (1999). *Brave dames and wimpettes: What women are really doing on page and screen.* New York: Ballantine.

Lippa, R. A. (2005). *Gender, nature, and nurture* (2nd ed.). Mahwah, NJ: Lawrence Erlbaum.

Maccoby, E. E. (1998). *The two sexes: Growing up apart, coming together.* Cambridge, MA: Harvard University Press.

Mussen, P. H., & Eisenberg-Berg, N. (1977). *Roots of caring, sharing, and helping: The development of prosocial behavior in children.* San Francisco: Freeman.

Nucci, L. P. (2001). *Education in the moral domain.* Cambridge, UK: Cambridge University Press.

Olweus, D. (1993). *Bullying at school: What we know and what we can do.* Cambridge, MA: Blackwell.

Osofsky, J. D. (1997). *Children in a violent society.* York, PA: Guilford Press.

Pipher, M. (1994). *Reviving Ophelia: Saving the selves of adolescent girls.* New York: Ballantine.

Pollack, W. S. (1999). *Real boys: Rescuing our sons from the myths of boyhood.* New York: Henry Holt.

Slaby, R. G., et al. (1995). *Early violence prevention: Tools for teachers of young children.* Washington, DC: National Association for the Education of Young Children.

Staub, E. (2003). *The psychology of good and evil: Why children, adults, and groups help and harm others.* New York: Cambridge University Press.

Thorne, B. (1993). *Gender play: Girls and boys in school.* New Brunswick, NJ: Rutgers University Press.

Turiel, E. (2002). *The culture of morality: Social development, context, and conflict.* Cambridge, UK: Cambridge University Press.

Appendix: Core Concepts of Development and Socialization

1. Human development is shaped by a dynamic and continuous interaction between biology and experience.
2. Culture influences every aspect of human development and is reflected in child-rearing beliefs and practices designed to promote healthy adaptation.
3. The growth of self-regulation is a cornerstone of early childhood development that cuts across all domains of behavior.
4. Children are active participants in their own development, reflecting the intrinsic human drive to explore and master one's environment.
5. Human relationships, and the effects of relationships on relationships, are the building blocks of healthy development.
6. The broad range of individual differences among young children often makes it difficult to distinguish normal variations and maturational delays from transient disorders and persistent impairments.
7. The development of children unfolds along individual pathways whose trajectories are characterized by continuities and discontinuities, as well as by a series of significant transitions.
8. Human development is shaped by the ongoing interplay among sources of vulnerability and sources of resilience.
9. The timing of early experiences can matter, but more often than not, the developing child remains vulnerable to risks and open to protective influences throughout the early years of life and into adulthood.
10. The course of development can be altered in early childhood by effective interventions that change the balance between risk and protection, thereby shifting the odds in favor of more adaptive outcomes.

Source: From *Neurons to Neighborhoods: The Science of Early Childhood Development* http://books.nap.edu/catalog/9824.html. Copyright © 2003 National Academy of Sciences. All rights reserved. This executive summary plus thousands more are available at http://www.nap.edu.

Glossary

abuse maltreatment that includes physical abuse, sexual abuse, and psychological or emotional abuse

accommodation a Piagetian term for mental adaptation to one's environment by reconciling differences of experiences

accountability making schools and teachers responsible for student learning or achievement outcomes

achieved status social class, rank, or position determined by education, occupation, income, and/or place of residence

achievement motivation the motivation to achieve mastery of challenging tasks

adaptation the modification of an organism or its behavior to make it more fit for existence under the conditions of its environment

advocacy speaking or writing in support of a person, a group, or a cause

affective having to do with feelings or emotions

aggression unprovoked attack, fight, or quarrel

alcoholism a chronic, progressive, and potentially fatal disease characterized by excessive tolerance for alcohol and by physical dependence and/or pathologic organ changes

altruism voluntary actions that are intended to help or benefit another person or group of people without the actor's anticipation of external rewards

antisocial behavior any behavior that harms other people, such as aggression, violence, and crime

apprenticeship a process in which a novice is guided by an expert to participate in and master tasks

ascribed status social class, rank, or position determined by family lineage, gender, birth order, or skin color

assimilation a Piagetian term for mental adaptation to one's environment by incorporating experiences

assumptive reality a theory about reality assumed to be true without examining or evaluating contradictory data

attachment an affectional tie that one person forms to another person, binding them together in space and enduring over time

attitude a tendency to respond positively (favorably) or negatively (unfavorably) to certain persons, objects, or situations

attributions explanations for one's performance

authentic assessment evaluation based on real performance, rather than test performance, showing mastery of a task

authoritarian a style of parent-centered parenting characterized by unquestioning obedience to authority

authoritative a style of democratic parenting in which authority is based on competence or expertise

autocracy a society in which one person has unlimited power over others

autonomous morality Piaget's stage of moral development in which children realize that rules are arbitrary agreements that can be changed by those who have to follow them

behavior what one does or how one acts in response to a stimulus

behaviorism the theory that observed behavior, rather than what exists in the mind, provides the only valid data for psychology

bilingual/multicultural education education in the student's native language as well as English, respect for the student's culture and ethnicity, and enhancement of the student's self-concept

binuclear family family pattern in which children are part of two homes and two family groups

Caldecott Medal award given yearly for the most distinguished picture book for children

care moral perspective views people in terms of their connectedness with others; others' welfare is intrinsically connected to one's own

charter school a school formed by a group of parents, teachers, or other community members with a shared educational philosophy, that is authorized and funded by a public school district

chronosystem temporal changes in ecological systems producing new conditions that affect development

classism the differential treatment of people because of their class background and the reinforcing of those differences through values and practices of societal institutions

cliques friends who view themselves as mutually connected and do things together

cognitive conceit Elkind's term for children in Piaget's stage of concrete operations who put too much faith in their reasoning ability and cleverness

cognitively oriented curriculum a curriculum that attempts to blend the virtues of purposeful teaching with open-ended, child-initiated activities

collectivism emphasis on interdependent relations, social responsibilities, and the well-being of the group

community a group of people sharing fellowship and common interests; a group of people living in the same geographic area who are bound together politically and economically

community ecology the psychological and practical relationships between humans and their social, as well as physical, environment

competence involves behavior that is socially responsible, independent, friendly, cooperative, dominant, achievement-oriented, and purposeful

competitive goal structure students working against each other to achieve goals that only a few students can attain

concrete operations the third stage in Piaget's theory of cognitive development (ages 7–11), in which the child can apply logical, systematic principles to specific experiences, but cannot distinguish between assumptions or hypotheses and facts or reality

contagion the phenomenon in which an individual exposed to a suggestion will act on it

conventional level Kohlberg's stages of moral reasoning in which the individual can look beyond personal consequences and consider others' perspectives

cooperative goal structure students working together to accomplish shared goals

crowds loosely organized reference groups of cliques

cultural assimilation the process whereby a minority cultural group takes on the characteristics of the dominant cultural group

cultural pluralism mutual appreciation and understanding of various cultures and coexistence in society of different languages, religious beliefs, and lifestyles

culture the knowledge, beliefs, art, morals, law, customs, and traditions acquired by humans as members of society

curriculum the goals and objections of an educational program, the teacher's role, the equipment and materials, the space arrangement, the kinds of activities, and the way they are scheduled

day care the care given to children by persons other than parents during the parts of the day that parents are absent

deductive reasoning reasoning from a general principle to a specific case, or from a premise to a logical conclusion

democracy a society in which those ruled have equal power with those who rule

desensitization the gradual reduction in response to a stimulus after repeated exposure

developmental appropriateness involves knowledge of children's normal growth patterns and individual differences

developmental interaction curriculum a curriculum that is individualized in relation to each child's stage of development while providing many opportunities for children to interact with peers and adults

developmental task a task that lies between an individual need and a societal demand

direct instruction curriculum a curriculum based on behaviorist principles

disability reduction in the functioning of a particular body part or organ, or its absence

discipline involves punishment, correction, and training to develop self-control

ecology the science of interrelationships between organisms and their environments

economics the production, distribution, and consumption of goods and services

egalitarian family family in which both sides of the extended family are regarded as equal

egocentrism the cognitive inability to look at the world from any point of view other than one's own

empowerment enabling individuals to have control over resources affecting them

equilibrium a Piagetian term for the state of balance between assimilation and accommodation, thereby allowing knowledge to be incorporated

ethnicity an attribute of membership in a group in which members identify themselves by national origin, culture, race, or religion

exosystem settings in which children do not actually participate, but which affect them in one of their microsystems (for example, parents' jobs, the school board, the city council)

experience-dependent the neural connections that develop in response to experience

experience-expectant the neural connections that develop under genetic influence, independent of experience, activity, or stimulation

extended day care care provided for children before or after school hours or during vacations

extended family relatives of the nuclear family who are economically and emotionally dependent on each other

external locus of control perception that others or outside forces are responsible for one's fate

extinction the gradual disappearance of a learned behavior following the removal of the reinforcement

family any two or more related people living in one household

family of orientation the family into which one is born

family of procreation the family that develops when one marries and has children

feedback evaluative information, both positive and negative, about one's behavior

fixation a Freudian term referring to arrested development

folktale a legendary or mythical story originating and handed down among the common people

formal operations the fourth stage in Piaget's theory of cognitive development (ages 11 and up), in which the child can think logically about abstract ideas and hypotheses as well as concrete facts

gang a group of people who form an alliance for a common purpose and engage in unlawful or criminal activity

gemeinschaft communal, cooperative, close, intimate, and informal interpersonal relationships

gender role the qualities that an individual understands to characterize males and females in his or her culture

generativity interest in establishing and guiding the next generation

genotype the total composite of hereditary instructions coded in the genes at the moment of conception

gesellschaft associative, practical, objective, and formal interpersonal relationships

goodness-of-fit accommodation of parenting styles to children's temperaments

guidance involves direction, demonstration, supervision, and influence

handicap something that hampers a person; a disadvantage, a hindrance

handicapism assumptions and practices that promote the deferential and unequal treatment of people because they are different physically, mentally, or behaviorally

heteronomous morality Piaget's stage of moral development in which children think of rules as moral absolutes that cannot be changed

high-context macrosystem culture generally characterized by intuitiveness, emotionality, cooperation, group identity, and tradition

humanism a system of beliefs concerned with the interests and ideals of humans rather than of the natural or spiritual world

ideology concepts about human life and behavior

imaginary audience the beliefs that others are as concerned with one's behavior and appearance as one is oneself

impairment physical damage or deterioration

incest sexual relations between persons closely related

inclusion the educational philosophy that all children are entitled to participate fully in their school and community

individualism emphasis on individual fulfillment and choice

individualized education program (IEP) a form of communication between school and family, developed by the group of people (teacher, parent, and other involved personnel) responsible for the education of a child with special needs

individualized goal structure one student's achievement of the goal is unrelated to other students' achievement of that goal

inductive reasoning reasoning from particular facts or individual cases to a general conclusion

information processing the way an individual attends to, perceives, interprets, remembers, and acts on events or situations

internal locus of control perception that one is responsible for one's own fate

justice moral perspective emphasizes the rights of the individual; when individual rights conflict, equitable rules of justice must prevail

laissez-faire a policy of letting people do as they please; permissive

latchkey children children who carry their own key and let themselves into their homes

learned helplessness the perception, acquired through negative experiences, that effort has no effect on outcomes

learner-directed curriculum a curriculum in which the learning activities emerge from individual interests and teacher guidance

learning style a consistent pattern of behavior and performance by which an individual approaches educational experiences

literacy the ability to communicate through reading and writing

locus of control one's attribution of performance, or perception of responsibility for success or failure; may be internal or external

low-context macrosystem culture generally characterized by rationality, practicality, competition, individuality, and progress

macrosystem the society and subculture to which the developing person belongs, with particular reference to the belief systems, lifestyles, patterns of social interaction, and life changes

magnet school a public school that offers special educational programs, such as science, music, or performing arts, and draws students from different neighborhoods by choice

maltreatment intentional harm to or endangerment of a child

marriage a legal contract with certain rights and obligations

mass media newspapers, magazines, books, radio, television, movies, videos, and other means of communication that reach large audiences via an impersonal medium between the sender and the receiver

mastery motivation the inborn motive to explore, understand, and control one's environment

matriarchal family family in which the mother has formal authority and dominance

maturation developmental changes associated with the biological process of aging

melting pot the idea that society should socialize diverse groups to blend into a common culture

mesosystem linkages and interrelationships between two or more of a person's microsystems (for example, home and school, school and community)

microsystem activities and relationships with significant others experienced by a developing person in a particular small setting such as family, school, peer group, or community

modeling a form of imitative learning that occurs by observing another person (the model) perform a behavior and experience its consequence

modern society a society that looks to the present for ways to behave and is thus responsive to change

Montessori curriculum a curriculum based on individual self-directed learning with the teacher as facilitator; materials provide exercises in daily living, sensory development, and academic development

morality of constraint behavior based on respect for persons in authority

morality of cooperation behavior based on mutual understanding between equals

morals an individual's evaluation of what is right and wrong

motives needs or emotions that cause a person to act

negative reinforcement the termination of an unpleasant condition following a desired response

neglect maltreatment involving abandonment, lack of supervision, improper feeding, lack of adequate medical or dental care, inappropriate dress, uncleanliness, and lack of safety

Newbery Medal award given yearly for the most distinguished contribution to American literature for children

norms rules, patterns, or standards that express cultural values and reflect how individuals are supposed to behave

nuclear family a family consisting of a husband and wife and their children

operant producing an effect

parenting the implementation of a series of decisions about the socialization of children

patriarchal family family in which the father has formal authority and dominance

peers individuals who are of approximately the same gender, age, and social status and who share interests

perception a biological construct that involves interpretation of stimuli from the brain

permissive a style of child-centered parenting characterized by a lack of directives or authority

personal agency the realization that one's actions cause outcomes

physical abuse maltreatment involving deliberate harm to the child's body

play behavior enjoyed for its own sake

pluralism the presence of more than one belief system

political ideology theories pertaining to government

positive reinforcement a reward, or pleasant consequence, given for desired behavior

postconventional level Kohlberg's stages of moral reasoning in which the individual considers and weighs the values behind various consequences from various points of view

preconventional level Kohlberg's stages of moral reasoning in which the individual considers and weighs the personal consequences of the behavior

prejudice an attitude involving prejudgment; the application of a previously formed judgment to some person, object, or situation

preoperational the second stage in Piaget's theory of cognitive development (ages 2–7), in which the child uses symbols to represent objects, makes judgments based on appearances, and believes that everyone has the same viewpoint as he or she

preventive services programs that seek to lessen the stresses and strains of life resulting from social and technological changes and to avert problems

prosocial behavior behavior that benefits other people, such as altruism, sharing, and cooperation

Protestant ethic belief in individualism, thrift, self-sacrifice, efficiency, personal responsibility, and productivity

psychological or emotional abuse maltreatment involving a destructive pattern of continual attack by an adult on a child's development of self and social competence, including rejecting, isolating, terrorizing, ignoring, and corrupting

punishment physically or psychologically painful stimuli or the temporary withdrawal of pleasant stimuli when undesirable behavior occurs

reality testing testing assumptions against facts

reasoning giving explanations or causes for an act

rehabilitative services programs that enable or restore people's ability to participate in the community

reinforcement an object or event that is presented following a behavior and that serves to increase the likelihood that the behavior will occur again

religion a unified system of beliefs and practices relative to sacred things

resilience the ability to recover from, or adjust easily to, misfortune or change

risk endangerment; vulnerability to negative outcomes

rites of passage rituals that signify changes in individuals' status as they move through the cycle of life

ritual a ceremonial observation of a prescribed rule or custom

routines repetitive acts or established procedures

selective attention choosing stimuli from one's environment to notice, observe, and consider

self-concept an individual's perception of his/her identity as distinct from others

self-efficacy the belief that one can master a situation and produce positive outcomes

self-esteem the value one places on his/her identity

self-regulation the ability to control one's impulses, behavior, and/or emotions until an appropriate time, place, or object is available for expression

sensorimotor the first stage of Piaget's theory of cognitive development (ages $1\frac{1}{2}$–2), in which the child uses senses and motor abilities to interact with the environment and understands only the here and now

sex typing classification into gender roles based on biological sex

sexual abuse maltreatment in which a person forces, tricks, or threatens a child in order to have sexual contact with him or her

shaping the systematic immediate reinforcement of successive approximations of the desired behavior until the desired behavior occurs and is maintained

social cognition conceptions and reasoning about people, the self, relations between people, social group's roles and rules, and the relation of such conceptions to social behavior

social competence behavior informed by an understanding of others' feelings and intentions, the ability to respond appropriately, and knowledge of the consequences of one's actions

social support resources (tangible, intellectual, social, emotional) provided by others in times of need

socialization the process by which individuals acquire the knowledge, skills, and character traits that enable them to participate as effective members of groups and society

sociocentrism the ability to understand and relate to the views and perspectives of others

socioeconomic status rank or position within a society, based on social and economic factors

sociometry techniques used to measure patterns of acceptance, neglect, and rejection among members of a group

sociotherapy an intervention to help children who have trouble making and keeping friends learn to relate to others

standard a level or grade of excellence regarded as a goal or a measure of adequacy

standardized tests tests in which an individual is compared to a norm on scientifically selected items

stereotype an oversimplified representation of members of a particular group

stress any demand that exceeds a person's ability to cope

supportive services programs that maintain the health, education, and welfare of the community

symbols acts or objects that have come to be generally accepted as standing for something else

tabula rasa the mind before impressions are recorded on it by experience; a blank slate

teacher-directed curriculum a curriculum in which the learning activities are planned by the teacher for all the children

temperament the innate characteristics that determine an individual's sensitivity to various experiences and responsiveness to patterns of social interaction

theory an organized set of statements that explains observations, integrates different facts or events, and predicts future outcomes

tradition customs, stories, and beliefs handed down from generation to generation

traditional society a society that relies on customs handed down from past generations as ways to behave

transductive reasoning reasoning from one particular fact or case to another similar fact or case

uninvolved a style of insensitive, indifferent parenting with few demands or rules

values qualities or beliefs that are viewed as desirable or important

values clarification the process of discovering what is personally worthwhile or desirable in life

violence behaviors that intentionally threaten, attempt, or inflict harm on others

zone of proximal development (ZPD) Vygotsky's term for the space between what a learner can do independently and what he or she can do while participating with more capable others

References

Aaronson, L. S., & MacNee, C. L. (1989). Tobacco, alcohol and caffeine use during pregnancy. *Journal of Obstetrics, Gynecology and Neonatal Nursing, 18*, 279–287.

Aber, J. L., Brown, J. L., & Jones, S. M. (2003). Developmental trajectories toward violence in middle childhood: Course, demographic differences, and response to school-based intervention. *Developmental Psychology, 39*(2), 324–348.

Aboud, F. (1988). *Children and prejudice*. Cambridge, MA: Basil Blackwell.

Abramovitch, R., & Grusec, J. E. (1978). Peer interaction in a natural setting. *Child Development*, 49, 60–65.

Adams, G. R., & Crane, P. (1980). Assessment of parents' and teachers' expectations of preschool children's social preferences for attractive or unattractive children and adults. *Child Development, 51*, 224–231.

Adams, G. R., Gullotta, T. P., & Markstrom-Adams, C. (1994). *Adolescent life experiences* (3rd ed.). Pacific Grove, CA: Brooks/Cole.

Adler, P. A., & Adler, P. (1998) *Peer power: Preadolescent culture and identity*. New Brunswick, NJ: Rutgers University Press.

Agne, K. J. (1992). Caring: The expert teacher's edge. *Educational Horizons, 70*(3), 120–124.

Ainsworth, M. D. S. (1973). The development of infant–mother attachment. In B. M. Caldwell & H. N. Ricciuti (Eds.), *Review of child development research* (Vol. 3). Chicago: University of Chicago Press.

Ainsworth, M. D. S. (1979). Infant–mother attachment. *American Psychologist, 34*, 932–937.

Ainsworth, M. D. S. (1982). Attachment: Retrospect and prospect. In C. M. Parkes & J. Stevenson-Hinde (Eds.), *The place of attachment in human behavior*. New York: Basic Books.

Ainsworth, M. D. S., & Bell, S. M. (1970). Attachment, exploration, and separation: Illustrated by the behavior of one-year-olds in a strange situation. *Child Development, 41*, 49–67.

Ainsworth, M. D. S., Blehar, M., Waters, E., & Wall, S. (1978). *Patterns of attachment: A psychological study of the strange situation*. Hillsdale, NJ: Erlbaum.

Alexander, J. E., & Tate, M. A. (1999). *Web wisdom*. Mahwah, NJ: Erlbaum.

Alsaker, F. D. (1992). Pubertal timing, overweight, and psychological adjustment. *Journal of Early Adolescence, 12*, 396–419.

Amato, P. (1998). More than money? Men's contributions to their children's lives. In A. Booth & A. C. Crouter (Eds.), *Men in families. When do they get involved? What difference does it make*? Mahwah, NJ: Erlbaum.

Amato, P. R. (2000). The consequences of divorce for adults and children. *Journal of Marriage and the Family, 62*, 1269–1287.

American Academy of Child and Adolescent Psychiatry. (1997a). *Facts for families: Children of alcoholics*. http://www.aacap.org/

American Academy of Child and Adolescent Psychiatry. (1997b). *Facts for families: The influence of music and rock videos*. http://www.aacap.org/

American Academy of Child and Adolescent Psychiatry. (1999). *Facts for families: The adopted child*. http://www.aacap.org/

American Academy of Pediatrics. (1995). The role of schools in combating substance abuse. *Pediatrics, 95*(5), 784–785.

American Academy of Pediatrics. (1996). The impact of music lyrics and music videos on children and youth. Policy Statement. *Pediatrics, 98*(6), 1219–1221.

American Academy of Pediatrics. (2002). *Peer groups and cliques*. http://www.aap.org/

American Association of University Women. (1991). *How schools shortchange girls*. Washington, DC: American Association of University Women Educational Foundation.

Anastasiow, N. J. (1973). *Educational psychology: A contemporary view*. New York: Random House.

Anderson, D. R., Huston, A. C., Schmitt, K. L., Linebarger, D. L., & Wright, J. C. (2001). Early childhood television viewing and adolescent behavior: The recontact study. *Monographs of the Society for Research in Child Development, 66*(1, Serial No. 264).

Anderssen, N., Amlie, C., & Ytteroy, E. A. (2002). Outcomes for children with lesbian or gay parents: A review of studies from 1978 to 2000. *Scandanavian Journal of Psychology, 43*(4), 335–351.

Andreasen, M. (2001). Evolution in the family's use of television: An overview. In J. Bryant & J. A. Bryant (Eds.), *Television and the American family* (2nd ed.). Mahwah, NJ: Erlbaum.

Apter, A., Galatzer, A., Beth-Halachmi, N., & Laron, Z. (1981). Self-image in adolescents with delayed puberty and growth retardation. *Journal of Youth and Adolescence, 10,* 501–505.

Arensberg, C. M., & Niehoff, A. H. (1975). American cultural values. In J. P. Spradley & M. A. Rynkiewich (Eds.), *The Nacirema: Reading on American culture*. Boston: Little, Brown.

Aries, P. (1962). *Centuries of childhood: A social history of family life.* New York: Knopf.

Arnett, J. (1991). Adolescents and heavy metal music: From the mouths of metal heads. *Youth and Society, 33*(1), 76–98.

Aronfreed, J. (1968). *Conduct and conscience: The socialization of internalized control over behavior.* New York: Academic Press.

Aronson, E., & Patenoe, S. (1996). *The jigsaw classroom: Building cooperation in the classroom.* Reading, MA: Addison-Wesley.

Arvey, R. D., & Chapman, J. E. (1982). The employment interview. *Personnel Psychology, 25,* 281–290.

Asch, S. E. (1958). Effects of group pressure upon the modification and distortion of judgments. In E. E. Maccoby, T. M. Newcomb, & E. L. Hartley (Eds.), *Readings in social psychology.* New York: Holt, Rinehart & Winston.

Asendorpf, J. B., & Baudoniere, P. (1993). Self-awareness and other-awareness: Mirror self-recognition and synchronic imitation among unfamiliar peers. *Developmental Psychology, 29,* 88–95.

Asher, S. R. (1982). Some kids are nobody's best friend. *Today's Education, 71*(1), 23.

Asher, S. R., & Coie, J. D. (1990). *Peer rejection in childhood.* New York: Cambridge University Press.

Asher, S. R., Gottman, J. M., & Oden, S. L. (1977). Children's friendships in school settings. In E. M. Hetherington & R. D. Parke (Eds.), *Contemporary readings in child psychology.* New York: McGraw-Hill.

Aslin, R. N., Jusczyk, P. W., & Pisoni, D. B. (1998). Speech and auditory processing during infancy: Constraints on and precursors to language. In W. Damon (Ed.), *Handbook of child psychology* (5th ed., Vol. 2). New York: Wiley.

Atkin, C., & Gibson, W. (1978). *Children's nutrition learning from television advertising.* Unpublished manuscript, Michigan State University, East Lansing.

Atkinson, A. H., & Green, V. P. (1990). Cooperative learning: The teacher's role. *Childhood Education, 67*(1), 8–11.

Atkinson, J. W. (1964). *An introduction to motivation.* Princeton, NJ: Van Nostrand.

Ausubel, D. P. (1957). *Theory and problems of child development.* New York: Grune & Stratton.

Avery, C. D. (1971). A psychologist looks at the issue of public versus residential school placement for the blind. In R. L. Jones (Ed.), *Problems and issues in the education of exceptional children.* Boston: Houghton Mifflin.

Azar, S.T. (2002). Parenting and child maltreatment. In M. H. Bornstein (Ed.), *Handbook of parenting* (2nd ed., Vol. 4). Mahwah, NJ: Erlbaum.

Azrin, N. H., & Foxx, R. H. (1976). *Toilet training in less than a day.* New York: Basic Books.

Bagwell, C. L., Coie, J. D., Terry, R. A., & Lochman, J. E. (2000). Peer clique participation and social status in preadolescence. *Merrill-Palmer Quarterly, 46*(2), 280–305.

Bagwell, C. L., Newcomb, A. F., & Bukowski, W. M. (2000). Preadolescent friendship and peer rejection as predictors of adult adjustment. In W. Craig (Ed.), *Childhood social development.* Malden, MA: Blackwell.

Bain, S., Holliman, B., & McCallum, R. S. (1989). Children's self-predictions and teachers' predictions of basic concept mastery: Effects of socioeconomic status, locus of control, and achievement. *Journal of Psychoeducational Assessment, 7,* 235–245.

Baker, A. K., Barthelemy, K. J., & Kurdek, L. A. (1993). The relation between fifth and sixth graders' peer-rated classroom social status and their perceptions of family and neighborhood factors. *Journal of Applied Developmental Psychology, 14,* 547–556.

Baker, C. H., & Young, P. (1960). Feedback during training and retention of motor skills. *Canadian Journal of Psychology, 14,* 257–264.

Balk, D. E. (1995). *Adolescent development.* Pacific Grove, CA: Brooks/Cole.

Ball, S. J., & Bogatz, G. (1970). *The first year of* Sesame Street: *An evaluation.* Princeton, NJ: Educational Testing Service.

Ballantine, J. H., & Spade, J. Z. (2004). *Schools and society: A sociological approach to education* (2nd ed.). Belmont, CA: Wadsworth.

Bandura, A. (1965). Influence of models' reinforcement contingencies on the acquisition of imitative responses. *Journal of Personality and Social Psychology, 1,* 589–595.

Bandura, A. (1973). *Aggression: A social learning analysis.* Englewood Cliffs, NJ: Prentice-Hall.

Bandura, A. (1974). Behavior theory and the models of man. *American Psychologist, 29,* 859–869.

Bandura, A. (1986). *Social foundations of thought and action: A social cognitive theory*. Englewood Cliffs, NJ: Prentice-Hall.

Bandura, A. (1989). Social cognitive theory. In R. Vasta (Ed.), *Annals of child development: Vol. 6. Six theories of child development: Revised formulations and current issues*. Greenwich, CT: JAI Press.

Bandura, A. (1991). Social cognitive theory of moral thought and action. In W. M. Kurtines & J. L. Gewirtz (Eds.), *Handbook of moral behavior and development* (Vol. 1). Hillsdale, NJ: Erlbaum.

Bandura, A. (1997). *Self-efficacy: The exercise of control*. New York: Freeman.

Bandura, A. (2000). Self-efficacy. In A. Kazdin (Ed.), *Encyclopedia of mental health* (Vol. 3). San Diego: Academic Press.

Bandura, A. (2001). Social cognitive theory: An agentic perspective. *Annual Review of Psychology, 52*, 1–26.

Bandura, A., Ross, D., & Ross, S. (1963). Imitation of film-mediated aggressive models. *Journal of Abnormal and Social Psychology, 66*, 3–11.

Bandura, A., Ross, D., & Ross, S. (1965). A comparative test of status, envy, social power, and secondary reinforcement theories of identificatory learning. *Journal of Abnormal and Social Psychology, 67*, 527–534.

Bandura, A., & Walters, R. H. (1963). *Social learning and personality development*. New York: Holt, Rinehart & Winston.

Bangert-Drowns, R. L., Kulik, C. C., Kulik, J. A., & Morgan, M. (1991). The instructional effect of feedback in test-like events. *Review of Educational Research, 61*, 213–238.

Banks, J. A. (2002). *Introduction to multicultural education* (3rd ed.). Boston: Allyn and Bacon.

Barber, B. R. (1996). *Jihad vs. McWorld: How globalism and tribalism are reshaping the world*. New York: Ballantine Books.

Barclay, K., Benelli, C., & Curtis, A. (1995). Literacy begins at birth: What caregivers can learn from parents of children who read early. *Young Children, 50*(4), 24–28.

Barker, R. G., & Gump, P. G. (1964). *Big school, small school: High school size and student behavior*. Stanford, CA: Stanford University Press.

Barnett, D., Manley, J., & Cicchetti, D. (1993). Defining child maltreatment: The interface between policy and research. In D. Cicchetti & S. Toth (Eds.), *Child abuse, child development, and social policy*. Norwood, NJ: Ablex.

Barnett, R. C., & Hyde, J. S. (2001). Women, men, and family: An expansionist theory. *American Psychologist, 56*(10), 781–796.

Baron, R. (1970). *Anonymity, deindividuation and aggression*. Unpublished doctoral dissertation, University of Minnesota.

Barry, H., Child, I. L., & Bacon, M. K. (1957). Relation of child training to subsistence economy. *American Anthropologist, 61*, 51–63.

Bar-Tal, D., Raviv, A., & Lesser, T. (1980). The development of altruistic behavior: Empirical evidence. *Developmental Psychology, 16*, 516–524.

Basow, S. A. (1992). *Gender stereotypes and roles* (3rd ed.). Pacific Grove, CA: Brooks/Cole.

Basow, S. A., & Rubin, L. R. (1999). Gender influence on adolescent development. In N. G. Johnson, M. C. Roberts, & J. Worell (Eds.), *Beyond appearance: A new look at adolescent girls*. Washington, DC: American Psychological Association.

Baumrind, D. (1966). Effects of authoritative parental control on child behavior. *Child Development, 37*, 887–907.

Baumrind, D. (1967). Child care practices anteceding three patterns of preschool behavior. *Genetic Psychology Monographs, 74*, 43–88.

Baumrind, D. (1971). Current patterns of parental authority. *Developmental Psychology, 4*, 1–101.

Baumrind, D. (1973). The development of instrumental competence through socialization. In A. Pick (Ed.), *Minnesota symposium on child psychology* (Vol. 7). Minneapolis: University of Minnesota Press.

Baumrind, D. (1977, April). *Socialization determinants of personal agency*. Paper presented at the biennial meeting of the Society for Research in Child Development, New Orleans.

Baumrind, D. (1989). Rearing competent children. In W. Damon (Ed.), *Child development today and tomorrow*. San Francisco: Jossey-Bass.

Baumrind, D. (1991). Effective parenting during the early adolescent transition. In P. A. Cowan & E. M. Hetherington (Eds.), *Family transitions*. Hillsdale, NJ: Erlbaum.

Baumrind, D., & Thompson, R. A. (2002). The ethics of parenting. In M. H. Bornstein (Ed.), *Handbook of parenting* (2nd ed., Vol. 5). Mahwah, NJ: Erlbaum.

Bauserman, R. (2002). Child adjustment in joint custody versus sole custody arrangements. A meta-analytic review. *Journal of Family Psychology, 16*(1), 91–102.

Beane, J. A. (1991). Sorting out the self-esteem controversy. *Educational Leadership, 49*(1), 25–30.

Bednar, R. L., Wells, M. G., & Peterson, S. R. (1989). *Self-esteem*. Washington, DC: American Psychological Association.

Beez, W. V. (1968). Influence of biased psychological reports on teacher behavior and pupil performance. *Proceedings of the 75th APA Annual Convention*. Washington, DC: American Psychological Association.

Begley, S. (1997, Spring/Summer). How to build a baby's brain. *Newsweek*, 28–32.

Behrman, R. E. (Ed.). (1997a). Executive summary: Children and poverty. *The Future of Children, 7*(2).

Behrman, R. E. (Ed.). (1997b). Executive summary: Welfare to work. *The Future of Children, 7*(1).

Behrman, R. E. (Ed.). (1999). Executive summary: When school is out. *The Future of Children, 9*(2).

Behrman, R. E. (Ed.). (2002). Children and welfare reform: Analysis and recommendations. *The Future of Children, 12*(1), 5–25.

Bell, P. A., Greene, T. C., Fisher, J. D., & Baum, A. (2001). *Environmental psychology* (5th ed.). Fort Worth: Harcourt.

Belle, D. (1989). Studying children's social networks and social supports. In D. Belle (Ed.), *Children's social networks and social supports*. New York: Wiley.

Belle, D. (1999). *The after-school lives of children: Alone and with others while parents work*. Mahwah, NJ: Erlbaum.

Belsky, J. (1988). The "effects" of infant day care reconsidered. *Early Childhood Research Quarterly, 3*, 235–272.

Belsky, J. (1992). Consequences of child care for children's development: A deconstructionist view. In A. Booth (Ed.), *Childcare in the 1990s: Trends and consequences*. Hillsdale, NJ: Erlbaum.

Belsky, J. (1993). Etiology of child maltreatment: A developmental–ecological analysis. *Psychological Bulletin, 114*, 413–434.

Belsky, J., & Rovine, M. (1988). Nonmaternal care in the first year of life and infant–parent attachment security. *Child Development, 59*, 157–167.

Bem, S. L. (1981). Gender schema theory: A cognitive account of sex-typing. *Psychological Review, 88*, 354–364.

Bengston, V. L. (2001). Beyond the nuclear family: The increasing importance of multigenerational bonds. *Journal of Marriage and Family, 63*, 1–16.

Bengtsson, H. (2003). Children's cognitive appaisal of others' distressed and positive experiences. *International Journal of Behavioral Development, 27*, 457–466.

Bennett, C. I. (2003). *Comprehensive multicultural education: Theory and practice* (5th ed.). Boston: Allyn and Bacon.

Bennett, W. J. (1993). *The book of virtues: A treasury of great moral stories*. New York: Simon & Schuster.

Bereiter, C., & Engelmann, S. (1966). *Teaching disadvantaged children in the preschool*. Englewood Cliffs, NJ: Prentice-Hall.

Berenda, R. (1950). *The influence of the group on the judgment of children*. New York: King's Crown Press.

Berg, M., & Medrich, E. A. (1980). Children in four neighborhoods: The physical environment and its effects on play and play patterns. *Environment and Behavior, 12*(3), 320–346.

Berger, E. H. (2003). *Parents as partners in education: Families and schools working together* (6th ed.). Englewood Cliffs, NJ: Prentice-Hall.

Berk, L. E. (2003). *Child development* (6th ed.). Needham Heights, MA: Allyn and Bacon.

Berk, L. E., & Winsler, A. (1995). *Scaffolding children's learning: Vygotsky and early childhood education*. Washington, DC: National Association for the Education of Young Children.

Berndt, T. J. (1979). Developmental changes in conformity to peers and parents. *Developmental Psychology, 15*, 608–616.

Berndt, T. J. (1983). Correlates and causes of sociometric status in childhood: A commentary on six current studies of popular, rejected and neglected children. *Merrill-Palmer Quarterly, 29*, 439–448.

Berndt, T. J., & Ladd, G. W. (1989). *Peer relationships in child development*. New York: Wiley.

Bernhard, J. K., Lefebvre, M. L., Kilbride, K. M., Chud, G., & Lange, R. (1998). Troubled relationships in early childhood education: Parent–teacher interactions in ethnoculturally diverse childcare settings. *Early Education and Development, 9*, 5–28.

Berns, R. (1981). *When handicaps come in handy*. Washington, DC: Department of Health, Education and Welfare, National Institute of Education, Educational Resources Information Center. (ED 208621)

Bernstein, B. (1961). Social class and linguistic development: A theory of social learning. In A. H. Halsey, J. Floud, & C. A. Anderson (Eds.), *Education, economy and society*. New York: Free Press.

Berry, G. L., & Asamen, J. K. (2001). Television, children, and multicultural awareness: Comprehending the medium in a complex multimedia society. In D. G. Singer & J. L. Singer (Eds.), *Handbook of children and the media*. Thousand Oaks, CA: Sage.

Best, R. (1983). *We've all got scars: What boys and girls learn in elementary school*. Bloomington: Indiana University Press.

Bettelheim, B. (1976). *The uses of enchantment: The meaning and importance of fairy tales*. New York: Random House.

Beyers, J. M., Bates, J. E., Pettit, G. S., & Dodge, K. A. (2003). Neighborhood structure, parenting processes, and the development of youths externalizing behaviors: A multilevel analysis. *American Journal of Community Psychology, 36*, 35–53.

Bhavnagri, N. P. (1997). The cultural context of caregiving. *Childhood Education, 74*(1), 2–7.

Bigler, R. S., Brown, C. S., & Markell, M. (2001). When groups are not created equal: Effects of group status on the formation of intergroup attitudes in children. *Child Development, 72,* 1151–1162.

Bigler, R. S., & Liben, L. S. (1990). The role of attitudes and interventions in gender-schematic processing. *Child Development, 61,* 1440–1452.

Bigner, J. (1979). *Parent–child relations.* New York: Macmillan.

Biklen, D., & Bogdan, R. (1977). Media portrayals of disabled people: A study in stereotypes. *Interracial Books for Children Bulletin, 6,* 4–9.

Biller, H. B. (1993). *Fathers and families: Paternal factors in child development.* Westport, CT: Auburn House.

Binion, V. J. (1990). Psychological androgyny: A black female perspective. *Sex Roles, 22,* 487–507.

Biskind, P. (1983). *Seeing is believing: How Hollywood taught us to stop worrying and love the fifties.* New York: Pantheon Books.

Bjorklund, D. F. (2005). *Children's thinking* (4th ed.). Belmont, CA: Wadsworth.

Black, C. (1991). *It will never happen to me!* (reissue ed.). Denver: M.A.C.

Blake, J. (1989). *Family size and achievement.* Berkeley: University of California Press.

Blas, A. (1990). Kohlberg's theory and moral development. In D. Schrader (Ed.), *New directions for child development* (No. 47). San Francisco: Jossey-Bass.

Block, J. H. (1973). Conceptions of sex role: Some cross-cultural and longitudinal perspectives. *American Psychologist, 28,* 512.

Block, J. H. (1984). The influence of differential socialization on the personality development of males and females. In A. Pines & C. Maslach (Eds.), *Experiencing social psychology* (2nd ed.). New York: Knopf.

Block, J. H., & Robins, R. W. (1993). A longitudinal study of consistency and change in self-esteem from early adolescence to early adulthood. *Child Development, 64,* 909–923.

Bloom, B. S. (1973). Individual differences in achievement. In L. J. Rubin (Ed.), *Facts and feelings in the classroom.* New York: Viking Press.

Bloom, B. S. (1982). *Human characteristics and school learning.* New York: McGraw-Hill.

Blume, J. (1970). *Are you there, God? It's me, Margaret.* New York: Dell.

Blume, J. (1974). *Blubber.* New York: Dell.

Bogenschneider, K., Wu, M., Raffaelli, M., & Tsay, J. C. (1998). Parental influences on adolescent peer orientation and substance use: The interface of parenting practices and values. *Child Development, 69,* 1672–1688.

Bolger, K. E., & Patterson, C. J. (2001). Developmental pathways from child maltreatment to peer rejection. *Child Development, 72,* 549–568.

Bornstein, M. H. (1995). Parenting infants. In M. H. Bornstein (Ed.), *Handbook of parenting* (Vol. 1). Hillsdale, NJ: Erlbaum.

Bornstein, M. H. (2002). Preface. In M. H. Bornstein (Ed.), *Handbook of parenting* (2nd ed.) Vol. 1. Mahwah, NJ: Erlbaum.

Bornstein, M. H., & Bradley, R. (Eds.). (2003). *Socioeconomic status, parenting, and child development.* Mahwah, NJ: Erlbaum.

Bossard, J. H. S., & Boll, E. S. (1954). The status of children in society. In J. H. S. Bossard & E. S. Boll (Eds.), *The society of child development.* New York: Harper & Row.

Bossard, J. H. S., & Boll, E. S. (1956). *The large family system.* Philadelphia: University of Pennsylvania Press.

Boswell, D. A., & Williams, J. E. (1975). Correlates of race and color bias among preschool children. *Psychological Reports, 36,* 147–154.

Bowlby, J. (1966). *Maternal care and mental health* (2nd ed.). New York: Schocken. (Original publication by U.N. World Health Organization, Geneva, 1952)

Bowlby, J. (1969). *Attachment* (Vol. 1). New York: Basic Books.

Bowlby, J. (1973). *Loss* (Vol. 2). New York: Basic Books.

Boyer, E. L. (1991). *Ready to learn: A mandate for the nation.* Princeton, NJ: Carnegie Foundation for the Advancement of Technology.

Boyer, P. J. (1983, March 15). TV grants kids a short shrift. *Los Angeles Times,* Part VI, p. 1.

Bradley, R. H. (2002). Environment and parenting. In M. H. Bornstein (Ed.), *Handbook of parenting* (2nd ed., Vol. 4). Mahwah, NJ: Erlbaum.

Bradley, R. H, Caldwell, B. M., & Rock, S. L. (1990). Home environment classification system: A model for assessing the home environments of developing children. *Early Education and Development, 1,* 237–265.

Bransford, J. D., Brown, A. L., & Cocking, R. R. (Eds.). (2000). *How people learn: Brain, mind, experience, and school* (expanded ed.). Washington, DC: National Academy Press.

Bray, S. H. (1988). Children's development during early remarriage. In E. M. Hetherington & J. D. Arasteh (Eds.), *Impact of divorce, single parenting and stepparenting on children.* Hillsdale, NJ: Erlbaum.

Brazelton, T. B. (1984). Working parents. *Newsweek, 15*(5), 66–70.

Bredekamp, S. (Ed.). (1986). *Developmentally appropriate practice*. Washington, DC: National Association for the Education of Young Children.

Bredekamp, S. (Ed.). (1993). *Developmentally appropriate practice in early childhood programs serving children from birth through age eight*. Washington, DC: National Association for the Education of Young Children.

Bredekamp, S., & Copple, C. (Eds.). (1997). *Developmentally appropriate practice in early childhood programs* (rev. ed.). Washington, DC: National Association for the Education of Young Children.

Brenner, J., & Von Moschzisker, M. (1971). *The school without walls*. New York: Holt, Rinehart & Winston.

Bria, G. (1998). *The art of family*. New York: Dell.

Bridges, K. B. (1933). A study of social development in early infancy. *Child Development, 4*, 36–49.

Bridges, L. J., & Grolnick, W. S. (1995). The development of emotional self-regulation in infancy and early childhood. In N. Eisenberg (Ed.), *Review of personality and psychology*. Newbury Park, CA: Sage.

Briggs, D. C. (1975). *Your child's self-esteem*. New York: Dolphin.

Brim, O. G. (1966). Socialization through the life cycle. In O. G. Brim & S. Wheeler (Eds.), *Socialization after childhood: Two essays*. New York: Wiley.

Britton, G., & Limpkin, M. (1983). Basal readers: Paltry progress pervades. *Interracial Books for Children Bulletin, 14*(6), 4–7.

Brody, G. H., & Flor, D. L. (1998). Maternal resources, parenting practices, and child competence in rural, single-parent African American families. *Child Development, 69*, 803–816.

Bromer, J. (1999). Cultural variations in child care: Values and action. *Young Children, 54*(6), 72–75.

Bronfenbrenner, U. (1970a). Reaction to social pressure from adults versus peers of Soviet day-school and boarding-school pupils in the perspective of an American sample. *Journal of Personality and Social Psychology, 15*, 179–189.

Bronfenbrenner, U. (1970b, November). *Who cares for American's children?* Address presented at the National Association of Educators of Young Children Conference, Boston.

Bronfenbrenner, U. (1977). Is early intervention effective? In S. Cohen & T. J. Comiskey (Eds.), *Child development: Contemporary perspectives*. Itasca, IL: Peacock.

Bronfenbrenner, U. (1979). *The ecology of human development*. Cambridge MA: Harvard University Press.

Bronfenbrenner, U. (1980). Reunification with our children. In P. Mussen, J. Conger, & J. Kagan (Eds.), *Readings in child and adolescent psychology: Contemporary perspectives*. New York: Harper & Row.

Bronfenbrenner, U. (1989). Ecological systems theory. In R. Vasta (Ed.), *Annals of child development* (Vol. 6). Greenwich, CT: JAI Press.

Bronfenbrenner, U. (1993). The ecology of cognitive development: Research models and fugitive findings. In R. H. Wozniak & K. W. Fisher (Eds.), *Development in context: Acting and thinking in specific environments*. Hillsdale, NJ: Erlbaum.

Bronfenbrenner, U. (1995). Developmental ecology through space and time: A future perspective. In P. Moen, G. H. Elder, Jr., & K. Luscher (Eds.), *Examining lives in context: Perspectives on the ecology of human development*. Washington, DC: American Psychological Association.

Bronfenbrenner, U., & Crouter, A. (1982). Work and family through time and space. In S. B. Kammerman & C. D. Hayes (Eds.), *Families that work: Children in a changing world*. Washington, DC: National Academy Press.

Bronfenbrenner, U., & Garbarino, J. (1976). The socialization of moral judgment and behavior in cross-cultural perspective. In T. Lickona (Ed.), *Moral development and behavior*. New York: Holt, Rinehart & Winston.

Bronfenbrenner, U., & Morris, P. A. (1998). The ecology of developmental processeses. In W. Damon (Ed.), *Handbook of child psychology* (5th ed., Vol. 1). New York: Wiley.

Brooks-Gunn, J., & Furstenberg, F. F., Jr. (1989). Adolescent sexual behavior. *American Psychologist, 44*(2), 249–257.

Brophy, B. (1989, August 7). Spock had it right: Studies suggest that kids thrive when parents set firm limits. *U.S. News & World Report*, 49–51.

Brophy, J. E. (1992). Probing the subtleties of subject matter teaching. *Educational Leadership, 49*(7), 4–8.

Brophy, J. E., & Good, T. L. (1986). Teacher behavior and student achievement. In M. Wittrock (Ed.), *Handbook of research on teaching* (3rd ed.). New York: Macmillan.

Brown, B. B., Clasen, D. R., & Eicher, S. A. (1986). Perceptions of peer pressure, peer conformity dispositions and self-reported behavior among adolescents. *Developmental Psychology, 22*, 521–530.

Brown, B. B., & Lohr, M. J. (1987). Peer group affiliation, adolescent self-esteem, and integration of ego-identity and symbolic-interaction theories. *Journal of Personality and Social Psychology, 52*(1), 47–57.

Brown, J., & Cantor, J. (2000). An agenda for research on youth and the media. *Journal of Adolescent Health, 278*, 2–7.

Brown, L. M., & Gilligan, C. (1990, March). *The psychology of women and the development of girls*. Paper presented at the meeting of the Society for Research on Adolescence, Atlanta.

Brown, M. W. (1947). *Goodnight moon*. New York: Harper and Row.

Bruer, J. T., & Greenough, W. T. (2001). The subtle science of how experience affects the brain. In D. B. J. Bailey, J. T. Bruer, F. J. Symons, & J. W. Lichtman (Eds.), *Critical thinking about critical periods*. Baltimore, MD: Paul H. Brooks.

Bruner, J. (1981). The art of discovery. In M. Kaplan-Sangoff & R. Y. Magid (Eds.), *Exploring early childhood*. New York: Macmillan.

Bryant, J., & Rockwell, S. C. (1994). Effects of massive exposure to sexually oriented prime-time television programming on adolescents' moral judgment. In D. Zillman, J. Bryant, & A. C. Huston (Eds.), *Media, children, and the family: Social, scientific, psychodynamic, and clinical perspectives*. Hillsdale, NJ: Erlbaum.

Bugental, D. B. (2000). Acquisition of the algorithms of social life: A domain-based approach. *Psychological Bulletin, 126*(2), 187–219.

Bugental, D. B., & Goodenow, J. J. (1998). Socialization processes. In W. Damon (Ed.), *Handbook of child psychology* (5th ed., Vol. 3). New York: Wiley.

Bukowski, W. M., Newcomb, A. F., & Hartup, W. W. (1996). Friendships and their significance in childhood and adolescence: Introduction and comment. In W. M. Bukowski, A. F. Newcomb, & W. W. Hartup (Eds.), *The company they keep: Friendship in childhood and adolescence*. New York: Cambridge University Press.

Bullock, J. R. (1992, Winter). Children without friends: Who are they and how can teachers help? *Childhood Education*, 92–96.

Burchinal, M. R., Peisner-Feinberg, E., Bryant, D. M., & Clifford, R. (2000). Children's social and cognitive development and child-care quality: Testing for differential associations related to poverty, gender, or ethnicity. *Applied Developmental Science, 4*(3), 149–165.

Burgess, K. B., Marshall, P. J., Rubin, K. H., & Fox, N. A. (2003). Infant attachment and temperament as predictors of subsequent externalizing problems and cardiac physiology. *Journal of Child Psychology and Psychiatry, 44*(6), 819–831.

Burhans, K. K., & Dweck, C. S. (1995). Helplessness in early childhood. The role of contingent worth. *Child Development, 66*, 1719–1738.

Burton, C. B. (1985). Children's peer relationships. *ERIC Digest*.

Buss, A. H., & Plomin, R. (1994). Temperament: Early developing personality traits. Hillsdale, NJ: Erlbaum.

Cain, K. M., & Dweck, C. J. (1995). The relation between motivational patterns and achievement cognitions through the elementary school years. *Merrill Palmer Quartery, 41*, 25–52.

Caldera, Y. M., Huston, A. C., & O'Brien, M. (1989). Social interactions and play patterns of parents and toddlers with feminine, masculine, and neutral toys. *Child Development, 60*, 70–76.

Caldwell, B. M. (1986). Education of families for parenting. In M. W. Yogman & T. B. Brazelton (Eds.), *In support of families*. Cambridge, MA: Harvard University Press.

Caldwell, B. M., & Bradley, R. H. (1984). *Manual for the home observation for measurement of the environment*. Little Rock: University of Arkansas Press.

Caldwell, B. M., & Crary, D. (1981). Why are kids so darned aggressive? *Parents, 56*(2), 52–56.

Campbell, J. (1968). *The hero with a thousand faces* (2nd ed.). Princeton, NJ: Princeton University Press.

Campbell, J. J., Lamb, M. E., & Hwang, C. P. (2000). Early child-care experiences and children's social competence between $1\frac{1}{2}$ and 15 years of age. *Applied and Developmental Science, 4*(3), 166–175.

Cantor, J. (1998). *"Mommy, I'm scared": How TV and movies frighten children and what we can do to protect them*. San Diego, CA: Harcourt Brace.

Carle, E. (1986). *The very hungry caterpillar*. New York: Putnam.

Carlsen, G. R. (1980). *Books and the teenage reader*. New York: Harper & Row.

Carlson, M., Charlin, V., & Miller, N. (1988). Positive mood and helping behavior: A test of six hypotheses. *Psychological Bulletin, 55*, 211–229.

Carpenter, C. J. (1983). Activity, structure, and play: Implications for socialization. In M. B. Liss (Ed.), *Social and cognitive skills: Sex roles and children's play*. New York: Academic Press.

Carpenter, C. J., Huston, A. C., & Hart, W. (1986). Modification of preschool sex-typed behaviors by participation in adult-structured activities, *Sex Roles, 4*, 603–615.

Cashdan, S. (1999). *The witch must die: How fairy tales shape our lives*. New York: Basic Books.

Caudill, W. (1988). Tiny dramas: Vocal communication between mother and infant in Japanese and American families. In G. Handel (Ed.), *Childhood socialization*. New York: Aldine de Gruyter.

Cebello, R., & McLoyd, V. C. (2002). Social support and parenting in poor, dangerous neighborhoods. *Child Development, 73*(4), 1310–1321.

Center for Communication and Social Policy. (1998). *National television violence study* (Vol.3). Thousand Oaks, CA: Sage.

Center for Media and Public Affairs. (1999). *I'm okay, you're dead! TV and movies suggest violence is harmless.* http://www.cmpa.com/pressrel/

Center for Media Education. (1997). *The deceiving web of online advertising.* http://www.cme.org/

Cesarone, B. (1994, January). Video games and children, *ERIC Digest.* (ED-PS-94-3)

Cetron, M. J. (1988, November/December). Class of 2000. *The Futurist*, 9–15.

Chafetz, J. S. (1974). *Masculine/feminine or human? An overview of the sociology of sex roles.* Itasca, IL: Peacock.

Chall, J. (2000). *The academic achievement challenge: What really works in the classroom.* New York: Guilford.

Chance, P. (1982). Your child's self-esteem. *Parents, 57,* 54–59.

Chang, J. (2005). *Can't stop won't stop: A history of the hip-hop generation.* New York: St. Martin's Press.

Chao, R. (1994). Beyond parent control and authoritarian parenting style: Understanding Chinese parenting through the culture notion of training. *Child Development, 65,* 1111–1119.

Chao, R. (2001). Extending research on the consequences of parenting style for Chinese Americans and European Americans. *Child Development, 72,* 1832–1843

Char, C. A., & Meringoff, L. K. (1981, January). The role of story illustrations: Children's story comprehension in three different media. *Harvard Project Zero Technical Report* (No. 22).

Chen, X., & Rubin, K. H. (1994). Family conditions, parental acceptance, and social competence and aggression in Chinese children. *Social Development, 3,* 269–290.

Chess, S., & Thomas, A. (1987). *Know your child.* New York: Basic Books.

Child Welfare League of America [CWLA]. (2002). *Fact sheet.* http://www.cwla.org/

Children Now. (May, 1998). *A different world: Children's perceptions of race and class in media.* Oakland, CA: Author.

Children's Defense Fund [CDF]. (2004). *The state of America's children, 2004.* Washington, DC: Author.

Chisholm, K. (1998). A three-year follow-up of attachment and indiscriminate friendliness in children adopted from Romanian orphanages. *Child Development, 69*(4), 1092–1106.

Chmielewski, C. (1997, September). Sexual harassment meet Title IX. *NEA Today, 16*(2), 24–25.

Chomsky, N. (1972). Stages in language development and reading exposure. *Harvard Educational Review, 42,* 1–33.

Christenson, P. G., Henriksen, L., & Roberts, D. F. (2000). *Substance use in popular prime-time television.* Washington, DC: Office of National Drug Control Policy.

Christenson, P. G., & Roberts, D. F. (1998). *Its not only rock & roll: Popular music in the lives of adolescents.* Cresskill, NJ: Hampton Press.

Cicchetti, D., & Lynch, M. (1993). Toward an ecological transactional model of community violence and child maltreatment: Consequences for children's development. *Psychiatry, 56,* 96–118.

Cillesen, A. H. N., & Bukowski, W. M. (2000). *Recent advances in the measurement of acceptance and rejection in the peer system.* San Francisco: Jossey-Bass.

Clarke-Stewart, K. A. (1987). Predicting child development from day care forms and features: The Chicago study. In D. A. Phillips (Ed.), *Quality in childcare: What does research tell us? Research Monographs of the National Association for the Education of Young Children* (Vol. 1). Washington, DC: National Association for the Education of Young Children.

Clarke-Stewart, K. A. (1988). The "effects" of infant day care reconsidered: Risks for parents, children, and researchers. *Early Childhood Research Quarterly, 3,* 293–318.

Clarke-Stewart, K. A. (1989). Infant day care: Maligned or malignant? *American Psychologist, 44*(2), 266–273.

Clarke-Stewart, K. A. (1992). Consequences of child care for children's development. In A. Booth (Ed.), *Childcare in the 1990s: Trends and consequences.* Hillsdale, NJ: Erlbaum.

Clarke-Stewart, K. A. (1993). *Daycare* (rev. ed.). Cambridge, MA: Harvard University Press.

Clark-Stewart, K. A., & Allhusen, V. D. (2002). Nonparental caregiving. In M.H. Bornstein (Ed.), *Handbook of parenting* (2nd ed., Vol. 3). Mahwah, NJ: Erlbaum.

Clausen, J. A. (1975). The social meaning of differential physical and sexual maturation. In S. E. Dragastin & G. H. Elder (Eds.), *Adolescence in the life cycle.* New York: Wiley.

Coates, B., Pusser, H. E., & Goodman, I. (1976). The influence of *Sesame Street* and *Mister Rogers' Neighborhood* on children's social behavior in the preschool. *Child Development, 47,* 138–144.

Coates, D. L. (1987). Gender differences in the structure and support characteristics of black adolescents' social networks. *Sex Roles, 17,* 719–736.

Cochran, M. (1993). Parenting and personal social networks. In T. Luster & L. Okagaki (Eds.), *Parenting: An ecological perspective.* Hillsdale, NJ: Erlbaum.

Cochran, M., & Henderson, C. R., Jr. (1986). *Family matters: Evaluation of the parental empowerment program.* Ithaca, NY: Cornell University. (ED 262862)

Cochran, M., & Niego, S. (2002). Parenting and social networks. In M. H. Bornstein (Ed.), *Handbook of parenting* (2nd ed., Vol. 1). Mahwah, NJ: Erlbaum.

Cohen, R., Bornstein, R., & Sherman, R. C. (1973). Conformity behavior of children as a function of group make-up and task ambiguity. *Developmental Psychology, 9*, 124–131.

Cohen, S., Glass, D. C., & Singer, J. E. (1973). Apartment noise, auditory discrimination, and reading ability in children. *Journal of Experimental Social Psychology, 9*, 407–422.

Coie, J. D., & Cillesen. A. (1993). Peer rejection: Origins and effects on children's development. *Current Directions in Psychological Science, 2*, 89–92.

Coie, J. D., & Dodge, K. A. (1998). Aggression and antisocial behavior. In W. Damon (Ed.), *Handbook of child psychology* (5th ed., Vol. 4). New York: Wiley.

Coie, J. D., Dodge, K. A., & Kupersmidt, J. B. (1990). Peer group behavior and social status. In S. R. Asher & J. D. Coie (Eds.), *Peer rejection in childhood*. New York: Cambridge University Press.

Colby, A., & Kohlberg, L. (1987). *The measurement of moral judgement: Vol. 1. Theoretical foundations and research validation*. Cambridge, UK: Cambridge University Press.

Colby, A., Kohlberg, L., Gibbs, J., & Lieberman, M. A. (1983). A longitudinal study of moral judgment. *Monographs of the Society for Research in Child Development, 48*(1–2, Serial No. 200).

Cole, D. A. (1991). Change in self-perceived competence as a function of peer and teacher evaluation. *Developmental Psychology, 27*, 682–688.

Cole, E., & Duva, J. (1990). *Family preservation: An orientation for administrators and practitioners*. Washington, DC: Child Welfare League of America.

Coleman, J. (1961). *The adolescent society*. New York: Macmillan.

Coleman, J. (1966). *Equality of educational opportunity*. Washington, DC: U.S. Government Printing Office.

Coleman, J. S. (1990). *Foundations of social theory*. Englewood Cliffs, NJ: Prentice-Hall.

Coletta, A. J. (1977). *Working together: A guide to parent involvement*. Atlanta: Humanics Limited.

Coll, C. G., & Szalacha, L. A. (2004). The multiple contexts of middle childhood: Children of immigrants. *The Future of Children, 14*(2), 81–97.

Collins, L. J., Ingoldsby, B. B., & Dellman, M. M. (1984). Sex-role stereotyping in children's literature: A change from the past. *Childhood Education, 60*(4), 278–285.

Collins, W. A., Harris, M. L., & Susman, A. (1995). Parenting during middle childhood. In M. H. Bornstein (Ed.), *Handbook of parenting* (Vol. 1). Mahwah, NJ: Erlbaum.

Collins, W. A., & Laursen, B. (2004). Parent–adolescent relationships and influences. In R. Lerner & L. Steinberg (Eds.), *Handbook of adolescent psychology* (2nd ed.). New York: Wiley.

Collins, W. A., Maccoby, E. E., Steinberg, L., Hetherington, E. M., & Bornstein, M. H. (2000). Contemporary research on parenting: The case for nature and nurture. *American Psychologist, 55*(2), 218–232.

Collodi, C. (1972). Pinocchio. In *The new Walt Disney treasury*. New York: Garden Press. (Original work published 1882)

Comer, J. P. (2004). *Leave no child behind: Preparing today's youth for tomorrow's world*. Hew Haven, CT: Yale University Press.

Comstock, G., & Paik, H. (1991). *Television and the American child*. San Diego, CA: Academic Press.

Comstock, G., & Scharrer, E. (1999). *Television: What's on, who's watching and what it means*. San Diego, CA: Academic Press.

Comstock, G., & Scharrer, E. (2001). The use of television and other film-related media. In D. G. Singer & J. L. Singer (Eds.), *Handbook of children and the media*. Thousand Oaks, CA: Sage.

Condry, J. (1989). *The psychology of television*. Hillsdale, NJ: Erlbaum.

Condry, J., Bence, P., & Scheibe, C. (1988). Non-program content of children's television. *Journal of Broadcasting and Electronic Media, 32*(3), 255–270.

Condry, J. C., & Simon, M. L. (1974). Characteristics of peer- and adult-oriented children. *Journal of Marriage and the Family, 36*, 543–546.

Conger, R. D., Xiaojia, G., Elder, G. H., Jr., Lorenz, F. O., Simons, R. L., & Whitebeck, L. B. (1994). Economic stress, coercive family process, and developmental problems of adolescents. *Child Development, 65*, 541–561.

Connors, L. J., & Epstein, J. L. (1995). Parent and school partnerships. In M. H. Bornstein (Ed.), *Handbook of parenting* (Vol. 4). Mahwah, NJ: Erlbaum.

Cooley, C. (1964). *Human nature and the social order*. New York: Schocken. (Original work published 1909)

Coontz, S. (1997). *The way we really are: Coming to terms with America's changing families*. New York: Basic Books.

Coopersmith, S. (1967). *The antecedents of self-esteem*. San Francisco: Freeman.

Corcoran, M. E., & Chandry, A. (1997). The dynamics of childhood poverty. *The Future of Children, 7*(2), 40–54.

Corsaro, W. A. (1981). Friendship in the nursery school: Social organization in a peer environment. In S. R. Asher & J. M. Gottman (Eds.), *The development of children's friendships*. Cambridge, UK: Cambridge University Press.

Cost, Quality, and Child Outcomes Study [COQ]. (1995). *Cost, quality, and child outcomes in child care centers: Executive summary* (2nd ed.). Denver: University of Colorado, Economics Department.

Cost, Quality, and Child Outcomes Study [COQ]. (1999). *The children of the cost, quality, and outcomes study go to school.* Denver: University of Colorado, Economics Department.

Council of Better Business Bureaus. (2000). *The children's advertising review unit. Self-regulatory guidelines for children's advertising.* http://www.bbb.org/advertising/caruguid.asp

Covington, M. V., & Beery, R. G. (1976). *Self-worth and school learning.* New York: Holt, Rinehart & Winston.

Cowan, P. A., Powell, D., & Cowan, C. P. (1998). In W. Damon (Ed.), *Handbook of child psychology* (5th ed., Vol. 4). New York: Wiley.

Cox, M. J., Owen, M. T., Henderson, V. K., & Margand, N. A. (1992). Prediction of infant–father and infant–mother attachment. *Developmental Psychology, 28*(3), 474–483.

Crawford, M. T., & Unger, R. (2000). *Women and gender: A feminist psychology* (3rd ed.). New York: McGraw-Hill.

Crespo, C. J., Smit, E., Troiano, R. P., Bartlett, S. J., Macera, C. A., & Anderson, R. E. (2001). Television watching, energy intake, and obesity in U.S. children. *Archives of Pediatric and Adolescent Medicine, 155,* 360–365.

Crick, N. R., Casas, J. F., & Ku, H.-C. (1999). Relation of physical forms of peer victimization in preschool. *Developmental Psychology, 35,* 376–385.

Crime Prevention Center. (1988). *Child abuse prevention handbook.* Sacramento: California Department of Justice.

Crnic, K., & Acevedo, M. (1995). Everyday stress and parenting. In M. H. Bornstein (Ed.), *Handbook of parenting* (Vol. 4). Mahwah, NJ: Erlbaum.

Crook, C. (1992). Cultural artifacts in social development: The case of computers. In H. McGurk (Ed.), *Childhood social development: Contemporary perspectives.* Hove, UK: Erlbaum.

Crouter, A. C., Bumpus, M. F., Maguire, M. C., & McHale, S. M. (1999). Linking parents' work pressure and adolescent's well-being: Insights into dynamics in dual-earner families. *Developmental Psychology, 35,* 1453–1461.

Crouter, A. C., & McHale, S. M. (1993). The long arm of the job: Influences of parental work on childrearing. In T. Luster & L. Okagaki (Eds.), *Parenting: An ecological perspective.* Hillsdale, NJ: Erlbaum.

Csikszentmihalyli, M. (1991). *Flow: The psychology of optimal experience.* New York: Harper Perennial.

Cubberley, E. P. (1919). *Public education in the United States.* Boston: Houghton Mifflin.

Cummings, E. M., & Cummings, J. S. (2002). Parenting and attachment. In M. H. Bornstein (Ed.), *Handbook of parenting* (2nd ed., Vol. 5). Mahwah, NJ: Erlbaum.

Curran, D. (1985). *Stress and the healthy family.* Minneapolis, MN: Winston Press.

Dahl, R. (1964). *Charlie and the chocolate factory.* New York: Knopf.

Daiute, C. (1983). Writing, creativity and change. *Childhood Education, 59*(4), 227–231.

Damasio, A. R. (1994). *Descartes' error: Emotion, reason, and the human brain.* New York: Putnam.

Damon, W. (1988). *The moral child: Nurturing children's natural moral growth.* New York: Free Press.

Damon, W. D. (1999). The moral development of children. *Scientific American, 281*(2), 72–78.

Daniels, D. H., Kalkman, D. L., & McCombs, B. L.(2001). Young children's perspectives on learning and teacher pactices in different classroom contexts: Implications for motivation. *Early Education and Development, 12,* 253–273.

Darling, S., & Westberg, L. (2004). Parent involvement in children's acquisition of reading. *The Reading Teacher, 57*(8), 774–776.

Davidson, E., & Schniedewind, N. (1992). Class differences: Economic inequality in the classroom. In D. A. Byrnes & G. Kiger (Eds.), *Common bonds: Anti-bias teaching in a diverse society.* Wheaton, MD: Association for Childhood International.

Davidson, P., & Youniss, J. (1995). Moral development and social construction. In W. M. Kurtines & J. L. Gewirtz (Eds.), *Moral development: An introduction.* Boston: Allyn and Bacon.

Dean, C. (1984). Parental empowerment through family resource programs. *Human Ecology Forum, 14*(1), 17–22.

Deax, K., & Wrightsman, L. J. (1988). *Social psychology* (5th ed.). Pacific Grove, CA: Brooks/Cole.

Decety, J., & Chaminade, T. (2003). Neural correlates of feeling sympathy. *Neuropsychologia, 41,* 127–138.

Deci, E. L., & Ryan, R. M. (1985). *Intrinsic motivation and self-determination in human behavior.* New York: Plenum.

Decker, L. E., & Decker, V. A. (2001). *Engaging families and communities: Pathways to educational success.* Fairfax, VA: National Community Education Association.

Dellman-Jenkins, M., Florjancic, L., & Swadener, E. B. (1993). Sex roles and cultural diversity in recent award-winning picture books for young children. *Journal of Research in Childhood Education, 7*(2), 74–82.

Dennison, B. A., Erb, T. A., & Jenkins, P. L. (2002). Television viewing and television in bedroom associated with overweight risk among low-income preschool children. *Pediatrics, 109,* 1028–1035.

DePanfilis, D., Holder, W., Corey, M., & Olson, E. (1986). *Child-at-risk field training manual.* Charlotte, NC: Action for Child Protection.

Derman-Sparks, L. (1989). *Anti-bias curriculum: Tools for empowering young children.* Washington, DC: National Association for the Education of Young Children.

Desmond, R. (2001). Free reading: Implication for child development. In D. G. Singer & J. L. Singer (Eds.), *Handbook of children and the media.* Thousand Oaks, Sage.

Desmond, R. J., Singer, J. L., & Singer, D. G. (1990). Family mediation: Parental communication patterns and the influences of television on children. In J. Bryant (Ed.), *Television and the American family.* Hillsdale, NJ: Erlbaum.

DeToledo, S., & Brown, D. E. (1995). *Grandparents as parents.* New York: Guilford.

Deutsch, B. (1952). The clever judge. In B. Deutsch & A. Yarmolinsky, *Tales of faraway folk.* New York: Harper & Row.

Devereaux, E. C. (1970). The role of peer group experience in moral development. In J. P. Hill (Ed.), *Minnesota symposia on child psychology* (Vol. 4). Minneapolis: University of Minnesota Press.

Dewey, J. (1944). *Democracy and education.* New York: Macmillan.

DeWolff, M. S., & van IJzendoorn, M. H. (1997). Sensitivity and attachment: A meta-analysis on parental antecedents of infant attachment. *Child Development, 67,* 3071–3085.

Dien, D. S. F. (1982). A Chinese perspective on Kohlberg's theory of moral development. *Developmental Review, 2,* 331–341.

Diener, E., Frasier, S. C., Beaman, A. L., & Kelem, R. T. (1976). Effects of deindividuation variables on stealing among Halloween trick-or-treaters. *Journal of Personality and Social Psychology, 33,* 178–183.

Dietz, T. L. (1998). An examination of violence and gender-role portrayals in video games: Implications for gender socialization and aggressive behavior. *Sex Roles, 38,* 425–442.

Dishion, T. J., McCord, J., & Poulin, F. (1999). When interventions harm: Peer groups and problem behavior. *American Psychologist, 54*(8), 755–764.

Dishion, T. J., Patterson, G. R., Stoolmiller, M., & Skinner, M. L. (1991). Family, school, and behavioral antecedents to early adolescent involvement with antisocial peers. *Developmental Psychology, 27,* 172–180.

Dobkin, P. L., Tremblay, R. E., Masse, L. C., & Vitaro, F. (1995). Individual and peer characteristics in predicting boys' early onset of substance abuse: A seven-year longitudinal study. *Child Development, 66,* 1198–1214.

Dodge, K. A. (1983). Behavioral antecedents of peer social status. *Child Development, 54,* 1386–1399.

Dodge, K. A. (1986). A social information processing model of social competence in children. In M. Perlmutter (Ed.), *Minnesota symposia on child psychology* (Vol. 18). Hillsdale, NJ: Erlbaum.

Dodge, K. A., Bates, J. E., & Pettit, G. S. (1990). Mechanisms in the cycle of violence. *Science, 250,* 1678–1683.

Dodge, K. A., & Pettit, G. S. (2003). A biopsychosocial model of the development of chronic conduct problems in adolescence. *Developmental Psychology, 39,* 349–371.

Dodge, K. A., Pettit, G. S., & Bates, J. E. (1994). Socialization mediators of the relation between socioeconomic status and child conduct problems. *Child Development, 65,* 649–665.

Doherty, W. J., Kouneski, E. F., & Erickson, M. F. (1998). Responsible fathering: An overview and conceptual framework. *Journal of Marriage and the Family, 60,* 277–292.

Dornbusch, S. M., Ritter, P. L., Leiderman, P. H., & Roberts, D. F. (1987). The relationship of parenting style to adolescent school performance. *Child Development, 58*(5), 1244–1257.

Dorr, A., & Rabin, B. E. (1995). Parents, children, and television. In M. H. Bornstein (Ed.), *Handbook of parenting* (Vol. 4). Mahwah, NJ: Erlbaum.

Dougherty, W. H., & Engle, R. E. (1987). An '80s look for sex equality in Caldecott winners and Honor books. *Reading Teacher, 40*(4), 394–398.

Downey, D. B., & Powell, B. (1993). Do children in single-parent households fare better with same-sex parents? *Journal of Marriage and the Family, 55,* 55–76.

Dreikurs, R., & Grey, L. (1968). *A new approach to discipline: Logical consequences.* New York: Hawthorn.

Dresser, N. (1996). *Multicultural manners: New rules of etiquette for a changing society.* New York: Wiley.

Dresser, N. (1999). *Multicultural celebrations.* New York: Three Rivers Press.

Dubowitz, H., & DePanfilis, D. (Eds.). (1999). *Handbook for child protection practice.* Thousand Oaks, CA: Sage.

Duncan, G. J., & Magnuson, K. A. (2005). Can family socioeconomic resources account for racial and ethnic test score gaps? School readiness: Closing racial and ethnic gaps. *The Future of Children, 15*(1), 35–54.

Duncan, G. J., & Raudenbush, S. W. (2001). Neighborhoods and adolescent development: How can we determine the links? In A. Booth & A. C. Crouter (Eds.), *Does it take a village?* Mahwah, NJ: Erlbaum.

Dunlop, K. H. (1977). Mainstreaming: Valuing diversity in children. *Young Children, 32*(4), 26–32.

Dunn, J. (1988). *The beginnings of social understanding.* Cambridge, MA: Harvard University Press.

Dunn, J. (1992). Siblings and development. *Current Directions in Psychological Science, 1*(1), 6–9.

Dunn, J. (1993). *Young children's close relationship: Beyond attachment.* Newbury Park, CA: Sage.

Dunn, J., Davies, L. C., O'Connor, T. G., & Sturgess, W. (2000). Parents' and partners' life course and family experiences: Links with parent–child relationships in different family settings. *Journal of Child Psychology and Psychiatry and Allied Disciplines, 41*, 955–968.

Dunn, L. M. (1968). Special education for the mildly retarded: Is much of it justified? *Exceptional Children, 35*(24), 5–22.

Durkheim, E. (1947). *The elementary forms of the religious life.* Glencoe, IL: Free Press.

Duska, R., & Whelan, M. (1975). *Moral development: A guide to Piaget and Kohlberg.* New York: Paulist Press.

Duster, T. (1971). Conditions for guilt-free massacre. In N. Sanford & C. Comstock (Eds.), *Sanctions for evil.* San Francisco: Jossey-Bass.

Dweck, C. S. (1975). The role of expectations and attributions in the alleviation of learned helplessness. *Journal of Personality and Social Psychology, 31*, 674–685.

Dweck, C. S. (1981). Social-cognitive processes in children's friendships. In S. R. Asher & J. M. Gottman (Eds.), *The development of children's friendships.* Cambridge, UK: Cambridge University Press.

Dweck, C. S., & Bush, E. S. (1976). Sex differences in learned helplessness: I. Differential debilitation with peer and adult evaluators. *Journal of Personality and Social Psychology, 12*, 147–156.

Dweck, C. S., Davidson, W., Nelson, S., & Enna, B. (1978). Sex differences in learned helplessness: II. The contingencies of evaluative feedback in the classroom: III. An experimental analysis. *Developmental Psychology, 14*, 268–276.

Dweck, C. S., & Gillard, D. (1975). Expectancy statements as determinants of reactions to failure: Sex differences in persistence and expectancy change. *Journal of Personality and Social Psychology, 32*, 1077–1084.

Dweck, C. S., & Leggett, E. L. (1988). A social-cognitive approach to motivation and personality. *Psychological Review, 95*, 256–273.

Dweck, C. S., & Reppucci, N. D. (1973). Learned helplessness and reinforcement responsibility in children. *Journal of Personality and Social Psychology, 25*, 109–116.

Eccles, J. (1983). Expectancies, values, and academic behaviors. In J. T. Spence (Ed.), *Achievement and achievement motives: Psychological and sociological approaches.* San Francisco: Freeman.

Eccles, J., Barber, B., Jozefowicz, D., Malenchuk, O., & Vida, M. (1999). Self-evaluation of competence, task values, and self-esteem. In N. G. Johnson, M. C. Roberts, & J. Worell (Eds.), *Beyond appearance: A new look at adolescent girls.* Washington, DC: American Psychological Association.

Eccles, J. S., & Bryan, J. (1994). Adolescence and gender-role transcendence. In M. Stevenson (Ed.), *Gender roles across the life span.* Muncie, IN: Ball State University Press.

Eccles, J. S., Wigfield, A., & Schiefele, U. (1998). Motivation to succeed. In W. Damon (Ed.), *Handbook of child psychology* (5th ed., Vol. 3). New York: Wiley.

Eder, D. (1995). *School talk: Gender and adolescent school culture.* New Brunswick, NJ: Rutgers University Press.

Eisenberg, N. (1998). Introduction. In W. Damon (Ed.), *Handbook of child psychology* (5th ed., Vol. 3). New York: Wiley.

Eisenberg, N. (2002). Emotion-related regulation and its relation to quality of social functioning. In W. W. Hartup & R. A. Weinberg (Eds.), *Minnesota symposium on child psychology: Vol. 32. Child psychology in retrospect and prospect.* Mahwah, NJ: Erlbaum.

Eisenberg, N., & Fabes, R. A. (1998). Prosocial development. In W. Damon (Ed.), *Handbook of child psychology* (5th ed., Vol. 4). New York: Wiley.

Eisenberg, N., Martin, C. L., & Fabes, R. A. (1996). Gender development and gender effects. In D. C. Berliner & R. C. Calfee (Eds.), *Handbook of educational psychology.* New York: Macmillan.

Eisenberg, N., & Murphy, B. (1995). Parenting and children's moral development. In M. H. Bornstein (Ed.), *Handbook of parenting* (Vol. 4). Mahwah, NJ: Erlbaum.

Eisenberg, N., & Mussen, P. (1989). *The roots of prosocial behavior in children.* Cambridge, UK: Cambridge University Press.

Elder, G. H., Jr. (1963). Parental power legitimation and its effect on the adolescent. *Sociometry, 26*, 50–65.

Elder, G. H., Jr. (1974). *Children of the Great Depression: Social change in life experience.* Chicago: University of Chicago Press.

Elder, G. H., Jr. (1979). Historical change in life patterns and personality. In P. Baltes & O. Brim (Eds.), *Life-span development and behavior* (Vol. 2). New York: Academic Press.

Elder, G. H., Jr. (1998). The life course and human development. In W. Damon (Ed.), *Handbook of child psychology* (5th ed., Vol. 1). New York: Wiley.

Elder, G. H., Jr., & Bowerman, C. E. (1963). Family structure and child-rearing patterns: The effect of family size and sex composition. *American Sociological Review, 30,* 81–96.

Elder, G. H., Jr., & Hareven, T. K. (1993). Rising above life's disadvantage: From the Great Depression to war. In G. H. Elder, Jr., J. Modell, & R. D. Parke (Eds.), *Children in time and space: Development and historical insights.* New York: Cambridge University Press.

Elder, G. H., Jr., Van Nguyen, T. V., & Casper, A. (1985). Linking family hardship to children's lives. *Child Development, 56,* 361–375.

Elders, J. (1994). Violence as a public health issue for children. *Childhood Education, 70*(5), 260–262.

Eldridge, S. (1999). *Twenty things adopted kids wish their adoptive parents knew.* New York: Dell.

Eley, T. C., Lichtenstein, P., & Stevenson, J. (1999). Sex differences in the etiology of aggressive and nonaggressive antisocial behavior: Results from two twin studies. *Child Development, 70,* 155–168.

Elkin, F., & Handel, G. (1989). *The child and society* (5th ed.). New York: Random House.

Elkind, D. (1981a). Egocentrism in children and adolescents. In D. Elkind (Ed.), *Children and adolescents: Interpretive essays on Jean Piaget* (3rd ed.). New York: Oxford University Press.

Elkind, D. (1981b). How grown-ups help children learn. *Education Digest, 80*(3), 20–24.

Elkind, D. (1988). *The hurried child: Growing up too fast too soon* (rev. ed.). Reading, MA: Addison-Wesley.

Elkind, D. (1994). *Ties that stress: The new family imbalance.* Cambridge, MA: Harvard University Press.

Elliot, E. S., & Dweck, C. S. (1988). Goals: An approach to motivation and achievement. *Journal of Personality and Social Psychology, 54,* 5–12.

Elliot, R., & Vasta, P. (1970). The modeling of sharing: Effects associated with vicarious reinforcement, symbolization, age, and generalization. *Journal of Experimental Child Psychology, 10,* 8–15.

Ellis, B. J., Bates, J. E., Dodge, K. A., Fergusson, D. M., Horwood, J. L., Pettit, G. S., et al. (2003). Does father absence place daughters at risk for early sexual activity and teenage pregnancy? *Child Development, 74,* 801–821.

Ellis, J. B. (1994). Children's sex-role development: Implications for working mothers. *Social Behavior and Personality, 22,* 131–136.

Ellis, S., Rogoff, B., & Cromer, C. C. (1981). Age segregation in children's social interactions. *Developmental Psychology, 17,* 399–407.

Emery, R. E. (1989). Family violence. *American Psychologist, 44,* 321–332.

Emmer, E., & Stough, L. (2001). Classroom management: A critical part of educational psychology with implications for teacher education. *Educational Psychologist, 36,* 103–112.

Epps, S., & Jackson, B. J. (2000). *Empowered families, successful children.* Washington, DC: American Psychological Association.

Epstein, J. L. (1983). Longitudinal effects of family–school–person interactions on student outcomes. In J. L. Epstein (Ed.), *Research in sociology of education and socialization* (Vol. 4). Greenwich, CT: JAI Press.

Epstein, J. L. (1995). School/family/community partnerships, for the children we share. *Phi Delta Kappan, 76*(9), 701–712.

Epstein, J. L. (2001). *School, family, and community partnerships: Preparing educators and improving schools.* Boulder, CO: Westview Press.

Epstein, J. L., & Sanders, M. G. (2002). Family, school and community partnerships. In M. H. Bornstein (Ed.), *Handbook of parenting* (2nd ed., Vol. 5). Mahwah, NJ: Erlbaum.

Erikson, E. H. (1963). *Childhood and society.* New York: Norton.

Erikson, E. H. (1980). *Identity and the life cycle.* New York: Norton.

Eron, L., Walder, L. O., & Lefkowitz, M. M. (1971). *Learning of aggression in children.* Boston: Little, Brown.

Escobedo, T. H., & Huggans, J. H. (1983). Field dependence–independence: A theoretical framework for Mexican American cultural variables? In T. H. Escobedo (Ed.), *Early childhood bilingual education: A Hispanic perspective.* New York: Teachers College Press.

Espeldge, D. L., Holt, M. K., & Henkel, R. R. (2003). Examination of peer-group contextual effects on aggression during early adolescence. *Child Development, 74,* 205–220.

Espin, O. M. (1993). Psychological impact of migration on Latinos. In D. R. Atkinson, G. Morten, & D. W. Sue (Eds.), *Counseling American minorities* (4th ed.). Dubuque, IA: Brown & Benchmark.

Esslin, M. (1982). *The age of television.* San Francisco: Freeman.

Estes, E. (1944). *The hundred dresses.* New York: Harcourt Brace Jovanovich.

Etzioni, A. (1993). *The spirit of community: The reinvention of American society.* New York: Touchstone.

Evans, E. D., & McCandless, B. R. (1978). *Children and youth: Psychosocial development.* New York: Holt, Rinehart & Winston.

Evans, E. D., Rutberg, J., Sather, C., & Turner, C. (1991). Content analysis of contemporary teen magazines for adolescent females. *Youth Society, 23*(1), 99–120.

Evans, G. W., & English, K. (2002). The environment of poverty: Multiple stressor exposure, psychophysiological stress, and socioemotional adjustment. *Child Development, 73*, 1238–1248.

Evans, G. W., Hygges, S., & Bullinger, M. (1993). *Psychology and the environment*. Unpublished manuscript, Cornell University, Ithaca, NY.

Evans, G. W., Palsane, M. N., Lepore, S. J., & Martin, J. (1989). Residential density and psychological wealth: The mediating effects of social support. *Journal of Personality and Social Psychology, 57*(6), 994–999.

Fagan, J. (1993). Drug selling and illicit income in distressed neighborhoods: The economic lives of street-level drug users and dealers. In G. Peterson & A. H. Washington (Eds.), *Drugs, crime, and social isolation*. Washington, DC: Urban Institute Press.

Fagot, B. I. (1977). Consequences of moderate cross-gender behavior in preschool children. *Child Development, 48*, 902–907.

Fagot, B. I. (1984). Teacher and peer reactions to boys' and girls' play styles. *Sex Roles, 11*, 691–702.

Fagot, B. I. (1985). Beyond the reinforcement principle: Another step toward understanding sex-role development. *Developmental Psychology, 21*, 1097–1104.

Fagot, B. I. (1995). Parenting boys and girls. In M. H. Bornstein (Ed.), *Handbook of parenting* (Vol. 1). Mahwah, NJ: Erlbaum.

Fagot, B. I., & Leinbach, M. D. (1987). Socialization of sex roles within the family. In B. Carter (Ed.), *Current conceptions of sex roles and sex typing: Theory and research*. New York: Praeger.

Falbo, T., & Polit, D. (1986). A quantitative review of the only child literature: Research evidence and theory development. *Psychological Bulletin, 100*, 176–189.

Fantz, R. L. (1965). Visual perception from birth as shown by pattern selectivity. *Annals of the New York Academy of Sciences, 118*, 793–814.

Farmer, S. (1989). *Adult children of abusive parents*. New York: Ballantine.

Farrington, D. P. (1991). Childhood aggression and adult violence: Early precursors and later life outcomes. In D. J. Pepler & K. H. Rubin (Eds.), *The development and treatment of childhood aggression*. Hillsdale, NJ: Erlbaum.

Farrington, D. P., & Loeber, R. (2000). Epidemiology of juvenile violence. *Juvenile Violence, 9*, 733–748.

Federal Interagency Forum on Child and Family Statistics. (2004). *America's children: Key national indicators of well-being, 2004*. Washington, DC: Author.

Feld, S. C. (1967). Longitudinal study of the origins of achievement strivings. *Journal of Personality and Social Psychology, 7*, 408–414.

Feldman, F. L., & Scherz, F. (1987). *Family social welfare*. New York: Atherton Press.

Feldstein, B. (1989). Selection as a means of diffusing censorship. In M. K. Rudman (Ed.), *Children's literature: Resources for the classroom*. Norwood, MA: Christopher Gordon.

Feurstein, R. (1980). *Instrumental enrichment*. Baltimore, MD: University Park Press.

Fick, A. L., Osofsky, J. D., & Lewis, M. L. (1997). Perceptions of violence: Children, parents, and police officers. In J. D. Osofsky (Ed.), *Children in a violent society*. New York: Guilford Press.

Field, T., Masi, W., Goldstein, S., & Perry, S. (1988). Infant day care facilitates preschool social behavior. *Early Childhood Research Quarterly, 3*, 341–359.

Fiese, B. H. (2005). Family routines and rituals: Family transactions and individual health. In D. Snyder & J. Simpson (Eds.), *Emotional regulation in families*. Washington, DC: American Psychological Association.

Fiese, B. H., Sameroff, A. J., Grotevant, H. D., Wamboldt, F. S., Dickenstein, S., & Fravel, D. H. (1999). The stories that families tell: Narrative coherence, narrative interaction, and relationship beliefs. *Monographs of the Society for Research in Child Development, 64*(2, Serial No. 257).

Fincham, F. D., & Cain, K. (1986). Learned helplessness in humans: A developmental analysis. *Developmental Review, 6*, 301–333.

Findley, M. S., & Cooper, H. N. (1983). Locus of control and academic achievement: A literature review. *Journal of Personality and Social Psychology, 44*, 419–427.

Finkelhor, D. (1984). *Child sexual abuse: New theory and research*. New York: Free Press.

Finn, J. D., & Achilles, C. M. (1990). Answers and questions about class size: A statewide experiment. *American Association Research Journal, 27*(3), 557–577.

Fischer, W. (1963). Sharing in preschool children as a function of amount and type of reinforcements. *Genetic Psychological Monographs, 68*, 215–245.

Fiske, E. B. (1980). School vs. television. *Parents, 55*(1), 54–59.

Fiske, E. B. (1992). *Smart schools, smart kids*. New York: Touchstone.

Flavell, J. (1986). The development of children's knowledge about the appearance–reality distinction. *American Psychologist, 41*, 418–425.

Flavell, J. H., Miller, P. H., & Miller, S. A. (2001). *Cognitive development* (4th ed.). Englewood Cliffs, NJ: Prentice-Hall.

Fletcher, A. C., Darling, N. E., Steinberg, L., & Dornbusch, S. M. (1995). The company they keep: Relation of adolescents' adjustment and behavior to their friends' perceptions of authoritative parenting in the social network. *Developomental Psychology, 31,* 300–310.

Fontana, D. J. (1992). *Save the family, save the child; What we can do to help children at risk.* New York: Dutton.

Forman, D. R., & Kochanska, G. (2001). Viewing imitation and child responsiveness: A link between teaching and discipline domains of socialization. *Developmental Psychology, 37,* 198–200.

Foss, R. D. (1983). Community norms and blood donation. *Journal of Applied Social Psychology, 13,* 281–290.

Foster-Clark, F. S., & Blyth, D. A. (1991). Peer relations and influences. In R. M. Lerner, A. C. Petersen, & J. Brooks-Gunn (Eds.), *Encyclopedia of adolescence* (Vol. 2). New York: Garland.

Fragin, S. (2000, November). Who cares for kids? *Working Mother,* 57–75.

Fraiberg, S. (1977). *Every child's birthright: In defense of mothering.* New York: Basic Books.

Francese, P. (1995). America at mid-decade. *American Demographics, 17*(2), 23–29.

Francke, L. B. (1983). *Growing up divorced.* New York: Fawcett/Crest.

Frankel, K. A., & Bates, J. E. (1990). Mother-toddler problem-solving. Antecedents in attachment, home behavior, and temperament. *Child Development, 61,* 810–819.

Frede, E. C. (1995). The role of program quality in producing early childhood program benefits. *The Future of Children, 5*(3), 115–132.

Freud, A. (1968). *The psychoanalytical treatment of children.* New York: International Universities Press.

Freud, S. (1925). Some psychical consequences of the anatomical distinction between the sexes. In J. Strachey (Ed. and Trans.), *The standard edition of the complete psychological works of Sigmund Freud.* London: Hogarth Press.

Freud, S. (1938). *The basic writings of Sigmund Freud.* New York: Random House.

Freud, S. (1999). The social construction of normality. *Families in Society: The Journal of Contemporary Human Services, 80*(4), 333–337.

Friedrich, L. K., & Stein, S. H. (1973). Aggressive and prosocial television programs and the national behavior of preschool children. *Monographs of the Society for Research in Child Development, 38*(Serial No. 151).

Fuligni, A. J., & Eccles, J. S. (1993). Perceived parent–child relationships and early adolescents' orientation toward peers. *Developmental Psychology, 29,* 622–632.

Fuligni, A. J., Tseng, V., & Lam, M. (1999). Attitudes toward family obligations among American adolescents with Asian, Latin American, and European backgrounds. *Child Development, 70,* 1030–1044.

Fulton, L. (1994). Peer education partners: A program for learning and working together. *Teaching Exceptional Children, 26*(4), 6–8, 10–11.

Funkhouser, J. E., & Gonzales, M. R. (1997). *Family involvement in children's education: Successful local approaches.* Washington, DC: U.S. Department of Education.

Furman, W. (1995). Parenting siblings. In M. H. Bornstein (Ed.), *Handbook of parenting* (Vol. 1). Mahwah, NJ: Erlbaum.

Furman, W., & Masters, J. C. (1980). Affective consequences of social reinforcement, punishment, and neutral behavior. *Developmental Psychology, 16,* 100–104.

Furrow, J. L., King, P. E., & White, K. (2004). Religion and positive youth development: Identity, meaning, and prosocial concerns. *Applied Developmental Science, 8*(1), 17–26.

Furstenberg, F. (1976). *Unplanned parenthood: The social consequences of teenage childbearing.* New York: Free Press.

Furstenburg, F. F., & Cherlin, A. J. (1991). *Divided families: What happens to children when parents part.* Cambridge, MA: Harvard University Press.

Galinsky, E. (1981). *Between generations: The six stages of parenthood.* New York: Times Books.

Galinsky, E. (1992). The impact of child care on parents. In A. Booth (Ed.), *Childcare in the 1990s: Trends and consequences.* Hillsdale, NJ: Erlbaum.

Gallay, L. S., & Flanagan, C. A. (2000). The well-being of children in a changing economy: Time for a new social contract in America. In R. D Taylor & M. C. Wang (Eds.), *Resilience across contexts: Family, work, culture, and community.* Mahwah, NJ: Erlbaum.

Galton, L. (1980). *Your child in sports.* New York: Watts.

Garbarino, J. (1977). The human ecology of child maltreatment: A conceptual model for research. *Journal of Marriage and the Family, 39,* 721–736.

Garbarino, J. (1986). Can American families afford the luxury of childhood? *Child Welfare, 65*(2), 119–128.

Garbarino, J. (1992). *Children and families in the social environment* (2nd ed.). New York: Aldine de Gruyter.

Garbarino, J. (1995a). *Building a socially nourishing environment with children.* San Francisco: Jossey-Bass.

Garbarino, J. (1995b). *Raising children in a socially toxic society.* San Francisco: Jossey-Bass.

Garbarino, J., & Eckenrode, J. (1997). *Understanding abusive families: An ecological approach to theory and practice*. New York: Jossey-Bass.

Garbarino, J., & Gilliam, G. (1980). *Understanding abusive families*. Lexington, MA: Heath.

Garbarino, J., Guttman, E., & Seely, J. W. (1986). *The psychologically battered child: Strategies for identification, assessment and intervention*. San Francisco: Jossey-Bass.

Garbarino, J., & Sherman, D. (1980). High-risk neighborhoods and high-risk families. *Child Development, 51*, 188–198.

Garcia, R. L. (1998). *Teaching for diversity*. Bloomington, IN: Phi Delta Kappa Educational Foundation.

Garcia-Coll, C. T. (1990). Developmental outcome of minority infants: A process-oriented look into our beginnings. *Child Development, 61*, 270–289.

Garcia-Coll, C. T., Meyer, E. C., & Britton, L. (1995). Ethnic and minority parenting. In M. H. Bornstein (Ed.), *Handbook of parenting* (Vol. 2). Mahwah, NJ: Erlbaum.

Gardner, H. (1999). *Intelligence reframed: Multiple intelligences for the 21st century*. New York: Basic Books.

Gardner, K. E., & LaBrecque, S. V. (1986). Effects of maternal employment on sex-role orientation of adolescents. *Adolescence, 21*(84), 875–885.

Gatz, I. L. (1975). On children and television. *Elementary School Journal, 75*(7), 415–418.

Gay, L. (1998). *The history of rock music*. http://orpheus.la.utk.edu/music

Geen, R. G. (1994). Television and aggression: Recent development in research and theory. In D. Zillman, J. Bryant, & A. C. Huston (Eds.), *Media, children and the family: Social scientific, psychodynamic and clinical perspectives*. Hillsdale, NJ: Erlbaum.

Gelfand, D., Hartman, D. P., Cromer, C. C., Smith, C. L., & Page, B. C. (1975). The effects of instructional prompts and praise on children's donation rates. *Child Development, 46*, 980–983.

Gellene, D. (1996, August 7). Scaring up lots of young readers. *Los Angeles Times*, pp. A1, 18–19.

Gerbner, G., Gross, L., Jackson-Beck, N., Jeffries-Fox, S., & Signorielli, N. (1978). *Violence profile* (No. 9). Philadelphia: University of Pennsylvania Press.

Gerbner, G., Gross, L., Morgan, M., & Signorielli, N. (2002). Growing up with television: Cultivation process. In J. Bryant & D. Zillman (Eds.), *Media effects: Advances in theory and research* (2nd ed.). Mahwah, NJ: Erlbaum.

Gesell, A., & Ilg, F. (1943). *Infant and child in the culture of today*. New York: Harper & Row.

Ghazvini, A., & Mullis, R. L. (2002). Center-based care for young children: Examining predictors of quality. *Journal of Genetic Psychology, 163*, 112–126.

Gibbs, J. C. (1995). The cognitive developmental perspective. In W. M. Kurtines & J. L. Gewirtz (Eds.), *Moral development: An introduction*. Boston: Allyn and Bacon.

Gifford-Smith, M. E., & Rabiner, D. L. (2004). Social information processing and children's social adjustment. In J. J. Kupersmidt & K. A. Dodge (Eds.), *Children's peer relations: From developments to interventions to policy: A Festschrift to honor John D. Coie*. Washington, DC: American Psychological Association.

Gilkeson, E. C., & Bowman, G. W. (1976). *The focus is on children*. New York: Bank Street Publications.

Gilligan, C. (1982). *In a different voice*. Cambridge, MA: Harvard University Press.

Gilligan, C. (1985, April). *Response to critics*. Paper presented at the biennial meeting of the Society for Research in Child Development, Toronto.

Ginsberg, G. S., & Bronstein, D. (1993). Family factors related to children's intrinsic/extrinsic motivational orientation and academic performance. *Child Development, 64*, 1461–1474.

Goff, B. G., & Goddard, H. W. (1999). Terminal core values with adolescent problem behaviors. *Adolescence, 34*, 47–60.

Goffin, S. G., & Lombardi, J. (1988). *Speaking out: Early childhood advocacy*. Washington, DC: National Association for Education of Young Children.

Golden, H. (1962). *You're entitled*. New York: Crest.

Goldman, J. (1994, January 23). Rose Kennedy, 104, dies; matriarch of a dynasty. *Los Angeles Times*, pp. A1, 20.

Goldstein, A. P. (1991). *Delinquent gangs: A psychological perspective*. Champaign, IL: Research Press.

Goleman, D. (1995). *Emotional intelligence*. New York: Bantam.

Gollnick, D. M., & Chinn, P. C. (2005). *Multicultural education in a pluralistic society* (7th ed.). Upper Saddle River, NJ: Merrill/Prentice-Hall.

Good, T. L., & Brophy, J. E. (1986). *Educational psychology* (3rd ed.). New York: Longman.

Good, T. L., & Brophy, J. E. (2003). *Looking in classrooms* (9th ed.). New York: Allyn and Bacon.

Goode, W. J. (1982). *The family* (2nd ed.). Englewood Cliffs, NJ: Prentice-Hall.

Goodlad, J. I. (1984). *A place called school: Prospects for the future*. New York: McGraw-Hill.

Goodman, G. S., Emery, R. E., & Haugaard, J. F. (1998). Developmental psychology and law: Divorce, child maltreatment, foster care, and adoption. In W. Damon (Ed.), *Handbook of child psychology* (5th ed., Vol. 4). New York: Wiley.

Gorn, G. J., & Goldberg, M. E. (1982). Behavioral evidence of the effect of televised food message on children. *Journal of Consumer Research, 9,* 200–205.

Gorsuch, R. L. (1976). Religion as a major predictor of significant human behavior. In W. J. Donaldson, Jr. (Ed.), *Research in mental health and religious behavior.* Atlanta: Psychological Studies Institute.

Gottfried, A. E., Gottfried, A. W., & Buthurst, K. (2002). Maternal and dual earner employment status and parenting. In M. H. Bornstein (Ed.), *Handbook of parenting* (2nd ed., Vol. 2). Mahwah, NJ: Erlbaum.

Gottman, J., Gonso, J., & Rasmussen, B. (1975). Social interaction, social competence, and friendship in children. *Child Development, 46,* 709–718.

Gould, W. S., & Gould, C. B. (1962). *Annotated Mother Goose.* New York: Clarkson N. Potter.

Gozali, H., Cleary, T. A., Walster, G. W., & Gozali, J. (1973). Relationship between the internal–external control construct and achievement. *Journal of Educational Psychology, 64,* 9–14.

Graves, N. B., & Graves, T. O. (1983). The cultural context of prosocial development: An ecological model. In D. L. Bridgeman (Ed.), *The nature of prosocial development: Interdisciplinary theories and strategies.* New York: Academic Press.

Greely, A. M. (2001, March/April). The future of religion in America. *Society,* 32–37.

Green, F. (1990, June 13). Officials say schools aren't prepared for first wave of crack babies. *San Diego Union,* pp. A1, A14, A15.

Greenberg, B. S. (1994). Content trends in media sex. In D. Zillman, J. Bryant, & A. C. Huston (Eds.), *Media, children and the family: Social scientific, psychodynamic, and clinical perspectives.* Hillsdale, NJ: Erlbaum.

Greenberger, E., & Chen, C. (1996). Perceived family relationships and depressed mood in early and late adolescence: A comparison of European and Asian Americans. *Developmental Psychology, 32,* 707–717.

Greenberger, E., & Goldberg, W. A. (1989). Work, parenting, and the socialization of children. *Developmental Psychology, 25*(1), 22–35.

Greenberger, E., O'Neil, R., & Nagel, S. K. (1994). Linking workplace and homeplace: Relations between the nature of adults' work and their parenting behaviors. *Developmental Psychology, 30,* 990–1002.

Greenfield, L. A. (Ed.). (1998, March). *Violence by intimates: Analysis of data on crimes by current or former spouses, boyfriends, and girlfriends.* Washington, DC: U.S. Department of Justice.

Greenfield, P. M. (1984). *Mind and media: The effects of television, video games and computers.* Cambridge, MA: Harvard University Press.

Greenfield, P. M., & Juvonen, J. (1999). A developmental look at Columbine. *APA Monitor Online, 30*(7).

Greenfield, P. M., Keller, H., Fuligni, A., & Maynard, A. (2003). Cultural pathways through universal development. *Annual Review of Psychology, 54,* 461–490.

Greenfield, P. M., & Suzuki, L. K. (1998). Culture and human development: Implications for parenting, education, pediatrics, and mental health. In W. Damon (Ed.), *Handbook of child psychology* (5th ed., Vol. 4). New York: Wiley.

Greenfield, P. M., Yut, E., Chung, M., & Land, D. (1990). The program-length commercial: A study of the effects of television toy tie-ins on imaginative play. *Psychology and Marketing, 7*(4), 237–255.

Grinder, R. E. (1964). Relations between behavior and cognitive dimensions of conscience in middle childhood. *Child Development, 34,* 881–891.

Grolnick, W. S., & Ryan, R. M. (1989). Parents' styles associated with children's self-regulation and competence in school. *Journal of Educational Psychology, 81,* 143–154.

Gronau, R. C., & Waas, G. A. (1997). Delay of gratification and cue utilization: An examination of children's social information processing. *Merrill-Palmer Quarterly, 43,* 305–322.

Groos, K. (1901). *The play of man.* New York: Appleton.

Grotevant, H. D. (1998). Adolescent development in family contexts. In W. Damon (Ed.), *Handbook of child psychology* (5th ed., Vol. 3). New York: Wiley.

Grusec, J. E., & Lytton, H. (1988). *Social development: History, theory, and research.* New York: Springer-Verlag.

Grusec, J. E., Saas-Korlsaak, P., & Simutis, Z. M. (1978). The role of example and moral exhortation in the training of altruism. *Child Development, 49,* 920–923.

Gunnar, M. R. (1980). Contingent stimulation: A review of its role in early development. In S. Levine & H. Ursin (Eds.), *Coping and health.* New York: Plenum.

Haefner, M. J., & Wartella, E. A. (1987). Effects of sibling coviewing on children's interpretations of television programs. *Journal of Broadcasting and Electronic Media, 31,* 153–168.

Haith, M. M. (1966). The response of the human newborn to visual movement. *Journal of Experimental Child Psychology, 3,* 235–243.

Hale, J. (1994). *Unbank the fire*. Baltimore, MD: Johns Hopkins University Press.

Hale-Benson, J. E. (1986). *Black children: Their roots, culture, and learning styles* (rev. ed.). Baltimore, MD: Johns Hopkins University Press.

Haley, G. E. (1989). Cited in J. Trelease, *The new read-aloud handbook*. New York: Penguin.

Hall, C. S. (1954). *A primer of Freudian psychology*. New York: New American Library.

Hall, E. T. (1964). *The silent language*. New York: Doubleday.

Hall, E. T. (1966). *The hidden dimension*. New York: Doubleday.

Hall, E. T. (1976). *Beyond culture*. New York: Doubleday.

Hall, E. T. (1983). *The dance of life*. New York: Doubleday.

Hallahan, D. P., & Kauffman, J. M. (2002). *Exceptional children: Introduction to special education* (9th ed.). Boston: Allyn and Bacon.

Haney, C., Banks, W. C., & Zimbardo, P. G. (1973). Interpersonal dynamics in a simulated prison. *International Journal of Criminology and Penology, 1*, 69–97.

Hardman, M., Drew, C. J., & Egan, M. W. (1999). *Human exceptionality: Society, school, and family* (6th ed.). Boston: Allyn and Bacon.

Hareven, T. K. (1989). Historical changes in children: Networks in the family and community. In D. Belle (Ed.), *Children's social networks and social support*. New York: Wiley.

Harms, T., & Clifford, R. M. (1980). *Early childhood environment rating scale*. New York: Teachers College Press.

Harris, J. R. (1998). *The nurture assumption: Why children turn out the way they do*. New York: Free Press.

Harris, M. (1970). Reciprocity and generosity: Some determinants of sharing in children. *Child Development, 41*, 313–328.

Harris, M. B., & Turner, P. (1986). Gay and lesbian parents. *Journal of Homosexuality, 12*, 101–113.

Harris, R. (1999). *A cognitive psychology of mass communication* (3rd ed.). Mahwah, NJ: Erlbaum.

Harrison, A., Serafica, F., & McAdoo, H. (1984). Ethnic families of color. In R. D. Parke (Ed.), *Review of child development research: Vol. 7. The family*. Chicago: University of Chicago Press.

Harrison, A. O., Wilson, M. N., Pine, C. J., Chan, S., & Buriel, R. (1990). Family ecologies of ethnic minority children. *Child Development, 61*, 347–362.

Hart, B., & Risley, T. R. (1995). *Meaningful differences in the everyday experiences of young American children*. Baltimore: Brookes.

Hart, C. H., DeWolf, D. M., & Burts, D. C. (1992). Linkages among preschoolers' playground behavior, outcome expectations, and parental disciplinary strategies. *Early Education and Development, 3*, 265–283.

Harter, S. (1990). Issues in the assessment of the self-concept of children and adolescents. In A. M. LaGreco (Ed.), *Through the eyes of the child: Obtaining self-reports from children and adolescents*. Boston: Allyn and Bacon.

Harter, S. (1998). The development of self-representations. In W. Damon (Ed.), *Handbook of child psychology* (5th ed., Vol. 3). New York: Wiley.

Harter, S. (1999). *The construction of the self: A developmental perspective*. New York: Guilford Press.

Harter, S., & Connell, J. P. (1984). A model of children's achievement and related self-perceptions of competence, control, and motivational orientations. In J. Nicholls (Ed.), *The development of achievement-related cognition and behavior*. Greenwich, CT: JAI Press.

Hartshorne, H., & May, M. (1978). *Studies in the nature of character: Vol. 1. Studies in deceit*. New York: Macmillan.

Hartup, W. W. (1964). Friendship status and the effectiveness of peers as reinforcing agents. *Journal of Experimental Child Psychology, 1*, 154–162.

Hartup, W. W. (1983). Peer relations. In P. H. Mussen (Ed.), *Handbook of child psychology* (4th ed., Vol. 4). New York: Wiley.

Hartup, W. W. (1989). Social relationships and their developmental significance. *American Psychologist, 44*(2), 120–126.

Hartup, W. W. (1996). The company they keep: Friendships and their developmental significance. *Child Development, 67*, 1–13.

Hartup, W. W., & Coates, B. (1967). Imitation of a peer group and rewardingness of the model. *Child Development, 38*, 1003–1016.

Haskins, R., & Rouse, C. (2005). Closing achievement gaps: School readiness: Closing racial and ethnic gaps. *The Future of Children, 15*(1), 1–7.

Hatcher, B., & Beck, S. S. (1997). *Learning opportunities beyond the school* (2nd ed.). Olney, MD: Association for Childhood Education International.

Haugland, S. W., & Wright, J. L. (1997). *Young children and technology*. Boston: Allyn and Bacon.

Hauser-Cram, P., Warfield, M. E., Shonkoff, J. P., & Krauss, M. W. (2001). Children with disabilities: A longitudinal study of child development and parent well-being. *Monographs of the Society for Research in Child Development, 66*(3, Serial No. 266).

Havighurst, R. (1972). *Human development and education* (3rd ed.). New York: McKay.

Hay, D. F. (1985). Learning to form relationships in infancy: Parallel attainments with parents and peers. *Developmental Review, 5,* 122–161.

Hay, I., Ashman, A. F., & Van Kraayenoord, C. E. (1998). Educational characteristics of students with high or low self-concepts. *Psychology in the Schools, 35,* 391–400.

Hayes, J. W., & Lipset, S. M. (1993/1994, Winter). Individualism: A double-edged sword. *The Responsive Community,* 69–80.

Hayton, J. C., George, G., & Zahra, S. A. (2002). National culture and entrepreneurship: A review of behavioral research. *Entrepreneurship: Theory and Practice, 26*(4), 33–53.

Hayward, D. G., Rothenberg, M., & Beasley, R. R. (1974). Children's play in urban playground environments: A comparison of traditional, contemporary and adventure playground types. *Environment and Behavior, 6*(2), 131–168.

Heady, E. B. (1968). *Men of different colors: When the stones were soft.* New York: Funk & Wagnalls.

Healy, J. (1990). *Endangered minds: Why children don't think and what to do about it.* New York: Touchstone Books.

Healy, J. (1998). *Failure to connect: How computers affect our children's minds and what we can do about it.* New York: Touchstone.

Heath, S. B. (1983). *Ways with words: Language, life and work in communities and classrooms.* Cambridge, MA: Harvard University Press.

Heath, S. B. (1989). Oral and literate traditions among black Americans living in poverty. *American Psychologist, 44*(2), 367–373.

Helburn, S. W., & Howes, C. (1996). Child care cost and quality. *The Future of Children, 6*(2), 62–82.

Helfer, M. E., Kempe, R. S., & Krugman, R. D. (Eds.). (1999). *The battered child* (5th ed.). Chicago: University of Chicago Press.

Henderson, A. T., & Berla, N. (Eds.). (1994). *A new generation of evidence: The family is critical to student achievement.* Washington, DC: National Committee for Citizens in Education.

Hermans, H. J. M., Terlaak, J. J. F., & Maes, P. C. J. M. (1972). Achievement and fear of failure in family and school. *Developmental Psychology, 6,* 520–528.

Hess, R. D. (1986). Family influences on school readiness and achievement in Japan and the United States: An overview of a longitudinal study. In H. Stevenson, H. Azuma, & K. Hakuta (Eds.), *Child development and education in Japan.* New York: W. H. Freeman.

Hess, R. D., & Holloway, S. D. (1984). Family and school as educational institutions. In R. D. Parke (Ed.), *Review of child development research: Vol. 7. The family.* Chicago: University of Chicago Press.

Hetherington, E. M. (1988). Parents, children, and siblings six years after divorce. In R. A. Hinde & J. Stevenson-Hinde (Eds.), *Relationships within families.* Oxford: Oxford University Press.

Hetherington, E. M. (1989). Coping with family transitions: Winners, losers, and survivors. *Child Development, 60,* 1–4.

Hetherington, E. M. (1993). A review of the Virginia longitudinal study of divorce and remarriage: A focus on early adolescence. *Journal of Family Psychology, 7,* 39–56.

Hetherington, E. M., & Clingempeel, W. G. (1992). Coping with marital transitions. *Monographs of the Society for Research in Child Development, 57*(2–3, Serial No. 227).

Hetherington, E. M., & Kelly, J. (2002). *For better or for worse: Divorce reconsidered.* New York: Norton.

Hetherington, E. M., & Stanley-Hagen, N. (2002). Parenting in divorced and remarried families. In M. H. Bornstein (Ed.), *Handbook of parenting* (2nd ed.). Mahwah, NJ: Erlbaum.

Heward, W. L. (2002). *Exceptional children: An introduction to special education* (7th ed.). Englewood Cliffs, NJ: Prentice-Hall.

Heward, W. L., & Orlansky, M. D. (1994). *Exceptional children: An introductory survey of special education.* (4th ed.). Columbus, OH: Merrill.

Hewitt, J. P. (2003). *Self and society: A symbolic interactionist social psychology* (9th ed.). Boston: Allyn and Bacon.

Hewlett, S. A., & West, C. (1998). *The war against parents.* Boston: Houghton Mifflin.

Higgins, A. (1995). Educating for justice and community: Lawrence Kohlberg's vision of moral education. In W. M. Kurtines & J. L. Gewirtz (Eds.), *Moral development: An introduction.* Boston: Allyn and Bacon.

Hilliard, A. (1992, Summer). Behavioral style, culture, and teaching and learning. *Journal of Negro Education, 61*(3), 370–371.

Hirschfield, L. (1997). The conceptual politics of race: Lessons from our children. *Ethos: Journal of the Society for Psychological Anthropology, 25,* 63–92.

Hochschild, A. R. (1989). *The second shift.* New York: Avon.

Hochschild, A. R. (1997). *The time bind.* New York: Metropolitan Books.

Hoff, E. (2003). The specificity of environmental influence: Socioeconomic status affects early vocabulary development via maternal speech. *Child Development, 74,* 1368–1378.

Hoff, E., Laursen, B., & Tardiff, T. (2002). Status and parenting. In M.H. Bornstein (Ed.), *Handbook of parenting* (2nd ed., Vol. 3). Mahwah, NJ: Erlbaum.

Hofferth, S. (1992). The demand for and supply of child care in the 1990s. In A. Booth (Ed.), *Child care in the 1990s: Trends and consequences*. Hillsdale, NJ: Erlbaum.

Hofferth, S. L. (1996). Child care in the United States today. *The Future of Children, 6*(2), 41–61.

Hoffman, L. W. (1989). Effects of maternal employment in the two-parent family. *American Psychologist, 44*(2), 283–292.

Hoffman, L. W. (2000). Maternal employment: Effects of social context. In R. D. Taylor & M. C. Wing (Eds.), *Resilience across contexts*. Mahwah, NJ: Erlbaum.

Hoffman, M. L. (1981). Is altruism part of human nature? *Journal of Personality and Social Psychology, 70*, 237–241.

Hoffman, M. L. (1983). Affective and cognitive processes in moral internalization. In E. T. Higgins, D. N. Ruble, & W. W. Hartup (Eds.), *Social cognition and social development*. Cambridge, UK: Cambridge University Press.

Hoffman, M. L. (1991). Empathy, social cognition, and moral actions. In W. M. Kurtines & J. L. Gewirtz (Eds.), *Handbook of moral behavior and development: Vol. 1. Theory*. Hillsdale, NJ: Erlbaum.

Hoffman, M. L. (2000). *Empathy and moral development*. New York: Cambridge University Press.

Hoffman, M. L., & Saltzstein, H. D. (1967). Parent discipline and the child's moral development. *Journal of Personality and Social Psychology, 5*, 45–57.

Hofstede, G. (1991). *Organizations and cultures: Software of the mind*. New York: McGraw-Hill.

Hogan, R., & Emler, N. (1995). Personality and moral development. In W. M. Kurtines & J. L. Gewirtz (Eds.), *Moral development: An introduction*. Boston: Allyn and Bacon.

Hohmann, M., & Weikart, D. P. (1995). *Educating young children: Active learning practices for preschool educators and child care programs*. Ypsilanti, MI: High/ScopePress.

Holmbeck, G. N., Paikoff, R. L., & Brooks-Gunn, J. (1995). Parenting adolescents. In M. H. Bornstein (Ed.), *Handbook of parenting* (Vol. 1). Mahwah, NJ: Erlbaum.

Honig, A. S. (1986). Stress and coping in children (Part I). *Young Children, 41*(4), 50–63.

Honig, A. S. (1993). Mental health for babies: What do theory and research teach us? *Young Children, 48*(3), 69–76.

Honig, A. S. (2002). Choosing child care for young children. In M. H. Bornstein (Ed.), *Handbook of parenting* (2nd ed., Vol. 4). Mahwah, NJ: Erlbaum.

Hopkins, H. R., & Klein, H. A. (1994). Multidimension self-perception: Linkages to parental nurturance. *Journal of Genetic Psychology, 154*, 465–473.

Horowitz, F. D., & Paden, L. Y. (1973). The effectiveness of environmental intervention programs. In B. M. Caldwell & H. N. Riccuiti (Eds.), *Review of child development research* (Vol. 3). Chicago: University of Chicago Press.

Horwitz, R. (1979). Psychological effects of the "open classroom." *Review of Educational Research, 49*, 71–86.

Howes, C. (1988). Peer interaction of young children. *Monographs of the Society for Research in Child Development, 43*(1, Serial No. 217).

Howes, C., & Matheson, C. C. (1992). Sequences in the development of competent play with peers: Social and social pretend play. *Developmental Psychology, 28*, 961–974.

Howes, C., Matheson, C. C., & Hamilton, C. E. (1994). Maternal, teacher, and child care history correlates of children's relationships with peers. *Child Development, 65*, 264–273.

Huck, C. S., & Helper, S. (Eds.). (1996). *Children's literature in the elementary school* (6th ed.). New York: WCB/McGraw-Hill.

Huesmann, L. R. (1986). Psychological processes promoting the relation between exposure to media violence and aggressive behavior by the viewer. *Journal of Social Issues, 42*, 125–139.

Huesmann, L. R., Eron, L. D., Klein, R., Brice, P., & Fisher, P. (1983). Mitigating the imitation of aggressive behavior by changing children's attitudes about media violence. *Journal of Personality and Social Psychology, 44*, 899–910.

Huesmann, L. R., Moise-Titus, J., Podolski, C., & Eron, L. D. (2003). Longitudinal relations between children's exposure to TV violence and their aggressive and violent behavior in young adulthood: 1977–1992. *Developmental Psychology, 39*(2), 201–221.

Hughes, F. P. (1999). *Children, play, and development* (3rd ed.). Boston: Allyn and Bacon.

Humphrey, J. H. (1993). *Sports for children: A guide for adults*. Springfield, IL: Charles Thomas.

Hunt, J. McV. (1961). *Intelligence and experience*. New York: Ronald Press.

Hurd, T. L., Lerner, R. M., & Barton, C. E. (1999). Integrated services. Expanding partnerships to meet the needs of today's children and families. *Young Children, 54*(2), 74–80.

Huston, A. C. (1983). Sex-typing. In P. H. Mussen (Ed.), *Handbook of child psychology* (4th ed., Vol. 4). New York: Wiley.

Huston, A. C., Carpenter, C. J., Atwater, J. B., & Johnson, L. M. (1986). Gender, adult structuring of activities, and social behavior in middle childhood. *Child Development, 57*, 200–209.

Huston, A. C., Duncan, G. J., Granger, R., Bos, J., McLoyd, V., Mistry, R., et al. (2001). Work-based antipoverty programs for parents can enhance the school performance and social behavior of children. *Child Development, 72*, 318–336.

Huston, A. C., McLoyd, V. C., & Coll, C. G. (1994). Children and poverty: Issues in contemporary research. *Child Development, 65*, 275–282.

Huston, A. C., & Wright, J. C. (1998). Mass media and children's development. In W. Damon (Ed.), *Handbook of child psychology* (5th ed., Vol. 4). New York: Wiley.

Huston, A. C., Zillman, D., & Bryant, J. (1994). Media influence, public policy, and the family. In D. Zillman, J. Bryant, & A. C. Huston (Eds.), *Media, children, and the family: Social scientific, psychodynamic, and clinical perspectives.* Hillsdale, NJ: Erlbaum.

Hutchison, R. (1987). Ethnicity and urban recreation: Whites, blacks and Hispanics in Chicago's public parks. *Journal of Leisure Research, 19*, 205–222.

Hyde, D. (1992). School–parent collaboration results in academic achievement. *NASSP Bulletin, 76*(543), 39–42.

Hymel, S., Bowker, A., & Woody, E. (1993). Aggressive versus withdrawn unpopular children: Variations in peer and self-perceptions in multiple domains. *Child Development, 64*, 879–896.

Iervolino, A. C., Hines, M., Golombok, S. E., Rust, J., & Plomin, R. J. (2005). Genetics and environmental influences on sex-typed behavior during the preschool years. *Child Development, 76*, 826–840.

Inhelder, B., & Piaget, J. (1958). *The growth of logical thinking from childhood to adolescence.* New York: Basic Books.

Inkeles, A. (1969). Social structure and socialization. In D. A. Goslin (Ed.), *Handbook of socialization theory and research.* Chicago: Rand McNally.

Isaacs, S. (1999). *Brave dames and wimpettes: What women are really doing on page and screen.* New York: Ballantine.

Iverson, T. J., & Segal, M. (1990). *Child abuse and neglect: An information and reference guide.* New York: Garland Publishing.

Jackson, R. K., & McBride, W. D. (1985). *Understanding street gangs.* Sacramento, CA: Custom.

Jacobs, J. S., & Tunnell, M. O. (1996). *Children's literature, briefly.* Englewood Cliffs, NJ: Prentice-Hall.

Jacobson, J. L., & Wille, D. E. (1986). The influence of attachment pattern on developmental changes in peer interaction from the toddler to the preschool period. *Child Development, 57*, 338–347.

Jaffe, M. L. (1998). *Adolescence.* New York: Wiley.

Jaffee, S., & Hyde, J. H. (2000). Gender differences in moral orientation: A meta-analysis. *Psychological Bulletin, 12*, 703–726.

Jaffee, S. R., Caspi, A. Moffitt, T. E., Polo-Thomas, M., Price, T. S., & Taylor, A. (2004). The limits of child effects: Evidence for genetically mediated child effects on corporal punishment, but not on physical maltreatment. *Developmental Psychology, 40*(6), 1047–1055.

James, M., & Jongeward, D. (1971). *Born to win.* Reading, MA: Addison-Wesley.

Jencks, C. (1979). *Who gets ahead?* New York: Basic Books.

Jensen, A. R. (1969). How much can we boost IQ and scholastic achievement? *Harvard Educational Review, 39*, 1–123.

Jensen, A. R. (1988). Speed of information processing and population differences. In S. H. Irvine & J. W. Berry (Eds.), *Human abilities in cultural context.* New York: Cambridge University Press.

Johnson, D. W., & Johnson, R. T. (1999). *Learning together and alone: Cooperative, competitive, and individualistic learning* (5th ed.). Boston: Allyn and Bacon.

Johnson, D. W., Johnson, R. T., & Maruyama, G. (1983). Interdependence and interpersonal attraction among heterogeneous and homogeneous individuals: A theoretical formulation and a meta-analysis of the research. *Review of Education Research, 53*, 5–54.

Johnson, J. A., Musial, D. L., Hall, G. E., Gollnick, D. M., & Dupuis, V. L. (2004). *Introduction to the foundations of American education* (13th ed.). Needham Heights, MA: Allyn and Bacon.

Johnson, P. A., & Staffieri, J. R. (1971). Stereotype affective properties of personal names and somatotypes in children. *Developmental Psychology, 5*(1), 176.

Johnson, R. (2002, July 24). Obituary: Chaim Potok. *Los Angeles Times*, p. B13.

Johnston, J., & Ettema, J. S. (1982). *Positive images: Breaking stereotypes with children's television.* Newbury Park, CA: Sage.

Jones, K. L., Smith, D. W., Ulleland, C. L., & Streissguth, P. (1973). Patterns of malformation in offspring of chronic alcoholic mothers. *Lancet, 1*, 1267–1271.

Jose, P. E. (1990). Just world reasoning in children's immanent justice judgments. *Child Development, 61*, 1024–1033.

Jung, C. G. (1938). *Psychology and religion.* New Haven, CT: Yale University Press.

Kagan, J. (1971). *Personality development.* New York: Harcourt Brace Jovanovich.

Kagan, J. (1975, September 22). The parent gap. *Newsweek.* (Reprinted *in Annual Editions: Readings in Human Development 76/77.* Guilford, CT: Dushkin)

Kagan, J. (1984). *The nature of the child.* New York: Basic Books.

Kagan, J. (1994). *Galen's Prophecy: Temperament in human nature.* New York: Basic Books.

Kagan, J. (1998). Biology and the child. In W. Damon (Ed.), *Handbook of child psychology* (5th ed., Vol. 3). New York: Wiley.

Kagan, J., & Moss, H. (1959). Stability and validity of achievement fantasy. *Journal of Abnormal and Social Psychology, 58,* 357–364.

Kagan, J., Reznick, J. S., & Gibbons, J. (1989). Inhibited and uninhibited types of children. *Child Development, 60,* 838–845.

Kagicibasi, C. (1996). *Family and human development across cultures: A view from the other side.* Mahwah, NJ: Erlbaum.

Kaiser Family Foundation. (1999). *Kids and media and the new millennium.* Menlo Park, CA: Author.

Kaiser Family Foundation. (2002). *Children and video games.* Menlo Park, CA: Author.

Kaiser Family Foundation. (2003). *Zero to six: Electronic media in the lives of infants, toddlers, and preschoolers.* Menlo Park, CA: Author.

Kaiser Family Foundation. (2004). *Tweens, teens, and magazines.* Menlo Park, CA: Author.

Kaiser Family Foundation. (2005a). *Generation M: Media in the lives of 8–18-year olds.* Menlo Park, CA: Author.

Kaiser Family Foundation. (2005b). *Sex-on-TV—4.* Menlo Park, CA: Author.

Kalichman, S. C. (1999). *Mandated reporting of suspected child abuse: Ethics, law, and policy* (2nd ed.) Washington, DC: American Psychological Association.

Kallen, H. M. (1956). *Cultural pluralism and the American ideal.* Philadelphia: University of Pennsylvania Press.

Kantrowitz, B. (1996). Gay families come out. *Newsweek, 128*(19), 50–57.

Kantrowitz, B., & Wingert, P. (1990). Step by step. *Newsweek, 94*(27), 24–34.

Kantrowitz, B., & Wingert, P. (1998). Learning at home: Does it pass the final test? *Newsweek, 132*(14), 64–71.

Kantrowitz, B., & Wingert, P. (2001). Unmarried with children. *Newsweek, 14*(11), 46–54.

Karoly, L. A. (Ed.) (1998). *Investing in our children: What we know and don't know about the costs and benefits of early childhood interventions.* Santa Monica, CA: Rand.

Kaslow, F. W. (2001). Families and family psychology at the millennium: Intersecting crossroads. *American Psychologist, 56*(1), 37–46.

Katchadourian, H. (1990). Sexuality. In S. S. Feldman & G. R. Elliot (Eds.), *At the threshold: The developing adolescent.* Cambridge, MA: Harvard University Press.

Katz, L. B. (1984). *More talks with teachers.* Urbana, IL: Elementary and Early Childhood Education.

Katz, P. A. (Ed.). (1975). *Toward the elimination of racism.* New York: Pergamon Press.

Katz, P., & Zalk, S. (1978). Modification of children's racial attitudes. *Developmental Psychology, 14*(5), 447–461.

Kaufman, J. (1989). The regular education policy: A trickle-down theory of education of the hard to teach. *Journal of Special Education, 23,* 256–278.

Kearny, M. (1999). The role of teachers in helping children of domestic violence. *Childhood Education, 75*(5), 290–296.

Keats, E. J. (1967). *Peter's chair.* New York: Harper & Row.

Kellam, S. G., Ling, X., Merisca, R., Brown, C. H., & Ialongo, N. (1999). The effect of the level of aggression in the 1st grade classroom on the course and malleability of aggressive behavior into middle school. *Development and Psychopathology, 10,* 165–185.

Kelly, J. B. (2000). Children's adjustment in conflicted marriage and divorce: A decade's review of research. *Journal of the American Academy of Child and Adolescent Psychiatry, 39,* 963–973.

Kelly, J. B., & Emery, R. B. (2003). Children's adjustment following divorce: Risk and resilience perspectives. *Family Relations, 52*(4), 352–362.

Keltikangas-Jarvinen, L., Terav, T., & Pakaslahti, L. (1999). Moral reasoning among Estonian and Finnish adolescents: A comparison of collectivist and individual settings. *Journal of Cross-Cultural Psychology, 30,* 257–290.

Kemple, K. M. (1991). Research in review: Preschool children's peer acceptance and social interaction. *Young Children, 46*(5), 47–54.

Kennell, J., Voos, D., & Klaus, M. (1976). Parent–infant bonding. In R. Helfer & C. H. Kempe (Eds.), *Child abuse and neglect: The family and the community.* Cambridge, MA: Ballinger.

Kerns, K. A., Contreras, J. M., & Neal-Barnett, A. M. (2000). *Family and peers: Linking two social worlds.* Westport, CT: Praeger.

Killen, M., & Nucci, L. P. (1995). Morality, autonomy, and social conflict. In M. Killen & D. Hart (Eds.), *Morality in everyday life: Developmental perspectives.* Cambridge, UK: Cambridge University Press.

Kim, J. E., Hetherington, E. M., & Reiss, D. (1999). Associations among family relationships, antisocial peers, and adolescents' externalizing behaviors: Gender and family type differences. *Child Development, 70,* 1209–1230.

Kimball, M. M. (1986). Television and sex-role attitudes. In T. M. Williams (Ed.), *The impact of television: A natural experiment in three communities.* Orlando, FL: Academic Press.

Kindermann, T. (1998). Children's development within peer groups: Using composite social maps to identify peer networks and study their influences. In W. M. Bukowski & A. H. Cillesen (Eds.), *New directions for child development* (No. 80). San Francisco: Jossey-Bass.

Kinman, J. R., & Henderson, D. L. (1985). An analysis of sexism in Newbery Medal award books from 1977 to 1984. *The Reading Teacher, 38*(9), 885–889.

Kinney, D. A. (1993). From nerds to normals. *Sociology of Education, 66*(1), 21–40.

Kirk, S., Gallagher, J. J., & Anastasiow, N. J. (2000). *Educating exceptional children* (9th ed.). Boston: Houghton Mifflin.

Kluckhohn, F. (1961). Dominant and variant value orientation. In C. Kluckhohn & H. Murray (Eds.), *Personality in nature and society.* New York: Knopf.

Kluckhohn, F., & Strodbeck, F. (1961). *Variations in value orientations.* Evanston, IL: Row Peterson.

Kluger, J., & Park, A. (2001). The quest for a super kid. *Time, 157*(7), 50–55.

Koblinsky, S., & Behana, N. (1984). Child sexual abuse: The educator's role in prevention, detection, and intervention. *Young Children, 39*(6), 3–15.

Kochanska, G. (1991). Socialization and temperament in the development of guilt and conscience. *Child Development, 62,* 1379–1392.

Kochanska, G. (1993). Toward a synthesis of parental socialization and child temperament in early development of conscience. *Child Development, 64,* 325–347.

Kochanska, G. (1995). Children's temperament, mothers' discipline, and security of attachment: Multiple pathways to emerging internalization. *Child Development, 66,* 597–615.

Kochanska, G. (1997). Multiple pathways to conscience for children with different temperaments: From toddlerhood to age 5. *Developmental Psychology, 33,* 228–240.

Kochanska, G., DeVet, K., Goldman, M., Murray, K., & Putnam, S. P. (1994). Maternal reports of conscience development and temperament in young children. *Child Development, 65,* 852–868.

Koff, E., Rierdan, J., & Stubbs, M. L. (1990). Gender, body image, and self-concept in early adolescence. *Journal of Early Adolescence, 10,* 56–68.

Kohl, H. (1967). *36 children.* New York: New American Library.

Kohl, H. (1984). *Growing minds: On becoming a teacher.* New York: Harper & Row.

Kohlberg, L. (1966). A cognitive developmental analysis of children's sex-role concepts and attitudes. In E. E. Maccoby (Ed.), *The development of sex differences.* Stanford, CA: Stanford University Press.

Kohlberg, L. (1969). Stage and sequence: The cognitive developmental approach to socialization. In D. A. Goslin (Ed.), *Handbook of socialization theory and research.* Chicago: Rand McNally.

Kohlberg, L. (1976). Moral stages and moralization. In T. Lickona (Ed.), *Moral development and behavior.* New York: Holt, Rinehart & Winston.

Kohlberg, L. (Ed.). (1980). *Recent research in moral development.* New York: Holt, Rinehart & Winston.

Kohlberg, L. (1984). *Essays on moral development: Vol.2. The psychology of moral development.* San Francisco: Harper & Row.

Kohlberg, L. (1985). The just community approach to moral education in theory and practice. In M. W. Berkowitz & F. Oser (Eds.), *Moral education: Theory and application.* Hillsdale, NJ: Erlbaum.

Kohlberg, L. (1986). A current statement on some theoretical issues. In S. Modgil & C. Modgil (Eds.), *Lawrence Kohlberg.* Philadelphia: Folmer.

Kohn, M. (1977). *Class and conformity: A study in values* (2nd ed.). Chicago: University of Chicago University Press.

Kohn, M. (1995). Social structure and personality through time and space. In P. Moen, G. H. Elder, & K. Luscher (Eds.), *Examining lives in context: Perspectives on the ecology of human development.* Washington, DC: American Psychological Association.

Kostelnik, M. J., Whiren, A. P., & Stein, L. C. (1986). Living with He-Man. *Young Children, 41*(4), 3–9.

Kounin, J. (1970). *Discipline and group management in the classroom.* New York: Holt, Rinehart & Winston.

Kozol, J. (1991). *Savage inequalities: Children in America's schools.* New York: Crown.

Krebs, R. (1967). *Some relations between moral judgment, attention and resistance to temptation.* Unpublished doctoral dissertation, University of Chicago.

Krononberger, L. (1966). Uncivilized and uncivilizing. *TV Guide, 14*(9), 15.

Krug, M. (1976). *The melting of the ethnics.* Bloomington, IN: Phi Delta Kappa.

Kuczen, B. (1987). *Childhood stress.* New York: Dell.

Kuczynski, L. (2003). Beyond bidirectionality: Bilateral conceptual frameworks for understanding dynamics in parent–child relations. In L. Kuczynski (Ed.), *Handbook of dynamics in parent–child relationships*. Thousand Oaks, CA: Sage.

Kuczynski, L., Kochanska, G., Radke-Yarrow, M., & Girnius-Brown, O. (1987). A developmental interpretation of young children's noncompliance. *Developmental Psychology, 23*, 799–806.

Kunkel, D. (2001). Children and television advertising. In D. G. Singer & J. L. Singer (Eds.), *Handbook of children and the media*. Thousand Oaks, CA: Sage.

Kunkel, D., Wilcox, B. L., Cantor, J., Palmer, E., Linn, S., & Dowrick, P. (2004). *Report of the APA Task Force on Advertising and Children*. Washington, DC: American Psychological Association.

Kupersmidt, J. B., Coie, J. D., & Dodge, K. A. (1990). The role of poor peer relationships in the development of disorder. In S. R. Asher & J. D. Coie (Eds.), *Peer rejection in childhood*. New York: Cambridge University Press.

Kurtines, W. M., & Gewirtz, J. (Eds.). (1991). *Handbook of moral behavior and development*. Hillsdale, NJ: Erlbaum.

Ladd, G. W. (1990). Having friends, keeping friends, making friends, and being liked by peers in the classroom: Predictions of children's early school adjustment. *Child Development, 61*, 1081–1100.

Ladd, G. W. (1999). Peer relationships and social competence during early and middle childhood. *Annual Review of Psychology*, 333–344.

Ladd, G. W., & LeSieur, K. D. (1995). Parents and peer relationships. In M. H. Bornstein (Ed.), *Handbook of parenting* (Vol. 4). Mahwah, NJ: Erlbaum.

Ladd, G. W., & Pettit, G. S. (2002). Parenting and the development of children's peer relationships. In M. H. Bornstein (Ed.), *Handbook of parenting* (2nd ed.). Mahwah, NJ: Erlbaum.

Laible, D. J., & Thompson, R. A. (2000). Mother–child discourse, attachment security, shared positive affect, and early conscience development. *Child Development, 71*, 1424–1446.

Lamb, M. E. (1977). The development of mother–infant and father–infant attachment in the second year of life. *Developmental Psychology, 13*(6), 637–648.

Lamb, M. E. (1998). Nonparental child care: Context, quality, correlates, and consequences. In W. Damon (Ed.), *Handbook of child psychology* (5th ed., Vol. 4). New York: Wiley.

Lamb, M. E. (2000). The effects of quality of care on child development. *Applied Developmental Science, 4*(3), 112–115.

Lamb, M. E. (Ed.). (2004). *The role of the father in child development* (4th ed.). New York: Wiley.

Lamb, M. E., Hwang, C. P., Ketterlinus, R. D., & Fracasso, M. F. (1999). Parent–child relationships: Development in the context of the family. In M. H. Bornstein & M. E. Lamb (Eds.), *Developmental psychology: An advanced textbook* (4th ed.). Mahwah, NJ: Erlbaum.

Lamb, M. E., Parker, F., Boak, A. Y., Griffin, K. W., & Peax, L. (1999). Parent–child relationship, home learning environment, and school readiness. *School Psychology Review, 28*, 413–425.

Lamborn, S. D., Mounts, N. S., Steinberg, L., & Dornbusch, S. (1991). Patterns of competence and adjustment among adolescents from authoritative, authoritarian, indulgent, and neglectful families. *Child Development, 62*, 1049–1065.

Landre, R., Miller, M., & Porter, D. (1997). *Gangs: A handbook for community awareness*. New York: Facts on File.

Langlois, J. H. (1986). From the eye of the beholder to behavioral reality: Development of social behavior and social relations as a function of physical attractiveness. In C. P. Herman, M. P. Zanna, & E. T. Higgins (Eds.), *Physical behavior: The Ontario Symposium* (Vol. 3). Hillsdale, NJ: Erlbaum.

Langlois, J. H., & Downs, A. C. (1980). Mothers, fathers, and peers as socialization agents of sex-typed behaviors in young children. *Child Development, 51*, 1217–1247.

Langlois, J. H., & Liben, L. S. (2003). Child care research: An editorial perspective. *Child Development, 74*(4), 969–975.

Lapsley, D. K. (1996). *Moral psychology*. Boulder, CO: Westview.

Larrick, N. (1975). Children of television. *Teacher Magazine, 93*, 75–77.

Larson, R. (1995) Secrets in the bedroom: Adolescents' private use of media. *Journal of Youth and Adolescence, 24*(5), 535–550.

Larson, R., Kubey, R., & Colletti, J. (1989). Changing channels: Early adolescent media choices and shifting investments in family and friends. *Journal of Youth and Adolescence, 18*(16), 583–599.

Larson, T. (1992). Understanding stepfamilies. *American Demographics, 14*, 360.

Lasker, J. (1972). *Mothers can do anything*. Chicago: Albert Whitman.

Lazar, I. (1977). The persistence of preschool effects: A long-term follow-up on fourteen infant and preschool experiments. *Final report to the administration on children, youth and families*. Washington, DC: U.S. Department of Health, Education, and Welfare, Office of Human Services.

Leach, P. (1994). *Children first*. New York: Knopf.

Leaf, M. (1936). *The story of Ferdinand*. New York: Viking/Penguin.

Leaper, C. (1994). Exploring the correlates and consequences of gender segregation: Social relationships in childhood, adolescence, and adulthood. In C. Leaper (Ed.), *New directions for child development* (No. 65). San Francisco: Jossey-Bass.

Leaper, C. (2000). Gender, affiliation, assertion, and the interactive context of parent–child play. *Developmental Psychology, 36*, 381–393.

Leaper, C. (2002). Parenting girls and boys. In M. H. Bornstein (Ed.), *Handbook of parenting* (2nd ed., Vol. 1). Mahwah, NJ: Erlbaum.

Lee, V. E. (2004). School size, and the organization of secondary schools. In J. H. Ballantine & J. Z. Spade (Eds.), *Schools and society: A sociological approach to education* (2nd ed.). Belmont, CA: Wadsworth.

Leershen, C., & Namuth, T. (1988). *Alcohol and the family, 111*(3), 62–68.

Leibert, R. M., Neil, M., & Davidson, E. S. (1973). *The early window: Effects of television on children and youth*. New York: Pergamon Press.

Leibert, R. M., & Poulos, R. W. (1976). Television as a moral teacher. In T. Lickona (Ed.), *Moral development and behavior*. New York: Holt, Rinehart & Winston.

Leibert, R. M., & Sprafkin, J. (1988). *The early window: Effects of television on children and youth* (3rd ed.). New York: Pergamon Press.

LeMasters, E. E. (1988). Blue-collar aristocrats and their children. In G. Handel (Ed.), *Childhood socialization*. New York: Aldine de Gruyer.

Lengua, L. J. (2002). The contribution of emotionality and self-regulation to the understanding of children's response to multiple risk. *Child Development, 73*, 144–161.

Lepper, M. R. (1983). Social-control processes and the internalization of social values: An attributional perspective. In E. T. Higgins, D. N. Ruble, & W. W. Hartup (Eds.), *Social cognition and social development: A sociocultural perspective*. Cambridge, UK: Cambridge University Press.

Lerner, J. V. (1993). The influence of child temperamental characteristics on parent behaviors. In T. Luster & L. Okagaki (Eds.), *Parenting: An ecological perspective*. Hillsdale, NJ: Erlbaum.

Lerner, J., Mardell-Czudnowski, C., & Goldberg, G. (1987). *Special education for the early childhood years* (2nd ed.). Englewood Cliffs, NJ: Prentice-Hall.

Lerner, R. M. (1998). Theories of human development: Contemporary perspectives. In W. Damon (Ed.), *Handbook of child psychology* (5th ed., Vol. 1.). New York: Wiley.

Leventhal, T., & Brooks-Gunn, J. (2000). The neighborhoods they live in: The effects of neighborhood residence on child and adolescent outcomes. *Psychological Bulletin, 126*(2), 309–337.

Lever, J. (1976). Sex differences in the games children play. *Social Problems, 23*, 478–487.

Lever, J. (1978). Sex differences in the complexity of children's play. *American Sociological Review, 43*, 471–482.

Levin, D. E. (1998). *Remote control childhood? Combating the hazards of media culture*. Washington, DC: National Association for Education of Young Children.

Levin, D. E., & Carlsson-Paige, N. (1995). The Mightly Morphin Power Rangers: Teachers voice concern. *Young Children, 50*(6), 67–72.

Levine, D. U., & Levine, R. F. (1996). *Society and education* (9th ed.). Needham Heights, MA: Allyn and Bacon.

LeVine, R. A. (1977). Child rearing as a cultural adaptation. In P. H. Leiderman, S. R. Tulken, & A. Rosenfeld (Eds.), *Culture and infancy*. New York: Academic Press.

LeVine, R. A. (1988). Human parental care: Universal goals, cultural strategies, individual behavior. In R. A. LeVine, P. M. Miller, & M. M. West (Eds.), *Parental behavior in diverse societies*. San Francisco: Jossey-Bass.

Lewin, K., Lippitt, R., & White, R. (1939). Patterns of aggressive behavior in experimentally created social climates. *Journal of Social Psychology, 10*, 271–299.

Lewit, E. M., & Baker, L. S. (1995). School readiness: Critical issues for children and youths. *The Future of Children, 5*(2), 128–139.

Liben, L. S., & Bigler, R. S. (2002). The developmental course of gender differentiation: Conceptualizing, measuring, and evaluating constructs and pathways. *Monographs of the Society for Research in Child Development, 67*(2, Serial No. 269).

Lickona, T. (1977). How to encourage moral development. *Learning, 5*(7), 36–43.

Lickona, T. (1991). *Educating for character*. New York: Bantam.

Limber, S. P., & Nation, M. A. (1998). Violence within the neighborhood and community. In P. K. Trickett & C. J. Schellenbach (Eds.), *Violence against children in the family and the community*. Washington, DC: American Psychological Association.

Linney, J. A., & Seidman, E. (1989). The future of schooling. *American Psychologist, 44*(2), 336–340.

Lionni, L. (1968). *The biggest house in the world*. New York: Pantheon.

Lippa, R. A. (2005). *Gender, nature, and nurture* (2nd ed.). Mahwah, NJ: Erlbaum.

Lippitt, R., & White, R. K. (1943). The social climate of children's groups. In R. G. Barker, J. S. Korinen, & H. F. Wright (Eds.), *Child behavior and development*. New York: McGraw-Hill.

List, J. A., Collins, W. A., & Westby, S. D. (1983). Comprehension and inferences from traditional and nontraditional sex-role portrayals on television. *Child Development, 54*, 1579–1587.

Logue, A. W. (1995). *Self-control: Waiting until tomorrow for what you want today*. Englewood Cliffs, NJ: Prentice-Hall.

Lohr, J. M., & Staats, A. (1973). Attitude conditioning in Sino-Tibetan languages. *Journal of Personality and Social Psychology, 26*, 196–200.

Long, L., & Long, T. (1982). The unspoken fears of latchkey kids. *Working Mother, 5*(76), 88–90.

Long, L., & Long, T. (1983). *The handbook for latchkey children and their parents*. New York: Arbor House.

Lonigan, C. J., Burgess, S. R., & Anthony, J. L. (2000). Development of emergent literacy and early reading skills in preschool children: Evidence from a latent-variable longitudinal study. *Developmental Psychology, 36*, 596–613.

Lorenz, K. (1966). *On aggression*. New York: Harcourt, Brace & World.

Lowenthal, B. (1999). Effects of maltreatment and ways to promote children's resiliency. *Childhood Education, 75*(4), 204–209.

Lull, J. (1980). The social uses of television. *Human Communication Research, 6*, 197–209.

Luster, T., & Okagaki, L. (1993). Multiple influences on parenting: Ecological and life-course perspectives. In T. Luster & L. Okagaki (Eds.), *Parenting: An ecological perspective*. Hillsdale, NJ: Erlbaum.

Lustig, M., & Koester, J. (1999). *Intercultural competence: Interpersonal communication across cultures*. New York: Longman Press.

Luthar, S. S., & Becker, B. E. (2002). Priveleged but pressured? A study of affluent youth. *Child Development, 73*, 1593–1610.

Lytton, H., & Romney, D. M. (1991). Parents' differential socialization of boys and girls: A meta-analysis. *Psychological Bulletin, 109*, 267–296.

Maccoby, E. E. (1990). Gender and relationships: A developmental account. *American Psychologist, 45*, 513–520.

Maccoby, E. E. (1998). *The two sexes: Growing up apart, coming together*. Cambridge, MA: Harvard University Press.

Maccoby, E. E. (2000). Perspectives on gender development. *International Journal of Behavioral Development, 24*, 398–406.

Maccoby, E. E., & Jacklin, C. N. (1974). *The psychology of sex differences*. Stanford, CA: Stanford University Press.

Maccoby, E. E., & Jacklin, C. N. (1987). Gender segregation in childhood. *Advances in Child Development and Behavior, 20*, 239–287.

Maccoby, E. E., & Martin, J. (1983). Socialization in the context of family: Parent–child interaction. In P. H. Mussen (Ed.), *Handbook of child psychology* (4th ed., Vol. 4). New York: Wiley.

Maccoby, E. E., & Mnooken, R. (1992) (Eds.). *Dividing the child*. Cambridge, MA: Harvard University Press.

MacDonald, K., & Parke, R. D. (1986). Parent–child physical play: The effects of sex and age of children and parents. *Sex Roles, 15*(7/8), 367–378.

MacLeod, A. S. (1994). *American childhood*. Athens: University of Georgia Press.

Madon, S., Jussim, L., & Eccles, J. (1997). In search of the powerful self-fulfilling prophecy. *Journal of Personality and Social Psychology, 72*, 791–809.

Madsen, M. C., & Shapira, A. (1970). Cooperative and competitive behavior of urban Afro-American, Anglo-American, and Mexican-American and Mexican village children. *Developmental Psychology, 3*, 16–20.

Maehr, M. L. (1974). *Sociocultural origins of achievement*. Monterey, CA: Brooks/Cole.

Maidman, F. (Ed.). (1984). *Child welfare: A sourcebook of knowledge and practice*. New York: Child Welfare League of America.

Main, M., & Solomon, J. (1990). Procedures for identifying infants as disorganized/disoriented during the Ainsworth Strange Situation. In M. T. Greenberg, D. Cicchetti, & E. M. Cummings (Eds.), *Attachment in the preschool years: Theory, research, and intervention*. Chicago: University of Chicago Press.

Malamuth, N. M., & Impett, E. A. (2001). Research on sex in the media. In D. G. Singer & J. L. Singer (Eds.), *Handbook of children and the media*. Thousand Oaks, CA: Sage.

Mann, J. (1982). What is TV doing to America? *U.S. News & World Report, 93*(5), 27–30.

Marcossen, M., & Fleming, V. (Eds.). (1978, November). *The children's political checklist*. Washington, DC: Coalition for Children and Youth.

Margolin, G. (1998). Effects of domestic violence on children. In P. K. Trickett & C. J. Schellenbach (Eds.), *Violence against children in the family and the community*. Washington, DC: American Psychological Association.

Margolis, C. (1971). The black student in political strife. *Proceedings of the 79th Annual Convention of the American Psychological Association, 10*, 395–396.

Marshall, P. L. (2002). *Cultural diversity in our schools.* Belmont, CA: Wadsworth.

Martin, C. L. (1989). Children's use of gender-related information in making social judgments. *Developmental Psychology, 25,* 80–88.

Martin, C. L., & Halverson, C. F. (1981). A schematic processing model of sex-typing and stereotyping in children. *Child Development, 52,* 1119–1134.

Martin, C. L., & Halverson, C. F., Jr. (1987). The roles of cognition in sex-roles and sex-typing. In D. B. Carter (Ed.), *Current conceptions of sex roles and sex-typing: Theory and research.* New York: Praeger.

Martin, C. L., Wood, C. H., & Little, J. K. (1990). The development of gender stereotype components. *Child Development, 61,* 1891–1904.

Martin, G. B., & Clark, R. D. (1982). III. Distress crying in neonates: Species and peer specificity. *Developmental Psychology, 18,* 3–9.

Martin, G., & Pear, J. (2003). *Behavior modification: What it is and how to do it* (7th ed.). Upper Saddle River, NJ: Prentice-Hall.

Martinez, R., & Dukes, R. L. (1991). Ethnic and gender differences and self-esteem. *Youth and Society, 3,* 318–338.

Mason, K. O., & Duberstein, L. (1992). Consequences of child-care practices and arrangements for the well-being of parents and providers. In A. Booth (Ed.), *Child care in the 1990s: Trends and consequences.* Hillsdale, NJ: Erlbaum.

Mason, M. A. (1998). *The custody wars: Why children are losing the legal battle—and what we can do about it.* New York: Basic Books.

Mason, M. G., & Gibbs, J. C. (1993). Social perspective taking and moral judgement among college students. *Journal of Adolescent Research, 8,* 109–123.

Maughan, A., & Cicchetti, D. (2002). Impact of child maltreatment and interadult violence on children's emotion-regulation abilities and socioemotional adjustment, *Child Development, 73,* 1525–1542.

Mayes, L. C., & Zigler, E. (1992). An observational study of the affective concomitants of mastery in infants. *Journal of Psychology and Psychiatry, 4,* 659–667.

McClelland, D. C. (1961). *The achieving society.* New York: Van Nostrand.

McClelland, D. C., Atkinson, J. W., Clark, R. A., & Lowell, E. L. (1953). *The achievement motive.* New York: Appleton-Century-Crofts.

McClelland, D. C., & Pilon, D. A. (1983). Sources of adult motives in patterns of parent behavior in early childhood. *Journal of Personality and Social Psychology, 44,* 564–574.

McCloskey, R. (1948). *Blueberries for Sal.* New York: Viking Press.

McCormick, L., & Holden, R. (1992). Homeless children: A special challenge. *Young Children, 47*(6), 61–67.

McGoldrick, M., Giordano, J., Pearse, J. K., & Giordano, J. (1996). *Ethnicity and family therapy* (2nd ed.) New York: Guilford.

McGuire, W. J. (1985). Attitudes and attitude change. In G. Lindzey & E. Aronson (Eds.), *Handbook of social psychology* (3rd ed., Vol. 2). New York: Random House.

McHale, J. P. (1995). Coparenting and triadic interactions during infancy: The roles of marital distress and child gender. *Developmental Psychology, 31,* 985–996.

McHale, S. M., Crouter, A. C., & Tucker, C. J. (1999). Family context and gender-role socialization in middle childhood: Comparing girls to boys and sisters to brothers. *Child Development, 70,* 990–1004.

McHale, S. M., Crouter, A. C., & Whiteman, S. D. (2003). The family contexts of gender development in childhood and adolescence. *Social Development, 12*(1), 125–148.

McHale, S. M., Updegraff, K. A., Helms-Erikson, H., & Crouter, A. C. (2001). Sibling influences on gender development in middle childhood and early adolescence: A longitudinal study. *Developmental Psychology, 37,* 115–125.

McHale, S. M., Updegraff, K. A., Jackson-Newsom, J., Tucker, C. J., & Crouter, A. C. (2000). When does parents' differential treatment have negative implications for siblings? *Social Development, 9,* 149–172.

McLanahan, S. (Ed.). (2005). School readiness: Closing racial and ethnic gaps. *The Future of Children, 15* (1).

McLanahan, S., & Carlson, M. J. (2002). Welfare reform, fertility, and father involvement. Children and Welfare Reform. *The Future of Children, 12*(1), 147–165.

McLanahan, S., & Sandefur, G. (1994). *Growing up with a single parent. What hurts, what helps.* Cambridge, MA: Harvard University Press.

McLane, J. B., & McNamee, G. D. (1990). *Early literacy.* Cambridge, MA: Harvard University Press.

McLoyd, V. C. (1990). The impact of economic hardship on black families and children. Psychological distress, parenting, and socioemotional development. *Child Development, 61,* 311–346.

McLoyd, V. C. (1998). Children in poverty: Development, public policy, and practice. In W. Damon (Ed.), *Handbook of child psychology* (5th ed., Vol. 4). New York: Wiley.

McLoyd, V. C., & Wilson, L. (1990). Maternal behavior, social support and economic conditions and predictors of distress in children. In V. C. McLoyd & C. A. Flanagan (Eds.), *Economic stress: Effects on family life and child development.* San Francisco: Jossey-Bass.

McLuhan, M. (1964). *Understanding media: The extension of man.* New York: McGraw-Hill.

McLuhan, M. (1989). A McLuhan mosaic. In G. Sanderson & F. Macdonald (Eds.), *Marshall McLuhan: The man and his message*. Golden, CO: Fulcrum.

McNally, L., Eisenberg, J., & Harris, J. D. (1991). Consistency and change in maternal child-rearing practices and values: A longitudinal study. *Child Development, 62*, 190–198.

McNeal, J. (1987). *Children as consumers*. Lexington, MA: Lexington Books.

McNeely, C. A., Nonnemaker, J. M., & Blum, R. (2002). Promoting student connectedness to school: Evidence from the National Longitudinal Study of Adolescent Health. *Journal of School Health, 72*(4).

Mead, G. H. (1934). *Mind, self, and society*. Chicago: University of Chicago Press.

Meadow-Orlans, K. P. (1995). Parenting with a sensory or physical disability. In M. H. Bornstein (Ed.), *Handbook of parenting* (Vol. 4). Mahwah, NJ: Erlbaum.

Mediascope. (1997). *National television violence study* (Vol. 2). Studio City, CA: Author.

Mednick, S. A., Moffit, M., Gabrielli, W., Jr., & Hutchings, B. (1986). Genetic factors in criminal behavior: A review. In D. Olweus, J. Block, & M. Radke-Yarrow (Eds.), *Development of antisocial and prosocial behavior: Research, theories, and issues*. Orlando, FL: Academic Press.

Medrich, E. A., Roizen, J. Rubin, V., & Buckley, S. (1981). *The serious business of growing up: A study of children's lives outside of school*. Berkeley: University of California Press.

Meisels, S. J., & Shonkoff, J. P. (Eds.), *Handbook of early childhood intervention*. New York: Cambridge University Press.

Meisels, S. J., & Wasik, B. A. (1990). Who should be served? Identifying children in need of early intervention. In S. J Meisels & J. P. Shonkoff (Eds.), *Handbook of early childhood intervention*. New York: Cambridge University Press.

Mercer, J. (1973). *Labeling the mentally retarded: Clinical and social system perspectives on mental retardation*. Berkeley: University of California Press.

Meringoff, L. K. (1980). Influence of the medium on children's story comprehension. *Journal of Educational Psychology, 72*, 240–249.

Meyers, J., & Kyle, J. E. (1998). The makings of a family-friendly city and municipal government's role. *Nation's Cities Weekly, 21*(28), 9–16.

Milgram, S. (1963). Behavioral study of obedience. *Journal of Abnormal and Social Psychology, 67*, 371–378.

Milgram, S. (1967). The small world problem. *Psychology Today, 61*(1), 60–67.

Miller, B. C., Christopherson, C. R., & King, P. K. (1993). Sexual behavior in adolescence. In T. P. Gullotta, G. R. Adams, & R. Montemayor (Eds.), *Adolescent sexuality*. Newbury Park, CA: Sage.

Miller, D. F. (1989). *First steps toward cultural differences: Socialization in infant/toddler day care*. Washington, DC: Child Welfare League of America.

Miller, D. R., & Swanson, G. E. (1958). *The changing American parent*. New York: Wiley.

Miller, J. G. (1995, March). *Culture, context, and personal agency: The cultural grounding of self and morality*. Paper presented at the biennial meeting of the Society for Research in Child Development, Indianapolis, IN.

Miller, J. G., & Bersoff, D. M. (1992). Culture and moral judgment: Resolved? *Journal of Personality and Social Psychology, 62*, 541–554.

Miller, J. G., & Bersoff, D. M. (1993, March). *Culture and affective closeness in the morality of caring*. Paper presented at the biennial meeting of the Society for Research in Child Development, New Orleans.

Miller, K. E., Sabo, D. F., Farrell, M. P., Barnes, G. M., & Melnick, M. J. (1998). Athletic participation and sexual behavior in adolescents: The different worlds of boys and girls. *Journal of Health and Social Behavior, 39*, 108–123.

Miller, K. S., Forehand, R., & Kotchick, B. A. (1999). Adolescent behavior in two ethnic minority samples: The role of family variables. *Journal of Marriage and the Family, 61*, 85–98.

Miller, L. B., & Dyer, J. L. (1975). Four preschool programs: Their dimensions and effects. *Monographs of the Society for Research in Child Development, 40*(5–6, Serial No. 162).

Minkler, M., & Roe, K. (1993). *Grandmothers as caregivers*. Newbury Park, CA: Sage.

Mintz, S. (1998). From patriarchy to androgeny and other myths. Placing men's family roles in historical perspectives. In A. Booth & A. C. Crouter (Eds.), *Men in families*. Mahwah, NJ: Erlbaum.

Minuchin, P. M. (1977). *The middle years of childhood*. Monterey, CA: Brooks/Cole.

Minuchin, P. M., & Shapiro, E. K. (1983). The school as a context for social development. In P. H. Mussen (Ed.), *Handbook of child psychology* (4th ed., Vol. 4). New York: Wiley.

Mischel, W. (1970). Sex typing and socialization. In P. H. Mussen (Ed.), *Carmichael's manual of child psychology* (Vol. 1). New York: Wiley.

Mischel, W. (1974). Processes in the delay of gratification. In L. Berkowitz (Ed.), *Advances in experimental social psychology* (Vol. 7). Orlando, FL: Academic Press.

Mischel, W. (1996). From good intentions to will power. In P. M. Gollwitzer & J. A. Bargh (Eds.), *The psychology of action*. New York: Guilford.

Mischel, W., Shoda, Y., & Peake, P. K. (1988). The nature of adolescent competencies predicted by preschool delay of gratification. *Journal of Personality and Social Psychology, 54,* 687–696.

Mistry, R. S., Vandewater, E. A., Huston, A. C., & McLoyd, V. C. (2002). Economic well-being and children's social adjustment: The role of family process in an ethnically diverse low-income sample. *Child Development, 73,* 935–951.

Mize, J., & Ladd, G. W. (1990). A cognitive social learning approach to social skill training with low-status preschool children. *Developmental Psychology, 26,* 388–397.

Mize, J., & Pettit, G.S. (1997). Mothers' social coaching, mother–child relationships, style, and children's peer competence: Is the medium the message? *Child Development, 68,* 312–332.

Montessori, M. (1967). *The absorbent mind.* New York: Holt, Rinehart & Winston.

Montgomery, K. C. (2000). Children's media culture in the new millenium: Mapping the digital landscape. Children and Computer Technology. *The Future of Children, 10*(2), 145–167.

Moore, S. G., & Bulbulian, K. N. (1976). The effects of contrasting styles of adult–children interaction on children's curiosity. *Developmental Psychology, 12*(2), 171–172.

Mosteller, F. (1995). The Tennessee Study of class size in the early school grades. *Critical Issues for Children and Youths, 5,* 113–127.

Mounts, N. S. (2002). Parental management of adolescent peer relationships in context: The role of parenting style. *Journal of Family Psychology, 16,* 58–69.

Murdock, G. P. (1962). Structures and functions of the family. In R. F. Winch, R. M. McGinnis, & H. R. Barringer (Eds.), *Selected studies in marriage and the family.* New York: Holt, Rinehart & Winston.

Murphy, S. (1999). *The cheers and the tears: A healthy alternative to the dark side of youth sports today.* San Francisco: Jossey-Bass.

Nadler, A. (1991). Help-seeking behavior: Psychological costs and instrumental benefits. In M. S. Clark (Ed.), *Prosocial behavior.* Newbury Park, CA: Sage.

Naisbitt, J. (2001). *High tech/high touch: Technology and our search for meaning.* London: Nicholas Braily.

Naisbitt, J., & Auberdene, P. (1990). *Megatrends 2000.* New York: William Morrison.

Nalley, R. (1973). Sociobiology: A new view of human nature. In H. E. Fitzgerald & T. H. Carr (Eds.), *Human development 83/84.* Guilford, CT: Dushkin.

National Association for the Education of Young Children [NAEYC]. (1984). *Accreditation criteria and procedures of the National Academy of Early Childhood Programs.* Washington, DC: Author.

NAEYC. (1988). NAEYC position statement on standardized testing of young children 3 through 8 years of age. *Young Children, 43*(3), 42–47.

NAEYC. (1996a). NAEYC position statement: Responding to linguistic and cultural diversity—Recommendations for effective early childhood education. *Young Children, 51*(2), 4–12.

NAEYC. (1996b). Public policy report: Be a children's champion. *Young Children, 51*(2), 58–60.

National Association of School Psychologists. (2001). *Helping children cope with loss, death, and grief: Response to a national tragedy.* Bethesda, MD: Author.

National Center for Education Statistics. (2004). *Revenues and expenditures for public elementary and secondary education: School year 2001–02.* Washington, DC: U.S. Department of Education.

National Center for Health Statistics. (2004). Births to 10–14 year-old mothers, 1990–2002: Trends and health outcomes. *National Vital Statistics Report, 53*(7).

National Clearinghouse on Child Abuse and Neglect (2002). http://www.calib.com/nccanch/

National Coalition Against Domestic Violence. (1999). *The Violence Against Women Act of 1999.* www.ncadv.org

National Commission on Children [NCC] (1991). *Beyond rhetoric: A new American agenda for children and families.* Washington, DC: U.S. Government Printing Office.

National Commission on Drug-Free Schools. (1990). *Toward a drug-free generation: A nation's responsibility.* Washington, DC: U.S. Government Printing Office.

National Commission on Excellence in Education. (1983). *A nation at risk: The imperative for educational reform.* Washington, DC: U.S. Government Printing Office.

National Education Association. (2001, June). Hate crime prevention. *Legislative Action Center.* http://www.nea.org/

National Education Goals Panel (1999). *The national education goals report: Building a nation of learners 1999.* Washington, DC: U.S Government Printing Office.

National Institute of Child Health and Development [NICHD]. Early Child Care Research Network. (1996). Characteristics of infant child care: Factors contributing to positive caregiving. *Early Childhood Research Quarterly, 11,* 269–306.

NICHD. Early Child Care Research Network. (1997). The effects of infant child care on infant–mother attachment security: Results of the NICHD study of early child care. *Child Development, 68,* 860–879.

NICHD. Early Child Care Research Network. (1998). Early child care and self-control, compliance, and problem behavior at twenty-four and thirty-six months. *Child Development, 69*, 1145–1170.

NICHD. Early Child Care Research Network (Eds.). (2005). *Child care and child development*. New York: Guilford.

National Institute of Child Health and Human Development. (2002). *Adventures in parenting.* Washington, DC: U.S. Government Printing Office.

National Institute on Media and the Family. (2001). *Fact sheet: Effects of video playing on children*. http://www.mediaandthefamily.org/

National Research Council. (1993). *Losing generations: Adolescents in high-risk settings*. Washington, DC: National Academy Press.

National Science Foundation. (1994). *Investing in human resources: A strategic plan for the human capital initiative: Executive summary*. Washington, DC: Author.

Nazario, T. A. (1988). *In defense of children: Understanding the rights, needs, and interests of the child*. New York: Scribner's.

Neuman, S. G. (1991). *Literacy in the television age: The myth of the TV effect*. Norwood, NJ: Ablex.

Nielson, A. C. (2000). *Nielson media research*. New York: Author.

Niles, F. S. (1981). The youth culture controversy: An evaluation. *Journal of Early Adolescence, 1*(3), 265–271.

Norton, D. E., & Norton, S. E. (2002). *Through the eyes of a child: An introduction to children's literature* (6th ed.). Upper Saddle River, NJ: Merrill.

Norwood, R. (2005, August 6). NCAA to crack down on "hostile" nicknames. *Los Angeles Times*, pp. A1, A20.

Nowicki, S., & Segal, W. (1974). Perceived parental characteristics, locus of control orientation, and behavioral correlates of locus of control. *Developmental Psychology, 10*, 33–37.

O'Brien, M., & Huston, A. C. (1985). Activity level and sex-stereotyped toy choice in toddler boys and girls. *Journal of Genetic Psychology, 146*, 527–534.

O'Brien, S. J. (1984). *Child abuse and neglect: Everyone's problem*. Wheaton, MD: Association for Childhood Education International.

O'Dea, J. A., & Abraham, S. (1999). Association between self-concept and body weight, gender, and pubertal development among male and female adolescents. *Adolescence, 34*, 64–79.

Oden, S., & Asher, S. (1977). Coaching children in social skills for friendship making. *Child Development, 48*, 495–506.

Ogbu, J. U. (1994). From cultural differences to cultural frames of reference. In P. M. Greenfield & R. R. Cocking (Eds.), *Cross-cultural roots of minority child development*. Hillsdale, NJ: Erlbaum.

Ogg, A., & Upshal, D. (1999). *The hip-hop years: A history of rap*. London: Channel 4 Books.

Olsen, G., & Fuller, M.L. (2003). *Home–school relations: Working successfully with parents and families* (2nd ed.). Boston: Allyn and Bacon.

Olweus, D. (1986). Aggression and hormones: Behavioral relationship with testosterone and adrenaline. In D. Olweus, J. Block, & M. Radke-Yarrow (Eds.), *Development of antisocial and prosocial behavior: Research, theories, and issues*. Orlando, FL: Academic Press.

Olweus, D. (1993). *Bullying at school: What we know and what we can do*. Cambridge, MA: Blackwell.

Oppenheimer, T. (2003). *The flickering mind: The false promise of technology in the classroom and how learning can be saved*. New York: Random House.

Orellana, M. F., Dorner, L., & Pulido, L. (2003). Accessing assets: Immigrant youths work as family translators or "para-phrasers." *Social Problems, 50*, 505–524.

Ornstein, A. C., & Levine, D. U. (1982). Multicultural education: Trends and issues. *Childhood Education, 58*(4), 245.

Ornstein, A. C., & Levine, D. U. (1989, September/October). Social class, race and school achievement: Problems and prospects. *Journal of Teacher Education, 40*(4), 17–23.

Osler, S. F., & Kofsky, E. (1965). Stimulus uncertainty as a variable in the development of conceptual ability. *Journal of Experimental Child Psychology, 2*, 264–279.

Pagano, A. I. (1997). Community service groups enhance learning. In B. Hatcher & S. S. Beck (Eds.), *Learning opportunities beyond the school* (2nd ed.). Olney, MD: Association for Childhood Education International.

Pagelow, M. D. (1982). Children in violent families. Direct and indirect victims. In S. B. Hill & B. J. Barnes (Eds.), *Young children and their families*. Lexington, MA: D. C. Heath.

Paik, H., & Comstock, G. (1994). The effects of television violence on antisocial behavior: A meta-analysis. *Communication Research, 21*, 516–546.

Palladrino, G. (1996). *Teenagers: An American history*. New York: Basic Books.

Papert, S. (1993). *The children's machine: Rethinking school in the age of the computer*. New York: Basic Books.

Papert, S. (1999). *Mindstorms: Children, computers, and powerful ideas* (2nd ed.). New York: Basic Books.

Park, H. (2001). The history of children's use of electronic media. In D. G. Singer & J. L. Singer (Eds.), *Handbook of children and the media*. Thousand Oaks, CA: Sage.

Park, H., & Comstock, G. (1994). The effects of television violence on antisocial behavior: A meta-analysis. *Communication Research, 21*, 516–546.

Park, K. A., & Waters, E. (1989). Security of attachment and preschool friendships. *Child Development, 60*, 1076–1080.

Park, L. S. (2001). *A single shard*. Boston: Clarion/Houghton Mifflin.

Parke, R. D. (1982). On prediction of child abuse: Theoretical considerations. In R. Starr (Ed.), *Prediction of abuse: Policy implications*. Philadelphia: Ballinger.

Parke, R. D. (1990, Fall). Family–peer systems: In search of a linking process. *Newsletter: Developmental Psychology*. Washington, DC: American Psychological Association (Division 7).

Parke, R. D. (2002). Fathers and families. In M. H. Bornstein (Ed.), *Handbook of parenting* (2nd ed., Vol. 3). Mahwah, NJ: Erlbaum.

Parke, R. D., & Buriel, R. (1998). Socialization in the family: Ethnic and ecological perspectives. In W. Damon (Ed.), *Handbook of child psychology* (5th ed., Vol. 3). New York: Wiley.

Parke, R. D., & Lewis, N. G. (1981). The family in context: A multilevel interactional analysis of child abuse. In R. Henderson (Ed.), *Parent–child interaction*. New York: Academic Press.

Parke, R. D., & Slaby, R. B. (1983). The development of aggression. In P. H. Mussen (Ed.), *Handbook of child psychology* (4th ed., Vol. 4). New York: Wiley.

Parker, J. G., & Asher, S. R. (1987). Peer relations and later adjustment: Are low-accepted children "at risk"? *Psychological Bulletin, 102*, 357–389.

Parker, J. G., & Gottman, I. M. (1989). Social and emotional development in a relational context: Friendship interaction from early childhood to adolescence. In T. J. Berndt & G. W. Ladd (Eds.), *Peer relations in child development*. New York: Wiley.

Parker, S. T. (1984). Playing for keeps: An evolutionary perspective on human games. In P. K. Smith (Ed.), *Play in animals and humans*. Oxford: Basil Blackwell.

Parkhurst, J. T., & Asher, S. R. (1992). Peer rejection in middle school: Subgroup differences in behavior, loneliness, and interpersonal concerns. *Developmental Psychology, 28*, 231–241.

Parsons, J. E., Adler, T. F., & Kaczala, C. M. (1982). Socialization of achievement attitudes and beliefs: Parental influences. *Child Development, 53*, 310–321.

Parten, M. (1932). Social play among preschool children. *Journal of Abnormal and Social Psychology, 27*, 243–269.

Pate-Bain, H., Achilles, C. M., Boyd-Zaharias, J., & McKenna, B. (1992). Class size does make a difference. *Phi Delta Kappan, 74*(30), 253–256.

Patterson, C. J. (2002). Lesbian and gay parenthood. In M. H. Bornstein (Ed.), *Handbook of parenting* (2nd ed., Vol. 3). Mahwah, NJ: Erlbaum.

Patterson, C. J., Kupersmidt, J. B., & Vaden, N. A. (1990). Income level, gender, ethnicity, and household composition as predictors of children's school-based competence. *Child Development, 61*, 485–494.

Patterson, G. R. (1982). *Coercive family processes*. Eugene, OR: Castilia Press.

Patterson, G. R., & Capaldi, D. (1991). Antisocial parents: Unskilled and vulnerable. In P. A. Cowan & M. E. Hetherington (Eds.), *Family transitions: Advances in family research* (Vol. 2). Hillsdale, NJ: Erlbaum.

Patterson, G. R., DeBaryshe, D., & Ramsey, E. (1989). A developmental perspective on antisocial behavior. *American Psychologist, 44*(2), 329–335.

Patterson, G. R., & Dishion, T. J. (1988). Multilevel family process models: Traits, interactions, and relationships. In R. A. Hinde & J. Hinde-Stevenson (Eds.), *Relationships within families*. Oxford: Oxford University Press.

Patterson, G. R., Littman, R. A., & Bricker, W. (1976). Assertive behavior in children: A step toward a theory of aggression. *Monographs of the Society for Research in Child Development, 32*(Whole No. 113).

Patterson, G. R., Reid, J. B., & Dishion, T. J. (1992). *Antisocial boys*. Eugene, OR: Castilia.

Pavao, J. M. (1999). *The family of adoption*. Boston: Beacon Press.

Pearce, M. L. (1978). *Child advocacy in 10 easy steps: A resource guide*. Sacramento: California Association for the Education of Young Children.

Pearl, D. (1984). Violence and aggression. *Society, 21*(6), 17–22.

Perry, D. G., Perry, L. C., & Rasmussen, P. (1986). Cognitive social learning mediators of aggression. *Child Development, 57*, 700–711.

Perse, E. M. (2001). *Media effects and society*. Mahwah, NJ: Erlbaum.

Peterson, G. W., Steinmetz, S. K., & Wilson, S. M. (2003). Introduction: Parenting styles in diverse perspectives. *Marriage and Family Review, 34*, 1–4.

Peterson, L. (1983). Influence of age, task competence, and responsibility focus on children's altruism. *Developmental Psychology, 19*, 141–148.

Peterson, R. R. (1996). A re-evaluation of the economic consequences of divorce. *American Sociological Review, 61,* 528–536.

Pettit, G. S., & Mize, J. (1993). Substance and style: Understanding the ways in which parents teach children about social relationships. In S. Duck (Ed.), *Learning about relationships*. Newbury Park, CA: Sage.

Pham, A. (2002, November 9). A single-minded focus on multiple threads. *Los Angeles Times*, pp. C1, C3.

Phelps, L. A., Johnston, L. S., Jimenez, D. P., & Wilczenski, F. L. (1993). Figure preference, body dissatisfaction, and body distortion in adolescence. *Journal of Adolescent Research, 28,* 297–310.

Phillips, D. A. (1987). Socialization of perceived academic competence among highly competent children. *Child Development, 58,* 1308–1320.

Phillips, D. A. (1992). Child care and parental well-being: Bringing quality of care into the picture. In A. Booth (Ed.), *Child care in the 1990s: Trends and consequences*. Hillsdale, NJ: Erlbaum.

Phillips, D. A., & Howes, C. (1987). Indicators of quality in child care: Review of research. In D. A. Phillips (Ed.), *Quality in child care. What does research tell us?* Washington, DC: National Association for Education of Young Children.

Phillips, M. (Ed.). (1981). *Statement on child advocacy*. New York: Child Welfare League of America.

Phinney, J. S., & Chavira, V. (1992). Ethnic identity and self-esteem: An exploratory longitudinal study. *Journal of Adolescence, 13,* 171–183.

Phinney, J. S., & Rotheram, M. J. (Eds.). (1987). *Children's ethnic socialization: Pluralism and development*. Newbury Park, CA: Sage.

Piaget, J. (1952). *The origins of intelligence in children* (M. Cook, Trans.). New York: New American Library.

Piaget, J. (1962). *Play, dreams, and imitation in childhood* (C. Gattegno & F. M. Hodgson, Trans.). New York: Norton.

Piaget, J. (1965). *The moral judgment of the child* (M. Gabain, Trans.). New York: Free Press.

Piaget, J. (1974). *The language and thought of the child* (M. Gabain, Trans.). New York: New American Library.

Piaget, J. (1976). *To understand is to invent: The future of education*. New York: Penguin Books.

Pinderhughes, E. E., Dodge, K. A., Bates, J. E., Pettit, G. S., & Zelli, A. (2000). Discipline responses: Influences of parents' socioeconomic status, ethnicity, beliefs about parenting, stress, and cognitive emotional processes. *Journal of Family Psychology, 14*(3), 380–400.

Pipher, M. (1994). *Reviving Ophelia: Saving the selves of adolescent girls*. New York: Ballantine.

Pitcher, E. G., & Schultz, L. H. (1983). *Boys and girls at play: The development of sex roles*. New York: Bergin and Garvey.

Pleck, E. H. (2000). *Celebrating the family: Ethnicity, consumer culture, and family rituals*. Cambridge, MA: Harvard University Press.

Plomin, R., & Asbury, K. (2002). Nature and nurture in the family. *Marriage and Family Review, 33,* 275–283.

Poinsett, A. (1997, March). *The role of sports in youth development*. Report of Carnegie Corporation Meeting. New York: Carnegie Corporation.

Pollack, W. S. (1999). *Real boys: Rescuing our sons from the myths of boyhood*. New York: Henry Holt.

Pomerantz, E. M., & Saxon, J. L. (2001). Conceptions of ability as stable and self-evaluative processes: A longitudinal examination. *Child Development, 72,* 152–173.

Postman, N. (1982). *The disappearance of childhood*. New York: Dell.

Postman, N. (1985). The disappearance of childhood. *Childhood Education, 61*(4), 288–293.

Postman, N. (1986). *Amusing ourselves to death*. New York: Penguin Books.

Postman, N. (1992). *Technopoly: The surrender of culture to technology*. New York: Vintage.

Power, T. G. (1987). Parents as socializers: Maternal and paternal views. *Journal of Youth and Adolescence, 18,* 203–220.

Powlista, K. K., Serbin, L. A., & Moller, L. C. (1993). The stability of individual differences in gender typing: Implications for understanding gender segregation. *Sex Roles, 239*(11/12), 723–737.

Prinsky, L. E., & Rosenbaum, J. L. (1987). Leerics or lyrics? *Youth and Society, 18,* 384–394.

Proctor, P. C. (1984). Teacher expectations: A model for school improvement. *Elementary School Journal, 84*(4), 469–481.

Provenzo, E. F. (1991). *Video kids: Making sense of Nintendo*. Cambridge, MA: Harvard University Press.

Putnam, L. (1986). Reading program decisions: The connection between philosophy and practice. *Childhood Education, 62*(5), 330–336.

Putnam, P. C. (1983, February). *A descriptive study of two philosophically different approaches to reading readiness, as they were used in six inner-city kindergartens*. Washington, DC: George Washington University. (ERIC Document Reproduction Service. ED 220 807/808)

Putnam, S. P., Sanson, A. V., & Rothbart, M. (2002). Child temperament and parenting. In M. H. Bornstein (Ed.), *Handbook of parenting* (2nd ed., Vol. 3). Mahwah, NJ: Erlbaum.

Radke-Yarrow, M., & Zahn-Waxler, C. (1986). The role of familial factors in the development of prosocial behavior: Research findings and questions. In D. Olweus, J. Block, & M. Radke-Yarrow (Eds.), *Development of antisocial and prosocial behavior: Research, theories, and issues.* Orlando, FL: Academic Press.

Radke-Yarrow, M., Zahn-Waxler, C., & Chapman, H. (1983). Prosocial dispositions and behavior. In P. H. Mussen (Ed.), *Handbook of child psychology* (4th ed., Vol. 4). New York: Wiley.

Ramirez, M., & Castaneda, A. (1974). *A cultural democracy, bicognitive development and education.* New York: Academic Press.

Ramsey, P. G. (2004). *Teaching and learning in a diverse world: Multicultural education for young children* (3rd ed.). New York: Teachers' College Press.

Rawlings, M. K. (1938). *The yearling.* New York: Scribner's.

Raywid, M. (1999). *Current literature on small schools.* Charleston, WV: ERIC Clearinghouse on Rural Education and Small Schools.

Reid, J. B., Patterson, G. R., & Snyder, J. (2002). *Antisocial behavior in children and adolescents: A developmental analysis and model for intervention.* Washington, DC: American Psychological Association.

Rheingold, H. L., & Cook, K. V. (1975). The content of boys' and girls' rooms as an index of parent behavior. *Child Development, 46,* 459–463.

Rice, F. P., & Dolgin, K. G. (2002). *The adolescent: Development, relationships, and culture* (10th ed.). Boston: Allyn and Bacon.

Rice, M., & Grusec, J. (1975). Saying and doing: Effects on observer performance. *Journal of Personality and Social Psychology, 32,* 584–593.

Rice, M. L., Huston, A. C., Truglio, R., & Wright, J. C. (1990). Words from *Sesame Street*: Learning vocabulary while viewing. *Developmental Psychology, 26,* 421–428.

Rich, D. (1992). *Megaskills* (rev. ed.). Boston: Houghton Mifflin.

Rich, M., Woods, E. R., Goodman, E., Emans, S. J., & DuRant, R. H. (1998). Aggressors or victims: Gender and race in music video violence. *Pediatrics, 101*(4, Pt.1), 669–674.

Rich, Y., & Golan, R. (1992). Career plans for male-dominated occupations and female seniors in religious and secular high schools. *Adolescence, 27,* 73–86.

Richman, A. L., LeVine, R. A., New, R. S., & Howrigan, G. A. (1988). Maternal behavior to infants in five cultures. In R. A. Levine, P. M. Miller, & M. M. West (Eds.), *Parental behavior in diverse societies.* San Francisco: Jossey-Bass.

Rickel, A. U., & Becker, E. (1997). *Keeping children from harm's way: How national policy affects psychological development.* Washington. DC: American Psychological Association.

Rilling, J. K., Gutman, D. A., Zeh, T. R., Pagnoni, G., Berns, G. S., & Kilts, C. D. (2002). A neural basis for social cooperation. *Neuron, 35,* 377–405.

Ritts, V., Patterson, M. L., & Tubbs, M. E. (1992). Expectations, impressions, and judgments of physically attractive students: A review. *Review of Educational Research, 62,* 413–426.

Rivkin, M. S. (1995). *The great outdoors: Restoring children's right to play outside.* Washington, DC: National Association for the Education of Young Children.

Roberts, D. E., & Maccoby, E. E. (1985). Effects of mass communication. In G. Lindsey & E. Aronson (Eds.), *Handbook of social psychology* (3rd ed., Vol. 2). New York: Random House.

Roberts, D. F., & Christenson, P. G. (2001). Popular music in childhood and adolescence. In D. G. Singer & J. L. Singer (Eds.), *Handbook of children and the media.* Thousand Oaks, CA: Sage.

Roberts, D. F., & Foehr, U. G. (2004). *Kids and the media in America.* New York: Cambridge University Press.

Rodin, J. (1976). Crowding, perceived choice and response to controllable and uncontrollable outcomes. *Journal of Experimental Social Psychology, 12,* 564–578.

Rogers, C. (1969). *Freedom to learn.* Columbus, OH: Merrill.

Rogoff, B. (1990). *Apprenticeship in thinking: Cognitive development in social context.* New York: Oxford University Press.

Rogoff, B. (2003). *The cultural nature of human development.* New York: Oxford University Press.

Rogosch, F. A., Cicchetti, D., Shields, A., & Toth, S. L. (1995). Parenting dysfunction in child maltreatment. In M. H. Bornstein (Ed.), *Handbook of parenting* (Vol. 4). Mahwah, NJ: Erlbaum.

Rose, A. J., & Asher, S. R. (2004). Children's strategies and goals in response to help-giving and help-seeking tasks within a friendship. *Child Development, 73,* 749–780.

Rosen, B. C., & D'Andrade, R. G. (1959). The psychosocial origins of achievement motivation. *Sociometry, 22,* 185–218.

Rosenberg, M. (1975). The dissonant context and the adolescent self-concept. In S. E. Dragastin & G. H. Elder, Jr. (Eds.), *Adolescence in the life cycle: Psychological change and social context.* New York: Wiley.

Rosenhan, D., & White, G. (1967). Observation and rehearsal as determinants of prosocial behavior. *Journal of Personality and Social Psychology, 5,* 424–431.

Rosenkoetter, L. I., Huston, A. C., & Wright, J. C. (1990). Television and the moral judgment of the young child. *Journal of Applied Developmental Psychology, 11*, 123–127.

Rosenthal, R., & Jacobson, L. (1968). *Pygmalion in the classroom*. New York: Holt, Rinehart & Winston.

Rosner, B. A., & Rierdan, J. (1994, February). *Adolescent girls' self-esteem: Variations in developmental trajectories*. Paper presented at the meeting of the Society for Research on Adolescence, San Diego, CA.

Ross, H., & Sawhill, I. (1975). *Time of transition: The growth of families headed by women*. Washington, DC: The Urban Institute.

Ross, J. L. (1988). Challenging boundaries: An adolescent in a homosexual family. *Journal of Family Psychology, 2*(2), 227–240.

Ross, R. P., Campbell, T., Wright, J. C., Huston, A. C., Rice, M. L., & Turk, P. (1984). When celebrities talk, children listen: An experimental analysis of children's responses to TV ads with celebrity endorsement. *Journal of Applied Developmental Psychology, 5*, 185–202.

Rothbart, M. K., & Bates, J. E. (1998). Temperament. In W. Damon (Ed.), *Handbook of child psychology* (5th ed., Vol. 3). New York: Wiley.

Rotter, J. B. (1966). Generalized expectancies for internal versus external control of reinforcement. *Psychological Monographs, 80*(Whole No. 609).

Rotter, J. B. (1971). Who rules you? External control and internal control. *Psychology Today, 5*, 37–42.

Rovenger, J. (2000). Fostering emotional intelligence. *School Library Journal, 46*(2), 40–43.

Rubenstein, J., & Howes, C. (1976). The effects of peers on toddler interaction with mothers and toys. *Child Development, 47*, 597–605.

Rubin, J. Z., Provenzano, F. J., & Luria, A. (1974). The eye of the beholder: Parents' views on sex of newborns. *American Journal of Orthopsychiatry, 43*, 720–731.

Rubin, K. H., Bukowski, W., & Parker, J. G. (1998). Peer interactions, relationships, and groups. In W. Damon (Ed.), *Handbook of child psychology* (5th ed., Vol. 3). New York: Wiley.

Rubin, K. H., & Coplan, R. J. (1992). Peer relationships in childhood. In M. H. Bornstein & M. E. Lamb (Eds.), *Developmental psychology: An advanced textbook* (3rd ed.). Hillsdale, NJ: Erlbaum.

Rubin, K. H., Stewart, S. L., & Chen, X. (1995). Parents of aggressive and withdrawn children. In M. H. Bornstein (Ed.), *Handbook of parenting* (Vol. 1). Mahwah, NJ: Erlbaum.

Rubin, K. H., & Thompson, A. (2003). *The friendship factor*. New York: Penguin.

Ruble, D., & Martin, C. L. (1998). Gender development. In W. Damon (Ed.), *Handbook of child psychology* (5th ed., Vol. 3). New York: Wiley.

Ruopp, R., Travers, J., Glantz, F., & Coelen, G. (1979). *Children at the center: Final results of the national day care study*. Cambridge, MA: Abt Associates.

Rushton, J. P., Fulker, D. W., Neal, M. C., Nias, D. K. B., & Eysenck, H. J. (1986). Altruism and aggression: The heritability of individual differences. *Journal of Personality and Social Psychology, 50*, 1192–1198.

Rust, J., Golombok, S., Hines, M., Johnson, K., & Golding, J. (2000). The role of brothers and sisters in the gender development of preschool children. *Journal of Experimental Child Psychology, 77*, 292–303.

Rutter, M. (1971). Parent–child separation: Psychological effects on the children. *Journal of Child Psychology and Psychiatry, 12*, 233–256.

Rutter, M., Giller, H., & Hagell, A. (1998). *Antisocial behavior by young people*. Cambridge, UK: Cambridge University Press.

Rutter, M. & O'Connor, T. G. (2004). Are there biological programming effects for psychological development? Findings from a study of Romanian adoptees. *Developmental Psychology, 40*(1), 81–90.

Rutter, V. (1994, May/June). Lessons from step families. *Psychology Today, 27*, 30–33, 60, 62, 64, 66, 68–69.

Ryan, R. M., & Deci, E. L. (2000). Intrinsic and extrinsic motivations: Classic definitions and new directions. *Contemporary Educational Psychology, 1*, 54–67.

Saarni, C., Mumme, D. L., & Campos, J. J. (1998). Emotional development: Action, communication, and understanding. In W. Damon (Ed.), *Handbook of child psychology* (5th ed., Vol. 3). New York: Wiley.

Sadker, D., & Sadker, M. (2003). *Teachers, schools, and society* (6th ed.). New York: McGraw-Hill.

Sadker, M., & Sadker, D. (1994). *Failing at fairness: How America's schools cheat girls*. New York: Scribner's.

Sadker, M., Sadker, D., & Klein, S. (1991). The issue of gender in elementary and secondary education. *Review of Research in Education, 17*, 269–334.

Saltzstein, H. D. (1975, April). Role taking as a method of facilitating moral development. *Symposium on Role-Taking and Moral Development*. Paper presented at the meeting of the Eastern Psychological Association, New York.

Saltzstein, H. D. (1976). Social influence and moral development: A perspective on the role of parents and peers. In T. Lickona (Ed.), *Moral development and behavior*. New York: Holt, Rinehart & Winston.

Sameroff, A. J. (1987). The social content of development. In N. Eisenberg (Ed.), *Contemporary topics in developmental psychology*. New York: Wiley.

Sameroff. A. J. (1994). Developmental systems and family functioning. In R. D. Parke & S. G. Kellan (Eds.), *Exploring family relationships with other social contexts*. Hillsdale, NJ: Erlbaum.

Sampson, R. J. (1983). Structural density and criminal victimization. *Criminology, 21,* 276–293.

Sampson, R. J., & Laub, J. H. (1994). Urban poverty and the family context of delinquency: A new look at structure and process in a classic study. *Child Development, 65,* 523–540.

Sandler, I. N., Miller, P., & Short, J., & Wolchik, S. A. (1989). Social support as a protective factor for children in stress. In D. Belle (Ed.), *Children's social networks and social supports*. New York: Wiley.

Sandler, I. N., Tein, J. Y., & West, S. G. (1994). Coping, stress, and the psychological symptoms of children of divorce: A cross-sectional and longitudinal study. *Child Development, 64,* 1744–1763.

Sandstrom, M. J., & Coie, J. D. (1999). A developmental perspective on peer rejection: Mechanisms of stability and change. *Child Development, 70,* 955–966.

Sanford, N., & Comstock, C. (Eds.). (1971). *Sanctions for evil*. San Francisco: Jossey-Bass.

Santrock, J. W., & Sitterle, K. A. (1987). Parent–child relationships: Stepmother families. In K. Pasley & M. Ihinger-Tallman (Eds.), *Remarriage and stepparenting: Current research and theory*. New York: Guilford Press.

Santrock, J. W., & Warshak, R. A. (1979). Father custody and social development in boys and girls. *Journal of Social Issues, 35,* 112–125.

Santrock, J. W., Warshak, R. A., & Eliot, G. (1982). Social development and parent–child interaction in father-custody and stepmother families. In M. E. Lamb (Ed.), *Nontraditional families*. Hillsdale, NJ: Erlbaum.

Savage, D. G. (1983, February 15). Freeway noise linked to poorer test scores. *Los Angeles Times,* Part I, p. 1.

Scarr, S. (1984). *Mother care/other care*. New York: Basic Books.

Scarr, S. (1992). Theories for the 1990s: Developmental and individual differences. *Child Development, 63,* 1–19.

Scarr, S., & McCartney, K. (1983). How people make their own environments: A theory of genotype–environment effects. *Child Development, 54,* 424–435.

Schaefer, E. S. (1991). Goals for parent and future-parent education. *The Elementary School Journal, 91*(3), 239–247.

Schank, R.C. (2004). *Making minds less well-educated than our own*. Mahwah, NJ: Erlbaum.

Scheibe, C. (1989). *Character portrayal and values in network TV commercials*. Unpublished master's thesis, Cornell University, Ithaca, NY. Cited in J. Condry, *The psychology of television* (Hillsdale, NJ: Erlbaum, 1989).

Schickedanz, J. (1986). *More than the ABCs: The early stages of reading and writing*. Washington, DC: National Association for the Education of Young Children.

Schickedanz, J. (1990). Preschoolers and academics: Some thoughts. *Young Children, 46*(1), 4–13.

Schneider, B. H. (2000). *Friends and enemies: Peer relations in childhood*. New York: Oxford University Press.

Schneider, B. H., Atkinson, L., & Tardif, C. (2001). Child–parent attachment and children's peer relations: A quantitative review. *Developmental Psychology, 37,* 86–100.

Schorr, L. B. (1997). *Common purpose: Strengthening families and neighborhoods to rebuild America*. New York: Anchor Books.

Schorr, L. B., Both, D., & Copple, C. (Eds.). (1991). *Effective services for young children: Report of a workshop*. Washington, DC: National Academy Press.

Schorr, L. B., with Schorr, D. (1988). *Within our reach: Breaking the cycle of disadvantage*. New York: Doubleday/Anchor Press.

Schramm, W., Lyle, J., & Parker, E. (1961). *Television in the lives of our children*. Stanford, CA: Stanford University Press.

Schunk, D.H. (2000). *Theories of learning* (3rd ed.). Upper Saddle River, NJ: Prentice-Hall.

Schweinhart, L. J., Montie, J., Xiang, Z., Barnett, W. S., Belfield, C. R., & Nores, M. (2005). *Lifetime effects: The High/Scope Perry Preschool Study through age 40*. Ypsilanti, MI: High/Scope.

Schweinhart, L. J., & Weikart, D. P. (1993). Success by empowerment: The High/Scope Perry Preschool study through age 27. *Young Children, 49*(1), 54–58.

Schweinhart, L. J., Weikart, D. P., & Larner, M. B. (1986). Child-initiated activities in early childhood programs may help prevent delinquency. *Early Childhood Research Quarterly, 1*(3), 303–312.

Seaver, W. B. (1973). Effects of naturally induced teacher expectancies. *Journal of Personality and Social Psychology, 28,* 333–342.

Sebald, H. (1986). Adolescents' shifting orientation toward parents and peers: A curvilinear trend over recent decades. *Journal of Marriage and the Family, 48,* 5–13.

Sebald, H. (1989). Adolescent peer orientation: Changes in the support system during the last three decades. *Adolescence, 24,* 937–945.

Sebald, H. (1992). *Adolescence: A social psychological analysis* (4th ed.). Englewood Cliffs, NJ: Prentice-Hall.

Segal, N. L. (1997). Genetic bases of behavior: Contributions to psychological research. In N. L. Segal, G. E. Weisfeld, & C. C. Weisfeld (Eds.), *Uniting psychology and biology*. Washington, DC: American Psychological Association.

Seligman, M. E. P. (1975). *Helplessness*. San Francisco: Freeman.

Seligman, M. E. P. (1990). *Learned optimism*. New York: Pocket Books.

Selman, R. L. (1980). *The growth of interpersonal understanding*. New York: Academic Press.

Selman, R. L., & Selman, A. P. (1979). Children's ideas about friendship: A new theory. *Psychology Today, 12*(4), 71–80.

Selye, H. (1956). *The stress of life*. New York: McGraw-Hill.

Sendak, M. (1963). *Where the wild things are*. New York: HarperCollins.

Sendak, M. (1970). *In the night kitchen*. New York: Harper & Row.

Serbin, L. A., O'Leary, K. D., Kent, R. N., & Tonick, I. J.(1973). A comparison of teacher response to the preacademic and problem behavior of boys and girls. *Child Development, 44*, 796–804.

Serbin, L. A., Powlishta, K. K., & Gulko, J. (1993). The development of sex typing in middle childhood. *Monographs of the Society for Research in Child Development, 58*(2, Serial No. 232).

Shantz, C. U. (1983). Social cognition. In P. H. Mussen (Eds.), *Handbook of child psychology* (4th ed., Vol. 3). New York: Wiley.

Shapira, A., & Lomranz, J. (1972). Cooperative and competitive behavior of rural Arab children in Israel. *Journal of Cross-Cultural Psychology, 3*, 353–359.

Shapira, A., & Madsen, M. C. (1974). Between- and within-group cooperation and competition among kibbutz and non-kibbutz children. *Developmental Psychology, 10*, 140–145.

Sherif, M. (1956). Experiments in group conflict. *Scientific American, 195*(2), 54–58.

Sherif, M., Harvey, O. J., White, B. J., Hood, W. R., & Sherif, C. W. (1961). *Intergroup conflict and cooperation: The robber's cave experiment*. Norman: University of Oklahoma, Institute of Group Relations.

Shields, M. A., & Behrman, R. E. (2000). Children and computer technology: Analysis and recommendations. *The Future of Children, 10*(2), 4–30.

Shonk, S. M., & Cicchetti, D. (2001). Maltreatment, competency, deficits, and risk for academic and behavioral maladjustment. *Developmental Psychology, 37*, 3–17.

Shonkoff, J. P., & Phillips, D. A. (Eds.). (2000). *From neurons to neighborhoods: The science of early childhood development*. Washington, DC: National Academy Press.

Shweder, R. A., Mahapatra, M., & Miller, J. G. (1987). Culture and moral development. In J. Kagan & S. Lamb (Eds.), *The emergence of morality in young children*. Chicago: University of Chicago Press.

Sigman, M., Neumann, C., Carter, E., & Cattle, D. J. (1988). Home interactions and the development of Embu toddlers in Kenya. *Child Development, 57*, 1251–1261.

Signorella, M. L., Bigler, R. S., & Liben, L. S. (1993). Developmental differences in children's gender schemata about others: A meta-analytic review. *Developmental Review, 13*, 147–183.

Signorielli, N. (1989). Television and conceptions about sex roles: Maintaining conventionality and the status quo. *Sex Roles, 21*(5/6), 341–360.

Signorielli, N. (1993). Television, the portrayal of women and children's attitudes. In C. L. Berry & J. K. Samen (Eds.), *Children and television: Images in a changing sociocultural world*. Newbury Park, CA: Sage.

Signorielli, N. (2001). Television's gender role images and contribution to stereotyping: Past, present, future. In D. G. Singer & J. L. Singer (Eds.), *Handbook of children and the media*. Thousand Oaks, CA: Sage.

Silverstein, L. B., & Auerbach, C. F. (2001). The myth of the "normal" family (© Society for the Advancement of Education). Reprinted in *Annual Editions 02/03: The Family* (Guilford, CT: McGraw-Hill/Dushkin), pp. 13–15.

Simeonsson, R. J., & Bailey, D. B. (1986). Siblings of the handicapped child. In J. J. Gallager & W. Vietze (Eds.), *Families of handicapped persons*. Baltimore, MD: Brookes.

Singer, D. G. & Singer, J. L. (1980). Television viewing and aggressive behavior in preschool children: A field study. *Forensic Psychology and Psychiatry, Annals of the New York Academy of Science, 347*, 289–303.

Singer, D. G., & Singer, J. L. (1990). *House of make-believe*. Cambridge, MA: Harvard University Press.

Singer, D. G., Singer, J. L., & Zuckerman, D. M. (1990). *The parent's guide: Use TV to your child's advantage*. Reston, VA: Acropolis Books.

Skeels, H. M. (1966). Adult status of children with contrasting early life experiences. *Monographs of the Society for Research in Child Development, 31*(3, Whole No. 105).

Skinner, B. F. (1948). *Walden two*. New York: Macmillan.

Skinner, B.F. (1968). *The technology of teaching*. Englewood Cliffs, NJ: Prentice-Hall.

Skinner, E. A. (1995). *Perceived control, motivation, and coping*. Thousand Oaks, CA: Sage.

Sklaroff, S. (2002). One nation under a groove. *U.S. News & World Report, 133*(2), 20–21.

Skolnick, A. (1987). *The intimate environment: Exploring marriage and the family* (4th ed.). Boston: Little, Brown.

Slaby, R. G., Roedell, W. C., Arezzo, D., & Hendrix, K. (1995). *Early violence prevention: Tools for teachers of young children*. Washington, DC: National Association for the Education of Young Children.

Slavin, R. E. (1991). Synthesis of research on cooperative learning. *Educational Leadership, 48*(5), 71–82.

Slavin, R. E., Devries, D. L., & Hutten, B. H. (1975). *Individual vs. team competition: The interpersonal consequences of academic performance*. Baltimore, MD: Johns Hopkins University Center for Social Organization of Schools. (Report No. 188)

Sleek, S. (1998). Isolation increases with Internet use. *APA Monitor, 29*(9), 1, 30–31.

Small, J. (Ed.). (1987). *Children of alcoholics: A special report*. Washington, DC: National Institute on Alcohol Abuse and Alcoholism.

Small, S., & Luster, T. (1994). Adolescent sexual activity: An ecological risk-factor approach. *Journal of Marriage and the Family, 56*, 181–192.

Small, S. & Supple, A. (2001). Communities as systems: Is a community more than the sum of its parts? In A. Booth & A. C. Crouter (Eds.), *Does it take a village?* Mahwah, NJ: Erlbaum.

Smetana, J. G. (1981). Preschool children's conceptions of moral and social rules. *Child Development, 52*, 1333–1336.

Smetana, J. G. (1985). Preschool children's conceptions of transgressions: Effects of varying moral and conventional domain-related attributes. *Developmental Psychology, 21*, 18–29.

Smetana, J. G. (1989). Toddlers' social interactions in the context of moral and conventional transgressions in the home. *Developmental Psychology, 25*, 499–508.

Smith, A. B., Dannison, L. L., & Vach-Hasse, T. (1998, Fall). When "grandma" is "mom." *Childhood Education, 75*(1), 12–16.

Smith, D. D., & Bassett, D. (1991). The REI debate: A time for a systematic research agenda. In J. Lloyd, A. C. Repp, & N. N. Sing (Eds.), *Perspectives on integration of atypical learners in regular education settings*. Sycamore, IL: Sycamore Press.

Smith, P. K., & Drew, L. M. (2002). Grandparenthood. In M. H. Bornstein (Ed.), *Handbook of parenting* (2nd ed., Vol. 3). Mahwah, NJ: Erlbaum.

Smith, P. K., & Dutton, S. (1979). Play and training indirect and innovative problem solving. *Child Development, 60*, 830–836.

Smolensky, E., & Gootman, J. A. (Eds.). (2003). *Working families and growing kids: Caring for children and adolescents*. Washington, DC: National Academies Press.

Snow, M. E., Jacklin, C. N., & Maccoby, E. E. (1981). Birth order differences in peer sociability at thirty-three months. *Child Development, 52*, 589–596.

Snyder, J. J., & Patterson, G. R. (1995). Individual differences in social aggression: A test of a reinforcement model of socialization in the natural environment. *Behavior Therapy, 26*, 371–391.

Soldier, L. L. (1985). To soar with the eagles: Enculturation and acculturation of Indian children. *Childhood Education, 61*(3), 185–191.

Solomon, C. (1999, October 2). The Gen-P gold mine. *Los Angeles Times*, pp. F1, F18.

Spence, S. H. (2003). Social skills training with children and young people: Theory, evidence, and practice. *Child and Adolescent Mental Health, 8*(2), 84–96.

Spencer, M. B. (2001). Resiliency and fragility factors associated with the contextual experiences of low resource urban African American male youth and families. In A. Booth & A. C. Crouter (Eds.), *Does it take a village?* Mahwah, NJ: Erlbaum.

Spitz, E. H. (1999). *Inside picture books*. New Haven, CT: Yale University Press.

Spitz, H. R. (1992). Early childhood intervention. In T. G. Sticht, M. J. Beeler, & B. A. McDonald (Eds.), *The intergenerational transfer of cognitive skills*. Norwood, NJ: Ablex.

Spitz, R. (1946). Hospitalism: An inquiry into the genesis of psychiatric conditioning in early childhood. In A. Freud (Ed.), *Psychoanalytic studies of the child* (Vol. 1). New York: International Universities Press.

Spock, B. (1946). *The common sense book of baby and child care*. New York: Duell Sloan Pearce.

Spock, B. (1957). *The pocket book of baby and child care*. New York: Pocket Books.

Spock, B. (1968). *Baby and child care*. New York: Pocket Books.

Spock, B. (1985). *Raising children in a difficult time* (2nd ed.). New York: Pocket Books.

Sprafkin, J. M., Liebert, R. M., & Poulos, R. W. (1975). Effects of a prosocial example on children's helping. *Journal of Experimental Child Psychology, 20*, 119–126.

Sroufe, L. (1978). Attachment and the roots of competence. *Human Nature, 1*, 50–57.

Sroufe, L. A. (1996). *Emotional development*. Cambridge, UK: Cambridge University Press.

St. Peters, M., Marguerite, F., Huston, A. C., Wright, J. C., & Eakins, D. J. (1991). Television and families: What do young children watch with their parents? *Child Development, 62*, 1409–1413.

Stabiner, K. (1993, August 15). Get 'em while they're young. *Los Angeles Times Magazine*, pp. 12, 14, 15, 16, 38.

Stainback, S., Stainback, W., East, K., & Sapon-Shevin, M. (1994). A commentary on inclusion and the development of a positive self-identity by people with disabilities. *Exceptional Children, 60*(6), 486–490.

Stallings, J. (1974). *Follow through classroom observation evaluation, 1972–1973: Executive summary*. Menlo Park, CA: Stanford Research Institute.

Starr, R. H., Jr. (1990, June). The lasting effects of child maltreatment. *The Word and I,* 484–499.

Staub, E. (1970). A child in distress: The effect of focusing responsibility on children on their attempts to help. *Developmental Psychology, 2,* 152–153.

Staub, E. (1971). The use of role playing and induction in children's learning of helping and sharing behavior. *Child Development, 42,* 805–816.

Staub, E. (1986). A conception of the determinants and development of altruism and aggression: Motives, the self, and the environment. In C. Zahn-Waxler, E. M. Cummings, & R. Iannotti (Eds.), *Altruism and aggression: Biological and social origins*. Cambridge, UK: Cambridge University Press.

Steinberg, L. (1986). Latchkey children and susceptibility to peer pressure: An ecological analysis. *Developmental Psychology, 22,* 433–439.

Steinberg, L. (1987). Single parents, step parents, and the susceptibility of adolescents to antisocial peer pressure. *Child Development, 58,* 269–275.

Steinberg. L. (1993). *Adolescence*. New York: McGraw-Hill.

Steinberg, L. (1996). *Beyond the classroom: Why school reform has failed and what parents need to do*. New York: Touchstone.

Steinberg, L. (2001). We know some things: Adolescent parent relationships in retrospect and prospect. *Journal of Research on Adolescence, 11,* 1–19.

Steinberg, L., Elmen, J. D., & Mounts, N. S. (1989). Authoritative parenting, psychosocial maturity, and academic success among adolescents. *Child Development, 60,* 1424–1436.

Steinberg, L., Lamborn, S. D., Darling, N., Mounts, N., & Dornbusch, S. M. (1994). Over-time changes in adjustment and competence among adolescents from authoritative, authoritarian, indulgent, and neglectful families. *Child Development, 65,* 754–770.

Steinberg, L., & Morris, A.S. (2001). Adolescent development. *Annual Review of Psychology, 52,* 83–110.

Steinberg, L., Mounts, N. S., Lambourn, S. D., & Dornbusch, S. M. (1991). Authoritative parenting and adolescent adjustment across various ecological niches. *Journal of Research on Adolescence, 1,* 19–36.

Stendler, C. B. (1950). Sixty years of child training practices. *Journal of Pediatrics, 36,* 122–134.

Stepfamily Association of America (2000). www.saafamilies.org

Stephens, M. W., & Delys, P. (1973). External control expectancies among disadvantaged children at preschool age. *Child Development, 44,* 670–674.

Stevenson, H. W. (1972). *Children's learning*. New York: Appleton-Century-Crofts.

Stevenson, H. W., & Lee, S. Y. (1990). Contents of achievement: A study of American, Chinese, and Japanese children. *Monographs of the Society for Research in Child Development, 55*(1–2, Serial No. 221).

Stevenson, H. W., Stigler, J. W., Lee, S. Y., Kitamura, S., & Kato, T. (1986). Achievement in mathematics. In H. Stevenson, H. Azuma, & K. Hakuta (Eds.), *Child development and education in Japan*. New York: W. H. Freeman.

Stewart, E. C., & Bennett, M. J. (1991). *American cultural patterns: A cross-cultural perspective* (rev. ed.). Yarmouth, ME: Intercultural Press.

Stinnett, N., & Defrain, J. (1985). *Secrets of strong families*. Boston: Little, Brown.

Stipek, D. (1996). Motivation and instruction. In D. C. Berliner & R. C. Calfee (Eds.), *Handbook of educational psychology*. New York: Macmillan.

Stipek, D., Recchia, A., & McClintic, S. (1992). Self-evaluation in young children. *Monographs of the Society for Research in Child Development, 57*(1, Serial No. 226).

Stomfay-Stitz, A. M. (1994). Pathways to safer schools. *Childhood Education, 70*(5), 279–282.

Strasburger, V. C. (2001). Children, adolescents, drugs, and the media. In D. G. Singer & J. L. Singer (Eds.), *Handbook of children and the media*. Thousand Oaks, CA: Sage.

Strasburger, V. C., & Wilson, B. J. (2002). *Children, adolescents, and the media*. Thousand Oaks, CA: Sage.

Streitmatter, J. (1994). *Toward gender equity in the classroom: Everyday teachers' beliefs and practices*. New York: State University of New York Press.

Strouse, J. S., Buerkel-Rothfuss, N., & Long, E. C. J. (1995). Gender and family as moderators of the relationship between music video exposure and adolescent sexual permissiveness. *Adolescence, 30*(119), 505–522.

Subrahmanyam, K., Kraut, R. E., Greenfield, P. M., & Gross, E. F. (2001). New forms of electronic media. In D. G. Singer & J. L. Singer (Eds.), *Handbook of children and the media*. Thousand Oaks, CA: Sage.

Sue, D. W. (1989). Ethnic identity: The impact of two cultures on the psychological development of Asians in America. In D. R. Atkinson, G. Morten, & D. W. Sue

(Eds.), *Counseling American minorities* (3rd ed.). Dubuque, IA: Wm. C. Brown.

Sunley, R. (1955). Early nineteenth-century American literature on child rearing. In M. Mead & M. Wolfenstein (Eds.), *Childhood in contemporary cultures*. Chicago: University of Chicago Press.

Sutton-Smith, B. (1971). Children at play. *Natural History, 80*, 54–59.

Sutton-Smith, B. (1972). *The folkgames of children*. Austin: University of Texas Press.

Sutton-Smith, B. (1982). Birth order and sibling status effects. In M. E. Lamb (Ed.), *Sibling relationships: Their nature and significance over the lifespan*. Hillsdale, NJ: Erlbaum.

Swick, K. J. (1986). Locus of control and interpersonal support as related to parenting. *Childhood Education, 62*, 41–50.

Swick, K. J. (1997). Learning about work: Extending learning through an ecological approach. In B. Hatcher & S. S. Beck (Eds.), *Learning opportunities beyond the school* (2nd ed.). Olney, MD: Association for Childhood Education International.

Taishido Study Group. (1984/1985). Generations of play in Taishido. *Children's Environment Quarterly, 1*(4), 19–28.

Tamis-LeMonda, C. S., & Cabrera, N. (1999). Perspectives on father involvement: Research and policy. *Society for Research in Child Development, 12*(2).

Teale, W. H. (1984). Reading to young children: Its significance for literary development. In H. Coleman, A. Oberg, & F. Smith (Eds.), *Awakening and literacy*. Portsmouth, NH: Heinemann.

Teasley, S. D., & Parker, J. G. (1995, March). *The effects of gender, friendship, and popularity on the targets and topics of adolescent gossip*. Paper presented at the Biennial Meeting of the Society for Research in Child Development, Indianapolis, IN.

Tharp, R. G. (1989). Psychocultural variables and constraints: Effects on teaching and learning in schools. *American Psychologist, 44*(2), 349–359.

Thiederman, S. (1991). *Bridging cultural barriers for success: How to manage the cultural work force*. New York: Lexington Books.

Thoma, S. J., Rest, J. R., & Davidson, M. L. (1991). Describing and testing a moderator of the moral judgment and action relationship. *Journal of Personality and Social Psychology, 61*, 659–669.

Thomas, A., & Chess, S. (1977). *Temperament and development*. New York: Brunner/Mazel.

Thomas, A., & Chess, S. (1980). *The dynamics of psychological development*. New York: Brunner/Mazel.

Thomas, A., Chess, S., & Birch, H. S. (1970). The origin of personality. *Scientific American, 223*, 102–109.

Thompson, K. P. (1993). Media, music, and adolescents. In R. M. Lerner (Ed.), *Early adolescents: Perspectives on research, policy, and intervention*. Hillsdale, NJ: Erlbaum.

Thompson, M., Cohen, L. J., & Grace, C. O. (2002). *Best friends, worst enemies: Understanding the social lives of children*. New York: Ballantine Books.

Thompson, R. A. (1994). Social support and the prevention of child maltreatment. In G. B. Melton & F. Barry (Eds.), *Safe neighborhoods: Foundations for a new national strategy on child abuse and neglect*. New York: Guilford.

Thompson, R. L., & Larson, R. (1995). Social context and the subjective experience of different types of rock music. *Journal of Youth and Adolescence, 24*(6), 731–744.

Thompson, S. H. (1998). Working with children of substance-abusing parents. *Young Children, 53*(1), 34–37.

Thompson, W. E., & Dodder, R. A. (1986). Containment theory and juvenile delinquency: A reevaluation through factor analysis. *Adolescence, 21*, 365–376.

Thornburg, H. D. (1981). The amount of sex information learning obtained during early adolescence. *Journal of Early Adolescence, 1*, 171–183.

Thorne, B. (1993). *Gender play: Girls and boys in school*. New Brunswick, NJ: Rutgers University Press.

Thuy, V. G. (1983). The Indochinese in America: Who are they and how are they doing? In D. T. Nakanishi & M. Huano-Nakanishi (Eds.), *The education of Asian and Pacific Americans: Historical perspectives and prescriptions for the future*. Phoenix, AZ: Oryx Press.

Tizard, J., Schofield, W. N., & Hewison, J. (1982). Collaboration between teachers and parents in assisting children's reading. *British Journal of Education, 52*, 1–15.

Tobin, J. J., Wu, D. Y. H., & Davidson, D. H. (1989, April). How three key countries shape their children. *World Monitor*, 36–45.

Toch, T. (1996, October 7). Schools that work. *U.S. News & World Report, 66*, 58–64.

Toffler Associates Inc. (2000–2003). Toffler Associates@toffler.com

Tonnies, F. (1957). *Community and society* (Gemeinshaft und Gesellshaft) (C. P. Loomis, Trans.). East Lansing: Michigan State University.

Took, K. J., & Weiss, D. S. (1994). The relationship between heavy metal and rap music and adolescent turmoil: Real or abstract? *Adolescence, 29*(115), 613–623.

Toufexis, A. (1991). Innocent victims. *Time, 137*(19), 56–60.

Tozer, S. E., Violas, P. C., & Senese, G. (2002). *School and society: Historical and contemporary perspectives* (4th ed.). New York: McGraw-Hill.

Travers, P. L. (1997). *Mary Poppins.* Orlando, FL: Harcourt Brace. (Original work published 1934)

Trelease, J. (2001). *The read-aloud handbook* (5th ed.). New York: Viking.

Triandis, H. C. (1994). *Culture and social behavior.* New York: McGraw-Hill.

Triandis, H. C. (1995). *Individualism and collectivism.* Boulder, CO: Westview Press.

Troy, M., & Sroufe, L. A. (1987). Victimization among preschoolers: Role of attachment relationship history. *Journal of the American Academy of Child and Adolescent Psychiatry, 26,* 166–172.

Trumbull, E., Rothstein-Fisch, C., Greenfield, P. M., & Quiroz, B. (2001). *Bridging cultures between home and school.* Mahwah, NJ: Erlbaum.

Tubman, J. G. (1993). Family risk factors, parental alcohol use, and problem behaviors among school-age children. *Family Relations, 42,* 81–86.

Tuchscherer, P. (1988). *TV interactive toys: The new high tech threat to children.* Bend, OR: Pinnaroo.

Tucker, L. A. (1983). Self-concept: A function of self-perceived somatotype. *Journal of Psychology, 14,* 123–133.

Turiel, E. (1983). *The development of social knowledge: Morality and convention.* Cambridge, UK: Cambridge University Press.

Turiel, E. (1998). The development of morality. In W. Damon (Ed.), *Handbook of child psychology* (5th ed., Vol. 3). New York: Wiley.

Turiel, E. (2002). *The culture of morality: Social development, context, and conflict.* Cambridge, UK: Cambridge University Press.

Turnbull, A. P., & Turnbull, H. R. (2001). *Families, professionals, and exceptionality: Collaborating for empowerment* (4th ed.). Upper Saddle River, NJ: Prentice-Hall.

Turner-Bowker, D. M. (1996). Gender stereotyped descriptors inchildren's picture books: Does "Curious Jane" exist in the literature? *Sex Roles, 35,* 461–488.

Tyler, R. (1992, May). Prenatal drug exposure: An overview of associated problems and intervention strategies. *Phi Delta Kappan,* 705–708.

Uba, L. (1999). *Asian Americans: Personality patterns, identity, and mental health.* New York: Guilford Press.

Uchida, Y. (1999). Momotaro: Boy of the peach. From *The Dancing Kettle and Other Japanese Folk Tales.* New York: Harcourt Brace Jovanovich.

Ungar, M. T. (2000). The myth of peer pressure. *Adolescence, 35*(137), 167–171.

U.S. Bureau of the Census. (2003). *Statistical abstract of the United States.* Washington, DC: U.S. Government Printing Office.

U.S. Department of Education. (1989). *What works: Schools without drugs.* Washington, DC: U.S. Government Printing Office.

U.S. Department of Education. (1991). *Preparing children for success: Guideposts for achieving our first national goal.* Washington, DC: U.S. Government Printing Office.

U.S. Department of Education. (1994). *Strong families, strong schools: Building community partnerships for learning.* Washington, DC: U.S. Government Printing Office.

U.S. Department of Health and Human Services. (2001). *Healthy people 2000: National health promotion and disease prevention objectives.* Washington, DC: U.S. Government Printing Office.

U.S. Department of Health and Human Services. (2002). *HHS invests in America's children.* Washington, DC: Author.

U.S. Department of Justice. (2000, August). Youth gangs in school. *Juvenile Justice Bulletin.* Washington, DC: U.S. Government Printing Office.

Valkenburg, P.M. (2001). Television and the child's developing imagination. In D. G. Singer & J. L. Singer (Eds.), *Handbook of children and the media.* Thousand Oaks, CA: Sage.

Van Ausdale, D. & Feaginb, J. R. (2001). *The first R: How children learn race and racism.* Lanham, MD: Rowman and Littlefield.

Vandell, D. L., & Mueller, E. C. (1995). Peer play and friendship during the play years. In H. C. Foot, A. J. Chapman, & J. R. Smith (Eds.), *Friendship and social relations in children.* New Brunswick, NJ: Transaction.

Vandell, D. L., & Su, H.-C. (1999). Child care and school-age children. *Young Children, 54*(6), 62–71.

Vanderslice, V. J. (1984). Empowerment: A definition of process. *Human Ecology Forum, 14*(1), 2–3.

Vander Zanden, J. W. (1995). *Sociology: The core* (3rd ed.). New York: McGraw-Hill.

Vasquez, J. A. (1990). Teaching to the distinctive traits of minority students. *The Clearing House, 63,* 299–304.

Vasquez-Nutall, E., Romers-Garcia, I., & DeLeon, B. (1987). Sex roles and perceptions of femininity and masculinity of Hispanic women: A review of the literature. *Psychology of Women Quarterly, 11,* 409–425.

Vaughn, S., Bos, C. S., & Schumm, J. S. (1997). *Teaching mainstreamed, diverse, and at-risk students in the general education classroom.* Boston: Allyn and Bacon.

Verdugo, R., Kuttner, A., Seidel, S., Wallace, C., Sosa, M., & Faber, M. (1990). *Safe schools manual: A resource on making schools, communities, and families safe for children.* Washington, DC: National Education Association.

Vigil, J. D. (1980). *From Indians to Chicanos: The dynamics of Mexican-American culture.* Prospect Heights, IL: Wave Press.

Vincze, M. (1971). The social contacts of infants and young children reared together. *Early Child Development and Care, 1,* 99–109.

Vorrath, H. H., & Brendtro, L. K. (1985). *Positive peer culture* (2nd ed.). New York: Aldine.

Vosler, N. R., & Robertson, J. G. (1998). Nonmarital co-parenting: Knowledge-building for practice. *Families in Society: The Journal of Contemporary Human Services, 79*(2), 149–157.

Vygotsky, L. S. (1978). *Mind and society: The development of higher psychological processes* (M. Cole, V. John-Steiner, S. Scribner, & E. Souberman, Eds.). Cambridge, MA: Harvard University Press.

Wachs, T. D., & Bates, J. E. (2001). Temperament. In G. Bremmer & A. Fogel (Eds.), *Blackwell handbook of infant developmental psychology.* Madden, MA: Blackwell.

Walker, L. J. (1991). Sex differences in moral development. In W. M. Kurtines & J. Gewirtz (Eds.), *Handbook of moral behavior and development* (Vol. 2). Hillsdale, NJ: Erlbaum.

Walker, L. J., & Taylor, J. H. (1991). Family interaction and the development of moral reasoning. *Child Development, 62,* 264–283.

Walker, L. S., & Greene, J. W. (1986). The social context of adolescent self-esteem. *Journal of Youth and Adolescence, 15*(4), 315–323.

Wall, J. A., Power, T. G., & Arbona, C. (1993). Susceptibility to antisocial peer pressure and its relation to acculturation in Mexican-American adolescents. *Journal of Adolescent Research, 8,* 403–418.

Wallach, L. B. (1993). Helping children cope with violence. *Young Children, 48*(4), 4–11.

Wallerstein, J. S., Corbin, S. B., & Lewis, J. H. (1988). Children of divorce: A ten-year study. In E. M. Hetherington & J. D. Arasteh (Eds.), *Impact of divorce, single parenting and stepparenting on children.* Hillsdale, NJ: Erlbaum.

Wallerstein, J. S., & Kelly, J. B. (1996). *Surviving the breakup: How parents and children cope with divorce.* New York: Basic Books.

Wang, A. Y. (1994). Pride and prejudice in high school gang members. *Adolescence, 29,* 279–291.

Wang, J., & Wildman, L. (1995). The effects of family commitment in education on student achievement in seventh grade mathematics. *Education, 115,* 317–319.

Wang, M. C. (2000). Preface. In R. D. Taylor & M. C. Wang (Eds.), *Resilience across contexts: Family, work, culture, and community.* Mahwah, NJ: Erlbaum.

Ward, C. (1978). *The child in the city.* New York: Pantheon.

Warren, R. (1983). The community in America. In R. L. Warren & L. Lyon (Eds.), *New perspectives on the American community.* Homewood, IL: Dorsey Press.

Wartella, E. A. & Jennings, N. (2000). Children and computers: New technology—old concerns. *The Future of Children, 10*(2), 31–43.

Waters, E., Posada, G., Crowell, J., & Keng-ling, L. (1993). Is attachment theory ready to contribute to our understanding of disruptive behavior problems? *Development and Psychopathology, 5,* 215–224.

Watkins, S. C. (2005). *Hip-hop matters: Politics, pop culture and the struggle for the soul of a movement.* Boston: Beacon Press.

Weber, M. (1930). *The Protestant ethic and the spirit of capitalism.* London: Allen.

Weiner, B. (1992). *Human motivation: Metaphors, theories, and research.* Newbury Park, CA: Sage.

Weiner, M., & Wright, F. (1973). Effects of undergoing arbitrary discrimination upon subsequent attitudes toward a minority group. *Journal of Applied Social Psychology, 3,* 94–102.

Weinstein, C. S. (1991). The classroom as a social context for learning. *Annual Review of Psychology, 42,* 493–525.

Weiss, L. H., & Schwarz, J. C. (1996). The relationship between parenting types and older adolescents' personality, academic achievement, adjustment and substance use. *Child Development, 67,* 2101–2114.

Weiss, M. F. (1994). Children's attitudes toward the mentally ill: An eight-year longitudinal follow-up. *Psychological Reports, 74,* 51–56.

Weissbourd, R. (1996). *The vulnerable child: What really hurts America's children and what we can do about it.* Reading, MA: Addison-Wesley.

Weissbrod, C. (1976). Noncontingent warmth, induction, cognitive style, and children's imitative donation and rescue effort behaviors. *Journal of Personality and Social Psychology, 34,* 274–281.

Weitzman, L. J. (1972). Sex-role socialization in picture books for preschool children. *American Journal of Sociology, 77,* 1125–1150.

Wells, G. (2001). *Action, talk, and text: Learning and teaching through inquiry*. New York: Teachers College Press.

Wen-Jui, H., Leventhal, T., & Linver, M. R. (2004). The Home Observation for Measurement of the Environment (HOME) in middle childhood: A study of three large-scale data sets. *Parenting, 4*(2–3), 189–210.

Wentzel, K. A., & Erdley, C. A. (1993). Strategies for making friends: Relations to social behavior and peer acceptance in early adolescence. *Developmental Psychology, 29,* 819–826.

Werner, E. E. (1993). Risk, resilience, and recovery: Perspectives from Kauai longitudinal study. *Development and Psychopathology, 5,* 503–515.

Werner, E. E., & Smith, R. S. (1992). *Overcoming the odds: High risk children from birth to adulthood*. Ithaca, NY: Cornell University Press.

West, M. M. (1988). Parental values and behavior in the outer Fiji Islands. In R. A. Levine, P. M. Miller, & M. M. West (Eds.), *Parental behavior in diverse societies*. San Francisco: Jossey-Bass.

White, B. L. (1971, October). *Fundamental early environmental influences on the development of competence*. Paper presented at Third Western Symposium on Learning: Cognitive Learning, Western Washington State College, Bellingham.

White, B. L. (1995). *The new first three years of life*. New York: Simon & Schuster.

White, B. L., & Watts, J. C. (1973). *Experience and environment: Major influences on the development of the young child* (Vol. 1). Englewood Cliffs, NJ: Prentice-Hall.

White, L. (1960). Symbol, the basis of language and culture. In W. Goldschmidt (Ed.), *Exploring the ways of mankind*. New York: Holt, Rinehart & Winston.

White, R. W. (1959). Motivation reconsidered: The concept of competence. *Psychology Review, 66,* 297–333.

White, S., & Tharp, R. G. (1988, April). *Questioning and wait-time: A cross-cultural analysis*. Paper presented at the annual meeting of the American Educational Research Association, New Orleans.

Whitebook, M., Howes, C., & Phillips, D. (1989). *Who cares? Child care teachers and the quality of care in America: Final report, National Child Care Staffing Study*. Oakland, CA: Child Care Employee Project.

Whitehurst, G. J., & Lonigan, C. J. (1998). Child development and emergent literacy. *Child Development, 69,* 848–872.

Whiting, B. B., & Edwards, C. P. (1988). *Children of different worlds: The formation of social behavior*. Cambridge, MA: Harvard University Press.

Whiting, B. B., & Whiting, J. W. M. (1973). Altruistic and egoistic behavior in six cultures. In L. Nader & T. W. Maretski (Eds.), *Cultural illness and health: Essays in human adaptation*. Washington, DC: American Anthropological Association.

Whiting, B. B., & Whiting, J. W. M. (1975). *Children of six cultures: A psychoanalysis*. Cambridge, MA: Harvard University Press.

Whittaker, J. K. (1983). Social support networks in child welfare. In J. K. Whittaker & J. Garbarino (Eds.), *Social support networks: Informal helping in the human services*. New York: Aldine.

Wiesner, D. (2001). *The three pigs*. Boston: Clarion/Houghton Mifflin.

Wigfield, A., & Eccles, J. S. (2002). The development of competence beliefs and values from childhood through adolescence. In A. Wigfield & J. S. Eccles (Eds.), *Development of achievement motivation*. San Diego, CA: Academic Press.

Williams, G. (1982). *The rabbit's wedding*. New York: HarperCollins.

Williams, R. M. (1960). Generic American values. In W. Goldschmidt (Ed.), *Exploring the ways of mankind*. New York: Holt, Rinehart & Winston.

Wilson, B. J., & Weiss, A. J. (1993). The effects of sibling coviewing on preschoolers' reactions to a suspenseful movie scene. *Communication Research, 20,* 214–248.

Wilson, S., & Mishra, R. (1999, April 28). In high school, groups provide identity. *Washington Post,* p. A1.

Wilson, W. J. (1987). *The truly disadvantaged: The underclass and public policy*. Chicago: University of Chicago Press.

Wilson, W. J. (1995). Jobless ghettos and the social outcome of youngsters. In P. Moen, G. H. Elder, & K. Luscher (Eds.), *Examining lives in context: Perspectives on the ecology of human development*. Washington, DC: American Psychological Association.

Winn, M. (1977). *The plug-in drug*. New York: Bantam.

Winsler, A., & Wallace, G. L. (2002). Behavior problems and social skills in preschool children: Parent–teacher agreement and relations with classroom observations. *Early Education and Development, 13,* 41–58.

Woititz, J. G. (1990). *Adult children of alcoholics: Common characteristics* (Expanded ed.). Hollywood, FL: Heath Communications.

Wolery, M., & Wilbers, J. S. (1994). Introduction to the inclusion of young children with special needs in early childhood programs. In M. Wolery & J. S. Wilbers (Eds.), *Including children with special needs in early childhood programs*. Washington, DC: National Association for the Education of Young Children.

Wolf, N. (1991). *The beauty myth: How images of beauty are used against women*. New York: Anchor.

Wolfe, D. A. (1994). The role of intervention and treatment services in the prevention of child abuse and neglect. In G. B. Melton & F. Barry (Eds.), *Safe neighborhoods: Foundations for a new national strategy on child abuse and neglect.* New York: Guilford.

Wolfenstein, M. (1953). Trends in infant care. *American Journal of Orthopsychiatry, 23,* 120–130.

Women's Sports Foundation. (1989). *Minorities in sports.* New York: Author.

Wright, J. C., Huston, A. C., Reitz, A. L., & Piemymat, S. (1994). Young children's perceptions of television reality: Determinants and developmental differences. *Developmental Psychology, 30*(2), 229–239.

Wright, J. C., St. Peters, M., & Huston, A. C. (1990). Family television use and its relation to children's cognitive skills and social behavior. In J. Bryant (Ed.), *Television and the American family.* Hillsdale, NJ: Erlbaum.

Yogman, M. W., & Brazelton, T. B. (1986). The family: Stressed yet protected. In M. W. Yogman & T. B. Brazelton (Eds.), *In support of families.* Cambridge, MA: Harvard University Press.

Young, E. (1992). *Seven blind mice.* New York: Putnam.

Young, T. W., & Shorr, D. N. (1986). Factors affecting locus of control in school children. *Genetic, Social, and General Psychology Monographs, 112*(4).

Youniss, J. (1981). Moral development through a theory of social construction: An analysis. *Merrill-Palmer Quarterly, 27,* 385–403.

Youniss, J., & Volpe, J. (1978). A relational analysis of children's friendship. In W. Damon (Ed.), *Social cognition.* San Francisco: Jossey-Bass.

Zahn-Waxler, C., & Radke-Yarrow, M. (1990). The origin of empathetic concern. *Motivation and Emotion, 14,* 107–130.

Zahn-Waxler, C., Radke-Yarrow, M., & King, R. A. (1979). Child-rearing and children's prosocial initiations toward victims of distress. *Child Development, 50,* 319–330.

Zahn-Waxler, C., Radke-Yarrow, M., Wagner, E., & Chapman, M.(1992). Development of concern for others. *Developmental Psychology, 28,* 126–136.

Zahn-Waxler, C., Robinson, J., & Emde, R. (1992). The development of empathy in twins. *Developmental Psychology, 28,* 1038–1047.

Zajonc, R. B. (1976). Family configuration and intelligence. *Science, 912,* 227–236.

Zarbatany, L., Hartmann, D. P., & Rankin, D. B. (1990). The psychological functions of preadolescent peer activities. *Child Development, 61,* 1067–1080.

Zaslow, M., Tout, K., Smith, S., & Moore, K. (1998). Implications of the 1996 welfare legislation for children: A research perspective. *Social Policy Report, 12*(3).

Zhou, Q., Eisenberg, N., Losoya, S. H., Fabes, R. A., Reiser, M., Guthrie, I. K., et al. (2002). The relations of parental warmth and positive expressiveness to children's empathy-related responding and social functioning: A longitudinal study. *Child Development, 73,* 893–915.

Zill, N., & Schoenbom, C. (1990). Developmental, learning, and emotional problems. *Advance data.* National Center for Health Statistics (No. 190). Washington, DC: U.S. Department of Health and Human Services.

Zimmerman, B. J. (2000). Self-efficacy: An essential motive to learn. *Contemporary Educational Psychology, 23,* 82–91.

Zion, G. (1956). *Harry the dirty dog.* New York: Harper & Row.

Zussman, J. U. (1980). Situational determinants of parental behavior: Effects of competing cognitive activity. *Child Development, 51,* 792–800.

Index